Addison-Wesley Publishing Company
Reading, Massachusetts
Menlo Park, California
London • Amsterdam
Don Mills, Ontario • Sydney

Leonard D. Goodstein
University Associates, Inc.

James F. Calhoun
University of Georgia

Understanding Abnormal Behavior

Description, Explanation, Management

Acquisitions Editor:	*Stuart W. Johnson*
Development Editor:	*Tess Palmer*
Production Editor:	*Stephanie Argeros-Magean*
Designer:	*Lauri Slawsby*
Design Coordinator:	*Herb Caswell*
Illustrators:	*Herb Bowes, Art Ciccone*
Art Coordinator:	*Loretta Bailey*
Cover Designer:	*Richard Hannus*
Cover Photographer:	*Talbot Lovering*

Library of Congress Cataloging in Publication Data

Goodstein, Leonard David.
Understanding abnormal behavior.

Bibliography: p.
Includes index.
1. Psychology, Pathological. 2. Psychotherapy.
I. Calhoun, James F. II. Title.
RC454.G594 616.89 81-17669
ISBN 0-201-04078-6 AACR2

ISBN 0-201-04078-6
ABCDEFGHIJ-RN-898765432

Preface

This book has two major goals: The first is to provide readers with as clear a picture as possible of the field of abnormal psychology—a field that has high intrinsic appeal, yet is unable to provide clear answers to the many implicit and explicit questions generated by the subject. The second goal is to set the study of abnormal psychology in the cultural, social, and political context in which it must be viewed if it is to be truly understood. As part of this goal, we would like to break down the "we-they" distinction that mainstream society has for so long applied to those persons who exhibit "strange," "deviant," or "abnormal" behavior.

In presenting our picture of the field, we shall focus on three major issues that we regard as critical to understanding abnormal behavior in general and each of the specific abnormal conditions considered here. The first issue is *description*—the behavior patterns defined as abnormal, the problems involved in making such judgments, the classification scheme we presently use to describe these states. The second is *explanation*—what psychologists and researchers have learned about the causes of abnormal behavior, how the various approaches explain abnormality, why there are so many different theories. The last issue is *management*—how mainstream society deals with people who exhibit abnormal behavior, how management strategies stem from our notions of causation, and why so many of our strategies are ineffective. We have chosen the term *management* rather than *treatment* or *therapy* because not all attempts to cope with abnormal behavior are (or should be) directed solely at the afflicted person, nor can all cases be significantly helped by medical or psychological intervention.

A separate chapter will be devoted to each of these three central issues. These same issues will then provide the organizational framework for the eleven chapters on different abnormal states. Our last chapter deals with present and projected efforts to prevent abnormal behavior.

We believe that our organization of this volume is unique—and that our focus on description, explanation, and management will provide each reader with a valuable conceptual map in an often elusive and difficult field. A second quality unique to this book—at least it is at the time of this writing—is that its content and nomenclature are based on the third edition of the *Diagnostic and Statistical Manual of Mental Disorders* (DSM-III) published in 1980 by the American Psychiatric Association. We recognize that psychologists are ambivalent at best about the DSM-III, but we also recognize that virtually all mental health treatment facilities and insurance programs issuing reimbursement for mental health services are required to use this guide. It seems appropriate, therefore, that we systematically base our book on the DSM-III—but also that we point out the still untested quality of the DSM-III as well as its potential limitations.

Our second goal is to set abnormal psychology in the cultural, social, and political context in which it can be understood. In many ways, the history of dealings with the abnormal is the history of human society. Approaches to unusual behavior always reflect, at least to some extent, the times out of which they arise. Much of our literature—from the Bible to the tragedies of Shakespeare, from *One Flew Over the Cuckoo's Nest* to *I Never Promised You a Rose Garden*—reflects the context as well as the emotions of the times. We have tried to provide such contextual cues where appropriate.

We believe that in our own time and culture, the context amply supports the view that abnormal behavior is not by and large different in kind from normal behavior. Rather, normal and abnormal are best understood as different points along a continuum, subject to the same challenges of definition, understanding, and control.

In writing this volume, we have strived for an informal, straightforward approach. Our heaviest emphasis is not on research findings and research methodology. Although these are critically important issues for professionals in the field, we believe that social context is the more important consideration for the average reader. Where research findings strongly illuminate a point of discussion, or where the weight of research evidence justifies a conclusion, we have decided to include such findings. Unfortunately, most of our research literature is neither that illuminating nor that clear.

To inform readers about the realities of abnormal states, we have made extensive use of brief case histories and examples. We have also included a glossary of important terms at the end of the text, along with a general bibliography. The instructor's manual includes teaching aids, test questions, and other materials that will aid the instructor in presenting the material to students. The student guide includes self-tests and additional readings that will assist students in grasping the material more quickly and determining their understanding of the information.

Another noteworthy feature of the book is the Conversations—in-depth discussions with persons who have been deeply affected, either directly or indirectly, by abnormal behavior. We believe these Conversations provide an unusual and valuable set of insights into abnormality and the diverse problems it poses.

There are a number of persons without whose help this book would not have come about. Stuart Johnson, our acquisitions editor, had the imagination, energy, and faith to initiate and support this undertaking. Our development editor, Tess Palmer, served as tireless adoptive mother to our child and raised it with hard work and loving care. The writers of the original drafts of the chapters on the individual disorders deserve special credit and recognition for sharing their special expertise with us. Carol Verburg took the rough draft of many of these chapters and marshalled them into a unified and readable whole. Finally, we gratefully thank our spouses, Jeanette and Judy, who were patient, understanding, and supportive as we moved in and out of the special abnormal world of the textbook author.

We are grateful for the thoughtful criticisms and suggestions of the following reviewers:

James Curran, Brown University Medical School
Carl Dodrill, University of Washington
Jerry Dodson, Boise State University
George Domino, University of Arizona
James Hooke, Virginia Commonwealth University
Jack Jenkins, University of Georgia
Richard P. Lanyon, Arizona State University
Marian MacDonald, University of Massachusetts
Paul McNeely, Lock Haven State College
Scott Moss, Federal Correctional Institute, Lompoc, California
Eric Nelson, University of Missouri
Ron Prinz, University of South Carolina
Kathryn K. Rileigh, Pembroke State University
Rochelle Robbins, University of Florida
Nancy Robinson, University of Washington
Brenda Townes, University of Washington
Jeffrey Webster, University of Mississippi Medical School
Amos Zeichner, University of Georgia

San Diego, California L.D.G.
Athens, Georgia J.F.C.
November 1981

Chapter drafts were contributed by the following people:

Chapter 5,	Deborah Kearney, VA Medical Center, San Francisco Faye Sultan, University of Georgia James Calhoun, University of Georgia
Chapter 6,	Faye Sultan, University of Georgia Deborah Kearney, VA Medical Center, San Francisco
Chapter 7,	Alan Glaros, Wayne State University
Chapter 8,	Antonette Zeis, Arizona State University
Chapter 9,	Marilyn Sperling, private practice
Chapter 10,	Douglas Payne, University of Georgia
Chapter 11,	Ronald Prinz, University of South Carolina
Chapter 12,	Dean Funabiki, Washington State University
Chapter 13,	Gordon Chelune, University of Georgia
Chapter 14,	Peter Toscano, private practice
Chapter 15,	Thomas Harrell, Florida Institute of Technology
Chapter 16,	Alan Rosenbaum, Syracuse University

Contents

13 *Organic Mental Disorders and Mental Retardation* 393

14 *Disorders of Childhood and Adolescence* 433

Note to the Reader

As you read through this text, you will notice a few sections that, like this page, are printed against a tinted background. These are the six Conversations, interviews with people who have been directly or indirectly affected by a mental disorder. Three of the Conversations are with more than one person—a homosexual couple, a woman paralyzed by polio and her husband, and an alcoholic and his family; three involve only a single individual—a schizophrenic woman, the sister of a twenty-four-year-old mentally retarded man, and a mental health counselor.

We feel that the personal insights revealed in these Conversations reflect the philosophy of our text: that the difference between normal and abnormal is usually one of degree, not of kind. Each one of the individuals that we interviewed have had to deal with extraordinary—even life-threatening—circumstances. Some of them have overcome their problems with professional help or by sheer willpower; some are still struggling.

These people have confronted painful and bewildering life situations with fear, anger, unhappiness, and frustration, the emotions we all feel at some point in life. Yet clearly their problems are extraordinary ones that most of us luckily will never have to face. We hope their experiences will enhance your awareness of the human qualities we all share.

Part One

Introduction

CHAPTER 1

An Overview of Abnormal Psychology

THE QUESTION OF ABNORMALITY

Some General Criteria

The Social Context

What Should We Call It?

ALTERNATIVE APPROACHES TO PSYCHOLOGICAL DISORDERS

The Statistical Model

The Biological Model

The Disease Model

The Absolute Model

THE FIELD OF ABNORMAL PSYCHOLOGY

Limitations of the Field

Issues in the Field

The Behavior Continuum

POSITIVE MENTAL HEALTH

Arnold is a part-time delivery man for a luncheonette in one of the seamier neighborhoods of a large city. He spends most of his days out on the street, delivering coffee, BLTs, and doughnuts to shops and offices in the area. But there's something different about Arnold. It's partly his gaze—he has dark, piercing hawk eyes that rarely blink, and he examines people with unusual intensity as they pass him by. It's partly the way he dresses—tattered half-laced sneakers, baggy khaki trousers, an oversized T-shirt. Most of all though, Arnold seems drunk or high on something. He shuffles when he walks; often he mutters to himself. Sometimes he stops in the middle of one of his deliveries to see if he is still wearing his white socks. Strangers tend to sidestep Arnold on the street and hurry past him, although there is nothing sinister about him.

He lives in a run-down residential hotel, where every morning he washes, dresses, shaves, and does some laundry in his sink before setting off to his job. His employers give him breakfast when he arrives. Arnold works for tips, usually a quarter for each delivery; on a good day he makes five dollars. He lives on this money plus a monthly supplement security income check, a kind of welfare for the disabled that is part of the federal social security program. By the time he pays his rent and buys dinner, his only other meal of the day, Arnold ends up with about two to three dollars a day for clothes and spending money.

Arnold is one of the thousands of chronically mentally ill people who have been "deinstitutionalized," that is, discharged from a mental hospital in a state of "remission," not because they have been cured. This means that as long as Arnold takes regular doses of his medicine, his behavior can be expected to stay fairly normal. On his regular monthly visit to the hospital, he sees a therapist for about fifteen minutes; most of the interchange is about whether he is still taking his medication and whether it is causing any serious side effects, such as internal bleeding or nausea. If Arnold doesn't mention any problems, he receives his monthly allocation of pills and returns to his hotel room.

Although Arnold's existence is somewhat grim, he prefers it to his old life. As a young man, Arnold's bizarre behavior—unpredictable bursts of shouting and gesticulating, babbling in sentences no one but he could understand—embarrassed his family and upset his employers. At least half a dozen times Arnold was admitted to a state mental hospital with a diagnosis of chronic schizophrenia. The last time, he slept in a ward with 75 other patients—a ward intended for 30. The beds were less than a foot apart, and the snoring and moaning were so loud that many patients could not sleep. After twenty years of life in and out of institutions, Arnold is glad to be "making it" on the outside.

Elaine spends most of her waking time sitting at the kitchen table of her modest suburban home. She stares into space, occasionally twisting the half-empty cup of coffee on the table in front of her. Dressed in a flannel nightgown and a worn chenille robe, with no makeup and uncombed hair, she looks older than her 44 years.

Elaine used to be a meticulous housekeeper, but she now seems unaware of the dirty dishes piled up in the sink, the unmade beds, the dust on the furniture, and the general clutter that has collected around the house. When the telephone or the doorbell rings, she is momentarily startled but rarely answers them. Every once in a while she does stand up—but only to pace around the kitchen, wringing her hands and exclaiming over and over, "Oh, God, oh my God!" If no one is home to lead her back to the table, her pacing can continue for over an hour.

Elaine's occasional bursts into action remind her troubled family of the energetic person she used to be. She was always a busy woman, involved in a variety of civic and church activities, committed to being a good wife and mother. About a year ago, she started to complain of feeling overburdened, tired, and depressed. Things that used to interest and excite her, like the annual spaghetti dinner for the high school marching band, no longer seemed worth the effort. Instead of popping out of bed in the morning to fix breakfast for her husband and two children, she began asking them to fend for themselves—first apologetically, then defensively. Now she typically gets out of bed long after the others have left home for the day. Once or twice recently, the task of getting up was just too difficult, and she wound up spending the day in bed.

Initially, Elaine's family was concerned about the changes in her behavior. Her husband, Ralph, insisted on taking her to their family physician, who examined her and found nothing physical to account for the dramatic changes. After a variety of tranquilizers and antidepressants failed to bring her back to her old self, the doctor gave up on medical treatment. His final recommendation was a referral to the staff psychiatrist at the local community hospital.

No one in either Elaine's or Ralph's family had ever been to a psychiatrist. The very thought of such a drastic action made Ralph nervous. What if their friends found out? He reassured himself that everybody has "down" periods; no doubt Elaine would snap out of hers soon. It wouldn't help anything to have some psychiatrist treating her as if she were crazy!

When Elaine did not change, the family began to accommodate her. Ralph has lately begun spending more and more time at the office, finding it easier to catch a bite to eat in town than to deal with Elaine and the mess at home. Their son is away at his first year of college. Their daughter has no trouble finding friends to invite her home for dinner—and when that doesn't work out, there's always the local pizza place. She and Ralph always make sure Elaine gets something to eat—usually a hamburger or some fast-food snack. But Elaine tends to find even such a simple meal more than she can manage. Both her husband and daughter are angry and bewildered at her failure to eat—and at her behavior in general. How can she do this to them? What's the matter with her? What should they do? Sometimes Ralph wonders if he should follow the doctor's advice and take Elaine to a psychiatrist. But he always backs off. Surely she'll begin to perk up tomorrow—or next week at the very latest.

Although Tommy is barely three years old, the impact he has had on his family has been enormous. Even as an infant, Tommy never seemed to care about being cuddled or held. When his parents picked him up, he stayed stiff and rigid, never relaxing against their bodies as their other children had. Both Bob and Myrna secretly feared that Tommy didn't like them, although the idea of an infant disliking its parents seemed absurd. Nor was Tommy as interested in being fed as the other children had always been. He ignored his siblings and their attempts to play with him, and eventually they stopped trying.

When Tommy was about six months old, Bob and Myrna began to share their concerns about him. Was something physically wrong? Could Tommy be deaf or visually handicapped? If not, why was he so unresponsive? They consulted their pediatrician, but she could find no physical abnormality that might explain Tommy's odd behavior. The most noteworthy feature of each of their repeated visits to her was that Tommy screamed almost the entire time.

Over the next several months, Tommy showed more and more clearly that he preferred to be left alone. He was unresponsive to approaches from his parents and siblings, and he actively resisted any changes in his environment. Visits to the doctor's office or to his grandparents', strangers coming to the house, even rearrangements of the furniture—all resulted in fits of screaming and crying. Only when he was alone again in his crib did Tommy seem content, but he remained aloof and uninterested in his surroundings.

Now at three, Tommy has still never developed any conversational speech. He repeats a few words and phrases, sometimes for minutes on end. But he remains uninterested in any social contact; he shows little desire to explore the world around him and has resisted all his parents' efforts at toilet training. Tommy learned to crawl and then to walk with little difficulty—indeed, to see him running in the backyard makes it easy to forget his behavioral problems. Alone in his room, however, Tommy sits on the floor for hours, rocking back and forth, and sometimes banging his head against the wall or the floor until he bruises himself.

Repeated visits to a variety of specialists have been of little help. Most recently, the team at the local community mental health clinic decided that Tommy is a classic case of early infantile autism. But when Bob and Myrna asked for more explanation, they learned only that there are some other children who share Tommy's odd combination of behaviors—and that there is no effective treatment.

THE QUESTION OF ABNORMALITY

What do Arnold, Elaine, and Tommy have in common? Each of them clearly exhibits **abnormal behavior**—in other words, behavior that is different either in kind or in degree from that of most people in our society. Arnold gives the impression of being a generally bizarre individual; his gaze, his clothes, his living situation, and his long history of hospitalization all mark him as different. Elaine, on the other hand, leads a typical middle-class life, except that her moodiness and depression are much more extreme than the blues most of us get from time to time. Tommy, in contrast, is strikingly different from other children, because of his violent tantrums, emotional unresponsiveness, and self-destructive behavior. A major point thus becomes obvious from these brief case studies: Abnormality is highly diverse; Arnold, Elaine, and Tommy are far more different from each other than alike. What qualities do they share that make them appropriate subjects for this book?

Some General Criteria

Most mental health specialists agree on three general characteristics that indicate significantly abnormal behavior:

1. *The behavior is markedly different from what is ordinarily seen in people of similar age, sex, background, and situation.* The emphasis here is on our expectations. That is, for a middle-aged woman like Elaine, staying inside all the time, rarely getting out of bed, and almost never talking is abnormal; but the behavior would be perfectly normal for a four-month-old baby. If a man suddenly started chasing someone, shoving and knocking over bystanders in his way, we would consider that abnormal—but not if he were a player in a football game. What we label abnormal thus depends on some accepted standard of what is normal. That standard is different for different individuals, not only within our culture but from one culture to another and from one historical period to another.

2. *The behavior impairs the individual's ability to function normally, sometimes to a great degree.* That is, the behavior in question causes other abnormal behaviors or prevents normal behaviors. Many people are mildly afraid of dogs; but some people are so terrified of meeting a dog that they are reluctant to go out of the house. One behavior—avoiding dogs—thus keeps them from engaging in other activities appropriate to their age, sex, situation, and so forth.

3. *The behavior is disturbing to other people, and often to the individual who has the problem as well.* One characteristic shared by Arnold, Elaine, and Tommy is that they persist in behaviors that bring unhappiness to themselves and others. Most of us attempt to maximize the happiness and reduce the unhappiness in our lives. Individuals with markedly abnormal behavior patterns do this less than people in general. Often they appear insensitive to opportunities for pleasure—or rather unwilling to make the effort that most of us would make to take advantage of such opportunities.

To put it another way, many abnormal behaviors do not appear to be acquired or maintained according to the general principles of learning. Arnold's preoccupation with his white socks, Elaine's staring into space, and Tommy's banging his head against the floor are not rewarded in a consistent or straightforward fashion. On the contrary, these behaviors have negative consequences for the person and everyone else involved. Many of the behaviors we will encounter and describe in this book seem to defy logic in this same way; for some of them no one, not even professionals who have had a great deal of experience in this area, can offer an explanation that really works.

Failing to seek happiness is, of course, a rather subjective issue. Perhaps Arnold, Elaine, and Tommy are being reinforced in ways that are not obvious to us. Or perhaps they are responding to rewards that are different from those that we seek. If their conception of what is rewarding is abnormal, it follows that their behavior would also be abnormal. As we shall later see, researchers have found evidence supporting both possibilities.

Communal bathing, a relaxing and acceptable pastime in Japan, would shock many Americans. Such diverse reactions emphasize how standards of normal and abnormal behavior vary from one culture to another.

The Social Context

No matter how we approach the question of abnormality, we find our expectations playing a central role. But do all of us really have the same expectations about what is normal? To the extent that we do, how are these expectations determined?

No society has a list of behaviors it considers normal and abnormal, but all societies distinguish between the two. And in most cases, "abnormal" also means "unacceptable." As we have seen, the label "abnormal" is usually applied to those behaviors that do not serve the best interests of the person—or other people. Banging your head against the wall is abnormal because most people don't do it; most people don't do it because it hurts and may cause serious injury. Thus, it is unacceptable not just because it is odd but because it is **maladaptive**—it decreases the person's chances of surviving and thriving.

Norms

What a society considers acceptable is usually rooted in the survival needs of the individual and of the larger group. The resulting standards of behavior, or **norms,** are typically expressed, taught, and monitored by the society's major institutions: family, church, schools, government. In some societies, the norms are fairly specific and strict, so that the range of acceptable behaviors is quite narrow. In other societies, including our own, the norms are less re-

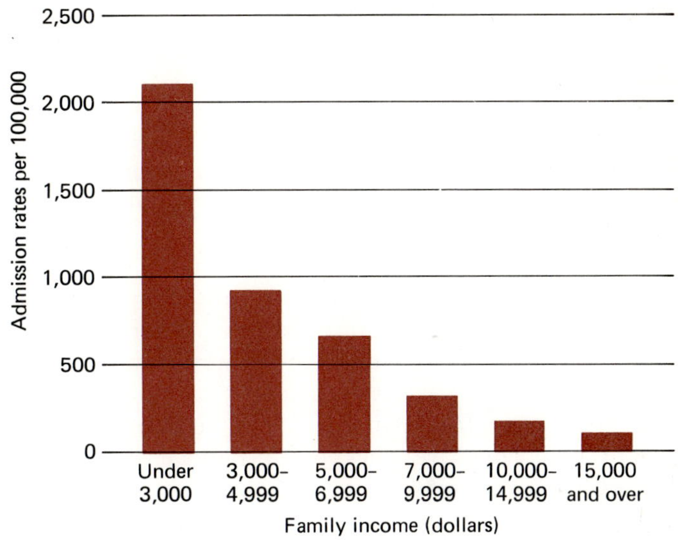

Figure 1.1. *The link between social class and mental health is indicated by the number of admissions to outpatient psychiatric services, which are greater for the poor. From the National Institute of Mental Health, 1978.*

strictive. Our culture currently permits a relatively wide band of behaviors. For example, it tolerates sexual preferences and activities that would have scandalized our grandparents and that are today prohibited in some other parts of the world; it allows a greater range of political behavior than many other cultures do; the roles it prescribes for men and women are fairly flexible. Furthermore, our society is comparatively tolerant of deviation. Someone like Arnold, whose behavior differs from the norm in so many respects, is nevertheless encouraged to be a participating member.

This is not to underestimate the restrictions placed on us by the established norms in our society. What the law allows still may be taboo according to the church; what a textbook says is socially acceptable may not be tolerated in all American homes. In addition, we are restricted by the numerous subcultures, each with rules of its own, that exist within the general diversity of our culture. The part of the country a person lives in has a strong influence on standards of conduct. Indeed, even the neighborhoods of a single city will vary. Socioeconomic class, ethnic background, educational level, and a variety of other factors influence our views of what is normal. Compare, for instance, the principles expressed in Abbie Hoffman's *Steal This Book* with those in Amy Vanderbilt's *Everyday Etiquette*. And socioeconomic class, ethnic background, and educational level also influence the ways in which people respond to behavior that is considered abnormal.

Socialization

Wherever and however we live, we all learn certain behavioral codes as we grow up—a process called **socialization**. The norms transmitted to us by our social group reflect its dominant values and long-term concerns. They also provide a framework within which we can develop effective ways to interact with other people and can learn the skills we need for survival and success. In addition, we acquire a social conscience—that is, the ability to distinguish right from wrong and to feel at least some distress if we violate the norms.

There are five areas of behavior for which

socialization is common in all cultures: feeding, elimination (toilet training), sexuality, aggression, and independence (learning the social and emotional skills needed to separate from parents and the childhood environment). Different cultures often establish different norms around these points, for example, the taboo against pork and shellfish that is observed in Jewish communities. Some norms are more universal, for instance, the taboo against eating human flesh that is common to most societies. Youngsters everywhere are taught to recognize and avoid whatever behaviors their society considers inappropriate. Interestingly, these inappropriate behaviors are very often natural impulses—one reason why the socialization process is typically so long and intense. Toddlers, for instance, do not distinguish between a right and a wrong time, place, or way to eat or to urinate. If adults fail to make this distinction, their behavior is likely to be considered abnormal and unacceptable.

The power of norms is so great that adults who do engage in deviant behavior generally try to keep it secret, and as a result suffer another punishment: *anxiety*. Anxiety may take many forms—a guilty conscience, fear that Mom or the police will find out, fear of going to Hell. It can also contribute to a wide range of physical problems, including ulcers, migraine headaches, asthma, hypertension, acne, and warts. But anxiety does more than punish us for violating society's rules. It also functions as a preventive measure to restrain us from committing unacceptable acts. That is, just *thinking* about doing something wrong—violating an important norm—usually generates enough anxiety to keep us from going any further. The role of anxiety in human behavior is too complex to summarize here, but we will return to the subject over the course of this book.

Of course, anxiety cannot prevent all deviant acts. Most of us occasionally overcome our consciences enough to defy social norms. Some people violate norms regularly—criminals, for instance, blatantly ignore the legal and moral codes that govern aggression. Still, even those who scorn society's norms cannot completely escape them—usually they accept society's ideas of success (wealth, power, status), though they use deviant means to achieve it. Many an underworld "hit man" still goes to church on Sundays.

What about the individual whose deviant behavior is not directed toward any apparent goal? We noted that Elaine, Arnold, and Tommy do not appear to gain anything from their violations of social norms. Yet the peer pressure, fear of punishment, and conscience pangs that keep most of us in line most of the time have little effect on them. They neither conceal their abnormal behavior nor enjoy it, as far as anyone can tell. Therefore, we conclude, their mental processes must differ from ours in some important respect. They must be—what? Mentally ill? Emotionally disturbed? Crazy?

What Should We Call It?

Just about every area of abnormal psychology involves some controversy or another; and certainly one of the most central issues is what to call the people who are its subjects. We have skirted this question so far by emphasizing two things: behavior and social standards. On one hand, we have focused on the idea that these individuals can be identified by their unusual actions; on the other hand, we have said that what is unusual is a matter of what socialization leads us to expect.

This approach has its limits. In stressing observable behavior, we neglect unobservable mental and physiological processes. In stressing social criteria, we ignore the role of biological factors, early childhood development, individual learning, and other influences. All approaches deserve attention. Our aim up to this point has been to avoid the negative connotations that often distort discussions of abnormality.

What we call a behavior pattern often depends on what we believe to be its cause. Lunacy comes from the Latin word for moon, *luna*, which explains why the actions of "lunatics" were once thought to be inspired by the moon. Mental illness, in contrast, implies a disease of the mind, and nervous breakdown suggests a mechanical failure—as if, under too much stress, the person has "burnt out."

Other terms are primarily descriptive. *Psychopathology* means "dysfunction of behavior"; *abnormal* simply means "not normal"; *deviant behavior* is "behavior deviating from the norm"; *disordered* means "not ordered" or "not organized in an orderly way." In this book, descriptive terms will be generally preferred to those that imply a theory of causation. Choosing the term "abnormal behavior," as limited as that concept is, keeps us from getting tangled up in such terms as "craziness," "nervous breakdowns," "mental illness," and the varied terminology sometimes applied to people like Tommy, Arnold, and Elaine.

We will have more to say about terminology when we consider the definition of abnormal behavior patterns. For the moment, it is worth emphasizing that this issue is not a trivial one. An individual who is labeled mentally ill, for example, is viewed as having a disease that prevents normal **cognition**—that is, normal thinking—and therefore also normal behavior. Thus, even when there is reason to suspect that a certain behavior pattern might actually reflect a disease of the mind, as is the case with schizophrenia, we urge caution in applying that label. How much of Arnold's behavior is actually due to schizophrenia, and how much has developed as a function of being treated as a schizophrenic? Carrying the label of schizophrenia is a kind of license to act peculiarly—no one expects mental patients, or even former mental patients, to behave completely normally. It is quite possible that some of Arnold's odd ways are the result of a self-fulfilling prophecy.

Thomas Eagleton was dropped as George McGovern's running mate from the 1972 Democratic ticket soon after it was revealed that he had at one time undergone electric shock treatment. Because of the emotionalism surrounding the term "mentally ill," the label is one that should not be used lightly.

ALTERNATIVE APPROACHES TO PSYCHOLOGICAL DISORDERS

The issue of terminology is related to the larger question of how we interpret psychological disorders. There are many ways of distinguishing abnormal behavior from mere eccentricity and of determining who among us is suffering from a disorder. We listed the three criteria mental health professionals often use in classifying a behavior pattern as significantly abnormal: showing marked difference from the norm, impairing the person's ability to function, and causing distress. Such an approach might be called the *psychological model.* In general, there are four other categories of models: *statistical, biological, disease,* and *absolute.*

The Statistical Model

The statistical approach is based on the fact that most human characteristics—appearance, intelligence, personality traits—are distributed according to what is called the *bell curve of standard distribution* (see Fig. 1.2). This means that most people have similar amounts of each of these traits (the sharp rise in the middle)—in other words, most people are average in height, weight, strength, and so on. Of course, some people are shorter, thinner, and weaker than average, and

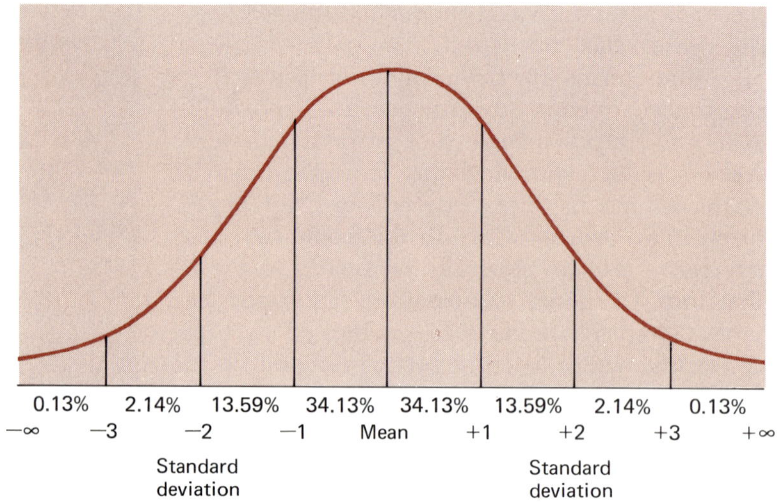

Figure 1.2. *The bell curve of standard distribution.*

others are taller, heavier, and stronger. For each characteristic, the above-average and the below-average groups are represented by the two ends of the curve. The distribution pattern thus formed resembles a bell.

At the center of the distribution curve is the **mean,** which is the arithmetic average. A score falling below or above the average *deviates from the mean.* It turns out that human characteristics tend to cluster in fairly predictable groupings, called **standard deviations** (marked on the figure). Thus only about 15 percent of the general population is below average in strength, intelligence, etc. (−1 standard deviation), and 15 percent is above average (+1 standard deviation). Among these individuals, most (almost 14 percent) will be only slightly below or above the average; the remainder will fall progressively farther from the mean (+2, +3, −2, −3, etc.).

The statistical approach to abnormal psychology thus defines a behavior as abnormal if it falls outside the normal range of the distribution curve. This approach is attractive because of its directness and simplicity, but it has the disadvantage of defining any uncommon behavior as abnormal, regardless of its social impact. While this may not be a drawback for such biological characteristics as height, it causes serious interpretive problems for most psychological characteristics. For example, people with IQs of 145 and above and those with IQs of 55 and below are equally abnormal in the statistical sense (in each case such scores occur in less than 0.13 percent of the general population), but categorizing both ends of the curve as abnormal raises more questions than it answers. On the whole, although the statistical approach is a way of identifying the frequency of various behaviors, it offers little help in suggesting how we should regard the people who exhibit them.

Another problem with the model is its implication that "statistically average" is the same as "normal." Most Americans have head colds each year, yet it is strange to think of being sick as normal. In a more relevant area, the initial findings of the Midtown Manhattan Study (Srole, et al., 1962) suggested that out of a large random sample of local residents, less than 20 percent of them could be considered psychologically healthy. The remaining 80 percent all showed at least some signs of psychopathology, and over 20 percent had marked impairment. Using the statistical model, the one fifth who were free of disturbance would be classified as abnormal, and those with problems would be considered normal. Such paradoxes are inherent in the use of the statistical model.

Therefore the major limitation of the statistical model is its inability to accord any value to the social and psychological impact of behaviors. Dangerous deviations are lumped together with harmless or desirable ones. If behaviors with negative consequences, such as reckless driving and alcoholism, become widespread enough, they would by definition become statistically normal. Likewise, statistically rare behavior, such as fluency in several foreign languages and artistic creativity, would become deviant. Given these problems, we should question the viability of the statistical model. Its simplicity and the importance of standard distribution in theorizing about behavior account for its continued use, but we need to be sensitive to its potential misuse.

The Biological Model

The biological approach simply assumes that all organisms, including humans, have biologically natural functions—eating, sleeping, growing, adapting, reproducing, and so on—and that when something interferes with these functions, an abnormal state develops. Like physical illness, abnormality is seen as a deviation from the structural and functional integrity of the body and its workings.

A central concept in the biological model is that of **homeostasis,** the inherent tendency of an organism to maintain balance among its many internal units and systems. As long as such equilibrium exists, survival of the individual and therefore of the species is more probable. Some biologically oriented writers (Miller, 1965) take this point of view even further. They argue that living organisms also strive to maintain an equilibrium with their environments that guarantees the food supply, fresh air, shelter, and other factors required for a steady internal state. Therefore both the internal functioning of living organisms and their interactions with the environment can be regarded as either normal or abnormal, depending on whether or not homeostasis is achieved.

According to this approach, a multitude of behaviors clearly fall into the abnormal category. Overeating and undereating, not sleeping

According to the biological model, an ordinary behavior such as the consumption of alcohol is labeled abnormal when it becomes self-destructive. Thus the family enjoying wine during Passover and the alcoholic on the street are at different points on the normal/abnormal continuum.

and sleeping too much, exercising too little and overexercising—these are just a few of the physical behaviors that can put the body off balance. Not getting adequate love and attention or mourning too long over a loss can create a psychological imbalance.

The notion that any behavior deviating from biological standards is abnormal appears to be simple, but it is rather difficult to put into practice. How can we determine which behaviors are biologically normal? Observation of humans and other animals provides very contradictory data. If we set a norm for heartbeats per minute, how do we categorize the low rates of superb athletes? Is it normal to eat the flesh of other animals or to drink fermented grape juice? What about having more than one mate or being sexually stimulated by a person of the same gender? Despite such drawbacks, the biological model has strong supporters. There are many who argue against homosexuality on the grounds that only cross-gender sexuality is biologically appropriate, and that any deviation from this path is automatically abnormal. These proponents tend to overlook the considerable evidence indicating that many animals engage in homosexuality.

Perhaps the greatest value of the biological model is in its reminder that we should examine the adaptive consequences of our behavior much more closely than we do. It is difficult to disagree with the argument that knowingly harmful biological actions should be seen as negative. After all, who favors poor nutrition, obesity, alcoholism, and other self-destructive behaviors? At the same time, however, how many of us can resist stuffing ourselves at a holiday feast, or drinking a little too much at a party on occasion?

The Disease Model

The disease approach—an offshoot of the biological model—states that deviations from the homeostatic normal state are best regarded as illnesses and should therefore be treated as medical problems. It is this model that currently dominates abnormal psychology and has given us such terms as "mental illness." As we shall see in later chapters, psychological problems, such as schizophrenia and the affective disorders, do seem to fit that model, at least in part. However, a number of other serious conditions, such as phobias, compulsions, and alcoholism, do not. Take alchoholism as a case in point. Although there is no question that alcoholism has strong physiological components, what do we gain by calling it a disease? The evidence for a purely biological explanation for why some people begin to drink too much is slim; psychological and social factors appear to play a much more important role. Labeling this problem as a disease has the benefit that alcoholics are now more likely to be taken to a hospital than to jail, but it does little to enlarge our understanding of this widespread condition.

Another problem with the disease model is the shortage of supporting evidence in the diagnosis of a condition. According to this approach, mental disorders are a subset of medical diseases that have primarily behavioral manifestations. In medical diseases, the behavioral manifestations (such as delirium from a high fever) are supported by independent evidence of some underlying organic disease process (such as bacteria found in a throat culture). When the disease model is applied to psychological problems, there is no such secondary evidence. Thus, when we say that Arnold is withdrawn because he is schizophrenic, we have no evidence beyond his visible symptoms to support the notion that a disease is in progress. Indeed, to argue that Arnold is withdrawn because he is schizophrenic amounts to circular reasoning, since we already have labeled him schizophrenic because he is withdrawn.

Perhaps the strongest opponent of the disease model has been psychiatrist Thomas Szasz. Szasz (1960) insists that no disease process is involved in most maladaptive behavior; rather, the patient has "problems in living" that are manifesting themselves as behavioral deviations from society's norms. He argues that mental illness is a myth, perpetuated by the mental health professionals to maintain and strengthen their own power. Szasz contends that what we have been calling "symptoms" are best seen as patients' communications about themselves and their world. Rather than the result of some underlying organic process, Szasz sees abnormal behavior as purposive, as the necessary and inevitable result of the tensions between individuals and the society in which they live. To regard such behaviors as something other than problems in living removes from patients the obligation to be responsible, and to be seen as responsible, for their own behavior.

Accepting the disease model has another consequence that is quite independent of its conceptual quality or its final validity. This approach makes the diagnosis and management of abnormal behavior the more-or-less exclusive province of the medical profession. The argument runs something like this: Abnormal behavior is the result of some organic disease process; physicians understand and know how to diagnose and treat disease; therefore, physicians are the only (or the best) ones to understand, diagnose, treat, and manage abnormal behavior. Szasz and other critics of this view contend that the medical profession's vested interest in the continued existence of mental illness makes them the least, not most, qualified judges of abnormality.

Similar concern has been raised about the management of patients suffering from physical disease. Some critics insist that we place far too much reliance on physicians in the treatment of heart disease, cancer, arthritis, and other diseases. Physicians tend to see only the disease, not the person with the disease, thereby neglecting such critically important considerations as the patient's attitude or acceptance of a dependent role, for instance. The limitations of the medical viewpoint are clearly illustrated by the story of Norman Cousins and his dramatic fight to overcome cancer: Told by all the specialists that the only route was chemotherapy and a long hospital stay, Cousins rebelled. He left the pallid atmosphere of the hospital and went home to a supportive and caring family. There, following an impulse, he immersed himself in comedy and proceeded to laugh himself well (Cousins, 1979).

The Absolute Model

Perhaps the oldest approach to determining the criteria of deviance is to use moral absolutes, such as those of various religious doctrines. Virtually all organized religions provide a set of rules for behavior—strengthened by the presumption that any violation is sinful in the eyes of God and will surely be punished. Although the rules vary somewhat in each religion, this model has a great impact on how society views particular behaviors. For instance, masturbation and homosexuality have long been considered abnormal in Western cultures because they violate the word of God as stated in the Bible.

THE FIELD OF ABNORMAL PSYCHOLOGY

Abnormal psychology has emerged as a field of study out of all these and many other attempts to understand abnormal behavior. The field's major concerns fall into three general categories:

1. Defining abnormal behavior, in terms of recurrent patterns of symptoms.
2. Explaining the development of such behavior patterns, with an eye toward possible prevention.
3. Managing the behavior, for both the individual concerned and others who must cope with it.

As we examine various psychological disorders in later chapters, we will consider each problem in terms of these three categories.

Let us first make certain that the issues themselves are clear by looking back at our three opening cases. How do we decide that Arnold, Elaine, and Tommy are to be regarded as abnormal rather than as normal? Each of us knows people with peculiarities or eccentricities. Are Arnold, Elaine, and Tommy significantly different from them? Defining behavioral deviance sets a dividing line between behavior that is considered within the bounds of normality and behavior that falls outside those bounds. As we have noted, this line is set legally by legislation, morally by various religions, and historically by custom. In the final analysis, it is also set personally by each of us in terms of the impact that the behavior of others has on us. Thus the answer to the question of what constitutes deviance is almost always relative and always changing.

The question of explaining abnormal behavior in our three cases is equally complex. Were Tommy, Arnold, and Elaine born the way they are, or did some set of events or experiences cause them to go off the track? Are they behaving strangely because of bad genes or are biological or nutritional deficiencies involved? This list of questions could easily be continued, but the point should be clear. There is no single answer to explain abnormal behavior; there are many possible answers, none of which suit all cases and none of which are universally accepted. Even the kinds of explanations that are preferred, both by professionals in this area and by the society at large, change from time to time. This general lack of agreement not only complicates our understanding but also interferes with efforts to carry out careful and thorough research on the causes of abnormal behavior.

The final issue is management. Assuming we could agree that Elaine, Tommy, and Arnold are indeed disturbed and that there are some reasonable explanations for their disturbance, then what should we do with them? Here again a range of possibilities exists. We could simply ignore the behavior and segregate the affected individuals from the rest of society, or we could actively work to change the abnormal behavior. The form of management we choose usually depends on how we explain the cause of a behavior. That is, if we believe the behavior results from the presence of a devil, then the treatment will involve getting rid of that evil spirit; if we believe that overwork and stress have caused the behavior, then rest and quiet will be the treatment chosen.

Limitations of the Field

Ideally then, definition, explanation, and management are closely related. Establishing a pattern of symptoms leads to a theory of **etiology** (cause), and that theory in turn suggests an appropriate treatment. In practice, however, things frequently proceed in a less orderly fashion. An effective treatment is often discovered by chance, and investigating why it works yields clues to the etiology of the problem. For example, the discovery that amphetamines can be useful in treating hyperactive children was accidental. But the success of this treatment gave researchers the idea of seeking a biological basis for hyperactivity.

Moving backward from a treatment technique to a theory of what causes the disorder is typically a long and difficult process. Many of the drugs currently prescribed for various psychological disorders work for reasons that are still unknown. In a sense, even the definition of the problem is affected. Once a biological cause is identified, the problem is no longer classed as a psychological one. When the behavioral disturbances due to vitamin deficiency were clearly identified, they became routine medical disorders treated by general physicians, not by mental health specialists. When penicillin was found to destroy the microorganism responsible for impairing brain function in syphilis, this disorder also became treatable as an ordinary medical problem. Many experts are convinced that similar physical etiology will eventually be discovered for all the psychological disorders—but such a development is a long way off.

Since abnormal behavior has existed as long as human beings, you might expect that most disorders would have been explained by now. This is far from the case. As far as we can tell, the incidence of psychological disorder has been fairly constant throughout history. Most forms of psychological disturbance have turned up in all parts of the world; where differences do exist, they often appear to be due to diagnostic practices or to the degree of social acceptability of a particular disorder within a given culture. Yet explanations and treatments still vary according to the prevailing social, religious, and scientific beliefs. Nor are the most "scientific" cures always the most effective. Rituals designed to drive out devils have had impressive success rates in cultures where evil spirits are viewed as the cause of abnormal behavior. It often appears that the most important factor in a patient's recovery is belief in the treatment.

In short, our understanding of psychological disorders is tentative and incomplete, as is our ability to cure them. With some disorders, total recovery is possible: The patient resumes the former level of functioning and goes home to a normal life. In other cases, partial recovery or arresting the progress of the disorder is a more realistic goal. The person may have to continue medication or psychotherapy indefinitely, and even then may never regain all the abilities needed to be self-sufficient. In some instances, the most that can be hoped for is to help the person as well as the family and friends involved adjust to the problem. It is for these reasons that we have chosen the term management rather than cure or treatment as the third phase after describing and explaining a disorder.

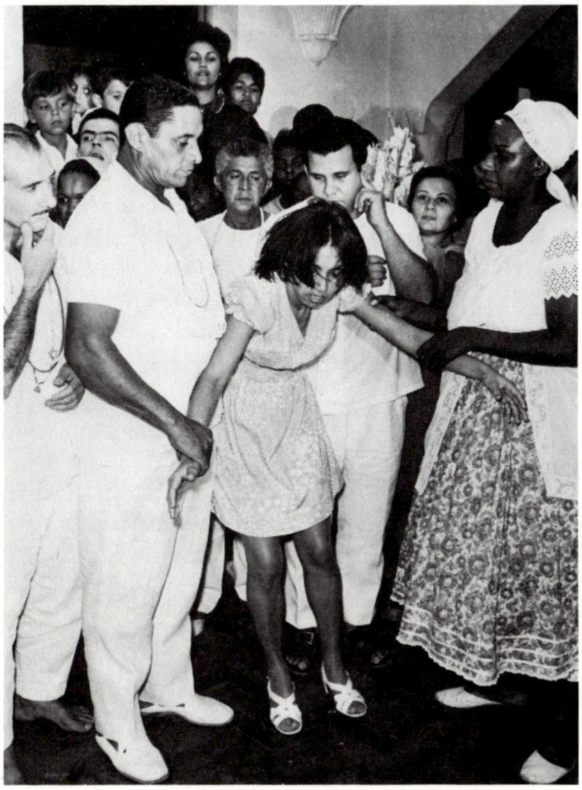

A *"possessed" Brazilian teenager collapses during a voodoo ceremony. In cultures where abnormal behavior may be attributed to evil spirits, the victim's belief in the supernatural may be a crucial factor in both illness and recovery.*

Issues in the Field

From our discussion to this point, it may seem that mental health professionals do agree generally on the nature of abnormal behavior—despite their differing views on causes or treatment. Actually, this is not the case. It's true that, as our society changes, certain behaviors can glide in and out of the abnormal category; therefore the nature of any single act is hard to pinpoint as essentially normal or abnormal. But some professionals, like Szasz, go further than this. They believe that the *concept* of abnormality is false—that insanity doesn't exist. This issue, and others, form another aspect of the field of abnormal psychology.

Do disorders really exist?

The considerable gaps in our knowledge have led to some skepticism about the value and even the validity of abnormal psychology as a field. If we can't be sure what causes psychological disorders, how can we be sure that that is in fact what they are? Indeed, even professionals disagree constantly about whether or not one problem or another is a disorder, let alone what kind. Perhaps the most dramatic example is the conflict over homosexuality. Reflecting the dominant view in this country, the American Psychiatric Association's *Diagnostic and Statistical Manual* (DSM) for years classified homosexuality as a disorder. But as a growing segment of society came to dispute this view, the association voted to delete homosexuality from its list. In the third edition of the DSM, homosexuality is classified as a disorder only when the person is disturbed by it and wants to change. This move did not by any means end the controversy, however. It is quite possible that future editions of the DSM will contain still other interpretations.

Is abnormality a false concept?
Some critics believe that the whole concept of disorder is artificial. Theorists such as R. D. Laing argue that abnormal behavior is actually a rational response to an irrational society. In a world that is contradictory and confusing, we should not be surprised that some people choose to create an alternative reality. Nor do we have any good reason to view their reality as less valid than ours. In fact, Laing in particular feels that the people we call "crazy" and "schizophrenic" are actually on the road to a better understanding of themselves and a truer vision of our world (1967). He therefore encourages them along this journey, interpreting their bizarre behavior as an attempt to wade through the cultural claptrap that encumbers all of us, which only they have perceived realistically.

Nevertheless, the prevailing opinion in abnormal psychology is that disorders do exist—the historical record alone is enough to convince most observers. Laing and others do raise some important points though. One is that it is dangerous simply to regard any view that conflicts with the social consensus as an indication of insanity. The Soviet practice of branding political dissidents "mentally ill" is an extreme example, but the problem has existed for centuries. A classic case is Joan of Arc, who was executed for the heresy of hearing voices that told her she could lead the army of France to victory over the British. Of course, the charge of heresy was not made until she proved her point with decisive action, and it was her pro-British Burgundian captors who denounced her and burned her at the stake.

Another point is that disordered behavior is not necessarily without logic. The alternative reality created by some schizophrenics, for example, is rich, detailed, and internally coherent. However, it is usually also a source of unimaginable torment to the schizophrenic. As we mentioned earlier, the current practice is to classify a behavior pattern as disordered not merely when it is different, but when it causes anguish to the individual or to others who try to deal with the problem.

Does abnormality serve a purpose?
Some observers have suggested that the strange behavior of the few may be valuable to the rest of us. Perhaps individuals who flout social norms are actually reinforcing those norms by dramatizing the consequences of right and wrong behavior (Doobs, 1971). According to this view, disturbed people become much like the exotic freaks that perform in the sideshow of a circus. They are the bag ladies, drunks, and other "weirdos" that we observe with curiosity and amusement, secretly relieved and even a little proud that *we* aren't like that! These individuals are acting out our own hidden urges to rebel against the norms, and so they alleviate our own need to rebel. Indeed, it has been suggested that people who feel threatened rather than amused or compassionate when they encounter deviant behavior may be showing a lack of confidence in their own normality. The "macho" man who loudly insists that he hates "faggots" is a classic example: His real concern may be a fear that he, too, can be attracted to other men.

The Behavior Continuum

We can see how someone like Arnold might function as part of the human sideshow. Arnold is visibly different from the rest of us. But what about Elaine? Her husband believes she is just suffering from a temporary depression—no need for professional help! If we noticed Arnold lifting his pants leg to check on his white socks, we might laugh at his odd behavior. But if we looked in through Elaine's kitchen window, we probably would not be amused. Elaine could too easily be the woman next door, or Aunt Helen, or even Mom.

The contrast between Arnold and Elaine raises a major question in abnormal psychology: Is the difference between normal and abnormal behavior a difference in kind or in degree? That is, are psychological disorders just an extreme form of the eccentricities all of us have, or is there a fundamental difference between the disordered person and the normal one? If we believe there is such a gap, then we must expect

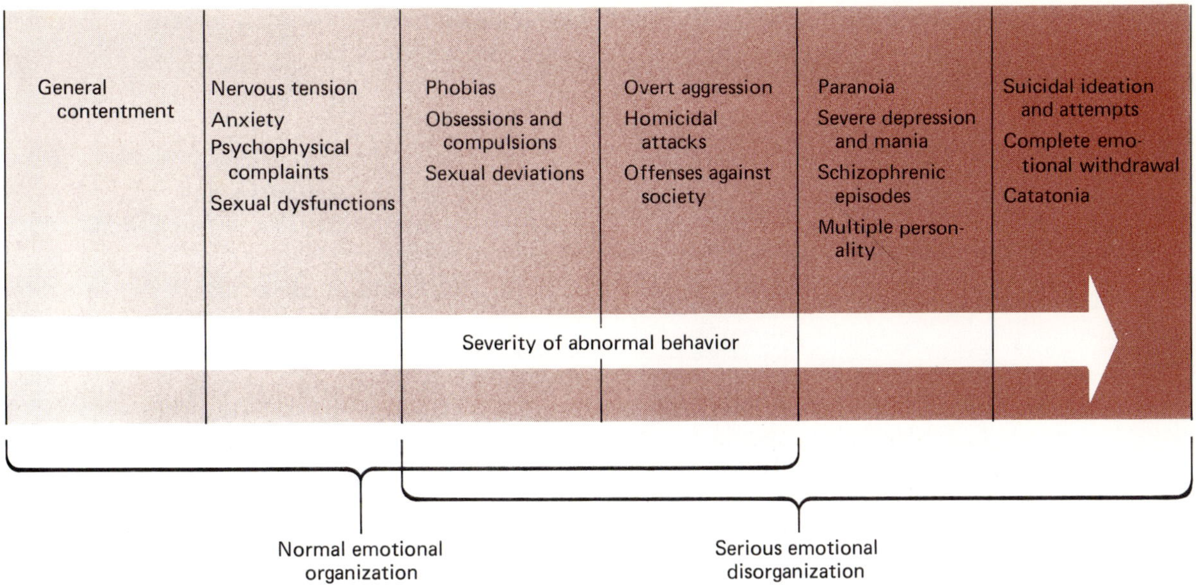

Figure 1.3. *The behavior continuum.*

to find fundamental differences in the mental and/or physiological processes underlying these two sets of behaviors. In contrast, if normal and abnormal are more accurately viewed as different positions on a **continuum of behavior,** then we can apply our understanding of normal behavior toward explaining the not-so-normal.

One way of answering this question is by working backward—looking first at what is considered normal. Most disorders, we find, do seem to fit with the same models psychologists use to explain normal behavior. For example, the mood swings that most of us experience are similar to the mood swings of manic-depression, though far less extreme. Most of those who study abnormal behavior believe that a thorough understanding of what causes normal mood swings will help to explain the manic-depressive syndrome. By the same token, identifying the factors underlying manic-depressive cycles should further our understanding of normal mood swings.

Also in support of the continuum theory is the fact that many of the symptoms of psychological disorder can be produced experimentally in otherwise normal people. For example, the loss of sensation that characterizes the conversion disorder can be produced by hypnosis (Hilgard, 1965). Similarly, hallucinations and depersonalization are common experiences for those who take certain drugs, such as LSD. While we do not fully understand the mechanisms that cause these symptoms, the fact that they occur both on their own and in the laboratory suggests that they are variants of normal behavior rather than unique to psychopathology. The prevailing view among psychologists is that psychological disorders are best seen as falling at one end of a continuum of behavior, with positive mental health at the other end. We can move step by step along this continuum from severe mental disturbance to limited personal distress to complete emotional satisfaction. Among the milder forms of disturbance might be the fear of flying that hampers an executive's travel schedule; the severe shyness that socially restricts a college student; the compulsion of a woman to wash her hands several times a day. Closer to the positive end is where most of us fall, though we tend to shift back and forth on the scale: sometimes shy or fearful, sometimes happy and confident.

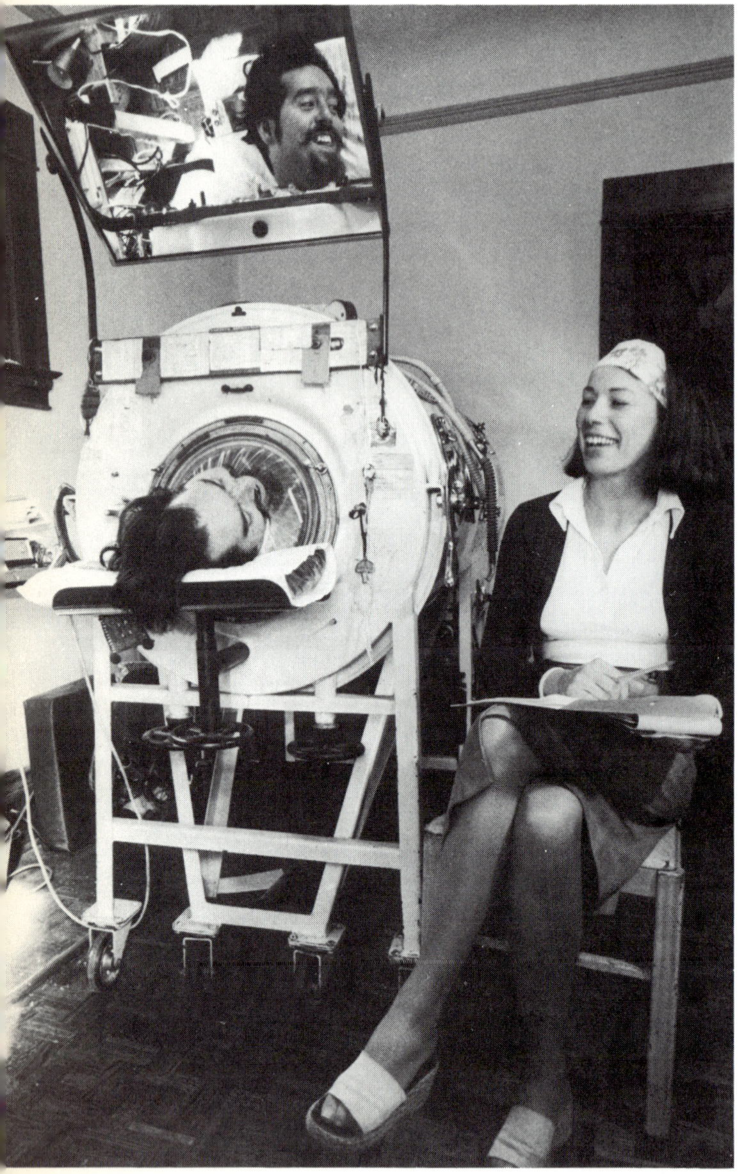

An outstanding example of an individual who rose beyond his physical limitations is Edward V. Roberts, appointed in 1975 as manager of California's Department of Rehabilitation. Roberts has been paralyzed for over twenty years and spends eleven hours a day in an iron lung. With the aid of an assistant, a special telephone, and a mirror, he has successfully coped with his handicap.

POSITIVE MENTAL HEALTH

Perhaps it seems strange to have a section on **positive mental health** in a book devoted to abnormal behavior. However, we have indicated that the definition of abnormal depends pretty much on the definition of normal—that is, *healthy*. We have also shown that societal definitions of normal and healthy are constantly changing, so it is almost as difficult to get a satisfactory definition of positive mental health as it is to define abnormal behavior. Nevertheless, several theorists have tried to establish exact standards for the positive end of the continuum, most of them agreeing that there are several necessary criteria, but agreeing less on just what the criteria are. Jahoda (1958), for instance, offers six:

1. Awareness, acceptance, and correctness of self-concept
2. Mastery of the environment and adequacy in meeting the demands of life
3. Integration and unity of personality
4. Autonomy and self-reliance
5. Perception of reality and social sensitivity
6. Continued growth toward self-actualization

According to this theory, a mentally healthy person should have a high degree of each characteristic; one or more deficiencies would indicate some degree of abnormality.

In a similar vein, Shoben (1957) sees positive mental health as a reflection of the unique human capacity for symbolization and social involvement. Specifically, Shoben lists:

1. The aptitude for capitalizing upon past experience
2. Self-control
3. The ability to envisage ideals
4. Social reliability
5. The capacity to act independently while still acknowledging the need for relationships with others

Close-up: *Mental Health Professionals*

In recent years, psychotherapy has become a rapidly expanding, diverse field that has given rise to a varied group of mental health entrepreneurs, each vigorously supporting a particular technique or method. While residents of rural areas may simply turn to a friend, a family doctor, or a clergyman for advice, urban dwellers may be confronted by a confusing array of options—ranging from astrologers and masseurs to social workers and psychiatrists.

Therapeutic approaches can be separated into three broad methods: those that examine the root of current psychological problems, those that emphasize modifying behavior rather than analyzing its causes, and those that seek to enhance personal growth, improve interpersonal interactions, and increase one's sense of well-being. Often, practitioners combine various methods. But, although techniques may overlap, it is important in choosing a therapist to clarify your own particular needs and to know the background and training of the professional you deal with.

Psychiatrists are medical doctors who have special training—including several years of residency training in a psychiatric hospital—in the diagnosis and treatment of mental disorders. They are licensed to prescribe medication and should be knowledgeable about mood-altering drugs and when to use them. Psychiatrists who specialize in Freudian theories and methods are often called psychoanalysts. In addition to their M.D. or Ph.D., they have spent several years studying psychoanalytical techniques and receiving in-depth analysis themselves.

Most clinical psychologists have a Ph.D. in psychology and have served a one-year internship in a psychiatric hospital or mental health center. Training has been geared to the diagnosis and treatment of mental disorders. In addition to administering and interpreting psychological tests, they may also be active in research. Although counseling psychologists usually have a Ph.D. in psychology, they tend to specialize in the treatment of problems that are not generally classified as mental disorders—for example, personal adjustment and marital conflict.

The professional social worker gains clinical experience in a mental health setting while earning a master's degree or doctorate. Special training in interviewing and information gathering may lead the social worker to go beyond face-to-face discussions with the individual patient to treatment programs for the family and community. The psychiatric nurse is yet another mental health professional. The requirements for such a position are an R.N. plus specialized training in the handling and treatment of mental patients.

People who need help should seek the expertise of the professional specializing in the area that applies to their specific problem. And, if the life crisis that impels them to seek help also clouds their decision-making ability, a good start might be a mental health or family service agency, a hotline, or a local hospital. Time commitment, money, and an affinity of temperament between therapist and patient are all important factors to consider. Unfortunately, there is no magic "cure," and many therapists and clients agree that the most effective treatment is the one that works best for the individuals involved.

Since definitions like these are extremely difficult to apply to particular behaviors, there is no reliable way to measure how much positive mental health an individual demonstrates at any given time. Researchers do agree, however, that good mental health is more than just freedom from dysfunction, personal distress, and illness. After all, most people encounter such problems at some point in their lives, but we would certainly not call them disturbed because of it. We agree with the theorists who say that in very general terms good mental health consists of two elements:

1. The ability to face and cope with our own limitations in meeting the demands of everyday life
2. A positive attitude toward ourselves and the world at large

These two elements are not all we need to keep us afloat during bad times. But they can go a long way in helping us maintain a peaceful sense of inner balance.

SUMMARY

Abnormal behavior is behavior that is markedly different from the behavior of most people in society. In addition, it impairs the individual's ability to function normally and is disturbing to others. Behaviors considered to be abnormal are usually maladaptive for the survival of the individual and often for the society in general. Through the process of socialization, we learn our society's norms, or standards of behavior, which help us differentiate between what our culture says is normal and abnormal.

The name we give to the people who have mental problems affects the way society responds to and treats those people. In turn, the way society feels about the issue affects the afflicted person's self-image and can greatly influence the course of recovery and even eventual rehabilitation and acceptance into mainstream society.

Although we prefer the psychological model of defining abnormal behavior, other models have been cited: the statistical, the biological, the disease, and the absolute. Currently, the disease model has a great deal of influence on how society treats mental problems. However, this and all the other models have major limitations. The field of abnormal psychology, which developed from all these different approaches, attempts to define, describe, explain, and manage the various forms of psychopathology.

Some psychologists argue that abnormality is a false concept. They contend that what we call insanity is simply an unorthodox way of coping with the problems and the stress of everyday living. Some theorists contend that madness is actually an essential process in rediscovering the true self, which has been buried beneath the masks that society makes us wear in order to succeed. An opposing idea is that abnormality does indeed exist and that it serves a purpose: to keep the rest of us in line and content to be normal.

Most theorists believe that abnormal behavior operates by the same natural laws governing normal behavior; understanding one will thus further our understanding of the other. Behavior is seen in terms of a continuum, with severe disturbance at one end and positive mental health at the other, the place where most of us fall, even though we may at times move around on the scale. Positive mental health is just as difficult to define as abnormality, but most psychologists agree that it includes more than mere freedom from disorder or personal distress.

CHAPTER 2

Classification and Assessment

In Chapter 1, we set the stage for our discussion of abnormal behavior by defining criteria and describing some general characteristics of psychopathology. This is a necessary first step because only when we share a common conception of this problem can we deal with it in any practical sense. However, simply stating that behavioral deviance is unusual, infrequent, and disturbing to those afflicted and to society—even setting precise limits on these characteristics—is not enough. Arnold, Elaine, and Tommy all behave abnormally but in very different ways. Obviously then, there are varying types or categories of abnormal behavior.

A classification system is quite helpful in obtaining the fullest knowledge possible about all the different forms of abnormality—and therefore about the very broad category of behavioral deviance itself. In fact, classification may even be essential, since most of the forms require different management methods. And, of course, if a problem is to be adequately treated, it must first be defined.

Once we have established a comprehensive classification scheme, the next step is to devise some sort of assessment techniques—that is, a way of determining the type of abnormal behavior present and how severely it is affecting the individual. The last point is important because the severity of certain disorders can also determine the treatment, as is the case with medical problems. A physician would not hospitalize a man with congested sinuses and a chest cough. However, if that man had congested sinuses, a chest cough, and a persistent high fever that did not respond to simple home treatment, hospitalization would probably be called for.

After the assessment has yielded the initial **diagnosis,** or identification of the problem and its severity, treatment (if there is to be any) may begin. Another factor of the assessment process is that each evaluation of a person's condition is regularly compared with the first assessment, which thus provides a way to measure both the person's progress and the adequacy of the management method being used.

The focus of this chapter will be on the classification and assessment of abnormal behavior. We will first discuss the historic development of reliable systems of categorization, concluding with the latest revision of the *Diagnostic and Statistical Manual* (III, 1980), which is considered to be the most comprehensive ever published. In the second half of the chapter, the most widely used assessment methods will be presented.

CLASSIFICATION SYSTEMS

The first step in any science is **classification**—that is, the organization of observations about various phenomena into some reasonably similar groups. Organizing data in this fashion allows for two things: communication and prediction. If we classify something or someone within a clearly defined category, then we have quickly communicated a good bit of information about that object or person simply by placing it there.

For example, if you say "I have a dog" to a person who shares your definition of dog, you have communicated a great deal of basic data. The other person knows that you are speaking of a domesticated animal of varying size that walks on all fours and eats meat. You could further classify your pet as an Irish setter, which would provide more specific data. Now your listener knows that your dog is fairly large (for dogs) and has long and silky reddish hair.

Obviously, classification makes things easier for us. We can provide maximum information with minimum output. But what if you had to describe a dog to someone who had never seen one and had no concept of how they looked or acted? And what if you had to constantly go through this same procedure for every subject, with every person you met? You can see how difficult it would be to try to communicate without the benefit of classification.

The second purpose of classifying data is prediction. An Irish setter, in addition to having certain characteristics that it shares with other dogs and some that are unique to its own breed, has a predictable life history. It will stay a setter and never become a beagle. Of course, some living things do undergo more-or-less complete metamorphosis, as for example, when caterpillars become butterflies. In these few cases, the change becomes an integral part of the classification scheme for that specific category. Consequently, when you refer to a caterpillar, your listener implicitly understands that you are speaking of a creature that changes its form.

Nevertheless, no classification scheme is perfect. We cannot make all of the correct predictions from a single classification. Classifying a whale as a mammal rather than as a fish imparts the information that it breathes air, has a self-regulating body temperature, and nurses its young, among other things. But we probably would not predict that it lives all its life in water, which is much more typical of fish. Still, a whale has more of the characteristics typically associated with other mammals than with fish, so the predictive advantages of classifying it as a mammal are greater. Therefore, although a good classification scheme can provide a clear description of the phenomenon (whether an animal or a behavior) in its present and future forms, the system may never be as complete as we would like. As William James, the noted American psychologist, once observed, "Most cases are mixed cases, and we should not treat our classifications with too much respect" (1902, p. 148).

Different Approaches

Throughout history, a number of different approaches to the classification of abnormal behavior have been suggested and attempted in order to heighten the quality of our communications and the accuracy of our predictions. The most popular approach has been based on *overt symptoms*—that is, the particular behaviors that warranted professional help. Since observable data are used, this kind of system would seem to be reliable, and would enable different observers to agree upon what had been observed and, therefore, on the category. Indeed, basing the category on clearly observable behaviors—the **empirical** approach—is traditional among the other sciences and is the most common approach used today. We will return to a more detailed analysis of this kind of categorization after examining some alternatives.

One alternative classification scheme involves using *known causes* of the behaviors. We could, for instance, have categories resulting from various factors: genetics, viral infections of the brain, traumatic brain injury, and so forth. Unfortunately, there are no explanations for most psychopathological conditions (Woodruff, Goodwin, and Guze, 1980). Woodruff and his colleagues further contend that once the etiology has been established the disorder is no longer regarded as psychopathological. When vitamin deficiency was clearly identified as the cause of certain behavioral disturbances, these became routine medical disorders to be treated by physicians, not by mental health specialists. When it was discovered that general paresis (a certain form of behavioral deviance) was linked to syphilis, this too became an "ordinary" medical problem. Some psychologists are convinced that some physical cause will eventually be discovered for all the psychopathological disorders, but as we noted earlier, we are still a long way from such a development.

Therefore it is simply not possible to routinely use an approach based on causes. At the same time, we do know or strongly suspect the etiology of some disorders, and this information is included in our current classification scheme. For example, the behavioral symptoms of organic mental disorders—confusion, disorganization, memory loss, irritability, and diminished energy—are common to many forms of psychopathology, but in this category the cause is physiological damage to the brain. Of course, this fact must be verified either by clear-cut historical data (if the person was in an accident, for example) or by medical laboratory evidence (from X rays, brain scans, electroencephalograms, etc.). Once verified, the diagnosis of organic mental disorder can be made. Thus the current classification scheme, while mainly based on overt symptoms, is not purely behavioral.

A second alternative classification scheme involves a *theoretical model of behavior,* which contrasts sharply with the empirical approach of the behavioral classification system. An example of such a model is Sigmund Freud's psychoanalytic theory (see page 74). Freud postulated that all individuals mature by stages—the oral, anal, phallic, latency, and genital stages of psychosexual development. However, maturation can be *fixated* (halted) during any stage; in fact, the particular stage at which a person is fixated determines the particular mental disorder that develops as a consequence. This type of classification scheme has many demands, including an in-depth understanding of psychoanalytic theory. A listing of observable characteristics must be made to sort people reliably into the various maturational levels. Despite the widespread popularity of Freud's model—and despite its enormous impact on our present theories—the reality is that it has not achieved that level of diagnostic reliability.

A third alternative to classification by overt behavior is to base the scheme on a *standardized task* or a *psychological test,* such as the one proposed by McLemore and Benjamin (1979), based on Leary's International Checklist (1957). Other diagnostic models, such as those based on the Minnesota Multiphasic Personality Inventory, have also been proposed. The score combinations on these tests are used to form individual psychological profiles, which are then grouped by similarity. In fact, evidence from empirical studies has consistently confirmed that individuals with similar profiles exhibit similar psychopathological behavior. Nonetheless, this particular approach is not popular because only psychologists who have had extensive experience with these diagnostic models and the instruments on which they are based can use this approach.

The drawbacks of these alternatives to a classification system based on overt symptoms are fundamental, making it even clearer why the empirical approach is predominant. Its scientific validity has been reaffirmed throughout history, in this and other areas of study, and it is today the most widely used and reliable system for categorizing the different psychopathological disorders. Knowing the historical development of our current system is an essential part of understanding why the new DSM is so important—and so controversial. The next section provides a brief summary of this history.

Historical Development of DSM-III

Classification systems are not something new. They go back to the time theorists first tried to understand the workings of nature and the actions of people, both individuals and groups. In fact, trying to fit things we don't understand into some orderly scheme could almost be called an innate human response; it just comes naturally to the species. Of course, as our knowledge has increased, the schemes we've devised have become much more sophisticated. Still, the very first attempts to distinguish the different types of abnormal behavior were quite an achievement.

Early categories

Hippocrates was the first to apply an empirical approach to the problem—more than 2000 years ago in Ancient Greece. He established three categories—*mania, melancholia,* and *phrenitis*—basing these on behavior he had actually witnessed during the close observation of his patients. Galen, a Roman physician, went on to distinguish various forms by etiology, in this case either physical or mental. These two individuals and others who followed gradually expanded the body of knowledge then in use. However, it was not until the late nineteenth century that a truly comprehensive system was attempted. In the intervening years—especially in the seventeenth century—many advances were made that profoundly affected that first system.

In the seventeenth century, a number of significant discoveries concerning the body's natural functioning sparked a keener interest

(a)

(b)

(c)

(d)

Following Hippocrates, some medieval scholars held that all human beings were composed of four humors, one of which was dominant and determined a person's emotional character. The humors were (a) sanguine (confident and cheerful), (b) melancholic (dejected, like the one-legged man), (c) choleric (hot-tempered), and (d) phlegmatic (apathetic, like the lazy fellow in bed).

in the then-young sciences of chemistry, anatomy, neurology, and medicine. In return, it was found that there was very often a simple organic cause behind physical illnesses, which led to more concerted (and more effective) efforts to cure problems. The success of this reasoning led many people to assume that, as it was with physical illness, so it must be with mental disorders. In this case, however, the pathology was assumed to be localized in the brain.

This may have fostered an interest in the brain that took hold at this time. There was a growing awareness that the brain has a critical role to play in every aspect of human functioning. We today are so accustomed to accepting the brain's importance as fact that it is difficult to believe this is a fairly recent realization. In 1757, Albrecht von Haller suggested that dissecting the brains of dead mental patients might provide clues about what had caused their disturbance. In 1845, William Griesinger presented the argument that all abnormal behavior was indeed caused by organic malfunction of the brain. But it was not until 1883 that one of Griesinger's students developed a systematic classification scheme that linked psychological problems with the organic diseased-brain model.

Kraepelin's classification system

Emil Kraepelin was the first to systematize the prevailing belief that behavioral disturbances should be regarded as diseases. Believing firmly in Griesinger's theory, Kraepelin wanted his system to validate that organic viewpoint. His central task was to describe and classify the various mental disturbances, the basis of his scheme being empirical—that is, it was based on overt behavior, since Kraepelin was naturally concerned with the reliability of his categories.

Emil Kraepelin, a German psychiatrist, believed behavioral disturbances were diseases and created a classification system based on overt behavior.

Many regard the work of Kraepelin as the start of the scientific age in understanding mental illness, and he is often termed the "father of modern psychiatry." Although others may disagree, the fact is that our current diagnostic scheme is a logical outgrowth of his early accomplishment: DSM-III is clearly based on Kraepelin's model. Specifically, Kraepelin's argument had two major points:

1. People should be sorted into groups based on similar observable symptoms or problematic behaviors.
2. Only those symptoms that occurred regularly, alone or in combination with others, and in a predictable sequence should be used.

Drawing from data he had collected, Kraepelin devised two primary categories that together accounted for roughly two thirds of all the patients then in mental hospitals: **manic-depressive psychosis** and **dementia praecox**.

Manic-depressive psychosis. This syndrome involved two opposite states: depression and mania, or elation. Using hospital records as well as empirical studies, Kraepelin observed that episodes of each of these states seemed to alternate in the same individual. Both states began abruptly, ended spontaneously, and were highly likely to recur. There was no progressive mental deterioration, however, nor was there any physiological pathology; both body and mind seemed to work normally, except for the mood states.

Dementia praecox. Kraepelin's name for this category signified its two major characteristics: *dementia,* complete mental deterioration, and *praecox,* onset at an early age, generally before the age of 25. Deterioration was steady, and the disorder was usually incurable. The final stage was not necessarily death, but rather the very lowest level of social and psychological functioning. And, as in the manic-depressive psychosis, physiological malfunction did not occur.

Kraepelin believed that his two diagnostic categories met the criteria of a useful classification scheme: They were fully descriptive and they aided in determining the **prognosis**, or final outcome. He further believed that, since the disorders had been identified, it would soon be possible to discover their causes. He himself had some ideas on the subject. He thought that manic-depressive psychosis probably resulted from a metabolism dysfunction; that dementia praecox was the result of a dysfunction of the sex glands. Despite his and countless other attempts to find specific etiologies for these two major disorders, to this day no exact cause has been identified for either problem. Nevertheless, Kraepelin's two categories are still as useful today as when he first developed them.

Support for Kraepelin's system received a boost in his own day. A series of independent medical discoveries undertaken about that same time linked the distinct psychological disorder known as general paresis to the organic disease syphilis. First, the distinguishing symptoms of general paresis were established; then those who exhibited these symptoms were grouped together according to Kraepelin's guidelines. Viennese psychiatrist Richard von Krafft-Ebing then made the conclusive experiment: He demonstrated that people with general paresis were immune to syphilis, which indicated that they had already been infected. Eventually, it was fully understood that general paresis was actually an advanced stage of the syphilitic infection of the central nervous system. Ultimately, a cure (penicillin) was discovered as well.

The beautiful simplicity of the general paresis case had another effect: It led most clinicians of that time to agree with Kraepelin that all mental disorders were essentially organic diseases. They were convinced that, with time, grouping people according to Kraepelin's scheme would lead to the discovery of both the organic cause and the organic cure for the full spectrum of mental illness. This belief in the disease model of psychopathology is an important factor in the development of both our current classification scheme and our present management techniques.

The validity of the disease model

It would be hard to overestimate the influence of Kraepelin's classification system. Today's most widely used diagnostic tool—the listing of all mental disorders that is published by the American Psychiatric Association—is based directly on his initial work. Indeed, although the several revisions of the DSM have all listed more than just two categories of disturbance, the similarities are still apparent:

1. Kraepelin's two categories, dementia praecox and manic-depression, although given new names (schizophrenia and the affective disorders), are still the most serious and frequently seen forms of disturbance.

2. The symptom patterns that he distinguished for these two groups have remained essentially unchanged.

3. New categories that were added as a result of our growing knowledge about psychopathology are still grouped by overt behavior, as Kraepelin advised.

4. Both categories classify mental disorders as a subset of organic disease—that is, they assume the validity of the disease model.

It would be equally hard to overestimate the influence of the disease model of approaching abnormal behavior, the model largely responsible for placing abnormal psychology within the jurisdiction of general medicine. The popular psychoanalytic theory proposed by Freud changed the emphasis of that perspective from the body in general to the mind in particular, but the underlying conviction of an organic cause was still indicated by the requirement, maintained today, that psychiatrists first obtain a medical degree and then specialize in mental disease, the way dermatologists specialize in diseases of the skin or ophthalmologists in disorders of the eye.

This bias toward a medical viewpoint brings up two rather controversial questions:

1. Is the disease model truly valid for understanding psychopathology?
2. Should the diagnosis and treatment of abnormal behavior be the more-or-less exclusive province of medicine?

These two issues are not a direct result of the DSM alone. As we noted in the previous chapter, the disease model received wide approval long before DSM-I was first developed in 1952. But the different versions of this classification system—especially the most recent—represent an approach that enlarges the role of medicine, as will be shown in our discussion of DSM-III.

The term mental illness reinforces the impression that abnormal behavior is a medical problem. It must be handled by a mental specialist, of course, but it is still a medical illness. However, in physiological illness there is always some underlying organic malfunction to account for the behavior that the ill person exhibits. Thus, when a child with a high fever complains of a very sore throat, it is highly possible that streptococcus bacteria will be found in a microscopic examination of the throat culture, a condition commonly called strep throat.

Unfortunately, the same formula cannot be applied to mental disorders, because there is no such corroborating physiological evidence. True, there is research, which will be detailed in later chapters, showing some clear links between certain forms of abnormal behavior and what appear to be breakdowns in the neurological functioning of the brain. But this is not true in every case—in fact, it's not true for the majority of cases. For most disorders, as we have said before, there is no clearly apparent cause. Therefore, although we do not wish to reject the disease model out of hand, we question its complete acceptance. We also question whether it is appropriate to place abnormal behavior within the realm of general medicine.

The Diagnostic and Statistical Manual

The first *Diagnostic and Statistical Manual of Mental Disorders* was published by the American Psychiatric Association in 1952. It and its two subsequent revisions (1968 and 1980) have been accepted by the World Health Organization as the official international classification system and are part of the WHO International Classification of Diseases. Clearly, they have proved to be useful. Nevertheless, as Woodruff, Goodwin, and Guze point out (1980), such diagnostic schemes are conventions and may not truly represent anything that exists in nature. They also remind us that there is no guarantee that our present mental or physical illnesses will consist of the same symptoms a hundred years from now. In fact, they believe that as we learn more about diseases, our future descriptions will be so much more accurate that they may not be recognizable to us today, but the categories will probably be much more effective. For now, the DSM occupies a central place in theory and practice—in hospitals and clinics, insurance companies and courtrooms, and, of course, in the study of psychopathology.

Why was it necessary to revise Kraepelin's original scheme? Indeed, if it was based on something as empirically sound as Kraepelin's system proved to be, why was it necessary to revise it twice in less than thirty years? The answer is poor reliability.

The problem of reliability. The value of any classification system can be judged by its **diagnostic reliability**—the likelihood that whatever behavior is exhibited by an individual will be correctly classified. Zubin (1967) suggested three methods to evaluate reliability:

1. Determine the likelihood that a number of different professionals would give the same diagnosis for the same person at the same time (*interjudge reliability*).
2. Determine the likelihood that, over time, the diagnosis given to an individual by one or more professionals would hold (*temporal reliability*).
3. Determine the likelihood that, over time, different professionals would classify large comparable groups of people who exhibited the same symptoms into the same categories.

We find serious problems in applying the last two methods, however. In the second, agreement between initial and subsequent diagnoses requires almost no change in the individual's behavior over time. This does sometimes occur, but certainly not in every case. In the third method, the clinician must assume that the groups of people have been taken from the same population, when in fact they have not been. Therefore the first evaluation method, finding the interjudge reliability, is really the only practical one.

According to any one of these three methods, however, the diagnostic reliability of DSM-I and DSM-II has been shown to be poor. Zubin (1967) reviewed several studies of the interjudge reliability of DSM-I and found that although agreement on major categories was reasonable there was little agreement on subgroup classification. For example, six out of ten clinicians might diagnose a patient as schizophrenic, but of those six, perhaps only two would agree on the specific type of schizophrenia exhibited.

Table 2.1
The DSM-II Classification

MENTAL RETARDATION

Borderline
Mild
Moderate
Severe
Profound
Unspecified
With each: Following or associated with
Infection or intoxication
Trauma or physical agent
Disorders of metabolism, growth or nutrition
Gross brain disease (postnatal)
Unknown prenatal influence
Chromosomal abnormality
Prematurity
Major psychiatric disorder
Psycho-social (environmental) deprivation
Other condition

ORGANIC BRAIN SYNDROMES (OBS)
A. PSYCHOTIC OBS

Senile and pre-senile dementia
Senile dementia
Pre-senile dementia

Alcoholic psychosis
Delirium tremens
Korsakov's psychosis
Other alcoholic hallucinosis
Alcohol paranoid state
Acute alcohol intoxication
Alcoholic deterioration
Pathological intoxication
Other alcoholic psychosis

Psychosis associated with intracranial infection
General paralysis
Syphilis of central nervous system
Epidemic encephalitis
Other and unspecified encephalitis
Other intracranial infection

Psychosis associated with other cerebral condition
Cerebral arteriosclerosis
Other cerebrovascular disturbance
Epilepsy
Intracranial neoplasm
Degenerative disease of the CNS
Brain trauma
Other cerebral condition

Psychosis associated with other physical condition
Endocrine disorder
Metabolic or nutritional disorder
Systemic infection
Drug or poison intoxication (other than alcohol)
Childbirth
Other and unspecified physical condition

B. NONPSYCHOTIC OBS

Intracranial infection
Alcohol (simple drunkenness)
Other drug, poison, or systemic intoxication
Brain trauma
Circulatory disturbance
Epilepsy
Disturbance of metabolism, growth or nutrition
Senile or pre-senile brain disease
Intracranial neoplasm
Degenerative disease of the CNS
Other physical condition

PSYCHOSES NOT ATTRIBUTED TO PHYSICAL CONDITIONS LISTED PREVIOUSLY

Schizophrenia
Simple
Hebephrenic
Catatonic
Catatonic type, excited
Catatonic type, withdrawn
Paranoid
Acute schizophrenic episode
Latent
Residual
Schizo-affective
Schizo-affective, excited
Schizo-affective, depressed
Childhood
Chronic undifferentiated
Other schizophrenic

Major affective disorders
Involutional melancholia
Manic-depressive illness, manic
Manic-depressive illness, depressed
Manic-depressive illness, circular
Manic-depressive, circular, manic
Manic-depressive, circular, depressed
Other major affective disorder

Paranoid states
Paranoia
Involutional paranoid state
Other paranoid state

In another interesting study (Kendall et al., 1971), comparison was made between diagnoses given by American, British, and Canadian psychiatrists, all using DSM-II as adopted by the World Health Organization. After viewing videotapes of the same set of patients, the professionals were asked to diagnose the problems they had seen. As suspected, there was little agreement among the many individual diagnoses, but there was another unexpected result:

Table 2.1 (continued)

Other psychoses
Psychotic depressive reaction

NEUROSES
Anxiety
Hysterical
Hysterical, conversion type
Hysterical, dissociative type
Phobic
Obessive compulsive
Depressive
Neurasthenic
Depersonalization
Hypochondriacal
Other neurosis

PERSONALITY DISORDERS AND CERTAIN OTHER NONPSYCHOTIC MENTAL DISORDERS

Personality disorders
Paranoid
Cyclothymic
Schizoid
Explosive
Obsessive compulsive
Hysterical
Asthenic
Antisocial
Passive-aggressive
Inadequate
Other specified types

Sexual deviation
Homosexuality
Fetishism
Pedophilia
Transvestism
Exhibitionism
Voyeurism
Sadism
Masochism
Other sexual deviation

Alcoholism
Episodic excessive drinking
Habitual excessive drinking
Alcohol addiction
Other alcoholism

Drug dependence
Opium, opium alkaloids and their derivatives
Synthetic analgesics with morphinelike effects
Barbiturates
Other hypnotics and sedatives or "tranquilizers"
Cocaine
Cannabis sativa (hashish, marihuana)
Other psycho-stimulants
Hallucinogens
Other drug dependence

PSYCHOPHYSIOLOGIC DISORDERS
Skin
Musculoskeletal
Respiratory
Cardiovascular
Hemic and lymphatic
Gastro-intestinal
Genito-urinary
Endocrine
Organ of special sense
Other type

SPECIAL SYMPTOMS
Speech disturbance
Specific learning disturbance
Tic
Other psychomotor disorder
Disorders of sleep
Feeding disturbance
Enuresis
Encopresis
Cephalalgia
Other special symptom

TRANSIENT SITUATIONAL DISTURBANCES
Adjustment reaction of infancy
Adjustment reaction of childhood
Adjustment reaction of adolescence
Adjustment reaction of adult life
Adjustment reaction of late life

BEHAVIOR DISORDERS OF CHILDHOOD AND ADOLESCENCE
Hyperkinetic reaction
Withdrawing reaction
Overanxious reaction
Runaway reaction
Unsocialized aggressive reaction
Group delinquent reaction
Other reaction

CONDITIONS WITHOUT MANIFEST PSYCHIATRIC DISORDER AND NONSPECIFIC CONDITIONS

Social maladjustment without manifest psychiatric disorder
Marital maladjustment
Social maladjustment
Occupational maladjustment
Dyssocial behavior
Other social maladjustment

Nonspecific conditions
Nonspecific conditions

No mental disorder
No mental disorder

Source: *Diagnostic and Statistical Manual of Mental Disorders.* 2nd ed. Washington, D.C.: American Psychiatric Association, 1968. Reprinted by permission of the American Psychiatric Association.

There were few differences in the diagnoses of psychiatrists grouped by nationality. For instance, in one case, only 2 percent of the British professionals diagnosed one person as schizophrenic, yet 69 percent of the American clinicians did so; the Canadian group fell somewhere between these two extremes. This indicates that the culturally different groups of professionals had defined certain behaviors in a similar fashion.

The difficulty of getting experts to agree on a diagnosis is illustrated by the case of convicted multiple murderer Ted Bundy, here conferring with his defense team in Miami in 1979. Prior to a previous trial, an examining team concluded Bundy was neither psychotic nor suffering from a personality disorder. But at the Florida trial, two psychiatrists testified he was a dangerous psychopath with a history of antisocial behavior.

In 1974, Spitzer and Fleiss gave their report on the diagnostic reliability of DSM-II. They found that reliability was never uniformly high for any single category but that three classifications had satisfactory reliability: mental deficiency, organic brain syndrome, and alcoholism. Spitzer and Fleiss also found that there had been no significant improvement in reliability since the first studies of the DSM had been run in the mid-1950s. They therefore concluded that DSM-II had not proved to be as helpful as had been hoped.

What was wrong with these two diagnostic aids? It was first thought to be mainly a problem of specificity: If more detailed descriptions of behavioral symptoms were supplied, more accurate diagnoses would result. Many assumed this meant adding more major categories to the list (which was done in revisions), even though the old categories had always had the best reliability. And although it was shown that the more detailed DSM-II did not increase reliability over DSM-I, specificity remained a primary objective.

.Another problem lies not with the DSM, but with a different part of the diagnostic process, the initial clinical interview. When an individual is first seen for a problem, the mental health professional usually asks several questions, which are designed to get the maximum information about that patient and the onset of the problem so that a diagnosis can be made. However, there is no standardized interview format for all clinicians to follow. Instead, each professional devises a very personal approach, and sometimes several different approaches. No two clinicians are likely to ask the same questions in the same order; therefore, it's not surprising that different conclusions are drawn.

There are a number of structured interview formats that could be used to get the initial diagnosis. The procedure is then quite ordered, with a set number of questions in a given sequence. Spitzer and Fleiss (1974) found that the diagnoses obtained by using standardized formats were more reliable than those obtained through the traditional, less formalized interview. However, most clinicians who have different backgrounds and attitudes still prefer to rely on their own personal approaches.

Blum (1978) reported on the pattern of initial diagnoses made in a single large psychiatric clinic from 1954 to 1974. Of eight categories selected for the study, five showed statistically significant changes. For example, during that period the number of male inpatients diagnosed as having an affective disorder increased from 7.4 percent to 21.9 percent. Meanwhile, the number diagnosed as neurotic showed an even greater change, decreasing from 25.2 percent to 4.5 percent. Yet Blum found that the symptoms exhibited in most of these cases were not drastically different, and the population base of the community had remained essentially the same. He therefore concluded that these dramatic differences in the way doctors diagnosed the same symptoms were the result of differences in the attitudes and viewpoints of the professional staff.

Specificity, lack of a standardized interview format, and variations in attitude on the part of the mental health professionals are probably not the only causes of low reliability. All of the factors underlying this problem with our most widely used diagnostic tool will probably never be identified. We feel that the outlook for higher reliability is not too bright—unless there is more agreement about the descriptions of the various categories, a standardized diagnostic procedure, and the development of clear-cut decision rules that do not rely so heavily upon the personal judgment of the clinician.

DSM-III

The developers of the latest revision of the DSM were quite aware of the limitations of the earlier versions. Therefore the task force that produced the final document was careful to be as comprehensive as possible—the hope being that this alone would increase the reliability of the diagnoses. Research on the effect of this new revision has, of course, only begun, so it will be a while before any results are available. However, the true test is not whether DSM-III will prove to be reliable in carefully controlled research studies, but rather whether it will prove reliable in everyday clinical practice.

Completed in 1980 after seven years of writing and two years of field trials, DSM-III has several features that mark it as unique. As just mentioned, its specificity is much greater than either of its predecessors. For example, it more than doubles the total number of listed disorders. DSM-III lists a total of 230; DSM-II listed only 100.

A multiaxial approach

One of the most striking changes in DSM-III is the development of what is termed a *multiaxial* approach to diagnosis. This means that each diagnosis requires information on five independent axes, or dimensions, which are designed to assist in classifying, in planning treatment, and in predicting the outcome. Rather than simply assigning an individual to a diagnostic category, five separate judgments, one on each axis, must be made about each individual. The five axes are:

- Axis I: Clinical psychiatric syndromes and other conditions
- Axis II: Personality disorders (adults) and specific developmental disorders (children and adolescents)
- Axis III: Physical disorders
- Axis IV: Severity of psychosocial stressor
- Axis V: Highest level of adaptive functioning during the past year

The disturbances traditionally included in previous editions of the DSM are now listed in Axes I and II. Axis I includes schizophrenia, the behavioral disturbances caused by brain dysfunction and by substance abuse, paranoia, the affective (emotional) disorders, the anxiety disorders, and several less prevalent conditions. Axis II lists the various adult personality disturbances and a variety of developmental problems, such as mental retardation and attention deficits.

The separation of the clinical syndromes into Axes I and II allows for the diagnosis of more than one problem in the same individual. For example, it is now possible to diagnose an individual as exhibiting depression (Axis I) and also as having a compulsive personality (Axis II). Previously, such dual diagnoses were so complicated to produce that most professionals avoided trying. Of course, the present rules do still allow for single axis decisions to be made.

Axis III identifies any current physical disorder (except for those that lead directly to a behavior disturbance) that could have a bearing on the abnormal behavior. Thus brain trauma and substance abuse are placed in Axis I, and such medical conditions as diabetes and physical deformities, which often play an important role in the development of a mental health problem, are placed in Axis III. It's also important to know of any physiological problems that may point out inappropriate treatments; for example, it may happen that a deeply depressed woman, who also has a large and disfiguring goiter that probably adversely affected her emotional state, may not be able to take certain

Table 2.2
A Short Form of the DSM-III Classification

DISORDERS USUALLY FIRST EVIDENT IN INFANCY, CHILDHOOD OR ADOLESCENCE

Mental retardation

Mild mental retardation
Moderate mental retardation
Severe mental retardation
Profound mental retardation
Unspecified mental retardation

Attention deficit disorder

with hyperactivity
without hyperactivity
residual type

Conduct disorder

undersocialized, aggressive
undersocialized, nonaggressive
socialized, aggressive
socialized nonaggressive
atypical

Anxiety disorders of childhood or adolescence

Separation anxiety disorder
Avoidant disorder of childhood or adolescence
Overanxious disorder

Other disorders of infancy, childhood or adolescence

Reactive attachment disorder of infancy
Schizoid disorder of childhood or adolescence
Elective mutism
Oppositional disorder
Identity disorder

Eating disorders

Anorexia nervosa
Bulimia
Pica
Rumination disorder of infancy
Atypical eating disorder

Stereotyped movement disorders

Transient tic disorder
Chronic motor tic disorder
Tourette's disorder
Atypical tic disorder
Atypical stereotyped movement disorder

Other disorders with physical manifestations

Stuttering
Functional enuresis
Functional encopresis
Sleepwalking disorder
Sleep terror disorder

Pervasive developmental disorders

Infantile autism
Childhood onset pervasive developmental disorder
Atypical

Specific developmental disorders

Developmental reading disorder
Developmental arithmetical disorder
Developmental language disorder
Developmental articulation disorder
Mixed specific developmental disorder
Atypical specific developmental disorder

ORGANIC MENTAL DISORDERS

Section 1. Organic mental disorders whose etiology or pathophysiological process is listed below

Dementias arising in the senium and presenium

Primary degenerative dementia, senile onset
with delirium
with delusions
with depression
uncomplicated
Primary degenerative dementia, pre-senile onset
Multi-infarct dementia

Substance-induced

Alcohol
intoxication
idiosyncratic intoxication
withdrawal
withdrawal delirium
hallucinosis
amnestic syndrome
dementia associated with alcoholism

Barbiturate or similarly acting sedative or hypnotic
intoxication
withdrawal
withdrawal delirium
amnestic syndrome

Opioid
intoxication
withdrawal

Cocaine
intoxication

Amphetamine or similarly acting sympathomimetic
intoxication
delirium
delusional syndrome
withdrawal

Phencyclidine (PCP) or similarly acting arylcyclohexylamine
intoxication
delirium
mixed organic mental disorders

Hallucinogen
hallucinosis
delusional disorder
affective disorder

Cannabis
intoxication
delusional disorder

Tobacco
withdrawal

Caffeine
intoxication

Other or unspecified substance
intoxication
withdrawal
delirium
dementia

Table 2.2 (continued)

amnestic disorder
delusional disorder
hallucinosis
affective disorder
personality disorder
atypical or mixed organic mental disorder

Section 2. Organic brain syndromes whose etiology or pathophysiological process is either noted as an additional diagnosis or is unknown

Delirium
Dementia
Amnestic syndrome
Organic delusional syndrome
Organic hallucinosis
Organic affective syndrome
Organic personality syndrome
Atypical or mixed organic brain syndrome

SUBSTANCE USE DISORDERS

Alcohol abuse
Alcohol dependence (Alcoholism)
Barbiturate or similarly acting sedative or hypnotic abuse
Barbiturate or similarly acting sedative or hypnotic dependence
Opioid abuse
Opioid dependence
Cocaine abuse
Amphetamine or similarly acting sympathomimetic abuse
Amphetamine or similarly acting sympathomimetic dependence
Phencyclidine (PCP) or similarly acting arylcyclohexylamine abuse
Hallucinogen abuse
Cannabis abuse
Cannabis dependence
Tobacco dependence
Other, mixed or unspecified substance abuse
Other specified substance dependence
Unspecified substance dependence
Dependence on combination of opioid and other non-alcoholic substance
Dependence on combination of substances, excluding opioids and alcohol

SCHIZOPHRENIC DISORDERS

Schizophrenia
disorganized
catatonic
paranoid
undifferentiated
residual

PARANOID DISORDERS

Paranoia
Shared paranoid disorder
Acute paranoid disorder
Atypical paranoid disorder

PSYCHOTIC DISORDERS NOT ELSEWHERE CLASSIFIED

Schizophreniform disorder
Brief reactive psychosis
Schizoaffective disorder
Atypical psychosis

AFFECTIVE DISORDERS

Major affective disorders

Bipolar disorder
mixed
manic
depressed
Major depression
single episode
recurrent

Other specific affective disorders

Cyclothymic disorder
Dysthymic disorder

Atypical affective disorders

Atypical bipolar disorder
Atypical depression

ANXIETY DISORDERS

Phobic disorders

Agoraphobia with panic attacks
Agoraphobia without panic attacks
Social phobia
Simple phobia

Anxiety states

Panic disorder
Generalized anxiety disorder
Obsessive compulsive disorder

Post-traumatic stress disorder

acute
chronic or delayed

Atypical anxiety disorder

SOMATOFORM DISORDERS

Somatization disorder
Conversion disorder
Psychogenic pain disorder
Hypochondriasis
Atypical somatoform disorder

DISSOCIATIVE DISORDERS

Psychogenic amnesia
Psychogenic fugue
Multiple personality
Depersonalization disorder
Atypical dissociative disorder

PSYCHOSEXUAL DISORDERS

Gender identity disorders

Transsexualism
Gender identity disorder of childhood
Atypical gender identity disorder

Paraphilias

Fetishism
Transvestism
Zoophilia
Pedophilia
Exhibitionism
Voyeurism
Sexual masochism
Sexual sadism
Atypical paraphilia

Table 2.2 (continued)

Psychosexual dysfunctions
Inhibited sexual desire
Inhibited sexual excitement
Inhibited female orgasm
Inhibited male orgasm
Premature ejaculation
Functional dyspareunia
Functional vaginismus
Atypical psychosexual dysfunction

Other psychosexual disorders
Ego-dystonic homosexuality
Psychosexual disorder not elsewhere classified

FACTITIOUS DISORDERS
Factitious disorder with psychological symptoms
Chronic factitious disorder with physical symptoms
Atypical factitious disorder with physical symptoms

DISORDERS OF IMPULSE CONTROL NOT ELSEWHERE CLASSIFIED
Pathological gambling
Kleptomania
Pyromania
Intermittent explosive disorder
Isolated explosive disorder
Atypical impulse control disorder

ADJUSTMENT DISORDER
with depressed mood
with anxious mood
with mixed emotional features
with disturbance of conduct
with mixed disturbance of emotions and conduct
with work (or academic) inhibition
with withdrawal
with atypical features

PSYCHOLOGICAL FACTORS AFFECTING PHYSICAL CONDITION
Psychological factors affecting physical condition

PERSONALITY DISORDERS
Paranoid
Schizoid
Schizotypal
Histrionic
Narcissistic
Antisocial
Borderline
Avoidant
Dependent
Compulsive
Passive-Aggressive
Atypical, mixed or other personality disorder

CONDITIONS NOT ATTRIBUTABLE TO A MENTAL DISORDER
Malingering
Borderline intellectual functioning
Adult antisocial behavior
Childhood or adolescent antisocial behavior
Academic problem
Occupational problem
Uncomplicated bereavement
Noncompliance with medical treatment
Phase of life problem or other life circumstance problem
Marital problem
Parent-child problem
Other specified family circumstances
Other interpersonal problem

Source: *Diagnostic and Statistical Manual of Mental Disorders.* 3rd ed. Washington, D.C.: American Psychiatric Association, 1980. Reprinted by permission of the American Psychiatric Association.

drugs proved effective against depression because they may also inflame her goiter.

Axis IV is used to determine any significant social and psychological factors that may have instigated or intensified the problem behavior. In most cases, there must be rather clear-cut evidence that these factors were operating during the past year, although they can be future rather than present events. For instance, knowing that retirement will soon occur can be seen as a psychosocial stressor, even though it has not yet occurred. In judging the severity of these stressors, the clinicians use their own idea of what an average person from a similar background would experience under the same circumstances. In addition, the developers of DSM-III have issued a list of guidelines that can be followed. But it must be recognized that reactions to stressors are highly individual. Going away to college may not be stressful for most people, but it may be highly stressful for some and thus contribute to a major disturbance. In judging psychosocial stress, DSM-III suggests examining the following areas:

Conjugal (marital and nonmarital): engagement, marriage, divorce

Parenting: becoming a parent, illness of a child, problems with a child

General interpersonal: problems with friends, neighbors, fellow employees

Occupational: problems at work, school, in homemaking, in retirement

Living circumstances: changes in residence, geographical changes, homelessness

Financial: inadequate finances, changes in financial circumstances

Legal: arrest, involvement in a lawsuit, imprisonment

Developmental: poor adjustment to puberty, midlife crisis, menopause

Physical illness or injury: illness, accident, surgery

Other psychosocial stressors: natural disasters, war, persecution, rape

Note that if there is a physical illness or injury, its psychological impact on the individual's personality, not its overall impact on functioning,

Sensitive to his dwarfish stature, famed impressionist painter Toulouse-Lautrec channeled his frustrations creatively. Many of his works depict other outcasts of Parisian society.

is listed on Axis IV. Its impact on overall functioning is included on Axis III. Obviously, there will be many cases in which a physical illness or injury will be included on both.

This listing is valuable not only for understanding DSM-III, but also for getting an overview of what society currently regards as critical social and psychological stressors. Since many of these stressors act together, DSM-III suggests that not more than four be included in any given diagnosis, and these should be rank-ordered in importance.

The amount of stress experienced by the individual is rated on a seven-point scale, ranging from 1 (no apparent psychosocial stress) to 7 (a catastrophic level). There is also a rating of 0 for cases in which data on stress is unavailable. An important way Axis IV data can be used is to locate the stressors that may have precipitated the disturbance so that they can be removed and avoided in the future.

Axis V calls for a judgment of the individual's highest level of adaptive functioning during the past year. For DSM-III, adaptive functioning involves three areas of human life: social relationships, occupational performance, and use of leisure time. In rating the level of functioning in these three areas, both the range of activities and their quality need to be considered. Most clinicians would give somewhat greater weight to social relationships because of their strong influence on prognosis. These ratings are on a six-point scale, ranging from 1, superior adaptive functioning, to 6, grossly impaired adaptive functioning; again, a rating of 0 indicates that no information was available.

Applying the multiaxial system

We opened this book with a description of three people who exhibited distinct forms of abnormal behavior—Arnold, schizophrenic; Elaine, depressed; and Tommy, autistic. To illustrate how DSM-III is applied in clinical practice, we will evaluate these three cases using this system.

Arnold. A clinician would probably determine the following about Arnold:

Axis I: Residual schizophrenia, chronic*
Axis II: Disturbance limited to Axis I
Axis III: No physical disorders
Axis IV: No apparent psychosocial stress
Axis V: Fair level of adaptive functioning during the past year (4)

Residual schizophrenia is a term for a controlled condition of the disorder. It means that, at some previous time, Arnold was very definitely out of touch with the real world (schizophrenia), but now is more able to function normally (residual, in remission). However, his condition is permanent (chronic). Axes II, III, and IV list no problems, which indicates that the major difficulty is the schizophrenia. Axis V states that he's doing fairly well at coping with life, a fact we know from the description of his case at the beginning of Chapter 1. He holds a job and keeps his appointments, but his social relationships are very inadequate. Clearly, a good bit of Arnold's present behavior, his ordinary pattern of social interactions, and his current level of functioning are rather well described by this categorical scheme.

Elaine. If Ralph were to finally get her to a clinician, her diagnosis might be the following:

Axis I: Major depressive disorder, severe
Axis II: Disturbance limited to Axis I
Axis III: No physical disorder
Axis IV: Minimal psychosocial stress—early stages of menopause (2)
Axis V: Grossly impaired level of adaptive functioning during the past year (6)

These data indicate that Elaine is uncommunicative, feels hopeless, and is apparently absorbed in some inner torment. Like Arnold, she has no problems to be listed on Axes II and III. The minimal psychosocial stressor referred to (menopause), although often implicated in depression in women, is not a known cause, and it's hard to see the connection between the first

* Axes I and II identify each disorder by a code number, which is used primarily for statistical analysis and record keeping; we have deleted them here.

beginnings of menopause and a depression of this order. Her symptoms are so severe, in fact, that within the past year her adaptive functioning dropped from superior to grossly impaired.

Tommy. Tommy's clinical profile would probably read like this:

Axis I: Infantile autism
Axis II: Developmental language disorder
Axis III: No physical disorder
Axis IV: No apparent evidence of psychosocial stress (1)
Axis V: Grossly impaired level of adaptive functioning during the past year (6)

From this we learn that Tommy is not responsive to other people, cannot communicate verbally, and in general behaves in a very strange manner, all of which developed before he was 30 months old. Tommy seems off in a world of his own, unable—but more than that, unwilling—to interact with people. His family members feel like strangers—until a real stranger enters Tommy's territory. Then his behavior proves that his cold and oblivious attitude is reserved for those he knows and values. No stressor or physical injury or defect has been found that could have initiated his bizarre behavior. Autism, by definition an extremely debilitating disorder, means that his adaptive functioning is very low.

These three cases were not selected with the DSM-III classification scheme in mind, but because they are straightforward examples of the people seen in ordinary clinical practice. Most cases are not as easy to diagnose or as simple as these, however; for many people, there are problems on both Axis I and Axis II, or a physical disability, or (especially) at least one stressor. Nevertheless, the DSM-III categories are highly descriptive of these three, and we would naturally assume that if they are indeed reasonably typical cases, the DSM-III classification will do an equally good job of prediction. Of course, not every case will fit a common pattern, no matter how detailed the scheme or complete the data, but this should not detract from the overall usefulness of the classification system—unless it develops that there are many such cases. However, the comprehensiveness of DSM-III and its development as a working tool make this possibility unlikely.

Emphasis on behavior

Another unique feature of DSM-III is its emphasis on behavior. For each of the 230 categories, the system lists the symptom syndrome, all the various behaviors currently known to be associated with the disorder, dividing them into three groups:

1. **Essential features**—the behaviors that distinguish the disorder
2. **Associated features**—the behaviors that are usually, but not always, present
3. **Diagnostic criteria**—the behaviors that *must* be present for the disorder to be diagnosed

Each section also contains information on how to distinguish between disorders that have very similar symptom clusters—that is, information on how to arrive at a **differential diagnosis**. Also present is a description of other elements of a typical case: usual age of onset, general course of the disorder, degree of impairment, factors that lead to greater susceptibility, prevalence of the disorder, genetic risk factors (whether it seems to run in families). Although causes are mentioned if they are known, speculations about etiology are not present.

The developers of DSM believe that giving comprehensive and detailed descriptions of the behavioral clusters is a much fairer and surer way of classifying the disorders and one that can't help but improve the reliability of the manual. Although, as we stated, this has yet to be proved, it does seem likely. However, the emphasis on behavior also led to other departures from the earlier versions, some of which are as controversial as the removal of homosexuality from the list of disorders.

The neurosis issue. One of these changes—probably for the better—is that the term **neu-**

rosis has been removed from the classification. DSM-II listed a wide range of problems under the heading of Neurotic Disorders. DSM-III dropped the heading—deciding that it implied a psychological cause that had never been validated. According to Freud, who coined the term, neurosis was caused by a build-up of anxiety, which was itself created by the repression of strong desires.

It is unfortunate that the term neurotic previously held such an important place in the psychological terminology. The term was such a common one among the general population that it may be hard for people to stop using it. We suspect that even professionals will have difficulty deleting it from their vocabulary.

New disorders. The addition of a number of new developmental disorders under Axis II is a move that we feel is not nearly as well justified. We doubt that the problems belong there; in fact, we question the assumption that they are mental disorders at all.

At issue are such listings as Specific Reading Disorder, Specific Arithmetical Disorder, Separation Anxiety Disorder, and Shyness Disorder, to name a few. Clearly, some children and youths do have serious problems in these areas. However, more often than not these are temporary problems experienced by many—if not most—children at some point in their maturation process. Why have they been included?

Since all the developmental disorders involve thought, it could be argued that psychological dysfunction may be to blame, which therefore qualifies these problems for inclusion. But is this a logical progression? If it is, then not knowing how to speak French fluently after several years of study also qualifies. But we certainly would not—and should not—call it a disorder. As it is now, children who experience difficulties in these areas—and few children will not—stand a good chance of being diagnosed as mentally disturbed.

In this case, we feel that DSM-III has inappropriately followed the statistical approach to defining abnormal behavior that we discussed in Chapter 1. The publication actually goes so far as to point out that any unacceptable condition that can be described clearly and distinctly may be included as a disorder if a significant number of people have that condition. The reasons behind this policy statement are at once admirable and frightening, and so are its possible implications.

Mental illness and social policy

A consideration that motivated this move toward a statistical approach was essentially pragmatic in nature. It was an attempt to maximize the ability of mental health professionals to help people and still prosper within our social system. If a problematic behavior is officially listed as a mental disorder, the problem will be covered by insurance. Even Medicaid and Medicare will pay for treatment—if the problem is officially listed as one. On the surface, this seems to help the general public. If the statistical approach is used, more and more unwanted behaviors will be defined as disorders, and more and more problems will be treated at no extra cost to the sufferer. There are at least two frightening implications, however:

1. People will have to pay another price for their inexpensive treatment: being labeled as mentally disturbed.
2. Trouble will almost certainly arise from the issue of who gets to decide which behaviors are included.

Labeling. We mentioned in Chapter 1 that labeling can be a problem in and of itself. When discussing mental illness, there is a whole spectrum of social reactions to consider. Admittedly, our society is today much more accepting than it used to be, but that really isn't saying much. People are just as likely as they ever were to react negatively to the label of mentally ill; they just may not react as openly as in the past.

Labeling has a definite effect on the person labeled. First of all, being labeled abnormal is like having a license to act peculiarly. Everybody expects strange behavior from someone who is labeled as strange, so why disappoint them? This brings up a second point: How much of

Moondog—eccentric poet, itinerant musician, and colorful vagabond—enjoyed a brief period of popularity during the psychedelic sixties. To what degree might his strange behavior have been encouraged by the counterculture?

the strange behavior is a true manifestation of a psychological problem, and how much has been learned from interactions with people who expect weirdness?

As we stated earlier, Szasz (1960) is an outspoken critic of labeling. He prefers to view mental disorders as behaviors arising from problems in living: Many people have serious problems in everyday life; some people, for whatever reasons, have less ability to cope with them. Szasz feels that the concept of mental illness is a myth that has been perpetuated by mental health professionals simply to maintain their own power. He goes on to suggest the political uses of labeling that are possible, and the case of Zhores Medvedev (see Close-up, page 44) indicates that his ideas are not without basis. Indeed, we can see the interaction of mental illness and politics to a lesser degree here in the United States.

Lobbying. In 1976, the American Psychiatric Association voted to remove homosexuality from the list of psychological disorders. This action was motivated in part by a general belief that homosexuality was not a mental problem but merely a sexual variant. Twenty years ago that belief would never have been accepted, but in light of today's different norms it was seen as valid, at least by the majority of psychologists who voted. Perhaps another factor may well have been the fact that homosexuals, as a united group, exerted enough influence themselves—much like lobbyists—to have the DSM changed.

Sometimes, the degree to which a behavior disturbs others—or the number of people who are disturbed—can be the true determining factor in whether an act will be considered abnormal. If that act is in any way personally debilitating or harmful, the case against it is strengthened. This suggests amazing possibilities: What if teetotalers lobbied to have all alcoholic consumption listed as a disorder? After all, it's an indisputable fact that excessive drinking is harmful, but you can't drink to excess if you never drink. You may scoff at such a possibility, but DSM-III already lists tobacco dependence as a disorder. It's unlikely that a heartless husband could ever get his chain-smoking wife "put away" for her habit, but now he can give it a try.

Close-up: Repression by Psychiatry

On the afternoon of May 29, 1970, three Soviet police officers and two psychiatrists forcibly entered the home of biochemist Zhores Medvedev, badgered him with questions about his nerves for a few hours, and then, while his wife, younger son, and several colleagues watched helplessly, dragged him out of his house into a waiting car. Medvedev was taken to a small, provincial mental hospital where a panel of professionals who had never before seen him diagnosed him as an "incipient schizophrenic" with "paranoid delusions of reforming society." He was then admitted as a patient for psychiatric treatment.

Medvedev's particular form of "insanity" can be easily explained. A scientific paper that he had written eight years earlier had recently been published by Columbia University Press in New York. The paper refuted the work of a once-eminent, pro-Stalinist geneticist in Russia, a man who still held enough power to exact retribution for this "insult." He was presently writing another paper focusing on the difficulties of sharing information within the worldwide scientific community. Both publications were enough for the psychiatric panel to declare him clearly "dangerous" to himself and to others.

However, in its eagerness to eliminate Medvedev and whatever threat he might personify, the Soviet government underestimated the response of its own academic leaders as well as those of other countries. Medvedev's twin brother Roy rallied support within Russia from the likes of Andrei Sakharov, the father of the Soviet H-bomb, and Nobel Prize winning novelist Alexander Solzhenitsyn. It wasn't long before word of Medvedev's plight was spread among scientists and academics around the world.

Confronted with the possibility of an extremely embarrassing international incident, the Soviet government suddenly did an about-face: Three weeks after Medvedev's admission to the psychiatric hospital, he was suddenly and very quietly released. Asked not to reveal what had taken place inside the institution, Medvedev nevertheless decided to tell the world his story. He and his brother together wrote an account of those fearful weeks entitled *A Question of Madness,* which was published in London in 1971 while they were still in Russia.

It will clearly take time to determine whether the apparent advantages of DSM-III outweigh its apparent disadvantages. On the whole, it seems to be an improvement over past versions, and the flaws we've pointed to could be eliminated with relative ease. Nonetheless, the real proof will be its diagnostic reliability in everyday clinical practice. But remember that there is more involved in the initial diagnosis than merely placing the behavioral symptoms that an individual presents into their proper category. Even though DSM-III's multiaxial system seems to cover all the bases—psychological disorder, physical problems, social stress, adaptive functioning—it's sometimes a good idea to supplement this information in order to get as complete a picture as possible about the individual and the various problems involved. In order to achieve this end, many psychologists also use a number of techniques to help determine the true psychological state of those people who come to them for professional help. These various assessment techniques will be presented next.

ASSESSMENT TECHNIQUES

Assessment is the term used to describe what goes on in a clinician's office that enables the diagnosis of problems. Through assessment, the clinician should be able to classify a problem, determine how severe it is, and decide how to deal with it in the most effective way. As we mentioned earlier, DSM-III has tried to make this process easier and more accurate by listing diagnostic criteria for each disorder. Theoretically, the clinician would simply try to match the presenting signs (that is, the client's problematic behaviors) with the diagnostic criteria for disorders listed in the manual.

It's not that simple, however. Few cases ever match perfectly. Therefore the clinician must also rely on personal judgments of how the client responds. This involves interpretations of the client's behavior, which again lead to possible problems in reliability. Nevertheless, the completeness of the DSM-III listings should help mitigate this problem.

The process generally begins with a rather lengthy interview, during which the psychologist tries to get a maximum amount of data about the client. From there, the client may be asked to take a psychological test, of which there are several types. Many college students may be familiar with the type that evaluates a person's career interests and aptitudes. The psychological tests most often used to diagnose abnormal behavior fall into three categories: (1) personality tests, (2) intelligence tests, and (3) tests for neurological impairment. Sometimes, the clinician will also request a full physiological examination.

The Initial Interview

The initial interview is probably the oldest and most widely used assessment technique, and still a very valuable one. It is basically a conversation with a purpose—ascertaining the problem. The interview can be structured, following a tested format of specific questions asked in a certain order, with guidelines for rating the person's responses; or it can be unstructured, as is usually the case. In an unstructured interview, the clinician may simply ask questions spontaneously, or perhaps let the client do most of the talking, under the assumption that important points will surface naturally if the client takes the lead. Some clinicians may follow a set format of questioning that they have devised themselves—a sort of semistructured interview—but only field-tested formats are considered to be truly structured. As we mentioned earlier, structured formats do seem to improve interjudge reliability.

There are three types of interview: *intake, case history,* and *therapeutic.* An intake interview is an initial meeting between client and therapist, its purpose being to find out the client's immediate history—that is, what led to the appointment. Case history interviews work toward getting a picture of the person's life span. The clinician tries to get an overview of the distant as well as the recent past. Therapeutic interviews are the periodic treatment sessions that are subsequently scheduled to try to root out the problem. We will discuss only intake and case history interviews in this chapter; treatment will be discussed in Chapter 4.

The interview is usually conducted with just the therapist and the client present; sometimes another member of the client's family may join in, especially if the client is a child. The therapist will try to get as much information as possible in one session, but often one or more sessions are necessary before the diagnosis can be made.

The information that the psychologist asks for is covered in the following list:

1. Identifying data—name, age, sex, marital status
2. Present problems—the problematic behavior
3. Family history—relationships with family members and any history of physical or mental illness
4. Education—highest level attained
5. Medical history—present and past states of health
6. Occupational record—career stability and interests
7. Sexual history—kind and frequency of intimate relationships
8. Social relations—quality of friendships

Table 2.3 *A Sample from the Current and Past Psychopathology Scales*

The left column lists questions to ask; the right column gives scoring criteria.

INTERVIEW GUIDE	SCALES
Original Complaint *If a psychiatric patient:* Now I would like to hear about your problems or difficulties and how they led to your coming to the (hospital, clinic).	*The time period for this section is the past month.*
General Condition Tell me how you have been feeling recently. (Anything else been bothering you?)	
Physical Health How is your physical condition? Does any part of your body give you trouble? Do you worry much about your health?	**Physical Health** 214 **Somatic Concerns** Excessive concern with bodily functions; preoccupation with one or more real or imagined physical complaints or disabilities; bizarre or unrealistic feelings or beliefs about body or parts of body. *Do not include mere dissatisfaction with appearance.* ? 1 2 3 4 5 6
If necessary, inquire for doctor's opinion about symptoms or illnesses. When you are upset do you react physically . . . like [stomach trouble, diarrhea, headaches, sick feelings, dizziness]?	215 **Conversion Reaction** Has a motor or sensory dysfunction which conforms to the lay notion of neurological illness, for which his doctors can find no organic basis (e.g., paralysis or anesthesia). ? 1 2 3 4 5 6
	216 **Psychophysiological Reactions** Is bothered by one or more psychophysiological reactions to stress. Examples: backache, headaches, hypertension, dizziness, asthma, spastic bowel. *Note: the reaction may or may not involve structural change.* ? 1 2 3 4 5 6

If the client is a child, the clinician will ask the parent about the child's developmental history—for example, if the formative physical and social growth stages were unusually rough for the child.

As we mentioned earlier, a structured interview has been shown to be of great help in obtaining the initial diagnosis and securing interjudge reliability (Helzer et al., 1977). Such formats list specific questions in a set sequence and give precise ratings for the answers. Two examples are the Brief Psychiatric Rating Scale and the Current and Past Psychopathology Scales; the latter, which was developed by Spitzer and Endicott in 1971, has even been adapted for use with computers.

Table 2.3 (continued)

INTERVIEW GUIDE	SCALES
Appetite-Sleep-Fatigue *Disturbances in these areas are often associated with Depression, Anxiety, or Somatic Concerns.* What about your appetite for food? Do you have any trouble sleeping or getting to sleep? (Why is that?) How easily do you get tired?	
Mood *This section covers several moods. The interviewer must determine to what extent the symptoms are associated with either one or the other or several of the dimensions.* What kinds of moods have you been in recently?	**Mood** 217 **Elated Mood** Exhibits or speaks of an elevated mood, exaggerated sense of well being or optimism, or feelings of elation. Examples: Says "everything is great," jokes, witticisms, silly remarks, singing, laughing, or trying to get others to laugh or smile. ? 1 2 3 4 5 6
What kinds of things do you worry about? (How much do you worry?) What kinds of fears do you have? (Any situation . . . activities . . . things?) How often do you feel anxious or tense? (When you are this way, do you react physically . . . like sweating, dizziness, cramps?)	218 **Anxiety** Remarks indicate feelings of apprehension, worry, anxiety, nervousness, tension, fearfulness, or panic. When clearly associated with any of these feelings, consider insomnia, restlessness, physical symptoms (e.g., palpitations, sweating, dizziness, cramps), or difficulty concentrating, etc. ? 1 2 3 4 5 6

Source: R. L. Spitzer and J. Endicott. *Current and Past Psychopathology Scales* (New York: New York State Psychiatric Institute and Biometrics Research, 1968). Reprinted by permission.

Observation

While the question-and-answer session is in progress, or while the person is being tested, the psychologist also tries to glean clues from observations of how the client behaves during the interview. The questions asked in the interview elicit information about the past and present; the behavior exhibited by the client while in the clinician's office directly reflects the present. A sloppy appearance, incoherent speech, or extreme sadness or nervousness, for example, is indicative of the kind of problem afflicting the individual.

In a way, the interview is a form of *situational observation:* The clinician can look at the entire interview session as a test to which the

(a) 

(a) A clinical psychologist administering a Thematic Apperception Test. (b) A psychologist giving a Rorschach Test to a college student. (c) A typical entry from the Children's Apperception Test, designed to help the therapist understand a child's significant relationships and emotions. The subject is asked to create a story based on the picture.

person responds. Therefore the behavior exhibited during the session is just as important as the answers to the interview questions or to any tests that may be given. The clinician can also exert different degrees of control over this situation by determining the setting. There are three basic settings:

1. *Natural*—The clinician and client sit down together and discuss the important points. Some clinicians have the client's family present as well, feeling that their interactions may have a bearing on the client's problem.

2. *Contrived*—The clinician exerts more control in this situation by setting up a specific environment in which the client responds. This is the basis for play therapy, in which children are put in a toy-filled room and their actions are observed.

3. *Laboratory*—Obviously, this is the most controlled situation, but it is used little for individual assessment.

The clinician can also call on others to help in observation. Parents of a child, for instance, can be asked to observe the child's behavior in spe-

(b/c)

cific situations at home. The clients themselves can be requested to keep track of all their different actions and feelings for a specified period of time. All such reports add to the psychologist's own observations and help determine the diagnosis. When the session is over, most interviewers will generally try to analyze their own reaction to the client: Did they establish rapport or was there an undercurrent of hostility?

Psychological Tests

Like interviews, psychological tests are designed to analyze a small sample of the client's behavior and attitudes. Also like interviews, some are quite structured and others are less so. **Intelligence tests**, for instance, are specifically formulated to show the degree of deviation that a person exhibits from certain norms. **Personality tests**, on the other hand, ask the client to respond to more subjective stimuli. We will discuss the types of psychological tests in turn.

Personality tests

The object of personality tests is to obtain a fairly clear picture of the feelings and attitudes clients have about themselves, other people, and the world at large. There are two different types of personality tests: (1) *projective tests,* and (2) *self-report inventories*. Projective tests are the least structured of the two. In projective tests, the possible answers are quite numerous, the goal being that unconscious fantasies and other private material will surface in the client's response.

Projective tests. The basic idea behind this form is that when people are asked questions that have no clear-cut right or wrong answer, they will generally respond according to their own personality—that is, their answers will reflect certain characteristics that are a fundamental part of those people. Projective tests force clients to deal with ambiguous situations, so their responses are assumed to be fairly representative of their overall behavior. Essentially, the way clients respond to the test is another indication of how they think and feel. The clinician gets two views at once: the answer to the test and whatever behavior is exhibited with that answer. Several different tests have developed from this idea, but the two primary ones are the Rorschach Test and the Thematic Apperception Test (TAT).

The Rorschach Test—which asks the client to describe in detail what each of ten different inkblots looks like—was devised by Swiss psychiatrist Hermann Rorschach (1884–1922) in 1921. While responses to the inkblots alone cannot in any way yield a full diagnosis, they do provide insight into certain aspects of the client's personality. Guidelines for interpreting the client's responses, such as the Beck method (1972), have been developed, and research indicates that they improve interjudge reliability (Exner, 1974).

In the more structured TAT, the client must make up a story for each of up to 30 different pictures that show one or more persons doing something. These cards are less ambiguous than the Rorschach inkblots because their content guides the person in a general direction. For instance, a card showing the faces of two women could hardly be described as "two bugs biting each other," which is how one inkblot was described. Yet there is still opportunity for the client to project—hence the name projective—personal views onto the scene: The women could be talking, or arguing, or plotting, for example.

A modification of this test, the T-TAT, was devised for use with black clients (Thompson, 1949). Its originator thought that blacks would respond more to scenes showing other black people, which has been shown to be the case (Fanon, 1967; Grier and Cobbs, 1971). Another modification, the CAT, is especially for children. Like the Rorschach, interpretation guidelines, such as the Henry method (1956), have improved the TAT's usefulness as a reliable diagnostic aid.

However, the major factor is the clinician's interpretation of the responses. This is not an easy task. Clinical psychologists need several years of training before they can correctly interpret projective test data—and even then their subjective feelings and thoughts can influence

Close-up: The Rorschach Inkblots

In diagnosing response to inkblots, clinicians generally do not concentrate on content alone; usually, other aspects of a person's response are given equal weight. For instance, did the person use the whole picture in formulating a response, or was there a focus on isolated parts? Was there any reaction to the shading or the color? As each inkblot is shown, the clinician looks for any themes that may be indicative of a problem. If the client consistently uses such words as "struggling," "fighting," and "attacking" to describe any activity seen in the inkblot, that can be a clue to a possible personal conflict. If only nonhuman objects are seen, this may indicate an attempt to disown any exposed feelings.

Here are several different responses to the inkblot shown here. What do you see?

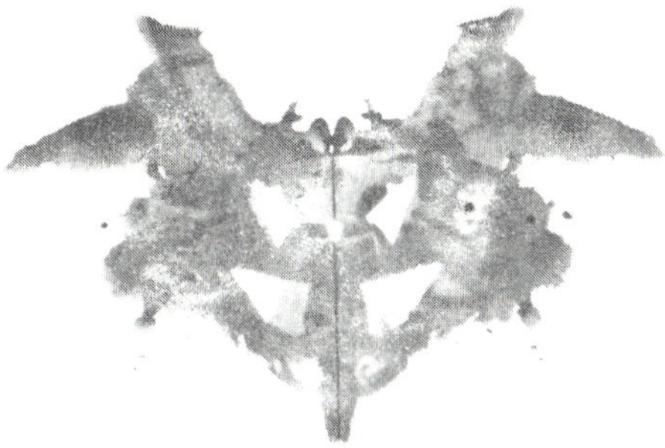

"A terrible face—a demon face."
"Bones—the backbone with the hips sticking out."
"A pelvis."
"Two dogs with their backs together."
"Birds, and a lake, and a beetle."
"An owl."
"Two animal skeletons back to back."
"The beginnings of a butterfly."
"A bat."
"A bug flattened out."
"Birds."

the interpretation. Nevertheless, these tests are still fairly popular.

Self-report inventories. These tests collect the same basic descriptive information, but they ask the client to do the assessing. Many of the questions asked about the client require only a yes or no answer, such as those listed in Table 2.4. These are from the Self-Assessment Psychological Inventory (SAPI), which asks people to evaluate their emotional status. Clearly, this type of self-inventory requires honest answers, but even scrupulously honest people can be too self-critical, yielding a negative assessment.

One of the most widely used inventories is the Minnesota Multiphasic Personality Inventory (MMPI), developed by Hathaway and McKinley (1943). It lists almost 600 statements that clients can categorize as True, False, or Cannot Say, depending on how they feel the statements fit their own behavior. A major problem with self-report inventories is that people can either lie about themselves or simply not be aware of their true state, which causes some researchers to question the validity of these tests. In response, the MMPI has attempted to deal with the problem by incorporating three control scales—that is, three distinct sets of questions that will clearly indicate basic discrepancies in the answers. There is, in fact, strong empirical support backing the MMPI as an effective classifier of personality characteristics (Dahlstrom and Dahlstrom, 1972), especially diagnostic categorization.

The Q-sort test developed by Butler and Haigh (1954) tries to ascertain the client's self-concept through the self-report format. Specifically, it tries to obtain a description of the client's idea of both the "real self" and the "ideal

Table 2.4 The Self-Assessment Psychological Inventory (SAPI)

I am sometimes anxious about my personal capabilities.	True	False
There have been moments when I have doubted my sanity.	True	False
My sexual adjustment has sometimes been problematic.	True	False
I have trouble understanding some of my moods.	True	False
My aspirations are often unrealistic.	True	False
Some of my friends would be shocked at the real "me."	True	False
I have occasionally feared losing my mind.	True	False
I tend to be very critical of myself.	True	False
I have occasional nightmares.	True	False
My fantasies are often unreasonable.	True	False
I am very concerned about people liking me.	True	False
There have been moments in which I wondered whether things were "real."	True	False
I sometimes get depressed.	True	False
I sometimes have trouble making decisions.	True	False
I worry a lot.	True	False

After table 1-1 (p. 5) in *Abnormal Psychology: Perspectives on Human Variance* by Michael J. Mahoney. Copyright © 1980 by Michael J. Mahoney. Reprinted by permission of Harper & Row, Publishers, Inc.

self." Carl Rogers, a humanist clinician, reported that the difference between the real and the ideal generally lessened as therapy progressed (1959); therefore, repeated use of the Q-sort can be valuable.

Intelligence tests

These tests measure the client's **intelligence quotient**, or **IQ**. They are used primarily to determine the presence and degree of intellectual dysfunction, especially mental retardation. Other disorders, however, are also characterized by deteriorated cognitive functioning. Schizophrenia, for instance, causes a decline in the ability to reason and problem solve—as was the case with Arnold in Chapter 1. Arnold's reduced cognitive functioning, and some of his idiosyncratic ideas, would be revealed in his answers to intelligence test items. Deteriorated cognitive functioning is a symptom of autism as well, but severely autistic children like Tommy are untestable.

There are two major intelligence tests: the Stanford-Binet Intelligence Scale and the Wechsler Intelligence Scales. Each has a different version for children and adults, and the Wechsler now offers special tests for the elderly and for very young (preschool) children.

The Stanford-Binet intelligence scale. This is based on the early work of Alfred Binet, a French psychologist who originally devised the test as a way to distinguish mentally retarded children. Lewis Terman of Stanford University revised it to yield results at the opposite end of the spectrum. After extensive field trials in U.S. schools, the concept of **mental age** (MA) was established. Simply stated, this means that a person who functions intellectually at the level of most 12-year-olds has a mental age of 12, even if the person's chronological age (CA) is higher or lower. According to this scale, a person's IQ can be determined by the following formula:

$$IQ = \frac{MA}{CA} \times 100$$

To determine the mental age, each person is given a series of age-graded tests to perform.

For each test passed successfully, the person earns one month toward the MA. The total number of months is computed at the end, and this figure is used to get the IQ.

The Wechsler intelligence scales. David Wechsler, who developed the scales, believed that intelligence was related to the ability to cope with and adapt to the environment. His selection of test items reflects this approach. The several scales have also been revised to keep more current with cultural changes, and are therefore considered by many clinicians to yield more valid scores. In addition, the fact that there are separate scales for different age groups makes them very popular. As mentioned previously, there are four scales:

1. The Wechsler Preschool and Primary Scale of Inteligence (WPPSI), for children 4 to 6½
2. The Wechsler Intelligence Scale for Children—Revised (WISC-R), for children 7 to 16
3. The Wechsler Adult Intelligence Scale—Revised (WAIS-R), for adults 17 to 65
4. The Wechsler Intelligence Scale for the Elderly (WISE), for adults over 65 (a new scale, developed in 1981)

In the WAIS-R, there are eleven subtests, six that evaluate verbal skills and five that measure performance at problem-solving tasks. Three different IQs (verbal, performance, and full total score scale) are then obtained. In addition, the pattern of the subtest scores often indicates the presence of organic or other impairment. In general, this is the case when the person scores strikingly better on the verbal tests than on the performance tests. An inability to remember number sequences, for instance, may indicate damage to the temporal lobe of the brain.

Such intelligence tests have come under considerable fire in recent years. The chief complaint is that they don't actually measure intelligence. Instead, they measure the person's ability to succeed within the educational and social systems of the culture that devised the test. A person who is seldom exposed to the norms and values of that culture will almost certainly obtain a poor rating.

Most psychologists agree with this criticism, at least to some extent, and a lot of time and energy have been spent on trying to formulate a test that has no cultural bias. Of course, since most of the would-be developers are steeped in a similar basic cultural tradition—and, further, since the entire notion of testing is culturally biased—their attempts should be just as severely questioned. Still, the concept of IQ has taken firm hold. As proof, despite their inherent deficits, intelligence tests are still widely used to distinguish children who are mentally retarded and those who are gifted, so that they can be placed in classes geared to their special needs. They are also used for generally evaluating the intellectual level of the person being assessed in the intake interview.

Tests for neurological impairment

Many behavioral symptoms are produced by organic problems in the brain, as will be shown in Chapter 13. Therefore a clinician must sometimes verify that the problem is indeed psychological. While there are several medical tests that can do this, there are also some psychological methods of determining this fact. One of the most valuable is the Halstead Reitan Neuropsychological Battery, which can identify difficulties in auditory and visual perception, in motor skills, and in abstracting ability. For instance, the client may be asked to do the following:

1. Differentiate between rhythmic beats that are sometimes the same and sometimes different (for auditory perception).
2. Fit a variety of blocks into a formboard by feel, while blindfolded (for visual perception).
3. Tap with the index finger as frequently as possible in the space of ten seconds (for motor skills).
4. Group items by specific characteristics, such as shape, color, or size (for abstracting ability).

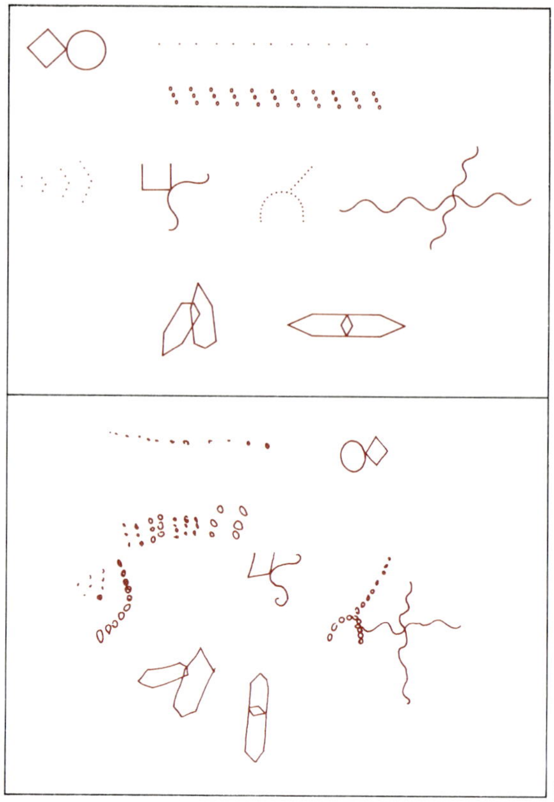

(a) (b)

Figure 2.1. *(a) The nine figures of the Bender Visual-Motor Gestalt Test. (b) Reproductions drawn by a ten-year-old boy of average IQ. The reversal of the square and circle and the vertical realignment of the last figure indicate organic brain impairment. Reproduced by permission of Dr. Lauretta Bender and the American Orthopsychiatric Association.*

Another test for organic impairment is the Bender Visual-Motor Gestalt Test, developed by Lauretta Bender (1938). In this test, clients are asked to draw freehand a set of designs shown to them on cards. Using tests like these, a clinician can assess brain functioning. Specific problems in reproducing the designs, such as turning a figure in another direction or being unable to draw a complex design, are suggestive of different kinds of brain impairment.

Physiological Examination

Sometimes a full medical exam is very helpful in diagnosis. Of primary importance in this kind of exam are the electroencephalogram (EEG), electrocardiogram (EKG), blood pressure tests, muscle tension tests, and X rays. An **EEG** is a graphic representation of brain wave activity. A normal pattern has certain known characteristics; the pattern of someone with epilepsy, for instance, looks quite different (see page 414). Indeed, many forms of organic brain dysfunction cause such distorted patterns. Therefore if a client's EEG is unusual, its pattern can be compared with those of other abnormal conditions to see which it most closely resembles.

An EKG and blood pressure tests can determine the status of the person's autonomic nervous system (ANS), part of which is involved in creating anxiety (see Chapter 7). This is true also of muscle tension. The muscles can be checked by a similar polygraph hook-up to see how tight they are.

X rays can reveal gross internal injuries that may cause behavior problems. For example, a brain tumor can enlarge to the point where it presses on certain sensitive areas in the brain, thus causing momentary blackouts (loss of consciousness), impaired speech, or confused thinking. In those cases where the symptom pattern is very similar to that of the known organic mental disorders, most clinicians will first request medical tests to rule out that possibility.

Problems in Assessment

The function of assessment, as we have stated, is to accurately classify the presenting problem and to determine its severity. Only when the problem has been assessed can an appropriate management method be selected and a prognosis made. Sometimes, despite all the different tests available to help this process, the diagnosis eludes the clinician. When that happens, some therapists will ask clients to admit themselves into an institution for a few days for observation. In this way, they can get the benefit of

Close-up: Computing Psychological Tests

The computer can be very useful in tabulating the results of certain self-inventory tests. One such test is the Strong-Campbell Interest Inventory, used to help people discover their primary career strengths based on like or dislike of certain scaled activities. A portion of a computerized summary report is shown here.

```
********* SUMMARY COPY OF RESULTS *********

        STRONG-CAMPBELL INTEREST INVENTORY

RESULTS FOR                                01/ 4/79     MALE

   GENERAL OCCUPATIONAL THEME SCORES AND PROFILE

         YOUR      3         4         5         6         7
SCALE    SCORE ....0.........0.........0.........0.........0....

C-THEME   65   *****************************************   (CONVENTIONAL)
R-THEME   64   ****************************************    (REALISTIC)
E-THEME   64   ****************************************    (ENTERPRISING)
I-THEME   53   *****************************               (INVESTIGATIVE)
A-THEME   48   ************************                    (ARTISTIC)
S-THEME   35   **********                                  (SOCIAL)

        BASIC INTEREST SCALE SCORES AND PROFILE

  THE SERIES OF DOTS BELOW INDICATE THE AVERAGE RANGE OF SCORES RELATIVE TO THE
SEX OF THE INDIVIDUAL. MINIMUM (MIN) AND MAXIMUM (MAX) POSSIBLE VALUES ARE LISTED.
```

BASIC INTEREST SCALES	YOUR SCORE	MIN-MAX
VERY HIGH INTEREST(66+)		
SALES	72	37-81
MECHANICAL	66	30-72
HIGH INTEREST (65-58)		
MATHEMATICS	65	31-67
MERCHANDISING	61	31-72
OFFICE PRACTICES	59	36-79
NATURE	58	17-67
BUSINESS MANAGEMENT	58	29-72
AGRICULTURE	58	30-68
AVERAGE INTEREST (57-43)		
SCIENCE	57	28-69
MUSIC/DRAMA	54	26-73
MEDICAL SERVICE	52	33-76
ADVENTURE	48	30-71
ART	47	26-68
MEDICAL SCIENCE	46	29-68
DOMESTIC ARTS	46	27-75
SOCIAL SERVICE	45	24-69
LOW INTEREST (42-35)		
MILITARY ACTIVITIES	41	41-76
ATHLETICS	38	27-70
PUBLIC SPEAKING	35	31-71
LAW/POLITICS	35	30-69
RELIGIOUS ACTIVITIES	35	31-68
VERY LOW INTEREST (34-)		
WRITING	33	26-66
TEACHING	26	23-67

other points of view, which may confirm their own suspicions or suggest an entirely new direction. Still, we see that the weak point in assessment is the dependence on the interpretation of the client's behavior given by the clinician.

By reviewing the client's responses to the interview questions and to whatever tests are administered as well as the client's overall behavior during the session, the clinician accumulates a list of important problematic behaviors or inappropriate emotional attitudes from which the final diagnosis is made. The way that the psychologist looks at these responses is very important—often just as important as the responses themselves. Essentially, they can be viewed in one of three ways:

1. As an accurate *sample* of the person's overall behavior
2. As a *correlate* of other behavior
3. As a *sign* of some underlying personality characteristic

The three ways require an increasing degree of interpretation on the part of the clinician, the first one requiring the least, the third one the most. The following examples will help clarify these three viewpoints.

Suppose Henry J. is shown the Rorschach inkblots during an intake interview. As Henry looks at them, he turns red in the face and looks very angry; in addition, he indignantly refuses to say what he thinks the various designs resemble. We can come up with three interpretations of Henry's behavior:

1. This is a sample of his widespread rage behavior when exposed to inkblots.
2. This is a correlate of his behavior in evaluative situations.
3. This is a sign of a major underlying personality characteristic, anger at experiencing ambiguity.

A clinician adopting the first viewpoint will probably develop a treatment program much different from a clinician who adopts the second or third.

For the most part, different psychological philosophies account for the varying ways of interpreting behavior. Therefore it is doubtful that this problem can be resolved. However, certain attempts have been made, one of them being diagnosis by computer.

Diagnosis by computer

This is the computer age, so it is hardly surprising to find that these versatile machines are involved in psychological assessment. As we mentioned earlier, at least one standardized interview format has been adapted for use with computers. And since standardized interviews yield better interjudge reliability, it would stand to reason that a computerized system would work at least as well. This has in fact been verified by Greist and associates (1976), who reported that computerization also shortened the process considerably. Because time is a commodity that everyone values, computer assisted diagnosis may become a popular assessment technique.

Personality test interpretations are also being computerized. The various elements of the tests can be programmed so that a profile is obtained when a person's responses are fed into the machine. The MMPI, in particular, lends itself to this process. And as is the case with the structured interview formats, the time savings can be considerable.

SUMMARY

If the many types of behavioral deviance are to be treated, they must be correctly identified and classified. Classification allows for quick and complete communication of information about a problem and for a fairly accurate prediction of its future course. Throughout history different methods of classification have been tried, including systems based on etiology, on a theoretical behavior model, and on a standardized psychological test. The most popular method and the one having the most validity is the empirical approach, the system based on overt symptoms.

Emil Kraepelin was the first to develop an empirical classification scheme; he listed two major categories: manic-depressive psychosis and dementia praecox. His system supported the idea that behavioral deviance should be regarded as disease and conformed to what is known as the disease model. This model has been followed by the APA in developing their widely used *Diagnostic and Statistical Manual.* However, there is little evidence in support of the theory that all mental disorders are caused by organic pathology.

The DSM has been revised twice since its first publication in an effort to improve its diagnostic reliability. The authors of DSM-III feel that the comprehensiveness of their version will lead to better interjudge agreement, which is the best method of evaluating diagnostic reliability. However, structured initial interviews are also necessary to improve the reliability of the system, but professionals prefer to use their own approaches.

DSM-III has a number of features that are unique and that its authors hope will make it more useful than its predecessors. First, it is much more comprehensive, listing more than 200 disorders. Second, it uses a multiaxial system, calling for diagnosis of an individual's immediate life situation to see how much bearing it has on the disorder. Third, it emphasizes behavior rather than etiology. Each disorder is listed by symptom syndrome—that is by the essential, distinguishing behaviors and those usually associated with the disorder as well as by those that must be present for the disorder to be diagnosed.

Assessment techniques still revolve around the initial interview, which concentrates on getting as much information as possible about the individual and the problem. In addition, several psychological tests are available to help diagnose the presenting problem. Intelligence tests, personality tests, and tests for neurological impairment are sometimes informative.

CHAPTER 3

Explaining Abnormal Behavior

THREE BASIC APPROACHES

HISTORICAL PERSPECTIVES

Ancient Explanations

The Rationalism of Classical Greece

The Middle Ages and the Renaissance

MODERN INTERNAL APPROACHES

The Biogenic View: The Disease Model

The Biogenic View: Genetics

The Biogenic View: Biochemistry

The Psychogenic View: Early Theories

The Psychogenic View: Psychodynamics

The Psychogenic View: Post-Freudian Theorists

The Psychogenic View: Humanistic Psychology

The Psychogenic View: Existential Psychology

The Psychogenic View: Cognitive Psychology

MODERN EXTERNAL APPROACHES

The Psychogenic View: Behavioral Psychology

The Sociogenic View: Social Forces

MODERN INTERACTIONAL APPROACHES

No matter how clearly we may define abnormal behavior and describe its many forms, there will always be still another question: Why, despite careful socialization of what is and what is not acceptable behavior, are there people who violate society's norms? What makes people engage in the innumerable deviant behaviors that society says are wrong? In short, how does society explain the presence of behavioral deviance?

Explanations of all phenomena are very much a product of history and culture, and the explanation of abnormality is no exception. Although it depends on when the question is asked and on who does the explaining, it will generally reflect how the society currently defines abnormal behavior, and in addition, what the underlying values of the society are at that particular point in its development.

Demonic possession, a fall from grace, premature weaning, toilet training, brain tumors, and weak nerves—all these and more have been accepted by our own society at one time or another as explanations of abnormal behavior. As we have moved toward rationalism and an empirical approach in our search for a better understanding of ourselves and our world, the explanations we propose have moved from the supernatural to the scientific. More and more people today see behavioral deviance less as a sign of God's eternal damnation and more as an unfortunate outcome of some cosmic game of chance. We no longer blame the stricken; we accept them—at least, to a much greater extent than in the past.

Likewise, our society has moved from regarding all deviance as a single problem with a single etiology to seeing it as a multitude of forms, each with its own possible cause. Later chapters will deal with various types of abnormal behavior and will examine in detail the explanations for those specific forms. This chapter is concerned with the broader issue of how the matter of etiology is generally approached.

THREE BASIC APPROACHES

Before discussing the historical development of our explanations of abnormal behavior, it is worth noting that the classification of deviance into various categories was itself an important step. Until the nineteenth century, there was little effort made to distinguish between the paupers, the criminals, and the lunatics. These people were simply society's waste products, and it was not worth the time to consider how they might differ or what accounted for their plight. Deviance was deviance. But with the reforms of the Age of Enlightenment came the recognition of different types of abnormality, which in turn spurred several attempts to explain them. All the explanations that were then offered—as well as previous explanations—can themselves be placed in three categories:

1. *Internal.* The focus here is on the internal operations of the individual. Physiological explanations, which emphasize genetics, biochemistry, or neurological changes, and the psychological explanations, which involve the mind and emotions, are both internal.
2. *External.* Changes within the individual originate in some external force. The focus, however, is on those external forces and how they influence behavior rather than on how they operate within the individual once they are experienced.
3. *Interactional.* The emphasis here is on the simultaneous operation of both internal and external factors. Thus a particular kind of behavior will occur only in persons with a particular kind of biochemistry (internal) who are also subjected to a particular kind of stress (external). Only when both of these conditions are met will the disorder develop.

We believe that the interactional approach is ultimately the one with the most validity, a fact that will become clear as you read this text. Since the interactional view is a blend of both internal and external factors, however, each of these approaches must be understood before it can be described. This holds for the very general study of etiology, to be discussed in this chapter, and also for the causes of specific forms.

It is also important to recognize that at any period of time there can be a wide variation among individuals in how completely they accept any of the societal theories of etiology. For example, today it is commonly known that certain forms of abnormal behavior are caused by an impairment of the brain's normal functioning, usually due to some organic pathology, such as a tumor or a blow to the head. Nevertheless, we often hear people say that the stricken person was working too hard, or dating too much, or drinking too heavily, or overeating—all these causes suggesting that the problem was a result of the person's negligence or moral impurity.

It seems our rationalism is really only a thin veneer. At the root of the idea that someone "was asking for it" is a deeply moralistic assumption: People are able to foresee all the consequences of their behavior and should therefore direct their actions to avoid such negative consequences. While this may be the way people ought to behave, there is little straightforward evidence to prove that this is the way they do behave. And what about those people who do not suffer because of their negligence or loose morals? Some people who drink a lot or work too hard are both successful and healthy. On the other hand, many perfectly moral people suffer like Job. A major problem of psychology is that it is impossible to predict with any accuracy which people will fall into which category.

HISTORICAL PERSPECTIVES

Using the internal-external conceptual model, we will briefly trace the historical development of our current viewpoints. You will see that society's explanation of abnormal behavior has constantly shifted back and forth between internal and external, but that is the story of our society's basic development as well.

Ancient Explanations

We have very little direct evidence of how prehistoric civilizations explained deviant behavior. However, their views were probably similar to those maintained by the few primitive cultures that exist today. Because of extreme geographical isolation, such groups have remained apart from mainstream society as we know it. The studies conducted by cultural anthropologists such as Margaret Mead indicate that most primitive people tend to place the blame for all misfortune on evil spirits. It's easy to conjecture

So-called primitive societies, isolated from the industrial world, may still blame misfortune on evil spirits and thus rely on magic for protection against evil. Here a shaman of the Huichole tribe in Mexico sprinkles holy water on the head of a tribesman about to set out on the peyote pilgrimage.

that people frightened by the strange actions of someone afflicted with something like schizophrenia would naturally assume the person's body was housing a different spirit—an evil spirit or devil—since the person's actions were bad and crazy.

Of course, it was equally possible to be possessed by good spirits, and this was generally how such behavior was explained when it could be used to further religious or mystical purposes. In ancient Greece, for instance, a person who could enter a trance state and predict the future was esteemed as an oracle. The Bible records many seizures, trances, and visions that were considered to be of divine origin. Even today such unusual behavior as *glossolalia,* or "speaking in tongues," is regarded as divinely inspired in pentecostal sects throughout the world.

Since most abnormal behavior involved norm violation, especially in the five primary areas of socialization, the consensus was that evil spirits or demons were in possession of the individual. Again, the Bible chronicles many behaviors that were regarded as the work of evil spirits. However, it is often unclear if the possession occurred first and resulted in norm violation, or if the norm violation occurred first and caused God to withdraw His divine protection, which then left the person open to the devil.

The Rationalism of Classical Greece

As early as the fifth century B.C., a strong rational movement had developed in Greece—a movement founded on the belief that human reason was able to understand nature. Such a rational approach led to the general theory that there were natural explanations for all things, the task of humankind being to discover these explanations. This led to a rejection of supernatural explanations for both physical and psychological disorders.

One of the leaders of the rational movement was the physician Hippocrates (460–377 B.C.), who has come to be regarded as the "father of modern medicine." While many of his contemporaries were insisting that physical and mental illness were controlled by the gods, Hippocrates developed a naturalistic set of internal explanations that would ultimately direct the course of today's system of medicine. The same search for rational, naturalistic causes of all diseases is the primary aim of every medical research laboratory in the contemporary Western world.

Three contributions

In addition, Hippocrates took three important steps that have greatly influenced our understanding of deviant behavior. In the first, he began his inquiry by actually observing the abnormal behaviors people presented—a practice so commonplace today that it seems ludicrous to mention it. The learned physicians of that time would discuss their ideas about how problems developed—ideas that were not based on any practical experience with the problem they discussed. Hippocrates argued that to understand any human phenomena, including behavioral problems, it was essential to start with careful observation. Following his own dictum, he provided the first rather complete empirical description of such conditions as epilepsy, phobias, and depression.

The second major step was Hippocrates' attempt to develop a classification system for the different abnormal mental states. He divided them into three major groups: (1) abnormal excitement, or **mania**; (2) abnormal depression, or **melancholia**; and (3) depravement of the brain, or **phrenitis**. Although modern research and theory have added to and rearranged his basic system, Hippocrates' identification of the three major psychopathological disorders is recognized as a lasting achievement.

The third step was the theory that the cause of abnormality was organic. In sharp contrast to the prevailing view, he asserted, "For my own part, I do not believe that the human body is ever befouled by a god." (Lewis, 1941, p. 37). Noting that injuries to the head sometimes caused serious behavioral and emotional changes, he concluded that other physiological causes, such as heredity and predisposition, probably accounted for the various forms of change.

By today's sophisticated standards, many of Hippocrates' organic explanations seem rather peculiar. For example, he believed that *hysteria,* the development of physical symptoms without physical disease, was caused by a wandering uterus: Not secured anywhere in the woman's body, the uterus was floating freely about, searching for children and causing strange behavior.

Hippocrates' notions about anatomy and physiology, and those of his peers, were very crude. Greek physicians placed very high value on the integrity of the human body and would not dissect it after death. Thus despite his commitment to empirical observation, Hippocrates actually knew very little about the body's inner working. He believed that four **humors**, or vital fluids, existed in the body, and that a balance of the four was necessary for normal functioning; an excess of any one would cause physical or mental disease. The four humors were *phlegm, blood, black bile,* and *yellow bile.* An excess of phlegm created indifference and sluggishness; too much black bile caused melancholia; an increase in yellow bile created irritability and aggressiveness; and a higher blood level caused quick mood changes. Today little remains of Hippocrates' humor theory except the terms—phlegmatic, bilious, choleric, and melancholic—but it foreshadowed our current interest in discovering physical causes of deviance and, as such, was a significant contribution to the development of our understanding.

Other Greek theories

Two of the greatest Greek philosophers, Plato and Aristotle, also developed theories of the causes of abnormal behavior. Plato (420–347 B.C.) suggested that "natural appetites," or physiological needs, motivate all living things, including humans. Human behavior was perceived as part of the natural order of things rather than as an exceptional case, an idea that resulted in a very different view of the human condition. Plato also held the rather modern view that society had an impact on the developing individual: He maintained that deviance was caused by a combination of factors—in this case, physical, moral, and divine. It is difficult to determine from Plato's writings exactly how these factors operated, but he did seem to be suggesting some kind of interactional etiology.

Aristotle (384–322 B.C.) rejected such a complex approach. Following Hippocrates, he strongly stressed internal, organic factors and took the position that an imbalance of the humors caused strange behavior. For instance, he believed that very hot bile stimulated passion and talkativeness.

The Roman Empire

The Greek notions of etiology were largely accepted in the emerging Roman Empire. The Hippocratic view of organic causation was dominant, as was the idea of classifying behavior problems by observed characteristics. Following Hippocrates' advice, Asclepiades, a Greek physician working in Rome during the first century B.C., noted the difference between *acute* (of recent onset) and *chronic* (long-term) disorders. He was also the first to clearly differentiate illusions, delusions, and hallucinations and to suggest how these could be used in distinguishing the various forms of disturbance.

Aretaeous, a colleague of Asclepiades, proposed the interesting idea that at least some psychological disturbances were simply exaggerations of normal psychological states. Melancholia was thus the extreme form of a generally serious and dour approach to life, while mania was an extension of ordinary joyfulness and excitement. Thus by the first century B.C., the concept that emotional disturbance was on a continuum with ordinary human functioning was developed.

A third Roman physician, Galen, continued this tradition by distinguishing between two causes of mental disturbance—physical and psychological. He listed as physical causes such things as head injuries and alcoholism, while unrequited love and unemployment were considered psychological. How familiar this logic appears, even after twenty centuries!

The Middle Ages and the Renaissance

By the fifth century A.D., the Roman Empire had been overrun and the Middle Ages began.

Although the Greek tradition continued for a time in the Moslem world, especially in Damascus and Baghdad, little rationalism survived in Western Europe. Instead, the ancient superstitions and beliefs again flourished, and the explanation of abnormal behavior became the exclusive province of the church. With good reason, then, is this period also known as the Dark Ages.

In medieval Europe, the clergy of the Christian church held tight control over the thoughts and beliefs of the people in an effort to guarantee the continued existence of their faith. That aim was achieved, but not without cost. The curiosity about nature and humanity that had been a large part of Greek rationalism was lost because the early church emphasized emotional states rather than intellectual attitudes. Mystical experiences, the miracles of saints, the ecstasy of martyrs—these were valued much more by the public because they brought people closer to the faith that in the Middle Ages was central to life.

A fundamental part of that faith was the idea that evil, personified by the devil and a multitude of minor demons, was always around and must be avoided at all costs. For those who did not fight temptation hard enough, eternal damnation awaited. In this atmosphere, it's easy to see how any behavior that did not fit in could be charged to the presence of Satan, and truly alarming means were used to get rid of that presence. It is extraordinary that under these conditions there seem to have been many more cases of madness and other examples of demonic possession, particularly in the late Middle Ages.

Chroniclers of the period wrote of several different types of abnormal behavior that were then common, such as *tarantism,* a state of frenzied dancing, and *lycanthropy,* the belief that some people at times become wolves. Considering the rather extreme methods that were used to get rid of any demons inhabiting a body, a growing population of possessed people seems an unlikely result. However, in addition to the enormous influence of the Roman Catholic Church on the emotional state of Europe, a good many other factors probably contributed as well to the generally chaotic climate of this era that spawned so much mass madness.

Social upheaval

Europe during this period was in an almost constant state of war. And between the continual battles, such devastating natural disasters as continent-wide famine and the infamous Black Death swept over the countryside, killing millions more. Nevertheless, despite all this social upheaval, by the fifteenth century the Renaissance had begun—a movement characterized by a return to greater rationalism that had begun to spread slowly across the continent. It was largely fostered by an economic upswing and a greater sense of social stability. However, one of its offshoots, the Protestant Reformation, once again plunged the populace into turmoil by challenging the supreme authority of the Roman Pope and seriously questioning the validity of what was still for most people the core of their existence—their religion. It was also during this "enlightened" time that the concept of *predestination* and the phenomenon of *witchcraft* were to arise.

Predestination. This notion was advanced by John Calvin, a Reformation leader, and it later became fairly well established in Puritan Colonial America. The basic idea behind predestination is that the fate of each person is determined by God, and nothing a person does can alter that fate. An extension of this is that worldly success is a sign of election into God's community, both in this life and in the next. Worldly failure, on the other hand, is a sign of predetermined damnation. And since demonic possession was still believed to cause abnormal behavior, this too was included in the second category—that is, a person who exhibited strange behavior was possessed, which was clear evidence that the person was damned (Rotenberg, 1978).

This led to an interesting situation. The Calvinists firmly believed in the principle that nothing could interfere with what was predestined, but that didn't stop them from trying. And since they were fighting against overwhelming odds, they used harshly punitive measures to exorcise the devils that were there by God's command. Although we today can see the paradox in this logic, those who devoutly followed Calvin's precepts apparently did not.

Witchcraft. Thus far we have differentiated only between two types of possession: that which occurs more or less accidentally and that which occurs because of some grand design. However, there is supposedly another form—that which comes about when a person voluntarily and intentionally signs a compact with the devil. Such people are called witches. This is a recurrent theme in Western literature, involving the notion that Satan actively recruits volunteers and, in return for a variety of personal gains, converts some people to evil. Witches were therefore seen as willing accomplices in the devil's never-ending attempt to destroy the social order.

An interesting point about witchcraft is its inherently antisexual—and especially antifemale—character. During this period, sexuality was considered to be a special temptation of the devil, and therefore evil. Temptation was also a woman's specialty, with Eve as the prototype. The natural extension of this belief was that women were essentially more wicked and more vulnerable to Satan. Consequently, it was assumed that almost all witches were women, and nearly every woman had to prove she was not a witch.

The Inquisition. Witches were plentiful in the Renaissance, and witch-hunting was a most popular sport. In 1484 Pope Innocent VIII announced dismay at the number of these evildoers and instituted an inquisition to root out the problem. This endorsement from the Church's highest authority was, for many people, practically a license to indict any behavior that was unusual—or merely disliked. Often, neighbors were accused in revenge for insignificant and even imagined slights.

Two monks—Heinrich Kraemer and Johann Sprenger—spearheaded this campaign to

A mid-nineteenth century engraving depicting a revel of witches and demons.

stamp out evil. They did not work without guidelines. Together, they devised a manual to aid their task, one that could be used by other inquisitors as well. Entitled *Malleus Maleficarum (The Witches' Hammer)*, it listed all the signs by which people could recognize witches, and it suggested the proper ways of handling them once they were caught. It was a very successful work, its popularity spanning the fifteenth, sixteenth, and seventeenth centuries. The witch-hunting craze was not to finally die down until after the infamous Salem witch trials of 1692.

It is quite probable that during those trials—as during earlier trials in Europe—many individuals who were put to death as witches were actually suffering from some kind of emotional disturbance. In fact, some mentally afflicted people may have even cooperated with their inquisitors, under the mistaken belief that they were indeed witches, since that was the only explanation they could find at the time for their own strange actions. Who knows how many ordinary people were handled in a similar fashion simply because of circumstantial evidence and the mass hysteria that gripped virtually every European community. In contrast with today's more tolerant view of the human sideshow, the deeply religious convictions of the time had little room for behavioral deviance.

It is interesting to note that in both predestination and witchcraft the explanation of demonology can be either internal or external. The key is whether or not there is some predisposing factor within the individual that opens that person to possession. Therefore predestination is an internal approach, while witchcraft is external: The devil makes advances and some people eventually yield to them. Thus we can see the issue of personal responsibility for misfortune again being raised, even in relatively early times, and the answer that our society provides today is still not very clear.

Opposing forces. Even while witch-hunting raged across Europe, a few people were risking their reputations, if not their very lives, by opposing the craze. Denouncing demonology, they instead suggested that people who behaved strangely were affected by much less evil influences. Two of these opponents were Paracelsus and Johann Weyer.

Paracelsus, a Swiss physician (1493–1541), asserted that the stars, and especially the moon, influenced behavior. In fact, as noted earlier, the term lunatic is derived from this idea. He argued that afflicted people were not to blame for their behavior, and that they needed special care, not torture and death (Zilboorg and Henry, 1941). A switch from demonoloy to astrology as an explanation for abnormal behavior may seem to be a very modest advance, but it was revolutionary for the period.

Johann Weyer (1515–1588) also challenged the existence of witches and demons. However, this German physician was convinced that people who exhibited strange actions were in reality mentally ill. Like Hippocrates, he based his argument on empirical evidence and advanced specific, humane medical treatments for various forms of disturbance that he witnessed. In 1563 he published the *Deception of Demons*, which attacked the points made in the *Malleus Maleficarum* and declared that demonology was offensive to both God and humanity. Weyer's close observation of afflicted people led him to conclude that disturbing inner conflicts and distorted social relationships were also involved in the origins of mental illness.

Unfortunately, neither Paracelsus nor Weyer convinced enough people that their views were valid. A similar fate befell others who attempted to turn people away from demonology. An eminent English physician, Sir Reginald Scot (1538–1588) and even St. Vincent de Paul (1576–1660) argued that behavioral deviance resulted from the disease process, but they too went largely unheard. However, it was the beginning of a change, and by the eighteenth century, the chief idea of these early physicians—that abnormality is an illness—had taken root.

MODERN INTERNAL APPROACHES

The eighteenth century saw the beginning of the Age of Enlightenment, the general move being toward more scientific ideas and practices. For instance, the revolutionary work of such people as Sir Isaac Newton (1642–1727), Johannes Kepler (1571–1630), and Rene Descartes (1596–1650), in the fields of mathematics, astronomy, and philosophy, became more widely accepted. In addition, as we mentioned in Chapter 2, several discoveries in various branches of medicine led to the very popular theory that all disease was caused by organic pathology. It was also finally recognized that the brain is central to all functioning—emotional and behavioral as well as physiological.

As we have seen, early opponents to the external explanation of demonology asserted that abnormal behavior was a manifestation of mental disease. Since this clearly agreed with the organic theory for all disease, the assumption that brain pathology in particular caused abnormal behavior seemed a logical extension. The work of von Haller and Griesinger—and especially Kraepelin's classification scheme—more or less cemented this belief in the disease models. This set the stage for one of the most longstanding disputes in psychology: the conflict between the **biogenic** and **psychogenic** approaches—that is, between the relative roles of organic and psychological factors in the development of abnormal behavior. As we noted earlier in this chapter, both of these approaches are essentially internal; they both concentrate on changes occurring within the individual that produce unusual behavioral symptoms. Therefore we will detail the development of each approach separately, beginning with the view that was most popular at the very beginning of that move toward a more modern perspective—the biogenic view.

The Biogenic View: The Disease Model

The disease model that finally displaced demonology as the primary explanation of behavioral deviance focused on internal biological malfunction. While an illness may be started by an external source, such as a virus, it is nevertheless clear that the disease operates internally. It was therefore believed that any abnormal behavior that developed was a result of changes in inner systems produced by the disease. One of the clearest illustrations—and supports—of the disease model is the connection between syphilis and general paresis.

The general paresis case

Syphilis is a very serious disease usually transmitted through sexual intercourse. Its cause is a spiral-shaped microorganism, the spirochete *Treponema pallidum,* which can attack one or several different inner systems once it enters the body. This attack always follows a clear and certain course in four stages. The first two stages occur shortly after infection, and both have clear physiological symptoms. During the third stage, the disease goes underground for as many as ten to thirty years. When the final stage occurs, the system or systems attacked by the microorganism begin to deteriorate.

One of the primary areas affected is the central nervous system. Because neurological functioning is impaired, this form of the disease is now called neurosyphilis as well as general paresis. However, it was not known until the nineteenth century that syphilis and general paresis were the same disease. In the past, general paresis referred to what was thought to be a psychological problem. Therefore when it was finally recognized that the two diseases were the same, the simple elegance of the explanation reinforced the belief in the disease model.

Unfortunately, belief in the disease model has not yet lead to the discovery of any organic pathology behind the two major mental disturbances, schizophrenia and the affective disorders; they are still etiological mysteries. However, researchers have turned their attention to relatively similar biogenic explanations, specifically in genetics and biochemistry. These areas have yielded some interesting findings and seem more promising than the idea that a virus invades the body and produces mental illness. Nevertheless, the disease model has left a strong legacy; mental illness, patient, mental hospital—these terms and others indicate its powerful influence.

The Biogenic View: Genetics

All living things transmit specific hereditary information from one generation to another. This

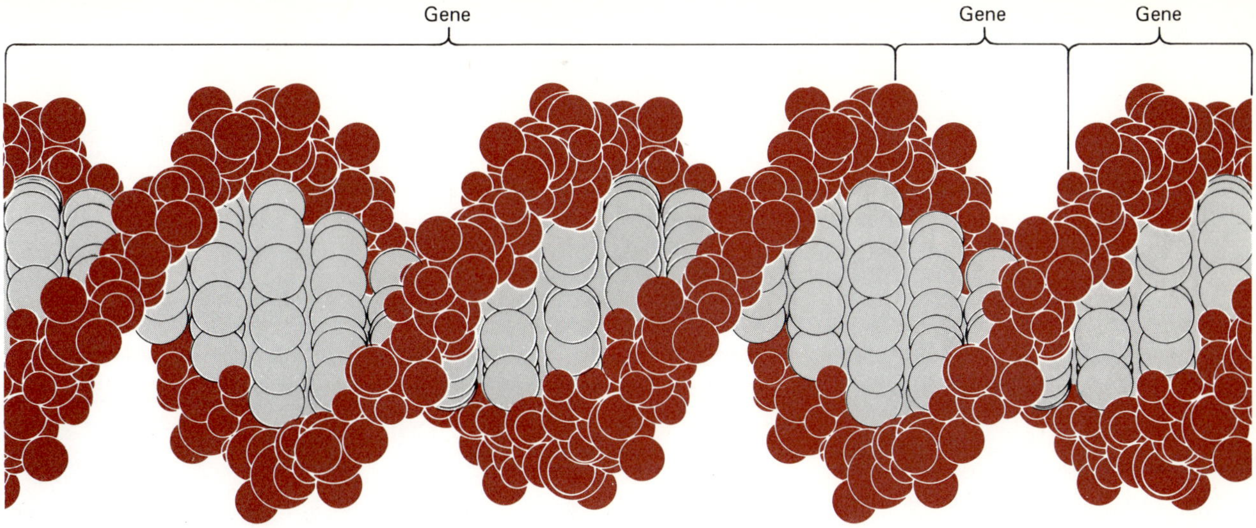

Figure 3.1. *The DNA double helix formation.*

information ranges from the very general (animal, primate, human) to the very specific (eye and hair color, shape of nose, height). In this way, each species is sure to reproduce more of itself, with individual variations included to aid the evolutionary process. This transmission of information takes place in a single cell at the moment of conception, when the entire genetic endowment for that person is set: the physical characteristics, the basic behaviors (crying, laughing), and the overall pattern of development throughout a rather predictable life cycle.

Chromosomes, tiny rod-like structures in that first and every other human cell, contain the genetic code that controls the pattern of development. Each cell contains 46 chromosomes, joined into 23 pairs. There is only a single exception: Sperm and egg cells contain only half of the total, so that when they unite, the new cell (the first cell of a new person) will have the required total of 46, having obtained 23 chromosomes from each parent. The determination of which chromosomes the sperm and egg cells will supply is a random process, and this accounts for the variations in genetic endowment. Geneticists estimate that there are over eight million possible combinations of chromosomes from the mating of a couple. It is therefore not very surprising that children of the same parents are often quite different in a number of ways.

We now know that each chromosome is made up of long molecules of *deoxyribonucleic acid (DNA),* which occur in interwoven strands called *double helixes.* Strung along each double helix, much like pearls on a necklace, are **genes**. These are the individual hereditary transmission units, and each contains specific information about traits—such diverse human characteristics as eye color, body size, and blood type. After fertilization, the genes line up in pairs, one from each parent.

Dominant and recessive traits

Certain genes are stronger than others, or **dominant**, while others are weaker, or **recessive**. For example, if one parent has given a gene for blue eyes and the other has given one for brown eyes, their child will have brown eyes, because in the determination of eye color, brown is dominant over blue. But remember that this brown-eyed child has a recessive gene for blue eyes. Therefore if it married another brown-eyed person with a recessive blue-eyed gene, they could produce a blue-eyed child. Random combinations can and do match these hidden traits. Clearly, recessive genes make the hereditary process more complex than it might initially appear.

What important behavioral characteristics are inherited? No answer to this question is generally accepted, and the question of whether abnormal behavior is transmitted from generation to generation has a similarly clouded answer. However, several specific types of behavioral deviance appear to have some hereditary component, the chief among these being schizophrenia, the affective psychoses, antisocial behavior, and the anxiety disorders. Evidence in support of a genetic explanation will be presented in later chapters that will describe all the disorders. Here we will review the conceptual and methodological issues involved in determining just how big a role heredity plays in the etiology of mental disorders.

Family studies

The traditional way of studying genetic factors has been to compare the incidence of abnormal behavior in persons of varying blood relationships. For instance, the incidence of schizophrenia in the general population is 1 percent (Slater, 1968), a figure that stays more or less the same for different socioeconomic and geographical groups. However, it is now reasonably well established that children of schizophrenic parents are fifteen times more likely to develop schizophrenia than are children of nonschizophrenic parents (Shields, 1968). Similar findings have been reported for other disorders.

However, there is a problem with this emphasis on the parent-to-child relay: An abnormal behavior could be either passed on genetically or taught by example, usually unintentionally, as part of the socialization process. But the biggest point against it is that most deviant persons do not have deviant parents. For example, more than 90 percent of adults whose behavior has been diagnosed as schizophrenic do not have a schizophrenic parent (Mosher et al., 1973). More impressive evidence has been collected from studies of very close family members—twin siblings.

Twin studies

Researchers have studied pairs of twins, both **monozygotic** (identical, from a single egg) and **dizygotic** (fraternal, from two eggs). The object is to determine two things:

1. The **concordance rate**—the percentage of twin pairs in which both twins have the same mental disorder.
2. The **discordance rate**—the percentage of twin pairs in which one twin is deviant but the other is not.

Monozygotic twins, born with the same genetic material, are the focus of much scientific research seeking to sort out the influences of heredity and environment on behavior.

These studies have shown that the concordance rate for schizophrenia among monozygotic twins is from three to six times higher than it is for dizygotic twins. In addition, the concordance rate for dizygotic twins is no higher than for regular siblings (Rosenthal, 1971). If the genetic explanation is valid, we would naturally expect a 100 percent concordance rate among identical twins who inherited the very same genetic material. This is not the case, but we cannot reject the genetic theory altogether because there is evidence indicating that it does make a fairly substantial difference.

Adoption studies

Perhaps the strongest evidence for the importance of genetic factors comes from the studies of children born to deviant people who were, at birth or shortly thereafter, adopted by psychologically more healthy parents. In one comparison, a control group of adopted children born to normal mothers was matched with children of schizophrenic mothers (Heston, 1966). The results: Five members of the schizophrenic-mother group were themselves diagnosed as schizophrenic; none of the control group was. Similar findings have been reported by other investigators (Karlsson, 1966; Rosenthal et al., 1968). Indeed, David Rosenthal, one of the authorities on the genetics of psychopathology, has stated that "the evidence . . . so strongly reinforces the probability of a genetic contribution to schizophrenia that such a view [that genetic factors are unimportant] no longer seems tenable." (1971, p. 104).

On one level, hereditary explanations are attractive in their simplicity. They suggest that some kind of completely internal mechanism underlies the behavior, so no additional reasons need to be offered. But what exactly is inherited? Our current understanding of genetics is very incomplete, and we do not know if the genes pass on complex behavior patterns, both normal and abnormal, or if they pass on a brain defect, or even the disease itself in a latent form (if a disorder is, indeed, a disease). Most geneticists doubt that complex behavior patterns are inherited, however; such patterns are thought to emerge slowly, as the person develops, in response to the environment. Given this dilemma, it is highly unlikely that any simple hereditary explanation will suffice. But one strong possibility is that the factor transmitted by heredity is a biochemical flaw.

The Biogenic View: Biochemistry

The brain is an intricate and complex network in which electrical impulses are constantly transmitted. In order for these impulses to be conducted—and therefore interpreted and acted upon—several different **neurotransmitter substances** are required. Researchers once assumed that nerve impulses jumped between neurons much the way electrical sparks jump. But now we know that these neurotransmitters, which are specialized biochemicals, move brain messages from neuron to neuron in the nervous system. We are still learning about this neurotransmission process, but what we already know is fascinating. Some neurotransmitters seem to carry only excitatory impulses; others conduct only inhibitory messages; still others carry both. But we have yet to discover what makes a neurotransmitter either excitatory or inhibitory.

Most theories about the role of biochemical influences on deviance have focused on this transmission process. For instance, it has been proposed that the cause of schizophrenia is the production of an abnormal neurotransmitter substance in the brain (Osmond and Smythies, 1952; Kety, 1967). Another hypothesis focuses on a class of neurotransmitters called *catecholamines,* which includes *norepinephrine* and *dopamine.* These two neurotransmitters are spread irregularly throughout the brain.

Many drugs that cause hallucinations and other cognitive disturbances, such as LSD and mescaline, are chemically very similar to dopamine. It is an easy step to then theorize that since these drugs cause similar symptoms, perhaps an imbalance in the system's natural chemical supply is producing abnormal mental states. There is some support for this argument. Many published reports assert that traces of specific hallucinatory chemicals have been found in the blood or urine of diagnosed schizophrenics. However, none of these studies have ever been adequately substantiated and as yet no conclusive proof has been shown.

Another line of research is a bit more promising. Many of the drugs used to control psychotic behavior, such as the irregular thought patterns of schizophrenia, are now known to block dopamine *receptors*—that is, the neurons that accept impulses carried by dopamine (Carlsson and Lindquist, 1963). Later studies (Creese et al., 1978) have shown that the effectiveness of antipsychotic drugs depends on their capacity to block dopamine receptivity in the brain. These findings rather strongly support the idea that the neurotransmission process is an important factor in at least some disorders. This in turn has excited strong interest in studying the influence of other neurotransmitters on the different forms of behavioral deviance.

The disease model, genetics, and biochemistry are currently the primary biogenic explanations. Although we have discussed them independently, they are, as you can see, quite interrelated. In fact, they cannot be viewed independently because they all operate within the human body, where every system interacts with—and sometimes even depends on—at least one other system. These explanations are clearly involved in the creation of abnormal behavior, but exactly how and to what degree has yet to be established. They are nonetheless very important parts of our modern conception of how behavioral deviance develops.

The Psychogenic View: Early Theories

There is another side to the internal model—the psychogenic side. As we stated earlier, this centers on the idea that abnormal behavior is created by the mind, as an entity separate from the physiological brain. Although a few of the ancients believed that the psyche played an important role in behavioral deviance, it was not until this century that any complete theories were developed. Before that, however, a few individuals did formulate some rather intriguing ideas. In this section we will outline the history of the psychogenic explanations and briefly discuss the major theories involved.

As mentioned earlier, Plato was an early advocate of a psychological foundation for deviant behavior, suggesting that moral factors influenced the development of abnormal behavior. He also felt that the interaction between individuals and society was another important factor. The Roman physician Galen asserted that there were clear psychological causes of deviance, such as unfulfilled love or the poverty and loss of status and self-esteem resulting from unemployment. Both of these foreshadowed the interest in the mind that began to grow during the Age of Enlightenment.

Mesmer and the Nancy school

One of the more unusual people to spur this interest in the mind was Friedrich Anton Mesmer (1733–1815), an Austrian who worked in both Vienna and Paris. He was greatly influenced by Paracelsus' theory that the planets and stars affect human behavior. Expanding on this theme, he insisted that irregular shiftings of a universal magnetic fluid, which he called "animal magnetism," were responsible for how people felt, and that this magnetism was controlled by the astral bodies. Mesmer further believed that it was possible to intervene in this process by using a treatment that he had perfected. Known popularly as "*mesmerism,*" this surprisingly successful treatment, which will be described in the next chapter, was said to be especially good for hysteria. Nevertheless, Mesmer was regarded as a charlatan by his medical colleagues and was forced into obscurity. However, the problem of explaining the success of mesmerism remained, and this puzzle excited much interest.

Eventually, an entire school of thought was formed around this subject. Called the "Nancy school," because of its location in that French city, this school was based on the work of two physicians, Ambrose Liébeault (1823–1904) and Hippolyte Bernheim (1840–1919). Liébeault had found that he could induce in some people a state resembling sleep that nevertheless allowed them to respond to spoken suggestion, a state we call **hypnosis**. Using this method, Liébeault successfully treated a patient of Bernheim's who had failed to respond to more traditional methods. A new team was thus formed. They advanced the theory that hypnosis could not only cure hysteria but also produce hysterical symptoms. They were also able to show that *anesthesia,* the loss of sensation in a part of the body, could be produced by hypnosis—a fact put to practice today by some physicians, who use hypnosis as an alternative to chemical anesthetics in surgery.

Liébeault and Bernheim concluded that hysteria was most probably caused by some kind of self-hypnosis. Extrapolating further, they hypothesized that other kinds of mental disorders were more than likely caused by a similar psychological phenomenon.

This revolutionary idea aroused a good bit of opposition, much of it led by Jean Charcot (1825–1893), a prominent French neurologist and the Director of La Salpêtriére Hospital, one of the largest mental institutions in Paris. Charcot upheld the disease model, insisting that organic brain changes lay at the root of hysteria. The Nancy school won this battle, however, when Charcot eventually agreed with their ideas and became part of their tradition. But until that reconciliation occurred, the often-heated arguments between these opponents aroused both popular and scientific interest in the role of psychological factors, an interest—and a debate—that still exists today.

The Psychogenic View: Psychodynamics

There is yet another reason for our interest in the Nancy school. One of the many people who came to observe and study with Charcot after his conversion was a young Viennese physician, Sigmund Freud (1856–1939). After learning the methods of the Nancy group, Freud returned to Vienna, where he collaborated with Josef Breuer (1842–1925), another physician interested in hypnosis. Breuer had already

Sigmund Freud, at the age of 52, poses in a group photograph taken at Clark University, Worcester, Massachusetts, in 1908. Top row: A. A. Brill, Ernest Jones, Sandor Ferenczi; Bottom row: Sigmund Freud, G. Stanley Hall, Carl G. Jung.

learned that certain patients would discuss their symptoms and their lives more freely when they were in a hypnotic state. Disclosures made under hypnosis provided clues to the development of their symptoms, and in addition, simply talking about the problem seemed to have some therapeutic effect.

Together, Freud and Breuer began to explore this "talking cure," also called the "cathartic method." In 1895 they published *Studies in Hysteria*, which argued that certain forms of mental disorders were caused by internal conflicts that the patient was not aware of except under hypnosis. Once the conflicts were allowed to surface to consciousness, they no longer caused any symptoms.

The relationship between Freud and Breuer eventually turned sour, however, as did many of Freud's later relationships with colleagues and students. One point of difference was Freud's growing disenchantment with hypnosis as the primary therapeutic technique. He developed a procedure called *free association,* in which the patient lies on a couch and says whatever comes to mind, especially reports of dreams and childhood memories. This process, and the analyst's interpretation of these associations, make up the core of modern *psychoanalysis*, a topic to be discussed in more detail in the next chapter. At the same time that he was developing the therapeutic technique of psychoanalysis, Freud was using these same free associations of his patients to formulate two theories that were to profoundly affect society: the **psychoanalytic**, or **psychodynamic**, **theory** of the mind and the theory of the psychosexual stages of development. Freud maintained that these two theoretical constructs could be used to explain the development of all the various forms of behavioral deviance.

Psychoanalytic theory

Central to this theory is the concept that the human personality is formed by the interaction of three different facets of the mind: the **id**, the **ego**, and the **superego**.

The id. Encompassing instinctual drives, such as eating and reproducing, the id is present in each individual at birth and is, in fact, the primary characteristic of infant personalities. Freud defined the id as having two wholly opposite natures: constructive and destructive. The constructive side centers on the **libido**, which is basically an urge toward self-gratification in all areas, but especially in sexual matters. The destructive side represents an urge toward death called **thanatos**.

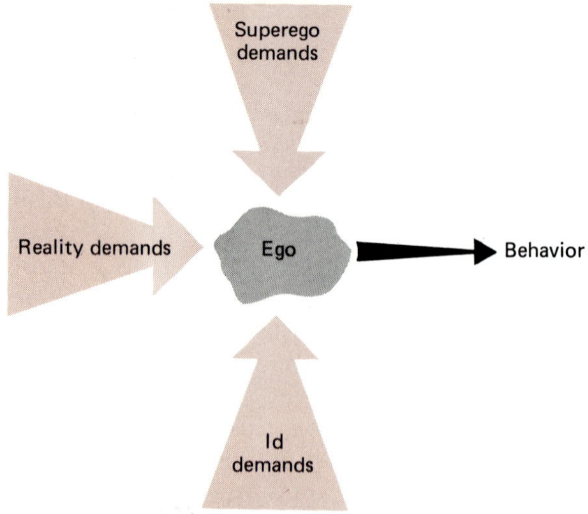

Figure 3.2. *Freud's three-part personality. The ego, under pressure from strong id, superego, and reality demands, must respond appropriately.*

In most people the urge for life is much stronger than the urge for death; therefore the id concentrates on meeting its libidinal needs. To this end it is very selfish, not being confined by moral or social limits—or even by reality, in some cases. Freud called this the **pleasure principle**. The id generates fantasies that let the individual become aware of what the id desires, but it cannot act itself to satisfy them.

The ego. This part of the mind mediates between the desires of the id and the demands of the real world. Ideally, the desires of the id should be obtained without jeopardizing the individual's well-being or continued survival, meaning, of course, that reasoning must be used to constantly keep the personality balanced. Therefore the ego operates under the **reality principle**, and it reflects all the norms and laws of society.

Freud theorized that this facet of the personality starts to develop in infancy but is not fully functional for a few years. This follows the idea of socialization: As the child grows, it learns from experience which actions provide pleasure with no unpleasant consequences and which provide pleasure that is outweighed by the punishment that follows. When the child acts to avoid the punishment, the ego is in operation.

The superego. At some point in the development of almost everyone, society manages to instill the concepts of right and wrong. Tied in with this is the development of the superego, or *conscience,* which makes people avoid actions not out of expediency but out of a sense of morality. This too reflects the norms and laws of society, particularly its most basic standards. The superego operates through the ego to place even more limitations on the id, its moral opposite. However, it is as blind to reality as the id is; it simply asks for the moral ideal rather than the pleasurable ideal.

The ego must work to satisfy as much as possible the demands of both the id and the superego. This task is never easy, but at certain times—for example, when a great conflict in demands arises—the ego may not be able to resolve the problem. The result, Freud asserted, is psychological dysfunction.

The unconscious. Another concept basic to psychoanalytic theory is that the conscious mind is actually only a very small portion of the entire mind. Freud perceived instead three different levels of consciousness. Those pieces of information currently in use for everyday functioning he termed the **conscious**. Anything that could be recalled at will but was not at the forefront of memory was called the **preconscious**. At the base of these two was a vast reservoir of hidden memories, thoughts, and desires called the **unconscious**. This store of information includes those things forgotten because of simple disuse and those things deliberately pushed out of awareness by the conscious mind—an action he termed *repression.* Freud contended that most of the memories, thoughts, and desires in the unconscious are simply too painful or upsetting for people to face, which is why they are repressed in the first place.

Freud asserted that repressing painful thoughts is not the same as permanently eradicating them. They are always ready to surface in the conscious mind whenever ego controls weaken—in dreams, in fantasies, under hypnosis, under extreme stress. Furthermore, he felt that they are the silent motivators behind many conscious acts and thoughts. This situation, he argued, also leads to the kind of conflict that can trigger a mental problem.

Freud viewed repression as an attempt to ward off the "psychic pain," or anxiety, caused by constantly suppressing either the id or the superego. Anxiety is a core element of psychoanalytic theory. Freud distinguished three types of anxiety: (1) *reality,* caused by real and present danger; (2) *neurotic,* caused by uncontrollable id impulses that would lead to punishment; and (3) *moral,* caused by conflict between a proposed action and the individual's superego. To avoid feeling anxiety of any type, he theorized, people developed **defense mechanisms**—a way of protecting their egos by irrational methods, repression being one of the ten he identified. The major defense mechanisms are:

Projection. Imagining that other people feel the way you feel.

Displacement. Directing your feelings (especially anger) toward a substitute object, not toward the thing or person that has made you angry.

Denial. Pretending that there is nothing wrong; ignoring the problem.

Reaction formation. Expressing a feeling opposite to what you really feel.

Rationalization. Justifying your behavior and emotion on some "logical" grounds.

Intellectualization. Refraining from emotional involvement; maintaining your objectivity.

Repression. Burying the problem in your unconscious and forgetting it.

The stages of psychosexual development

The three-faceted personality and the levels of consciousness work in concert with another major theory advanced by Freud—the idea that the personality is also formed by growing through a series of five developmental stages based on sexual impulses, with each level centering on gratification from a particular body area. In each stage, the child must find a compromise between its own desire for gratification and society's desire to instill appropriate behavior. This represents the insoluble conflict between the id and the superego.

The idea that sexual drives motivate the behavior of very young children was at first not well received by Victorian Europe—quite the opposite. Freud was actually trying to suggest that infant pleasure, such as that derived from feeding, had the same libidinal base as adult sexual pleasure. Furthermore, he was convinced that adult sexuality did not suddenly appear at adolescence, but rather that it developed slowly, as the child's body matured. The stages Freud identified were an attempt to trace this psychosexual development. However, the public viewed such theories as an affront to society.

The oral stage. According to Freud, stimulation around the mouth is what gratifies the id impulses during infancy, from birth to approximately one year or whenever weaning begins. Therefore anything that a baby eats satisfies not just hunger and nutritional needs, but the libido as well. This is also true of everything else babies try to put in their mouths. Infants seem to derive a lot of pleasure from sucking on such non-nutritional objects as teething rings, rubber nipples and other kinds of toys. When weaning begins, however, the infant faces the first confrontation between its own desires (to continue sucking) and those of society (to start drinking from a glass). The same thing happens to thumb-sucking children.

The anal stage. As its name suggests, in this stage the child receives pleasure from the bodily sensations associated with control over bowel movement. It is at this point that toilet training begins, a process Freud considered another crucial turning point: the second confrontation between the child's desires and those of society. Freud thought that the ego could experience anxiety from these early conflicts, and that, if the anxiety level were high enough, fixation could result.

The phallic stage. At about age three, Freud thought, a child's interest again shifts, this time to the genitals. This stage is characterized by a sort of sensual narcissism: The child is absorbed with discovering the pleasurable feelings that can be derived from stroking and handling its own body, especially through masturbation. Freud suggested that this stage is very important for the proper development of a sense of an independent self. But here again society can intervene, saying, as it has in the past, that masturbation is not appropriate or moral behavior.

This stage was the arena for several other unique ideas. Freud believed that all children at this level have an incestuous urge to get rid of their same-sex parent and to take that parent's place. This arouses *castration anxiety* in boys—the belief that the father will seek revenge by cutting off the child's penis. The guilt and fear aroused by this situation is termed the **Oedipal complex**, after King Oedipus of Greek mythology. Separated at birth from his natural parents, he later killed his father and married his mother, all without knowing their true relationship. The feminine counterpart of this syndrome was called the **Electra complex**. Freud also thought that girls experience *penis envy*. This makes their desire to take over the wife/mother role even stronger, because they can then have the penis vicariously, through the husband/father.

The latency stage. Freud theorized that from the ages of six to twelve the id impulses are (or seem to be) dormant. In fact, he hypothesized that children at this level are essentially asexual. He believed that the fear of revenge aroused by their incestuous desires is so strong that it prevents them from showing any kind of sexual expression. During this period, the major involvement is with mastering other areas, such as social skills and learning.

During latency, both sexes eventually resolve the problem of incestuous urges by identifying with the same-sex parent. The child should at this time incorporate that parent's sexual orientation and may even take on the parent's mannerisms—walking the same way, for instance. Simultaneously, the morals and standards of the parent that are absorbed will help the child to build a superego.

The genital stage. When the child enters puberty, the fifth and final stage has been

According to Freud's theory, as a result of the anxiety in the phallic stage children identify with parents of the same sex during the latency stage.

reached. The narcissistic tendencies of earlier stages end, and adolescents begin to view other people as individuals with their own needs. In addition, the id reawakens and through puberty merges with this newfound altruistic love to become mature sexuality. By this, Freud meant not just a healthy heterosexual desire but also other typically adult aspects, such as responsibility and independence.

Psychodynamics and psychopathology

Freud's psychoanalytic theory of the development of abnormal behavior is based on the belief that the three parts of the mind—id, ego, and superego—are not balanced. When the id is in control, the gratification of any and every desire is the core of the person's existence. Alternatively, when the superego is in control, the ego exerts all its powers to suppress the id's desires, and ego defense mechanisms begin to obstruct normal functioning. The ego is the weak link; it is also what keeps the individual attuned to the real world. Therefore as the ego loses strength, contact with reality gets equally weak. The final collapse of the ego—the complete loss of contact with reality—Freud termed **psychosis**.

How does the personality get off-balance? Freud claimed that this could happen in either of two ways. First, some highly traumatic incident, such as experiencing a horrible plane crash or an earthquake, could put so much stress on the person that the ego loses control. Second, and much more likely to occur, was that the personality had developed incorrectly—that some great disturbance in an early psychosexual stage (that is, pregenital) had left its mark by tilting the power balance in a certain direction.

For instance, a young man who never resolved the Oedipal conflict of his phallic stage must constantly repress (or deny or sublimate or use some other defense mechanism) his id's desire to replace his father in his mother's affections. Consequently, his superego, in retaliation for such offensive thoughts, is always trying to keep him in line about anything sexual. At the same time, that unresolved Oedipal conflict has resulted in **fixation**—an arrest of normal emotional growth—at the phallic stage, meaning that sexual gratification, which he is not getting, is of primary importance. His id is doubly denied and fights harder to get its needs met. His ego works overtime and eventually weakens.

The influence of Freud

Freud's impact on the theories and research of both normal and abnormal behavior was profound. His was the first systematic attempt to show that deviance could result from purely psychological functions rather than organic brain dysfunctions. Furthermore, just as the disease model replaced demonology, his psychoanalytic theory replaced the disease model, at least among his followers.

Many of Freud's concepts have come under fire today. Critics claim, for instance, that his theories (1) place far too much emphasis on the sex drive; (2) are biased, in that they reflect a primarily male psychology; (3) neglect the effect that environment can have on development; and (4) lack sufficient research evidence in their support. Nevertheless, the psychoanalytic model made many valuable contributions to the understanding of behavioral deviance.

Major contributions. Freud developed many theories—besides those that emphasized the mind in the development of mental disorders—that added new insights into the whys and wherefores of human behavior. The idea that *motivation*—that is, the reasoning behind a behavior—could be unconscious was revolutionary. That people act to satisfy a desire or impulse of which they are not aware was a concept that excited the imagination of many psychologists. It also led to a quite innovative therapeutic technique, the "talking cure." The idea that emotional problems could be solved by simple conversation was revolutionary. Dream interpretation, which will be discussed in the next chapter, was another Freudian innovation.

Freudian theory also highlighted the impact that early childhood experiences can have on later personality and adjustment problems. His use of the term sex, although used originally in a broader sense, did help free that formerly taboo area for more discussion and research. Finally, the idea that mental disorders are essentially exaggerated attempts to defend the ego from problems it cannot resolve was also unique. Furthermore, this meant that the psychological principles underlying normal behavior applied as well to psychopathology, which helped remove some of the stigma that had always been attached to mental illness.

The Psychogenic View: Post-Freudian Theorists

Freud's hypotheses served to launch numerous other psychological theories of behavioral deviance. Many were produced by his students, or by their students. In effect, these were variations on Freud's own themes, since most of his students accepted at least some part of their teacher's ideas. However, some psychologists rejected the psychodynamic theory and eventually worked out their own models, which we will examine shortly. First we will discuss the changes made by those who, in essence, agreed with Freud's basic concepts.

Carl Jung (1875–1961). Jung expanded the idea of the unconscious to a concept he termed the **collective unconscious**. This included what might be called "primal memories"—that is, inherited instinctual memories that have been common to all humanity from the beginning of our existence. He also developed the idea of *inner self-experience* as of equal value in the determination of individual personality makeup.

Jung thought that Freud placed too much value on the psychosexual aspects of motivation. The libido, the life force that Freud believed was sexual in nature, Jung considered to be an undifferentiated energy that could be turned outward or inward. Individuals whose energy turned outward were called *extroverts;* he described them as outgoing, adventurous, and friendly, which was in contrast to *introverts,* who were reflective, shy, and cautious.

Alfred Adler (1870–1937). Like Jung, Adler rejected the emphasis on sexual development and instead asserted that the desire for power was a stronger motivator. He believed that all people developed an **inferiority complex** (a term he coined) during infancy, and then spent the remainder of their lives trying to overcome it. However, Adler's major difference was in his insistence that social factors must be included as determinants of personality. In fact, he maintained that social elements were more important than the biologically inherited foundation on which they worked.

Karen Horney (1885–1952). Considered to be a neo-Freudian psychologist, Horney rejected the biological orientation of Freud. Instead, she expanded Adler's theme of sociocultural influence. In her view, anxiety originated in poor interpersonal relationships, especially inadequate parenting. The result was a feeling of helplessness, of having to face a hostile world all alone. In order to cope with this anxiety, children develop one of three strategies for dealing with people:

1. *Compliance:* being submissive and dependent—a conformist
2. *Aggression:* being competitive and covertly hostile—a rebel
3. *Withdrawal:* being reserved and distant—a loner

Once one of these patterns has proved successful, the child will generally rely on it for all situations, and this will continue into adulthood. But what is successful for children is not always appropriate adult behavior. When the favored strategy stops being so successful, the person's whole coping response breaks down. The result is abnormal behavior.

Erik Erikson (1902–). Erikson is what has been called an *ego psychologist.* That is, he belongs to a group who viewed Freud's idea of the ego as being too limited—the ego being caught between a rock (the id) and a hard place (the superego), with no purpose of its own. Erikson feels that the ego has its own energy, drive, and purpose, separate from its mediating tasks, as evidenced in the human ability and desire to reason, to know, to learn, to solve problems. This group focuses on improving the adaptational responses of all people.

Erikson's concept of the personality is also different. To Freud, the personality was set in childhood and did not alter significantly after that. To Erikson, the personality never stops growing and changing. He has expanded Freud's psychosexual development stages from five to eight, moving on into adulthood. He also maintains that psychosocial maturity is at least as important as the psychosexual, and his stages stress this. For each level, he describes a psychosocial crisis that, if not successfully resolved, can lead to emotional breakdown.

Three other important post-Freudians deserve mention: Anna Freud (1895–), the daughter of Sigmund, Karl Menninger (1893–), and Erich Fromm (1900–1980). All three of these psychologists are proponents of the basic psychodynamic model. Anna Freud elaborated on her father's discussion of the ego defense mechanisms and finalized them in her book, *The Ego and the Mechanisms of Defense* (1937). Menninger, who founded the Menninger Clinic in Topeka, Kansas, compiled evidence from his own research at the clinic that supports Freud's original hypotheses. Fromm called his own brand of therapy *humanistic psychoanalysis,* which placed him halfway into the camp of a group of psychologists who offered various internal psychological explanations for behavioral deviance that were not in full agreement with Freudian theory.

The Psychogenic View: Humanistic Psychology

One group of psychologists—the **humanists**—rejected Freudian theory because they thought it had an unwarranted, pessimistic opinion of human nature. They felt it was better to emphasize the good aspects of each individual and to stress the potential for personal growth. Abraham Maslow was an early leader in this group, formulating a theory of motivation that was quite different from the idea of the id. Carl Rogers, the preeminent humanist therapist today, devised *client-centered therapy,* which will be discussed in the next chapter. Fritz Perls developed a different approach to treatment, *gestalt therapy,* which he practiced at the Esalen Institute in California.

General theory

Humanistic psychology is based in part on the idea of **self-concept**, as first proposed by American psychologist William James (1842–1910). This self-concept is formed by the conceptions individuals have of themselves as well as their relationship to the world, with one conception helping to formulate the other. In addition, each individual's unique view of self and world mandates a **phenomenological approach**, which means that each person's perceptions must be regarded as reality. Essentially, the therapist must try to see things in the same way that each different client sees things.

Another important foundation of humanism is a positive view of human nature. According to this view, if individuals are allowed to develop naturally, unencumbered by social restraints, they will develop positive characteristics, such as creativity, sensitivity, and honesty. The role of the therapist is to help people realize their full potential as rational and emotional human beings—that is, to help people along the road to **self-actualization**.

The many different humanistic psychologists have each added to the general theory in specific ways. Maslow and Rogers in particular contributed greatly to this movement, so we will briefly discuss their viewpoints.

Abraham Maslow (1908–1970). Maslow's unique motivation theory was based on needs that he thought all humans had in varying degrees. He established a **hierarchy of needs**—that is, a ranked series of five different kinds of human needs:

Table 3.1 *Some Major Internal Theorists*

THEORIST	PHILOSOPHY	VALUES	GOALS
Carl Jung	Psychodynamics	Collective unconscious	Continuous personality development
Abraham Maslow	Humanism	Human needs	Self-actualization
Carl Rogers	Humanism	Self-concept	A realistic and positive self-image
Fritz Perls	Humanism	Wholeness	Self-acceptance
Rollo May	Existentialism	Being a subject rather than an object	Accepting responsibility for choices
R.D. Laing	Existentialism	Constructive quality of personality disintegration	The true self

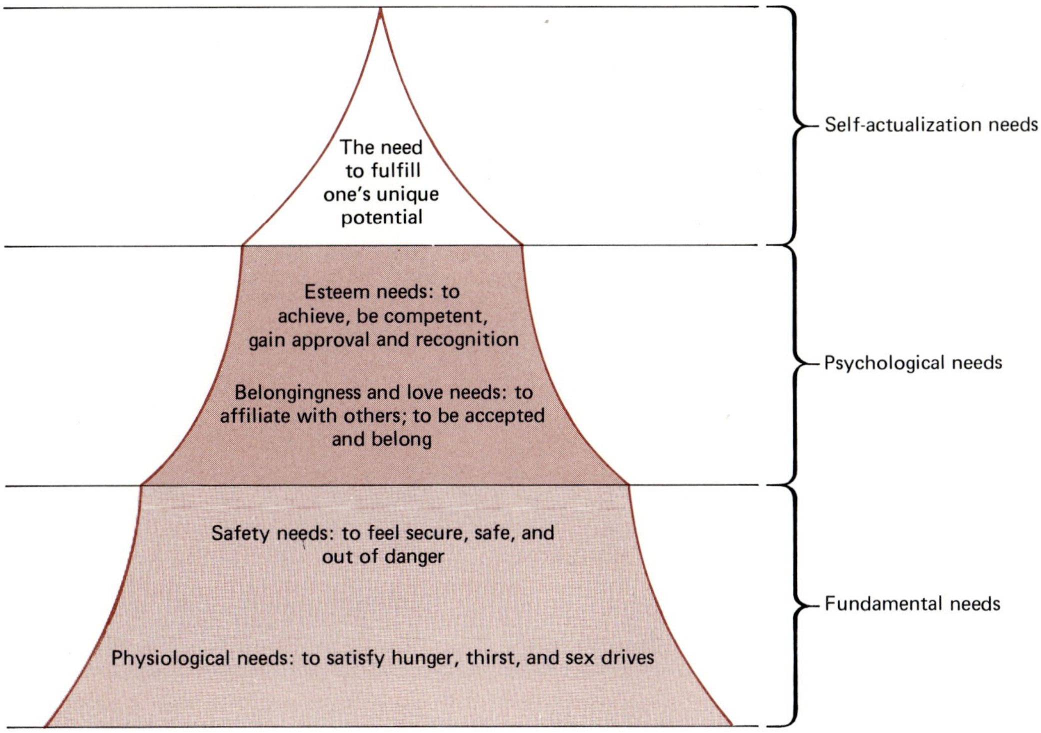

Figure 3.3. *Maslow's hierarchy of needs.*

1. Basic biological needs
2. Safety and security needs
3. Belongingness and love needs
4. Self-esteem needs
5. Self-actualization needs

Maslow believed that unless lower-rank needs were met there could be no significant movement to upper-rank levels. For instance, a woman who had an extremely deprived childhood may as an adult be overly concerned with fulfilling her safety and security needs. Consequently, she may devote all her time and money on food, stocking up on items she isn't even likely to use. The chances of her reaching the top of the hierarchy are slim, because her basic needs are never satisfied.

To Maslow, this kind of "stuck in a rut" living was at the foundation of abnormal behavior. He even developed the notion of the "psychopathology of the normal." This means that people who live up to all their various role expectations (as parent, citizen, lover, friend, etc.) can still find their lives to be empty and feel alienated.

Carl Rogers (1902–). Rogers' major contribution to the theory of humanistic psychology is his idea that self-regard is of utmost importance in attaining self-actualization. This self-regard, however, depends largely on the respect of others. The son of highly demanding and rarely satisfied parents will have less self-respect as an adult because he will come to accept their opinion of him as his own. Conversely, a person offered more acceptance and respect will have a much more positive self-concept. More to the point, however, that person will develop a much more *real* self-concept.

Carl Rogers, shown here conducting a therapy session, emphasizes the importance of developing a positive self-concept in order to achieve self-actualization.

If parents or other important adult figures continually place conditions on a child's behavior in order for that child to gain their love and acceptance, chances are that the child, when grown, will continue in that pattern. A young girl whose parents always denied her desire to run and play, like a tomboy, and instead accepted her only as a "little lady," may grow up in that very limited role, never allowing herself to yield to her inner urges because she is sure she will be rejected for it. This clearly blocks self-actualization and in Rogers' view, leads directly to abnormal behavior.

The Psychogenic View: Existentialist Psychology

This branch of psychology is founded on the writings of Sören Kierkegaard (1813–1855), Martin Heidegger (1889–1976), and Jean-Paul Sartre (1905–1980). Their philosophy—*existentialism*—gave birth to a new explanation of abnormal behavior, **existentialist psychology**. Its chief proponents today are Rollo May, Viktor Frankl, and R. D. Laing.

General theory

Existentialists feel that it is impossible to consider human beings separately from the world in which they live. They believe that the relationship between an individual and the world is an intrinsic part of that person's existence. For this reason, we have included existential psychology with the internal models. A satisfactory existence requires living by a number of principles that, at best, are difficult to follow; but in our unfeeling modern world it is even harder. Three of these precepts are **authenticity, freedom and responsibility of choice,** and **becoming**.

Authenticity. This refers to going through life in a way that is consistent with the "real" person that exists inside everyone. This is not an easy task. Society constantly asks for and rewards conformity to its version of what is true and real. Individuals who always stick to their personal principles will almost inevitably experience conflict with someone having different ideas of what is right. Therefore most people hide their true selves deep inside, never expressing real feelings and living behind a false front—a situation that leads to stagnation and a waste of life.

Choice. Every individual has the freedom to choose how to live and the responsibility for whatever choice is made. Opportunities to choose between living authentically and following the group are constantly provided, and individuals must learn not to make these choices blindly. Individuals are always aware of choosing against their inner principles. Nevertheless even knowing that, in the long run, it is not to their advantage, they will often select the wrong course. They build their own lives and, in effect, choose to be unhappy. As Sartre said, "I am my choices."

Becoming. Each day brings a fresh chance to express the real self. If individuals choose at each opportunity to live as authentically as possible within the confines of an intrinsically natural social interaction, they are then becoming. This is a continual growing process, a constant striving for a self-definition that gets progressively clearer. It is a hard road, but it leads to self-fulfillment.

Some individuals lack the courage to choose authenticity. Living behind their false fronts leads to a feeling of emptiness and to the realization that their lives are devoid of anything meaningful. They recognize that they are nothing and have nothing ahead in the future except the ultimate nothing—what existentialists call **nothingness**—which is death. The despair of knowing that they have in essence chosen spiritual death without ever having truly lived is called **existential anxiety**, and this is manifested in abnormal behavior.

Laing views abnormal psychology somewhat differently, as we briefly mentioned in Chapter 1. He feels that society is no longer constructive—in fact, he considers it to be destructive. The limitations under which we are forced to live, the cultural goals we are expected to attain, the overwhelming depersonalization of an increasingly technological society—these and other characteristics, he says, describe a society that is itself sick. Those we call mentally ill have chosen to go back to living authentically. What we who have conformed to the "sick society" see as madness is in actuality an attempt to rediscover the true self. Laing felt this to be especially true for schizophrenia, and most of his research and theory focus on this idea (see Chapter 11).

The Psychogenic View: Cognitive Psychology

As we explained earlier, cognition refers to the thinking processes that people use, the way people interpret information and put it to use. Cognitive psychologists therefore believe that behavioral deviance results from a way of thinking that somehow gets off the normal track. Aaron Beck was one of the first to propose this theory, and he used it primarily to explain clinical depression. Albert Ellis is another cognitive psychologist whose ideas of what causes this "thought derailment" are quite popular.

General theory

According to cognitive theorists, we all talk to ourselves, at least nonverbally and what is said in those private conversations has a lot of bearing on our self-concept and how we interact with other people. For example, a young woman whose date is 30 minutes late might think "Gee, I hope nothing has happened to Bob," or she might think "I'm not going to date this creep again!" But another woman might think "Bob obviously doesn't like me; if he shows up at all it's because his roommate forced him to come." All three different interpretations of Bob's absence will lead to different behaviors once Bob finally arrives. But that third alternative also leads to a specific way that woman will look at herself.

Basically, she blames herself for the date's late arrival. Something is wrong with her, she tells herself, that makes Bob not want to be around her. The first and second thoughts, on the other hand, place the blame on external factors or on Bob, either of which would probably be a more logical assumption to make. Cognitive theorists would say that the self-demeaning line of reasoning is an inappropriate inner punishment, which reinforces behaviors that lead to psychopathology.

Ellis contends that this kind of thought pattern results from what he terms "irrational beliefs," which are simply assumptions with no basis in fact. He gives as very common examples the beliefs that we must be loved (or at least liked) by everyone we know and meet, and that, if we make a mistake, the sky will fall. Anyone who lives under either of these assumptions is clearly doomed to a very trying and frustrating life. No sense of that person's real self will ever be shown and many emotions and thoughts will never be expressed—until they explode in abnormal behavioral symptoms.

Beck believes that some people develop in childhood a whole system of thinking that is self-defeating. He calls such a pattern a **negative cognitive set**. This includes a generally pessimistic view of the world as well as a very poor self-image. Beck has noted in particular three tendencies shared by people with a negative cognitive set:

1. They exaggerate obstacles in life.
2. They attach major significance to trivial negative incidents.
3. They magnify the negative elements of other people's statements.

This theory is examined more thoroughly in Chapter 12.

The biogenic view of etiology and the psychogenic views presented here are clearly classified as internal approaches to explaining abnormal behavior. They focus on changes, whether neurological, genetic, emotional, or cognitive, that occur within the individual. And with one exception, they stipulate that treatment should focus on this internal change. The exception, R. D. Laing's idea that society—not the person—is sick, offers no treatment to counteract what others call insanity. Instead, he views it as a necessary process in recovering the true self. Other theorists, however, have a totally different view of the development of abnormal behavior, one that emphasizes external factors.

MODERN EXTERNAL APPROACHES

Many psychologists feel that human behavior is not motivated from within. Instead, it is more or less determined by external situations or by single elements in those situations. To these theorists, all behavior is pretty much a function of present circumstances and past learning. Thus under certain conditions or in specific surroundings we respond in certain set ways. We can understand what prompts our responses by looking at our learning history and then at present external events.

Different external approaches focus on various elements. Some concentrate on how we learn from specific experiences and how this helps determine future responses. Others focus on the human reactions to enormous societal forces. However, they are all psychogenic because they view the learning and changing of behavior as being dependent on psychological factors.

The Psychogenic View: Behavioral Psychology

This movement grew out of a desire to make psychology more scientific. It is founded on the empirical tradition of basing ideas on clearly observable data, in contrast with the highly introspective model of Freud's psychodynamic approach. The major behavioral theorists also believed that every behavior has a clearly observable (and therefore a clearly identifiable) cause. To them, all behavior—normal and abnormal—is learned, through one of the two basic forms of learning: (1) **classical conditioning**, discovered by Ivan Pavlov, and (2) **operant conditioning**, formulated by B.F. Skinner.

Pavlov and the conditioned reflex

Just after the turn of the century, an experiment conducted by the Russian physiologist Ivan Pavlov (1849–1936) yielded unusual re-

Ivan Pavlov and staff demonstrating the phenomenon Pavlov termed a conditioned reflex.

sults. While studying the salivation of dogs, he noticed that they began salivating even when no food was produced, simply because other things associated with feeding (the person who brought in the bowl or the bowl itself) were present. He then tried an experiment in which he sounded a bell tone immediately before feeding the dogs. The result: the dogs started salivating whenever the tone sounded, even when no food was offered. Pavlov termed this phenomenon a **conditioned reflex**. This meant that the dogs had been taught to respond with an automatic action (salivation) to a stimulus not generally associated with that automatic response. The form of learning that Pavlov demonstrated has since been referred to as *respondent* conditioning as well as classical conditioning.

The elements of this system revolve around the fact that animals (including humans) respond automatically to certain stimuli. A light flashed in your eyes will make you blink, for instance; likewise, a tap on the kneecap makes you jerk your knee. The light and the tap are examples of **unconditioned stimuli**; the responses we make to them (blinking and jerking) are **unconditioned responses**.

If a light flashed—or two golden arches appeared—whenever we were offered food, we would probably start to associate the light (or the arches) with eating. Like Pavlov's dogs, we might then salivate whenever we saw either of these two stimuli. The light and arches are **conditioned stimuli**—that is, stimuli to which we have been taught (conditioned) to respond. Since salivation is not an automatic response to either a flashing light or a golden arch, it is, in this case, now termed a **conditioned response**. If the conditioned stimulus (the flashing light or an arch) were not repeated, the conditioned response to it would eventually disappear, a process that is called **extinction**.

Two important features of respondent conditioning are **generalization** and **discrimination**. Generalization refers to the fact that once a person has been conditioned to respond a certain way to a specific stimulus, that person may respond the same way to similar stimuli without any further conditioning. For instance, if a young woman is conditioned to dislike the feel of mink, her response (dislike) might generalize to any fur, so that she cannot even touch dogs and cats. However, she has the ability to discriminate the original conditioned stimulus (mink) from similar things. Using discrimination, she can learn to avoid mink, and this will still leave her a wide range of furs for a warm coat. In addition, she can have a pet, if she likes.

The early behaviorists

In America, three developments helped further the empirical approach first taken by Pavlov: (1) the publication of John B. Watson's writings, (2) the formulation of behavioral laws by E.L. Thorndike, and (3) the restatement of these laws into a more universal formula, a contribution of B.F. Skinner.

John B. Watson (1878–1958). Watson was convinced that psychology would gain validity as an exact science only by focusing on clearly observable features. He felt that Pavlov's conditioning offered a method of studying human actions that was truly scientific and ordered. His perspective, which he termed **behaviorism** (thus giving the movement its name), saw society as the primary conditioner of human behavior.

The results of his famous experiments with Albert, a baby boy who liked animals, clearly indicated that *phobias,* or irrational fears, could be developed through conditioning. In the study, whenever Albert tried to touch a white rat, a loud noise sounded, which made the child fearful. Gradually, Albert began to associate the white rat with the startling noise, and then with fear. Eventually, the baby cried at the sight of any furry animal, without the added stimulus of the loud noise. This phenomenon eventually generalized to include anything furry. A few years later, another researcher, Mary Cover Jones, reversed this process, removing another child's fear of rabbits by using similar conditioning techniques.

E. L. Thorndike (1874–1949). Thorndike's experiments approached learning, or conditioning, from a different angle. Instead of using painful or pleasant stimuli to induce a certain behavior, he offered them *after* the behavior was performed to see how this affected learning. In his experiments, a cat was placed in a trap-like box, from which it had to figure out the escape route. In successive trials, Thorndike observed that the cat took less and less time to escape when food was offered as a reward each time it gained its freedom.

From this foundation Thorndike formulated his **law of effect:** Behaviors that have a pleasant consequence will more likely be repeated than those that have an unpleasant consequence, or even no consequence at all. Thorndike's experiments with rewards led directly to the highly influential work of B.F. Skinner, who set down the rules of operant conditioning.

Skinner and operant conditioning

B.F. Skinner (1904—) agreed that external stimuli, not internal thoughts, desires, or needs, are the more important factors determining behavior. But Thorndike's law of effect prompted him to conclude that since external stimuli can be manipulated, human behavior can be manipulated as well.

Reinforcement. Skinner's first move was to restate the law of effect, calling it instead the **principle of reinforcement**. He insisted that human behavior can be controlled by *reinforcers,* which strengthen responses—that is, they increase the likelihood that a certain response to a given stimulus will occur. He listed two different types of reinforcers, positive and negative. Both positive and negative reinforcers heighten the chance that a desired response will be repeated, but they work in different ways.

Positive reinforcers are desirable ends in themselves. They strengthen behavior by occurring after the correct response has been given. For example, a young child given a cookie for putting away her toys is likely to learn that each time she puts away her toys she will be rewarded. Since she wants cookies, this may encourage her to be neat. A negative reinforcer is generally something unpleasant; a response will occur by avoiding or removing it. If the same child were made to take care of her fussy brother until she cleaned her room, she might hurry to put her toys away in order to get away from her little brother.

Now suppose that same little girl hit her baby brother and was consequently spanked, a typical punishment. Punishment doesn't have to be unpleasant, and the behavior it follows doesn't have to be inappropriate or undesirable, but punishment must reduce the likelihood that the behavior will recur. If spanking does not discourage the child from hitting her brother, it is not an effective punishment.

Skinner's contention was that with the right reinforcers he could instigate, control, and extinguish complex human behaviors by operating (hence the name operant) on the environment in which they are learned. Operant conditioning, unlike respondent conditioning, is concerned with what happens after the responses are made. Thus we must learn by trial and error what consequences to expect from which operant behaviors.

Dr. B. Frederick Skinner, experimental psychologist at Harvard University, trained a rat in a "Skinner box" to press a lever in order to receive a reward of food. The experiment illustrated the principle of reinforcement.

To a certain extent, we all experience operant conditioning. As children, we learn to eat our vegetables in order to get dessert, to be quiet in a movie theater in order to get popcorn and soda. As adults we learn to be punctual and efficient so that we can keep our jobs and our salaries. In each of these cases, the probable consequence (getting popcorn or getting fired) increases the likelihood that our behavior will be appropriate (being quiet or being a good employee). Notice that the stimulus is withheld until after we exhibit the correct response.

The behavioral explanation of any form of deviance is that it has been learned and systematically reinforced, just like any normal behavior. Behaviorists suggest that there are two ways to account for the development of abnormal behavior:

1. There were inadequate opportunities to learn the appropriate behaviors.
2. The inappropriate behaviors were deliberately or accidentally taught.

This theory is supported by research on children reared from infancy in institutions. Spitz (1945) reported on children who had been brought up in orphanages with minimal contact with adults. As a consequence, these children had learned very few of the behaviors considered normal for children their age. In fact, their actions—especially eating, toileting, talking, relating to others, and other major areas of socialization—were more like those of children half their age.

The theory regarding accidental or deliberate teaching has support, too. Fagin, the rascally leader of the troop of pickpockets in *Oliver Twist,* inculcates immoral and illegal behaviors to sustain his life style. However, most teaching of deviant behavior is not intentional. Usually, it occurs because the parents of a child are themselves troubled, and they unwittingly socialize their children into similar behavior.

Clearly, this approach is quite the opposite of the disease model. Modern behaviorists, such as Ullmann and Krasner (1975), insist that it is as ridiculous to search for the "bug" that causes abnormal behavior as it is to search for the "bug" that causes problems with learning a foreign language.

Bandura and social learning

Although respondent and operant conditioning are two important methods of learning, there is a third way in which we learn behavior, a method demonstrated by Albert Bandura. Essentially, he feels that people learn by imitation, a process he has termed **modeling**. In modeling, children in particular observe the actions of adults (models) and then imitate their behavior. Bandura does not deny the importance of reinforcement in his social learning theory; indeed, his own research proves again how strong the concept of reward is. In one experiment, he asked three groups of children to watch different films showing aggressive behavior (Bandura, et al., 1963). The groups that saw aggression being rewarded or saw that it elicited no consequences were much more apt to respond with aggressive behavior than the group that saw it being punished.

A contribution of modeling is that it demonstrates how complex behaviors or skills—such as playing tennis, cooking, driving a car—can be learned. According to this view, not every behavior must be reinforced before it can be learned. Furthermore, we can observe a model today and still be able to engage in the particular behavior days, weeks, even years later. Social learning also suggests that there are some internal processes at work—that is, there is more to learning than simply responding to external stimuli. In his latest writings (1977), Bandura devotes a good deal of attention to possible cognitive processes involved in learning. Nevertheless, he continues to focus on the external factors that determine behavior, which places him within the behavioral school of thought.

The Sociogenic View: Social Forces

A number of psychologists see abnormal behavior as a problem caused by broad and widespread social forces. Individuals caught up in these forces are like the powerless pawns on a chess board. Behind them, moving them around, are strong cultural currents, especially poverty and social disorder. People who live in abject poverty and in chaotic social conditions are reminded daily how the other half lives: That life is glorified on billboards and in almost every TV show and movie. The poor encounter well-dressed people on city streets (at least in the "better" sections) and must then face their own world: poor food, inadequate clothing and shelter, filthy living conditions, street crime, and a "don't trust anybody" attitude that leaves them virtually isolated. There is no way to brighten this picture—and no way out. Angry, confused, depressed, they eventually give way to despair.

Support for this idea was provided by the research findings of a study conducted by Faris and Dunham (1939). They reported that in the Chicago areas the highest admission rates for schizophrenia came from the central city, the section with the lowest socioeconomic status. They also discovered that the admission rate declined as they moved away from this area into the more affluent suburbs. Jaco (1960) found the number of psychotic admissions in urban areas to be three times greater than in rural zones. Although rural areas are often poorer than city slums, they are in general less frag-

The continuation of cultural traditions, such as this celebration of the Chinese New Year in New York City, acts as a unifying force in the ethnic sections of urban areas.

mented, with a stronger supportive community based on a firmer value system.

Another interpretation is offered for this concentration of psychopathology at the low end of the economic ladder: the **drift hypothesis**. People who exhibit abnormal behavior have drifted downward because they cannot cope effectively with the social demands of a higher class. They cannot hold jobs with much responsibility, which limits their income; with a small income, they cannot afford the trappings of the affluent class: home, car, expensive clothes. Without all these things, they are unwelcome anywhere but the inner city, which is much more tolerant of differences. Several studies (Goldberg and Morrison, 1963; Turner and Wagonfeld, 1967) have found support for this theory.

Other theorists feel certain that the stress of living in the inner city contributes to the development of psychopathology. The **social support hypothesis** points at the lack of support groups that is characteristic of low-income, low-status areas. There is no unifying force: The family group is no longer strong, and religion is no longer the stabilizing influence it once was.

Because the inner city is an ethnically and culturally mixed area, support is more likely to be offered to persons having similar cultural backgrounds; therefore it is not surprising that fragmentation is so widespread. Mintz and Schwartz (1971) found evidence in support of this idea: Among Italian Americans who had an ethnically similar support group, there were fewer hospital admissions for serious mental problems than among those who had limited contact with people from the same culture.

A related set of findings was reported by Brenner (1973). He found that the rate of hospital admissions increased during periods of economic recession. One obvious interpretation is that jobs are a clear social support that fails in times of economic crisis. Without work and the money it supplies, people become more alienated. In addition, the greater numbers of people being affected strain those outside systems of support normally available (such as welfare relief programs), which are overburdened and unable to help as much as usual.

To a certain extent, Laing's notion of the sick society fits here, his belief being that the breakdown of the social structure contributes to psychopathology. However, he ultimately believes that personal choice also has a large role in the development of abnormal behavior, and he also sees schizophrenia, in particular, as an essential step for personal growth. The psychologists who argue for the sociogenic view see individuals as unwilling but essentially will-less victims. They clearly believe that abnormal behavior is caused by external forces.

MODERN INTERACTIONAL APPROACHES

As we have seen, there is at least some support for both the internal and the external approaches to explaining deviant behavior. It should come as no surprise therefore that some theorists have attempted to integrate these two approaches into a single interactional theory. The interactional approach has been most fully developed for schizophrenia, where the evidence for both alternatives is strongest and at the same time clearly contradictory. But there is no reason to believe that the approach is not equally valid for all forms of abnormal behavior. In fact, an interactional explanation can be formulated for most of the disorders described in this book.

One interactional theory was advanced by American psychologist Paul Meehl for the etiology of schizophrenia (1962). Meehl argued that an inherited brain defect is necessary for the development of schizophrenia. This genetic predisposition, *schizotaxia,* involves a defect in neural integration. However, he also stipulated that environmental events must trigger the development of the disorder. Meehl's idea is that schizotaxia is like a seed planted in deep earth. Given the right conditions, it will develop into the full-blown disorder, much as the seed will sprout and grow if given enough sunlight and water. But without severe biological, psychological, or social stress to trigger it, people with schizotaxia exhibit only schizotypic behavior, such as withdrawal and inappropriate emotional expression. They do not exhibit true, diagnosable schizophrenia.

A somewhat different view is that the genetic predisposition to any mental disorder can range from weak to strong, as can the external stressors. In other words, when the combined factors cross some threshold, the clinically detectable form of abnormal behavior will emerge. One such explanation is the **diathesis-stress model**. A diathesis is a predisposing biological factor, usually hereditary; the stress can again be biological or psychosocial. With a strong diathesis, even a modest amount of stress can precipitate the disorder; with a weak diathesis, only a long series of strong and diverse stressors (or possibly one cataclysmic event) will elicit the clinical form.

There is a somewhat more complex interactional view, the **transactional approach** (Sameroff and Zax, 1973). This involves a never-ending spiral of interacting external and internal events. For example, the hereditary predisposition produces a young boy who is a little different, perhaps quiet and withdrawn—a dreamer whose fantasy life is quite vivid and real. Other children cannot participate in the dreams and they reject this slightly peculiar child. Their rejection further inhibits him, and he withdraws more. Clearly, his chances of developing adequate social skills are extremely limited. Without the appropriate social skills, he will never develop adequate peer relationships at any growth stage. In addition, his somewhat peculiar personality combined with low social skills will make it difficult to find and keep a fundamental part of adult independence—a responsible job. Alone and unable to take care of himself, he finally retreats completely. The result is a mental disorder.

In the final analysis, we believe that some type of interactional theory is probably the most likely explanation of how abnormal behavior develops. Almost daily, new discoveries indicate ever more clearly how the brain functions, and that there is a unity between mind and body. Although we may try to separate our thoughts and emotions from their physiological housing—the brain—we are now more aware than ever that this is a false, if not impossible, way to study behavior.

SUMMARY

Explanations of abnormal behavior can be categorized as internal, external, and interactional. Internal explanations focus on the physiological and psychological functioning of an individual; external theories focus on outside forces; interactional explanations combine the principles of internal and external explanations. The major theories of today are internal, but in the past major theories switched between the internal and external approach, ranging from demonic possession to simple disease. Hippocrates was a major influence on a more rational view of abnormal behavior, but his ideas were to be replaced by the more superstitious attitudes of the Middle Ages.

The Age of Enlightenment saw many new scientific advances and a return to more rational explanations of psychopathology. The disease model in particular was favored, which set the stage for the dispute between biogenic and psychogenic theories. There is some support for various biogenic views, especially the genetic and biochemical theories. However, there is also support for the various psychogenic theories that became prominent after the work of Sigmund Freud was popularized.

Freud advanced an intricate psychoanalytic explanation of the development of abnormal behavior. The ego has lost its ability to maintain proper balance between the mind's three facets. Consequently, either the id or the superego rules the personality. Defense mechanisms such as repression eventually impair normal functioning. The ego can be so weakened that it finally collapses and loses all contact with the real world, a condition Freud called psychosis.

Post-Freudian theorists accepted many of Freud's basic premises, but most of them felt he placed too much emphasis on sexual motivation and too little on social factors. Humanistic and existential psychologists both see psychopathology as a manifestation of the inability to attain self-fulfillment. Cognitive theorists blame behavioral problems on the thinking process, which somehow gets off-track and becomes very negative and self-destructive.

Behavioral psychologists see the cause as external. They focus on the learning process and contend that abnormal behavior is like any other behavior—it has simply been learned and positively reinforced. Social learning theorists believe that people learn deviant actions by modeling the behavior of other deviant individuals, usually those they admire. Still other external explanations see psychopathology as the result of poverty and social disorganization.

A few psychologists have proposed interactional theories. The diathesis-stress hypothesis, for example, suggests that a physiological predisposition, probably inherited, is triggered by environmental stress. Such interactional explanations are probably the most accurate, since they do not conflict with the basic unity of mind and body.

CHAPTER 4

Managing Abnormal Behavior

THE ISSUE OF MANAGEMENT

Society's Response

HISTORICAL PERSPECTIVES

Ancient Management Methods

The Methods of Classical Greece

Medieval Methods

Beginnings of Reform

Moral Therapy

Human Warehouses

THE MENTAL HEALTH MOVEMENT

Efficacy of the Disease Model

New Medical Treatments

PSYCHOLOGICAL MANAGEMENT: INTERNAL APPROACHES

Mesmerism

Psychoanalysis

Humanistic Methods

Existentialist Methods

Cognitive Methods

PSYCHOLOGICAL MANAGEMENT: EXTERNAL APPROACHES

Behavior Therapy

Social Methods

IS PSYCHOLOGICAL MANAGEMENT EFFECTIVE?

The Community Mental Health Center

Success of the Mental Health Centers

In the preceding three chapters, we have attempted to relate all the difficulties associated with defining, describing, and explaining abnormal behavior. Clearly, it is a very complex process, integrating concepts that are formed at the very lowest level of social organization—the single individual—with those formulated by the intricate meshings of society—and with those of many different societies. It is made even more complicated by a necessary final question: How do we manage the problem? What do we—and what *should* we—do with people who exhibit abnormal behavior?

THE ISSUE OF MANAGEMENT

The term "management" may seem a little inappropriate in this particular context. It sounds too businesslike, a little cold and uncaring. After all, aren't we talking about mental *patients*? Shouldn't we be discussing treatment, or cure, or at least intervention?

We have chosen the term management instead of treatment for two reasons. First, treatment implies an ability to overcome the problem, to "cure the patient." In actuality, our present treatment methods have never been that complete or that successful. At best, we treat symptoms; we certainly do not cure. No one knows why or for how long these treatments work. We do know, however, that they often create other problems that are almost as bad as the disorders they treat.

Second, treatment implies a more caring attitude than has generally been shown. It would be false to say that we have never been caring about those troubled with mental disorders. However, it is not false to say that our first concern has always been for mainstream society, not for the mentally disturbed, a point that will be illustrated in the last chapter, which discusses prevention. History proves that management—that is, coping with the problem, trying to get around it in order to get on with living—is really the most appropriate term.

Perhaps our attitudes result from the fortunate fact that the incidence and prevalence of most mental disorders are low compared with, say, the number of divorces, which can also disrupt lives—even though there is no way of telling how many divorces are the result of some mental problem. And of course, the more the public is aware of any issue as a widespread problem, the more willing it is to cooperate in trying to solve it.

As we said, humanity has not been *un*responsive. Many times in the past there has been a real desire to eradicate the problem of psychopathology once and for all. Many attempts were made to improve the situation, and many succeeded. This chapter will take a look at what we have done to and for individuals who are mentally ill.

Society's Response

At the most general level, the societal response to abnormal behavior is determined by the culture—by its nature and beliefs about what causes the phenomenon. These factors in turn affect how the people close to an afflicted person—family, neighbors, colleagues, friends—will respond. In addition, societal beliefs also influence the person's own self-image.

As we mentioned previously, the treatments used for abnormal behavior will depend in large part on the explanation that is currently in vogue. If possession by devils is the prevailing explanation, then whatever is required to exorcise those devils is clearly the appropriate treatment. If unconscious conflicts are to blame, then bringing them into consciousness so they can be faced and resolved is in order. If the problem is simply a result of poor social skills, then training in social competence will set matters aright. Since society supports only one explanation at a time (usually), the preferred treatment tends to change only when the explanation changes. A major problem with this attitude is that it overlooks the very strong possibility that the different kinds of abnormal behavior have different etiologies and require different treatments.

The range of past and present societal responses is enormous, from relative indifference—ignoring anything but the most destruc-

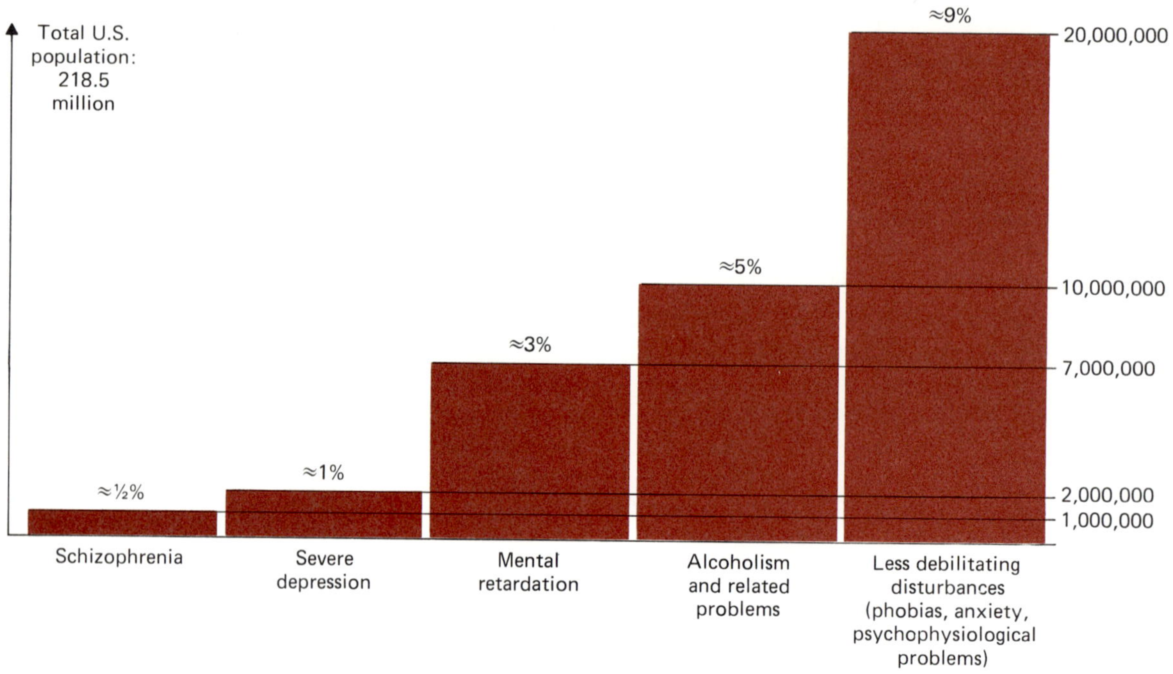

Figure 4.1. *The estimated incidence of several disorders. From the National Institute of Mental Health, 1978.*

tive or bizarre behavior—to ruthless action—executing anyone who is too different. In small, traditional societies that strongly value the nuclear family (father, mother, and children), dear old Aunt Agatha, with her strange ideas of religious persecution and damnation, will probably be seen as a problem for the family—not for society—to manage. Aunt Agatha's family would never consider sending her away! But in urban areas and highly technological societies, the size and importance of the traditional family have eroded. There is little room—too often literally—and even less patience for maintaining mentally disturbed family members at home. The "village idiot," once the source of humor and pity, is now safely ensconced in a state school or hospital for the retarded and is securely out of mind.

Research conducted by Kitano (1969) clearly illustrates this point. In Hawaii, Japanese Americans are divided into three major groups: Issei, first-generation immigrants from Japan; Nisei, the second generation, born in Hawaii of first-generation parents; and Sansei, Japanese Americans born in Hawaii of Hawaiian-born parents. Of these groups, the Sansei are much more acculturated to a typically American way of life. The Issei, on the other hand, still hold to the more traditional Japanese culture.

Kitano studied hospitalization patterns for mental disorders for all three groups. As expected, the Issei had a much lower rate than the Nisei and Sansei—in fact, it was even lower than that of other ethnic groups living in Hawaii. It was very close to the hospitalization rate of mainland Japan, where the cultural response is still "take care of your own." The Issei who were hospitalized were severely disturbed, which meant they stayed there longer and were less likely to be discharged. In addition, the typical hospitalized Issei was an elderly, single male with few or no family ties. Among the Sansei, the rate was virtually the same as that for any other ethnic group in Hawaii, and much higher than the Issei and even the Nisei. Clearly, this group had adopted a more "modern American" attitude toward and way of responding to abnormal behavior.

HISTORICAL PERSPECTIVES

A review of how behavioral deviance has been managed over recorded history is interesting and provides support for our major contention—that the societal response to abnormal behavior reflects the prevailing theories of cause. The management issue will also be made clearer by such a review.

Ancient Management Methods

The primary view of abnormal behavior during ancient times was that the person was possessed by evil spirits. It followed, therefore, that bringing the person back to normal required getting rid of these spirits. The only problem was to figure out how this could best be accomplished. Records of the time show that there was a good bit of conflict on this point.

For example, fossilized skulls indicate that some prehistoric tribes practiced *trephining*—a procedure in which a hole was made in the skull so that the evil spirit or spirits could make their escape more easily. It is not known how many patients did not outlive their exorcism, but many did apparently survive. Of course, it is not known whether these survivors became normal or remained possessed. In any event, the method didn't survive, as later cultures became much more progressive.

The Bible records conflicting management techniques: In the Book of Samuel, King Saul's evil spirit was relieved by the music from David's harp; in Leviticus, the recorder wrote that the only way to exorcise spirits was to stone their host to death. Prayer, incantations, starvation, and torture had their proponents, too. The modern notion of the "snake pit" comes from the ancient belief that evil spirits were so terrified of snakes that placing possessed people in a pit filled with poisonous snakes was certain to drive the spirits out. Such conflicting ideas of management did not seem to disturb anyone. If people were killed by any of these "cures," the healers could not be blamed; they had, after all, only the best intentions.

Some theorists speculate that King Saul's intense headaches were caused by a disorder such as migraine and that David brought him relief by playing soothing music on his harp.

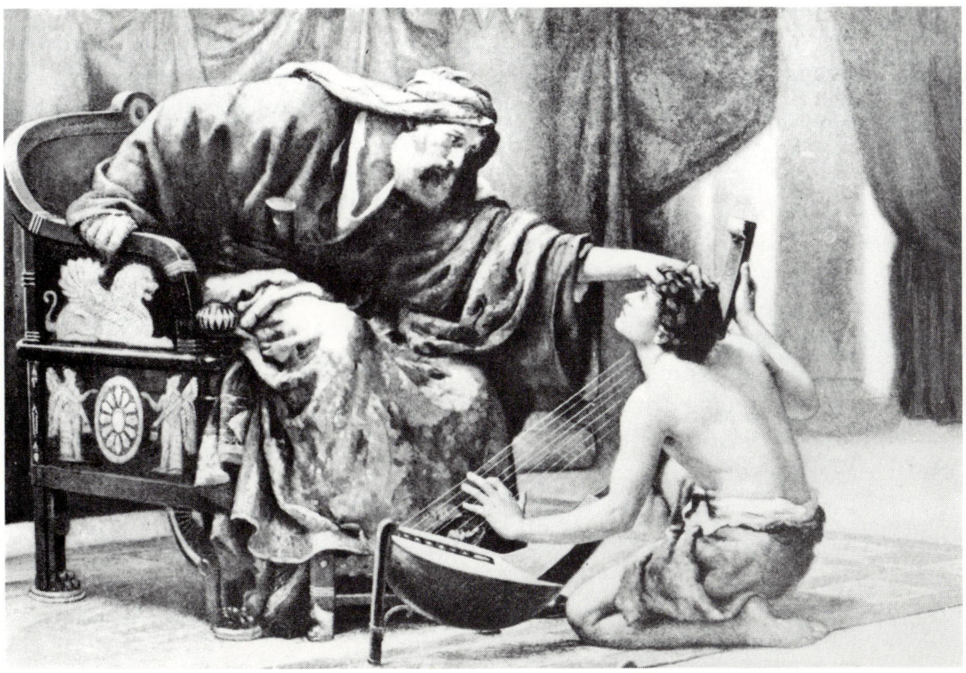

The Methods of Classical Greece

Hippocrates developed a rather different view of the etiology of mental disturbances. His insistence upon a rational, more naturalistic approach was very much the beginning of the modern disease model, or medical model, of abnormal behavior. However, Hippocrates' ideas about etiology and treatment were hampered by the understanding of human anatomy and physiology that then prevailed—a situation that is equally true today. However, the ancient Greek understanding was severely limited. They were very reluctant to perform autopsies or to otherwise "defile" the body, so their ideas of bodily functions were based on not-too-well-educated guesses. Consequently, they came up with some peculiar, although interesting, notions.

Recall that Hippocrates explained deviant behavior as the result of an imbalance of four bodily humors—blood, black bile, yellow bile, and phlegm. An obvious approach to treatment was to restore this balance. Unfortunately, Hippocrates didn't know how to do this—at least not directly; instead, he recommended indirect treatments. He suggested, for example, that pursuing a low-key life, abstaining from alcohol, meats, and sexual encounters, and exercising regularly would improve the balance, suggestions that seem quite modern. It is worth noting that despite his insistence on a physical etiology, Hippocrates stressed environmental controls in his treatments, a management paradox that still exists.

Although Hippocrates' recommendations were somewhat vague, they were quite humane. They led to the later development in Greece of *asylums*—places that housed mentally ill people, away from the rest of society, where they were exposed to regular rest, exercise, soothing music, and affectionate care. These benign settings were actually special temples dedicated to the god Saturn, who was thought to be responsible for these unfortunates.

Medieval Methods

When Rome fell to barbarian invaders in the fifth century, the rational approach to treatment fell with it. In the Middle Ages, old superstitions about demonology reappeared, beliefs that were readily accepted by the then-struggling church. People who behaved strangely were believed to be possessed either by Satan or by lesser evil spirits, and their care was clearly the province of the clergy. Monasteries were frequently used both as refuges and as places for confinement and treatment.

Treatment at the monasteries generally started with the monks hurling insults at the spirits who possessed the body. This practice sprang from the belief that Satan's pride had led to his fall from grace. But everyone knew that getting rid of the devil was not easy; so if pages-long curses did not work, there was always torture.

Torture, especially the more horrible and excruciating forms, always produced some results. The person invariably confessed to allowing the possession to take place (everyone was convinced that Satan enters only those people who have paved his way by committing some wickedness). Of course, some people died. Since the belief was that the body was not as important as the immortal soul, which was now free to go to God, the deaths did not concern many people. The torturers were doing their duty, and all of them were certain that what they did was beneficial to those they treated and to the community at large.

This kind of treatment was also popular for witches, a phenomenon of the late Middle Ages and early Renaissance. However, witches did not merely commit some evil deed that made Satan's entry easier; they actually *invited* him to enter and possess their bodies and minds. Blasphemy on this order naturally demanded death as the necessary treatment, once torture had wrung out a confession.

Torture was an almost universal management method in the western civilizations of the fourteenth, fifteenth, and sixteenth centuries. But there were pockets of more humane treatment. As we mentioned, certain monasteries believed that their mission was to care for the mentally disturbed. They opened their asylum doors, offering food, shelter, and escape from attack by hysterical mobs. Eventually, these asylums became badly overcrowded, filthy, and ridden with vermin. Those exhibiting the most severe symptoms were often chained and shackled in an attempt to maintain some order. The conditions at Bethlehem Hospital, a monasterial asylum in London, were so chaotic and horrible that our word *bedlam* is derived from that name. It was not at all uncommon for those in charge of these institutions to sell tickets to the general public so that they could see the "crazies" perform; the attendants made sure the patients gave the audience a good show.

The belief in demonic possession gradually subsided, and by the middle of the eighteenth century an interest in the disease model was beginning to appear. However, the care and management of disturbed people remained atrocious. Many continued to wander about, living squalid lives as beggars, undergoing constant harassment. They were generally looked upon as being subhuman, less valuable even than farm animals. There was no differentiation between felons, paupers, and the mentally disturbed; all were regarded in about the same light and treated similarly. But late in the eighteenth century there came a dramatic reversal.

Beginnings of Reform

The Age of Enlightenment saw a number of radical changes in people's beliefs. Old superstitions were replaced with a spirit of scientific inquiry, and the result was a better understanding of how the body functions. There was a return to a more rational view of psychopathology, and a sense of humanitarianism emerged. Reforms in treatment soon followed, both in Europe and in the New World.

Reforms in Europe

One of the most important figures in the European reform movement was Philippe Pinel (1745–1826), a French physician. He decided to devote his life to the study and treatment of insanity after the death of one of his friends, who after going mad had run into the woods and was killed by wild animals. In 1792, in the middle of the French Revolution, he was appointed director of La Bicêtre, a mental hospital in Paris. He took the unprecedented and initially unpopular step of unchaining the patients, some of whom had not been out of their cells for more than 30 years. He also did away with such violent treatment methods as bleeding, purging, and blistering. Instead, he insisted upon humane and moral treatments, which simply involved rest, proper food, a regular routine, and kind care. All of this sounds, like Hippocrates' suggestions, quite ordinary, but it was revolutionary for Pinel's time. Not surprisingly, just being unchained wrought positive effects on the patients, many of whom wept with joy.

Pinel's reforms were then instituted with equally satisfying results at other French hospitals, such as La Salpêtrière. Jean Esquirol (1772–1840), Pinel's colleague and successor, continued Pinel's work and was able to establish ten new hospitals in France for the care of mental patients. This made France the center of humane and moral treatment in the Western world.

Similar developments were occurring in England, where William Tuke (1732–1822), an English Quaker, founded the York Retreat. This hospital for the mentally disturbed was based on the Quaker principles of human kindness and respect. The work of Tuke and his son, Henry, was greatly aided by the reports from France of the success of Pinel and Esquirol. England thus joined France in improving the care of the mentally disturbed and in implementing the disease model by turning the asylums into hospitals. For instance, in 1841, trained nurses were used for the first time in Gloucester Asylum, further cementing the idea that these were indeed hospitals, not prisons.

The Gheel community in Belgium also deserves mention. This was not a new idea; Gheel had existed as a shrine for the mentally disturbed ever since the thirteenth century. Thousands visited it yearly, hoping to be cured. Many pilgrims were taken into the homes of local families for the duration of their stay, a custom that gradually expanded: As people grew less fearful about the disturbed, more and more pilgrims ended up staying and living with the people who had taken them in. Thus normal and abnormal lived peacefully together, each group benefiting from the other's presence. What is most remarkable is that the Gheel colony is still thriving today, a fact that merits much more acclaim than it has received.

Reforms in America

The reform movement swept the New World as well. One of the truly extraordinary figures in the American movement was Benjamin Rush (1745–1813). A well-known physician, he was also a signer of the Declaration of Independence, a delegate to the Continental Congress, the surgeon general of Washington's army, a treasurer of the U.S. mint, founder of the first free medical clinic in the United States, and the author of the first American psychiatric textbook, *Medical Inquiries and Observations upon Diseases of the Mind*, published in 1812. Rush used leeches to bleed patients, believing that abnormal behavior resulted from a blood overload in the brain, caused by overexcitement. He also developed a method called *tranquilizing,* which involved strapping patients into a strange device and then plunging them into ice cold water. Both of these interventions were intended to reduce the flow of blood to the brain, not to harm the patients.

As part of his treatment, Rush advocated a considerate and humane attitude toward the disturbed. He believed that proper nutrition was essential and even encouraged the hospital staff to bring fruits and sweets to the patients. He insisted on hiring only compassionate and intelligent staff members, who would be able to converse with patients, read to them, and participate in their activities—a set of injunctions that also holds for today's mental health personnel. Clearly, Rush's title as the "father of American psychiatry" is well deserved.

Another important figure in the reform movement was Dorothea Dix (1802–1887), who spent her early adulthood as an unheralded Boston school teacher. She was forced to retire early because of illness, and in 1841 began teaching Sunday school in jails, poorhouses, and asylums. In 1848 she submitted a petition to Congress stating that she had seen almost 10,000 people, primarily mentally disturbed and retarded adults, "bound with galling chains, bowed beneath fetters and heavy iron balls attached to drag chains, lacerated with ropes, scourged with rods and terrified beneath storms of excretion and cruel blows; now subject to jibes and scorn and torturing tricks; now abandoned to the most outrageous violations" (Zilboorg and Henry, 1941, pp. 583–584).

For four decades, Dix singlemindedly campaigned in the United States, Canada, and England for the humane management of mental patients. She spoke before most of the state legislatures, convincing some fifteen states as well as Canada and Scotland of the need to build and staff more suitable institutions for the mentally disturbed. Considering the times and the apathy of most politicians to such an issue, her success is astounding: She is personally credited with initiating the construction of 32 mental hospitals. A great heroine in the war against inhumanity, superstition, and ignorance, she was honored in 1901 by the U.S. Congress.

Dix's work was followed by that of Clifford Beers, a graduate of Yale University who suffered a breakdown and was hospitalized as a result. In 1908 he published his now-famous book, *A Mind that Found Itself*, which recounted his breakdown and the horrible treatment he received in three typical institutions of the period. Beers graphically portrayed the inhumanity of physical restraints, especially straitjackets, which were used to control excited patients. He finally recovered after a compassionate and friendly hospital attendant took him home and treated him with affectionate care.

With this book Beers began his lifelong efforts to humanize the management of the disturbed and to educate the American people about the problems that are posed by the mentally ill—regarding themselves and the entire society. His work led to the formulation of what is today the National Association for Mental Health, which continues to struggle for the same goals.

Moral Therapy

A common feature in all these humanitarian reforms was kindness to the patient. Seeking to gain the confidence of the patients and instill in them a sense of hope, Pinel and his followers developed what has since become known as **moral therapy**. This involved creating a totally therapeutic environment—social, psychological, and physical. Moral therapy assumed that the problem was psychological and therefore that it could be cured through understanding, patience, kindness, and proper care directed at the patient's psychological state. Each patient had an individualized treatment program based on personal needs. Another feature of this new approach was that the patient actively participated in the treatment process. Especially important in moral therapy was placing the patients in a new and different environment, so that patterns associated with their past history could be broken. This last idea came from some new theories in psychology that stressed the influence of the environment on emotional and mental states.

The beneficial aspects

Samuel Woodward (1787–1850), an American physician and the first president of what is now the American Psychiatric Association, was one of the people interested in the effects of environment. Although he believed that mental dis-

An innovative treatment for nervous ataxia practiced during the nineteenth century at Salpêtrière Hospital in Paris, which exemplified the reform concept that patients should actively participate in therapy.

orders were the symptoms of a somatic disease, he felt that human beings were governed by unchangeable natural laws that provided a guide to proper living. If these laws were followed, both a healthy mind and a healthy body resulted; if not, neither the body nor the mind could function normally. Therefore he felt that psychopathology, although organically caused, could have psychological elements as well.

According to this view, insanity was at least partially self-inflicted. By ignoring the straight and narrow road of the natural laws governing health, people placed themselves instead on the road to mental illness. Woodward named intemperance, ill health, masturbation, religiosity, personal disappointments, and even the routine pressures of the business and commercial world to be unnatural and the leading causes of insanity. By removing these elements he believed that both the symptoms and the disease itself would disappear; and the sooner it happened, the better the person's chances for recovery.

Close-up: "Enlightened" Nineteenth-Century Therapies

The nineteenth century saw several unusual methods of dealing with mental disorder, many of them holdovers from ancient times; both bloodletting and sudden shocks from either cold water or electric current (Galen had used live eels) were among the treatments still widely used. But some new techniques were gaining popularity.

Because masturbation was long believed to lead to insanity, extreme measures were sometimes taken to discourage the practice. One method utilized a male "chastity belt," which consisted of a metal plate attached to a leather waist belt. The penis was inserted through an opening in the plate, at the rim of which was a sharp prong that issued a sharp jab if the wearer had an erection. This method was, however, a good deal milder than the operations that desensitized or removed the sex organs of "stubborn" cases.

Quite an opposite approach was taken by James Graham, who billed himself as James Graham, O.W.L. (Oh! Wonderful Love!). His treatment (for all problems) consisted of having the person (or persons) spend the night in the "Magnetico-Electrico" bed he had built in a highly ornamented, domed temple. The bed was 12 feet by 9 and rested on 40 glass pillars. Blue lights shone overhead, while music and incense wafted up from below. Graham asserted that sleeping in his "celestial bed" would cure any physical or mental problem; in addition, any children conceived during this therapy would live gloriously trouble-free lives.

The therapy that drew the most attention, however, was phrenology, the determination of personality and intelligence by examining the shape of the skull. Viennese physician Franz Joseph Gall originated this theory after noticing that his most brilliant students had bulging eyes. He then examined many hundreds of skulls—those of prisoners and patients in insane asylums as well as those of his most gifted colleagues. From these studies he derived a map of the areas of the brain that supposedly affected mental and emotional faculties. A typical diagnosis was that a woman with a hysterical pregnancy had been overstimulated in the region that controlled love for children. Vienna found Gall's ideas too unorthodox and he was forced to leave. But one of his students, John Caspar Spurzheim, was given a tumultuous welcome in the United States.

Removing the person to a place where moral therapy could be provided clearly enhanced this possibility.

The development in Massachusetts of the Worcester State Mental Hospital under Woodward's leadership provided exactly such a setting. There, in the days of Woodward's charge (1833–1846), the patients were provided with a substantial but simple diet, kind and respectful staff members, and the freedom to use the hospital grounds and even to go into the city without supervision. Woodward apparently established close personal relationships with nearly every patient, all of whom came from a background similar to his—middle-to-upper-class, educated, Protestant, New England-born and bred. Woodward's treatment program, clearly based on his own notions of etiology, was both integrated and cohesive.

How successful was moral therapy? According to Grob (1965), Woodward's own research reported that over 50 percent of the initial admissions to the hospital were discharged as recovered. An independent follow-up study found that 58 percent of those who were discharged never had a relapse. These findings are very impressive when compared with today's figures, but they're even more incredible when we realize that the discharged group included a great many chronic (that is, long-term) cases. We must conclude that the family atmosphere of this small hospital, with its humanistic care and hopeful attitude, produced a therapeutic environment that had lasting and beneficial effects on its patients.

The reasons for decline

This brings up a critical question: If moral therapy was so successful in producing therapeutic gains, even for chronic patients, why did it decline and virtually disappear as a valid management approach in the next century? Apparently, a number of factors played an important role in this change.

Lack of leadership. The individuals who initiated moral therapy—Pinel, Esquirol, Tuke, and Woodward, for instance—were charismatic leaders who generated to their subordinates an extraordinary enthusiasm. There is little doubt that these intellectual pioneers had a personal vision, a deep commitment, and an energy level that exhausted their followers. Unfortunately, their successors had a more pedestrian style, a more limited vision, and a lot less energy. Consequently, they found it difficult to generate as much enthusiasm for the project—both in themselves and in others—as had the previous generation of leaders.

Overpopulation. The very success of moral therapy may have contributed to its decline. Worcester State, for instance, built up a solid and well-founded reputation, but then faced more and more petitions for admission. In the period from 1833 to 1852, the patient population more than quadrupled. With over 500 inmates, the strain on the facilities and staff was unbearable. As the population grew, the hospital became less able to provide proper care. For example, from 1834 to 1853, the physician-to-patient ratio rose from 1:58 to 1:140, a situation that caused the close, kindly relationship between physician and patient to disappear. Grob (1965) notes that many patients had no physician entries in their records for as long as three to five years; meanwhile, any consultations that did occur were superficial and brief, a state of affairs that is all too frequent today.

Different patient mix. The original patient population, consisting of nonviolent cases from typical New England stock was suddenly changed by two elements. The first was a growing tendency for families to have more dangerously violent people committed. The knowledge that their seriously disturbed loved ones were in a hospital, receiving moral therapy, was much more comforting than the thought of them locked away in prison or on a county poor farm.

The second was that New England was being overwhelmed by foreign immigrants, for the most part poor Irish Catholics—farmers fleeing the devastating potato famine. The New England they flooded had a wholly different character: strong ties with England and its class distinctions; a primarily middle- and upper-class society of tradespeople, educators, and artisans; a predominantly Protestant—in fact,

Puritan—tradition, which included a deep anti-Catholic sentiment. The immigrants, traumatized by destitution, by the move to an alien culture, by the switch from rural life to an urban and industrial life style, were prime candidates for mental health problems. They were hospitalized in droves. Grob (1965) estimates that in the late nineteenth century, about 70 percent of the patients in Massachusetts hospitals and asylums were Irish immigrants.

Clearly, these extreme ethnic differences did not help the already deteriorating situation in the hospitals. Establishing a close therapist-patient relationship was much harder when the two came from such different worlds. The very negative feelings toward the immigrants that pervaded the native population also made it difficult for the support staff to be kind and considerate.

Staff problems. Overpopulation and a more difficult patient group led to an overworked but underpaid nonprofessional support staff. Eventually, most of them left. Their replacements were neither well educated nor committed to the success of the hospitals. Consequently, the annual turnover rate was very high—almost half of the staff at some points (Grob, 1965).

The contact these nonprofessionals had with the patients increasingly became the only interaction the patients received. Such a support staff might have been able to function as lay-therapists, a kind of responsibility that might in turn have improved their sense of commitment, if they had received training in the precepts and techniques of moral therapy. But none of them did because treatment was still considered to be the exclusive province of the physicians. After all, the heart of moral therapy was the physician-patient relationship; any intrusion into this relationship was considered to be harmful for therapy. Lay personnel could simply not be trusted to administer such complex programs. If not enough physicians were available, the obvious conclusion was that moral therapy simply could no longer be provided.

All of these diverse factors resulted in the decline of moral therapy. During the latter part of the nineteenth century and for most of the twentieth as well, this management method virtually disappeared. Instead, restraints, both physical and chemical, reappeared. Seclusion rooms, straitjackets, and bed bindings were reinstituted. Drugs to produce a quiet stupor, especially morphine and opium, became common. Working in the hospital—on the farm, in the laundry, in the kitchen—replaced occupational therapy, which had previously formed an important part of treatment. But two thirds to three quarters of the patients were too feeble or too disturbed to be trusted at such work, so the hospital became a custodial institution, where simply keeping the patients under control became the criterion of success. This change of the therapeutic hospital into a custodial institution was not reversed until after World War II.

It is interesting to note that the failure to establish the close relationships essential to moral therapy was never seen as an inadequacy on the part of the physicians. The blame for this was placed elsewhere. Some psychiatrists attributed it to the unreachability of the patients from low socioeconomic backgrounds or different cultures, saying that these patients simply couldn't understand or respond. Others argued that the patients had inborn character defects, which accounted for both their low status and their deviant behaviors. Still others argued, not without reason, that the overcrowded and poorly staffed mental hospitals made moral therapy impossible; only custodial care was feasible under such bad conditions.

Human Warehouses

By the end of the nineteenth century, the prevailing attitude was that abnormal behaviors, especially the psychotic varieties, could not be treated effectively. Consequently, the importance of psychological factors, either in etiology or treatment, was rejected. The completely somatic point of view—the disease model—again became popular. The role of the mental hospital was simply to warehouse patients, until such time as some underlying organic cause was found to provide the cure.

And human warehouses they were: large and grim buildings removed from urban cen-

By the late nineteenth century, mental hospitals had become little more than human warehouses. Benign neglect might best describe the policy at such institutions.

ters and cut off from the surrounding communities by walls, fences, and guardhouses. The treatment in practice was "benign neglect." Low budgets, inadequately trained professional and nonprofessional staffs, and the waning enthusiasm for reform led to even more overcrowding and even worse conditions.

Fox (1978) provides a fascinating picture of the inmates of these warehouses in his historical report of 1,229 people committed as insane to California's state mental hospitals early in this century. The legal criterion for commitment at the time was that a person be "so disordered in mind" as to be "dangerous . . . at large"; however, this was apparently interpreted quite loosely. The report indicates that less than one third of the inmates were dangerous or even severely disturbed. The rest were "imbeciles, dotards, idiots, drunkards, simpletons, fools, the aged, the vagabond, the helpless." Especially at risk for commitment were male adults from blue-collar backgrounds who had no strong family or other social support systems.

Fox argues that this overinclusiveness in the California definition of deviant behavior accounts for California's having the highest rate of commitment in the United States. Interestingly, his findings are very much like those of Kitano (1969), discussed earlier in this chapter. They both support the idea that commitment to a mental hospital relieves society of having to deal with peculiar people who have no one else to look after them—the bothersome rather than the dangerous.

THE MENTAL HEALTH MOVEMENT

For decades workers in the mental health movement have been trying to persuade the general public to accept the biogenic view—the idea that mental illness is just like any other illness. An underlying assumption of this movement has been that the therapeutic attitudes toward somatic illness would be transferred to mental illness, thereby removing the stigma of being called mentally ill. The quality of care would also improve: Public interest would be heightened and more public funds would be available; the caliber of personnel attracted to this field would then improve, and more attention would be given to identifying and eliminating those factors that cause mental disturbance. Many among the lay leadership of the National Association for Mental Health honestly believe that if mental illness were regarded in exactly the same light as physical illness, several major management problems would be solved and society could focus on prevention, which they see as the goal of the next mental health revolution. However, we seriously doubt that a strictly medical model could ever be that completely effective.

Efficacy of the Disease Model

Even if most of the disorders listed in DSM-III do eventually turn out to be organically caused, our view of those with these problems (that is, whether they are ultimately considered to be acceptable to society) will still help to determine how they are managed and treated. In addition, society's attitude will influence the attitudes of these individuals toward their illness, the degree of their handicap, and the way they are able to fit in with the rest of us. And these attitudes will have tremendous effects on recovery and rehabilitation. In other words, a positive societal attitude could mean the difference between a person's becoming an emotional cripple, even though clinically normal again, and a vibrant and active individual.

Suppose a medical cure for schizophrenia were to be developed tomorrow. How would we respond to someone like Arnold in Chapter 1? Would he suddenly become a competent person in our eyes, able to cope with the complexities of today's society? Hardly! Even if his peculiarities were to vanish, the social skills that he has been so sadly lacking throughout his adult life would not suddenly appear, and the social and economic resources needed to rehabilitate him into the mainstream would be almost nonexistent.

Studies indicate that the response to the Arnolds of our society, regardless of how much they have recovered, is not very positive. It has also been shown that the crusade of public acceptance of the medical model of behavioral deviance has failed (Cumming and Cumming, 1957; Nunnally, 1961; Phillips, 1963). The general public has not been persuaded that illness is an appropriate way to regard abnormal behavior. While there is a general willingness to tolerate and accommodate the less bizarre overt behaviors, there is still a strong stigma attached to having experienced any mental disorder. The history of our shoddy management of the mentally disturbed is additional proof of how we really feel about the problem, no matter what the cause. The asylums and mental hospitals we've established were built primarily to protect the rest of us from the "weirdos." They did not change our negative feelings, and they certainly did not endear any former patients to mainstream society.

What is even more interesting is that those who minister to the mentally ill—psychiatrists, psychologists, psychiatric nurses, social workers, and so on—also tend to get the same negative response. There seems to be a fascination with mental health professionals—or rather, with what is popularly believed they can do, which is to more or less "read minds." Of course, existing alongside that fascination is the very real fear that they will uncover something dreadful about us that we don't want anyone to know—and probably don't want to face ourselves. With such ambivalent feelings on the part of most of the population, it seems that the mental health movement has taken on a giant task in trying to change the cultural attitude.

Despite the failure of the moral crusade to alter the feelings of the public toward abnormal behavior, two events that occurred in the past three decades drastically changed our outlook regarding management and the techniques used and also gave the disease model a lot of support: first, the development of a variety of treatments, especially psychoactive drugs, that altered behavior; and second, another reshaping of the role of the mental hospital to more closely fit the goals of the mental health movement.

New Medical Treatments

Thus far in this chapter we have been concerned with the issue of managing behavioral deviance—that is, with the efforts that have been used to control the mentally disturbed at the societal level, especially using the currently in favor medical model. But management has another aspect: treatment, which involves using remedies to try to cure the problem. This is clearly part of an overall management strategy, but it is not directly related to prevention, public attitudes, or rehabilitation—all of which are implied in the concept of management. Although we have in the past tried, more or less unsuccessfully, to deal with the problem of management, until very recently little has been done about actual treatment.

However, the dominance of the disease model led to the establishment of a number of research laboratories, which were created for the special purpose of discovering the cause of abnormal behavior. As we have noted, it was assumed that finding the cause of mental illness would automatically lead to discovering the cure. A famous laboratory founded in Worcester, Massachusetts, had a long-term partnership with the Worcester State Mental Hospital discussed earlier in this chapter.

Antipsychotic drugs

Despite all our efforts, no clear-cut etiology of any of the major disorders has yet been pinned down. Nevertheless, major breakthroughs were made in the treatment of two severe forms of mental disturbance: schizophrenia and the affective disorders (depression and manic-depression). Specifically, a number of **antipsychotic drugs** were synthesized—drugs that reduce psychotic symptoms. Some nonchemical treatments were also developed that had almost as great an impact. Because they clearly illuminate both the benefits and problems of the medical model, we will briefly review these discoveries.

Reserpine. For untold centuries, *pagla-kadawa,* which means "insanity herb" (actually, the snakeplant root, *rauwolfia*), had been used in India to treat a variety of conditions, from snakebite to high blood pressure to insanity (Snyder, 1974). Finally, in 1931, two Indian physicians conducted the first formal study of rauwolfia in the treatment of high blood pressure (hypertension) and psychosis. For twenty years little attention was given to this report, until a Swiss pharmaceutical company became interested while trying to find a treatment for hypertension.

Dr. Nathan Kline, an American psychiatrist strongly committed to the disease model, knew vaguely about rauwolfia. When it became commercially available as a treatment for hypertension, he began to experiment with **reserpine**, the pure chemical synthesized from the plant, as a treatment for schizophrenia. In his first research report, published in 1954, he stated the following:

> Since the advent of reserpine . . . patients have undergone a metamorphosis from raging, combating, unsociable persons to cooperative, friendly, cheerful, sociable, relatively quiet persons who are admittable to psychotherapy and rehabilitative measures. Hyperactive patients have become quiet, sedate, and cooperative in their behavior. Noisy patients have become quiet, while withdrawn and depressed patients have become alert and cheerful in their demeanor. (Snyder, 1974, p. 18)

Chlorpromazine. At about the same time another discovery was made. A French chemist, Paul Charpentier, developed **chlorpromazine**, a drug that leaves patients calm and tranquil but still alert. It also had few negative side effects. Chlorpromazine is derived from *anti-*

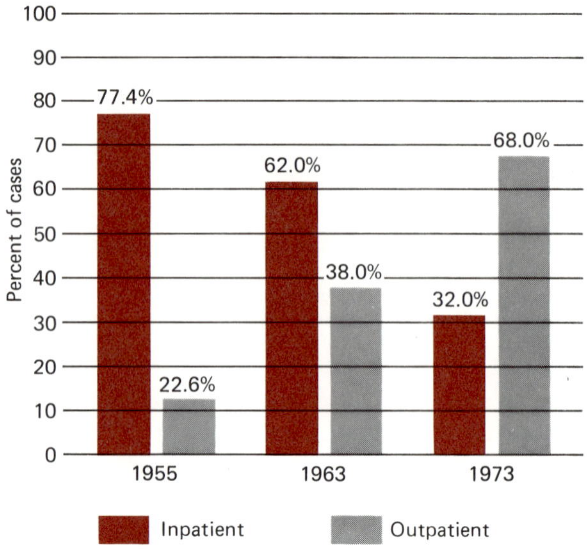

Figure 4.2. *Total psychiatric cases treated in both inpatient and outpatient facilities in 1955, 1963, and 1973. From Ozarin et al., 1976.*

histamines, which in turn are structurally similar to phenothiazine, a drug first synthesized in Germany in 1880. Early in 1940 the basic phenothiazine structure was used to create one family of antihistamines, which were used to treat allergies and to prepare patients for surgery, since the drugs make people sleepy. They also lower anxiety without affecting blood pressure.

Chlorpromazine was the first of a long series of phenothiazine drugs that are specifically antischizophrenic agents. Reserpine, which is chemically different from the phenothiazines, has more negative side effects, so when chlorpromazine was developed, reserpine fell out of favor. By 1952, chlorpromazine and its derivatives were the preferred treatment, a turn of events that had enormous consequences for the management of schizophrenia.

It is fascinating to think that both discoveries were accidental, both occurred about the same time, and both contributed to a revolutionized concept of management for schizophrenia. What is equally interesting is that the "cure" was found before the cause. Of course, there is no clear agreement on why reserpine or the phenothiazines work. Nevertheless, there is little doubt that the phenothiazines especially are effective. The fact that they are specifically good for schizophrenia alone (termed **therapeutic specificity**) is proved by their inability to lessen anxiety and depression.

Before the introduction of chlorpromazine, most people with schizophrenia, close to half a million, were hospitalized. In fact, nearly one half of all the mental hospital beds in the country were filled by people diagnosed as schizophrenic (Taube and Redick, 1973). But the introduction of chlorpromazine sharply reversed this trend; by 1971, there were only 330,000 hospitalized mental patients. In addition, the length of hospital stay for the patient diagnosed as schizophrenic dramatically declined, from years to months.

The overwhelming majority of schizophrenic patients are now hospitalized briefly and then returned to society. As long as they regularly take their chlorpromazine, they can maintain a fairly normal life outside of the hospital, much in the manner of Arnold, our case study from Chapter 1. It can be argued on the one hand that he and those like him are neither fully normal nor cured; on the other hand the lives they lead are certainly an improvement over life in a mental hospital before the introduction of drug treatment; furthermore, there are significant financial benefits to taxpayers as well.

Minor tranquilizers. The discovery of drugs that could control a major psychosis such as schizophrenia encouraged researchers to redouble their efforts to find drugs that could control other disorders. A new class of drugs, the **minor tranquilizers,** (as opposed to the major tranquilizers), was developed to reduce and control anxiety. The three most common are meprobamate (Miltown or Equanil), chlordiazepoxide hydrochloride (Librium), and diazepam (Valium). At the time of this writing, Valium was the most widely prescribed medication in the United States.

The minor tranquilizers are very effective in reducing both the acute anxiety of severe stress and chronic anxiety. They have even helped reduce the behavioral symptoms of some psychosomatic disorders. However, these drugs do have negative side effects, and when taken with alcohol can be extremely dangerous. There is also strong evidence suggesting that they are addictive: After heavy or prolonged use, withdrawal symptoms such as insomnia, hallucinations, delusions, tremors, and even convulsions can occur. Clearly, the minor tranquilizers should not be taken casually or without medical supervision.

If the attempt to humanize our management efforts was the first mental health revolution, surely the widespread use of antipsychotic drugs constitutes the second. It dramatically changed the character of psychiatric care for the mentally disturbed. None of these new drugs really "cure," but they do seem to have quite positive effects. More important, however, they have made most disturbed patients enormously more manageable, which opened the door to alternative management strategies, especially psychologically oriented strategies.

Electroconvulsive therapy

The discovery of various specific therapies for the affective disorders was equally haphazard. The first breakthrough was the development of **electroconvulsive therapy (ECT)** (also known as *electroshock therapy,* or *EST*). It had been noted that persons with epilepsy had a much lower incidence of schizophrenia than did the general population. It was therefore thought that artificially induced epileptic convulsions would eliminate or reduce schizophrenic symptoms. Although more careful observation clearly indicated that epilepsy did not prevent schizophrenia, the research with ECT continued. Psychiatrists began to experiment with ways to induce seizures. Various drugs were tried, but they posed a number of problems, especially a long lag time between injection and convulsion and difficulties in controlling the length and intensity of the seizure. But in 1938 it was found that small doses of electrical current sent through the forebrain would result in epileptic-like convulsions that could be controlled more readily.

After the introduction of ECT in the early 1940s, it was routinely used for treating all sorts of mental problems. It was not uncommon to find schizophrenic patients who had had hundreds of ECT treatments. But careful research revealed that this therapy is truly beneficial for only certain forms of depression. Although the media, especially such popular movies as *One Flew Over the Cuckoo's Nest,* present an almost sinister view of ECT, the data on its effects are rather clear. No one knows why ECT works, but it does work. However, ECT does not cure depression or any other disorder; it simply eliminates the symptoms. A fuller discussion of its application and the pros and cons of its use are presented in Chapter 12.

There have also been advances in the chemical treatment of the affective disorders. One drug, *iproniazid,* was developed initially to treat tuberculosis, but one of its side effects was to make patients more cheerful and optimistic. This led eventually to the development of other artificially synthesized mood-elevating drugs. A more thorough review of the current status of drug therapy in treating the affective psychoses will also be found in Chapter 12.

Psychosurgery

Much more negative is the collective data on **psychosurgery**, a procedure that involves cutting, removing, or otherwise destroying parts of the brain, especially in the frontal lobe. This procedure was first developed in the nineteenth century, but it did not become popular in the United States until the 1940s and 1950s. It was used especially to treat severe and otherwise untreatable schizophrenia, and initial reports were positive. This procedure transformed violent, unmanageable patients into cooperative and responsive ones. However, later reports indicated a reduction not only in negative and violent behaviors but in virtually *all* voluntary behaviors. After recovering from surgery, patients were markedly unresponsive and resembled nothing more than the "zombies" of horror movies. Some patients treated in this way developed epilepsy; others died. Interest in psychosurgery dropped considerably after the advent of the major tranquilizers, but some neurosurgeons and other medical personnel still contend that the procedure should not be overlooked.

PSYCHOLOGICAL MANAGEMENT: INTERNAL APPROACHES

The aim of the mental health movement was to have society accept mental disorders as simple medical illness. The hope was that this would make it easier for mainstream society to accept those who had suffered from mental problems—at least after the experience, if not during. Clearly, the medically based treatments just discussed gave a lot of support to this disease model. But what about the psychogenic view? What was being done in the way of psychological management?

Many of the psychological theorists discussed in Chapter 3—both internal and external—developed management techniques that reflected their own particular views of etiology. Of course, each of these theorists saw the emotional yet rational mind, not the biological brain, to be the primary element. However, each school of psychology believed that the development of abnormal behavior was caused by slightly different factors requiring different treatment. Mesmer and Skinner, for example, both used psychological treatments, but widely varying ones.

In the next section, we will present the different modern psychological managements that have been developed. As in the previous chapter, the first to be discussed are the internal approaches; external approaches will follow. Finally, we will take a look at the most recent interactional management method.

Mesmerism

It is interesting to note that at just about the same time that Pinel was unchaining patients at La Bicêtre and La Salpêtrière, and that Benjamin Rush was plunging patients in cold water to "tranquilize" them, Anton Mesmer was practicing his own particular brand of psychological treatment. **Mesmerism**, which had quite a following, was a unique therapy.

The setting was important: a room bathed in soft light, with music playing in the background. People—especially hysterical women—seeking cures for their emotional complaints sat around a large tub from which metal rods extended. When everything was ready, Mesmer made his entrance, dressed in a long, flowing robe and carrying a wand. He would then walk around the tub, touching each person in various places with his hands or wand, or with a rod.

This treatment supposedly redistributed the magnetic fluid inside each person, thus correcting the problem. Actually, Mesmer had sim-

Patients at one of Mesmer's sessions sit around the baquet, a specially constructed table filled with water, iron filings, ground glass, and empty bottles. Each patient holds an iron rod, which extended through the table surface into the fluid that was supposed to establish a magnetic connection between the participants.

ply found a good way to hypnotize people—to put them in a trance-like state in which they were highly suggestible. Then he simply told them to get well, and they did. Despite his eventual banishment from practicing in either Paris or Vienna, he and his exotic methods were nevertheless credited with effecting a good many cures. However, his chief importance lies in the fact that he demonstrated that hypnotism was a valuable treatment, a treatment that was finally adopted by more traditional psychologists. Among them was Sigmund Freud, who developed from hypnotism the methods he collectively termed psychoanalysis.

Psychoanalysis

The form of therapy that Freud developed, **psychoanalysis**, was designed to help patients gain insight into the many different motivators underlying their behavior. For this reason it is also sometimes called *insight therapy*. The chief aim of psychoanalysis is to bring unconscious thoughts and conflicts into the conscious mind so they can be resolved. Then the person's energies can be used to work for a full and rewarding life, not to keep up ego defenses. At first, Freud used hypnosis to release repressed material, but he eventually dropped it in favor of other methods.

Free association

In **free association**, the client simply talks—about anything, saying whatever comes to mind. The therapist may ask questions to clarify points but generally does not intrude into what is essentially a monologue. It is assumed that sooner or later important points will be revealed—long forgotten memories of childhood, deeply repressed fantasies, and so on. In short, all the things that blocked that person's adult growth and caused the mental disturbance will come spilling out in the "talking cure."

To aid this process, Freud suggested that the client lie on a couch facing away from the analyst, thus making it easier for the person to talk about private matters. The method put the client at ease and gave an impression of solitude, an impression reinforced by the analyst's basically silent role of interpreter. Freud believed that this kind of session should ideally be repeated four or five times a week, each session lasting about an hour, for as long as necessary. Freud also thought that most people would require years—not months—of treatment.

Modern psychoanalysts do not hold strictly to these rules. Today, the client usually sits facing the therapist, who is no longer so silent. In fact, it is not unusual for the analyst to initiate topics for discussion and to direct the conversation much more than Freud would probably have thought advisable. And while childhood experiences are still the most important focus, present life events—especially interpersonal relationships—are no longer ignored.

Dream interpretation

Another aid in retrieving unconscious thoughts and wishes is **dream interpretation**. Freud asked his patients to try to remember their dreams, his belief being that dreams held keys to their problems. He believed that behind the story told by the dreamer (the *manifest content* of the dream) was a deeper meaning, a true view of the inner workings of that individual. This was termed the *latent content* of the dream, and it was determined by the correct interpretation of the symbols that appeared in the manifest content.

For instance, suppose a woman related a dream in which she felt extreme fear and agitation after seeing the Stars and Stripes wave high up on a flag pole. During free association she mentions the following things: North Star, Star of Bethlehem, Bethlehem Steel, and crime. From this it might be interpreted that the woman has stolen something and she now fears the vengeance of Christ.

Freud also believed that there are universal symbols—symbols that always hold the same meaning in every context. Tall buildings, he claimed, and anything similar in shape resemble a penis and therefore represent sexual urges. Boxes and circles, on the other hand, symbolize the womb. This idea was disputed by the majority of later researchers, although some of the symbols (the phallic, for example) seem to have caught on so strongly—among the general public, at least—that they survived.

Resistance and transference

Two concepts that appear as therapy progresses should be mentioned here: **resistance** and **transference**. Although they are not part of the therapy program, recognizing and dealing with them is crucial if the treatment is to be successful.

Resistance. Freud theorized that this phenomenon occurs whenever something that is potentially painful or threatening is about to be dredged up from the unconscious. The client uses a variety of tactics to avoid facing such a revelation: suddenly changing the subject, forgetting past experiences, making jokes or getting irritated, and missing appointments. The important thing for the therapist is to recognize the behavior for what it is, to point it out to the person, and to try to discover what the threatening material is.

Transference. According to Freud, during the course of therapy the client will start to act as if the therapist were a parent or some other significant person. He determined that this was most probably caused by the simple fact that during treatment the therapist does have a role that is at least partially parental: listening to and trying to help solve the person's problems. The fact that psychoanalysts reveal little about themselves during sessions increases the likelihood that patients will attribute to them the same magic qualities that small children attribute to their parents. These intense feelings constitute the *transference neurosis*. Again, the analyst must identify this phenomenon and help the person work through these feelings. Otherwise, it is doubtful that the therapy program will succeed.

The impact of psychoanalysis

Both psychoanalysis and the view of emotional development on which it is based profoundly influenced the field of psychology, and Freud's pioneering views opened the door to subsequent theories. Despite this great impact, it must be stated that psychoanalysis alone has not played a major role in managing abnormal behavior. There is a popular image of a gray-bearded psychoanalyst who finally confronts a client's conscious impulses after years of treatment, waits patiently for the dramatic emotion to subside, and then congratulates the individual on being cured. Unfortunately, the image is not based on fact.

First, very few mentally disturbed people are treated in this manner. Because psychoanalysis requires frequent sessions over a long time span, only small hospitals (which are generally private and quite expensive) are able to institute this kind of treatment. Large public institutions having too many patients are unable to undertake such a long-term program. Hence, only the very wealthy are exposed to psychoanalysis. The vast majority of the disturbed population may never come in contact with it.

Second, as will be illustrated in later chapters, psychoanalysis has not proved to be effective against the most severe forms of disorder. Even when drugs have been used to decrease any bizarre symptoms and to allow the patients to understand and comply with a therapist's requests, psychoanalysis has not been as valuable as other psychological management methods. However, it has had some success with less serious problems, such as generalized anxiety and certain psychophysiological disorders.

Nevertheless, psychoanalysis has left an indelible mark on modern management. Most psychotherapists in private practice use at least some of the psychoanalytic methods, although they usually borrow from other theoretical models as well. But probably its biggest influence was that it led, through the humanistic and existentialist groups, to the many experiential techniques that flourish today, such as encounter groups and transactional analysis.

Humanistic Methods

The humanistic branch of psychology rejects the negative image of individuals driven by irrational, barely controllable id impulses. This group wanted to focus more on the good points that people possess and on their ability to grow in self-awareness. Self-concept is an important part of this theory, and the humanistic methods of management reflect this emphasis. Most of the clinicians who developed these methods were originally trained in classical psychoanalysis and then altered that formal model to fit their new theoretical approach. Two distinct treatment forms in particular emerged from humanistic psychology: **client-centered therapy**, developed by Carl Rogers, and **gestalt therapy**, developed by Fritz Perls.

Client-centered therapy

The chief concern of this therapy is the development of a healthy and positive view of the self. Rogers (1951) believes that for this to be achieved it is essential to give clients unconditional acceptance and positive regard. As a phenomenologist, Rogers suggests that the therapist adopt the client's perspective because only that particular frame of reference is valid for that particular person. In this way, the person's ideas and opinions are never judged; instead, the therapist tries to reinforce the positive aspects of these attitudes.

Therapists who use client-centered counseling feel that as a patient receives more and more unconditional regard, the actual self becomes more similar to the ideal self; in other words, the self-concept becomes more realistic. The client slowly begins to shed the defenses that were erected for protection. In turn, the actual self is expressed more easily, and this opens the way to self-actualization.

To determine the person's actual and ideal selves, some client-centered therapists use the Q-sort technique. Clients are asked to prioritize some statements according to how they believe they really are and how they would like to be. After counseling, the process is repeated. The differences between the two sets reflect the influence of the therapy; ideally, the statements for actual and ideal should be more alike.

A major criticism of this method is that it creates an environment that is completely unrealistic, based on a client-therapist relationship that is artificial. Chances are that most therapists cannot always be sincere in their feelings toward the client. Therefore the positive regard would sometimes be a lie. Some people question the value of never having therapists express their true feelings.

Gestalt therapy

Fritz Perls was convinced that the whole person (which is the meaning of "gestalt") must be involved for therapy to work. This necessitates that clients become aware of their full range of mental, emotional, and physical reactions. This is based on the contention that what individuals say—and even what they think they believe—is often contradicted by an unconsciously triggered physical response, such as a movement, or a rigid stance, or a staring expression.

Perls (1970) suggested several techniques to help individuals recognize how they are truly feeling and behaving. One of these is to have the client act out dreams and fantasies, not to simply tell the story. Another is to have the client focus on a physical response—that is, to magnify the action and then do anything else that seems to follow naturally. For instance, a woman who has been unknowingly clenching her fists may eventually also clench her teeth, shut her eyes tight, and scream with rage when focusing on her fists.

Perls stressed what Naranjo (1971) has called the "moral injunctions of gestalt therapy." The following instructions represent the most important precepts of the therapy:

1. Live now. Be concerned with the present rather than the past or future.
2. Live here. Deal with what is present rather than what is absent.
3. Stop imagining. Experience the real.

Gestalt therapy encourages group members to exaggerate their physical behavior in the hopes of releasing intense, pent-up emotions.

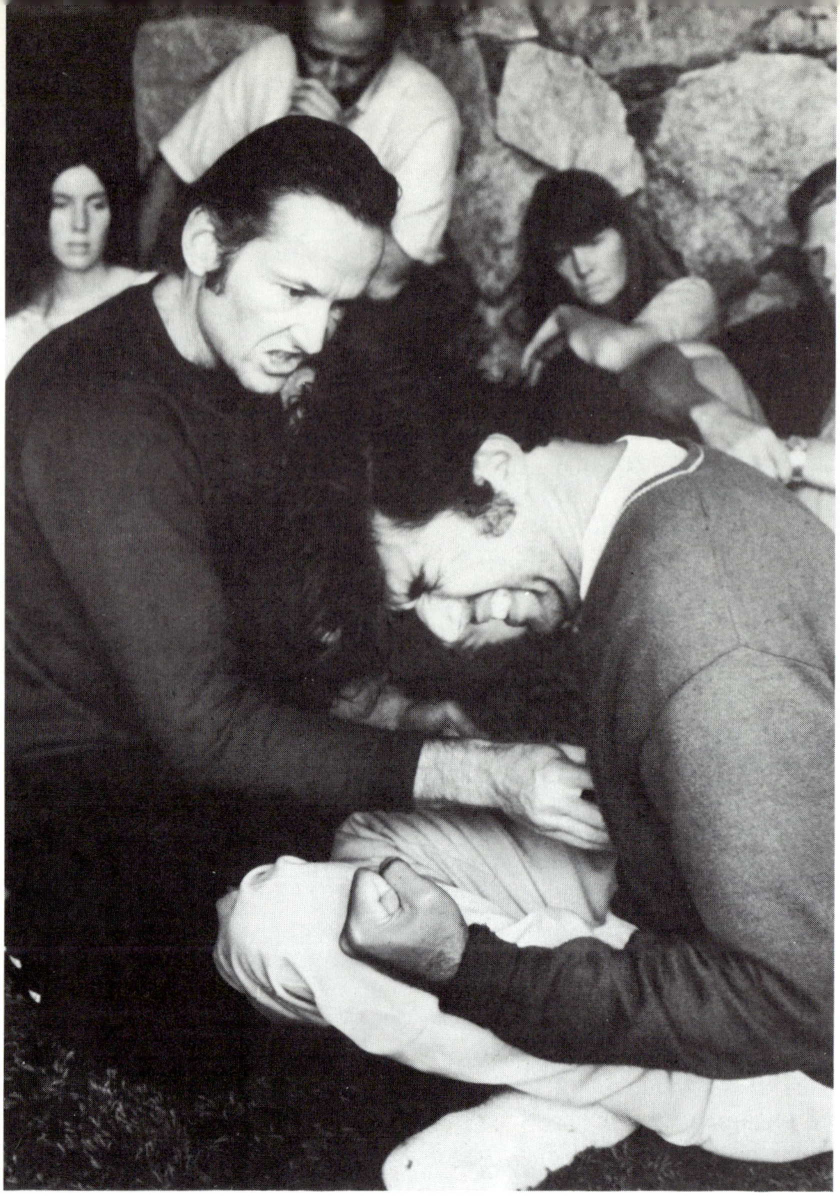

4. Stop unnecessary thinking. Rather, taste and see.
5. Express rather than manipulate, explain, justify, or judge.
6. Give in to unpleasantness and pain just as to pleasure. Do not restrict your awareness.
7. Accept no "should" or "ought" other than your own. Adore no graven image.
8. Take full responsibility for your actions, feelings, and thoughts.
9. Surrender to being as you are.

Gestalt therapy blends key points from psychoanalysis (working through unfinished conflicts) and behaviorism (focusing on overt behavior) with its humanistic emphasis on awareness and growth. For this reason it is a very widely used—and popular—management method.

Existentialist Methods

Many existentialist psychologists have also been trained originally as psychoanalysts, and they too have altered that basic therapy model to fit the tenets of their theory. The emphasis is no longer on the past, but on the present and the future; the stress is on what people choose to become, not what makes them the way they are.

Existentialist self-fulfillment depends on growth in awareness, which in turn relies on expressing the true self. The focus of therapy is to discover the true self, which does not have society's approval and which therefore has been masked and buried.

Unlike client-centered therapists, existentialist therapists strive at all times to express their true selves. In seeking their goal of authentic living, they are urged to open up to clients, to share their feelings and thoughts. In this way, they set an example for their clients, who may then find it a little easier to become authentic themselves. Viktor Frankl added something he calls *logotherapy,* which is designed to deal with moral issues in the client's life. However, it is R.D. Laing who developed the one unique existentialist therapy for dealing with what society calls schizophrenia.

Laingian therapy

According to Laing, the bizarre behaviors of schizophrenia are caused not by illness or by an overpowering id impulse, but rather by the person's inability to keep up the false self shown to society. When the facade is gone, the person tries to find the true self buried underneath, and this attempt is what we call insanity. From Laing's point of view, the process does not require treatment to set the person right again because the process itself is the only way to set the person right. Therefore the role of the therapist is to encourage that process.

Laingian therapists are sometimes described as guides on a journey. To a certain extent this is valid, although in actuality the individual makes the move and the therapist must keep pace. The important thing is to not interfere with whatever actions the person takes. Instead, the therapist must try to see these actions as purposeful—and even as beneficial—and to support them, no matter how strange they may seem.

This kind of therapy was offered at Kingsley Hall, a residential treatment facility established by Laing in London in 1965. Successes were achieved, including the rehabilitation of Mary Barnes, who subsequently became a well-known artist. But the neighborhood grew increasingly unhappy with the residents and with what they had always regarded as, at best, a bad risk. Community pressure ultimately forced Kingsley Hall to close. Its U.S. equivalent, Soteria House in San Jose, California, operates on the same principles. A chief qualification for the staff is the ability to "tune in" to the residents, to understand at a very basic level what they're trying to communicate about their experiences.

Cognitive Methods

Cognitive psychologists believe that the normal thinking process has been thrown out of kilter, thus causing the abnormal thought patterns that then lead to abnormal behavior. Their goal is therefore to correct the client's way of thinking. The major cognitive therapies are (1) **rational-emotive therapy**, (2) **cognitive restructuring**, and (3) **stress-inoculation training**.

Rational-emotive therapy

Developed by Albert Ellis, this program focuses on the irrational beliefs that he feels are at the root of abnormal behavior. He contends that life events alone don't cause problems, but the way that people interpret those events does. And those interpretations depend in large part on personal beliefs. A young woman who believes she must be perfect, that she must never make a mistake or else no one will like her, is liable to feel devastated and worthless when she does something wrong, as she inevitably will.

Ellis (1970) compiled a list of different irrational beliefs that he felt caused most mental disturbances. Among these are the following:

1. We must be loved by everyone for everything we do.
2. We must always be competent, intelligent, and achieving.
3. We must have complete self-control.
4. We need something stronger or more powerful on which to rely.
5. Certain acts are wicked and call for severe punishment.
6. It is better to avoid problems in life than to face them.

These beliefs, and others, lead to a negative sense of self-worth, which in turn leads to abnormal behavior.

Rational-emotive therapists try to uncover these unrealistic beliefs and root them out in order to give the client a better self-image. The major method is to dispute the beliefs, denying their validity outright, sometimes rather bluntly. This kind of frontal attack helps break down the beliefs faster. Once that is accomplished, the next step is to rehearse with the client more realistic ways of thinking.

Cognitive restructuring

According to Aaron Beck, some people have developed a negative cognitive set. In particular, they tend to magnify the negative side of every situation or statement, especially as it pertains to them, and this, he theorized, leads to depression. To overcome this negative thought pattern, he tries a different approach: testing the beliefs in a logical way. To this end, therapist and client together devise a plan that will allow for a check on how well these beliefs hold up.

The therapist usually divides this plan into smaller units, assigning the easier units first so that they serve as positive reinforcement for the more complex units. In most cases, activities are devised to have as much action as possible, since inactivity tends to deepen the depression. Referring regularly to the Pleasant Events Schedule (see page 374), the therapist may try to include a maximum number of those things that the client has indicated were pleasurable. With such a scheme, the client begins to see how unrealistic the previous thought pattern was.

Stress-inoculation training

Also known as *self-instructional training,* this management method is a relatively new one. According to Donald Meichenbaum (1977), the developer of the theory, behavioral problems really revolve around the self-statements that are made in stressful situations. Like the young woman in Chapter 3 whose date was late, most of us have private conversations with ourselves, and in stressful situations, what we say can affect our responses. This program, which attempts to alter those statements so that different actions result, is divided into three phases: (1) cognitive preparation, (2) skills acquisition and rehearsal, and (3) application and practice.

Cognitive preparation. In this initial stage, the therapist determines the problematic attitudes and beliefs, then points out how the inner conversations have worked against the client in the past and how they can work for the client in the future. Together, therapist and client formulate new, more adaptive self-statements for the client to use.

Skill acquisition and rehearsal. The client must now start to use the new self-statements, preferably in nonstressful times so that they become second nature. The following are examples of self-statements to reduce fear:

1. You can reason this fear away.
2. It will all be over very soon.
3. Don't concentrate on the fear, focus on what you're doing, or on the surroundings, or on other people.

Application and practice. Eventually, the client is required to use the newly acquired stress-inoculation skills in actual stressful situations. Again, only slightly stressful events will be tried at first, in order to gain positive reinforcement from successful applications.

This technique has been used with particularly good results in the management of anxiety (Meichenbaum, 1977) and has even been used in the control of pain (Turk, 1974).

PSYCHOLOGICAL MANAGEMENT: EXTERNAL APPROACHES

As we stated in the previous chapter, certain schools of thought feel that external agents cause behavioral deviance. The most prominent members in this group are the behaviorists, who feel that abnormal behavior is a learned response to a stimulus that has been applied either accidentally or deliberately. Other theorists in this group contend that social forces are responsible. Neither of these views focuses on the inner "doings" of the individual; instead, they both feel that people are "done to." Despite their common focus, the management methods advocated by these two groups differ.

Behavior Therapy

Although several different techniques fall into the behavioral category, all are based on the conditioning models, as used by Pavlov (classical conditioning) and by Skinner (operant conditioning). These processes begin with the same premise: Either the person never learned more adaptive responses or the maladaptive responses that were learned are still being reinforced. Behaviorists are not very concerned with how or why the behaviors began. They work first to change unwanted responses to more adaptive behaviors, and to teach the client how to control the desired responses once they are attained.

The first step in behavior therapy is to indicate, in specific detail, the exact behavior or behaviors that the client wants to change or lose. The therapist must also identify those adaptive behaviors, if any, that need to be learned to replace the lost ones or to supplement the newly acquired ones. The term "in specific detail" means just that: Not the general—Paul wants to have more social interactions—but the specific—Paul wants to increase his ability to initiate conversations with strangers. This, of course, requires some research to determine Paul's baseline of social interactions.

Once the situation has been analyzed, there are a number of techniques that can be used to effect a change. Paul may receive positive reinforcement (pleasure, praise, and so on) for initiating conversations; he may lose social approval, the chance to meet people, if he fails to initiate conversations. However, if Paul avoids meeting people because he panics in social situations, his behavior (being panicked) is a much more complex problem. To change it, several methods are popular.

Subjects are learning not to fear dogs through a systematic desensitization process. The patients are helped to relax while viewing a series of progressively more frightening pictures of dogs. Once they are able to remain relaxed while viewing the pictures, they should be able to generalize this response to the real world.

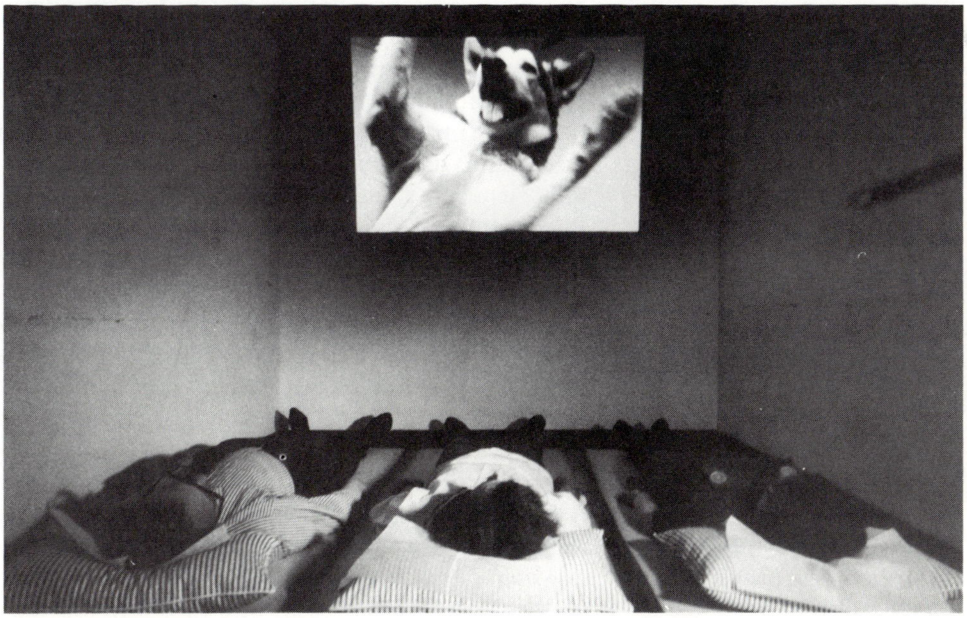

Systematic desensitization

Systematic desensitization is primarily used to reduce the fear and anxiety some people experience when faced with certain stimuli, which is essentially what Mary Cover Jones (1924) did when she desensitized a small child's fear of rabbits (see Chapter 3). But it was Joseph Wolpe (1958) who formalized the technique, dividing it into three steps.

1. *Relaxation.* This step consists of training in how to relax. During the first few sessions, the client is taught Jacobson's (1938) exercises in *progressive muscle relaxation,* in which all the muscles are systematically contracted and then relaxed. This teaches the person how to reduce body tension and, consequently, how to cope with the tension that accompanies anxiety.

2. *Fear hierarchies.* The client and therapist establish a hierarchy of fears—that is, a list of anxiety-provoking situations arranged from least to most fearful. For example, a young man who is afraid of cats might list the following:
   a. Seeing pictures of cats
   b. Seeing a live cat sitting in a window sill
   c. Talking with someone who is holding a cat
   d. Being in a room alone with a cat
   e. Holding a cat

3. *Desensitization.* This step consists of a combination of the first two. Under relaxation, clients are asked to imagine the anxiety-provoking situations on their list, beginning at the lowest level. They continue going through scenes of anxiety-provoking stimuli until they indicate that they are experiencing anxiety. They are then told to stop imagining the scenes and to concentrate on regaining the relaxed state. That accomplished, they then re-imagine the scene in which relaxation gave way to anxiety before. (Sometimes, a client will be asked to go back a level or two in the hierarchy and again work up.) This process is repeated until clients can stay relaxed while imagining the most fearful situation in the hierarchy.

A lot rests, of course, on the imaginative powers of the client—and on whether the response will work as well for the real stimulus as for the imagined one. Research indicates that it does (Wolpe, 1958, 1976), but some therapists now use **in vivo desensitization**—that is, desensitizing the person to the actual stimulus or situation. Either way, systematic desensitization has proved to be remarkably effective, especially for phobias, anxiety, and even certain psychosexual dysfunctions and deviations.

Implosive therapy and flooding

These two treatments operate under a principle totally opposite that of desensitization. Instead of gradually replacing anxiety with relaxation, the aim here is to quickly bring the person's anxiety level up to its highest point and to maintain it there until the stimulus loses its power to evoke that response.

In **implosive therapy**, the therapist takes an active role, describing in graphic and dramatic detail scenes that the client finds incredibly terrifying. This is continued until the anxiety level drops, and then repeated as often as necessary. Stampfl, one of the originators of this treatment, reported a case in which a young woman was so afraid of water "that she wore a life preserver when she took a bath" (1975, p. 66). Her therapist told her to imagine bathing in a bottomless bathtub and sinking in the water. She was also given homework: to imagine herself drowning. Stampfl records that her anxiety lessened considerably, so that by the fourteenth session she could bathe without the life jacket.

Flooding is essentially the same, except for one major difference. Like *in vivo* desensitization, it uses the real stimulus, not imagery. Rachman and colleagues (1973) reported the effectiveness of flooding on obsessive-compulsive rituals. In a typical case, the person is prevented from engaging in the ritual, a technique that usually requires close, round-the-clock supervision. Therefore flooding usually takes place in a hospital or clinic.

Aversion therapy

Aversion therapy uses punishment to modify responses, whereby an undesired behavior is gradually associated with something painful or at least very unpleasant. Kantorovich (1930), who was reportedly the first to use this method, treated alcoholics by pairing an electric shock with the sight, taste, and smell of alcohol. Other therapists used this method with good success on such disorders as sexual deviations and drug abuse.

The electric shock used in aversion therapy should not be confused with ECT, however; it is milder and is never administered directly to the brain. Nevertheless, many clinicians feel that any shock is a bit drastic and they have tried to substitute other negative stimuli, such as nausea-producing drugs. Sometimes, just having the client imagine nausea or something equally unappealing works well, too. This is called **covert sensitization**. Still, shock has been found to work in certain cases where nothing else has—for instance, to stop the self-mutilating behaviors of autistic children (Bucher and Lovaas, 1968), a situation that is certainly more drastic than the treatment.

Response shaping

The behavior therapy processes described up to now are used to remove an already-established response, either an emotion or a behavior prompted by that emotion. But sometimes therapy calls for learning a new response. When this is the case, conditioning rewards are used, usually under a specific program. This method is called **response shaping**, because through the systematic use of positive reinforcement, the person's behavior (the response) is shaped into a more adaptive form. We will discuss some of the most widely used programs.

Contracts. Under this program, the people involved agree on the desired behavior or behaviors and on the reward to be used for each. A **behavior contract** is drawn up and everyone must abide by it. This is a useful system in two-party disputes—between husband and wife or between parents and truant children, for instance. The weakness is that both sides must work for the success of the contract. If one side imposes unreasonable demands from the beginning or just refuses to comply with the agreed-upon terms, the contract clearly will not succeed.

Token economies. In a **token economy**, which is widely used in institutions, the resident patients earn the right to have certain privileges by behaving correctly. For each right action performed, a token is rewarded; wrong behaviors receive nothing. Since essential aspects of the person's life must be paid for in tokens, a patient who does not respond correctly may not be able to watch TV, or listen to records, or eat certain foods. This has proved to be a highly effective way to modify the behavior of most participants in the program (Paul and Lentz, 1977). It has several advantages:

1. The tokens do not tend to lose their incentive value.
2. The way they are spent is almost totally up to the patient.
3. The system is very much like the monetary system used outside the institution, which may help patients make the adjustments to living in the community.

While there is little doubt that token economies improve the adjustment of patients to the hospital regime, there is some question about the transfer of these behaviors to nonhospital settings. Some studies on token economies have concluded that the learned behaviors often persist only as long as the token system is maintained. Therefore some researchers doubt that token economies actually increase the motivation to change, which is clearly essential. But one study showed that token economies do seem to bridge the gap from hospital to community. Paul and Lentz (1977) followed 84 patients for six years, from assessment and treatment to a follow-up contact a year and a half after their release from the hospital. One third of this number had lived under a token economy; the other two thirds were given milieu therapy and traditional hospital management. The token economy group had the best rehabilitation record: Over 90 percent had remained continuously in the community.

A number of other programs integrate token economies with milieu therapy to guarantee the development of both motivation and skill (Fairweather et al., 1969; Greenberg et al.,

Table 4.1 *A Behavior Contract*

PRIVILEGES	RESPONSIBILITIES	PENALTIES
Watch TV from 2 to 4 p.m.	Make bed every morning before breakfast	Misses 1 morning: no TV that afternoon Misses 2 mornings: no TV that afternoon and the next Misses 3 or more mornings: no TV for 7 days from second morning missed
Walk Spot each morning	Vacuum and dust room once a week	Misses 1 week: no walk for 2 days Misses 2 weeks: no walk for 1 week
Join group activities during recreation hour	Help wash lunch dishes 3 times a week, as scheduled	Misses 1 time: no group participation that day Misses 2 times: no group participation for three days from second time missed Misses 3 times: no group participation for 1 week from second time missed
Take pottery classes every afternoon	Help with laundry 3 times a week, as scheduled	Misses 1 time: no class attendance for the next class Misses 2 times: no attendance for the next three classes
Go on unsupervised trips to the shopping mall with one or two other residents	Help cook 4 meals a week, as scheduled	Misses 1 time: no trip that week Misses 2 times: no trip for 2 weeks
Go to the library once a week with the group	Clean up the workshop after each private potting session	Misses 1 time: no trip that week Misses 2 or more times: no trip for 5 weeks

1975). Fairweather and colleagues moved patients through a three-step process: (1) in-hospital treatment and skills training, (2) sheltered workshop, and (3) living arrangements in the community. Three years after the program terminated, the patients in Fairweather's group had made a significantly better adjustment to the outside world than had a more traditionally treated group.

Civil rights groups have lately expressed concern that token economies revoke essential human rights. They feel that forcing patients to earn basic privileges is inhumane and should be stopped. Many people may wonder why a system that encourages people to earn a special dessert, or some time to watch TV, or a chance to go out to a movie is considered heartless and controversial. The fact is that most of the severely disturbed patients in institutions respond better—at least, at first—to the most fundamental of privileges, such as eating dinner. They must learn to appreciate the more sophisticated privileges—like going to the movies or shopping with friends—and to want to earn tokens for them.

As the problem becomes clearer one may wonder if it is wrong to take away such fundamentals as food in order to help a person improve in the long run. Under this system individual behavior can and does gradually change—from the outrageously bizarre to the more adaptive. And when this happens, the situation improves for all in the residence. Therefore although we understand the concern of the civil rights advocates, our feeling is that the effectiveness of token economies far outweighs any problems that may be encountered in the application of this management method.

Modeling. The social learning approach, an outgrowth of behaviorism, advocates this method. Bandura, an eminent theorist, believes that responses are learned through imitation as well as through reinforcement. Therefore the desire to act like another person can make us model that person's way of walking or talking, for example. Therapeutic modeling has enjoyed great success in overcoming phobias (Rosenthal and Bandura, 1978) and in teaching social skills (Sarason, 1976).

Social Methods

There are theorists who maintain that overwhelming social forces are to blame for abnormal behavior and that only the broadest social and economic changes will eradicate mental disorders. When social instability and poverty—the root of the problem—are eliminated, most human ills will then disappear. Many people believe that a more equitable distribution of wealth and a worldwide commitment to peace would go a long way toward making a much saner and healthier world. We doubt, however, that mental disturbance would be eliminated, just as we doubt that physiological disease would disappear.

First of all, as we have indicated, many forms of mental disorder have a clear biological component. No one is yet certain what it is, but it is there. Since that is the case, no amount of social change will remove it—except perhaps over the incredibly long time spans necessary for evolution. Second, attitude—what we think about ourselves and others—also has an influence on the development of disorders. Furthermore, there is no proof that a world without war and poverty would also be a world without personal prejudice.

IS PSYCHOLOGICAL MANAGEMENT EFFECTIVE?

In 1952, a scathing attack on the effectiveness of psychotherapy was published by British psychologist Hans Eysenck. He compared the effectiveness of five previously published, large-scale studies of psychoanalysis and nineteen studies of eclectic styles of psychotherapy. His results? Only 44 percent of the patients treated by psychoanalysis showed any improvement, while 64 percent of those treated eclectically improved. But more important was his report that 72 percent of a group of *untreated* hospital cases showed improvement, a clear suggestion that treatment has little or no positive impact—and it may possibly lead to a negative impact!

There have been any number of rebuttals to Eysenck's criticism and various deficiencies pointed out: that the patients in these studies were hardly similar; that the degree of improvement was difficult to ascertain; that most studies of untreated hospitalized patients show a 30-percent improvement figure. A 1977 research report on the effectiveness of psychotherapy reaches a more positive conclusion. In their review of nearly 400 research studies, Smith and Glass took into account the most plausible idea that certain types of psychotherapy have positive effects on certain types of disorder. They found that this was indeed the case. They also concluded that *any* treatment approach was more effective than no treatment at all. We agree.

The Community Mental Health Center

The twentieth century in particular has seen some amazing advances in the possible ways to manage behavioral deviance. From the discovery of reserpine to the establishment of token economies, it is clear that the care of the mentally disturbed has undergone some major rethinking. Most important, all of these new advances led to the "rediscovery" of the problem of mental illness.

The increased use of antipsychotic drugs, a growing social awareness of the plight of the mentally disturbed, and a return to a more humanitarian spirit led to the Community Mental Health Centers Act of 1963. This legislation was passed by Congress in response to President John F. Kennedy's demand for a "bold new approach" to the management of abnormal behavior. Much of the impetus for these changes came from the work of the Joint Commission on Mental Illness and Health, which articulated the following goals in its 1961 report:

> (1) To save the patient from the debilitating effects of institutionalization. . . . (2) To return a hospitalized patient to home and community life as soon as possible. . . . (3) To maintain him in the community as long as possible.

All of these points work toward a single objective: To help disturbed people live a fairly normal life despite their handicap. To this end, the Joint Commission recommended that rehabilitative after-care be provided by every available source—full-care hospitals, after-care clinics, public health nursing services, convalescent nursing services, foster family care, and others.

The intent of the community mental health program was to reduce the barriers between the disturbed and their communities in order to

Close-up: Foster Respite Care

Have you ever considered caring for a mentally disturbed person in your own home? What would it be like to act as a foster family for someone with emotional problems? A few years ago these questions would probably have never been asked. Today, however, attitudes are changing, and the result is a community mental health program that truly involves the community.

Taking a cue from the centuries-old success of the Gheel community in Belgium, a similar program for the mentally disturbed was established in Denver, Colorado nine years ago: Individuals with mental health problems are "adopted" for short periods by families in the community. This program has since spread to other areas in the United States.

Under this system, families receive a small stipend for accepting a person with psychiatric problems for temporary care. The stay is rarely longer than two weeks, since most of the people in this program are ER cases—that is, people suffering situational crises who end up at the emergency room of the local hospital. Usually they need space and time in order to adjust to whatever stressor has upset their lives. If in the two weeks they remain in the family's home no progress has been made toward a resolution of the crisis, more permanent arrangements are made.

The program has been quite successful in Denver, and seems to be working well in New England, too. But it's not for everyone. One family who cared for a "defiant and hostile" woman decided to drop out of the program after that unnerving experience. Still, they were full of admiration for the goals of the program and for those families who can continue to provide care.

Milieu therapy teaches patients to assume some responsibility for their lives and thus enhance their self-image.

facilitate normal behavior. This was moral therapy in a new form. The emphasis on avoiding hospitalization, on discharging hospitalized patients as soon as possible, on using partial hospitalization, and on maintaining community contact all meld to produce a management approach that is more humane and more interactive.

The funding provided by this legislation led to the development of over 500 community mental health centers. Each center was to be accessible to the community, in contrast with the isolated hospitals of the past, and each was to provide a variety of services, including the following:

1. *Inpatient care* for those who require short-term hospitalization.
2. *Partial hospitalization,* including *day hospitals* for those who require intensive care during working hours but can return home at night and on weekends, and *night hospitals* for those who require continued care but are well enough to work during the day.
3. *Outpatient care* for those who require only continued but brief treatment.
4. *Emergency mental health care* on a 24-hour basis.
5. *Consultation and education services* on mental health problems to other community agencies, such as schools and the police.

Many centers offer a number of additional services, such as crisis intervention hot lines and rape victim counseling programs.

The older, traditional mental hospitals still exist, but the values and attitudes of the community mental health movement have had an impact on them. Of course, the most important change in traditional institutions is the one brought about by the antipsychotic drugs, making patients both more accessible and more responsive. However, the change to a more concerned attitude, is best exemplified in the establishment of a **therapeutic community** (Jones, 1953) in some institutions. This is the clearest successor to moral therapy. It is based on the premise that mental patients need to actively participate in the planning and execution of their own treatment programs and possibly in those of other patients as well. A major difference between the traditional hospital and the therapeutic community is the blurring of professional roles. There are no uniforms for either patients or staff and the atmosphere is very relaxed and casual. Attendants, nurses, patients, psychiatrists, psychologists, and social workers all attend regular "community meetings," in which they openly discuss the various issues posed by individual patients and make decisions about their programs.

Milieu therapy, as this treatment is sometimes called, provides an atmosphere in which patients can once again learn to accept some responsibility for their own lives and to rebuild their self-concept. But more than attitudes are required to resocialize many patients into a more normal life. Skills are required—social skills and occupational skills. Therefore another important change in the management of patients hospitalized in the large state institutions is the use of behavior therapy, especially token economies. Combined with milieu therapy, behavior therapy produces incredible results.

Success of the Mental Health Centers

How successful has the community mental health program been? Unfortunately, its success has been very limited. The programs we have described are the ideals; the actual programs have never been developed as originally planned.

The major problem is financial: All of the community mental health programs are costly. They involve considerable staff time, and the kind of staff required must be well trained and is therefore expensive. The cost of most of these programs has now gone beyond what most state legislative bodies are willing to pay. Changes in national priorities—specifically the loss of interest in social programs and an emphasis on lower taxes—have severely reduced the commitment for reform that initiated the movement. Federal funding was expected to "seed" later funds from local and state sources; instead, as federal funds dried up, many programs were either sharply curtailed or completely eliminated. And the amount of federal money for new programs has, of course, also been sharply reduced. Now there is a tendency to return to the old model of "benign neglect."

But even here the picture is not quite the same as it used to be. The widespread use of antipsychotic drugs has led to what has been termed the "revolving door" approach to treatment. Patients like Arnold in Chapter 1 are now only briefly hospitalized and then returned to the community. This **deinstitutionalization** seemingly satisfies all the wonderfully humanitarian goals set by the Joint Commission on Mental Health in 1961. However, the Arnolds of the world need more than drugs to succeed in our complex society—which is why they often wind up back in the hospital. Each time this happens they are stabilized with a new prescription, cleaned up, reoutfitted with just enough clothing to look presentable, and sent out to try again. This is the "revolving door."

Still, few among us would disagree that this process, regardless of the many problems it poses, is still an improvement on earlier attempts to manage abnormal behavior. The reduced patient load in most hospitals has made them more humane places, in which it is now possible to obtain caring, individual attention. And few patients enter under what once amounted to a life sentence for the crime of being different. In our opinion, the "revolving door" is clearly preferable to the locked ward.

SUMMARY

Although management may seem an inappropriate way to refer to the care of mentally disturbed people, in actuality it is the most appropriate term. The history of our treatment of those who exhibit abnormal behavior is proof that our first priority is to protect the normal in the population. The ways that we have coped with the problem of abnormal behavior have varied with the prevailing belief in what causes the problem, but we have rarely been caring.

Past methods of coping with abnormal behavior have varied dramatically: insulting the demons in possession, killing the disturbed person, plunging the person in water in order to tranquilize the nerves, using leeches to lessen the blood flow to the brain. When the scientific advances of the Age of Enlightenment were finally accepted, reform movements spread throughout Europe and the New World. The revolutionary treatment then instituted in many hospitals was called moral therapy, and it involved a sympathetic environment and a strong relationship between therapist and client.

Societal changes—and success—led to the decline of moral therapy. By the turn of this century, most institutions were warehousing patients—holding them with little or no treatment until a medical cure was discovered. This situation had developed naturally from the attempts of the mental health movement to get the public to accept the premise that mental disturbance is a disease. But medical discoveries made in this century, chiefly in the early 1950s, did change the management program of most hospitals.

The antipsychotic drugs, especially, decreased bizarre symptoms and made patients much more manageable. Soon the number of people institutionalized—and the average length of time spent in the hospital—dropped considerably. More importantly, however, this also allowed psychological treatment to be tried. The major psychological treatments now used are psychoanalysis, humanistic and existential therapies, and social learning and behavior therapies. Psychoanalysis has not proved as successful as some other therapies, particularly in dealing with severe disorders. Behavior therapies, on the other hand, have had great success, from getting rid of phobias to eliminating bizarre schizophrenic symptoms.

All these different methods were incorporated in the move to establish community mental health centers, which was begun in the 1960s. Community centers were set up to provide different types of treatment and to cover the various needs of the people served. The milieu therapy now provided in many such centers and in more traditional institutions, is very similar to the original moral therapy. Although this plan has never been fully implemented in its entirety—and may never be—because of financial and social limitations, it remains a standard for future efforts at management.

Conversation 1

Many young people elect careers in psychology because it blends the opportunity to help people in a very direct way with the ever-fascinating study of the human psyche. But what is it like to work as a counselor? This interview is with Anne, a young woman who "burned out" after several years in the field in different positions. Her experiences are not typical; nevertheless, her advice is sound.

This is the first of six Conversations, a special feature of this book. All of these are in-depth interviews with persons who have been involved, either directly or indirectly, with abnormal behavior. Three of the Conversations are with more than one person—a homosexual couple, a woman paralyzed by polio and her husband, and an alcoholic and his family—and three involve only a single individual—a schizophrenic woman, the sister of a 24-year-old mentally retarded man, and a mental health counselor. Each of these interviews reveals a person or persons who have had to deal with extraordinary—even life-threatening—circumstances. Their attempts to cope with them have been variably effective. Some have overcome their problems—with professional help, or by sheer will power—and some are still struggling.

Interviewer: What fostered your interest in social work?

Anne: I knew that I wanted to help people; I had a sort of "save the world" idealism. But for the most part, I saw psychology as *the* field that helped people solve their problems. I saw myself as having a lot of insight and sensitivity, so psychology seemed the best way. And I wanted to get really involved with the person, so my interest was in doing clinical work as opposed to, say, being a researcher or teacher.

Int.: What kind of training did you go through? What were your typical college courses?

Anne: I took the standard psychology courses: Intro, Personality, Abnormal, Child Development, Psychology and Education. I also took courses in delinquency, family therapy, statistics (of course), and research. And in research I began to focus on special education—working with mentally retarded and autistic people, developing programs, working with their families. My volunteer work also focused on special education. I would say that the more specialized training I got was a result of my own initiative: I volunteered to work in a center for autistic children; I volunteered to develop a behavior modification program for twelve mentally retarded adults at a local school. Even before college I had done volunteer work for a hotline dealing with all sorts of adolescent issues—runaways, sex counseling, etc. In college the focus changed to special education because I am physically handicapped and I felt I would have a better understanding. But I stayed away from working with the physically handicapped because that issue was too touchy.

Int.: When you got out of college, what kinds of positions did you hold?

Anne: When I graduated I looked specifically for a position in mental retardation. I had found autism too difficult and too frustrating. Some autistic people are abusive, but more than that, you're never really sure that you're getting through. I think results are seen much more clearly and sooner with the mentally retarded, through a good behavior modification program and good support systems. And that's part of my personality: I need to see results; if I don't, I get frustrated.

Int.: We all respond better that way.

Anne: Exactly. Anyway, when I came out of college the big movement to deinstitutionalize was in full force. There was also a move to mainstream, so a lot of community group homes were coming about. I got a position in an apartment setting, where the retarded residents really had an opportunity to interface with the rest of the community. It was very radical, because generally they were put in a separate home that became a mini-institution.

That position was very frustrating. I lived in, so there was no clear separation between work and personal life. There were four live-in and four live-out counselors; a live-out had to cover for you if you left overnight, which was very difficult to coordinate. I'd have plans to go away for the weekend and then my cover person would call to say "I can't come."

And we were supposed to work a normal week, but you really couldn't do that. I would sometimes find myself working 80 hours, not 40. Because of all my volunteer work, I had more experience with special needs people than most of the other counselors—I knew how to handle them better. So I got an increasing amount of responsibility to supervise the staff, develop the program, and work with the patients. A lot of the counselors were not very good—one wasn't caring at all and could not work effectively with any of our patients. He only took the job because he couldn't find anything else.

That's a problem I've come across with *all* special needs programs, but especially at the community level: In most of the group homes I visited, the counselors were not very caring and not very well trained. These are very low-paying positions, and the counselors tend to view them as jobs that provide room and board and let them save money. Out of all of us at the group home where I worked, I think only I and one other person had a sincere interest in working with this population.

In behavior modification programs, one important thing is consistency: Every counselor must say the same thing when an inappropriate behavior is observed. That means the counselors have to be dedicated and patient. That wasn't happening. They didn't care enough to follow the program—or maybe they were just too frustrated with the overall situation.

Int.: How long did this last?

Anne: Eight months. And another problem there was that our population included everything: We had women and men, ages 16 to 22. We had a range of profoundly retarded to borderline. We had different levels of skills, especially verbal skills. Two were blind; one of them was also borderline schizophrenic. One was self-abusive. Another was abusive towards the counselors. One wasn't even toilet trained! Yet the focus was to try to have them work as a team. Just trying to coordinate a sensible behavior modification program was almost impossible at times.

You take all these things together and work day to day with them, and after a while the frustration builds up: the constant pressure, the patience that's needed, the fact that you can't get away from it. That program has changed since I left: Counselors leave the premises at night and someone else comes on.

Int.: Does the director live in?

Anne: No, and that's another reason why I burned out. I didn't feel I had the support of my director. She didn't see a lot of what was happening; she didn't see that I was being overwhelmed and overburdened. There were also differences about administrative policies—how this or that should be done, etc.

So after eight months I began to evaluate the fact that I cared too much, I got too involved, I couldn't separate myself from my job. You have to be a caring person, but you have to be able to disassociate yourself. A sort of depersonalization needs to take place—ideally it shouldn't, but in reality it must if you want to stay with it and be effective.

And towards the end I really felt that I had an equal interest in the administrative role. I had also demonstrated a good deal of ability in that area, so it seemed best to move out of clinical interaction. My next position was administrative within a clinical setting.

Int.: Where were you working then?

Anne: At a clinic dealing with alcoholism. I still got involved—I took an interest in some of the patients and I did have to cover at times in terms of crisis intervention and triage—but direct clinical interaction didn't happen as often. Still, social work is very demanding—emotionally and in terms of work hours—even at the administrative level. And I became frustrated with the bureaucracy of the system—with the inability to keep people from just passing patients from department to department instead of doing something to help.

So it did indicate to me that I don't have the personality for social services. I have the interest to be damn good, but in terms of my personal needs, no, it's not the field for me. I realized that I had different priorities: I need to be in a more results-oriented setting; I need to make money. I later abandoned the field because it pays very little. But I also discovered that I really liked business activities.

Int.: So it was a several step process: You first realized that it was difficult to disassociate yourself from your clients. Then it was too frustrating—there weren't enough results to reward your efforts. Finally, it was too demanding and low paying even in areas where you didn't have to interact with the cases.

Anne: Correct. And there was one other problem for me. When you work in special education, at least, you tend to lose a lot of your social skills because you rarely interact with regular people. After a while you forget how to talk to someone who's not mentally retarded. I have a friend who teaches severely disturbed children eight hours a day. She's very shy and withdrawn, but what can you expect? She doesn't really interact with adults or "normal" people. I'm very social—I like to interact with people. I need to have that in my career.

But I also had to face other issues. I realized that my great interest in psychology was an effort to resolve certain personal issues. Once those were confronted—I wouldn't say resolved—then I could look at myself in terms of what career best meets my needs.

I think it's important to know that not everybody burns out. Some people are able to disassociate; others have as their first priority the need to stay in the field. That friend of mine who teaches disturbed children didn't burn out. The people who have the dedication and the ability and the need to work in social services don't care about the money or the frustrations—or else these issues are not as important.

Int.: They are getting more rewards than frustrations.

Anne: Exactly. And I was not—I was getting more frustrations. The principle on which I operate, right or wrong, is that the minute I see more frustration than reward I leave. I don't want to abandon social services totally, though. My objective is to serve on a supervising committee such as those that govern group homes like the one where I was employed. At that committee level, I can be involved with the overall program and with decisions made to improve it, but I won't be too closely associated with the patients.

I think that people who want to stay in the field must learn to set limits, especially if they have any clinical contact. They have to develop some mechanism for disassociating from the cases. But they have to be caring if they're going to get results. It's very difficult. And they should realize that they're going to get frustrated—they're not always going to like it. But when they seem to be getting more frustrations than rewards, that's when they need to step away and really look at the situation.

Part Two

The Disorders

CHAPTER 5

Normal and Abnormal Reactions to Stress

DEFINING STRESS

The General Adaptation Syndrome

Other Reactions to Stress

EXPLAINING STRESS

The Social Readjustment Rating Scale

Limitations of Life Change Scales

POST-TRAUMATIC STRESS DISORDER

The Disaster Syndrome

ADJUSTMENT DISORDER

DISSOCIATIVE DISORDERS

Psychogenic Amnesia

Psychogenic Fugue

Multiple Personality

Depersonalization

MANAGING STRESS

Biological Methods

Psychological Methods

Mike Boston, 33 . . . has been unemployed since 1977 and has suffered several emotional breakdowns. Today, he shakes and sweats as he talks. . . . [Boston's] psyche might have been mortally wounded March 23, 1967, on a ridge in Vietnam known as "The Rockpile." A mortar shell exploded near his head, shooting a piece of hot, jagged metal into his face. It severed an artery, and he watched helplessly as his blood pumped into the soil of Vietnam.

He says a friend, a radio man, was "kind of crouched up in a way he shouldn't be. I jerked him backwards but there was nothing much left of the front of him." Mike crawled to a helicopter, leaving a shining trail of blood behind him. He does not remember much after that, except for waking up in a tent hospital in Dong Ha with a bandage taped to his face. . . .

"A doctor told me I was being sent to Japan, but instead they sent me to Da Nang for twelve days and then I was ordered back into combat," says Boston. "The bandage was still soaked with pus and blood and I had a plastic tube in my face to drain the wound, but I was back on patrol."

Instead of being discharged early, which was done in some cases at the end of thirteen months of combat duty, he was assigned to guard duty at Parris Island, South Carolina, in late 1967.

He opened his eyes one morning, he said, stared at the ceiling of his barracks, and "knew" he was dead. He left his bed only to go to the bathroom, living on peanuts and Coca-Cola from a vending machine. "I had wonderful dreams of death, and that gave me great relief. When I woke up, I was in hell again, reliving the frustration and helplessness of seeing friends killed and not being able to do anything about it.

Andrew Blake, *The Boston Sunday Globe*
July 27, 1980. Reprinted by permission.

Most of us are lucky enough never to have experienced the kind of stress that has disabled Mike Boston. It has been said that every person has a breaking point; during catastrophes such as war and natural disasters, many ordinary, well-adjusted people learn the truth of that statement. If you have ever been seriously ill or injured, or involved in a crisis such as a fire, flood, or auto accident—and even if you have not—you can probably empathize, or at least sympathize, with Mike Boston.

All of us have to deal with stress from time to time—and most of us are usually able to adjust to it. But occasionally some individuals are hit by so much stress at one time that they are no longer able to cope. This is a common occurrence during wartime and after natural disasters, but it can also happen less dramatically: One mishap follows another until the cumulative result is too much to endure. In the case of Mike Boston and many other war veterans, the stress brought on by combat was both immediate and delayed, beginning in the field but continuing long after the war is over.

Stress can be cited as the direct cause of several disorders, and the indirect cause of nearly every psychiatric illness—and of many physical ailments as well. Stress is a sort of common denominator of illness. DSM-III treats disorders related to stress in several places. In this chapter we will focus first on defining stress and stressors. We will then investigate two categories of stress-related disorders, the reactive and the dissociative disorders. The **reactive disorders** involve fairly direct responses to more-or-less identifiable stressors. They include post-traumatic stress disorder (the reactions of an otherwise normal person to some abnormally traumatic event), and adjustment disorder (maladaptive reactions to a particular stressor or set of stressors). The **dissociative disorders** involve a breakdown in the person's normal patterns of functioning, a break that is manifested in an alteration of consciousness, identity, or motor behavior. Unlike the reactive disorders, the person is usually unaware of either the alteration or the stress. This group of disorders includes

Figure 5.1. *Selye's General Adaptation Syndrome. Note that each additional stressor decreases both the resistance to stress and the time lapse to exhaustion. From Goldstein et al., 1980.*

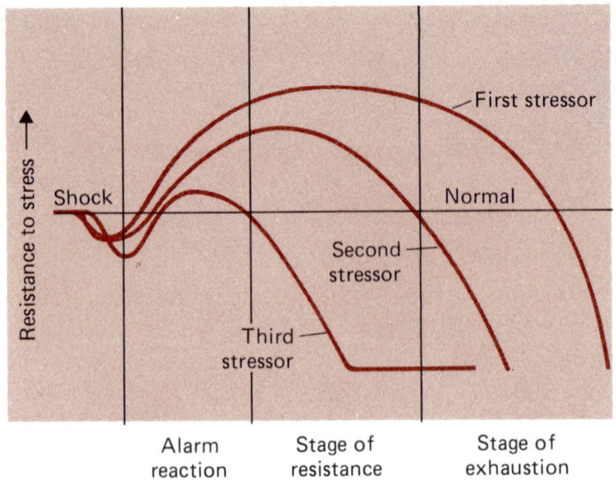

psychogenic amnesia, psychogenic fugue, multiple personality, and depersonalization.

In Chapter 6, we shall discuss anxiety disorders, which can be briefly summed up as chronic abnormal reactions to normal stressors. In Chapter 7, we shall consider reactions to stress that involve unusual physical symptoms. Stress has also been implicated in depression, which will be examined in Chapter 12.

DEFINING STRESS

The term **stress** commonly means a variety of things: an emphasis, a strain, an unpleasant situation. In psychology, it generally refers to the state characterized by emotional and cognitive changes that occur as a consequence of a stressor. A **stressor** is an event, situation, or thing that disrupts the status quo and necessitates adaptation. Cofer and Appley have described stress as "a state where the well-being (or integrity) of an individual is endangered, and he must devote all of his energies to its protection" (1964, p. 463). This rather general description is a good definition of the stress Mike Boston experienced in Vietnam. Other writers include less drastic elements. Lawrence Hinkle (1973), for instance, has observed the following:

> The ordinary activities of daily life—the ingestion of food, or the failure to ingest food; muscular activity, or the absence of muscular activity; breathing, or not breathing; sleeping, or not sleeping—all affect the dynamic steady state. . . . It has been aptly said that "to be alive is to be under stress." (p. 43)

Hinkle's concept of stress is close to an operational definition that could be used in laboratory research. This approach reflects the pioneering work of physiologist Hans Selye, who took a similar tack in his extensive investigations of stress. Since the physiological aspects go hand in hand with the psychological, we will first look at how the organic systems of the body respond to stressors.

The General Adaptation Syndrome

Selye's view is that stress is a state that can be inferred from specific physiological changes within a biological system (for example, the circulatory system). It can be induced by any stimulus, situation, or event that creates an imbalance in one or more of the body's systems. Our physiological reactions to stress are basically a mobilization of our internal defense forces—an attempt to fight back and right the balance. Selye calls this set of reactions the **general adaptation syndrome**, or GAS (1956).

The first phase of the GAS is the *alarm reaction*: The body encounters a stressor and realizes it must rally its forces. Some event sets off internal receptors; in response, chemical signals are sent out to the nervous system and endocrine glands. An example would be the shock you would feel if you were to dive off a boat into the cold ocean.

To deal with the stressor, the body enters

Close-up: *Distress vs. Eustress*

Hans Selye, the noted researcher on bodily reactions to stress, felt that all change resulted in the physiological response that we call being under stress. However, he did distinguish between different types of stressors—or rather between ways people respond behaviorally to them.

Specifically, some stressors result in dysfunction. If, for instance, you are so apprehensive about failing a certain exam that, when the test is given, you cannot concentrate enough to answer the questions, you are experiencing *distress.* On the other hand, if the apprehension urges you to study twice as much as usual, to get tutored in uncertain areas, and to generally prepare to the point where you feel confident, you are experiencing functional stress, or—in Selye's terms—*eustress.* The prefix "eu" comes from the Greek for "good." Euphoria—"good feelings"—is a similar word.

The notion of eustress comes from Selye's view that all that we do and accomplish is due to our being stressed or motivated to act. Thus, the greatest achievements in human history—from art, music, and sculpture to democracy and penicillin—come from eustress. In short, our very survival and ultimate growth result from eustress.

---

the stage of *resistance*, manning the barricades and fighting back or readying the body for flight from the stressors. The nervous system and endocrine glands direct emergency hormone activity, monitor blood pressure, and control other physiological changes aimed at fighting "wear and tear" in the body. After your plunge into the ocean, your body would make the necessary adjustment, and you would gradually get used to the cold water.

If resistance fails to get rid of the stressor or if the body cannot adapt to the stressor, the body will pass into the stage of *exhaustion:* Resources have been depleted, the body is ready to surrender. Defenses cease, and the organism dies. If you do not climb out of the water back onto your boat, you would eventually succumb to the prolonged cold. Selye (1956) offers the following summary:

> The response to stress has a [threefold] mechanism consisting of: (1) the direct effect of the stressor upon the body; (2) internal responses which stimulate tissue-defense; and (3) internal responses which stimulate tissue-surrender by inhibiting defense. *Resistance and adaptation depend on a proper balance of these three factors.* (p. 47)

A good illustration of the GAS is a study in which Selye and his colleagues tested the responses of rats to stress induced by cold (Selye, 1956). After 48 hours in a refrigerated room, the rats showed typical physiological signs of the alarm reaction—enlarged adrenal glands, shrunken thymuses, and stomach ulcers. Another group of rats stayed in the room for five weeks, at which point they had reached the resistance stage and had adapted to the cold. Moved to an even colder chamber, they survived temperatures that would have killed ordinary rats. But after several months, exhaustion set in. Then the rats could not live even in the moderately cold temperatures of the first room. This illustrates an important aspect of the alarm reaction: When the body's resources have been mobilized for a long time, its resistance goes down, and its ability to fight additional stressors is greatly decreased.

Two points about this research are worth noting. When Selye repeated this experiment with a variety of stressors, which included in-

Clinging to her few remaining possessions, a Vietnamese mother flees the fighting in Saigon. When confronted with a stressful situation, the nervous system rallies the body's physical resources in the fight or flight response.

tense exercise and toxic drugs, he got the same results. This supported his idea that the body responds in essentially the same way to any stressor. Selye also observed that this phenomenon can be related to the commonly heard advice doctors give to patients—get plenty of rest, keep warm, avoid strenuous exercise, eat only easily digestible food. Such basic strategy helps because the body that is already under stress (responding to a particular ailment) is less able to react as it ordinarily would to additional stressors (not enough sleep, chills, etc.). In Selye's study, animals that were under stress from one source, such as infection, did not develop the normal coping response (inflammation from white blood cells trying to fight that infection) when subjected to a second stressor. This also supports Selye's contention that stress can build to the point where it totally debilitates the body's physiological defenses and can lead to death.

Other Reactions to Stress

Selye's findings are reflected in other aspects of the human response to stressors. Imagine a man who learns that he is about to lose his job. When he first hears the news, he has a rush of adrenaline that causes increased heart rate, clammy palms, rapid breathing, and a flow of blood to his cheeks. Following this alarm reaction, he settles into resistance: His nervous and endocrine systems are hard at work, though outwardly he may appear calm. As his efforts to hold onto his job show no signs of succeeding, he eventually becomes exhausted—he develops a nervous twitch, perhaps, or an ulcer, and he is no longer able to resist. He manifests the physiological reactions Selye described, as well as cognitive, emotional, and behavioral responses. On the cognitive level, he is faced with assessing the situation: Is it a no-fault layoff or a firing? What are his chances of persuading his superiors to change their minds? Can he get another job? Emotionally, he is likely to be anxious, fearful, hurt, and angry. Depending on his cognitive evaluation, he may also feel guilty, embarrassed, or outraged.

His behavior will be based on both his cognitive and emotional perceptions. Does he want to fight for his job or just give in? If he decides to fight, he must take action—talk to his superiors, write memos, and in general act enthusiastic and determined about his work. If he decides to give in, his behavior is likely to involve withdrawal—avoiding contact with his colleagues, perhaps coming in to work late and leaving early.

This is the psychological side of the "fight or flight" response to stressors. In our society, most people do not have the option of simply fighting or fleeing (Cannon, 1936). The man faced with losing his job cannot literally fight with his superiors about it, nor can he run away and forget the whole thing. Instead, he is likely to suppress his anxiety and frustration and try to act normally—a masquerade that typically adds even greater stress to an already difficult situation. In an animal study of the development of stomach ulcers in response to electric shock, Weiss (1971) found that as long as two rats could react to the shock by attacking each other, even if a barrier kept them from actually landing any blows, they did not develop ulcers. Those rats with no such outlet did. Humans very rarely have such an opportunity of direct attack—and they often do develop ulcers in response to stress.

Aaron Antonovsky (1972), writing about stress and coronary heart disease in humans, described a four-part sequence in people's reactions to stressors: confronting a problem, responding with tension, managing the tension (that is, resolving the problem), and stress (which is defined as a state of drawing on extra energy to deal with unresolved problems). This sequence is similar in concept to Selye's GAS model, although Antonovsky's is more psychological—stress in his model being viewed as a consequence of poor tension management. Antonovsky uses the term *resistance resources* to describe the power a person can apply to resolve problems and avoid stress. Individuals with high resistance resources are least susceptible to stress and the various physical and psychological illnesses often associated with it. These are the people who survive such traumas as confinement in concentration camps without developing stress-related disorders. Antonovsky's model is also similar to the diathesis-stress theory discussed in Chapter 3. The difference is that Antonovsky depicts resistance resources as positive—a capacity for managing stress—whereas a diathesis is considered to be negative—a vulnerability to stress.

EXPLAINING STRESS

Just as different researchers define stress in different terms, there are several different approaches to explaining stress and its effects. Selye's work laid a physiological foundation: He studied measurable physiological changes in animals responding to specific stimuli. But to understand stress in humans, it is necessary to consider the psychological aspects as well. This means finding out what events or situations cause people to respond with the set of phys-

Table 5.1

The Social Readjustment Rating Scale

RANK	LIFE EVENT	MEAN VALUE
1	Death of spouse	100
2	Divorce	73
3	Marital separation	65
4	Jail term	63
5	Death of close family member	63
6	Personal injury or illness	53
7	Marriage	50
8	Fired from job	47
9	Marital reconciliation	45
10	Retirement	45
11	Change in health of family member	44
12	Pregnancy	40
13	Sex difficulties	39
14	Gain of new family member	39
15	Business readjustment	39
16	Change in financial state	38
17	Death of close friend	37
18	Change to different line of work	36
19	Change in number of arguments with spouse	35
20	Mortgage over $10,000	31
21	Foreclosure of mortgage or loan	30
22	Change in responsibilities at work	29
23	Son or daughter leaves home	29
24	Trouble with in-laws	29
25	Outstanding personal achievement	28
26	Spouse begins or stops work	26
27	Begin or end school	26
28	Change in living conditions	25
29	Revision of personal habits	24
30	Trouble with boss	23
31	Change in work hours or conditions	20
32	Change in residence	20
33	Change in schools	20
34	Change in recreation	19
35	Change in church activities	19
36	Change in social activities	18
37	Mortgage or loan less than $10,000	17
38	Change in sleeping habits	16
39	Change in number of family get-togethers	15
40	Change in eating habits	15
41	Vacation	13
42	Christmas	12
43	Minor violations of the law	11

Reprinted by permission from "The social adjustment rating scale," by T.H. Holmes and R.H. Rahe, *Journal of Psychosomatic Research,* 11(1967): 216, Table 3.

iological, behavioral, cognitive, and affective changes that are symptoms of stress.

The Social Readjustment Rating Scale

If you wanted to measure the stress in someone's life, you might count the number of stressors that had recently been encountered by that person. You could further refine the tally by assigning each stressor a value—say, 1 for breaking a fingernail, 5 for a minor car accident, 10 for a broken arm, and so on. This was in fact done by T. H. Holmes and R. H. Rahe (1967), who developed the Social Readjustment Rating Scale (SRRS), which is illustrated in Table 5.1. Their hypothesis is that stress is cumulative: The higher a person's score on the scale, the greater the amount of life stress, and the greater the likelihood that the person will have physical or psychological difficulties. We can see in this concept the influence of Selye's idea that response to one stressor lowers resistance to others.

Another idea in the SRRS that originated with Selye is that what makes a life event stressful is not necessarily its negative impact but the simple fact that it causes change. A stressor does not have to be a catastrophe or even a physical stimulus—any life change can cause stress. Furthermore, a positive event may be more stressful than a negative one. Note, for instance, that the SRRS considers marriage to be more stressful than the death of a close friend. The implication is that the amount of behavioral change involved is the critical variable, not the painfulness of the event itself.

Holmes and Rahe include 43 items on the SRRS "whose advent is either indicative of or requires a significant change in the ongoing pattern of the individual" (1967, p. 217). The items are ranked and weighted on the basis of how much readjustment respondents thought they would require. Someone being tested with this scale would receive a score that reflects the

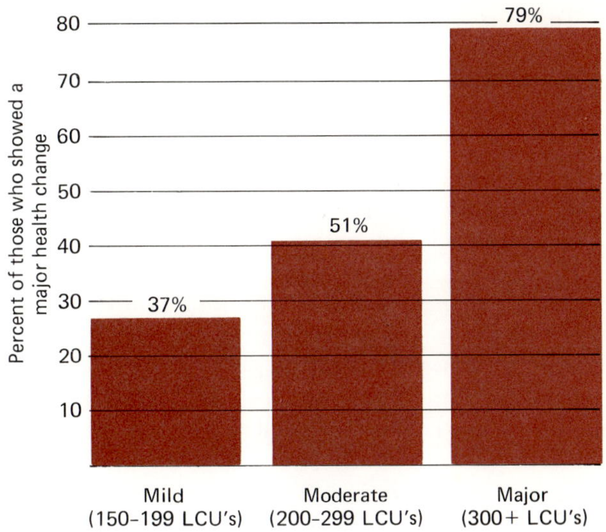

Figure 5.2. *This graph indicates that life stress, as measured on the Social Readjustment Rating Scale in life change units (LCU's), does have an effect on health. From Holmes and Masuda, 1974.*

total amount of change encountered in the recent past. Holmes and Rahe found that people who scored 300 or above on the scale had a 79 percent risk of developing a major illness within the next two years.

Characteristics of stressors

Numerous variations of the SRRS have since been created, and a range of populations have been tested with it. Although subsequent findings have not always confirmed Holmes and Rahe's initial results, as we shall see, the ranking of the items does appear to hold fairly well for both urban and rural dwellers, for whites as well as blacks, and for Mexican Americans, Japanese, Western Europeans, and other ethnic groups. From these and other data, psychologists have been able to draw some conclusions about what makes a situation or event stressful. Among the important characteristics of a stressor are its nature, duration, intensity, directness, and suddenness and predictability.

Nature. The stressfulness of a situation can be physical, psychological, or social. Physical stressors include personal illness or injury, sex difficulties, and changes in sleeping habits. Psychological stressors include the death of a close family member, losing your job, and an outstanding personal achievement. Social stressors include marriage, divorce, separation, trouble with in-laws, and a change in residence. Most stressors have elements of all three components: Pregnancy, for example, might involve the physical stress of carrying a child, the psychological stress of impending motherhood and related changes in life style, and the social stress of dealing with friends who are unable or do not want to have children.

Duration. As we saw in the case of Mike Boston, the duration of an unpleasant situation greatly affects its stressfulness. Long-term stressors might include a drastic change in financial status, a business readjustment, or a jail term. One of the most anxiety-provoking aspects of many long-term stressors is not knowing when they will end or improve—a point often raised by those who argue against indeterminate prison sentences. Brown and colleagues (1973 a, b) found that depression was not linked to events posing a short-term (one day) threat to subjects; however, events whose impact was still felt a week after their occurrence did correlate with depression.

Intensity. The whole idea of a ranked scale is that some stressors are more intense than others. The SRRS rates death of spouse as more intense than death of a close family member, which in turn is more intense than death of a close friend. Obviously, intensity is largely subjective; but extensive testing has confirmed that most people agree with Holmes and Rahe's rankings. Research also indicates that one very intense stressor has more impact than several minor ones on the development of a disorder.

Directness. The impact of a direct stressor, such as personal injury or illness, is typically greater than that of an indirect stressor, such as a change in the health of a family member. Of course, many stressors have both direct and indirect effects. A child's illness, for example, is likely to cause the parents not only sympathetic worry but additional work, loss of sleep, and perhaps a financial burden.

Indirect stressors can also lower a person's resistance to direct stressors. A study of data collected in New York state for more than a century indicates that the rate of admissions to mental hospitals has been directly related to the condition of the national economy (Brenner, 1973).

Suddenness and predictability. Another major factor in the stressfulness of a situation is whether it was possible to prepare for it. Bruce Dohrenwend (1974) suggests that the subject's control or lack of control over an event can affect its impact. Even uncontrollable events vary in stressfulness according to whether they are anticipated. The death of a child from a sudden accident is likely to be more shattering than death that occurs after the child has suffered a long, incurable illness. A surprise quiz causes sharper stress than an expected final exam. The stresses of surgery, divorce, parenthood, old age, and many other life changes can be lessened by advance preparation. On the other hand, these same situations can be *more* stressful than they need to be if the individual anticipates them with fear. Apprehension is a factor that the SRRS does not account for, but it has been significant in the treatment of stress, as we shall see later.

Limitations of Life Change Scales

The SRRS and similar scales have been used in a vast number of studies. On the whole, the results have supported a connection between stress (as measured by life changes) and psychiatric as well as physical disorders. Paykel (1974) offers this summary:

> The amount of preceding stress, its time relationship to onset, and, to a limited extent, the types of event involved, vary from disorder to disorder. . . . The most marked differences appear to be in amount of stress. . . . Suicide attempters report the most events, depressives the next highest number, then schizophrenics. (p. 148)

Nonetheless, research has brought out some important problems with such scales. Probably the most central one is that the SRRS depends on retrospective data—that is, subjects are asked to identify what life changes have preceded an illness that has already developed. This is far more practical than trying to find people who have recently undergone life changes and then waiting a few years to see if they become ill. However, it creates some obvious drawbacks, especially in dealing with psychiatric illnesses. For one, determining which is cause and which is effect is a complex process. The usual assumption is that the stress led to the illness: George lost his job, his wife left him, he went to pieces, and here he is in the hospital. But in most cases, it is equally possible that the life changes (and therefore the stress) were precipitated by the illness: George started acting a little weird, his boss got nervous and fired him, his wife was frightened and left him, and that finally convinced him to seek medical help.

A related problem is that symptoms of mental illness are stressors. Dohrenwend (1974), testing a sample that included some psychiatric patients, found that the most recent major events those patients reported in their lives usually were changes in their psychological condition. Dohrenwend concluded that if we are simply interested in predicting illness, we should use a scale that includes items related to psychiatric distress. The SRRS has been accused of being just such a scale. According to Hudgens (1974, p. 131), "By my count, 29 of 43 events . . . are often the symptoms or consequences of mental illness."

There is also a tendency among both patients and psychologists to put more emphasis than is warranted on past events in order to identify the cause of a problem—the patient in order to make sense of the illness, the psychologist in order to treat it. This may bias both the patient's report and the psychologist's interpretation. If you have ever been seriously upset, you probably remember looking back and picking out several events that might have contributed to your difficulties. A disordered person faced with a checklist of possible reasons for the

According to some researchers, a positive life change, such as this college graduation, can be just as stressful as a negative change.

illness may well be inclined to overemphasize the incidence and importance of life changes in the preceding two years.

The SRRS and similar scales have also been called into question because of the factors they *fail* to consider. Although the relationship between negative events and behavior problems holds to some degree, this does not seem to be the case with positive events (Sarason et al., 1978). Gersten and her colleagues (1974) have also disputed the idea that change is as significant as undesirability. While agreeing that anxiety may be a response to any change, they feel that "the appearance of other forms of disturbed behavior, however, such as aggression, antisocial behavior, or withdrawn behavior, may depend on the quality of the life event and not the fact that it introduces *change* per se" (p. 161).

Gersten and colleagues drew two other interesting conclusions about the validity of change as a stressor from their research with children and young adults in New York City. First, they found that a certain amount of life change is evidently necessary for adaptive and integrated behavior. People seemed to develop problems when their lives included either too much change or too little. Second, stress can be caused by things that fail to happen as well as by those that do—a desired event that is anticipated but does not come through, such as a Sunday picnic that is rained out or a vacation that has to be cancelled. Another cause of stress is more general deprivation—not having a girlfriend, not getting into college. This failure to achieve a desired object is not measured by the SRRS and other scales.

Another factor typically left out of scales of stressful events is the *context* of the stressor. An individual's social situation is crucial to the perception of an event as stressful or not. Brown's London studies of life change and depression (Brown et al., 1973 a, b) were constructed to take account of what Brown calls "contextual measures of threat."

> We started with the general notion that we should look for the reasons for different responses to life changes not so much in the meaning that is given by men and women, young and old, low- and middle-class, and so on, to an event as such, but in the particular circumstances surrounding it; and we should then go on to correlate social positions such as class status with these circumstances. Perhaps it is not so much that two women react with different meaning in the sense of emotions and understanding to, say, the fact that they have been told their husband has inoperable cancer; both may react with equal amounts of distress and be equally aware of the consequences. But it may be critical to know that one has no close tie other than her husband, has no security of tenure on her house, and was for a long period led to believe the symptoms were of minor significance, whereas the other has had the reverse expectation. (p. 230)

Unfortunately, procedures for weighing context are considered too cumbersome to be practical for most research situations.

Individual responses

Discussing the different social contexts that can influence a person's response to a stressor brings up again the question of individual differences. Is it reasonable to say, for instance, that all divorces carry a relative weight of 73, and all sex difficulties a weight of 39? Common sense says no, and so do most psychologists. Harold Wolff made the following assertion more than thirty years ago: "Regardless of the apparent magnitude, the capacity of a given stress to evoke a protective reaction is a function of its significance to the implicated individual" (1950, p. 1079). But what determines the significance of an event to the individual, and hence its stressfulness?

Demographic characteristics. Quite a bit of stress research has focused on the importance of demographic characteristics—age, sex, race, social class, level of education, geographic area, and so on. Stress-related disorders are considerably more common among people of low socioeconomic status, a fact that has led investigators to try to find out why. Bruce and Barbara Dohrenwend (1969) hypothesized that people of low social status are exposed more often to stressful life events. In a later study, Barbara Dohrenwend (1973) found support for this idea with regard to low educational level and sex (that is, women reported more stressors than men), but not with regard to ethnic group. Another study yielded no support at all for the Dohrenwend's hypothesis. Markush and Favero (1974) concluded that this discrepancy appeared to involve the scale the Dohrenwends used: "It seems likely that the list of events that is psychologically significant for one geographic area or demographic subgroup is different from that appropriate for another" (p. 185). For instance, losing a job may be more traumatic in an area where unemployment is high than in an area where numerous jobs are available. The effects of having a child are different for a 25-year-old woman and a 45-year-old woman. In other words, as Brown emphasizes, the context of the event has a strong bearing on its stressfulness. On the whole, however, research has tended to substantiate the Dohrenwend hypothesis: Members of the lower socioeconomic groups do experience more major life changes than other people.

Desirability vs. undesirability. There is considerable evidence that the stressfulness of a situation depends to a great degree on whether the person experiences it as positive or negative. To a woman who is bored with her job, for example, an increase in workload might be a welcome change, whereas to a woman who is overworked, such an increase would be unwelcome (Cobb, 1974). In a summary of research linking stress to several different disorders, Paykel states, "Events that can be regarded as desirable do not appear to occur excessively before any of the psychiatric disorders examined, but undesirable events do" (1974, p. 148).

Loss. Paykel goes on to add, "Exits precede depression but entrances do not." That is, events

Close-up: Work and Stress

Most people realize that just being on the job can create stress, but many of us may not know how much. A lot of attention has been given lately to such jobs as air traffic controller because of the obvious pressure produced by such a great responsibility. Police officers—and fire fighters, too—might logically be placed at the top of a list of stressful occupations because they never know when a life-and-death situation is going to hit.

However, a two-year study of the health records of more than 22,000 American workers turned up some surprising results. Completed in 1978 by the National Institute for Occupational Safety and Health, the study covered 130 different jobs and their link to stress-related problems. Listed below are the ten jobs that were found to be the most stressful.

1. Manual laborer
2. Secretary
3. Inspector
4. Waitress-waiter
5. Clinical lab technician
6. Farm owner
7. Miner
8. Office manager
9. House painter
10. Manager

involving loss—leaving a job, the death of a friend—seem to have negative effects, whereas neutral events or those involving an addition to the person's life do not. This point will come up again when we look more closely at depression in Chapter 12.

Another issue here is that of *perceived* loss. For example, an advertising account executive loses a big client to the competition; she feels that she has lost status, and her self-esteem drops. Even if her colleagues feel that she did the best that she could under the circumstances, her own poor attitude toward her abilities may create stress, which in turn may lead to a worse performance.

Immediate situation. As Brown has pointed out, no scale that rates the stressfulness of events can take account of all the factors affecting individual perceptions. Consider the following:

Both Joyce and Teri have entered their campus literary magazine's annual poetry contest. Joyce is busy every evening rehearsing for the class play and consulting with her adviser about the short stories she is writing for her honors project. Teri has just broken up with her boyfriend; she spends her evenings writing melancholy blank verse and fantasizing about how sorry her ex-boyfriend will be when she becomes a famous poet. When the news comes that neither Joyce nor Teri has won the contest, Joyce shrugs it off—a minor disappointment. Teri, in contrast, is so devastated that she considers dropping out of school.

If Joyce were asked to list recent major changes in her life, she might not even think of listing the poetry contest. Teri certainly would. Why is the same event highly stressful for Teri and hardly stressful for Joyce? Demographically, both students are identical. Variables such as desirability and actual loss are the same. The differences here lie in more subtle factors, the primary one being perceived loss.

First, Teri was already under stress because of a previous stressful experience—breaking up with her boyfriend—which probably made her more vulnerable to additional stress than Joyce. Second, Joyce counted less on winning the contest than Teri did. Other activities—her acting, her short stories—were apparently more important to her. Therefore Joyce probably did not build up many hopes about winning the poetry contest, so the bad news did not hit her as hard as it did Teri. Being able to transfer her energy to so many other activities may have kept Joyce from dwelling on her failure after it was announced. Furthermore, Joyce had no dreams of winning back anyone's lost regard by becoming a famous poet, so her self-esteem probably was not tied to the contest. (Note the element of perceived loss.) And the social support Joyce got from her fellow participants in the class play and from her adviser may have reduced any possible stress, a factor that has empirical support (Webb and Colette, 1975).

An important variable in any discussion of stress and stressors is the person on the receiving end. The impact of any stressor depends greatly on how it is perceived by the person it affects. When your life is going well and your self-confidence is high, you are least vulnerable to stress. Your personal fears also play a large part in determining what you find stressful. An event that touches one of your special fears or ambitions—not getting into medical school, for example—may cause more stress to you than being involved in an auto accident; another person may react with opposite feelings. Individual circumstances, such as those just discussed, therefore determine *how much* stress a person experiences in response to a stressor. In addition, they are a main reason why one person reacts to stress with temporary tension while another develops amnesia and blocks out all recollection of the stressor.

Biological as well as psychological susceptibility appears to be significant in individual responses to stress. Numerous studies have examined the possible function of genetic and other physical factors in specific stress-related illnesses. Susceptibility to depression, for example, appears to be influenced by having a psychiatrically ill parent and by having a medical disorder likely to cause disability or death as well as by stress (Hudgens, 1974). We shall return to the question of biology when we consider another group of stress-linked problems, the anxiety disorders (Chapter 6), and when we discuss depression (Chapter 12).

POST-TRAUMATIC STRESS DISORDER

On a February morning in 1972, a dam gave way and sent over 130 million gallons of water rushing into the Buffalo Creek Valley in West Virginia. Deluged by a 20- to 30-foot tidal wave of water and coal sludge, the valley's sixteen small communities were wiped out. More than 125 people were killed immediately; 4000 more were left homeless. Roland Staten woke up to the sound of people screaming and the roar of the oncoming water. By the time he and his wife could get from their bedroom to the living room, they were in water up to their necks.

> As I was climbing out, the water just sort of picked me up and I was on the roof before I even knew it with that boy of mine. My wife, she was hanging on the edge of the roof, and she—as I tried to help her up, she was kind of heavy—she was about five and a half months pregnant. . . . I lost my grip . . . and by that time the water was so deep and so much force, why, I was 20 or 30 feet from her. When I looked back and saw her she said, "Take care of my baby. . . ." That's the last time I saw her. (Stern, 1977, pp. 43–44)

James Titchener, Frederick Kapp, and the other psychiatrists called in to help in the aftermath of the flood found that of the 613 survivors they interviewed, only 9 showed no psychological impairment. Of the rest, 115 were mildly impaired, 301 were moderately impaired, 182 were severely impaired, and 6 were incapacitated. Symptoms included psychological difficulties, such as anxiety, depression, phobia,

Close-up: The Legacy of Vietnam

In 1978, former Vietnam helicopter pilot Michael Tindal was arrested in Gloucester, Massachusetts, for smuggling narcotics and marijuana into the country. He and some other ex-Nam buddies sailed a boat to Morocco, picked up the drugs, and then sailed back. Apparently, they made very little money for their enormous effort, but when they were caught, all said that they would certainly do it again—and for nothing. Why?

One counselor working with Vietnam veterans in an outreach program has termed Tindal an "action junkie." During the Vietnam War he was constantly involved in—and was able to survive—exciting, life-and-death struggles that probably earned him a strong sense of mastery. When he returned home, he had trouble finding any work, much less something to give him the same kind of emotional satisfaction. Therefore Tindal turned to anything that offered a challenge, an adventure—from parachuting and hang gliding to crime.

In 1980, veteran Henry Brown was killed by Washington, D.C., police when he tried to kill the enemy he was convinced had surrounded his house. For nearly three days, just prior to this confrontation, he had forced his alarmed family to stay with him in a makeshift "bunker" in their living room.

Many of the problems experienced by Vietnam veterans are a result of post-traumatic stress, which often lies dormant until some crisis—in Tindal's case, being rejected for a job—releases all the repressed feelings. There seem to be a number of reasons why Vietnam veterans have had a rougher time adjusting to life at home than veterans from other wars:

1. The average soldier in Vietnam was only 19 years old—seven years younger than the average soldier of World War II, and consequently less experienced and emotionally mature.
2. Most soldiers served only brief stints rather than staying with one outfit until either victory or defeat was achieved, as was the usual policy in earlier conflicts. Therefore they never became hardened to the situation, and when they did leave—alive—they felt guilty about turning their backs on their friends.
3. Once they left the field, they were often home within days, leaving little chance to "decompress"—to talk out their experience of war with other returning buddies. In fact, since companies didn't stick together for the duration, they often didn't know anyone on the jet that carried them home.
4. Probably most important was the anger and resentment that greeted them on their return: It seemed as though half the population was convinced they were fools and killers to have served at all; the other half was equally sure that they were traitorous and crazed addicts who had let the Viet Cong run over America's reputation. Why should anyone bother to help them?

Intensive treatment can overcome all the deleterious effects of having served in a war that had so little support. The problem is that there aren't many treatment centers for Vietnam vets. Max Cleland, former head of the Veterans Administration and himself a Vietnam veteran—as well as a paraplegic—started the outreach programs, which have done what they could for as many as they can reach. The question is, with the recent cutbacks in federal funding, will such programs survive?

sexual dysfunctions, and sleep disturbances; physical problems, such as headaches, backaches, and fatigue; and such problems as alcohol addiction and developmental deviation (Stern, 1977).

The disorder developed by survivors of the Buffalo Creed flood is labeled **post-traumatic stress disorder**, DSM-III's category for the reactions of an otherwise normal person to some unusual and cataclysmic event. DSM-III (p. 236) elaborates:

> The stressor producing this syndrome would evoke significant symptoms of distress in most people, and is generally outside the range of such common experiences as simple bereavement, chronic illness, business losses, or marital conflict. The trauma may be experienced alone (rape or assault) or in the company of groups of people (military combat). Stressors producing this disorder include natural disasters (floods, earthquakes), accidental man-made disasters (car accidents with serious physical injury, airplane crashes, large fires), or deliberate man-made disasters (bombing, torture, death camps).

The Disaster Syndrome

The typical sequence of immediate reactions to a catastrophe has been called the **disaster syndrome**. During the first stage—the *shock* stage—people tend to act stunned and disoriented. They may wander around haphazardly, unable to make sense of what is happening or to exert themselves to cope with it. In his book *Welcome to Hard Times*, E.L. Doctorow describes the reaction of a man who has just learned that the town he founded and built is about to collapse:

> I wrote slowly . . . thinking Now isn't this queer how I got through these motions with my hands of ice, how peculiar to be doing business; like I once saw a man who was shot in the heart, he was as dead as you can be but he walked around awhile before he lay down. (p. 191)

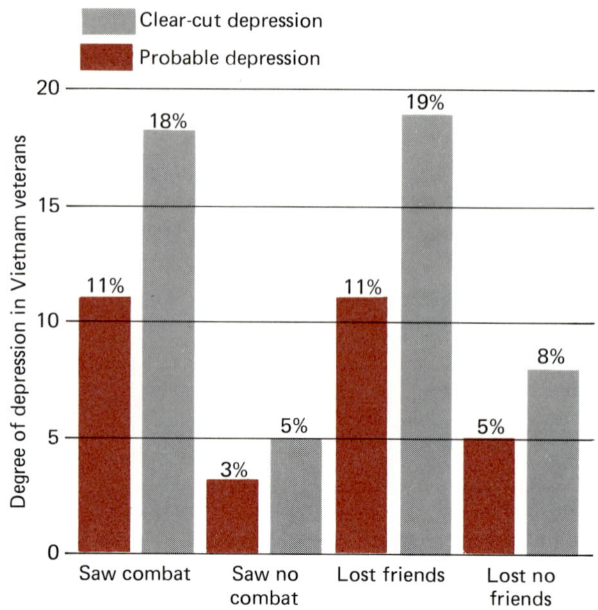

Figure 5.3. *The incidence of depression among different groups of Vietnam veterans. From Helzer et al., 1976.*

During the next stage—*suggestibility*—people become passive and compliant, glad to take orders from anyone capable of giving them but still too dazed to be of much help. The last stage is *recovery*, when people begin to think clearly again and to initiate constructive action. They are still likely to be tense and fearful, hypersensitive to anything startling, and irritable; they may also talk a great deal about the disaster, as if to work through it by telling others what happened.

The disaster syndrome is a series of typical reactions to a short-term stressor, such as a natural disaster. People who pass through all three phases and return to normal functioning within six months are said to have had the *acute* form of post-traumatic stress disorder. As we saw in the case of Vietnam veteran Mike Boston, however, it may take months or even years for the symptoms of the disorder to come on. When onset is six months or more after the stressor, the disorder is classed as *delayed*. If symptoms persist longer than six months, the disorder is considered *chronic*.

Symptoms of post-traumatic stress

Robert Lifton reported that every survivor of the Buffalo Creek flood showed some or all of the same symptoms he had noted among survivors of the bombing of Hiroshima (Stern, 1977, p. 236):

1. *Death imprint.* Flood victims were haunted by visions of the death and destruction they had witnessed. They remained fearful, viewing their environment as threatening and feeling painfully conscious of the uncertainty of life and their own vulnerability. Many relived the disaster in nightmares.

2. *Death guilt.* Numerous survivors seemed unable to forgive themselves for having lived when so many others died and for failing to save lost relatives and friends. This irrational sense of guilt was intensified by their relief at being alive.

3. *Psychic numbing.* Probably the most widespread response to the disaster was a decreased capacity for feeling. This was partly an extension of the shock stage of the disaster syndrome, a defense against painful memories, death imprint, and guilt. Typically it involved apathy, depression, and withdrawal from social groups and activities. A few people reacted in the opposite way, becoming overactive till they exhausted themselves.

4. *Impaired human relationships.* Even as they clung to each other for support, survivors grated on each other's nerves, as if closeness reminded them of their dependency and vulnerability. Many seemed irritable and suspicious of life and other people.

5. *Need to seek significance.* This common response to disaster—rationalizing it as God's will or beyond the influence of human power—was thwarted for flood victims by their awareness that the dam's bursting was the result of human negligence. DSM-III notes of post-traumatic stress disorder, "The disorder is more severe and longer lasting when the stressor is of human design."

People with this disorder frequently show behavioral reactions as well. Hearing a car backfire, an ex-soldier might drop to the ground.

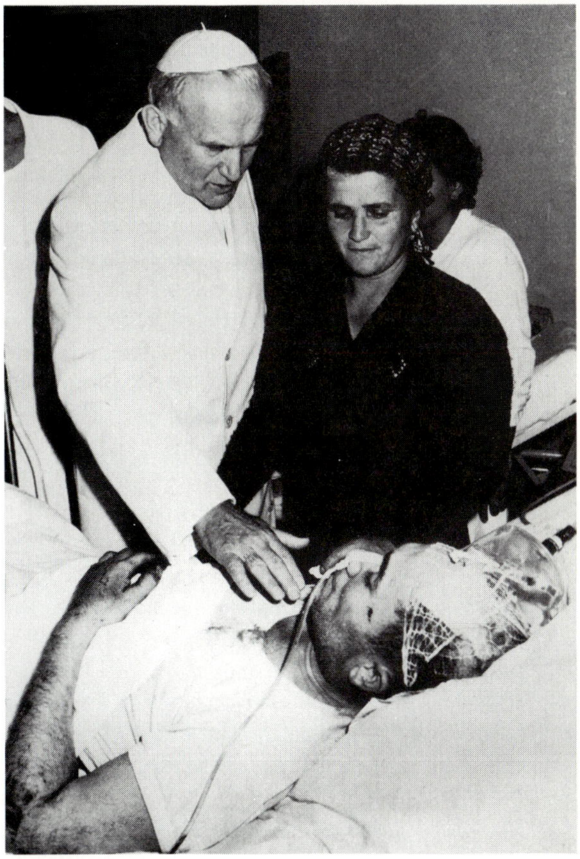

Pope John Paul comforts a victim of the 1980 earthquake that left thousands homeless in southern Italy. Many people are able to cope with a natural disaster by rationalizing it as God's will.

Their decisions may be colored by their fears: Someone seriously injured in an accident in a small car replaces it with the largest car available. Many individuals with this disorder act impulsively, sometimes aggressively.

Most cases of the disorder eventually clear up by themselves once the stressful situation is over. Apparently, talking about and visualizing the traumatic event, as agonizing as it may be at first, causes the unpleasant memories to lose their painfulness over time (Horowitz, 1969). Psychotherapy—the sooner the better—can often help by providing victims with reassurance and an opportunity to "talk out" their stress and their reactions to the stress. Sedatives may also be useful to eliminate sleeping problems. Many victims of the delayed and chronic forms of the disorder still suffer from some symptoms years after the event, however.

ADJUSTMENT DISORDER

According to the DSM-III, an **adjustment disorder** is "a maladaptive reaction to an identifiable psychosocial stressor, which occurs within three months after the onset of the stressor" (p. 299). Like post-traumatic stress disorder, an adjustment disorder is reactive, precipitated by a specific stressful event or situation. The central difference is that the stressor is usually less severe, and the person's reaction to it is disproportionate. That is, something about this particular stressor hits a vulnerable spot in the individual that causes an overreaction.

The precise symptoms vary according to the stressor and the person involved. Adjustment disorder with depressed mood is diagnosed when the individual's primary symptoms are tearfulness and hopelessness—for example, a woman who cannot adapt to life alone after her husband leaves her. A boy who suddenly starts picking fights, driving recklessly, and cutting school after the death of his father would be classed as having adjustment disorder with disturbance of conduct. Someone who finds it impossible to work or study after a traumatic experience is suffering from adjustment disorder with work (or academic) inhibition. DSM-III lists eight types of adjustment disorder. What they all have in common is onset immediately or soon after a stressor, and a pattern of behavior that (1) impairs the person's social or occupational functioning and (2) exceeds the "normal and expectable" response.

Sam P. is an ambitious young writer whose first play opened in New York to respectable success. During the first few days after the opening, when reviews were just coming in, Sam continued to haunt the theater as he had done during rehearsals, encouraging the actors and making occasional suggestions to the director, who was also a close personal friend. But as ticket sales began skyrocketing, Sam's spirits plummeted. He stopped appearing at the theater. He refused to attend any of the parties to celebrate the play's success. He brusquely turned down lunch and dinner invitations from friends. For periods of several days he would stop answering his telephone. When the director of the play went to his apartment to see what was wrong, Sam refused to let him in, saying he was not in the mood to talk to anyone. Finally, after nearly three weeks, Sam showed up again at the theater. His explanation for his unsociable behavior was that he had started a new play and was afraid of breaking his concentration. His mood was cheerful, although not as intensely so as before the play opened. He refused to say a word about the new play he was writing.

Sam's problem probably would be diagnosed as adjustment disorder with withdrawal. Apparently, after working so hard for so long on his first play, Sam found it hard to adjust to a situation in which he had nothing to worry about. He was able to make the transition at last by beginning a new project similar to the one he had just finished. For many people with adjustment disorder, adapting to new circumstances is more difficult. It is often necessary to change old habits rather than simply to find a new focus for them. It should also be kept in mind that Sam's stressor was a pleasant one. If his first play had failed and he had been forced to seek some other kind of work, the process of adjustment may have been considerably more stressful.

Like post-traumatic stress disorder, adjustment disorder usually fades away on its own once the precipitating stressor disappears or the person learns to adapt to it. Treatment can help the individual identify the source of the problem and develop a strategy for coping with it.

DISSOCIATIVE DISORDERS

This category includes some of the disorders that many novelists and filmmakers find so fascinating. They are called **dissociative disorders** because they are characterized by a break or dissociation between the individuals and their ordinary consciousness, identity, or motor behavior. Our hero is hit on the head and wakes

(a)

(b)

Peter Sellers as (a) Dr. Strangelove, (b) Inspector Clouseau, and (c) Chance the Gardener. An actor's ability to emphasize certain personality traits is essential to the creation of believable characters. In this context, fragmentation of the core personality is a useful function rather than a disorder.

(c)

up with no idea who he is. Only when the villain wallops him again, near the end of the story, does his memory miraculously return. Or a young woman's contradictory behavior puzzles her friends—until they realize she has not one but half a dozen different personalities.

Do such strange things happen in real life? Yes and no. Amnesia does occur, but it cannot be cured by a blow on the head. Multiple personality is extremely rare, but when it does happen, it may be every bit as dramatic as it is depicted on screen.

More important, dissociation can be very much like an extreme form of situational behavior, which plays a major role in most of our lives: At home or with friends, Hal is a pleasant and charming person. On the tennis court he turns into an unrelentingly fierce competitor. At school he is serious, efficient, and hardworking, known for his organizational ability. At a late night party, he may wind up dancing on the piano with a lampshade on his head; when he wakes up the morning after, he has no recollection of anything he did after midnight. This does not mean Hal needs to see a therapist; it is a very mild form of the same kind of dissociation as multiple personality disorder. The difference between the two is that Hal is conscious of most of his different attitudes—he purposely changes to suit his situation. What constitutes a disorder, in short, may not be so much the *nature* of the dissociation as its *degree*. Some dissociation is useful—perhaps essential—for normal functioning. Only in its extreme form, when it impedes the person's ability to cope, does it become a problem.

There are four dissociative disorders: psychogenic amnesia, psychogenic fugue, multiple personality, and depersonalization. Stress appears to play a key role in all four, although the connection is by no means as clear-cut as it is for post-traumatic stress disorder or adjustment disorder. In the reactive disorders, individuals are responding directly to an identifiable stressor, and their symptoms can be expected to disappear once the traumatic situation is over or once they have adapted to it. In contrast, a dissociative disorder is an attempt to *escape* from a stressor—a sort of evasive maneuver or camouflage. The stressor is often immediate and obvious, but it can also be indirect, perhaps rooted in some painful childhood experience or related to long-term dissatisfactions in the person's life. Most individuals are not aware that they are responding to anything—indeed, they may not even recognize that any change in behavior or consciousness has taken place.

Psychogenic Amnesia

Psychogenic amnesia is defined as the loss of memory caused by a psychological rather than physical factor. Four types of amnesia are included in this category. The most common is *localized* (or post-traumatic) amnesia: The person loses the memory of everything that happened during a specific period, usually the first few hours after a traumatic event. A man who comes home from work and finds his wife's murdered body might later be unable to tell the police anything that happened from that moment until they interrogated him the next morning. *Selective* amnesia, which is somewhat less common, involves forgetting some but not all of the events during a given period. The man might remember finding his wife's body, ordering a drink at a bar, and walking into a drugstore to look for a phone, but nothing in between. The least common forms are *generalized* amnesia, in which the entire life history is forgotten, and *continuous* amnesia, in which everything from a certain point in the past up through the present is forgotten.

Amnesia is fortunately rare; it happens most often in wartime or during a natural disaster, when it may accompany post-traumatic stress disorder. It comes on suddenly, usually after severe stress; typically, it disappears just as quickly.

Psychogenic Fugue

The term *fugue* comes from the Latin word for flight—and is also the root for fugitive. **Psychogenic fugue** is a person's sudden flight from home and identity. Hugo says he's going down to the corner to buy the evening paper but doesn't come back. Two weeks later he turns up playing honky-tonk piano in a bar in Topeka, with no idea how he got there. Whereas amnesiacs may wander about aimlessly, individuals in a fugue state seem to have a precise destination in mind, in spite of having forgotten where they came from. Most often the fugue lasts only a few hours to a few days and consists mainly of travel. If it continues longer, and the person goes as far as openly adopting a new game and identity to replace the forgotten ones, the new personality is likely to be more daring and outgoing than the old one.

Although a fugue is usually precipitated by a specific stressor, it appears to be a response to deeper dissatisfactions—often to a life that seems stifled and boring. It may be a way for the person to suppress the stress brought on by a traumatic event and at the same time to unleash impulses and personality traits not allowed expression in ordinary situations.

Fugues are rare. (They are also not always genuine—a man who leaves home in a fit of frustration may be reluctant to admit it once the anger wears off, claiming instead to have simply forgotten his identity and address. Such charades generally can be exposed if the person is interviewed under hypnosis or under the influence of sodium amytal.*) During a true fugue, the person will generally avoid situations that might lead to discovery. Hugo may come back home on his own in time, or he may be found months later and brought home by force, still not remembering his real identity. There is a quality of rebellion to fugue that may even include violent behavior; however, in most cases the person is unlikely to do anything that seriously conflicts with the normal personality. When memory does return, there will usually be no recollection of what happened during the fugue.

*Sodium amytal, sometimes called "truth serum," is a drug used to produce a groggy, "twilight" state that is followed by a period of deep sleep. During the twilight state, an individual can reenact traumatic experiences and discuss unpleasant subjects (Orr, 1949). Things deeply repressed may be remembered.

Multiple Personality

Eve White was 25 when she first sought treatment, a neat, colorless young woman whose main complaint was headaches. Only after many months did her real problem emerge:

> The brooding look in her eyes became almost a stare. Eve seemed momentarily dazed. Suddenly her posture began to change. Her body slowly stiffened until she sat rigidly erect. An alien, inexplicable expression then came over her face. This was suddenly erased into utter blankness. The lines of her countenance seemed to shift in a barely visible, slow, rippling transformation. . . . Closing her eyes, she winced as she put her hands to her temples, pressed hard, and twisted them as if to combat sudden pain. A slight shudder passed over her entire body.
>
> Then the hands lightly dropped. She relaxed easily into an attitude of comfort the physician had never before seen in this patient. A pair of blue eyes popped open. There was a quick reckless smile. In a bright unfamiliar voice that sparkled, the woman said, "Hi, there, Doc!" (Thigpen and Cleckley, 1957, p. 20)

One of the rarest disorders, **multiple personality** refers to the existence in a single individual of two or more distinct personalities that take turns as the dominant self. DSM-III explains the disorder further: "Each personality is a fully integrated and complex unit with unique memories, behavior patterns, and social relationships that determine the nature of the individual's acts when that personality is dominant" (p. 257). The personalities are nearly always very different—one may be a shy, polite young wife while another is a wild and promiscuous teenager. They may be of different family background, race, sex, and age—usually the same age or younger than the person's real age. Usually each personality has a name. Although the original personality is most often unaware of the others, the subpersonalities may be acquainted with each other. If they do interact, it is as separate individuals; they do not view each other as aspects of the same person. Flora Rheta Schreiber describes the case of the woman she calls Sybil Dorsett:

> Peggy and Sybil, although existing in the same body, had different memories, different moods, different attitudes, different experiences. The experiences that they shared were perceived differently. Their voices, their diction, and their vocabularies were different. They presented themselves in different ways. Even their ages were different. Sybil was 31, but Peggy . . . the doctor couldn't decide whether Peggy was a precocious child or an immature adult. Peggy was unselfconscious in a little-girl way, not easily embarrassed. Instead, she got mad. Instead of being like Sybil, circuitous, she gave vent to undisguised terror. And unmistakably Peggy carried some terrible burden that Sybil refused to face. (Schreiber, 1974, pp. 56–57)

The function of the subpersonalities seems to be to provide outlets for conflicting facets of the individual's core personality—facets that are

Close-up: *More Multiple Personalities*

Most readers recognize the famous cases of multiple personality—"Sybil" and "Eve" (Chris Sizemore) in particular because of the popular books published about their experiences. Multiple personality is a rare mental disorder, however—only 100 cases have been recorded in history, among them the following less publicized cases:

Mary Reynolds (1793–1854). Born in England but brought up in Pennsylvania, she is believed to be the first recorded case of multiple personality. At the age of 18, she began to suffer fits that left her blind and deaf and with no memory of recent events. After one severe attack she changed completely from a quiet, withdrawn young woman to one who was excitable, talkative, and robust. About eighteen years later, the more outgoing personality took over completely.

Ansel Bourne (1826–?). In January, 1887, Bourne disappeared from his Rhode Island farm. He "came to" in March in Pennsylvania, operating a small store under the name of Arnold Brown. Back home again, in 1890 he was hypnotized and the Brown personality again emerged, describing all that had occurred in those two missing months. Bourne's second personality, which never surfaced except under hypnosis, gradually faded.

Henry Dana Hawksworth (1933–). Hawksworth had six different personalities: Dana, Peter, Johnny, Phil, Jerry and Henry. Of these, Dana seemed the strongest—an ambitious worker who became a corporate executive. Peter was quiet and sensitive; Johnny was a brawler and womanizer. After therapy, the initial five merged into Henry, who then used his past disorder as a defense against an old drunken driving charge against Johnny—and won.

William Milligan (1955–). The personalities that surfaced in Billy Milligan were particularly unusual: Some of them were female, and one was a lesbian. A childhood as horrible as that of "Sybil" apparently fostered the fragmentation of Milligan's core personality. In the mid-1970s Milligan was charged with raping four coeds at Ohio State University. Like Hawksworth, he was acquitted because of his mental condition. Doctors say it appears likely that the lesbian personality, Adalene, was guilty of the rapes.

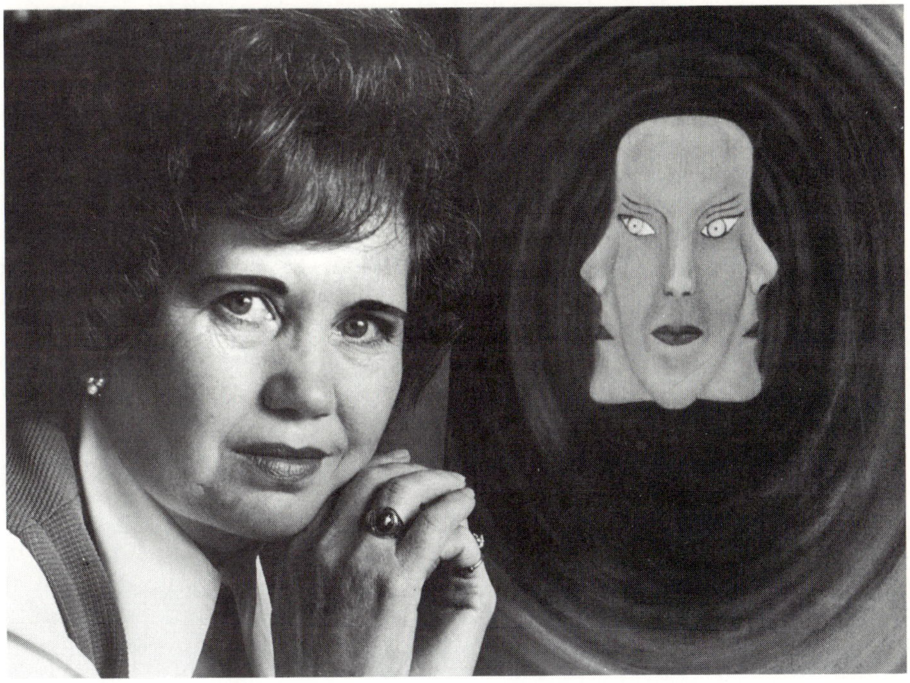

Chris Sizemore, the subject of the film The Three Faces of Eve, *shown with a work that she painted entitled* Three Faces in One.

otherwise impossible to reconcile in one identity. Multiple personality is more common in women than men. It may develop as early as childhood, although it is usually not diagnosed until adolescence or early adulthood. It often appears to be related to a severe emotional trauma the person suffered in childhood, such as abuse or the loss of a close friend or family member. Multiple personality is generally more persistent than the other dissociative disorders, and it is not as likely to disappear spontaneously. This may be because in most cases the main personality is not aware of the subpersonalities or of the memories and needs they conceal. When one of the subpersonalities takes over, the person typically experiences a blackout—or fails to recognize the loss of conscious control until "coming to" in an unexpected place.

Shifts from one personality to another usually are brought on by psychosocial stress. As the case of Eve White shows, the shift can be quite dramatic. A therapist may use hypnosis to induce a shift between personalities or to try to bring out other hidden personalities that have not yet shown themselves. Hypnosis also can help the therapist elicit the memories of the subpersonalities and bring them into the consciousness of the core personality. The goal of therapy is to integrate all the personalities into one strengthened self capable of coping with the person's past and present problems.

Corbett Thigpen and Hervey Cleckley described their treatment of Eve White's case in *The Three Faces of Eve* (1957). They note that authorities at the time were inclined to dismiss multiple personality as a flight of fancy that belonged to an earlier, less scientific age. The idea that therapists' attitudes and procedures, especially hypnosis, may actually encourage patients to show additional personalities is still being raised (Berman, 1975; Rycroft, 1978). Cornelia Wilbur, the psychiatrist who treated Sybil Dorsett, went on to diagnose five other cases of multiple personality in seven years. Does this remarkably high incidence of a supposedly rare disorder point to an over-eager therapist or to an overly conservative field?

Wilbur and others have documented distinctly different responses of patients' subpersonalities to a variety of psychological and physiological tests (Ludwig et al., 1972). The similarity between multiple personality, amnesia, and fugue suggests the possibility that some cases of the latter two disorders could be undiagnosed multiple personality. So far, there is too little information available to justify any definite conclusions.

Another confusing similarity of terms exists between the popular name for this disorder—"split personality"—and schizophrenia, a completely separate disorder that is identified by a word that literally means "split" between mind and body. It is probably still widely believed that a person with multiple personality disorder is schizophrenic. Although it may be possible for one (or more) of the different personalities that exist to show schizophrenic behavior, multiple personality and schizophrenia are two separate disorders.

Treatment of multiple personality usually involves creating a supportive relationship between the therapist and each of the separate personalities. This acceptance lessens the patient's alienation from those aspects of the personality that were previously so repellent they could not be faced. Wilbur used psychoanalytic techniques to uncover Sybil's traumatic early childhood, the painful memories of which were divided among her sixteen subpersonalities. Thigpen and Cleckley strove to give "uncritical acceptance and understanding" to Eve White and her opposite self, Eve Black, and above all to Jane, the new personality that emerged from their reconciliation. When last heard from, Sybil Dorsett had ceased dissociating and appeared happy and well adjusted. Eve, however, manifested additional personalities in the years after treatment, and finally wrote a book about her difficult experiences, *I'm Eve*, under her own name of Chris Sizemore.

Depersonalization

The symptoms of **depersonalization** are a lot like those experienced under the influence of certain drugs. Perceptions suddenly change: Hands and feet may look huge or tiny, the whole self may seem distant, mechanical, or dreamlike. The normal ability to control speech and actions may seem to vanish. Sensory perceptions may be altered or fragmented. Sometimes there is a feeling of being outside of the body.

An episode of depersonalization may be precipitated by drugs, or by some other change in consciousness, such as meditation or hypnosis. Or it may be brought on by severe stress or pain. The symptoms of depersonalization do not in themselves constitute a disorder; but when they become chronic, or when they or the problems they create impair the person's functioning, a disorder will be diagnosed. Treatment usually consists of trying to identify the stressor causing the problem and helping the patient to develop a less disruptive way of coping with it.

Some psychologists do not believe that depersonalization should be classified as a dissociative disorder, since it does not involve the loss of memory that typifies other syndromes in this group. DSM-III includes it in this category because it does involve a dissociation of the person from the normal sense of self.

MANAGING STRESS

With many disorders, therapy is limited by our inadequate knowledge of what causes the problem. With the stress-related disorders, the limitations are different: We can be fairly sure of the cause, but we cannot do much about it. Post-traumatic stress disorder is the response a normal, relatively well-adjusted person might have to an extremely traumatic experience. Adjustment disorder is somewhat more unusual, and the dissociative disorders are distinctly unusual, but they too appear to be essentially reactive. That is, as far as we can tell from existing evidence, all of these disorders are individual responses to external stressors. They do not run in the family—genetic factors do not appear to cause a predisposition for any one of them. If heredity plays a role, it probably takes the form of vulnerability to stress rather than to a specific disorder—or as Antonovsky theorized (1972), heredity provides fewer resistance resources for coping with stress.

We have seen over the course of this chapter that various techniques exist for helping people with post-traumatic stress disorder, adjustment disorder, and the dissociative disorders. Nearly always, the therapist's first goal is to identify the source of the stress that precipitated the disorder. Following this, patient and therapist work together to find ways the patient can confront the problems more directly and cope with them more productively. Usually, it is impossible to directly repair the effects of the original stressor—the war, the accident, the loss of a loved one, the abuse in childhood. If anything in the patient's environment seems to be continuing to cause stress, however, it may become a target for change. In many cases, the patient's family has unconsciously contributed to the disorder, and therapy can help them work out a more supportive pattern of interaction. For example, a husband may not realize that by forbidding his wife to go out with friends, he is repeating a pattern of repression and guilt begun years ago by her parents. If he can become more understanding of her need for independence, she will probably stop wandering off in a psychogenic fugue.

Strictly speaking though, the stressor is not the problem, the stress is. The therapist's primary aim is therefore to help the patient find a more adaptive way to manage the stress. Relaxation is usually crucial; so is self-confidence. Methods for managing stress may be biological, psychological, or both.

Biological Methods

The minor tranquilizers are probably the most common biological tactic against stress. (The major tranquilizers are antipsychotic drugs.) Valium, Librium, Miltown, and Equanil—drugs with these and other trade names are consumed by millions of people every day in the United States. Exactly how they work is unknown, but they do reduce anxiety, and they also typically cause drowsiness. If stress-related disorders are involved, they can help patients relax so that they can concentrate on a constructive approach to dealing with their disorder. For post-traumatic stress disorder, this may mean simply getting some sleep—to forget the disaster for a little while and to prevent possible exhaustion. For adjustment disorder, tranquilizers may help patients think less about their problems and more about the positive aspects of life. For the dissociative disorders, tranquilizers may lessen the anxiety felt about both the situation and the disorder so that the person can work on ways of preventing the disorder from recurring or continuing.

On the plus side, tranquilizers are usually effective at reducing the symptoms of stress. They are easy to take, they are relatively inexpensive, and they require little physician time to prescribe. On the minus side, the fact that they are easy to get and easy to use also makes them easy to abuse. An obvious drawback is that individuals may rely on tranquilizers rather than face their problems directly and try to resolve them. For instance, an executive under stress from a recent promotion might push herself too hard, rationalizing that she has a vacation coming up in three more months and until then she can get by on Valium. Aside from the wear and tear this causes to her body, the strain on her family and friends may get to be more than they are willing to put up with. If quarrels and separations result, that greatly increases her stress. Thus the tranquilizers may wind up having exactly the opposite effect of what was intended. Another, more dangerous result of too much reliance on tranquilizers is unintentional addiction. Withdrawal from these substances can be severe, and sometimes fatal.

A biological approach that has been gaining in popularity in recent years is an emphasis on physical activity. Sedentary Americans have been growing more and more aware that a healthy body is one of the best weapons against stress. Remember, stress is not just psychological tension but a set of physiological responses. The body can resist stress most effectively when its resources are in good shape. Two essential components of physical health are exercise and diet.

Exercise—jogging, cross-country skiing, roller-skating, tennis, yoga, aerobic dance, swimming, or whatever—does more than keep you thin. Among other benefits, it helps your heart function at its best, which maintains efficient blood circulation as well as a low heart rate and blood pressure. When the body reacts to a stressor with the general adaptation syndrome, heart rate increases and blood pressure rises. The person who exercises regularly has a lower heart rate and blood pressure to begin with and therefore is better able to take stress in stride.

A well-balanced diet also strengthens a person's physical capacity to resist the ill effects of stress. Hunt and Margie (1979) illustrated this point dramatically in their study on the control of sodium (in the form of salt) in 3500 patients with hypertension (high blood pressure). Of those patients whose diets included very little sodium, 51 percent to 85 percent regained a normal (unhypertensive) blood pressure. Little success was recorded in the group with the highest pretreatment blood pressure; the highest success rate was among those who had started with borderline hypertension. But among patients whose sodium intake approached the typical North American diet, only 0 to 13 percent achieved normal blood pressure. This is only one example of the many ways diet is related to the body's ability to combat stress.

Psychological Methods

One of the psychological approaches to managing stress is **biofeedback**, a technique in which information about physiological responses is fed back in an altered form to the individual. Information about muscle activity might be translated electronically into a tone whose pitch or intensity varies directly with muscle activity. Cardiovascular information, such as heart rate or blood pressure, might be indicated by a meter or a digital display. Whatever the form, the individual uses this feedback to understand and control the system being gauged. The experimenter may say, "This green light will go on when your brain is emitting a certain proportion of alpha waves. See if you can make the light go on—and then stay on." Through a process of operant conditioning, the person gradually learns how to keep the green light on most of the time. Biofeedback training can be used to teach people to control a variety of normally unconscious physiological functions—to relax muscles, to increase or decrease heart rate or blood pressure, and to produce particular brain wave patterns, for example. Interestingly, recent research suggests that biofeedback training performed under conditions of stress is more likely to retain its effectiveness than biofeedback training given under nonstressful conditions (Benthem and Glaros, 1981).

Researchers have often noted that a general effect of biofeedback training is relaxation. Several other more direct approaches to relaxation can also be useful in managing stress. One is *progressive muscle relaxation,* devised by Edmund Jacobson in 1938. Subjects learn to tense and relax the various parts of the body, paying attention to the subjective states that accompany muscular tension and relaxation. A variant of progressive relaxation is the *relaxation response,* developed by Herbert Benson. To generate the relaxation response, individuals need to be physically comfortable. They then adopt a passive attitude while focusing on a cue word, such as "calm."

Meditation is yet another relaxation method. The meditation techniques practiced by Zen and Yoga masters typically involve a focusing of attention plus control over breathing. To keep the mind from being diverted by thoughts, the meditator may repeat a meaningless word or phrase—a mantra—over and over. A similar focusing of attention and calm physical and psychological state can be achieved with hypnosis.

All these techniques help counter not only the psychological tension but the physiological arousal that accompanies stress. That is, the person may experience lowered muscle tension, slower respiration and heart rate, and other physical signs of relaxation. Practiced diligently, relaxation techniques can have long-lasting generalized effects.

By concentrating on a word or object, a person meditating may produce specific physiological changes and achieve a state of consciousness different from normal wakefulness.

To help relaxation techniques maintain their effectiveness, therapists often combine them with other self-control techniques. Many of these focus on the feelings and cognitions that accompany problem situations. One such self-control technique is termed rational-emotive therapy or RET (Ellis, 1973). This technique teaches the client first to recognize irrational thoughts and beliefs and then to counter these with more rational beliefs. For example, a man who believes that other people will despise him if he is not perfectly competent and successful in all possible respects would be shown how unrealistic that belief is. Since thoughts like these can have physiologically arousing consequences in stressful situations, RET can be useful in helping people deal with stress and related disorders.

Another self-control technique has been termed stress inoculation (Meichenbaum, 1977), a procedure that has several components, including relaxation training. A key element is graduated exposure of clients to particularly stressful situations while they remain calm and relaxed. Although the cognitive emphasis in stress inoculation is relatively strong, this technique has obvious similarities to systematic desensitization.

Finally, people who are prone to stress may need to make important life-style changes. The man who starts wishing he would get sick in order to slow down a little would do well to learn to unwind and not be so tied to his job or studies. Of course, this is often easier said than done. To significantly lower the level of stress in someone's life may require a major reworking of social patterns, occupation, and hobbies. But the hard-driving corporation president may not be willing to turn more responsibility over to other people. The divorced mother of several young children may not be able to afford to give up her job or to pay for day care. Most of us, though, can find ways to change our habits if we are convinced the results will be worth the effort.

Sometimes, as the Holmes-Rahe scale suggests, the way to lower stress is to aim for *less* change rather than more. A person who is starting a new job may be tempted to put the increase in income toward a better apartment. But the stress of moving could make it harder to meet the demands of the job. After the loss of a loved one, whether to death, divorce, or breaking up, it is a good idea to weigh the probable stress of remaining alone in the same surroundings against the stress of starting over in unfamiliar ones. As Brown's London study suggested, the impact of any stressor depends to a great degree on the person's expectations, degree of general stability, and other individual factors. A good therapist will encourage the person to consider these things when making a major decision.

SUMMARY

Stress is a state of psychological and physiological mobilization, the rallying of an organism's forces to combat a perceived threat. Stress is manifested by the general adaptation syndrome (GAS), which consists of the alarm reaction (the body's initial response to a stressor) followed by the stage of resistance, in which the body resists or retreats from the stressor, adapts to it, or both. If resistance is unsuccessful, the organism passes into the stage of exhaustion. In humans, stress also has behavioral, cognitive, and affective components.

Much of the research on the relationship between stress and illness has depended on the Social Readjustment Rating Scale (SRRS) and similar measures that assign a relative rank and weight to various stressors in order to gauge the amount of stress present in the life of a subject. Stress for this purpose is operationally defined as any change, positive or negative, requiring significant readjustment. High scores on the SRRS have been correlated with later development of major illness, though objections have been raised to both the design of such scales and the interpretation of resulting data.

Various characteristics determine the stressfulness of situations or events, among them their nature, duration, intensity, directness, suddenness, and predictability. The context of the stressor and the individual's perceptions of it are also highly significant. Demographic characteristics, the desirability or undesirability of an event, whether or not it represents a loss, and the person's general situation are particularly important. The failure of a desired event to occur also can be a stressor.

Post-traumatic stress disorder, a reactive disorder, is the response of otherwise normal people to an unusual and highly traumatic situation, such as war or a natural disaster. The subsequent pattern of reactions ordinarily occurs in three stages: shock, suggestibility, and recovery. Common symptoms include death imprint, death guilt, psychic numbing, impaired human relationships, and a need to seek significance for the event. Adjustment disorder, another reactive problem, is an individual's maladaptive reaction to an identifiable stressor, usually much less severe than the disasters that cause post-traumatic stress. Symptoms vary with the situation and the person involved, but they center on a reaction that exceeds the "normal and expectable" response to the stressor and impairs the person's social or occupational functioning.

The dissociative disorders involve sudden changes in a person's normal consciousness, identity, or motor behavior. Stress is a precipitating factor, but the stressor is generally not as direct or clear-cut as in the reactive disorders. Psychogenic amnesia involves a loss of memory that blocks out all or part of a traumatic experience or other unacceptable thought. In psychogenic fugue, individuals literally flee their surroundings and identity as part of the subconscious effort to forget. Multiple personality is still more dramatic. Spurred by trauma and internal conflicts, the individual develops one or more subpersonalities as vehicles for dealing with memories and expressing attitudes the main personality is unable to accept. These subpersonalities, which may possess the distinct characteristics and behavior of several different people, alternate control of the body. Depersonalization involves episodes of alienation from the normal sense of self.

Treatment of the reactive disorders usually focuses on helping the person to manage the stress and adjust to the change brought on by the stressor. Most often these disorders eventually fade once the stressful situation is over or the person has adapted to it. With the dissociative disorders, the therapist must first help the patient to identify the stressor before they can work toward means of adapting to it or finding other less disruptive strategies for coping. Because all stress-related disorders represent maladaptive attempts to deal with stress, successful therapy depends on developing adaptive alternatives.

An essential first step is for the individual to relax enough to take a constructive attitude toward the situation. Biological tactics include tranquilizers, to diminish the amount of stress perceived by the individual, and exercise and diet, to increase the capacity to cope with stress. Psychological approaches include biofeedback, progressive muscle relaxation, and the relaxation response, all of which try to help the person cope adaptively with tension. Meditation and hypnosis can also contribute to relaxation and the focusing of attention. Relaxation techniques are most effective against stress when they are combined with strategies for self-control, which include rational-emotive therapy, stress inoculation, and changes in life style. It is important to try to evaluate the effects of a change. Will a new situation reduce stress, or will it only serve to increase it?

Conversation 2

The young family in this interview is undergoing a stress that may never abate: Lee, now 27, contracted polio in 1979, when her infant son was just three months old. Almost completely paralyzed below the neck, her world turned upside down overnight. Her husband Don, 29, suddenly found that, in addition to pursuing his architectural career, he was now chief caretaker for the helpless Lee and baby Jay and responsible for keeping the household running smoothly. It has been rough, but they are managing.

Interviewer: Was it a sudden thing?

Don: Yes, it was. In a two-hour period the paralysis spread from her feet up to her knees, and then in another two hours it was at her waist.

Int.: What was your initial reaction?

Lee: I just thought it was a bad flu. I think I was too sick to be scared.

Int.: What was it like for you?

Don: Terrifically terrifying in every way, shape, and form! I mean, my wife was paralyzed to the waist! I was scared. It just seemed like the worst thing that could ever happen to me. Everything was perfect—it really was—in our lives. The initial shock was really the worst part, I think. I have a close friend, down in Louisiana, who's the first person I told. I was crying real hard. He said, "Well, you just gotta be strong and do what you have to do."

Int.: What was it like taking care of Jay?

Don: Not too bad. My mind really wasn't that much on him, you know. It was almost like tying your shoes. Jay is a super-good kid. That's made it a lot easier. I had offers to get Jay off my hands, but Jay was one of the things that made it OK for me to come home. I had a piece of Lee right here. An empty house would have been much harder.

Int.: Did you need to have a routine in your life?

Don: That was one of the key things! You've got to have some kind of stable ground when everything is topsy-turvy. I still managed to get into work—a place where everything wasn't changing.

Int.: That must have been a really rough time.

Lee: Oh, yeah. But the memory is slowly fading. I can remember the day they took me to intensive care, just in case I had trouble breathing. They were saying, "Don't be upset, there's no cause for alarm." Then as the night wore on I kept feeling this thing take over. One part of my brain was going crazy! And I knew that part was saying, "If you go to sleep, you're never going to wake up."

Int.: When did you realize the totality of it?

Lee: That was a long time afterwards—I'd say two months later.

Int.: What did you think then?

Lee: I felt like I'd been kicked in the stomach; like I was an air balloon and they just popped me. I cried and cried. My first reaction was it wasn't fair: Why am I being punished? What did I do wrong? Then I got angry for the first time in my life. I mean mad at God: How could You do this to me? Why didn't some old person in the bed over there get this?

Int.: How long did that last?

Lee: A couple of weeks. I talked to a priest, and we became really good friends. I saw him walking down the hall and said, "Nurse, please go get him. I have to talk to him." But I think I went through all the phases. First I was too sick to even think about what was going on. And then I think I dealt with it by saying it wasn't real. I would wake up and think, "When I open my eyes, I'm going to be able to move again. It's a bad dream; it'll go away." That happened for the longest time, and then finally one morning I woke up and said, "It's not a bad dream and it's not going to go away."

Don: You went through some pretty severe depression. I remember your parents leaving and you were trying to mouth the words "Kill me, kill me!" I said, "Listen, I'm just going to be selfish. You can't die. Jay and I need you too much—you *have* to stay here."

Lee: That hit home hard. And then anger comes in. Anger like I've never felt, like if I could punch my hand through that window I would. Damn it! I'm not going to be like this! I *am* going to get better! And such turmoil and agony inside, feeling like I just can't get through another day. But you do.

Don: We reinforced each other. I would look at Lee and consider any problem I had insignificant to hers.

Lee: The whole way through he's been like that. I cope with it by praying and calling someone to talk to whenever I feel depressed.

Int.: Faith seems to really support you.

Lee: Oh, yes. I say my prayers every night and during the day—I mean I'm always talking to Him. Just knowing that all the other people are praying for me—it's a constant reassurance.

Don: I think you operate on a much more spiritual level. You pray a lot; you can feel that it works. People we thought were spiritually in tune were the people we wanted around. You know right off what people are negative, and you just don't need those people around—doctors included.

Lee: There was one negative doctor. I said, "I don't want that person to touch me anymore; I don't want him around." But for the most part, we had excellent support systems.

Int.: What is the worst part?

Lee: Not being able to move! Not being able to do *anything*. I can't help my baby. If there's a bug on me I can't get it off. I'm a distance from everything. I'm a very affectionate person, and the thing that's killed me is I can't reach out for Don at night, I can't kiss him, I can't grab Jay.

Don: I think you lose all the little touches that occur in the course of the day. Whenever you touch a person, I think that has some kind of effect on you. I would tell people that were coming up here to see Lee, no matter what shape she was in, "Whatever you do, hug her and kiss her more than you want to, 'cause she can't get enough."

Int.: What kinds of things do you do for fun?

Lee: We have friends in Lexington with a pool; we've gone over there to visit. We invite friends here. Don's parents are always calling us to do something. They've taken us to the movies, they've taken us out to dinner.

Int.: Do you ever think of becoming an activist for the handicapped?

Lee: Yes, I would like to do something about that, but right now it's enough for me to run the house.

Don: Lee's a real manager!

Lee: The girl who helped me with my personal care and the house is leaving, and a new girl started today. Two of them here at once and I had to teach everything—at least a first-day run-through. I had to get dinner cooked, Jay taken care of, the house picked up, phone calls made, mail opened. My mind never stops!

Don: I put the pressure on her. I said, "Look. Things have to get done around here. I don't care how, but you're responsible."

Lee: I used to be scared to ask people for a piece of gum, and now I have to ask them to do *everything*. I've even had to fire a person.

Int.: Do you think that's a good change?

Lee: In a lot of ways it's been really good. I was outgoing, but I think I was always a follower. At times I've wanted to lead, but I just didn't know how. And now I'm really not scared of much.

Int.: How do you feel about that?

Don: Good change. We've worked on that since we've been married.

Lee: He's really tried to help me become independent.

Int.: How has it been financially?

Lee: Oh, well, we've coped. It's been heartrending sometimes. I feel we sell our soul half the time to keep above water.

Don: We've had various types of state aid. The main burden of the whole thing has been on insurance. Lee was a computer programmer before she had Jay—

Lee: And just happened to be under the thirty-day grace period.

Don: Our friends and family have helped.

Int.: How do you think this is going to affect Jay?

Lee: When I came home I felt like a stranger. I had very little rapport with Jay, and I had to be his mother! I yelled at him all the time—you know, just my own frustration of not being able to hold him or do anything for him. I've had to learn to touch. He sits in my lap and he's very good in the chair. Now that he's learned to climb out, of course, he knows he can get his freedom, but he does want to get up.

Don: He puts Lee's arms around him.

Lee: It hurts, and I have to remember not to scream "No!" every time. I don't want to discourage him from touching me. Other people can fend him off and play with him—I'm at his mercy.

Don: I suspect it might be a good influence on Jay.

Int.: What is the prognosis?

Lee: Based on what movement I had gotten back after three months and based on all the readings and on what the doctor was familiar with, it didn't look very hopeful. He just didn't think I had a great chance of getting everything back.

Int.: Has your relationship improved?

Don: It's much deeper and stronger. The odds are not good, though, of a family staying together after something like this happens. That's one of the first things counselors tell you.

Lee: They might last through the critical period, but afterwards it falls apart.

Don: I think having a really strong relationship going into the whole thing helped. We were at the peak of our relationship. You can't do it half way. You're either going to be totally committed to it or you're going to leave. A lot of people leave.

Int.: Are you happy?

Don: Oh, yeah! Super happy!

Lee: I could be happier sometimes—but yeah, basically I'm happy.

CHAPTER 6

Anxiety Disorders

DESCRIBING ANXIETY

Evaluation Difficulties

Generalized Anxiety Disorder

Panic Disorder

Phobic Disorders

Obsessive-Compulsive Disorder

EXPLAINING THE ANXIETY DISORDERS

Biological Explanations

Psychological Explanations

Social Explanations

Interactional Explanations

MANAGING THE ANXIETY DISORDERS

Biological Methods

Psychological Methods

Anna Michaels, 27 years old, was referred to a psychologist by her physician. She seemed extremely nervous during her first session—wringing her hands, crossing and uncrossing her legs, looking at the psychologist and looking quickly away, playing nervously with strands of hair. She described her stomach as feeling like an empty pit one second, a twisting, convulsing knot the next. Her heart, she said, was pounding so fast and hard she felt sure someone could hear it. Her hands felt cold, and the muscles in her neck were so tight that they often hurt. She would have her husband massage the muscles sometimes, she said, but lately he and she had been arguing more than usual and she guessed he was tired of her constant complaints about being anxious all the time.

She described feeling more and more tense throughout the day, as if something were about to happen that she could not prevent. She had given birth to a baby girl six months ago and since that time her anxiety had increased. At first, Anna just seemed a little nervous about having a new baby, and she thought with experience her nervousness would pass. But instead of decreasing, the anxiety increased. She spent more and more of her time worrying about whether she was a good mother, whether her baby was happy, whether she would accidentally hurt the baby, and so on. When she told her husband about her concerns, he chuckled and told her not to worry, that everything would be "just fine." But Anna did not see things that way. To her, everything seemed to be getting worse. When the phone rang, her heart would start pounding, her breathing would become faster, and a sense of impending doom would seem about to overwhelm her. If the doorbell rang, she would react the same way, grabbing up her baby before she answered the door as if she needed to protect the child from danger. Around people, even people she knew well, she stumbled on her words and felt as if the person she was talking to could tell what she was thinking. She began to avoid visiting friends and gradually isolated herself in her own home. She still worried about the baby constantly. Finally, as her husband became more and more impatient with her, she decided to seek help.

Anna would be diagnosed as having generalized anxiety disorder, a condition of persistent anxiety apparently unrelated to any specific cause. Anxiety is a normal response to threatening situations. What made Anna's anxiety noteworthy was its lack of apparent provocation: There was nothing specific threatening her. As her therapist probed into her past, nothing emerged that might have brought on the degree of fear and tension she reported. This accorded with Anna's own perception of her difficulty—"I just can't stop worrying, that's all!"

Before the third edition of the *Diagnostic and Statistical Manual* was published in 1980, the American Psychiatric Association used the term *neurotic disorders* to refer to four types of disorders that are now listed separately: the anxiety disorders, the dissociative disorders, the somatoform disorders, and the mild affective disorders. The anxiety disorders consist of (1) generalized anxiety disorder and panic disorder, which are mild to severe anxiety responses marked by the absence of any identifiable stressor; and (2) the phobic disorders and obsessive-compulsive disorder, which are extreme responses to specific but not extraordinary stressors. These are not the only stress-related problems. The disorders presented in Chapter 5, the disorders with specific and severe physiological problems discussed in Chapter 7, and the mild affective disorders discussed in Chapter 12 also include at least some element of stress.

DESCRIBING ANXIETY

As we have seen, stress is a state of physical and psychological arousal within an organism in response to a stressor. A stimulus (an approaching car, a surprise party) applies stress, and the body reacts in ways aimed at avoiding the stressor or adapting to it. **Anxiety** normally occurs as part of this reaction. It is a psychological state of generalized worry and tension characteristic of the stage of resistance. But anxiety can also arise in the absence of an identifiable stressor, or it can arise as an inappropriate response to a stimulus most of us would not regard as threatening. Either situation indicates the presence of an anxiety disorder.

Psychological anxiety is usually reflected in physical signs as well. Thoughts are apprehensive; the body reacts by readying itself for action—but what kind? The result of these ambiguous signals is that in addition to feeling nervous, fearful, and restless, the person may have a pounding heart, rapid breathing, clammy hands, and a dry mouth. There may be muscle tension, especially in the neck and upper shoulders, chest pains, and numbness or tingling in the extremities. Mild diarrhea, frequent urination, and sleep disturbances such as insomnia and nightmares may occur also. The person is irritable, on edge, and easily startled—and all these symptoms will persist. In a sense, the individual seems to be under siege by his or her own defense forces. An aroused mental and physical state keeps the body mobilized, but the person doesn't know what's causing the anxiety and can't make a move. Gradually, the sustained physiological resistance wears out the body's resources.

In addition, there are cognitive changes that can be very wearing. Because the body is constantly in the "fight or flight" stage, ready to respond to danger, the mind is exceptionally alert, always on the lookout for the stressor. However, this can cause a sort of "cognitive overload," in which the person finally just can't think straight any more—being constantly alert has worn out the ability to reason normally. After staying up all night working on a term paper, many people are confused and disoriented the next morning—their normal cognitive functions have been temporarily disrupted. In contrast, people with anxiety disorders are not afflicted for just a morning—their disruption lasts as long as all the other signs of their anxiety remain.

Numerous researchers have suggested that anxiety is related to the person's degree of control over a situation (Pervin, 1963; Neale and

Close-up: Night Terror

Jim had been asleep about an hour. Suddenly, he sat up and began talking wild, excited gibberish and flailing his arms. He jumped from the bed and started to move around the room as if avoiding something unseen, something terrible. A few minutes later, he climbed back in bed, much calmer, and went back to sleep. The next morning he had no recollection of the episode.

What Jim experienced was neither a nightmare nor a simple act of somnambulism. Researchers are now calling this special type of episode a night terror. It is distinguished from somnambulism by its emotional tone—extreme fear—and from nightmares by several factors.

First, nightmares are vivid dreams that people can generally recall very easily the next morning. After night terror, people remember either nothing at all or one very frightening image, such as the presence in the room of something evil. Of their own response there is often no memory. Second, the people who experience night terror are convinced themselves that it is not a dream; when asked if it was a nightmare they are scornful.

Most significantly, nightmares take place late in the sleep cycle, during the second half of the night. Night terror, on the other hand, occurs in the first three hours of sleep. Furthermore, the body's reaction to the two is quite different. The ANS response to nightmares is mild, but during a night terror the pulse and respiratory rate can double and there are changes in skin resistance, all characteristics of the "fight or flight" response.

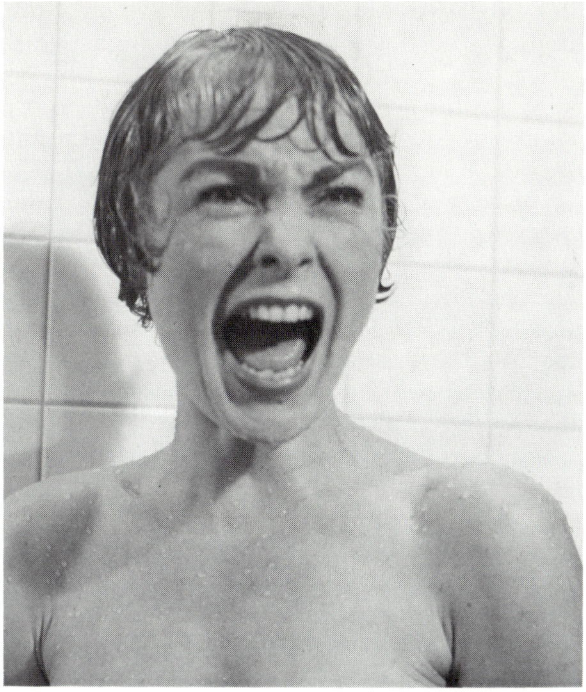

Janet Leigh in the terrifying shower scene from the movie, Psycho. *Hitchcock, a master at building suspense, focused the attention of his audience on the anticipation—rather than the graphic depiction—of a dreadful event.*

Katahn, 1968; Seligman, 1975). However, *actual* control may not be as important as *perceived* control (Geer et al., 1970). In studies on urban stress, Glass and Singer (1972) found that subjects exposed to loud noise performed poorly at proofreading, found the noise highly irritating, and gave up problem solving. If the subjects merely perceived that they could control the noise if they wished, their complaints and symptoms disappeared. In another example, if two people are traveling by car in hazardous weather, the driver is likely to be less anxious than the passenger. Similarly, some social learning writers have suggested that anxiety in a situation is related to whether the person expects to succeed and be positively reinforced, or to fail and be punished (Rotter, 1954). As an example, the man who goes to a party feeling attractive and interesting is likely to have a good time, while the man who expects that nobody will want to talk to him is likely to spend the evening feeling anxious.

In order to understand the nature of anxiety, it is helpful to contrast it with a closely related emotion—fear. Seligman (1975) believes that anxiety differs from fear mainly with regard to the predictability of the anticipated stressor. Film director Alfred Hitchcock perceived the importance of this difference; in his many successful suspense films, he made use of what he called the difference between shock and suspense. Imagine the following movie scene: A woman comes home to her empty apartment; when she opens the closet door to put away her coat, a man jumps out at her. We—the audience—react with shock, or in Seligman's terms, with fear. But if the filmmaker rearranges this scene—we first see the man climbing in through a window and hiding in the closet, and *then* the woman coming home and taking off her coat—we are caught in a grip of prolonged suspense until that closet door opens. Seligman (like Hitchcock) believes that anxiety—knowing something awful is about to happen, but not knowing when—causes more stress than confrontation with the threat itself.

Evaluation Difficulties

How many people have anxiety disorders? Although there are few data on this question, anxiety disorders appear to be among the most common psychological ailments. A good estimate is that between 2 and 4 percent of the general population have been diagnosed as having one of the four types of anxiety disorder. Interestingly, about 10 percent of cardiology patients have some kind of anxiety disorder (DSM-III, 1980). But this estimate is difficult to verify because certain anxiety disorders can be so easily misdiagnosed.

Anxiety and other problems

Sometimes it is difficult to recognize the severity of anxiety. Everyone feels anxious at one time or another, without necessarily needing a therapist. Since anxiety often accompanies more serious disorders, it often escapes notice and is not treated. The fact that anxiety can be defined as a negative emotional state, a physiological state of arousal, and a disruptive cognitive state complicates the picture and makes evaluation difficult. Self-report measures can be used, physiological arousal can be gauged, and behavior can be observed and evaluated; however, these measures can and often do yield contradictory evidence. Does a psychologist decide that a young man is anxious if he has a rapid heartbeat and other physiological indications of arousal yet reports feeling relaxed?

If the available data pertaining to a case are ambiguous, or if only one or two symptoms are present, the necessary next step is to gather more information. Has a specific traumatic event, such as separation from someone close, occurred in the near past? If not, the psychologist might try to find out how the person behaves and feels in certain situations generally considered anxiety-provoking (such as speaking in front of a large group), or what situations make the person feel anxious. If the source of anxiety can be pinpointed, a diagnosis of generalized anxiety disorder is not appropriate.

The picture becomes more complicated if the person uses alcohol, barbiturates, or other drugs. If alcohol is a major problem, most individuals would be diagnosed as having an alcohol abuse disorder rather than an anxiety disorder, even though they may have started drinking to ease their anxiety. If they are simply detoxified and sent home, the whole process is likely to start again. Likewise, someone who is taking tranquilizers may be using them to combat anxiety. But excessive use can also *cause* anxiety (see Chapter 9).

It is essential that the possibility of physical dysfunction be ruled out before a diagnosis is made. For example, thyroid problems, or simply an overdose of caffeine from drinking too much coffee, can cause symptoms similar to those of anxiety disorders. In addition, it may be necessary—especially in drug abuse cases—to look beneath the physical dysfunction (the abuse that's causing anxiety) to see what's at the bottom. In order for a diagnosis of anxiety disorder to be given, anxiety—measured physiologically, behaviorally, or through self-report—must be the primary difficulty, not the result of some other problem.

Generalized Anxiety Disorder

The essential feature of **generalized anxiety disorder** is strong and persistent anxiety that has lasted at least a month and is not due to a specific stressor. Physiologically, generalized anxiety shows up as hyperactivity of the **autonomic nervous system** (ANS), which plays a major part in emotional behavior, and specifically in anxiety. It governs activity in the heart, endocrine glands, and smooth muscles of the stomach, kidneys, and other major organs. There are two divisions included in the ANS: the **sympathetic** nervous system and the **parasympathetic** nervous system (see Figure 6.1). Although the distinction is not clear-cut, the sympathetic nervous system is believed to energize: to increase the heart rate, pump blood to the muscles, release adrenaline into the system, and generally prepare the person for activity. The parasympathetic nervous system orders everyday functions, such as digestion, in order to maintain homeostasis. It is these two divisions that ready the organism for "fight or flight" when it faces a stressful situation.

As happens in stressful conditions, in a generalized anxiety disorder the organism is mobilized to deal with whatever stressor threatens, but the point of fighting or fleeing never comes. Thus the person is likely to report feeling shaky, jittery, restless, jumpy, or irritable—in Selye's model, symptoms of the resistance phase moving toward exhaustion. Body aches or fatigue may occur in the muscles from continual tension and the inability to relax. The person often complains of sweating, hot or cold spells, dizziness or light-headedness, a lump in the throat, or discomfort in the pit of the stomach. Some people have cold, clammy hands and a pounding heart or a tingling feeling in their hands and feet. A feeling of apprehension that some-

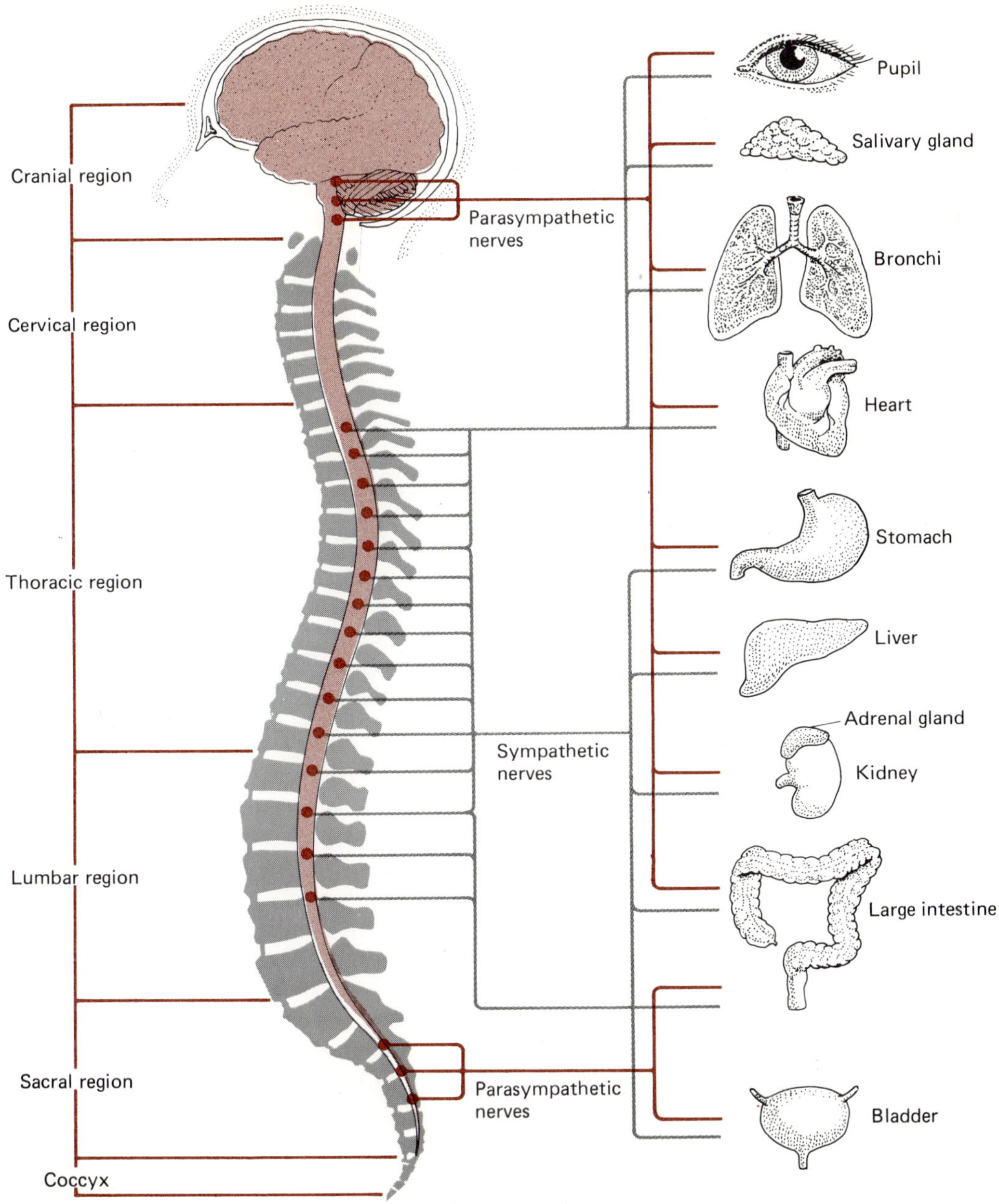

Figure 6.1. *The autonomic nervous system (ANS) is divided into a parasympathetic system, which originates in the brain and sacral vertebrae, and a sympathetic system, which originates in the vertebrae of the spinal cord. Both of these divisions affect each internal organ, but for different purposes. The parasympathetic system controls the organs under normal stress and maintains homeostasis. The sympathetic system goes into action when emergencies arise by stimulating the internal organs. Under extreme stress, the sympathetic system signals for the blood flow to be diverted to the brain and the muscles of the arms and legs. In addition, adrenaline is secreted into the bloodstream, which further prepares the body for action.*

The Shriek, *1896, a black and white lithograph by Edvard Munch. (Collection, The Museum of Modern Art, New York. Mathew T. Mellon Fund.)*

thing unpleasant is about to occur accompanies a variety of other symptoms, and mild depression is common.

People experiencing generalized anxiety may be most aware of its cognitive and affective aspects. They cannot say exactly what it is they fear, yet they remain in a state of dread. They spend their time consumed with worry and uneasiness. Even if life seems to be going in their favor, they feel tense and apprehensive. At night after going to bed, they may worry about the day's activities, about what they are going to do tomorrow, about the fact that they cannot get to sleep. Once they do slip into a restless sleep, they may dream that they are being shot or choked to death, or that they are trapped by a killer and can't move.

Daily functioning is difficult with so much to worry about—what mistakes they have made, what they meant to do but forgot, what friend or family member they might have offended. Being anxious so much of the time for no apparent reason interferes with decision making, concentration, and other thought processes that most of us take for granted as part of everyday life. Anxious people generally find themselves unable to think clearly, or cope with stressful situations, or solve problems. Then their fears are confirmed; they prove what they have always worried might be true—that they are inept. This further increases their nervousness, which contributes to greater physiological arousal and more cognitive interruptions. It is a truly vicious circle.

Sometimes anxious people even worry about worrying—"I can't get anything done because I worry all the time!" Such people may develop chronic nervous symptoms: aching muscles, high blood pressure, clammy hands, tingling sensations in their extremities, and indigestion. This secondary anxiety includes worrying that the anxiety will cause them to lose their jobs, alienate friends, get sick, or go crazy. Yet this recognition does not motivate a change. They are simply stuck, and each move seems to make the situation worse.

Panic Disorder

Charlie R., aged 43, was walking down the street in the small Minnesota town where he lived when he had his first panic attack. He was passing the store where his father had once worked and where his new son-in-law was now employed when suddenly he began to feel anxious. Something horrible was about to happen! Most alarming of all, he was overwhelmed with fear that he would lose control of his actions and do something crazy. Charlie's face paled; he felt hot, then cold. His heart racing, he found himself gasping for breath, choking, as if he were about to smother. He grew dizzy and faint. This can't be real, Charlie thought. But the panicky feeling would not go away, and he thought for sure he would pass out. He managed to get to a park bench; then, almost as suddenly as the attack had occurred, it subsided. Charlie felt as physically exhausted as if he had been engaged in strenuous physical labor. The whole thing had lasted only four minutes, but to Charlie it felt like a lifetime. And all through the attack, a terrible feeling that he was about to lose control had been with him.

The main feature of **panic disorder** is recurring **panic attacks**. As in Charlie's case, the attack usually comes on suddenly, mounts to a high level of intensity, and then subsides. During the attack, which can last from a few seconds to an hour or more, the person may experience a wide range of symptoms, including sweating, dizziness, shortness of breath, chest pain or tightness, choking or smothering sensations, shivering, increased pulse and pounding heart, an urge to urinate, gastric distress, alternating hot and cold flashes, tingling in the extremities, trembling, shaking, and feelings of unreality. The most overwhelming aspect of a panic attack is, however, the subjective feeling of impending doom. The person is certain that something awful that cannot be prevented is about to happen. People who have experienced such attacks later recall that they thought they were going to die, or lose control, or do something violent or obscene, or go crazy. The world was closing in on them and there was nothing they could do to stop it. Afterward, they felt exhausted, as if they had used up a tremendous amount of energy—which is indeed what happened.

Panic attacks can occur as part of the generalized anxiety disorder or in reaction to a phobic stimulus; they do not necessarily indicate panic disorder. A man with a cat phobia, for example, may experience a panic attack whenever he sees a cat or even suspects that one is nearby. According to DSM-III, panic disorder is diagnosed when the panic attacks are unpredictable and occur in the absence of a life-threatening situation, a phobic stimulus, or a period of marked physical exertion. Individuals with panic disorder may even wake from a sound sleep feeling anxious and go right into a panic attack. Between attacks they may seem calm, but mild anxiety is more usual because they are never certain when the next attack will occur. Because the attacks are uncontrollable and unpredictable, they may become afraid to leave their home or neighborhood. Panic attacks appear to be fairly common among the general population, as is panic disorder itself. According to DSM-III (1980), the disorder is diagnosed more often in women than men.

Phobic Disorders

Phobic disorders, more commonly called **phobias,** are characterized by overwhelming and persistent fear of a particular object, situation, or activity. A normal person's aversion to snakes or spiders is not a phobia. Only when someone reacts to a spider or a snake with incapacitating terror or repulsion is the problem considered a phobic disorder. In such a case, the fear of encountering the dreaded stimulus is so great that the person will go to almost any lengths to avoid it. Even the *thought* of having to confront the object is terrifying. The person's capacity to function is thus disrupted not so much by the stimulus itself as by the efforts made to avoid it.

Phobias interfere with people's lives to varying degrees, of course. A city-dwelling woman with a snake phobia probably would not find that this fear interrupted her daily routine; at worst, she might avoid a summer hike in the woods. A man with an elevator phobia, however, would find living and working in Manhattan extremely difficult. Not only would he be upset at having to ride in an elevator, but even seeing an elevator or hearing the sound of its doors closing might cause anxiety. The only solution for him would be to avoid entering any building with an elevator in it—a serious problem for an urban resident.

The effects of the phobia are exacerbated when the person generalizes beyond the original feared object to other similar stimuli. For instance, the woman with a fear of snakes might also avoid rubber hoses, pieces of rope, snakeskin belts and shoes, and all other objects resembling or associated with snakes.

In a study of several countries, it has been estimated that about 3 percent of all psychiatric outpatients suffer from phobic disorders (DSM-III, 1980). Most people with phobias admit that their fear is unreasonable, but this does not prevent them from feeling it. Many individuals will rationalize their behavior by saying that avoiding the phobic stimulus makes sense simply because not to do so would create anxiety too intense to handle.

A phobia often arises from a frightening experience early in life—being bitten by a dog, for example, could cause a child to grow up fearing dogs. Usually such a fear does not become a phobia, though, without some additional psychological influence. Perhaps the child's parents were afraid as well, and always pulled the child back in alarm when they encountered a dog; perhaps they used the threat that "a big bad dog will come and carry you away" to enforce discipline. If the child is bitten and the parents show extreme fear, their reaction may have a more profound effect than the bite itself.

A phobia can also be a way of displacing negative emotions from their real target. Imagine a young girl whose father spends all his spare time training his Doberman as an attack dog. Besides being terrified of the vicious dog, the child may feel unwanted and unloved because the dog is getting all the attention she feels should be hers. Years later, she falls in love with a man who owns a dog, and finds she is so frightened of his beloved pet that he finally has to get rid of it.

DSM-III divides phobic disorders into three categories: **agoraphobia, social phobia,** and **simple phobia**.

Agoraphobia

This disorder—by far the most incapacitating of the phobias—can be defined as an unreasonable fear of being alone or in a public place away from friends and familiar surroundings. The phobia often manifests itself after a round of panic attacks: As agoraphobic individuals become afraid that they may suddenly have a panic attack that will incapacitate them, they avoid going anywhere where they do not have access to immediate help and they are disinclined to venture outside familiar territory without someone they know. Even when accompanied by friends, they may avoid crowds, closed or open spaces, bridges, or tunnels. Being forced to face such a situation—or even to think about facing it—fills them with anxiety. The disorder thus is severely disruptive, since it limits normal activities and often keeps the person from going out of the house.

Agoraphobia is the most common of the phobic disorders. In a study of a small city population, it was found that 0.5 percent had at some time been agoraphobic (DSM-III, 1980). The disorder is diagnosed far more often in women than men, but it is not certain whether this represents an actual difference in occurrence. The incidence of agoraphobia is also higher among members of the same family than in the general population.

Social phobia

People who will do almost anything to avoid a public performance or exposure to scrutiny by other people are said to have social phobia. Their fear seems to be that they may do something ridiculous or inept and embarrass themselves. As a result, such individuals avoid situations ranging from public speaking to using

public restrooms. Because they are usually aware that the fear is irrational, they try to hide it from other people, which is likely to increase their anxiety. For example, a woman afraid of speaking to audiences may dread having her voice crack or quiver. This anxiety causes her voice to crack, impairs her performance, and proves to her that public speaking should indeed be avoided.

Simple phobias involve the fear and avoidance of certain objects or situations, such as spiders, snakes, or heights.

Simple phobia

Sometimes called a specific phobia, simple phobia can be defined as the fear and avoidance of specific objects or situations other than those involved in agoraphobia and social phobia. Among the simple phobias are *acrophobia* (fear of heights), *claustrophobia* (fear of enclosed places), *hydrophobia* (fear of water), *mysophobia* (fear of dirt or germs), and *ophidophobia* (fear of nonpoisonous snakes).

Afflicted individuals are afraid of something that may actually be slightly dangerous, such as dogs, snakes, insects, or high places. Encountering the feared stimulus can increase their level of distress and may also interfere with their functioning. The usual response is intense anxiety, with all the physiological symptoms noted previously—increased pulse, breathing difficulty, clammy hands, and so on. They may even experience a full-blown panic attack. Simple phobias are also reported more often in women than men. Most phobias, especially those involving animals, begin in childhood.

Obsessive-Compulsive Disorder

An **obsession** is a recurrent image, impulse, or thought that comes to mind involuntarily. A **compulsion** is a repetitive behavior the person feels compelled to carry through even though it causes no pleasure—rather, it is performed only to avoid intolerable anxiety. In both forms of the disorder, the individuals usually regard the thought or act as senseless or even undesirable. They yield to it only because resisting it results in so much tension. It is a little like playing the first seven notes of a scale—your ear is not satisfied until you play that eighth note.

We use the terms obsession and compulsion loosely in everyday language—"Nancy's obsessed with jazz." "Greg's really getting compulsive about his job." Thinking often about something that has meaning for you is not an obsession in the clinical sense, however. If you find that a line from a song is stuck in your head, or you can't stop mulling over plans for an upcoming trip, that does not mean you need a therapist. Similarly, it is not truly compulsive if you can't stop eating chocolate when you're depressed, or if you always turn off lights when no one is using them. The **obsessive-compulsive disorder** is diagnosed on the basis of a repetitive thought or act that serves no productive purpose except the prevention of anxiety in a situation that would not make most people anxious. It does not go away after a few hours or days, and its recurrence either causes the person serious distress or impairs normal functioning.

Obsessions

Many obsessions are sexual or violent in nature (though not all recurrent sexual or violent thoughts are obsessions). An example of an obsession is the case of a businessman who reported that he was spending much of the day preoccupied with the idea of raping his wife and then choking her. He wanted desperately to stop these thoughts, but he could not seem to keep his mind on anything else. Another case involves a mother who found herself constantly thinking about stealing her baby grandson, taking him to another town, and bringing him up

Table 6.1 *The Way Obsessive-Compulsives Feel About Their Rituals*

How sensible do the rituals seem?	Sensible 22%	Rather silly 13%	Absurd 65%
Does reassurance from others influence the rituals?	Definitely yes 27%	Some 15%	Definitely no 58%
Does the presence of others affect the rituals?	Occurs when alone 20%	Company irrelevant 76%	Occurs in company 4%
How much family distress do rituals cause?	Little or none 29%	Moderate 22%	A great deal 49%
Do you resist carrying out the rituals?	Definitely yes 32%	Somewhat 22%	Definitely no 46%

Stern and Cobb (1978), *Phenomenology of Obsessive-Compulsive Neurosis*, British Journal of Psychiatry, 182, 233–39. Reprinted by permission.

as her own child. In both cases, the individuals had attempted to block their obsessions, but they were unable to control their unacceptable thoughts. Not surprisingly, obsessions are typically accompanied by guilt and anxiety over the indecency and horror of the thoughts as well as a fear of carrying out the imagined behavior.

Another type of obsession involves contemplating and trying to resolve some problem, often an absurd one. Kolb (1973) illustrates with the case of the patient who was obsessed with trying to figure out why a chair had four legs instead of one. Sometimes normal behavior comes very close to disorder in this category. Take the case of the housewife who stays up round the clock designing a fabulous, one-of-a-kind dream house and neglecting her family in the meantime. A week later, she drops her pen and graph paper, kisses the baby, and starts doing the laundry that has accumulated while she was absorbed in floorplans. Is she normal or disordered? What if you knew she had no immediate plans to build—and in fact was not likely to have enough money for such a project for several years to come?

Compulsions

Compulsions, like obsessions, are an extreme form of a behavior that most of us demonstrate mildly from time to time. We check three times to make sure we have locked the car door or walk around ladders instead of under them. In contrast, the person with a pathological compulsion exaggerates this pattern into a meaningless habit. Rachman and colleagues (1973) identified two categories of compulsions: *checking rituals,* in which the person interrupts normal activities to check something again and again, and *cleaning rituals,* in which the person feels something is contaminated and must be cleansed. A man with a checking ritual might check to make sure the front door is locked before going to bed and then check it and the back door several more times before he is satisfied. A woman with a cleaning ritual might wash her hands three or four times after touching a dog for fear of the dirt and germs on its body. Another type of cleaning ritual involves "washing away" the moral "contamination" that some people believe results after a sexual act such as masturbation.

The case of Georgia M. is a good example of an obsessive-compulsive disorder. Georgia described her problem to her therapist as follows:

> I can't get to sleep unless I am sure everything in the house is in its proper place so that when I get up in the morning the house is organized. I work like mad to set everything straight before I go to bed, but, when I get up in the morning, I can think of a thousand things that I ought to do. I know some of the things are ridiculous, but I feel better if I get them done. . . . Once I found just one dirty shirt and washed, dried, and ironed it that day. I felt stupid running a whole wash for one shirt but I couldn't bear to leave it undone. It would have bothered me all day just thinking about that one dirty shirt in the laundry basket.
>
> What really bothers me is this whole business of sex. My husband acts like he wants it all the time and he always brings it up at times when it's impossible because I have so much to do. . . . I like to make preparations, too. I think we both ought to take a shower and the bed should have clean sheets on it. But he gets mad and says "the hell with it" and sulks. . . . Now he says he's going to leave me and that's the only reason I came to see you. (McNeil, 1967, pp. 27–28)*

Notice that although Georgia was aware that her compulsive neatness did not make sense, she did not view it as a problem. To Georgia, the problem was that her husband might leave her. To her husband, Bill, the problem was Georgia:

> I'll tell you what it makes me feel like. If I forget to leave my dirty shoes outside

*Elton B. McNeil, *The Quiet Furies: Man and Disorder.* © 1967. Adapted by permission of Prentice-Hall, Inc., Englewood Cliffs, N.J.

> the back door she gives me a look like I had just crapped in the middle of an operating room. . . . When we used to have people over for supper she would jitterbug around everybody till they couldn't digest their food. I hated to call them up and ask them over because I could always hear them hem and haw and make up excuses not to come. . . . I'm going out of my mind but you can't talk to her. She just blows up and spends twice as much time cleaning things. . . . I think the only reason she came to see you was because I told her I was going to take off and live in a pigpen just for laughs. (pp. 26–27)

Spurred by the threat of having her marriage break up, Georgia forced herself to change her habits. She began by doing the laundry every other day instead of every day and limiting herself to one shower a day. The anxiety caused by this "gross neglect" turned out to be less than she had expected, though at last report she and Bill still had a long way to go to a happy and comfortable life together.

EXPLAINING THE ANXIETY DISORDERS

We mentioned earlier that until the publication of the third edition of the *Diagnostic and Statistical Manual* in 1980, the anxiety disorders, the dissociative disorders, and the somatoform disorders were classified as neurotic disorders. These three groups of disorders still have much in common. They all involve extreme reactions to normal stressors, and for that reason their explanations have some similarities. Furthermore, research following the old classification of neurotic disorders often did not separate the three types. Some of what follows thus applies to the dissociative and somatoform disorders as well as the anxiety disorders. The major explanations of the anxiety disorders have tended to fall into four categories: biological, psychological, social, and interactional.

Biological Explanations

A number of researchers believe that biological factors play an important role in the anxiety disorders. It has been suggested that people who develop these disorders may have physical characteristics that in some way predispose them either to anxiety or to a particular strategy for coping with it. The two main areas of investigation have been genetic variations and possible physiological differences.

Genetic factors

The most common first step in genetic research on any disorder is to see whether its incidence is higher among blood relations than among comparable groups of unrelated persons. In a study of neurosis among the relatives of people who had already been diagnosed neurotic, Brown (1942) found the incidence in first-degree relatives—parents and siblings—to be 16.8 percent, compared with only 1.1 percent in a control group. More recent research has shown the incidence of anxiety disorders to be around 15 percent in first-degree relatives of subjects with anxiety disorders (Noyes et al., 1978).

Although these data support the genetic hypothesis, they do not provide conclusive evidence for it. It is difficult to be certain whether the influential factor really is genetic or whether it is based on learning dysfunctional behaviors from close family members. Research with identical and fraternal twins is one way of trying to sort out these influences. The idea behind twin research is that any pair of twins may share the same environment, but only identical twins share the same heredity. This is because identical (monozygotic) twins develop from the same egg and therefore have the same genetic material, whereas fraternal (dizygotic) twins develop from different eggs and are only as genetically similar as any other siblings. If heredity is a factor in a disorder, then the chance of both twins having the disorder would be greater for identical twins than for fraternal twins. This is usually expressed in terms of concordance rate. For instance, if identical twins

As the old adage advises, the best thing to do after falling off a horse is to climb right back on. The element of danger in most fears is real, however. In fact, most phobias concern situations that can actually cause harm.

show a concordance rate of 50 percent for a disorder, that means that when one twin has the disorder, there is a 50 percent chance the other twin will also have it.

In 1970, a review of twin studies up to that time for the neurotic disorders showed a 53 percent concordance rate for identical twins and a 40 percent concordance rate for fraternal twins (Rosenthal, 1970). This is consistent with a theory of genetic transmission, though it does not amount to proof for such a theory. Other research has had different results, however, with some studies showing a concordance rate as low as 25 percent (Eysenck, 1973a). After examining the available data, Cohen (1974) concluded that the evidence in favor of a genetic hypothesis was not strong enough to comprise an adequate explanation of anxiety disorders.

Of course, part of the problem is pinpointing just what it is about the anxiety disorders that may be inherited. The following section will review several possible physiological explanations for anxiety-related disorders, any of which could be genetically transmitted. We should bear in mind, too, that it is quite conceivable that the anxiety disorders have more than one cause. If that is the case, hereditary factors could be influential in a more complex way than family or twin research would necessarily indicate. This possibility will come up again in the section on interactional explanations.

Physiological explanations

Since the autonomic nervous system (ANS) is the primary bodily system involved in anxiety, it is not surprising that many physiological theorists seeking a biological explanation for the anxiety disorders focus on this branch of the nervous system. Remember that it is the ANS that is active in the body's responses to stress mentioned earlier in this chapter and in Chapter 5—increased heart rate, respiration difficulties, clammy hands and feet, sweating, and so on.

One physiological hypothesis, a form of the diathesis-stress theory, suggests that some people inherit more sensitive autonomic nervous systems than others (Lacey. 1967). Such hypersensitive individuals may respond more actively to stress than other people and thus may be more susceptible to chronic anxiety disorders.

Seligman (1971) has suggested that a hypersensitive ANS may be a factor in anxiety disorders, but he shies away from the idea that it is an inherited trait. Instead, he postulates that people develop ANS hypersensitivity from exposure to continual stress. That is, the ANS becomes more and more sensitive with each traumatic event until it finally becomes active at the slightest cue from the environment.

Seligman has also emphasized the possibility that people may innately fear certain things more than others (Seligman and Hager, 1972). For instance, most phobias involve objects or situations that have the potential to be dangerous—spiders, snakes, dogs, heights, and so on. People rarely develop a phobia of something totally unthreatening to them. Nevertheless, there are many such cases included in the literature, among them fear of dust, fear of virgins, and fear of sermons.

Psychological Explanations

Probably every school of psychology has at least one theory to offer about the anxiety disorders. Indeed, without this group of disorders, some of the major theoretical viewpoints might not exist. Whatever the role of biological factors in anxiety, there is little question that psychological influences are significant. In this section we will consider the various psychological interpretations of the anxiety disorders offered by psychodynamic, behavioral, cognitive, and social theorists.

Psychodynamic approaches

The milder disturbances have always been a central concern of psychodynamic theorists—and anxiety has always been viewed as central to these disturbances. Freud had a great deal to say about this group of disorders, although he changed his mind about them more than once. At this point, so many psychodynamically oriented theories exist that the most we can do is briefly summarize some of the major ones.

Freud believed that the source of adult anxiety is an unresolved childhood conflict that has been pushed into the unconscious. At some point during or after infancy, the person was frustrated by some ungratified urge related to sex or aggression. Later, during adulthood, the id keeps trying to push this sexual or aggressive impulse into consciousness, while the ego fights in vain to completely repress the impulse. The result is anxiety, as the person worries that the id will win out and the unacceptable impulse will become a reality—control will be lost and the horrible thought will be acted upon.

A good example of how Freud applied these ideas to actual cases of anxiety disorder is the case of Little Hans (Freud, 1955). At the age of five, Hans refused to go out into the street because he was afraid a horse would bite him. Freud interpreted this phobia as Hans's subconscious struggle between sexual desire for his mother and aggressive hostility toward his father—the Oedipal conflict. Afraid that his father would punish him by castration for coveting his mother, Hans displaced his intense anxiety and fear of his father onto horses. The size and strength of horses made them a good father symbol, and the boy's fear of being bitten seemed to Freud a clear sign of castration anxiety. Besides, his father sometimes played "horsie" with him. In Freud's view, Hans was attempting to alleviate his anxiety by avoiding horses.

Freud explained the other anxiety disorders similarly, as manifestations of repressed inner conflicts. Violent obsessions, such as the man's fantasy about raping and then strangling his wife, would thus represent aggressive id impulses that have come to the surface. People like Georgia M. with compulsions about cleanliness are said to be reacting to a repressed anal desire to soil things and be destructive.

Fundamental to Freud's ideas of neurosis are his theories about defense mechanisms. Briefly, a defense mechanism is a tactic for avoiding anxiety; usually it involves removing an unacceptable thought or impulse from consciousness, or transforming it into some more acceptable form. Little Hans, for example, was using both repression and displacement to escape his Oedipal anxiety, and the result was a phobia. According to Freudian theory, a neurosis typically develops when one or more defense mechanisms are inadequate to stave off anxiety.

Later psychodynamic theorists rejected Freud's emphasis on sexual and aggressive id impulses. Jung (1915) believed that the repressed anxiety and needs of the parents are an important factor in the child's development of an anxiety disorder. Adler (1917) viewed anxiety as the result of children's feelings of inferiority when they compare themselves to their bigger, more powerful, and wiser parents. Anxiety disorders were thus seen as growing out of attempts to compensate for these feelings of inferiority. Karen Horney (1937, 1939) did not reject the significance of early childhood experiences, but she felt that the person's present life situation is also important. In her view, a man who feels anxious around people in authority did not necessarily feel the same way about his parents; however, any such early feelings would influence the present situation and would therefore contribute to his anxiety.

Taking another viewpoint, Carl Rogers (1961) claims that the discrepancy between the ideal self individuals want to be and the real self they think they are creates anxiety. Rogers sees this discrepancy beginning in childhood, when children must live up to very high parental standards in order to gain love and acceptance. Failing this, they come to see themselves as incapable, inadequate, and unable to meet the demands of "successful living" in society. This makes them extremely anxious and leads to an even worse situation: They stop growing toward self-actualization. Limited by a narrow and negative self-concept, the anxious person cannot open up to growth-stimulating experiences. Thus in addition to being problems in themselves, the anxious symptoms and defenses prevent individuals from realizing their full potential.

It has also been suggested that anxiety may come from a perceived conflict in the person's wants and needs. Perhaps a man's parents always wanted him to join the family law firm, but he perceives his talents as lying in chemistry. Caught between his desire to please his parents and his wish to pursue his own interests, he becomes anxious. Another person may be torn by the need for financial security and a wish for self-fulfillment: Should I take this promotion even though I prefer the kind of work I'm doing now? Should I major in engineering instead of music because it will give me a better chance of getting a job? Anxiety can also result from a conflict between moral values and other needs. The Roman Catholic family facing questions of birth control or abortion is an excellent example of this type of anxiety.

Behavioral approaches

The behavioral explanation of anxiety disorders focuses on the present and follows a learning model. The classic behavioral example of phobia acquisition is John Watson's work (Watson and Raynor, 1920) with the child known as Little Albert, mentioned in Chapter 3. Just as Albert was conditioned to respond with fear to a white rat, behavioral theorists suggest that classical or operant conditioning is responsible for some phobias.

O.H. Mowrer (1948) elaborated on this model by introducing the concept of anxiety as part of a two-stage process. In the first stage, the person encounters certain neutral stimuli that, by being paired with an aversive stimulus, become anxiety-producing. For example, imagine a young man who for one reason or another has developed great embarrassment about his dancing ability. He goes to parties with friends, and every time he dances he feels extremely anxious. He soon learns to associate certain neutral stimuli connected with parties—dim lights, thick smoke, and loud music—with his anxiety. Mowrer referred to this process—learning to associate neutral stimuli with anxiety—as **sign learning**.

In Mowrer's second stage, the discomfort caused by the anxiety-producing stimuli is generalized to any situation characterized by the same signs. The young man who was anxious about dancing is now anxious about any situation where lights are dim, loud music is playing, and people are smoking cigarettes. He begins to stay away from *all* parties, not just those where he might be urged to dance; he even avoids restaurants with jukeboxes.

Notice that although the first stage of Mowrer's model involves respondent conditioning, the second stage involves operant conditioning. After learning the unpleasant association, the behavior is reinforced by temporary relief from anxiety, and avoidance is thus strengthened. Unless something happens to change this cycle, the person will continue to avoid the various stimuli (both unconditioned and conditioned) associated with the anxiety, and through generalization, may increasingly avoid similar stimuli if the anxiety is great enough.

Mowrer's model offers a plausible explanation for generalized anxiety, but how would the two-stage process create a disorder? A good example is Freud's case involving Little Hans. It was pointed out by later writers (Wolpe and Rachman, 1960; Bandura, 1969) that Hans had developed his fear of horses after being frightened by a serious accident involving a horse. His phobia seemed to be only of large horses pulling heavy wagons at fairly high speeds, which were the conditions of the accident. To apply Mowrer's theory to this case, Hans would have seen horses pulling wagons as neutral stimuli until they were paired with an unconditioned aversive stimulus, the pain of the accident. Then horses, wagons, and high speed became signs of a dangerous and therefore anxiety-provoking situation. By avoiding horses, Hans avoided the anxiety that originally was associated with the accident and afterwards was associated with those three signs.

Is it possible to learn to fear almost anything? Conditioning interpretations suggest that it ought to be. If a little girl at a circus was eating peanuts when the big top suddenly caught fire, wouldn't it be possible for her to be terrified of peanuts forever after? Some researchers have found, however, that in the laboratory it is not possible to condition people to fear just any object (Davison, 1968b).

Other anxiety disorders can also be explained in terms of conditioning, particularly if Mowrer's two-stage model is used. Compulsions can readily be seen as behaviors that are reinforced by the relief from anxiety they provide. Agoraphobia might be a means of avoiding aversive stimuli—including panic attacks—that the person fears encountering when going out.

Behavior theory doesn't seem to work as well for panic attacks and obsessions, however. It is difficult to imagine how people could have learned to have either of these disorders. In addition, obsessions seem to indicate the involvement of cognitive factors, and possibly emotional elements as well. Furthermore, investigating the histories of people with anxiety disorders very often fails to uncover any experience that might have involved conditioning.

Albert Bandura (1969) has suggested mod-

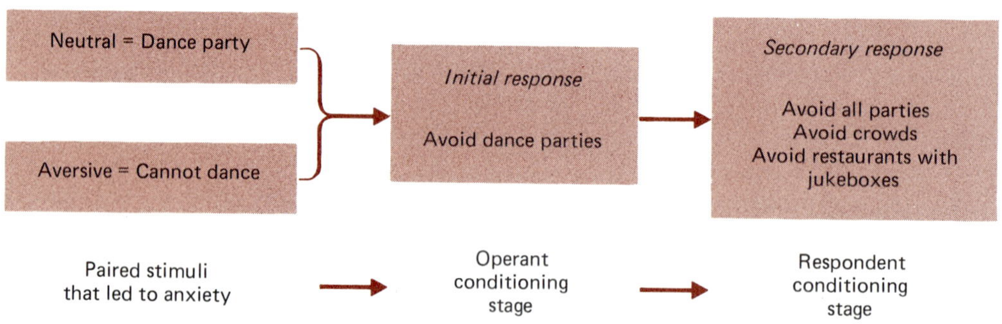

Figure 6.2. *Mowrer's two-stage conditioning model.*

eling as an alternative to direct experience. That is, people may be able to learn various responses—including anxiety and avoidance—indirectly, by observing the emotional reactions and behaviors of others, especially those who are important to the individual. A young girl who watches her mother scream and run for the house when she sees a snake in the garden may develop a snake phobia. Or a boy may observe his father washing his hands again and again after he has spent an anxious afternoon trying to repair the family car and conclude that the way to manage anxiety is with a washing ritual. Notice that the children in these examples have modeled the same-sex parent, a tendency for which there is strong evidence in research (Bandura, 1969).

Cognitive approaches

The cognitive view of anxiety is appropriately summed up in a statement originally made by Franklin D. Roosevelt: "We have nothing to fear but fear itself!" According to several theorists (Ellis, 1962; Beck, 1967, 1976; Meichenbaum, 1974), anxiety is not caused solely by external events; rather, it results from irrational expectations about those events. The anxious person is someone whose thinking about the world is distorted. One such distortion is exaggerating the danger of certain situations—for example, a woman may be afraid to fly in an airplane because of an exaggerated and irrational expectation that it will probably crash. In this case, her irrational perception (and resulting anxiety) prevents her from doing things that otherwise would be enjoyable. A similar distortion is exaggerating the likelihood that some unpleasant event will happen—for example, a man might devote a great deal of energy to installing several different alarm systems and special locks because he is afraid his house might be burglarized. In this case, the irrational perception *causes* action that otherwise would be recognized as unnecessary. Another common type of distortion involves doubting one's ability to handle a difficult situation. Consider a student who has to give a presentation to 40 classmates plus the teacher. As the time approaches, he becomes more and more anxious—his stomach churns, his heart rate increases, his hands feel clammy, and his forehead perspires heavily. According to cognitive theorists, these symptoms of anxiety are due not to the assignment but to the young man's distorted cognitions—"This is going to be a lousy presentation, and everyone in the class will think I'm boring," or, "If I mess up, the teacher will realize how stupid I am."

Social Explanations

Social explanations for anxiety and the anxiety disorders are currently in a speculative stage. One area of investigation is the family. Parents who view their marriage as a necessary evil and are constantly voicing their dissatisfactions with it may teach their children to become anxious about their own close heterosexual relationships. This is especially problematic if the parents use the children as weapons against each other. If the parents are unduly worried and preoccupied about health or their children's success at school, or if they place much importance on having their children carry out some goal that they achieved (or failed to achieve), the children may grow up anxious about that particular issue. While research has turned up some evidence for correspondences between the problems of parents and children (Dohrenwend and Dohrenwend, 1969; Ehrenwald, 1960; Jenkins, 1966), no distinction has been established between environmental and hereditary influences.

There is also evidence that the type of anxiety disorder a person develops may be related to cultural background. Cross-cultural research suggests that the disorders that are most common in a particular society depend to some extent on what kinds of behavior are considered acceptable. Consider the example of "hysteria." A hundred years ago, hysteria—a loss of memory or function with no organic basis—was apparently quite common. Now it is rarely diagnosed, and has been dropped from the DSM. No cure contributed to its decline; perhaps social influences did.

A study of Australian aborigines found that as their culture became more civilized by Western standards, the number of somatic complaints increased (Kidson and Jones, 1968). In general, hysteria is more common in underdeveloped areas, whereas in areas using more advanced technology, generalized anxiety and obsessive-compulsive disorders occur more often. Although the anxiety disorders occur at all educational and socioeconomic levels within Western society, generalized anxiety and obsessive-compulsive disorders tend to cluster in the middle and upper classes. The research data on these issues are insufficient to support any general conclusions; however, social conditions and environment do seem to affect the types of anxiety disorders people develop.

Interactional Explanations

Like the social explanation, the interactional explanation of anxiety disorders is speculative at this point. If you think back on the biological, psychological, and social explanations presented in this chapter, you will notice that each theory depicts anxiety as resulting primarily from either a characteristic of the person or an environmental factor. The personal characteristics, or *traits,* that have been pointed to by biological theorists and some psychological theorists include genetic factors, ANS sensitivity, learned avoidance patterns, and maladaptive cognitions. The situational factors, or conditions, that may explain anxiety disorders include any specific and temporary environmental stressor. Obviously, a long-term situation may cause a person to develop certain characteristics—for instance, some theorists believe that constant quarreling between parents may create chronic anxiety in their children. But psychologists generally discriminate between **state anxiety**, which is temporary and caused by a specific stressful situation, and **trait anxiety**, which is a long-term characteristic of an individual.

Mischel (1976) has advocated a diathesis-stress theory of anxiety disorders, proposing that most anxiety results from the interaction between states and traits. Along this line, a man who complains of generalized anxiety may have to be checked biologically (for a hypersensitive autonomic nervous system, say) and cognitively (for an anxiety-provoking cognitive set), to determine his traits. Then the therapist would check his life circumstances for stressors, to determine his current states.

MANAGING THE ANXIETY DISORDERS

As with stress and stress-related disorders, attempts to manage the anxiety disorders involve two different strategies. The first is identifying and attempting to alter the source of the person's anxiety. Jane has a dog phobia. Why? What can we do to change her attitude and eliminate her fear? The second is treating the manifestations of anxiety directly. When Jane reacts fearfully to a dog, how can we calm her down? Most of the psychological approaches to treatment take the former tack, while the biological approaches tend toward the latter.

Biological Methods

It is very likely that identifying causal factors will ultimately lead to more effective treatment techniques. At present, too little is known about any genetic or physiological causes of the anxiety disorders to allow biological treatment to attack the root of the problem. For the moment, however, the biological therapies for anxiety are not directly related to the genetic and physiological explanations we have described. One of the most prevalent therapies is a medical treatment commonly prescribed for all disorders—drugs. Another therapy is exercise, which is related to recent physical fitness trends in society and research interest in the effects of exercise on the psyche.

Minor tranquilizers and other treatments

As we saw in the previous chapter on stress, millions of people in our society use the minor tranquilizers to relieve tension and relax. One reason why tranquilizers are so widely prescribed is that a high proportion of people seeking medical help want relief from the aches and pains that accompany tension—headaches, stomachaches, general muscle tension. Most of these problems can be successfully treated with tranquilizers no matter what their cause. Two

Table 6.2 *Features of Some Common Antianxiety Drugs*

	BENZODIAZEPINES	MEPROBAMATES	PHENOTHIAZINES	BARBITURATES
Trade names	Librium Valium Serax Dalmane Tranxene	Equanil Miltown	Compazine Stelazine Trilafon Prolixin	Phenobarbital Butabarbital
Muscle relaxation	Extensive	Moderate	Slight	Slight
Habituation	Slight	Extensive	None	Slight
Possibility of physical dependence	Slight	High	None	Slight
Possibility of sleep disturbance	Slight	Moderate	Moderate	Moderate
Danger of overdose	Slight	High	Slight	Moderate

major classes of minor tranquilizers in particular are commonly prescribed: the meprobamates and the benzodiazepine derivatives. The first class, which includes Miltown and Equanil, reduces muscle tension and thus has a calming effect on many patients. The second class includes Librium (chlordiazepoxide), Valium (diazepam), Serax (oxazepam), Dalmane (flurazepam), and Tranxene (chlorazepate). These antianxiety drugs seem to reduce the experience of fear or anxiety without hurting the person's performance of most everyday tasks.

Statistics indicate that approximately 70 percent of patients with anxiety disorders (or "neurotic" characteristics) show at least some symptom relief following drug therapy (Covi et al., 1974; Engelhardt, 1974; Prusoff and Klerman, 1974). Unfortunately, the relief is not total. As noted earlier, drugs address only the outward signs of anxiety, not the underlying problem. Tranquilizers also have a wide range of undesirable side effects—in some people, simple drowsiness; in others, addiction.

Another recourse for anxious people is self-medication, most often with alcohol. After a day full of tension, many people decide that a couple of drinks after work will help them to relax, or that a nightcap will make it easier for them to sleep. People who rely on alcohol in this way are likely to find themselves drinking more and more in order to relax but having less and less success. Although alcohol is a sedative and can facilitate relaxation, it generally cannot alleviate an anxiety problem.

Other biological treatments for anxiety disorders have met with mixed results. **Electrosleep**—a state of relaxed sleep induced by passing low-intensity electric currents through the brain—has been successful in some cases and disappointing in others (Rosenthal and Wulfsohn, 1970). Muscle relaxation induced through biofeedback has also worked only sporadically with anxiety disorders.

Exercise

As we discussed in Chapter 5, a number of researchers, medical professionals, authors, and physical fitness enthusiasts advocate exercise as a method of coping with stress and anxiety. Many popular books testify to the advantages of exercising the body to help it relax and release pent-up tension. More and more therapists are recommending running or swimming to clients with anxiety disorders. Just how exercising provides relief from anxiety has not yet been explained. The effect may be related to chemical changes or to muscle relaxation that releases physical tension. Whatever the mech-

Many therapists are recommending that their patients take up jogging to reduce the physical tension related to anxiety.

anism, some people feel exercise helps reduce anxiety considerably.

Matthew L., a 51-year-old man with a generalized anxiety disorder, was advised by his therapist to take part in a six-week exercise class. The therapist reasoned that exercise might help her client focus on muscle tension in his body and possibly would facilitate relaxation. By the end of the exercise class, Matthew did report feeling somewhat less general tension. He decided on his own to try a program of running. He started with a half-mile at first and worked up to two miles a day. He reported to his therapist that he now seemed more capable of relaxing and in general felt less tense. He liked the time he had alone while running—he said he liked to think about his life while he ran. He also reported feeling more energetic, but without his previous anxiety.

Like any treatment technique, exercise does not work for everyone with an anxiety disorder. It does appear to be effective in treating some clients, however, and therefore it is worth pursuing as a treatment method.

Psychological Methods

Most psychological approaches to treating anxiety and the anxiety disorders depend heavily on the interaction between therapist and client. The goal of this interaction—talking, thinking, feeling, teaching, and learning—varies according to the orientation of the therapist. Nearly always, though, the central aim is for the patient to develop a less disruptive alternative to replace the disordered response to anxiety-provoking stimuli.

Psychodynamic therapy

The goal of psychoanalysis is to help the client uncover and resolve the unconscious intrapsychic conflicts that are causing the anxiety. With the conflicts resolved, the ego will not have to expend all its energy repressing those impulses that caused the conflicts, but can direct itself into more constructive and creative channels.

In one interesting case, a woman named Pauline James was terrified of small dogs for most of her life. Under hypnosis, with the help of her therapist, she discovered the cause (Moss and James, 1970, pp. 105–112).

P: My little sister and I are playing. And there is a little dog there. . . .

T: Whose little dog is it?

P: I don't know but it is staying with me.

T: It must have a name of some sort. All little dogs have a name.

P: I don't know it.

T: Now listen carefully; perhaps you can hear somebody call it by name. [*Claps.*]

P: My mother is at the door; she is calling the little dog "Rover." . . . It knocked my little sister over. . . . She fell on the wood.

T: It didn't really hurt her very much?

P: She has a scratch. [*Pause.*] *That seems to be all. . . . My mother thinks I knocked my sister over. . . . And so they are going to play a little game. My brothers, my big sister, and I are going to walk to the door, and when the one who knocked my sister over gets to the door, something will knock on the other side. . . . Well, when I go to the door, something knocks on the other side, but I didn't knock her over, but everybody thinks I did, and they don't believe me when I tell them. But I wouldn't hurt her.*

T: Was it there in the yard when they thought you knocked her over?

P: Yes, when she was running with the wood.

T: Actually, it was the little dog.

P: The dog was playing with her. . . . I was just watching it.

T: You got blamed for it?

P: I got blamed for it. I didn't do it.

T: Go on, tell me what happens next . . . the next day.

P: We're out by the woodpile again and I feel quite badly because they think I pushed my sister over and I didn't, and my little sister isn't out playing with me. She is ill. She's ill, I guess, and Dr. Donahue is coming. That's Dr. Donahue coming. Then there are a lot of people there. My mother seems to be crying and my dad too. My little sister just looks like she's asleep. . . . She is lying on a bed. She looks awfully pretty. Now everybody is in the parlor, they all start crying again. . . . Then I go back in by myself. I want to see her again. She looks so pretty lying there, so I think I'll pick her up. She doesn't hug me like she usually does, though. I am holding her and the dog is with me. He wants to see her too. Oh, he tore her dress!

T: How did he do that?

P: He was jumping up on her, just playing, and he tore her dress. . . . My mother won't like that!

T: What happens next?

P: My mother came into the room. She's mad at me. She told me I should know better. Somebody took the baby away from me.

T: You didn't want to give her up?

P: No, I wanted to hold her. It must be my Aunt Anna. She said I shouldn't have torn her dress. Oh, but I didn't tear her dress. I didn't do it.

T: [*Simulating the mother.*] *Somebody did! It's torn!*

P: I didn't do it.

T: Well, who did it?

P: Rover did it, but he didn't mean to. . . . Now they are going to put her in that box. I mustn't touch the box, but I can look over her if somebody is with me. I guess we are going some-

where now. Oh, yes, we are going [pause—sighs very deeply].

T: Going where?

P: Going behind Aunt Ethel's house to the cemetery. They are putting the box down in the ground. We are singing some kind of songs. I wish I could see her again, but I guess I won't.

T: Your little sister is gone now?

P: Uh-huh. It seems like it's later, some days later. I am on the back porch by myself. I wish she would come play with me.

T: You're lonely now?

P: Mother comes out the back door and she finds me crying. I don't want her to find me crying.

T: You don't want her to know how you feel?

P: No, she thinks I hurt her and I didn't.

T: Your mother blames you for what happened to your little sister?

P: She thinks I pushed her over. But I didn't. [Pause.] I don't seem to like my dog anymore.

T: He still wants to be friendly, doesn't he?

P: I don't want him to be friendly.

T: You don't like your little dog?

P: No, I don't like my little dog anymore. I want my sister. I don't want that little old dog.

T: Your little dog took your sister away from you?

P: I don't like him. I wish that they would take him *away.**

The course of treatment provided Pauline with new insights about herself, her childhood relationships with her mother and father, and her current role as a wife and mother. In addition, within a short period of time she was able to accomplish something she had thought impossible—buying a dog for her daughter.

There are many other forms of psychotherapy, some using techniques that are similar and some that are quite different. All of them help clients strengthen their defenses and recognize their ego functions. For example, suppose a man could not maintain successful relationships with women and sometimes felt extremely anxious around them. The therapist would help him recognize his fears and evaluate how each fear was functioning for him in his present circumstances.

Carl Rogers (1961) uses a different approach to modify anxiety. You will remember that Rogers considers the discrepancy between the ideal self and the real self to be the conflict that produces anxiety. In client-centered therapy, the therapist gives the client unconditional positive regard—that is, all clients are viewed as worthwhile no matter what they may have done. This makes it possible for clients to accept their real self and to explore that self without fear of ridicule or rejection. Rogers reasons that in this way clients can gain a sense that all parts of their self are valid and deserve attention. Thus the discrepancy between the ideal self and the real self diminishes, and the client's anxiety is alleviated.

Behavior therapy

Reflecting the theoretical orientation of behaviorism, behavioral therapists are more concerned with changing the problematic behaviors of patients with anxiety disorders than with discovering the source of the problem. Behavior modification techniques have been very successful in controlling certain anxiety-related disorders, particularly phobias.

Behaviorists use reinforcement principles to shape the clients' adaptive response to situations that initially produce anxiety. A behavior contract can use these principles to good effect. A man with a fear of high places who is learning to give a relaxed response to higher and higher buildings may have a reinforcement contract saying that for every story of a skyscraper that he reaches, one dollar will be taken off the therapy bill.

One of the most common approaches, and one that is supported by research, is systematic desensitization (Wolpe, 1973). The client first makes up a hierarchy of fear-provoking situations, ranking them from least anxiety-arousing to most anxiety-arousing. The client is then asked to imagine being in various situations,

*Reprinted by permission from *Black Rover, Come Over*, by C.S. Moss and P. James (Urbana: University of Illinois Press, 1970), pp. 105–111.

Table 6.3 *A Fear Hierarchy for Public Speaking*

1. Writing the speech.
2. Getting dressed for the presentation.
3. Walking onto the stage.
4. Sitting on the stage with the other speakers.
5. Waiting for my turn.
6. Hearing my name being called by the master of ceremonies.
7. Walking to the podium.
8. Beginning to speak.

gradually moving up the hierarchy while maintaining a state of relaxation. For example, a woman who fears heights might list looking out a window on the second floor of a building, standing on the roof of her home, standing at the edge of a high cliff looking down at the sea. While she is practicing progressive muscle relaxation, scenes from the fear hierarchy will be described to her. Even though relaxation is the usual technique used to deal with the anxiety response, it is not the only one—the important thing being to do something that counteracts anxiety. Such processes takes several therapy sessions. Once the therapy is complete—meaning that the person can imagine the most frightening scene without feeling anxious—the desensitization will usually generalize to everyday life.

A similar technique, *in vivo* desensitization, follows the same principles and methods, except that the person progresses through the fear-provoking hierarchy in real-life rather than imagined situations. For the woman with a fear of heights, the therapist would probably accompany her from the least to the most anxiety-provoking situation it was practical to find until she no longer felt anxious in high places. In both systematic and *in vivo* desensitization, clients build their own hierarchy and progress through it at their own pace.

Some cases of anxiety seem to be related to an inability to express feelings or needs. For example, a man may decide he wants to tell a friend he cares about her, but he becomes too anxious when they are together to say anything. Or a shopper who is overcharged on a purchase may want to bring the mistake to the salesclerk's attention but is too overcome by anxiety to mention it. **Assertiveness training**, a technique originated by Salter (1949), attempts to alleviate anxiety that is associated with specific social situations like these. Through graded assignments, clients learn to express their emotions and concerns without feeling anxious or embarrassed. Schwartz and Gottman (1976) have demonstrated that many nonassertive people do know how to express feelings directly, but they hold back because of a fear that others will not like them or that they will offend someone.

A behavioral technique that is especially appropriate for phobias and obsessive-compulsive disorders is modeling or modeling with rehearsal. The therapist models an appropriate or adaptive response to the problem situation; the client observes and then rehearses, or practices, the modeled response. Bandura, Blanchard, and Ritter (1969) have shown that modeling can be effective in helping people overcome snake phobias. Lazarus (1971) has used behavioral rehearsal to teach people with social anxieties how to handle difficult interactions.

Self-control strategies teach the client new skills for coping with stress. Modeling is one way someone can acquire new coping skills. In fact, modeling of coping may be more effective than modeling of mastery (Mahoney, 1972). That is, if the model is anxious but managing to deal with a difficult situation, the subject may learn coping skills more effectively than if the model is thoroughly competent and in control (Mahoney and Ainkoff, 1978). Another method of self-control is for clients to learn to make statements to themselves, silently or aloud, that express a more positive perspective on the situation. A woman who is anxious about calling people on the telephone might approach a phone call by talking to herself aloud. "It really will be fun to talk to Joyce, she'll probably be happy to hear from me, and maybe she's wishing right now that somebody would call her!"

Aversive conditioning extinguishes undesirable responses, such as obsessions, by pairing them with aversive stimuli. In the laboratory, clients may be given an electric shock while they are thinking the obsessive thought. The idea is for the person to learn to associate the undesirable thought with unpleasantness rather than with relief of anxiety. This principle is also used at home by numerous dieters, who paste pictures of overweight people on their cupboard doors and refrigerator in an effort to countercondition their compulsive munching. Aversive conditioning can also be used as a method of self-control (Bandura, 1969). Instead of being passively conditioned to avoid a particular stimulus by having the therapist pair it with shock or some other noxious stimulus, the client learns to use aversive self-stimulation. For example, a man with a checking compulsion might deliberately recall a nauseating image or experience whenever he has the urge to check.

Cognitive therapy

As we mentioned earlier, Ellis (1962) has postulated that anxiety is caused by distorted thoughts about an event. Therefore the goal of the cognitive therapist is to help clients identify their irrational cognitions or beliefs and, by challenging these beliefs, to teach them more adaptive cognitions to replace the old maladaptive ones. To test the client's belief system, the therapist may elicit the reasons for a given assumption, cite evidence in favor of or contradictory to the assumption, or set up an empirical demonstration whereby the assumption is tested and immediate feedback obtained about its validity.

Other psychologists who favor a cognitive model use the principles of behavior therapy to change cognitions directly (Meichenbaum, 1977; Mahoney, 1974). They view cognitions as unobservable internal behaviors (Ullmann, 1970), and anxiety is seen as a response to these internal states. Thus behavior reinforcement principles are used to modify these covert behaviors (self-statements or thoughts). In cognitive restructuring (Goldfried and Davison, 1976), the goal is to change the way patients view situations or events by modifying their labeling process. Once they learn to label potentially anxiety-producing situations more positively, it is assumed that their anxiety-related behavior will change.

Morita therapy (Kora and Ohara, 1973) has produced favorable results by combining biological measures and psychotherapy. First, the person is made to rest in bed for four to seven days, with no external stimuli allowed—reading, writing, visitors, television, all being banned. By the end of this period, external stimuli are usually very welcome to the person and can thus be used as positive reinforcement. A graded series of tasks is assigned next. The person may progress from light housework to heavier chores, such as washing windows. Lastly, therapy focuses on interpersonal relationships. In short, the person moves from no activity of any kind, to minimal physical activity, to full cognitive, emotional, and physical involvement.

SUMMARY

Until the publication of DSM-III, the anxiety disorders were classified with the neurotic disorders. There are four principal types of anxiety disorders: generalized anxiety disorder, panic disorder, phobic disorders, and obsessive-compulsive disorder. It has been estimated that 2 to 4 percent of the general population has at one time or another been diagnosed as having some kind of anxiety disorder. Anxiety can be defined as a state of physical tension and psychological fear that occurs as part of the general adaptation syndrome. Anxiety affects people in a number of physiological ways, and it can also interfere with cognitive abilities.

If a person experiences anxiety for an extended period and there is no identifiable stressor, a generalized anxiety disorder is said to exist. Panic disorder is characterized by recurring panic attacks, which come on suddenly, rise rapidly in intensity, and then subside quickly. The most overwhelming aspect of the attack is the feeling that something terrible is about to happen, and that self-control will be lost. Between attacks, the person may feel calm and function normally, although more often the unpredictability of the attacks adds to the general level of anxiety.

Phobic disorders are characterized by fear and avoidance of a specific object, situation, or activity. About 1 percent of the population has at some time been treated for a phobia. There are three basic types of phobias: agoraphobia, social phobia, and simple phobia.

The essential feature in the obsessive-compulsive disorder is either a recurrent, undesired thought (obsession) or behavior (compulsion). Attempts to resist increase the anxiety, which is relieved only when the person indulges in the obsessive thought or the compulsive ritual. Many obsessions involve unacceptable aggressive or sexual thoughts, while compulsions often involve checking rituals and cleaning rituals.

Biological explanations for these disorders focus on possible genetic influences and physiological bases. Genetic research points to the possibility of some hereditary influence, while physiological explanations are based on the hypothesis of a hypersensitive autonomic nervous system.

Numerous psychological explanations have been proposed for the anxiety disorders. The psychodynamic approach began with Freud, who postulated that anxiety is generated when unconscious sexual or aggressive id impulses threaten the ego. Usually individuals manage their anxiety through defense mechanisms, but if these fail, the result is what Freud labeled neurosis and DSM-III calls an anxiety disorder. Jung, Adler, Horney, Rogers, and other psychotherapists have proposed variations on Freud's model.

Behavioral explanations are based on various concepts of learning. Watson explained anxiety in terms of conditioning. Other theorists add that the person is reinforced when an aversive stimulus is avoided and no anxiety occurs. Modeling is another way people may develop anxiety disorders. The cognitive explanation postulates that anxiety is related to maladaptive or distorted beliefs.

Social explanations of anxiety disorders emphasize external events. Some theorists cite the pressures of living in a disadvantaged socioeconomic group as a major source of anxiety; others cite the effects of cultural influences.

Management of these disorders may be biological or psychological in approach. Probably the most common treatment is drugs, usually minor tranquilizers such as Valium and Librium; however, drug dependency may occur, and the person may ultimately fail to address the underlying problem. Other biological treatments include electrosleep, Morita therapy, and the various techniques for stress management described in Chapter 5, such as conscious relaxation, biofeedback, and exercise.

Psychotherapy tries to help the client discover and confront whatever is causing the anxiety. Behavior therapy concentrates on eliminating the undesirable behavior through a variety of methods. Systematic desensitization, *in vivo* desensitization, assertiveness training, and modeling are all used with good success. In addition, reinforcement principles can shape adaptive responses, and self-control strategies can teach the client new and useful skills for coping with stress.

CHAPTER 7

Psychophysiological and Somatoform Disorders

When I was 15, 16, even 25, I used to think that I could rid myself of [*migraine*] *by simply denying it, character over chemistry. "Do you have headaches sometimes? frequently? never?" the application forms would demand. "Check one." Wary of the trap, wanting whatever it was that the successful circumnavigation of that particular form could bring (a job, a scholarship, the respect of mankind and the grace of God), I would check one.* "Sometimes," *I would lie. That in fact I spent one or two days a week almost unconscious with pain seemed a shameful secret, evidence not merely of some chemical inferiority but of all my bad attitudes, unpleasant tempers, wrongthink.*

For I had no brain tumor, no eyestrain, no high blood pressure, nothing wrong with me at all: I simply had migraine headaches, and migraine headaches were, as everyone who did not have them knew, imaginary. . . . "Why not take a couple of aspirin," the unafflicted will say from the doorway, or "I'd have a headache, too, spending a beautiful day like this inside with all the shades drawn." All of us who have migraine suffer not only from the attacks themselves but from this common conviction that we are perversely refusing to cure ourselves by taking a couple of aspirin, that we are making ourselves sick, that we "bring it on ourselves." And in the most immediate sense, the sense of why we have a headache this Tuesday and not last Thursday, of course we often do.

Joan Didion, *The White Album,* pp. 168–171*

In DSM-II, migraine headaches were classified as a *psychophysiologic disorder*—a physical ailment caused, or at least heavily influenced, by psychological factors. Also included in this category were ulcers, asthma, and hypertension, among other ailments. As we saw in Chapter 5, however, recent research strongly suggests that psychological stress contributes to a much wider range of medical problems than these. Indeed, it has been estimated that three fourths or more of the physical disorders physicians are called on to treat have psychological origins. Accordingly, DSM-III has dropped the psychophysiologic category. Instead, it includes one called *psychological factors affecting physical condition.*

Disorders falling in this category are those commonly called **psychosomatic**—an earlier word for psychophysiological. Psychosomatic does *not* mean "It's all in your mind." Rather, the term suggests that mind and body work together, and the collaboration is not always to their mutual benefit. Gastric ulcers, for example, are *lesions* (sores) in the walls of the stomach that usually occur in people who are under stress. Ulcers involve damage to physical tissue, but they are brought on by psychological factors, particularly anxiety. People who have a psychosomatic disorder occasionally have a psychological disorder as well.

Because of the long history of misunderstanding behind the term psychosomatic, we shall use the term **psychophysiological** to refer to all disorders in this category. Common physical conditions that may be called psychophysiological include obesity, tension headache, migraine headache, angina pectoris, painful menstruation, sacroiliac pain, eczema, acne, rheumatoid arthritis, asthma, gastric ulcer, duodenal ulcer, cardiospasm, nausea and vomiting, ulcerative colitis, and frequent urination (DSM-III, 1980).

In contrast, the **somatoform disorders** involve physical symptoms that do *not* cause actual tissue damage but *do* indicate a psychological problem. Formerly called the *hysterias* or *hysterical neuroses,* they are physical complaints with no organic basis. DSM-III lists five categories of somatoform disorders: somatization disorder, conversion disorder, psychogenic pain disorder, hypochondriasis, and atypical somatoform disorder. These were classified in the DSM-I and DSM-II under the neuroses, along with the dissociative and anxiety disorders. Although their symptoms may include paralysis, blindness, numbness, and similar physical dysfunctions, they are still considered to be psychological disorders. They afflict the voluntary rather than

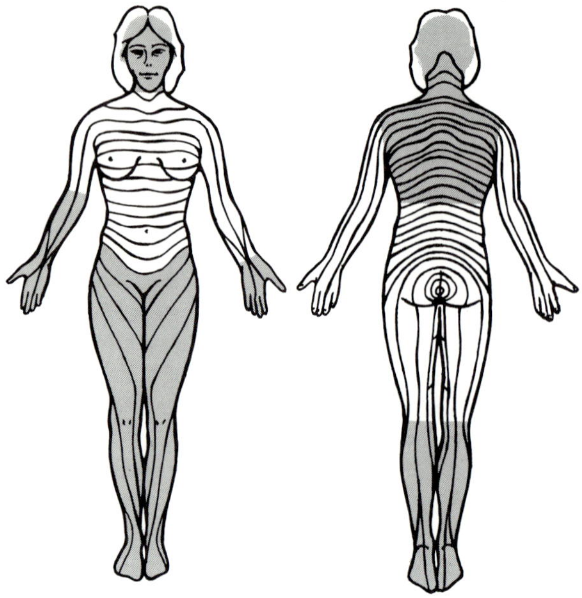

Figure 7.1. Body areas usually involved in somatoform disorders (shaded). Note that they do not necessarily correspond to typical neural patterns, as shown by the markings.

involuntary muscles, and usually they are confined to peripheral areas. That is, a somatoform disorder would be likely to involve the hands, feet, legs, or fingers, whereas a psychophysiological disorder might affect the heart, lungs, stomach or skin. Since there is no organic impairment, the somatoform disorders do not threaten the person's life (at least directly), as some psychophysiological disorders do. Probably the greatest danger from a somatoform disorder is that it may lead to an unnecessary operation or to dependence on painkilling drugs.

Not surprisingly, the explanation and management of the somatoform disorders usually emphasize the psychological conditions that underlie the physical symptoms. In the second half of this chapter, we shall describe some of the main somatoform disorders and then examine possible reasons why they occur and the methods psychotherapists use to treat them.

The psychophysiological disorders are a rather different story. Though they are precipitated by psychological stressors, the damage they do is very real and must be treated medically in most cases. A doctor might analyze the psychological factors that appear to be involved and attempt to deal with them, but usually the more immediate concern is improving the patient's physical condition. Because the physical aspects of each of these disorders are quite different, their explanations and management are different as well. We shall therefore first consider several of the psychophysiological disorders separately and then turn to more general explanations and to their separate management techniques.

DESCRIBING THE PSYCHOPHYSIOLOGICAL DISORDERS

The idea implied by psychophysiological disorders is that the mind and body are not two separate entities but two aspects of a unified organism. As Hans Selye's research demonstrated (see Chapter 5), stress affects the whole person—when we experience fear, our pulse rate increases, blood rushes to our cheeks, and our breathing becomes rapid and shallow. Numerous observers have debated about which set of responses cues the other. But whether our physical reaction dictates our emotional and cognitive reaction or vice versa, the two are clearly inseparable. The multiaxial diagnostic system of DSM-III attempts to take this unity into account.

Our response to a stressor does not depend entirely on its nature, as the previous chapter indicates. Still, both psychological stressors (such as losing a fortune) and physical stressors (such as meeting a bear) elicit a combination of psychological and physical responses. This is not to say that we respond in exactly the same way to every stressor—obviously, a loss causes sorrow, whereas encountering something frightening causes fear, and there are varying degrees of each emotion. Furthermore, each of us does not respond to the same stressor identically. If we did, this book would be unnecessary, and so would most mental health facilities. Indeed, one of the most intriguing questions to psychologists is why a similar set of circumstances makes person A develop high blood pressure, person B break out in hives, person C become chronically anxious, and person D flee to an island in the South Seas.

Before we investigate some of the general explanations that have been proposed for the psychophysiological disorders as a group, we shall look more closely at five conditions commonly classed as psychophysiological: hypertension, migraine headaches, asthma, ulcers, and bruxism (grinding the teeth).

Hypertension

Essential hypertension is chronically elevated blood pressure in an otherwise healthy individual. The term *blood pressure* refers to the pressure of the blood in the arteries. It is expressed as a ratio, such as 120/70, which compares the pressure during the pumping action of the heart (*systolic*) with the pressure during its resting state (*diastolic*). When the systolic pressure is over 140 and the diastolic pressure is over 90, diagnosable hypertension (or high blood pressure) exists.

Blood pressure can rise for a number of reasons. A narrowing of the *arterioles* (small blood-carrying vessels), increased viscosity of the blood, certain kidney disorders, and tumors of the adrenal gland can all raise the pressure. However, at least 90 percent of individuals with high blood pressure have chronic hypertension with no organic problem (Benson, 1975). Of this group blacks outnumber whites by about two to one. Roughly 15 percent of whites are clinically hypertensive, while over 30 percent of blacks are (Freis, 1973). Studies also suggest that

Table 7.1 *The Psychophysiological and Somatoform Disorders*

Category	Example	Characteristics
Psychophysiological	Hypertension Migraines Ulcers Asthma Bruxism Coronary disease	Organic impairment caused by a physiological response to psychological stress
Somatoform	Somatization	Exaggeration of nonsensical organic signs to take on patient status
	Hypochondriasis	Chronic exaggeration of real organic signs to take on patient status
	Conversion	Involuntary loss of motor or sensory functioning as a response to psychological stress
	Malingering	Faked organic impairment to help achieve clear goal
	Factitious	Faked organic impairment to receive care and attention of patient status

What range of emotions are portrayed on the faces of these roller coaster riders? Obviously, we do not all respond to the same stressful situation in the same way.

hypertension is slightly more common in men than women.

Not all hypertensive people are concerned about their condition, part of the reason being that hypertension rarely produces any symptoms, aside from a higher-than-normal blood pressure reading. When symptoms do occur, they tend to be relatively mild and undramatic—fatigue, tension, headaches. They rarely affect the person's day-to-day functioning, and they can fluctuate from one day to another. Thus, someone who is diagnosed as having hypertension, may react with an astonished "But I feel fine!"

Unfortunately, this lack of symptoms often leads patients to ignore the blood pressure control regimen their doctor prescribes. And individuals whose hypertension is not controlled increase their risk of a variety of more severe medical problems. The most important and frequent medical complication is cardiovascular disease, including heart attack (myocardial infarction), congestive heart failure, and stroke (cerebrovascular accident). Uncontrolled hypertension can also lead to kidney failure and to retinal bleeding. Finally, epidemiological data clearly suggest that the more elevated the blood pressure, the shorter the life span is likely to be (Lyght, 1966). This lack of initial symptoms in conjunction with decreased life expectancy is why hypertension is often called "the silent killer."

The role of stress in producing elevated blood pressure has been well established. Ruskin, Beard, and Shaffer (1948) examined the survivors of a tremendous explosion in Texas City, Texas, and found elevated blood pressure in over half the people they studied. Two weeks after the explosion, the blood pressure of many subjects was still higher than normal. Less dramatic stressors can also cause hypertension. Moving from a rural to an urban area can increase blood pressure (Gampel et al., 1962); so can performing arithmetic manipulations under pressur Brod, 1964), immersing a hand in ice water (Hilgard et al., 1974), and reading statements about painful personal experiences (Palmer, 1950).

Not all individuals who are exposed to stress develop hypertension, however. Some researchers have attempted to find personal characteristics that may explain why some people develop high blood pressure and others do not. Psychodynamic theorists have suggested that hypertensive individuals are generally aggressive but do not express their aggression overtly. Instead, their suppressed hostility is transformed into increased blood pressure. In a series of studies based on this suppressed rage hypothesis, Hokanson and colleagues placed college students in frustrating situations that increased their blood pressure. In one set of studies (Hokanson and Burgess, 1962; Stone and Hokanson, 1969), it was found that harassing students who were engaged in a complex cognitive task consistently increased their blood pressure. In an attempt to find out how quickly their blood pressure would return to normal, some of the students were given the opportunity to aggress against the person who had previously harassed them. The experimenters observed that the blood pressure of male students decreased more rapidly when they were able to give electric shocks to their tormentor than when they were not. Interestingly, aggression against a low-status opponent (another student) was more effective in reducing blood pressure than aggression against a high-status opponent (a visiting professor). For females, a different pattern developed: Their blood pressure returned to normal more quickly when they were able to *reward* the person who had harassed them.

These studies suggest that although aggression or frustration can bring on hypertension, socially acceptable means of expressing aggression may help to reduce it. Having a sense of control over potentially stressful conditions may also play a role (Hokanson et al., 1971). The reason aggression against a low-status tormentor reduced blood pressure more than aggression against a high-status tormentor may be that it was perceived as having a better chance of changing the person's behavior. In other words, yelling at someone at your own level is more likely to get results than yelling at someone who doesn't have to listen to you.

It appears that a predisposition for hypertension may be inherited. Some research has suggested that this may be why more blacks are hypertensive than whites. Schachter and colleagues (1974) found the heart rates of black infants to be substantially higher, by as much as six to nine beats per minute, than those of white infants several days after birth. Although the blood pressures were similar, the faster heart rates in some infants could be predictive of increased blood pressure. Since socioeconomic differences did not account for the differences in heart rate, a genetic predisposition may be the explanation.

Other evidence indicates that this predisposition, if it exists, may only be expressed under environmental stress. A study in Detroit compared black and white males living in high-stress areas—that is, areas characterized by high unemployment, poverty, crime, divorce, and family discord—and in low-stress areas, which were typical middle-class neighborhoods. Although blacks generally had higher blood pressure than whites, blacks in high-stress areas had higher blood pressure than blacks in low-stress neighborhoods.

Diet also seems to be significant in hypertension. For example, substantial evidence suggests that sodium (salt) intake is positively correlated with blood pressure (Hunt et al., 1979). When individuals lower their salt intake dramatically, their blood pressure usually declines as well. Unfortunately, controlling salt intake can be difficult. Aside from the many foods, such as certain cheeses, that are naturally high in sodium, many processed foods, canned foods, and fast foods contain additional salt. It is possible that some of the racial differences in blood pressure may also be related to diet.

Migraine Headaches

> Three, four, sometimes five times a month, I spend the day in bed with a migraine headache, insensible to the world around me. Almost every day of every month, between these attacks, I feel the sudden irrational irritation and the flush of blood into the cerebral arteries which tell me that migraine is on its way, and I take certain drugs to avert its arrival. . . . Once an attack is under way, however, no drug touches it. Migraine gives some people mild hallucinations, temporarily blinds others, shows up not only as a headache but as a gastrointestinal disturbance, a painful sensitivity to

> all sensory stimuli, an abrupt overpowering fatigue, a strokelike aphasia, and a crippling inability to make even the most routine connections. When I am in a migraine aura (for some people the aura lasts fifteen minutes, for others several hours), I will drive through red lights, lose the house keys, spill whatever I am holding, lose the ability to focus my eyes or frame coherent sentences, and generally give the appearance of being on drugs, or drunk. The actual headache, when it comes, brings with it chills, sweating, nausea, a debility that seems to stretch the very limits of endurance. . . . (Didion, 1979, pp. 168–171)

To people like writer Joan Didion who suffer from **migraine headache**, the pain ranks high on the roster of aversive experiences. Whereas most other headaches are caused by contraction of the muscles in the neck and scalp, migraine headaches are thought to be a vascular disorder. For reasons unknown, the mechanism that controls the major cranial arteries malfunctions, causing those blood vessels to first constrict, then dilate more than they should. Migraine pain tends to be *unilateral* (affecting only one side of the head) and is usually described as throbbing or stabbing. The headache is often accompanied by other systemic changes, including nausea and vomiting, diarrhea, dizziness, or fainting. About 5 percent of the population has migraines, the majority of sufferers being women (Adams, Feuerstein, and Fowler, 1980). Margaret Fuller, the nineteenth century literary critic and author, Mary Todd Lincoln, novelist George Eliot, Thomas Jefferson, Frederic Chopin, and Woodrow Wilson are all said to have been migraine victims.

(a)

(b)

Migraine headaches, more accurately labeled vascular headaches of the migraine type, can be divided into three categories on the basis of symptoms: classic migraine, common migraine, and cluster migraine (Dalessio, 1972). The **classic migraine** generally follows the pattern described by Joan Didion. In the earliest phase, called the *aura,* appear warning signs

(c)

Three famous migraine sufferers: (a) Thomas Jefferson, (b) Kareem Abdul Jabbar, and (c) Joan Didion.

that a migraine attack is about to occur. The individual may become especially sensitive to light or sound; spots may be seen in front of the eyes; jagged edges may be perceived around the periphery of the visual field. These *prodromal symptoms* appear to be caused by constriction of the cranial arteries. Individuals who are sensitive to and aware of these prodromal symptoms may be able to use certain drugs or psychological procedures to abort the headache. These measures are less effective once the arteries dilate and the pain phase of the migraine begins.

Common migraines are similar to classic migraines but lack an aura. Because they frequently appear after or during a period of environmental stress, they are sometimes called "weekend" or "Monday" headaches. Common migraines may be less unilateral than classic migraines, but they are often accompanied by the same nausea and vomiting.

Cluster migraines, in contrast, consist of a group of migraine-type headaches that occur in rapid succession. Attacks of cluster headaches can occur with punctual regularity (for instance, every two hours) for months at a time. During such a period, the pain is so severe that sufferers may contemplate suicide. Fortunately, remissions lasting months or years are common. Cluster migraines, like classic migraines, are unilateral but they are not usually preceded by a warning aura. They are more likely to be accompanied by sweating or a runny nose than by nausea and vomiting.

Investigations of the possible role of heredity in migraine headaches have had mixed results. Clinical evidence originally suggested that parents of migraine patients have a very high incidence of the disorder; but follow-up research on this question has turned up conflicts. A certain study that asked migraine patients whether one or both parents suffered from migraine headaches found that from 44 to 90 percent of patients said yes (Goodell et al., 1954). Reasoning that these data might be biased, Waters (1971) decided to interview the parents of migraine patients directly. They proved to have only a 10-percent incidence of migraines. Considering that parents of individuals who did not suffer from headaches showed a 5-percent incidence of migraines, it appears that familial factors are not as important as earlier reports suggested.

The autonomic nervous system appears to have an influence in the creation of migraine headaches. The pain of the headache appears to be related to the flow of blood through the temples (Graham and Wolff, 1938). Additionally, the nervous systems of migraine patients may be more reactive than the systems of other people to a variety of stimuli, both biochemical and behavioral (Bakal, 1975).

William Speed, a headache consultant for the Pain Treatment Center at Johns Hopkins Hospital, has described an individual who suffers migraine headaches as having a cocked gun in his head, ready to go off with little provocation. Joan Didion says, "Almost anything can trigger a specific attack of migraine: stress, allergy, fatigue, an abrupt change in barometric pressure, a contretemps over a parking ticket. A flashing light. A fire drill." (p. 169)

Personality factors also have been implicated in migraine headaches. The migraine patient is often described as tense, driving, and obsessional (Mitchell and Mitchell, 1971). Hostility is often mentioned as the most important predictor of migraine (Bakal, 1975). Others have characterized the "migraine personality" as ambitious, introverted, highly organized, and intolerant of error. Unfortunately, relatively little controlled research has examined the importance of personality factors in headache patients. In one of the more elaborate studies, Henryk-Gutt and Rees (1973) used a variety of psychometric tests and found more obsessional behavior in migraine patients than in controls. Other traits, such as anxiety and hostility, showed a more mixed pattern. Bakal (1975) has concluded that broadly based personality traits do not account for all migraine headaches.

Ulcers

An **ulcer** is a hole or lesion in the wall of the stomach or in the lining of the intestine. Generally, ulcers occur when there is an excess of digestive fluids (hydrochloric acid and pepsin) in the stomach and the mucous lining in the gastrointestinal (GI) tract fails to provide its usual protection. The digestive fluids literally eat away at the lining. The resulting ulcer causes pain and discomfort; in severe cases, it can also cause gastrointestinal bleeding.

Several types of ulcers have been identified. The most common ones are **gastric ulcers**, which occur in the stomach wall, and **duodenal ulcers**, which occur in the lining of the *duodenum,* a section of the intestine just below the stomach. Recent research has suggested that these two kinds of ulcers have some important differences. Gastric ulcers strike both sexes about equally, while duodenal ulcers are two to three times more common in men. Duodenal ulcers are often susceptible to medical and psychological treatment. A significant proportion of gastric ulcers, however, are associated with malignant diseases. The suspicion that someone has a gastric ulcer thus often leads to complex diagnostic procedures to rule out the possibility of more serious illness.

A third type of ulcer is **ulcerative colitis**, which occurs in the intestine and typically causes severe diarrhea, pain, and bloody stools. Though less common than gastric and duodenal ulcers, ulcerative colitis is also a psychophysiological disorder.

Like headaches, ulcers may be caused by physiological or psychological factors, or both. Research has recognized the importance of gastric secretions and suggests that people with unusually high levels of digestive fluids are ulcer-prone. Weiner and colleagues (1957) investigated this hypothesis by studying pepsinogen levels in the blood. They theorized that because pepsinogen is closely related to the digestive fluid pepsin, individuals with high pepsinogen levels would be more likely than others to develop ulcers under stress. They selected as their subjects more than 2000 inductees to the armed services—a situation stressful to most individuals. The researchers identified 120 inductees whose pepsinogen levels were significantly above or below average, only one of whom had an active ulcer before the start of basic training. By the end of basic training, nine inductees had developed ulcers, all of them in the high pepsinogen group.

One of the earliest studies noting the importance of gastric secretions and stress on ulcers was the case of Tom, reported by Wolf and Wolff (1947). Following surgery to his esophagus, Tom's stomach was opened for extended observation. The physicians noted that his stomach lining became inflamed when he was under stress, occasionally resulting in minor bleeding. Ordinarily the inflammation healed quickly; however, when the area was bathed in gastric secretions for several days, an ulcerative-type lesion appeared. When the lesion was protected by a salve, it quickly healed. This study showed not only that stress is related to ulcer formation but that ulcer formation may be more common than formerly believed. Some of us, under stressful conditions, may develop "mini-ulcers" that usually heal without causing any serious trouble.

Psychological theories on the causes of ulcers have concentrated on identifying personality traits related to ulcers. Ulcer patients are often described as tense, hard-driving individuals who push themselves to their limits—the ideal executive. This stereotype received apparent confirmation from the "executive monkey" studies of Brady and his colleagues (1958). In these studies, two monkeys were yoked in the same apparatus and given electric shocks. One monkey—the executive monkey—was able to control the occurrence of shocks by pressing a lever. The other monkey, the "worker monkey," had no control: When the executive monkey was shocked, the worker monkey was shocked as well. Many of the executive monkeys developed severe duodenal ulcers, while none of the worker monkeys showed signs of ulcers.

Other research using rats has, however, reversed these findings. Apparently the original selection procedures caused more aggressive animals to be cast in the executive role. In a series of studies in which rats were assigned roles randomly, Weiss (1971, 1977) found that rats in control of the shock (the executive rats) were *less* likely to develop ulcers.

Other investigators have described the "ulcer personality" as competitive, ambitious, success-oriented, and immature. Most of this research has examined the ulcer patient *after* the ulcer has developed, however, so it is not clear whether the observed traits are the cause of ulcers or whether they result from the discomfort and distress produced by the disorder. Perhaps the clearest finding of a personality trait related to ulcers has come from the Weiner study on pepsinogen levels, in which hostility was positively identified *before* ulcers were noted. It also appears that anxiety plays an important role in the development of ulcers (Baron, 1972).

Asthma

Asthma is a disorder of the respiratory system. A variety of symptoms may accompany an asthmatic attack: difficulty in breathing, a choking sensation, coughing, wheezing, and *rales*, a whistling sound that occurs during exhalation. An attack can last from a few minutes to several hours, and it can range from mild to severe. The frightening choking sensations produced by a severe attack can cause panic and make breathing even harder. Between attacks, asthmatic patients generally feel symptom-free; however, a careful examination by a physician can identify the necessary signs. For example, the asthmatic individual may take longer than normal to exhale, and forced heavy breathing will often bring on rales.

Asthma affects around 2 to 5 percent of the population. It strikes males more often than females and, unlike other psychophysiological disorders, is most common in children. Asthma attacks are produced by a narrowing of the major and minor airways in the respiratory system—in particular, the trachea, the bronchi, and the bronchioles. The cause may be increased mucous secretion, *edema* (fluid retention), spasms of the bronchial muscles, or collapse of certain parts of the respiratory system during exhalation. Three types of factors seem to precipitate attacks (Rees, 1964): (1) allergic factors, including pollen, dust, foods, and odors; (2) infectious factors, of which acute bronchitis is the most important; and (3) psychological factors, such as stress, emotional arousal, and family discord. Most asthma patients show some combination of these factors, not just one.

The possible role of heredity in asthma is unclear. According to Rees (1964), 86 percent of asthmatics had respiratory ailments before they developed asthma, whereas only 30 percent of a nonasthmatic control group showed respiratory problems. If this reflects a genetic vulnerability or diathesis, it could be to asthma, to respiratory problems in general, or simply to infections. Family studies (Konig and Godfrey, 1973) and twin studies (Edfors-Lubs, 1971) suggest that genetic factors play only a minor role in the development of asthma.

Nevertheless, family studies have strongly suggested that parental attitudes and behavior affect children's asthma. Research on anything as changeable and complex as family patterns is, of course, difficult to interpret. One study showed that only 44 percent of the parents of asthmatic patients were affectionate and accepting towards their children, compared with nearly double that percentage of a control sample of parents of hospitalized accident victims (Rees, 1963). But whether a parental attitude existed before the child's medical condition or arose in response to it was not determined.

Purcell and colleagues (1969) tried to separate the influence of parental attitudes from other aspects of the home environment. Purcell noted that asthmatic children removed from their homes often improved substantially—a change that could be due to leaving behind either allergens or a stressful family environment. To test these two possibilities, the researchers removed children's natural parents from their homes and briefly replaced them with substitute parents. Those children whose asthma was thought to be related primarily to psychological factors did improve; children whose asthma was thought to be related mainly to allergic factors did not improve. Whatever other affects this rather extraordinary study may have had on the children involved, it clearly implicated family stresses in some cases of asthma.

Determining how parental attitudes affect asthmatic children is even more difficult. One possibility is that parents inadvertently reinforce their children's "sick" behavior by giving them special attention when they have attacks. Or the influence may be less direct: By heredity, modeling, reinforcement, or some combination of these, parents may cause their children to develop personality traits that make them prone to asthma attacks. Asthma patients are often described as dependent, anxious, and perfectionistic (Rees, 1964), qualities that may not be unique to asthmatic children, however: Children with cardiac problems often show the same combination of traits (Kelly and Zeller, 1969).

Suggestion may also be important in producing asthmatic attacks. Asthma patients often trace their attacks to stressful events (Kleeman, 1967). As we saw in Chapter 5, what makes a situation stressful depends partly on the perceptions of the person involved. Furthermore, an individual's expectations of stress can influence the onset or end of an asthma attack. In one study (Luparello et al., 1971), 40 asthma patients were asked to inhale a substance that they were led to believe would bring on an asthma attack, though in fact it was nonallergenic. Twelve subjects did have an attack. When the same twelve were then asked to inhale what they thought was a bronchodilator (but was actually the same nonallergenic substance used in the earlier part of the study), the attacks ceased.

Bruxism

Bruxism is the nonfunctional gnashing and grinding of the teeth. Although it may occur during the day, it usually happens while the person is sleeping. More women report bruxism than men, but experimental research suggests that it occurs about equally often in both sexes, affecting about 5 percent of the population.

Although bruxism is most notable for the annoyance it creates for sufferers and those who have to sleep with them, it can also cause medical problems. In severe cases, bruxism can wear down the teeth (Glaros and Rao, 1977b); it can also contribute to gum disease. Sometimes it causes the masticatory (chewing) muscles of the jaw to develop abnormally, or impairs the working of the major jaw joint. Bruxism may lead to headache, earache, and other pains in the face and neck.

Most biological research on bruxism has focused on the *occlusion*, or bite, of the person involved. A bad bite (*malocclusion*) can prevent the jaw and teeth from attaining a proper relationship, creating discomfort that the person may try to relieve by grinding the teeth. Other researchers (Scandrett and Ervin, 1973) have suggested that stress may trigger some cases, since not all bruxists have malocclusions, and vice versa. Psychodynamic theorists, in contrast,

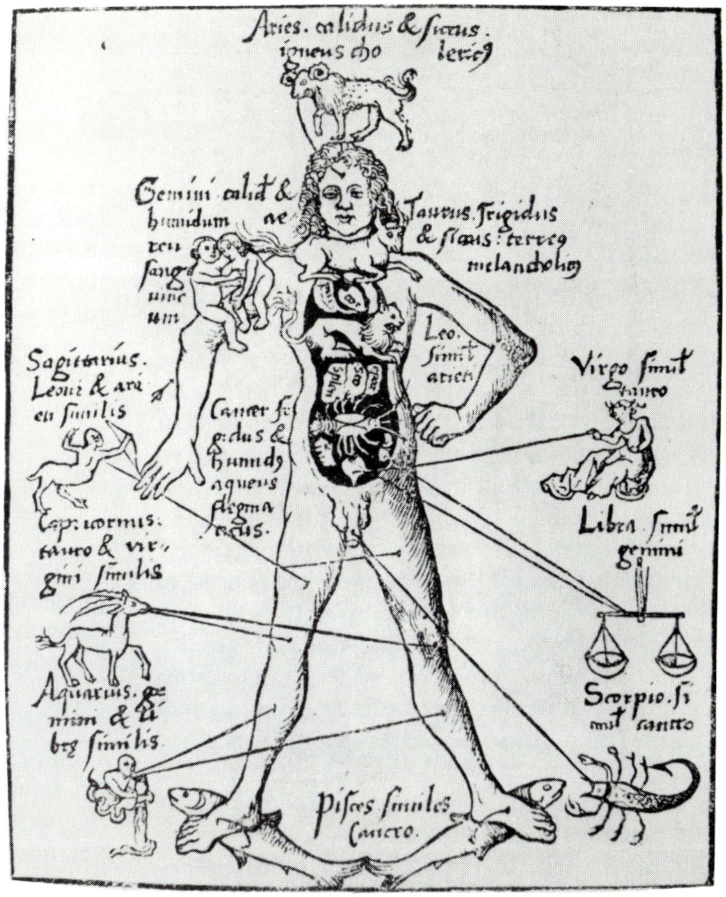

This sixteenth-century woodcut of the "blood-let man" shows the supposed influence of the position of stellar bodies on various human organs.

attribute bruxism to repressed oral aggression. Almansi has described bruxism as "a symptom of emotional illness [that] may represent the expression of . . . anger, anxiety, hate, aggression or sadism which the patient has strongly repressed from his consciousness" (1949, p. 101). Other psychoanalytically oriented theorists have proposed that two different types of bruxists exist: One is passive and dependent; the other is successful, perfectionist, obsessive, and domineering (Glaros and Rao, 1977a).

EXPLAINING THE PSYCHOPHYSIOLOGICAL DISORDERS

Hypertension, migraine headaches, ulcers, asthma, bruxism—these are only a small sample of the physical disorders affected by psychological factors. As we have seen, the physiology of each disorder is different; yet they all share some important characteristics. These similarities have prompted researchers to try to discover the common mechanisms underlying the etiology and development of these various disorders.

In general, approaches to the psychophysiological disorders fall into three categories: biological, psychological, and sociocultural. We shall concentrate on the first two, since the sociocultural factors involved in this group of disorders are essentially the same as those discussed in relation to stress in Chapter 5. In addition, because none of these approaches provide an adequate explanation of the available data, we shall consider an interactional perspective, in which biological, psychological, and sociocultural approaches are seen as inseparable parts of a whole.

Biological Explanations

One biological approach theorizes that a predisposition toward psychophysiological disorders can be inherited. Some of the evidence for genetic factors in psychophysiological disorders comes from examinations of infants shortly after birth. Presumably, newborn infants have had less chance to be affected by environmental and learning factors than the typical adult. For instance, infants with high levels of pepsinogen in their blood were found to come mainly from families that also had high pepsinogen levels. As the Weiner (1957) study of inductees noted, individuals with high pepsinogen levels tend to develop ulcers. Thus the infants with high pepsinogen levels may have inherited a tendency to develop ulcers. However, other explanations are also possible. For example, a variety of biochemical and hormonal changes during pregnancy, including the mother's diet and exposure to chemicals and pollutants, can significantly and permanently alter the fetus. Even though such permanent physical changes occur before birth, they are not hereditary but related to the fetal environment.

Other methods of investigating possible genetic factors in psychophysiological disorders have not produced strong evidence of hereditary influence. A limitation of most genetic theories is that they do not specify the precise nature of the inherited factor. Is a specific weakness in some organ responsible for the disorder? Do individuals inherit particular ways of reacting physiologically to environmental conditions? Is a hereditary inability to control physiological functioning involved? Each of these questions has led to specific theories that have been given some research attention; their results are worth examining.

The somatic weakness theory

We have already seen evidence that both biological and environmental factors can influence psychophysiological disorders. Given that, how is a particular organ or physiological system "selected" for a disorder? In other words, why do some people develop hypertension while others develop ulcers? The **somatic weakness theory** (also known as the *organ inferiority* or *weak organ hypothesis*) attempts to answer this question. According to this theory, a psychophysiological disorder develops at the organism's most vulnerable spot, just as a tire blows at its weakest spot. Each of us has different thresholds for the development of different disorders—in one person, the gastrointestinal system may be the most vulnerable to disease or damage, in another person the cardiovascular system may be the most vulnerable.

The somatic weakness theory is a hard one to test. About the only way to determine the presence of such a weakness is to see if the individual develops a disorder—but this would not in itself confirm the theory. To produce a weakness experimentally would mean causing serious tissue damage. Some support for the somatic weakness theory comes from studies of bruxism showing that this disorder relates to malocclusion, a "weakness" in jaw alignment—but not all cases of bruxism relate to malocclusion. This theory thus remains only speculative at present regarding those disorders that supposedly involve vulnerability in an organ or system.

We all know some individuals who become infuriated and upset at the slightest difficulty, and others who endure enormous tensions without showing any visible sign of stress. This points to another theory: that different people have different physiological reactions to stressors. The focus here is on variations in autonomic activity that may account for psychophysiological disorders. Some people may have a low threshold for stimulation, and their nervous systems may react to only slight disturbances. They would thus be likely to "crack" more easily than individuals whose nervous systems have a higher tolerance for stress. Expressed differently and from the point of view of the somatic weakness theory, the nervous system itself may be the vulnerable spot for such people.

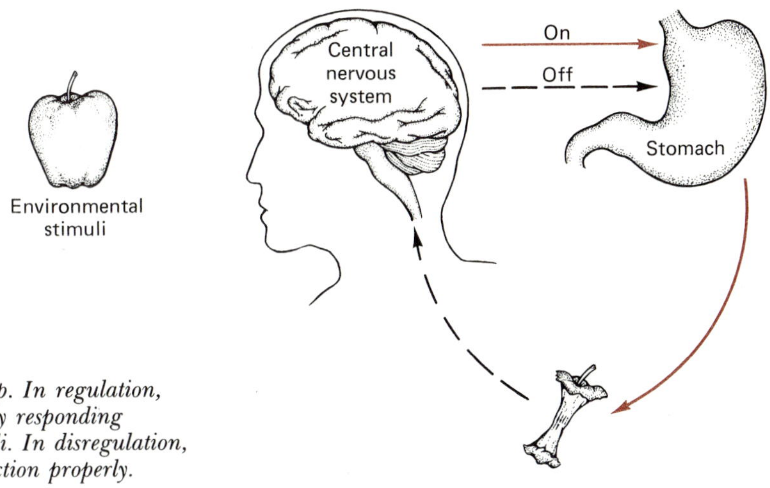

Figure 7.2. *A negative feedback loop. In regulation, the body controls internal functions by responding appropriately to environmental stimuli. In disregulation, something in this process fails to function properly.*

The disregulation model

One of the most promising attempts to explain the psychophysiological disorders is the **disregulation model**, which also implicates the nervous system. You recall that the autonomic nervous system (ANS), which controls the body's reactions to stress, has two branches: the sympathetic division and the parasympathetic division. When the body is under stress, the sympathetic branch is in control: pupils dilate, blood pressure and heart rate increase, adrenaline is released from the adrenal glands, and blood flow to the outer parts of the body is restricted. These and other responses prepare the body for a "fight or flight" reaction. The parasympathetic division produces the opposite effect: It prevents the organism from overreacting and calms it down, so to speak, once the stress has passed.

The actions of the sympathetic and parasympathetic branches of the ANS normally create a condition of stability, or **homeostasis**. Temperature control is a good example of a homeostatic mechanism. When we get too hot, we sweat more than usual to help lower our body temperature, which causes the evaporation of water off the skin. If we get too cool, we shiver in an attempt to raise body temperature. Regulation of body temperature thus involves a **negative feedback loop**. When body temperature gets too low, a temperature sensor in the brain sends a signal to the control mechanism (shivering) to produce more heat. When enough heat has been generated, the sensor signals that no more heat is needed—negative feedback—and shivering is shut off. Similarly, when body temperature gets too high, the sensor calls for sweating; as body temperature drops, the sensor calls for less and less sweating. Negative feedback loops are hypothesized to be the process by which the body maintains homeostasis throughout its systems.

What might happen if one of these feedback loops no longer functioned properly? The disregulation model, proposed by Gary Schwartz (1977), suggests that the result is likely to be a psychophysiological disorder. Schwartz believes there are four ways this can happen. First, environmental demands may keep the person from making use of the body's negative feedback. For example, a woman who is having a stressful conversation in a cold room may be unable to stop shivering even after putting on a sweater.

Second, the person may not utilize negative feedback properly. Lower back pain, for instance, can be minimized if the sufferer limits physical activity at the first signs of pain; but if such activities—running, gardening, or whatever—continue, the disorder will get worse.

When someone in a migraine aura ignores the prodromal symptoms and fails to take medication, a migraine attack will occur.

Third, the person may be physiologically incapable of responding appropriately to feedback. A study of heart patients (Lang, 1975) found that people with documented heart damage performed more poorly than normal individuals on a task of heart rate control. Damage to the organ involved thus may reduce the body's capacity to influence it through feedback.

Fourth, and finally, the negative feedback loop may not function properly. If either the sensor mechanism or the control mechanism fails to respond to the appropriate signals, the feedback loop breaks down. This is the case in some spastic disorders—the feedback loops controlling muscle activity do not work correctly, and the person's movements are jerky and uncontrolled as a result.

Of all the biological explanations of psychophysiological disorders, the disregulation model is the most comprehensive so far. It is a fairly new theory and therefore not well tested. However, its ability to deal with psychological as well as physical influences is a decided advantage.

Psychological Explanations

The theory explaining psychophysiological disorder is, of course, that the physical symptoms are caused by psychological as well as biological factors. That is, although someone may have a genetic or physiological predisposition for a particular disorder, biological factors alone are not usually enough to bring on an actual attack. The symptoms *imply* a biological cause—for instance, if a lesion like an ulcer appeared on someone's hand, we would assume it was caused by an accident or some other physical injury. But in this group of disorders (which, remember, can include many others besides those discussed here), the symptoms usually do not appear in force until some form of stressor precipitates them. Thus the psychophysiological disorders (or, as DSM-III calls them, psychological factors affecting physical condition) are an excellent example of the diathesis-stress theory in action.

Identifying the particular stressors behind any one instance of a psychophysiological disorder would be extremely difficult and, perhaps, not especially useful. As Joan Didion's description of her migraine headaches indicated, even the same disorder in the same person can be brought on by a different stressor every time. The question for psychologists therefore becomes not just what precipitated the disorder but also why did this particular disorder develop. There are three basic psychological explanations of psychophysiological disorders. One deals primarily with a possible link between certain emotions and specific disorders. The second focuses on the individual's overall approach to life situations—stressful or not. The third ascribes a major role to learning.

Specific attitude theory

That people differ in their reactions to stressful situations is undisputed. Given these differences, researchers have turned to psychological variables, such as personality traits, for an explanation of why person A develops high blood pressure while person B develops ulcers and person C does not seem to be at all affected. Investigations of this question have produced mixed findings. Some studies do report evidence of psychological differences between people who later develop a given disorder and those who do not (Weiner et al., 1957), while others have found no differences (Rao and Glaros, 1979). Graham, who developed the **specific attitude theory** (1962), suggested that certain attitudes can cause specific psychophysiological disorders. For example, a man who feels deprived of what was due to him and wants to get either justice or revenge is likely to get ulcers. Similarly, a hard-driving person who struggles to achieve a goal but then feels let down when the goal is reached is likely to develop a migraine.

Research into the specific attitude theory has produced interesting results. Using hypnosis, Graham and colleagues (1962) induced attitudes hypothesized to be related to hives (frustration, feeling helpless) and to hyperten-

Table 7.2 *Type A Characteristics*

Seems generally aggressive and hostile.
Tends to eat, move, and talk rapidly.
Frequently impatient about the rate at which most events take place.
Frequently tries to "save time" by doing two or more things simultaneously.
Tends to focus conversations on topics of personal interest.
Tends to feel guilty about relaxing or "doing nothing constructive."
Tends to overlook and/or forget aesthetic objects.
Seems preoccupied with "having" things rather than "being" or "becoming."
Shows a chronic sense of time urgency.
Tends to dislike other Type A people.
Has characteristic gestures and nervous "tics" (e.g., teeth grinding, fist clenching, etc.).
Believes that accomplishments are due to speedy execution, so is inclined to get things done faster.
Tends to evaluate everything and everyone in terms of numbers.

From Friedman and Rosenman, 1974.

sion (feeling threatened and perpetually on guard). The physiological responses of the subjects did change in ways associated with the appropriate disorder. Other research produced the skin temperature changes associated with Raynaud's disease, a disorder in which the blood flow to the hands decreases, by inducing an attitude of wanting to take hostile physical action (Gottlieb et al., 1967). Although these results are promising, they have also been difficult to replicate (Peters and Stern, 1971). At present, the specific attitude theory must be regarded as an interesting but poorly supported hypothesis.

The Type A personality

Another idea is the **Type A personality**. Recently, research on cardiovascular problems by two heart specialists concluded that a particular set of behaviors—known collectively as *Type A behavior*—is strongly associated with heart disease (Friedman and Rosenman, 1974). Type A individuals can be described as highly motivated, capable, and achievement-oriented, at best; at worst, they are aggressive, impatient, demanding, and compulsive. Unfortunately, such a strong direction toward goals leaves them with a limited repertoire of behaviors to choose from. In contrast is the relaxed, laissez-faire behavior of Type B individuals, who have more alternatives for coping with problematic situations—and a much lower risk of heart disease.

Evidence in support of the link between the Type A personality and coronary disease is fairly strong. One study of Type A and Type B men followed them for more than eight years and found that the Type A group had twice as much heart disease in that period (Rosenman et al., 1975). Jenkins, Zyzanski, and Rosenman (1976) concluded that Type A behavior is a very strong predictor of heart attacks.

Conditioning

Behavioral theorists emphasize the role of learning in psychophysiological disorders. There appear to be three ways people may develop or maintain psychophysiological disorders through learning: operant conditioning, respondent conditioning, and modeling.

Operant conditioning refers to learning that is controlled by its consequences; in other words, behavior that is reinforced (rewarded) becomes more likely to be repeated. Someone with a

By watching overweight family members and friends, children may learn patterns of behavior that lead to obesity.

psychophysiological disorder may receive attention from other people and freedom from responsibility that serve to reinforce the symptoms of the disorder. For example, a young boy who has an asthma attack may be allowed to stay home from school and be coddled by his parents. Operant conditioning appears to be an especially strong factor in the development of chronic pain. Fordyce (1973) has shown that although the pain is quite real, it also wins patients who have this problem the attention and sympathy of friends and family. When that reinforcement is removed, patients often report a dramatic reduction in pain and frequently can increase their physical activity to near-normal levels.

Although operant conditioning is often mentioned as a way sick behavior is *maintained* (Kluger, 1969), respondent, or classical, conditioning may explain how some psychophysiological disorders *develop*. A response that occurs naturally to certain stimuli—sneezing in reaction to pollen, for example—can become attached to a previously neutral stimulus if the two stimuli frequently occur at the same time. A woman who gets used to constantly sneezing every fall during pollen season may come to associate sneezing with falling leaves and a nip in the air; thus she may become asthmatic in the fall whether or not there is a high pollen count. Experimental attempts to condition such responses, however, have rarely succeeded. It is possible that only individuals with a predisposition toward a certain disorder are prone to develop it though classical conditioning. Furthermore, the ethical problems involved in establishing a psychophysiological disorder in anyone limits the kinds of investigations that can be carried out. It appears, though, that classical conditioning is the means by which at least some cases of psychophysiological disorder develop.

Perhaps the most potent source of learning psychophysiological symptoms is observational learning or modeling. Obesity, a common disorder among children and adolescents, often develops through modeling. Although many people seem able to maintain their weight at an appropriate level, some learn to override whatever mechanism is used in this process by watching family members and friends. We shall discuss obesity further in Chapter 14.

Other behavior patterns appear to be learned by modeling. We may learn Type A behavior from a friend whose accomplishments we admire, or we may learn the rewards of sickness from an acquaintance who is excused from a difficult assignment because he doesn't feel well.

In practice, it is difficult to separate the effects of operant conditioning, classical conditioning, and modeling. More often than not, these three learning mechanisms interact to produce changes in behavior that can cause and maintain psychophysiological disorders.

Interactional Explanations

Each of the theories just described takes into account only certain aspects of the whole problem. Biological, psychological, and sociocultural factors actually operate in conjunction, though we may try to separate them for purposes of explanation and research. The aim of an interactional explanation is to acknowledge this conjunction and to use it to describe both the development and the maintenance of psychophysiological disorders. An interactional perspective also allows for various "mixes" of the three types of theories at different points in the development of the disorder. For example, psychological factors may be the most important at one point, while biological factors may become more important at another point.

By applying an interactional perspective to bruxism, we can see how various factors play a role in one psychophysiological disorder. Genetic predispositions and somatic weakness can be seen in abnormalities of the bite, the jaw, or the surrounding muscles. Specific attitudes may play a role; anger and aggression seem to help initiate bruxism. In the earliest stages of the disorder, inability to deal effectively with environmental, interpersonal, and personal stressors is probably the most important factor. Conditioning may play a role in maintaining bruxism, if grinding the teeth relieves the discomfort of a bad bite or provides a release for anxiety about other matters. The role of sociocultural factors is unclear. Although other people generally react negatively to bruxism, that response alone is apparently not enough to motivate an attempt to stop. Perhaps the responses from others aren't as strong as whatever rewards are derived from bruxism. For example, if no one is likely to say "Stop that!" when a boy grinds his teeth while sleeping, he will maintain the behavior. After all, several hours of teeth grinding each night, uninterrupted, will probably override any attempts at control during the day.

MANAGING THE PSYCHOPHYSIOLOGICAL DISORDERS

Since it is possible to live a near-normal life in spite of having a psychophysiological disorder, many sufferers never seek treatment. Those individuals who do will generally consult a physician first, and medical treatment will probably be prescribed. If the physician suspects that psychological factors are involved, the patient may be referred to a psychologist or other mental health worker. Our discussion of the management of psychophysiological disorders will follow this course: First, we shall discuss biological approaches, then the approaches with a psychological component. Because many common techniques are aimed at the person's stress or anxiety, and have been covered in Chapters 5 and 6, we will emphasize treatments that address physical symptoms or the disorder as a whole.

The first task facing a physician confronted with a psychophysiological disorder is to see if the problem is due solely to some underlying organic cause. Even though the psychophysiological disorders are known to involve psychological factors, it is still important to rule out any possibility of medical illness. Once this is done, active treatment begins.

Very often, minor tranquilizers are prescribed to help relieve the stress related to the disorder. As Chapters 5 and 6 suggested, tranquilizers have both advantages and disadvantages: They are often effective, easy to prescribe and take, and relatively inexpensive, but they are also easy to abuse. They mask the disorder so that it appears to be gone. Consequently, the real problem—whatever caused the physical symptoms—is never faced and is likely to strike again and again. Tranquilizers would have to be prescribed more often; possibly, the dose would increase, as well. Clearly, the chances of

Close-up: Managing the Pain of Migraine

To date, there is no universal cure for migraine, a complex disorder that involves a combination of biological and psychological factors. The most effective treatment is one tailored to fit each patient's particular pattern of headaches, personality, and general health. Many migraine sufferers have been helped through biofeedback and simple dietary restrictions. For other migraine sufferers, research into the effects of several promising drugs offers the only hope of relief.

Several drugs are beneficial in preventing the onset of migraine: propranolol hydrochloride, Elavil, and Sansert. Propranolol hydrochloride is a vasoactive drug (one that affects the constriction or dilation of the blood vessels) that is currently used in treating certain heart conditions and high blood pressure. During treatment, heart, pulse rate, and blood pressure should be monitored periodically. Although most patients tolerate this drug well, possible side effects may include fatigue and gastrointestinal problems.

Some of the mood-altering drugs—tranquilizers and antidepressants—have also proved effective in preventing migraines. Elavil, for example, may have an anti-migraine effect when taken in relatively low dosages each night before sleeping. Side effects include dryness of the mouth, blurry vision, dizziness, and weight gain.

Sansert simulates the action of serotonin, a chemical found in the brain and other tissues that affects sleep patterns and mood and constricts some blood vessels and dilates others. A significant amount of current research focuses on the part serotonin levels may play in producing migraines. Unfortunately, Sansert can be dangerous when taken over long periods of time, producing scar tissue on such organs as the kidneys, lungs, and heart. Other side effects include impaired blood circulation, muscle cramps, stomach pains, dizziness, and hallucinations.

Drugs that constrict the dilated blood vessels of the migraine sufferer are generally prepared from the plant fungus ergot, which grows on several varieties of grain. The most commonly used form for treating migraine is called ergotamine tartrate, which can be administered either in tablet or suppository form or injected into the muscles. These drugs are usually taken to stop, rather than prevent, an attack and are more effective when taken at the very first sign of migraine. Adverse side effects of ergotamine may include nausea and vomiting, rapid heartbeat, leg cramps, and a numbing of the fingers and toes.

becoming dependent on these drugs is quite high.

Today, more physicians prefer to prescribe drugs designed for particular problems. Into this category fall anti-hypertensive medications, anti-ulcer medications (e.g., tagament), and asthma medications designed to relax bronchial spasms. Like tranquilizers, these medications may have side effects; for example, many anti-hypertensive drugs produce fatigue, depression, and changes in sexual responsiveness. It is important for the physician to make sure the prescribed medication does not have side effects that will keep a particular patient from using it.

Another part of medical treatment may address the patient's diet and exercise habits. Ulcer patients should avoid alcohol and certain

*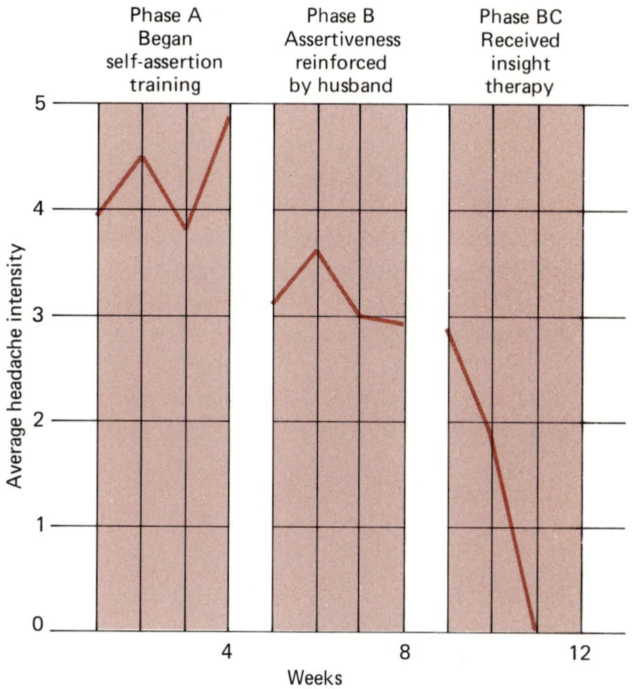

Figure 7.3. *Average intensity of migraine headaches during assertiveness training therapy. From Lambley, 1976.*

other foods. A person with hypertension is usually advised to restrict sodium intake. Heart problems often can be helped—or, better yet, avoided—with proper exercise.

The Psychological Side

As important as psychological factors are in most cases of psychophysiological disorder, both patients and physicians often are reluctant to confront them. After all, it's much easier to prescribe drugs that will be taken and appreciated for their effectiveness than to try to convince patients that the pain of their ulcers has a strong psychological component. This approach is likely to raise the psychosomatic issue once again, which most people wrongly assume means "imagined." The patient will probably not take kindly to this suggestion: "It's a pain in my stomach, damn it! It's not in my head!" However, as people become more aware of the wide-ranging effects of stress on the body, willingness to admit the influence of psychological factors will increase.

In treating the psychophysiological disorders, it is important to remember that the patient has developed these symptoms for a reason. Therefore it is generally necessary to go beyond simple medical treatments and to try to determine what's behind the physical symptoms. Once that has been done, certain techniques can be used to help prevent future problems—or at least, prevent serious attacks. Since these techniques have been described in Chapters 5 and 6, we shall simply list the major coping responses.

Biofeedback is a hybrid technique—part biological and part psychological. It has proved useful in the treatment of several psychophysiological disorders, such as Raynaud's disease, a disorder characterized by cold, painful fingers. Researchers have found that using skin temperature biofeedback to warm the hands is probably more effective than standard medical treatments (Freedman, 1980). Biofeedback also can be used effectively with some neurological disorders, particularly those involving spastic motor activity and epilepsy (Sterman, 1979). The particular physiological parameter that is fed back to the patient seems to significantly affect success. Migraine patients given feedback for temporal blood flow, for example, showed significantly more improvement than patients given muscle tension feedback (Adams et al., 1979).

Some researchers have reported success using assertiveness training. In one case (Lambley, 1976), the severe migraines suffered by a 38-year-old woman decreased in frequency and intensity during a three-phase therapy schedule. During Phase A, she worked on her ability to express strong negative feelings. In Phase B, the focus was on having her husband reinforce her assertiveness at home. Phase BC was devoted mainly to insight therapy—helping her see the connection between her difficulty in handling negative emotions and the intense headaches that had harassed her for years.

The results of this study are shown in Fig. 7.3. Assertiveness training alone did not help reduce the number or severity of the attacks, but in combination with the other techniques used, the effect was rewarding. Nine months after the study, the woman reported that she had not experienced a single migraine in five months.

DESCRIBING THE SOMATOFORM DISORDERS

A young man reports that his hand is paralyzed. The hand appears healthy—no sprain, broken bone, or nerve damage accounts for the problem. But while testing it, the physician finds that the hand does not respond to pinpricks or other stimuli. When the patient is asked to move his fingers, he seems to try but apparently cannot.

Psychophysiological disorders are characterized by observable physical symptoms, often including tissue damage. They appear not to have an organic cause, such as accident or infection, but evidently are brought on in some way by stress. The somatoform disorders also involve physical symptoms with no overt cause. The difference is that they typically do not reflect physiological damage or disability, and they often cannot be confirmed by objective measures.

Presented with a fairly serious physical symptom with no apparent cause, the physician must ask questions. Is the person telling the truth? To find out if the young man's hand is really paralyzed, the doctor can test his reflexes, but not all complaints can be checked so easily. What about the patient who complains of a terrible pain in the side? This is what philosophers call an *incorrigible proposition:* Whether or not you believe it, there's no way you can argue with it. If someone seeks treatment for pain, the physician is forced to assume—at least at first—that the pain exists. However, if the symptoms do not fit into a logical pattern, and if the ailment is serving some useful purpose for the person, the physician may suspect malingering.

Malingering and Factitious Disorders

Malingering is the intentional faking of physical symptoms in order to gain some reward or to further some purpose. An example of malingering would be a college student who goes to the infirmary complaining of stomach cramps because she has not finished a paper that is due the next morning. Some people go so far as to deliberately induce the symptoms of a real organic problem through some artificial means. Malingering may be suspected, for instance, if someone about to be drafted into the armed forces appears for his physical with nausea or stomach cramps. His symptoms are real, but it appears likely that he deliberately brought them on to avoid joining the service. On the other hand, if someone volunteered for the military and appeared satisfied with this decision, but then kept showing up at sick bay, the diagnosis might be a factitious disorder.

Factitious disorders are very similar to malingering. People with factitious disorders create the symptoms deliberately, but usually not with conscious intent—that is, they seem truly unaware of their own part in creating the symptoms—and the symptoms do actually exist. Unlike malingering, factitious disorders don't accomplish anything obvious for the person or serve some readily visible purpose. Rather, underneath the physical symptoms is a psychological conflict or problem that causes them to deliberately become ill. Some researchers speculate that there *is* a goal behind factitious disorders: to receive the attention, freedom from responsibility, and other privileges that come with being a patient. To achieve this, they unconsciously make themselves really ill. In serious cases, they may spend their whole life moving in and out of hospitals.

Once the physician has ascertained that the

distinguishing factor in the symptoms is involuntary control, which means that the person is not malingering, the most likely possibility may be a somatoform disorder. DSM-III lists five types: somatization disorder, conversion disorder, psychogenic pain disorder, hypochondriasis, and atypical somatoform disorder (for cases that do not fit into any of the first four categories).

Somatization Disorder

Originally described by Briquet in 1859, **somatization disorder** has been known as *Briquet's syndrome* ever since. Before DSM-III, it was classified under hysteria. The primary characteristic of this disorder is that the person has a multitude of different complaints—most patients report at least a dozen symptoms, and usually more are reported (especially by women). DSM-III warns that the symptoms must have caused the person to "take medicine (other than aspirin), alter his or her life pattern, or see a physician" (p. 243). Somatization disorder usually starts in the teens, and appears in all cases before age 30. It affects mostly women; often it begins with menstrual difficulties, though symptoms may involve nearly every organ and system in the body. To diagnose the disorder, the physician or psychologist obviously must first rule out a wide range of other possibilities. And care must be taken not to confuse the person's original complaints with any real physical damage that might have resulted from unnecessary surgery, other medical treatment, or self-treatment, such as overuse of alcohol or drugs.

Table 7.3 *The Top Twenty Somatization Disorders*

Problem	Patients with this complaint (%)
Nervousness	92
Back pain	88
Dizziness	84
Fatigue	84
Weakness	84
Pain in extremities and joints	84
Nausea and abdominal pain	80
Headache	80
Breathing difficulties	72
Chest pain	72
Physical incapacitation	72
Abdominal bloating	68
Depression	64
Constipation	64
Blurred vision	64
Anxiety attacks	64
Heart palpitations	60
Loss of appetite	60
Crying spells	60
Fainting spells	56

From Perley and Guze, 1962.

Conversion Disorder

Conversion disorder is characterized by an alteration in or loss of physical function that has no known organic basis. It differs from somatization disorder in that it involves one specific problem, such as paralysis or blindness, rather than a vague symptom or multiple complaints. Formerly known as hysterical neurosis—conversion type, conversion disorder occupies a significant place in the history of psychology. It is relatively rare nowadays, and is perhaps best and most interestingly discussed as a psychological issue rather than as an illness.

The issue of hysteria

Hysteria was studied by the Greek physician Hippocrates more than 2000 years ago. He believed that it was confined to women—specifically, childless women—and was due to a "wandering uterus" (the Greek word for uterus being hysteria). Hippocrates' theory was that the uterus traveled to various parts of the body, causing organic difficulties. To cure it, he prescribed marriage.

In the nineteenth century, hysteria came under the scrutiny of biogenic and psychogenic theoreticians, and served as a battleground for the debate between them. In fact, much of psychodynamic theory grew out of the study of

Charcot, famous Parisian neurologist and director of the Salpêtrière Hospital, delivering a lecture on hysteria. Although Charcot initially believed hysteria was caused by organic damage to the nervous system, he was eventually won over to the psychogenic theory.

hysteria. The success of Mesmer, Breuer, and Freud at using hypnosis to cure such hysterical symptoms as paralysis of the limbs and blindness laid the foundations for the theory of the unconscious. The fact that hypnosis, which was obviously not a physical treatment, could relieve physical symptoms suggested that the underlying ailment was not organic but was due instead to unconscious psychological factors. Freud, like Hippocrates, attributed the symptoms largely to sexual conflicts. These studies of hysteria paved the way for the acceptance of Freudian theory in the early twentieth century.

Primary and secondary gain

The term conversion disorder is based on the assumption that a psychological conflict is converted into a physical symptom and presented as a physical problem. This conversion serves two psychological purposes. First, it blocks out the person's awareness of the internal conflict, reducing the anxiety the conflict would otherwise arouse. This is called the *primary gain*. Second, the physical symptoms excuse the individual from blame and attract sympathy and attention from others. This is known as *secondary gain*.

One way conversion disorder can often be differentiated from an organic problem is by the afflicted individual's apparent lack of concern about such severely debilitating symptoms as blindness or paralysis. This phenomenon is known as **la belle indifference** ("the beautiful indifference"). Viscott (1972) describes a case of conversion disorder he encountered while working in the emergency unit of a general hospital. A girl named Charlotte was brought into the emergency unit by her boyfriend because she claimed she could not move her feet. They had been traveling from her home to a distant city. The following is an excerpt from

Viscott's interview with Charlotte:

V: Charlotte, what's wrong?
C: It's my feet, Doc. I can't move my feet.
V: You don't seem very worried about your feet.
C: Why should I, Doc? You're the doctor. It's your problem. I don't know nothing about no feet.
V: What happened at your Aunt's? I understand you had words.
C: Nothing, nothing.
V: Maybe we should talk about it. What did your Aunt say?
C: She didn't say nothing. She just talked to my mother on the telephone.
V: What did your mother say about your coming North?
C: That's my business.
V: It's important.
C: It may be important but it's none of your business.
V: Mothers sometimes see situations differently from their daughters.
C: We sure do. [Angry.] She thinks just because I'm going North with a man means I'm a tramp. . . . She wants me to get married.
V: And?
C: She says if I didn't get married I should consider myself a slut. . . .
V: I bet you wanted to say something to her.
C: Well, I didn't. I couldn't.*

From this interview, we can deduce a serious and unresolved conflict between Charlotte and her mother regarding her decision to move away with her boyfriend. It is interesting that Charlotte's conversion symptom was paralysis of the feet. This paralysis prevented her from traveling and symbolized her own inner conflict between wanting to move away with her boyfriend and knowing what the move meant to her mother.

People with conversion disorder actually do have the physical capacity believed to be lost. In many cases, they can be tricked into using this "lost" function; in addition, the paralysis usually disappears under hypnosis. Further evidence that no organic pathology is involved comes from the numerous individuals with conversion blindness who rarely bump into things, and from those with paralysis who can move their limbs in certain circumstances—for example, during sleep—but not in others. However, this does not mean that the person with a conversion disorder is consciously refusing to perform. On the contrary, the reaction is quite involuntary.

*From *Making of a Psychiatrist* by David S. Viscott, M.D. Copyright © 1972 by David S. Viscott. Used by permission of Arbor House Publishing Co.

Diagnostic difficulties

The fact that conversion disorders are neither deliberate nor organically based often makes them difficult to diagnose. Some cases are easier than others. For instance, the presenting symptoms may contradict what scientists know about the nervous system. In *glove anesthesia*, for example, the individual reports a numbness of the hands from the fingertips to the break in the wrist. If this loss of feeling represented a true physiological problem, there would be no such precise line between sensitive and insensitive areas. In other cases, where the symptoms are similar to those of a genuine organic disorder, the diagnostic task becomes more difficult.

It is important for physicians and psychologists to be extremely cautious in making a diagnosis of conversion disorder because the risk to the patient is enormous if the diagnosis is incorrect. Unfortunately, misdiagnosis is not unusual. Slater and Glithero (1965), conducting a nine-year follow-up study of patients diagnosed as having a conversion reaction, found that 60 percent had either died or developed serious physical disorders. In a similar study, Whitlock (1967) compared 56 patients with a diagnosis of conversion disorder and 56 patients diagnosed as having an anxiety reaction or depression. Of the conversion group, 61.5 percent had developed signs of organic brain impairment, compared with only 5.3 percent of the anxiety and depression group. These findings strongly suggest that many cases diagnosed as conversion disorder may in fact have been organic problems in the early stages of development.

Unfortunately, there are not many clues to look for to distinguish between true organic dysfunction and a conversion disorder. There are two signs of conversion disorder that professionals look for, but their reliability is not always complete: The first is "la belle indifference," mentioned earlier—the patient's odd lack of concern about the symptoms; the second is the speed with which the symptoms appear—genuine organic disorders tend to emerge more gradually.

Another diagnostic challenge is differentiating between conversion disorders and malingering. One sign mental health professionals can look for is the tendency of malingerers to be defensive and cautious about their symptoms, largely out of fear of being detected as fakers. People with true conversion reactions tend to be very candid and take delight in going on and on about their disabilities.

Psychogenic Pain Disorder

Psychogenic pain disorder, or *psychalgia,* is a complaint of severe aches and pains that cannot be attributed to any underlying mental or physical disorder. The pain symptoms are usually "neurological nonsense"; if they do parallel a known disease, diagnostic evaluation fails to detect any organic disturbance. The problem is judged instead to be psychological in origin, on the basis of one of the following criteria: (1) the pain began during or after a stressful situation or traumatic event; (2) the pain appears to be helping the person avoid some unpleasant activity; or (3) the person is receiving special support and attention because of the pain. In most cases, the person denies that psychological factors are playing any role in the illness.

Although psychogenic pain disorder may occur early or late in life, it usually begins in early adulthood. The symptoms appear suddenly and typically increase in severity over a few days or weeks. Their effect varies, from disturbing the person's everyday functioning mildly to causing total incapacitation. Individuals with this disorder tend to visit physicians frequently, seeking whatever aid is available, from drugs to surgery. They run the risk of becoming dependent on drugs and also of turning into perpetual patients.

Hypochondriasis

People with **hypochondriasis** live in constant fear of illness. Preoccupied with the condition and functioning of their bodies, they worry over every cough, every ache, and anything else that may possibly be a symptom. They may be afraid of some specific ailment or of disease in general, even though they do not in fact have any physical disability; nevertheless, their conviction that illness is imminent never fades.

Many hypochondriacs are constantly reading medical literature and making self-diagnoses. When physicians examine them and find them healthy, they are skeptical—or outraged. Hypochondriacs do not fake their symptoms; they really feel whatever pains they report. It is the significance they attach to these symptoms that is exaggerated.

The following letter (Menninger, 1945) illustrates one hypochondriac's preoccupation with pain and illness:

> Dear Mother and Husband:
>
> I have suffered terrible today with drawing in the throat. My nerves are terrible. My head feels queer. But my stomach hasn't cramped quite so hard. I've been on the verge of nervous chills all day, but I have been fighting it hard. It's night and bedtime, but, oh, how I hate to go to bed. Nobody knows or realizes how badly I feel because I fight to stay up and outdoors if possible. . . .
>
> Annie

EXPLAINING THE SOMATOFORM DISORDERS

By definition, this group of disorders is psychological and not organic in nature. That is, the physical symptoms of a somatoform disorder have no biological cause. However, this is not quite the same as saying that no biological factors are involved in the person's development of the disorder. There is general agreement that somatoform disorder is a way of responding to stress or anxiety; and as Chapters 5 and 6 indicated, both stress and anxiety may have important biological components. The fact that a large number of somatoform patients go on to manifest a physical ailment also suggests that the possible contribution of organic factors should not be overlooked.

Leaving aside the biological aspects of individual reactions to stress, we can view the somatoform disorders as having a psychological explanation. In the following section we shall look at different interpretations of these disorders: psychodynamic, behavioral, sociocultural, and interactional.

Psychodynamic Explanations

As we have seen, psychology's first attempt at explaining the somatoform disorders (which were then lumped together under hysteria) was Freud's psychodynamic theory. Freud believed that the surface symptoms of hysteria are a reflection of anxiety-provoking intrapsychic events, such as motives, drives, emotions, fantasies, and conflicts. To defend against these impulses—that is, to prevent them from entering awareness or from spurring overt action—we unconsciously convert them into a more acceptable physical form. Expressed another way, we use repression to protect ourselves from this urge, but the evil thoughts are too strong to be disposed of so easily. They emerge into consciousness in a different form, such as pain or paralysis. For example, conversion reactions are viewed as being rooted in the child's failure to resolve the sexual conflicts of the Oedipal (or Electra) complex. If the patient is a young woman, the repression of her early incestuous attachment to her father is thought to have produced both a preoccupation with sex and a tendency to avoid it. Later in her life, sexual excitement has reawakened those repressed impulses and converted them into physical symptoms. Psychodynamic theorists thus believe that the psychological factors affecting physical condition are repressed urges and conflicts that originated in the person's childhood.

Behavioral Explanations

Behavioral theorists emphasize the role of learning in establishing and maintaining the somatoform disorders. Someone who receives sympathy and attention for a real or imagined physical condition is likely to repeat that pattern of behavior. A somatization disorder or a similar chronic problem may develop as a result of operant conditioning; hypochondriasis, meanwhile, may reult from respondent conditioning. For example, a woman who has read or heard about another person's ailment may associate that problem with any slight abnormality in her own functioning.

Somatoform disorders may also be related to the avoidance learning hypothesis mentioned in Chapter 6. That is, physical symptoms become paired with relief from anxiety and thus are reinforced. Anything that provokes anxiety then becomes a stimulus for the conditioned response of physical pain. It is virtually impossible to extinguish the anxiety as long as avoidance continues; in fact, the anxiety is much more likely to increase than to disappear. It can thus be said that anxiety is not so much relieved as perpetuated and intensified by avoidance. Only repeated exposure to the avoided stimulus leading to the discovery that the original anxiety-producing event would not recur could end this pattern.

To see how an actual case of a somatoform disorder can be interpreted using this model, think back to the case of Charlotte, the girl whose legs were paralyzed. As became clear in Charlotte's conversation with the psychiatrist, if she could not walk, then she could not continue her journey with her boyfriend. By putting an end to their trip, Charlotte's symptoms provided a way for her to avoid the conflict and anxiety that arose from disobeying her mother, and they also enabled her to avoid a similar conflict with her boyfriend.

Ullmann and Krasner (1975) have proposed a slightly different explanation for conversion reactions. They focus on the fact that people with this disorder are necessarily behaving according to their conception of how a person who truly has this disability would act. This implies that they must have some experience with the role they are adopting. It also implies that they assume that by taking on the role, they will be rewarded. Individuals will feign a disability only if they expect it either to have positive consequences or to reduce stress. Ullmann and Krasner have evaluated several cases of conversion reactions in these terms, pointing out in each case both the rewards the person might have expected and previous opportunities to become familiar with the role.

Sociocultural Explanations

A number of observers have noted that the patterns and types of mental disorders vary from one society and cultural group to another. In the United States, for example, somatoform disorders are much more common among people with relatively little education and low socioeconomic status than in other segments of the population. Furthermore, the pattern of disorders has changed over time. The incidence of conversion reactions in the nineteenth century was reported to be quite high; today, physicians and psychological professionals rarely see anyone with this problem.

Several cultural factors have been cited as possible explanations for this discrepancy. A hundred years ago, very little was known about the relationship between psychological factors and physical symptoms, and it may have been easy for both patients and physicians to accept hysterical symptoms as signs of physical illness. Sudden, inexplicable pain or loss of function thus would have allowed the individual to escape from a stressful situation and to receive attention and sympathy from others. In addition, repressive sexual attitudes may also have been a contributing factor. Both lack of information and sexual conservatism still prevail among the population groups having the highest incidence of conversion disorders.

Another aspect of sociocultural explanations for the somatoform disorders involves the notion of social role. Society prescribes fairly specific professional and personal roles to each person. Individuals who behave in ways appropriate to their role in a given situation are given strong social reinforcement—and those who fail to behave as expected face strong social sanctions.

Individuals who are mentally ill are thus seen as unable to meet ordinary role demands. They have assumed a "sick role" that relieves them of most role responsibilities. Although most of us have at some time solved a problem or avoided a difficulty by "playing sick," the person with a somatoform disorder has serious trouble facing the problems of everyday life that most people can deal with. Not surprisingly, feelings of inadequacy are often a part of this pattern. Nor are these feelings necessarily unjustified. For example, imagine a young woman whose husband has deserted her and their three small children. Her role as a mother demands that she provide loving care for her children, as well as clean clothes, nourishing food, and a safe environment. Yet suddenly she must also take on the role of provider, though she has neither the time nor the skills and education to handle a full-time job. Faced with demands she cannot possibly meet, she may take refuge in illness to escape the guilt and frustration of her failure.

Interactional Explanations

Many mental health professionals believe the somatoform disorders are the result of an interaction between a person's individual characteristics and situational factors. Individual characteristics may include inherited biological traits, influential childhood events, general and specific learning, and social roles. Situational factors may include a recent stressful or traumatic event, or even social and cultural change.

When dealing with a disturbed individual, a therapist faces the complex task of assessing any or all of these components. In each case, of course, some factors will be more significant

Eddie Robinson, 62, the ex–truck driver who reportedly regained his sight and hearing after being struck by lightning. Experts have been unable to agree whether his disorders were brought on by physical injury or psychological trauma.

than others. For example, psychogenic pain disorder might be associated in one case with a recent move to a new neighborhood, in another case with long-standing depression, and in another with a family history of using minor physical problems as a means of winning attention within the family.

MANAGING THE SOMATOFORM DISORDERS

Treatment of this group of disorders is likely to focus on convincing the patient that there is actually nothing physiologically wrong. Thus, paradoxically, the best medicine may be no medicine at all. Biological methods, such as painkilling drugs or surgery, are more likely to harm the patient, since they are most often used when the disorder has been misdiagnosed as an organic problem. Furthermore, the person's ill behavior may be reinforced by the attention received, so that treatment increases the likelihood that symptoms will continue.

Psychoanalysis, including hypnosis, is still a widely used method of treating the somatoform disorders. Another method that has proved successful in a number of cases is behavior therapy. In most cases, the therapist arranges for the person's sick behaviors to cease being functional (that is, incapable of earning the rewards they used to). At the same time, it is essential that rewards be provided for behavior that is out of accord with the "sick role." Parry-Jones and colleagues (1970) devised a program to treat a 47-year-old woman who claimed to be blind but showed no apparent physical impairment. Opinion on the case was divided: Was the woman deliberately feigning blindness or was she afflicted with true hysterical blindness? Such questions were ignored and treatment that stressed giving the woman feedback and social reward (praise) for correctly responding to visual cues was begun. Her sight response was gradually "shaped," and eventually her vision returned to normal.

SUMMARY

The psychophysiological or psychosomatic disorders are conditions that have physical symptoms but no apparent organic cause. DSM-III, mindful of the role psychological factors can play in nearly any physical ailment, no longer includes this traditional group of disorders as a separate category. Rather, it refers to "psychological factors affecting physical condition." Certain disorders are particularly good examples of this interaction. Hypertension, or high blood pressure, has few overt symptoms but can lead to severe medical problems or death. It appears to be brought on and maintained by stress and to be affected by diet. An inherited predisposition may also be involved. Migraine headaches are severe, generally unilateral headaches often accompanied by such symptoms as nausea, vomiting, poor coordination, and distorted vision. Migraines are evidently caused by excessive constriction and dilation of the cranial arteries. The classic migraine is preceded by a warning aura. The person who heeds these prodromal symptoms and takes appropriate medication can often avert the attack. The common migraine has no aura. Cluster migraines occur in a series. There is little evidence that heredity plays a significant role, but a biological predisposition seems to be involved.

An ulcer is a lesion in the wall of the stomach or intestine. There are some differences between gastric and duodenal ulcers and ulcerative colitis, but all appear to be brought on by stress. Biological factors, including unusually high gastric secretions, may also be involved. Asthma is a disorder of the respiratory system. During an attack, breathing is impaired, a condition caused by a narrowing of the airways and perhaps precipitated by allergic factors, infectious factors, psychological factors, or (most often) a combination of all three. Bruxism, the grinding or gnashing of the teeth, is often associated with poor jaw alignment. These are not the only psychophysiological disorders; almost any body organ or system can be involved.

Most biological explanations for the psychophysiological disorders involve variations of the diathesis-stress theory. The affected individual may have a physical vulnerability to a particular disorder—a somatic weakness that causes one organ or system to "give" under stress. Or the person's nervous system may be physiologically reactive to an unusual degree. One of the most promising theories is the disregulation model, which hypothesizes that one or more of the body's negative feedback loops is impaired, so that stress severely disrupts the homeostasis of the system in which the disorder develops. One psychological explanation is specific attitude theory, which hypothesizes that specific personality traits may predispose certain individuals to various disorders. The Type A personality theory suggests that there is a personality type and an overall behavior pattern—for example, hard-driving, achievement-oriented, aggressive—strongly associated with heart disease. Another theory suggests that these disorders may be developed, maintained, or both, by classical conditioning and reinforcement. Modeling also may play a role. Interactional theories hold that the psychosomatic disorders are probably attributable to several of these factors acting together or in sequence rather than to any one of them alone.

Specific medications now exist for many of these disorders, but tranquilizers are still widely used to control the physical symptoms. The trouble with medical treatments is that they mask the real problem so that the person never has to face it. There are some psychological methods of dealing with the underlying conflict once it has been uncovered. Biofeedback has been very useful, as has assertiveness training. In general, the methods for coping with stress that were discussed in Chapter 5 and 6 are also good, since the person must learn better ways of coping to prevent a recurrence of the problem.

The somatoform disorders are psychological conditions that manifest themselves as physical symptoms. They are distinct from malingering, which involves deliberately faking illness for a particular purpose, and factitious disorders, which occur when the individual voluntarily (but unconsciously) creates an injury or illness for no apparent reason other than to be treated as a patient. The somatoform disorders have no known organic component, but neither are they deliberate. DSM-III lists five types: somatization disorder (the person complains of multiple and often unrelated aches and pains); conversion disorder (a loss of function, such as paralysis or blindness); psychogenic pain disorder (severe pain that has no neurological cause and appears to have begun in response to stress or to some personal need); and hypochondriasis (an unwarranted fear of disease).

The ancient Greeks attempted to explain this group of disorders by grouping them together under hysteria. Freudian psychoanalysis got its start from successfully treating these physical symptoms with hypnosis, thus establishing their psychological origin. Psychodynamic theorists still interpret the somatoform disorders as outward manifestations of inner conflicts the person is attempting to repress. Behaviorists believe the symptoms are maintained and possibly originated as a result of conditioning and reinforcement. Other observers suggest that sociocultural factors such as income and educational level and the demands of social roles also may be involved.

Treating these disorders is first a matter of helping the person understand that there is no physical illness. Then the maladaptive behavior must be extinguished and replaced with more adaptive habits. Traditional psychoanalysis is still a popular method for this, since hypnosis seems a very valuable aid in effecting behavior change. In contrast, behavior modification techniques try to end the cycle of reinforcement that has maintained the maladaptive "sick role" so that these behaviors will stop being functional. When the dysfunctional behaviors have been eliminated, it is again important to replace them with more adequate ways to cope with stress. The techniques discussed in Chapters 5 and 6 are most valuable.

CHAPTER 8

Sexual Dysfunctions and Deviations

SEXUAL AROUSAL

The Phases of Sexual Arousal

SEXUAL DYSFUNCTIONS

Inhibited Sexual Excitement

Premature Ejaculation

Inhibited Orgasm

EXPLAINING SEXUAL DYSFUNCTIONS

MANAGING SEXUAL DYSFUNCTIONS

The Masters and Johnson Program

SEXUAL DEVIATIONS

Paraphilias

Incest

Rape

Transsexualism

Ego-dystonic Homosexuality

Transvestism

EXPLAINING AND MANAGING SEXUAL DEVIATIONS

Preparations went forward for Scarlett's wedding and, almost before she knew it, she was clad in Ellen's wedding dress and veil, coming down the wide steps of Tara on her father's arm, to face a house packed full with guests. . . . But when the dancing and toasting were finally ended . . . then the dreamlike trance shattered like crystal before reality. The reality was the blushing Charles, emerging from her dressing room in his nightshirt, avoiding the startled look she gave him over the high-pulled sheet.

Of course, she knew that married people occupied the same bed . . . but she had never applied it to herself. . . . As he hesitatingly approached the bed she spoke in a hoarse whisper.

"I'll scream out loud if you come near me. I will! I will—at the top of my voice! Get away from me! Don't you dare touch me!"

Margaret Mitchell, *Gone with the Wind**

Scarlett O'Hara's shock and horror on her wedding night were not uncommon for women of the nineteenth century—and for much of the twentieth as well. Even after pioneers like Havelock Ellis and Sigmund Freud began breaking down the taboos of the Victorian era, the idea persisted that sexuality was part of the dark side of human nature. For women in particular, sex was primarily a duty, a means toward the noble end of having children. The possibility that it could also be a source of pleasure was a reality for only a small number of fortunate women; many women were never to experience that aspect of sex.

Given this history, our present-day ambivalence toward sexuality is not surprising. The work of Freud and his successors has taught us that sex is an integral part of our lives. Today we recognize that our sexuality helps shape our relationships with people of both sexes; it influences how we view ourselves; it can affect what kind of car we drive, what clothes we wear, and what toothpaste we buy. For most of us, sexuality is associated with the pleasures of physical contact, intimate sharing with a loved one, and procreation. Yet for some people, sexuality is frightening, a source of pain, guilt, and anxiety.

In this chapter we shall explore some of the problems associated with human sexuality, as well as their causes and treatment. The kinds of problems we shall discuss fall into two general categories: dysfunctions and deviations. Sexual dysfunctions can be defined as problems arising during the arousal sequence that interfere with the ability or desire to engage in sexual relations. Sexual deviations are somewhat harder to define. Cultural factors have a profound impact on what we consider "normal" and "deviant." In one culture, for example, anything but intercourse between husband and wife might be considered deviant, while in another culture any sexual activity between consenting adults would be acceptable. It might be more accurate to speak of sexual variations than of sexual deviance.

Havelock Ellis, British author and early sex researcher, reclining in a garden chair. In the 1920s he emerged as a champion of sex education.

* New York: Macmillan, 1936, p. 87.

Little was known about normal sexual behavior in the United States before 1949, the year that Alfred Kinsey published the first objective study of American sexual practices. In personal interviews, Kinsey and his colleagues asked hundreds of intimate questions about sexual activities, including many behaviors that until then had seldom even been mentioned aloud, let alone surveyed. Among Kinsey's findings was that by the age of eighteen over 90 percent of the white males in America had committed a sexual act that was then considered illegal! Kinsey's sample may not have been truly representative of the general population, and his interviewing technique may not always have elicited truthful responses, but his pioneering work laid the foundation for scientific research on human sexual behavior.

Dr. Alfred Kinsey (far right) and two members of his research staff.

At present, concepts of normal and deviant sexual behavior seem to be in a state of flux. Although we shall be using the categories from DSM-III in our discussion, this classification represents just one of many ways of looking at the issue of sexual variation. Remember, too, that for every problem generated by human sexuality, many pleasures and profound joys could be described as well—but that would be a different book.

SEXUAL AROUSAL

Before we can discuss dysfunction, it is important to first describe the normal physiological sexual response of humans. Twenty-five years ago, this would not have been possible: The taboo was still very strong, and no one had researched this area. Kinsey and his colleagues opened the door, but it was not until some twenty years later that Masters and Johnson became the first researchers to study sexual behavior directly in the laboratory. Their early finds were reported in *Human Sexual Response* (1966) and *Human Sexual Inadequacy* (1970), two books that still stand as cornerstones in sexual research. Besides generating a wealth of information, Masters and Johnson's extensive first-hand observations have profoundly changed the way we think about and treat sexual problems.

Before Masters and Johnson's pioneering work, the catchall terms *frigidity* and *impotence* were freely used to label almost all sexual dysfunctions. Men who failed to get an erection, ejaculated too quickly, got an erection but couldn't ejaculate, or got an erection only under certain conditions were all labeled impotent in the literature. Moreover, frigidity and impotence implied personality patterns that were assumed to be related to the sexual difficulties: The frigid female was believed to be cold, aloof, uncaring, and unresponsive; the impotent male was supposedly weak, submissive, and lacking in the manly virtues of courage and aggressiveness. Little attention was paid to assessing the specific and diverse problems people actually experienced. Instead, individuals with sexual problems were offered psychoanalysis or other therapy designed to change their personalities and thus resolve their sexual problems.

However, the data compiled by Masters and Johnson changed this situation. From their observations, they formulated a general sequence in sexual excitement that seems to be followed by most people. Problems such as erection fail-

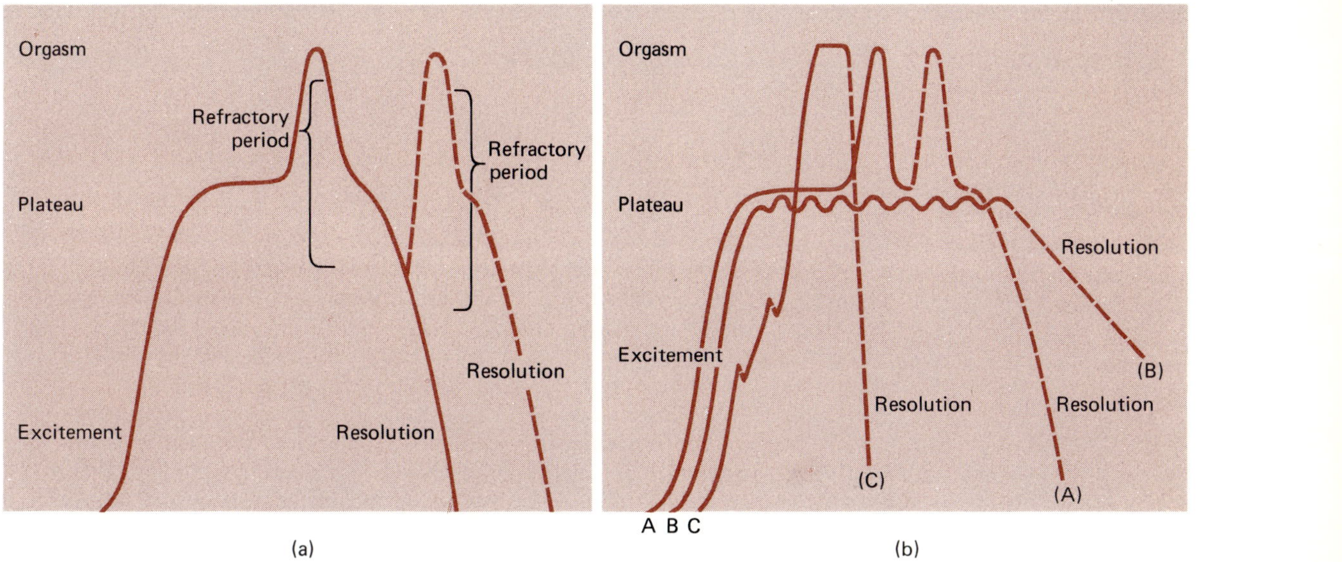

Figure 8.1. *(a) The male and (b) the female sexual response cycles. Reprinted by permission. W. H. Masters and V. E. Johnson,* Human Sexual Response. *Boston: Little, Brown, 1966.*

ure or inability to ejaculate, they discovered, stem from a dysfunction occurring at some point in the arousal sequence. Such a dysfunction could be caused by an organic problem or by psychological conflicts.

The Phases of Sexual Arousal

Masters and Johnson proposed that sexual arousal involves four phases: excitement, plateau, orgasm, and resolution. The **excitement phase** is the first response to sexual stimulation: The male reacts with a penile erection, while the female's clitoris, labia, and vagina become engorged and vaginal lubrication begins. For both, muscular tension, heart rate, blood pressure, and breathing rate increase. This gradually merges into the **plateau phase**, during which the diameter of the vaginal opening decreases by about a third while the inner portion of the vagina enlarges. In the male, the penis becomes completely erect, and the testicles increase in size and pull up tightly against the body.

The **orgasm phase** in the male begins as the ejaculate flows into the penis. Once this occurs, ejaculation is generally inevitable, although orgasm can sometimes occur without ejaculation. The penis begins throbbing rhythmically and soon the semen is propelled out through the penis in the ejaculate. For women, there is no point of orgasmic inevitability. Orgasm consists of a series of strong muscle contractions around the lower part of the vagina.

Orgasm is followed by the **resolution phase**. Blood flows away from the genital area, and pulse, breathing, and heart rates, as well as muscular tension, diminish almost immediately to normal levels. The male, but apparently not the female, experiences a **refractory period** during which he cannot be restimulated to orgasm.

Overall, the arousal sequence is remarkably similar for men and women. For both sexes, *vasocongestion*—the pressure created when blood flows into an area faster than it flows out—and *myotonia*—a generalized increase in muscle tension associated with voluntary and involuntary

Close-up: What Men Fear Most About Sex

Even in this era of sexual enlightenment, myths and fears about sex still persist. Wardell B. Pomeroy, a coauthor of the Kinsey Report and dean of the Institute for Advanced Study of Human Sexuality, compiled a list of the most common anxieties men have about lovemaking (1977). Here are the most prevalent fears, according to Pomeroy:

1. "Am I normal?" Men were concerned about whether their sexual behavior resembled that of other men and if what they did would be considered the "normal" way to have sex.
2. Anxiety about impotence. Most men experience sexual difficulty at some time and continuing anxiety about failing future performances can become a self-fulfilling prophecy.
3. Anxiety about premature ejaculation. A problem that can afflict men of all ages, premature ejaculation is often brought on by psychological factors. Again, fear of possible repetition of the problem can create a self-fulfilling prophecy.
4. Anxiety about general performance. Such anxiety is usually based on a fear of being rejected.
5. Anxiety over penis size. Concern about small penises is derived from the common but incorrect belief that the quality of lovemaking depends on penis size.
6. Anxiety about aging. Some men believe that their sex life will come to an automatic end by a certain age.
7. Anxiety about insatiable demands. Threatened by the image of the super lover depicted in novels and movies and by some of the rhetoric of the women's movement, some men feel they will never be able to satisfy the demands of the insatiable female.
8. Anxiety about latent homosexuality. Many men fear that some unforeseen event will cause latent homosexual desires to surface.
9. Anxiety that one's wife will become sexually involved with other men. The "macho" mentality, which encourages feelings of jealousy and possessiveness, may actually hide strong feelings of inadequacy.

muscle contractions—account for most of the manifestations of sexual arousal. Besides making intercourse possible, vasocongestion and myotonia increase sensory potential and thus the opportunity for pleasure from physical stimulation. Any interference with this process can lead to feelings of frustration. The sexual dysfunctions described in the next section result from such interference.

SEXUAL DYSFUNCTIONS

Sexual dysfunction is a general label for problems at any stage of the arousal sequence that prevent the sequence from following its natural course. These problems seem to be much more common than we might expect. In a recent study of 100 couples who were *not* in treatment for sexual problems, 40 percent of the men reported erectile or ejaculatory dysfunctions, while 64 percent of the women reported arousal or orgasmic dysfunction (Frank et al., 1978). Moreover, 50 percent of the men and 77 percent of the women reported having some significant difficulty that interfered with their ability to relax and enjoy sex. Despite these reports, however, over 80 percent of these couples decribed their relationship—including its sexual aspect—as happy and satisfying.

As these findings suggest, an important factor in many sexual dysfunctions is the expectations involved. Apparently some couples do not really expect much satisfaction from sex. Others may have conflicting expectations: A woman might place greatest value on the intimacy and closeness created during foreplay, while her partner's criterion for "successful" sex is simultaneous orgasms. As we shall see in a following section, an essential step in treating most sexual dysfunctions is recognizing the role of our cultural and individual assumptions—and putting them in perspective.

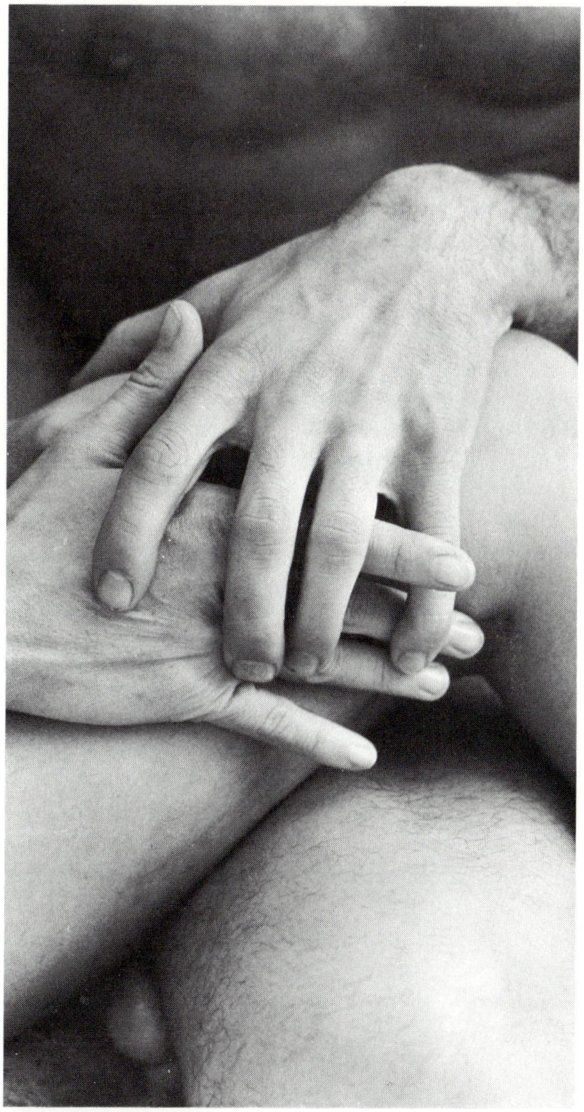

Although most people enjoy the emotional intimacy of sex, some have difficulty sustaining arousal during intercourse.

Inhibited Sexual Excitement

Karen was blushing; it appeared to the therapist that she was near tears. "I don't know what's wrong with me!" she blurted. "I really do want to have a normal sex life, but somehow nothing Jack does turns me on! Is there any kind of medicine I can take? Or am I just frigid?"

Karen's inability to respond to sexual stimulation is a problem that can afflict either men or women, although it seems to be more common in women. In **inhibited sexual excitement** there is a desire to have sex, yet there is trouble becoming or staying aroused. A woman might find that lubrication and genital swelling are inhibited; a man may have trouble achieving an erection. These are problems that everyone has sometimes, of course. They are considered dysfunctional only when the person wants to become aroused but persistently cannot, or when the person habitually fails to sustain arousal despite being stimulated.

Many clinical patterns fit into this general category. One man may easily get an erection while dancing or cuddling with his partner, but lose it after moving to the bedroom. Another man may never get an erection when he is with a woman but regularly awakens with an erection in the morning. Yet another may not achieve an erection under any circumstances. Likewise, one woman may enjoy the closeness and intimacy of sex but not feel much during intercourse. Another may feel anxious throughout stimulation and be distressed by her inability to become aroused. A third may eagerly begin sexual contact, rapidly grow aroused, but then get distracted by a noise or by thoughts of routine chores. For both men and women, dysfunctions in the early stages of arousal typically arise from the same problems: fear, performance anxiety, conscience pangs, or dissatisfaction with the partner. We will examine these problems more closely in a later section.

When the female partner loses her arousal, it is still possible for the couple to have intercourse. When the male partner cannot achieve or maintain an erection, intercourse is impossible. For this reason, *male erectile insufficiency* (the clincial term for impotence) has traditionally been taken more seriously than female arousal insufficiency. Occasionally though, the woman's inhibition does take a form that prevents intercourse. *Vaginismus,* an involuntary contraction of the muscles around the entrance to the vagina, can make penetration difficult or impossible. *Dyspareunia*—painful intercourse—is often due to a failure to lubricate; although it frequently has psychological origins, it may also result from infection or an irritation caused by douches, certain contraceptives, or other sources. It can occur in men as well as women, sometimes because of an injury. It is important for the therapist treating such cases to rule out physical difficulties before diagnosing either vaginismus or dyspareunia, both of which are fairly rare.

Premature Ejaculation

Difficulties at the orgasm phase of sexual arousal are quite prevalent and fall into two broad categories: Orgasm happens too soon or it doesn't happen at all. The question is what is "too soon"? Some people have been convinced by popular literature—such as *Ideal Marriage* by Van Der Velde—that orgasms are "wrong" if they do not occur simultaneously in both partners. However, most sex therapists feel that this is not only unnecessary but also a highly unrealistic expectation. Indeed, for one partner to make a habit of trying to wait for the other is likely to create more frustration than it solves.

Premature ejaculation is a dysfunction strongly related to this type of cultural expectation. Certainly if a man consistently ejaculates before, during, or immediately after penetration, this can create real difficulties for his partner. On the other hand, there is no reason to expect that he will always be able to last until she is satisfied. Few men are capable of such total control; and even to attempt it may destroy the pleasure that comes from the spontaneous and involuntary quality of sexual responses.

Masters and Johnson (1970) attempted to establish a realistic basis for dealing with premature ejaculation by avoiding the "clockwatching" approach of clinicians who set a fixed goal—such as thirty seconds—for maintaining an erection after penetration. Instead, they defined premature in terms of the female partner's response: If she fails to reach orgasm during intercourse at least 50 percent of the time, then her partner's erection is too brief. Although this approach avoids the problem of saying exactly how long is long enough, it raises other problems. Not only does it heighten the performance demands of sexuality, but it implies that the man is responsible for inducing his partner's orgasm before he is entitled to his own.

DSM-III alternatively proposes that ejaculation is premature if it occurs before the individual desires it. While solving both the "clockwatching" and "control tower" problems, this approach fails to provide reasonable guidelines for a couple's expectations. Is ejaculation premature if a man wishes to last three hours but only lasts for two? What is the value of determining that 36 percent of men in a recent study (Frank et al., 1978) reported that they ejaculated "too quickly" when no clear criteria for defining this dysfunction have been provided?

Although premature orgasm is not included as a dysfunctional category for women in DSM-III, 11 percent of the "normal" women in the same study reported that they reached orgasm "too quickly." It is too bad that we don't really know what the respondents meant by that; 11 percent is quite a large figure for a problem that is presumed to be nonexistent.

Inhibited Orgasm

The category of **inhibited orgasm** includes many different dysfunctional patterns for women. Some women never have an orgasm under any circumstances. Others experience orgasm infrequently or only with persistent effort using one very specific kind of stimulation or masturbatory technique. Whether or not to include in this last category those women who do not have orgasms during intercourse is a matter of considerable debate. Masters and Johnson (1970) refer to the absence of orgasm during intercourse as *coital orgasmic inadequacy*. Other sex researchers, including Hite (1976), argue that it is actually more usual for women not to achieve orgasm through intercourse, and that to consider this pattern dysfunctional is like saying that only marathon runners are physically fit. DSM-III is noncommittal, observing that sometimes this could be caused by pathology, but in other cases it is just a normal variation of the feminine response. Unfortunately, no criteria for distinguishing between these cases are proposed.

One thing we do know is that little support now exists for the long-held view stated by Freud, that orgasm is functional for the female only if it is a "vaginal" orgasm, occuring during intercourse. To say that all orgasms are alike would be to underestimate the variety of sensations women are capable of experiencing; but it is fairly clear that there is no special and different orgasm we can call "vaginal."

Many female researchers (for example, Hite, 1976; Hyde, 1979) are urging that women need to take responsibility for their own orgasms and should not feel that there is a right time and a right way to have them. Still, many women want to experience orgasm during intercourse and they continue to seek treatment to enable them to do so (Zeiss et al., 1977). Perhaps the absence of orgasm during intercourse should not be considered a dysfunction or a "pathological inhibition" as DSM-III suggests; but sexuality may be enhanced when both partners share orgasmic experiences while they are together.

Men can also have difficulty reaching orgasm. Inhibited male orgasm is defined in DSM-III as the delay or absence of ejaculation, or both. Because this problem is relatively rare, retarded ejaculation has received considerably less attention in the literature than premature ejaculation.

Because orgasm releases vasocongestion and myotonia, resolution can be quite prolonged and uncomfortable for male and female alike if stimulation is not followed by orgasm. Aside from that, few problems are associated with the resolution phase of the arousal sequence. Some researchers (Zilbergeld, 1978) have suggested that the refractory stage for men is a culturally induced condition and that men could be capable of multiple orgasms; however, this assertion has not received wide acceptance. Whereas many women can be restimulated to orgasm during the resolution stage, men generally find additional stimulation at that point to be unpleasant rather than erotic.

EXPLAINING SEXUAL DYSFUNCTIONS

Like sexual responsiveness, sexual dysfunction is highly individual: There is no one clear cause behind all cases. We do know that dysfunctions tend to escalate—a person who has problems in the orgasmic phase, for example, may begin to have trouble getting aroused and may eventually lose all interest in sex. This points to the crucial role of psychological factors in sexual dysfunction. In spite of the vivid physicality of sexual stimulation, sex is, like all sensory experiences, governed by the brain—witness the number of people who have erections or orgasms in their sleep. In considering the origins of any sex dysfunction, it is thus important to look not only at its physical manifestations but at the attitudes and experiences behind it. Hogan (1978) has classified the causes of sexual dysfunctions into six categories: physical factors, early learning experiences, lack of accurate information about sex, lack of a skilled partner, emotional and cognitive factors, and problems in the sexual relationship.

Physical factors. Injuries, infections, and illnesses are common causes of a change in sexual functioning. For example, spinal cord damage may have profound effects on the response of the nervous system to sexual stimulation. Diabetes affects peripheral blood circulation and may consequently affect vasocongestive responses to stimulation. Medication, too, can alter sexual responsiveness.

Throughout history people have been searching for a drug—a true aphrodisiac—that would dramatically enhance sexuality. So far, none has been found. Although certain drugs (alcohol, amyl nitrate, marijuana) seem to heighten the subjective experience of sex for some people, their effect may be due as much to the expectations of the drug-taker as to the physiological effect of the drug itself. For instance, marijuana may increase sexual responsiveness simply by decreasing inhibitions. Alcohol, in contrast, has negative physiological effects on the sexual response system even though it may be increasing the desire for sex. Many clinical cases of impotence begin with a failure brought on by alcohol—for example, when a drinker's expectations exceed physical capabilities.

Early learning experiences. It has been widely suggested that sexual patterns learned in childhood or adolescence set the stage for problems in adulthood. For example, Masters and Johnson (1970) argue that the teenage boy whose first sexual experiences are hurried encounters in the back seat of a car may learn a habit of rapid ejaculation that is hard to overcome later on. Why this common situation should lead to premature ejaculation in some adult men but not others, however, is unclear. Similarly, many dysfunctional adults were raped as children, or involved in incestuous relationships. All such encounters can leave deep emotional scars on children that may eventually affect their adult sexual lives; nevertheless, many children who have such experiences do not develop adult dysfunctions. It has also been suggested that if other adults learn of these experiences, their reactions (shock, horror) are likely to intensify the emotional scars of the children. This theory has never been substantiated, however.

Related to this is the influence of a strict moral (often religious) upbringing. It is common in our society for children to be taught that their genitals are private, meant to be covered at all times, and never touched or mentioned. Girls in particular are warned against any contact with boys that might be remotely sexual. The young woman who has been sheltered from her own sexuality until she is turned over as a virgin bride to her husband may find herself as terrified as Scarlett O'Hara on her wedding night. It is not surprising that such women may have difficulty reaching orgasm or even allowing themselves to become sexually aroused.

Lack of accurate information. Another aspect of our cultural taboo on sexuality is the ignorance it creates. The girl who has been warned since childhood against sex is not likely to know much about it. Even if she is able to overcome her fears, she may expect her husband—who may be equally inexperienced—to know exactly what to do to initiate both of them into the mysteries of sex. The pressure of such expectations on the young man is tremendous. He may find himself impotent in every sense of the word: unable to get an erection, and unable to comfort the frightened girl for whom he is suddenly responsible. With both partners embarrassed, ignorant, and afraid of failure, failure is very likely.

Misinformation can be just as damaging. Masters and Johnson (1970) reported a case in which a married couple who had been enjoying intercourse about once a day for three years were advised by a professional that such a high rate of sexual activity could cause the male partner to wear out rapidly. Worried about his imminent sexual demise, the husband began to have trouble getting an erection. He became impotent and remained so for seven years before seeking treatment.

Lack of a skilled partner. As we have noted, it is fairly common in our culture for a woman to look to her partner for guidance in the techniques of sex. Obviously, if she does so and he is inept, the couple will have difficulties. It has rarely been suggested, however, that the male may have problems because his female partner lacks experience. In short, the skill of the partner is a factor in sexual dysfunction only if the other person is not initiating anything. Moreover, to attribute dysfunction to the lack of a skilled partner is to suggest that sexual success is primarily a matter of knowing the right techniques for arousal. In fact, individuals vary tremendously with regard to the kind of stimulation they consider to be exciting. Probably the most important attribute of a skilled sexual partner is the ability to ask the question, "What would you like?"

Emotional and cognitive factors. We have already touched on the role emotional and cognitive factors play in dysfunction. Among these, performance anxiety has been strongly emphasized. Masters and Johnson (1970) argue that performance anxiety interferes with sexual response in two ways: It interferes with the processes of vasocongestion and myotonia (making sexual intercourse difficult or impossible), and it causes the anxious partner to take a "spectator" role. The anxious male may wonder, "What if I don't get an erection? What does she think of me? Am I doing the right things to please her?" The woman may wonder, "Does he like my body? Am I being too eager? Will I be able to have an orgasm?" As a spectator, each is distracted from the sensory experiences that would otherwise be arousing. While other psychological factors (such as guilt, fear of losing control, hostility, and fear of pregnancy) may play a role in sexual dysfunction, clinical evidence indicates that anxiety is the most pervasive problem.

Problems in the sexual relationship. This factor has been emphasized by all sex therapists. Certainly, two people who find each other disgusting or hateful are unlikely to have a successful sexual relationship. Although there seems to be little evidence to support a correlation between sexual dysfunction and marital (or partner) problems, there is little doubt that one can affect the other. The presence of a dysfunction—especially one of long standing—can certainly intensify any temporary disputes, and possibly turn them into long-term cold wars. Likewise, an argument over some nonsexual aspect of the partnership could conceivably lead to dysfunction, although most sexual problems caused by marital dispute are short-term. A woman who believes that her partner no longer cares about her but only wants to "get off," or a man who thinks his partner secretly despises him, may easily have trouble becoming aroused or reaching orgasm.

Sara Davidson (1977) describes a young woman's sudden discovery of the connection between her sexual dysfunction and her relationship with her partner. Through years of marriage and lovers, Susie never had an orgasm with her husband or any other man. She had given the idea up as an unrealistic hope until she met Russ:

> Once as he was swaying above her, he looked in her eyes with unaffected sweetness. "Hey lady, I love you." She felt a spinning in her head, and tingling all through her. "It wasn't like the orgasms I'd been giving myself with the vibrator but it was astounding." She thought about it for days and began to wonder if she had not been focusing on the wrong thing. "It wasn't just a penis, it was the context of the lovemaking. It hit me that to have orgasms with a man, I would have to deal with profound issues like surrendering, trusting and letting go." (p. 252)

This is not to say that every sexual failure means that a dysfunction can be made to vanish if the couple cares about each other enough. But "the context of the lovemaking," as Susie put it, can be crucial.

Masters and Johnson counseling a couple with sexual problems at their St. Louis clinic.

MANAGING SEXUAL DYSFUNCTIONS

According to Kaplan (1974), some 3 to 20 percent of dysfunction cases can be traced to a physical problem. Difficulties that arise from temporary conditions (such as a side effect of medication or a genital infection) usually resolve themselves when the condition clears up. Individuals with irreversible physical problems (such as spinal cord damage or impotence due to diabetes) may need to redefine their sexual goals and desires in order to achieve satisfaction within the existing framework of their physical capacities.

Sexual problems that do not have a physical basis often respond to direct treatment as well. LoPiccolo (1978) lists seven techniques that are accepted by most sex therapists: These are (1) encouraging the sexual partners to take mutual responsibility for overcoming their shared problem; (2) presenting both partners with information and education; (3) changing sexual and relationship attitudes and beliefs; (4) eliminating performance anxiety; (5) increasing communication between the partners and the effectiveness of their sexual techniques; (6) changing destructive life-styles and sex roles; and (7) prescribing changes in sexual behavior through "homework" assigned during the course of therapy.

The Masters and Johnson Program

According to Masters and Johnson (1970), sexual dysfunction is a failure in the relationship between two people, not a pathology that "belongs" to one of the partners. Working together as a male/female cotherapy team, Masters and Johnson see patients only at their St. Louis, Missouri, research center. They begin therapy with extensive interviewing and a medical examination to assess the nature of the problem. Following assessment, education begins with a feedback session. The therapists present a conceptualization of how the problem was created and how the couple will begin to solve it; the couple is encouraged to agree or disagree and to suggest any changes they think are appropriate. Misconceptions about sex are cleared up, and extensive information about sexual functioning is provided. The therapists then begin to assign "homework," consisting of prescribed sexual behaviors. For the duration of therapy, which comprises two weeks of daily sessions, the couple must do everything they are assigned, but no more than what they are assigned.

The first few of these graduated assignments are designed to eliminate performance anxiety and to improve communication skills. In these **sensate focus exercises**, the couple is told to take turns giving and receiving pleasure through sensual massage. At first the massage does not include the breasts or genitalia. The receiver has two tasks. The first is to learn to receive pleasure without feeling pressured to respond reciprocally. In allowing themselves to focus on their own natural responses to pleasure, the partners learn to let go of the demand to perform and the habit of being a spectator rather than a participant. The receiver's second task is to communicate constructively to the giver about what is most pleasurable. The receiver should be neither demanding nor punishing but should learn to guide the giver verbally and nonverbally to enhance pleasure. The giver also has two tasks. One is to focus on the pleasure of giving in a sexual relationship and to let go of the need to perform. The other is to try to respond to feedback from the receiver in order to learn how to give pleasure. The giver stops trying to read the receiver's mind and begins to communicate directly about sexual feelings.

The couple reports on progress and problems in therapy sessions. The therapists focus on any obstacles that may arise and suggest changes in the relationship that might enhance progress. Meanwhile, they continue to educate the clients and to alter any attitudes and beliefs that seem to contribute to the dysfunction.

The final component of therapy involves gradually building in homework assignments to alter the specific problem. A couple complaining about premature ejaculation, for example, might be taught the *squeeze technique,* in which the female partner squeezes the penis in such a way that the urge to ejaculate is painlessly controlled. Other techniques are used for specific dysfunctional problems to create an effective pattern of sexual interaction between the partners.

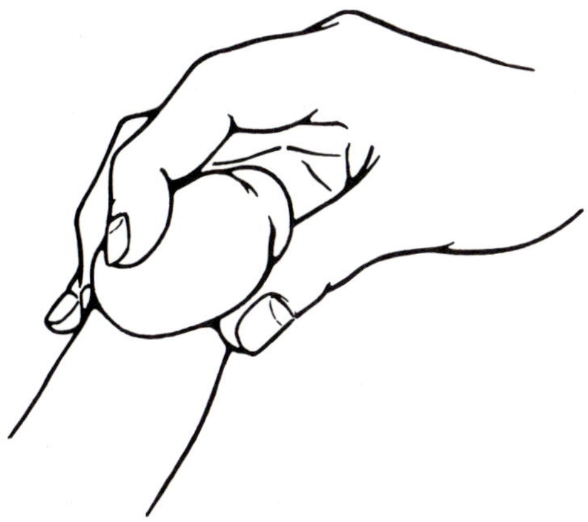

Figure 8.2. *The squeeze technique for eliminating premature ejaculation.*

This therapy operates simultaneously on several levels to alter the couple's sexual behavior, their relationship, their communication with each other, and their sexual beliefs and attitudes. Although the techniques may seem simple and straightforward, considerable skill is required of the therapists to function on these

Table 8.1 *Results of Masters and Johnson Treatment*

Problem	Couples treated	Immediate failures	Initial failure rate (%)	Treatment reversals	Overall failure rate (%)
Women					
Primary orgasmic dysfunction	193	32	16.6	2	17.6
Situational orgasmic dysfunction	149	34	22.8	3	24.8
Subtotal	342	66	19.3	5	20.8
Men					
Primary impotence	32	13	40.6	0	40.6
Secondary impotence	213	56	26.2	10	30.9
Premature ejaculation	186	4	2.2	1	2.7
Ejaculatory incompetence (inability to reach orgasm in intercourse)	17	3	17.6	0	17.6
Subtotal	448	76	16.9	11	19.4
Total, men and women	790	142	18.9	16	20.0

From Masters and Johnson, 1970, p. 367.

diverse levels and to deal with the idiosyncratic aspects of each case.

Masters and Johnson reported (1970) that their program proved to be very effective: Success rates ranged from 100 percent for women with vaginismus to 60 percent for men who had never experienced erection sufficient to complete intercourse. Overall, the program reported a success rate of 83 percent for problems of male sexual dysfunction and 80 percent for problems of female dysfunction. These statistics have recently been criticized (Zilbergeld and Evans, 1980). The chief complaint is that the high rates of success reported by Masters and Johnson are based on criteria that are not clearly defined, making any attempts to replicate their studies and confirm their statistics impossible.

Despite this criticism, most sex therapists who follow the guidelines formulated by Masters and Johnson report decent success rates, although they are lower than those reported by the St. Louis team. Some changes have been made in the basic treatment program by these other therapists. LoPiccolo and Lobitz (1972) developed alternative procedures for working with nonorgasmic women. It now seems conclusive that a cotherapy team is not essential (Franks and Wilson, 1974), nor is it necessary to concentrate therapy into daily sessions for two weeks; one weekly session occuring for a period of three or four months is quite adequate (LoPiccolo and Lobitz, 1972). In addition, some therapists see only one partner (Husted, 1972).

SEXUAL DEVIATIONS

In sexual dysfunctions, a person experiences a disruption in the arousal sequence, but the choice of sexual object and aim remain normal—that is, socially acceptable. In **sexual deviations**, the person's goal is something other than intercourse with a consenting adult (some would add "of the opposite sex"). This definition reflects the standards of our particular culture, not any sort of "natural order." Many societies in other parts of the world tolerate and even encourage sexual behavior that we would label deviant—sex between children, for instance, or open masturbation. Even in the United States, the definitions of normal and deviant have changed considerably over time. For most of our history, virtually any sexual act other than genital intercourse between a husband and wife was considered to be immoral and unnatural.

Kinsey and his associates (1949, 1953) reported that even between socioeconomic classes in the United States there are tremendous differences in what is viewed as normal. In the lower classes, for example, couples are more likely to avoid nudity; they may live out their entire married life without ever seeing their partner nude. In the middle and upper classes, nudity is more often considered a natural and pleasurable aspect of sexual activity. While the differences are probably less drastic today than they were at the time of Kinsey's research, sexual attitudes still vary greatly according to such factors as class, national region, and type of environment (urban, suburban, or rural).

Paraphilias

DSM-III refers to variations in sexual choice and aim as **paraphilias**. Some paraphilias, including voyeurism, exhibitionism, and pedophilia (child molesting), have been designated criminal acts because they involve sexual choices that one person imposes on another who is not a consenting partner or who is considered too young to make an intelligent choice to participate. Other paraphilias such as fetishism are victimless, but many people believe they should be treated as disorders because they interfere with the person's interest and ability to form normal sexual relationships. The range of paraphilias is as wide as the human imagination, and we shall thus not attempt to cover them all. Most of them, including *necrophilia* (an attraction to corpses) and *zoophilia* (a preference for animals as sexual partners) are too rare to warrant discussion. We shall treat here only a few of the most common paraphilias: voyeurism, exhibitionism, pedophilia, fetishism, sadism, and masochism.

Voyeurism

A compulsive desire to watch some unsuspecting person disrobing, nude, or engaging in sexual activity is called **voyeurism**. Although most people are aroused by such sights to some extent, the voyeur (almost invariably male) derives his primary sexual gratification from "peeping" to the exclusion of normal sexual relations. The woman he views is usually a stranger, and generally the voyeur does not want her to know she is being observed; if he is discovered, he cannot derive gratification. The voyeur will often masturbate to orgasm either while observing the woman or while remembering the incident later, and there is usually no further contact between him and the woman he observes.

Voyeurs tend to be young men, often married, who experience difficulty in establishing adequate peer and sexual relationships (Smith, 1976). Few voyeurs have records of serious criminality, but many have repeated arrests for peeping. Although voyeurs rarely harm the women they watch, some voyeurs may be dangerous. According to one study (Yalom, 1960), the more dangerous voyeurs were those who would enter a building to view a subject and who would try to make her aware that she was being observed. In this study, such voyeurs were more likely to attempt rape or assault.

Carl, a 21-year-old carpenter, and his wife were experiencing a great deal of stress during their first year of marriage, and their sex life was far from satisfactory. One day after a fight about sex, Carl went for a long walk. Sitting on a park bench, he began thinking about how seldom he had intercourse with his wife. He didn't realize he had begun masturbating until two teenage girls passed by and cried out when they saw him. Scared and confused, Carl was also very aroused. He ejaculated quickly and hurried off, swearing that this would never happen again. But he couldn't stop thinking about the incident, and he returned to the park the following weekend. Soon he began to go almost every day; he would find a quiet spot, unzip his pants, and masturbate. Always frightened, he felt totally alone and almost as if he were in a trance. He never spoke to the women who passed by or tried to draw their attention. As soon as someone saw him and reacted with fear, he quickly ejaculated and left. When Carl was arrested for indecent exposure, he made no attempt to escape. The arresting officer was impressed by Carl's gentleness and pleasant manners.

Exhibitionism refers to exposure of the genitals to an unsuspecting stranger for the purpose of sexual arousal, which the exhibitionist may experience either during or immediately after the act of exposure. Contrary to the popular stereotype, the exhibitionist is usually not a "dirty old man"; the average age at first conviction is in the mid-twenties to early thirties (Blair and Lanyon, 1981).

It should be noted that Carl represents an atypical case in certain respects. For one thing, he exposed himself to no one in particular; in contrast, most exhibitionists select someone to exhibit themselves to. For another, Carl masturbated to ejaculation even after being spotted. The majority of exhibitionists, generally stop masturbating if the observer takes some action.

Because gratification usually results from the emotional response of the observer, the most effective response to an exhibitionist may be to remain calm and not show a strong reaction. The exhibitionist typically desires no further contact with his victim and presents no danger to her. However, although most exhibitionists do not seek physical contact, about 10 percent of arrested exhibitionists have attempted or considered rape (Gebhard et al., 1965). Exhibitionism accounts for 23 to 35 percent of arrests for sexual offenses (Hughes, 1977).

Whether female exhibitionists exist is not known. Certainly, women have more socially approved ways to expose their bodies than men do; and a man might be less likely to report to the police that a woman exposed herself to him. The women who do "expose" themselves—whether it is by wearing revealing clothing in public, visiting a nude beach, or working as erotic dancers or strippers—report that their exposure does not result in sexual gratification (Skipper and McCaghy, 1970).

Today, men as well as women have more socially approved opportunities to expose their bodies. Many work as exotic "dancers" who routinely strip before an audience of strangers.

Pedophilia

Pedophilia, or *child molesting,* refers to a sexual preference for preadolescent children. Most pedophiles are heterosexual males who enjoy looking at and fondling the genitals of young girls. While heterosexual pedophiles rarely attempt intercourse, homosexual pedophiles may engage in mutual masturbation, fellatio (oral sex), and anal intercourse. Heterosexual pedophiles generally prefer girls aged eight to ten; homosexual pedophiles tend to prefer slightly older boys (DSM-III, 1980). The pedophile is very often a relative, family friend, or acquaintance; indeed, Katchadourian and Lunde (1975) report that the pedophile and the child already know each other in 85 percent of all cases.

Pedophiles tend to be older and more conservative than other sex offenders. Some 70 to 80 percent of arrested pedophiles are or have been married, and many have a history of sexual inadequacy, unsuccessful marital relations, and impotence. According to DSM-III, 13 to 20 percent of homosexual pedophiles and about half that many heterosexual pedophiles are repeat offenders. Although many of them express shame, guilt, and anxiety when they are caught, others maintain elaborate justifications for their behavior, insisting that they were sharing love with a disadvantaged youth or that they wanted to initiate the child into sexual behavior in a warm and supportive atmosphere. Nevertheless, pedophilia is deplored by the majority of heterosexuals and homosexuals alike. Convicted child molesters are particularly despised and often sexually abused by their fellow inmates in prison.

The impact on the child is not known, although we can speculate that it is usually not positive. Most children are pressured into the relationship with promises of rewards and assurances that it's really quite all right. The children are generally old enough to know that it's *not* quite right, yet they continue for a time—some are threatened with exposure, some derive real pleasure from the relationship. Conflict between the guilt of knowing it's wrong and the sexual pleasure or warmth that is occasionally experienced can lead to sexual difficulties in adulthood.

Fetishism

The regular and compulsive use of inanimate objects (such as articles of clothing) or, more rarely, a particular part of the body (such as feet or hair) for erotic excitement and gratification is called **fetishism**. While it is not abnormal to attach sexual connotations to certain objects or anatomical features, the fetishist (almost always male) usually fears rejection by women and focuses on a particular object or body part as a substitute for personal contact and interaction. His activities normally are not a matter of public concern unless he commits theft or burglary to obtain the object that attracts him. An interesting case of fetishism was brought to public attention recently when Seattle police apprehended a man who had assaulted many women on the street in order to steal from each a single shoe.

Sadism and masochism

Sadism is the infliction of physical pain or psychological suffering on another person in order to achieve sexual arousal or gratification. In **masochism**, individuals derive sexual excitement from their own suffering brought about through planned physical harm or the threat of physical punishment. Although a certain amount of biting or scratching during lovemaking can be considered normal, sadistic and masochistic behavior ranges from verbal abuse to the extremes of torture and even the planning of one's own murder. The function of receiving or inflicting pain varies among relationships: Some participants achieve orgasm during ritual while others use sadomasochistic activity merely as part of foreplay.

The more common behaviors involved in sadism and masochism include humiliation, bondage, biting, whipping, slapping, and pinching. Sadomasochistic behavior often involves the preplanned acting out of elaborate rituals that may focus on some real or imagined misdeed and the consequent physical punishment. Various devices and paraphernalia (such as tight-fitting black leather or rubber clothing, spike-heeled shoes and black net stockings, handcuffs, collars, hoods, ropes, chains, and whips) may be used as props.

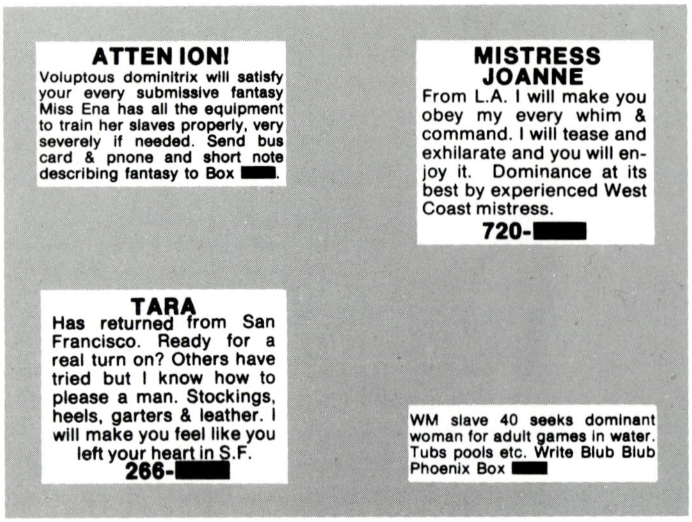

Figure 8.3. *"S & M" personal ads from a counterculture newspaper of a major city.*

Certain abnormal personality features, such as difficulty controlling hostility, seem to be common to both sadists and masochists. Indeed, sadistic and masochistic tendencies often exist side by side in the same person. These qualities usually show up first in childhood; by early adulthood most sadists and masochists have begun to display persistent patterns of deviance. If the sadist and masochist are opposite sexes, the male is most often the aggressor. In the subculture that has developed to help participants locate each other, male masochists value female sadists in particular.

Incest

Unlike the paraphilias, **incest**—sexual relations between close family members—does not represent a general sexual preference. Usually it is a matter of yielding to temptation in a particular situation. Incest most often occurs when one or both of the individuals involved have limited access to other more socially acceptable sexual outlets, or when the warmth and affection expressed within the family triggers a sexual reaction. In the vast majority of cases, of course, closeness between family members never goes beyond simple affection. But a man who feels inhibited about touching or even acting friendly toward women his own age may find it quite natural to hug and kiss his daughter. If his opportunities for sexual contact are limited or unsatisfying, he may find himself pushing this one close relationship farther than he intended. Likewise, a brother and sister who take baths together, play together, and sleep together are bound to be curious about their genitals, and they may engage in sexual exploration that could lead to incest. Incest is no longer thought to be rare, but few data are available on the subject.

The early work of Kinsey and his colleagues fails to discuss incest in any detail, and few systematic studies of this phenomenon have been conducted to date. According to Hunt (1974), brother-sister incest is more common than father-daughter incest: None of the nearly 2000 subjects Hunt interviewed reported having intercourse with a parent. The popular belief that father-daughter intercourse is the most common type may reflect the fact that most research on incest has been based on psychotherapy cases and prison samples.

Sexual intercourse between siblings seems to be neither as socially abhorrent nor as traumatic for the participants as parent-child incest. Studies by Meiselman (1978) and others suggest that sexual relations between father and daughter often result in negative long-term consequences for the daughter, especially in their effect on her subsequent relationships with men. Perhaps part of the outrage society feels about father-daughter incest stems from its similarity (in outward behavior, at least) to child molesting. The participants share the age difference of pedophilia, and they engage in most of the same sexual acts. However, the difference in initial motivation is great. Unlike the pedophile, who actively seeks the relationship, most of those involved in incest generally report that it "just happened."

Sexual relations between close family members have been punished in almost all human societies throughout history. While application of the incest taboo varies greatly from society to society, the ban on sexual relations within the nuclear family (excluding, of course, husband and wife) is virtually universal (Meiselman, 1978). The strength of this ancient prohibition in our culture today was demonstrated in 1979. *Newsweek* reported on a brother and sister who were separated as infants and adopted by different families, met again as adults, fell in love, and married. The powerful taboo on sexual relations between siblings rendered this marriage socially and legally unacceptable.

Rape

Rape is an act of violence in which a woman is forced to have sexual intercourse against her will. Although the legal definition of rape has traditionally excluded intercourse forced by a husband on his wife or by a woman on a man, these limitations have recently been challenged in some states. In a 1979 case in Oregon reported in *Time,* a woman charged her estranged husband with rape. Although the law in Oregon does define forced sexual intercourse, even with a legal spouse, as rape, the jury in this case acquitted the accused spouse. *Statutory rape* refers to intercourse with a female who is beneath the legal age of consent and is presumably incapable of making an informed choice.

Until recently, rape was assumed to be a result of uncontrollable passion; today it is understood to be an act of violent assault in which sexual arousal may play only a minor role. It also tends to be a repetitive behavior pattern rather than an isolated act. Researchers have found that 80 percent of all rapes are premeditated (Amir, 1971), and that aggression itself, rather than sexual gratification, is the major source of satisfaction for some rapists (Cohen et al., 1971). Some writers, such as Brownmiller (1975), argue that rape is an inevitable outcome of socializing males to be dominant and aggressive while socializing females to be nonassertive and nurturant.

This shift in the public perception of rape is demonstrated by the recent case of a Wisconsin judge who suggested that a young rapist should not be held entirely responsible for his actions, considering the sexual permissiveness of our society and the provocative way some women dress. This is by no means a new idea; indeed, it has contributed to the anguish of rape victims for many years. This time, though, public reaction was so negative that the judge was removed from office. It was pointed out that one might as well say a mugger should not be held entirely responsible for robbing someone at gunpoint, considering the permissiveness toward violence in our society and the fact that many wealthy men wear expensive suits that suggest they probably have fat wallets.

While there is no such thing as a "typical" rapist, studies suggest that most rapists are emotionally immature and physically unattractive young men from culturally deprived backgrounds (McCary, 1978). Usually they attack in their own neighborhood, which is typically urban. Most rapes take place at night, often in the victim's (and sometimes in the rapist's) home. In about half of all cases, the victim and the rapist are at least casual acquaintances. Forty-three percent of the rapes examined in one Philadelphia study involved more than one assailant, and in these cases the rapists were especially likely to have chosen a location in advance (Amir, 1971). The fact that 40 percent of rapists are married bolsters the view that aggression rather than sexual intercourse per se is the key factor in most rapes. Cohen and colleagues (1971) categorized rapists into three groups:

1. The *aggressive rapist,* who is interested primarily in aggression and uses sex merely to attain that goal.
2. The *inadequate rapist,* who desires sexual gratification and uses aggression as a means to achieve that goal.
3. The *psychopathic rapist,* who requires aggression to derive pleasure from sex—that is, sex is not gratifying to him unless it is in the context of rape.

Society has generally treated rape as a criminal act rather than as a mental disorder. In recent years, the number of reported rapes has increased: the FBI's statistics showed about 55,000 cases in 1974, and more than 63,000 in 1977—and these statistics probably represent only a quarter or so of the rapes that actually occur. Aside from the stigma of being a rape victim, women may fear possible reprisal from the rapist if he goes free (which he often does); and they may be unwilling to face the insensitivity, skepticism, and even harassment that have often characterized police investigations of rape. Rape crisis centers now exist in most large cities—staffed sometimes by female police officers and sometimes by independently trained counselors—to help women deal with the physical and emotional damage caused by the rape itself and the violence associated with it. These centers are also concerned with facilitating the arrest and conviction of the rapist but they try to minimize the negative emotional impact on the victim of the investigation and subsequent legal proceedings. A typical result of rape is **rape trauma syndrome** (Burgess and Holmstrom, 1974): strong feelings of fear, anxiety, guilt, and anger, accompanied by headaches, insomnia, stomach pains, and nausea. The anxiety may last long after the event, impelling the victim to move, change phone numbers, change jobs, or perhaps quit working. Although the rape trauma syndrome seems to be an unavoidable consequence of rape, counseling with a knowledgeable and supportive therapist can greatly facilitate a woman's adjustment.

Transsexualism

In **transsexualism**, gender identity—that is, the sense of being male or female—fails to coincide with sexual anatomy. The transsexual feels like a woman trapped in a man's body or a man trapped in a woman's body. DSM-III lists this as a *gender identity disorder.* Transsexuals have a long-standing dissatisfaction with their anatomic sex and wish to alter the offending genitals and live as a member of the opposite sex. A rare disorder, transsexualism has proved highly resistant to psychotherapy, and thousands of transsexuals have sought major sex reassignment surgery.

According to DSM-III, male-to-female transsexuals are estimated to greatly outnumber female-to-male transsexuals (by ratios that vary at different clinics from two to one to eight to one), but female-to-male transsexuals appear to be more psychologically and socially stable and better able to make long-range adjustments (with or without therapy) than male-to-female transsexuals. Transsexualism should not be confused with homosexuality or transvestism, although male-to-female transsexuals often go through stages of homosexuality and transvestism before deciding to seek sex-change surgery (Driscoll, 1971).

According to Money and Ehrhardt (1972), a person's gender identity is established by social and environmental influences between the ages of eighteen months and three years and is irreversible by age five or six. Many transsexuals report having been reared as members of the opposite sex—they cross-dressed as children and played mainly with children of the opposite sex. This background is not shared by all transsexuals, however (Luria and Rose, 1979). Money's assumptions also are challenged by a more recent study: A group of adult males whose genitals had failed to develop prenatally because of an inherited genetic deficiency were brought up as females from birth. Researchers found that seventeen out of eighteen made a successful shift to living as males in response to the natural biological changes that occur at puberty (Imperato-McGinley et al., 1979).

The overall failure of psychotherapy in treating transsexualism resulted in an increased demand for sex-change surgery. Several major hospitals in the United States offer a program of sex-change surgery based on careful personal assessment and preparation. After extensive psychological evaluation and counseling to weed out individuals for whom less drastic treatment might be appropriate, hormone supplements are administered to alter such secondary sex characteristics as breast development, facial hair, fat distribution, and voice quality. Some clinics require the surgery applicant to live as a member of the opposite sex for a period of six months to two years before deciding whether to go through with such expensive and major surgery.

For male-to-female transsexuals, the final phase of the sex-reassignment process is the removal of the male sex organs and their replacement with an artificial vagina. Although they remain incapable of bearing children, many are able to achieve orgasm through intercourse as women. The female-to-male transsexual usually has her breasts and sexual organs removed and may choose to have an artificial penis constructed as well. Such a penis may be used for urination and even for intercourse, but it lacks natural erectile and ejaculatory capabilities.

Many writers have expressed alarm at the proliferation of sex-change operations in recent years (for example, Stoller, 1973). Considering how little is known about the causes of transsexualism, surgery seems a drastic solution. Some researchers believe there may be a biological explanation for transsexualism. For example, Benjamin (1971) proposed that prenatal hormonal abnormalities may predispose certain individuals to a conflict in their gender identity. Nor is surgery the only successful alternative for transsexuals. One lifelong male-to-female transsexual immediately and permanently identified himself as a heterosexual male after a physician-faith healer exorcised 22 evil spirits from his body (Barlow, et al., 1977).

The popularity of gay resorts, such as this one in northern California, reflects a growing tolerance toward homosexuality.

Ego-dystonic Homosexuality

In December, 1973, the American Psychiatric Association removed **homosexuality**, the sexual preference for members of the same sex, from the official list of disorders in DSM-II. This move accorded with the long-held belief of most homosexuals (and some heterosexuals) that homosexuality is not a "sickness" but simply an alternative sexual preference. As you can imagine though, the APA's change of policy did not by any means end a controversy that has been going on for several thousand years. Public opinion on the subject still runs the gamut: At one extreme are those who cite the Bible's condemnation of homosexuals and insist that only heterosexuality is moral and healthy; at the other extreme are those militant lesbians who believe men are unnecessary, a destructive force in human life that ought to be stamped out as soon as the sperm banks are full.

DSM-III's approach to the question of homosexuality is to consider it a disorder *if* it distresses the person to the degree that he or she wants to change to a more heterosexual orientation—a condition that is referred to as **ego-dystonic homosexuality**. In keeping with our

Table 8.2 *Homosexual Relationship Patterns*

	MEN		WOMEN	
HOMOSEXUAL PARTNERSHIPS	White (574)	Black (111)	White (227)	Black (64)
1–4	1%	2%	27%	24%
5–24	8	15	57	55
25–99	17	24	13	19
100–499	32	26	2	4
500–999	15	14	0	0
1000 or more	28	19	0	0

From Bell and Weinberg, 1978.

policy of following the classification system of DSM-III, we treat ego-dystonic homosexuality as a sexual deviation. Because homosexuality is still highly controversial, as well as a source of considerable social, professional, and even sometimes legal discrimination, we have devoted a Close-up to it here.

Ego-dystonic homosexuals believe that their sexual preference—desiring partners of their own sex—is incongruent with the way they wish to be. Many seek therapy to try to change their sexual orientation; psychoanalysis, rational-emotive therapy, and various behavioral interventions may have all been tried. But whether or not mental health professionals should be involved at all in reorientation of the homosexual who wishes to become heterosexual is a highly controversial issue. Many researchers have observed that any therapies used to bring about a change in sexual orientation reflect an antihomosexual bias that is not appropriate for a psychotherapist. For instance, Davison (1976) argues that to offer sexual reorientation treatment is to reaffirm that homosexuality is a path-

Table 8.3 *Homosexual and Heterosexual Experiences*

Description of life experience to date	Men	Women
Exclusively heterosexual		
Single	53–78%	61–72%
Married	90–92	89–90
Previously married	—	75–80
Some homosexual experience	18–42	11–20
More than incidental homosexual experience	13–38	6–14
Homosexual as much as heterosexual	9–32	4–11
Mainly homosexual	7–26	3–8
Almost entirely homosexual	5–22	2–6
Exclusively homosexual	3–16	1–3

Note: Data for women apply only between ages 20 and 35; all percentages apply only to single individuals. From Kinsey et al., 1953.

Close-up: Homosexuals and Adjustment

When the APA voted in 1973 to eliminate homosexuality from its list of mental disorders, it lent tacit support to the argument that homosexuality is not pathological. However, that vote by no means disposed of the issue. A 1978 survey of 10,000 members of the APA conducted by the journal *Medical Aspects of Human Sexuality* indicates that many psychiatrists still believe that homosexuality is a disorder. Of the 2500 responses that were tabulated, 69 percent said they believed "homosexuality is usually a pathological adaptation, as opposed to a normal variation." Sizable majorities also said that homosexuals are generally less happy than heterosexuals (73 percent) and less capable of mature, loving relationships (60 percent). Seventy percent said homosexuals' problems are more a result of their own inner conflicts than of stigmatization by society.

Despite the opinions of these psychiatrists, the research tends to indicate that homosexuals manifest no greater personality maladjustment than heterosexuals. In a major study of male homosexuals, Weinberg and Williams (1974) found no evidence of significant differences in psychological well-being between homosexual and heterosexual males. Most homosexuals, it seems, are comfortable with their homosexual identity and are responsible members of society. Bell and Weinberg (1978) found that many homosexuals, especially women, form lasting interpersonal relationships with one other person. A few homosexual couples have even exchanged marriage vows, usually in ceremonies conducted by homosexual ministers, even though such marriages do not enjoy legal recognition.

A recent survey (Peplau et al., 1981) attempted to determine whether or not there were major differences between homosexual and heterosexual relationships and found them to be remarkably alike. In fact, more often than not, any differences that were discovered clustered around *gender,* not sexual preference. Women, whether lesbian or not, tended to value the same qualities in a partner and to have the same expectations about their relationship. This was true of the men as well.

In general, men and women of both camps preferred the intimacy and security of having one special partner but still found that this need conflicts with the desire for personal freedom. However, the homosexual couples, both male and female, seemed to have progressed a little further toward resolving that conflict by rejecting the traditional marriage model in which one partner (usually the male) is dominant. Homosexual relationships tended to be "best-friendships" with the addition of sex, and this seemed to lead to more equal and open partnerships.

ological condition, and he proposes that such treatment should be denied even to those who seek it. Such controversy points to a difficult ethical issue.

An alternative to changing the homosexual orientation is for individuals to become comfortable with their sexual preferences. Gay counseling groups argue that when homosexuality presents an emotional and psychological problem, it is largely because of cultural presuppositions about normal sexual behavior, and that the problems of the ego-dystonic homosexual are rooted in social and political issues rather than in pathology.

Transvestism

Mr. G., a 31-year-old traveling salesman who had been married for eight years, reported that his earliest interest in cross-dressing began at age four or five, when he would put on his mother's clothes and take them to bed. He recalled engaging in the same type of activity at age nine or ten, accompanied by sexual arousal. He also reported that while he was dating his wife prior to marriage, he would request to put on her panties, and would do so. Mrs. G. was able to recall these incidents with difficulty, and reported thinking nothing of them at the time. . . .

Mr. G.'s deviant behaviors were as follows. He would masturbate in the presence of women's clothing four and five times per week, and had been doing so almost all of his married life, and also prior to marriage. He would dress in the clothing whenever the opportunity was available, usually about half the time. For the remainder, he would fondle the clothing, which was mostly underwear. Mr. G. carried a supply of women's clothing in a shopping bag in his car. Also, he would go home during the day while his wife was working, and (he) kept another bag of clothing in the basement. He had also cross-dressed occasionally in the dressing rooms of clothing stores.

*At (this point), Mr. G. was seriously considering dissolving the marriage and becoming an open transvestite, . . . Mrs. G. had caught him (cross-dressing) three times . . . , and was reportedly shocked and amazed anew each time. She had sought psychiatric help over the matter, and had asked her husband also to go. The current treatment was seen by both as a "last-ditch" effort. Mr. G. reported that his wife was sexually conservative. . . . Mrs. G. believed that her husband was basically homosexual, (but) Mr. G. denied any homosexual interest or involvement, past or present. (Lanyon, 1979, pp. 5–7)**

In **transvestism** an individual—typically a man—achieves sexual arousal from dressing as a member of the opposite sex. The extent of such cross-dressing may range from occasionally wearing feminine undergarments under masculine clothes to completely cross-dressing in order to pass as a woman and participate in group activities with other transvestites. Most transvestites don their feminine garments secretly, usually at home, so that part of the excitement may be the thrill of doing something "forbidden." There is no evidence that women derive sexual stimulation from dressing as men, but then wearing masculine clothes is socially acceptable for women and is quite common.

Because transvestism is an uncommon disorder, it has not been studied widely enough for much reliable information to be available. As with other disorders, all that was known about it for many years was what therapists learned from their patients. In the early seventies, however, several studies (Buckner, 1970; Prince and Bentler, 1972) examined data from broader sources. One such source was subscribers to the magazine *Transvestia.* These reports turned up a number of interesting points. Most transvestites (89 percent) are heterosexual and either are or have been married (78 percent); about two thirds of married transvestites have children. Sometimes their wives find their cross-dressing upsetting enough to ask for a divorce, but more than half the wives accept or at least tolerate such predilections. (Here the nature of the sample may affect the data—presumably a man whose wife is distressed about his transvestism is less likely to subscribe to a magazine on the subject than one whose wife accepts it.) They come from a variety of social, educational, and religious backgrounds, and they work in a wide range of occupations. Their personalities do not appear to be much different from other men's, although other research suggests they are somewhat more controlled and reserved than average.

Transvestites often report that they were forced as children to wear girls' clothing, either as a punishment or because they looked "so cute." Some transvestites have had only limited and not very successful experience with women; some suffer from erectile failure. A fairly common case is the transvestite who at first becomes aroused by partial cross-dressing but gradually shifts toward complete dressing in women's clothes in order to feel sexually stimulated. He may find eventually that even as the behavior

* Reprinted by permission of the author.

A new bellhop at the Plaza Hotel in New York City and a "drag queen" in Provincetown, Massachusetts. For several decades women have enjoyed more freedom than men have in their choice of everyday apparel. While tailored pants and shirts are considered socially acceptable and stylish on women, a man dressed in female attire is regarded as deviant.

increases in frequency, it is no longer exciting and functions only as an antidote to anxiety.

EXPLAINING AND MANAGING SEXUAL DEVIATIONS

Attempting to explain the development of sexual variations, Freud theorized that all humans start life "polymorphously perverse," meaning that as infants they can receive sexual gratification from many sources. According to Freud, many of these sources of gratification are eliminated as the child develops, until the source of sexual gratification for the psychosexually mature adult is limited to heterosexual intercourse. However, fixation at an early stage of development—oral, anal, or phallic—prevents the early sources of gratification from consolidating into the adult genital stage, and this may result in the desire to use an abnormal stimulus for sexual gratification. Freud further postulated that when a person represses unresolved developmental conflicts, such conflicts manifest themselves through the development of either a neurosis or a sexual variation. This psychoanalytic theory of abnormalities is based on hypothesized processes and states that cannot be objectively measured, and it lacks empirical support.

In recent years, learning explanations for the development of deviant behavior have begun to gain acceptance. It was originally suggested that a person learns an abnormal pattern of sexual behavior from one such experience—the erotic success of the experience provides reinforcement, so that the person repeats the behavior. For example, a man happens to pass a window where a woman is undressing; he finds the sight stimulating and begins to seek out similar situations. A revision of this theory argues that it is not the original deviant experience that causes a pattern of deviation to develop but rather the person's masturbation to a memory or fantasy of that particular event (McGuire et al., 1965). That is, the man's first sight of a woman undressing provides fantasy or memory material, which he later uses as a stimulus when he masturbates; thus the fantasized stimulus of woman-in-window receives the powerful reinforcement of sexual arousal and orgasm. Basing their conclusions on a sample of 45 patients, these researchers speculated that the original incident was often the first real sexual experience for these individuals and that it therefore had strong stimulus value. They noted, furthermore, that fantasy or memory stimuli for masturbation need not exactly repeat the original experience. Any negative heterosexual experiences or feelings of social or sexual inadequacy could contribute to the development of the deviant pattern and cause the individual to believe that a normal sex life was not possible.

Individuals who practice sexual variations may seek treatment for any of several reasons. Some feel guilty about their behavior; others are concerned about negative effects on their family and social relationships or their professional standing; still others choose therapy as an alternative to criminal prosecution or imprisonment. The primary treatment used to be traditional psychoanalysis, which views the problem as one of basic personality organization. Unfortunately, psychodynamic therapy has had little success in treating sexual disorders.

Concurrent with the increased popularity of behaviorism, behavior therapies have received considerable emphasis, and they have shown remarkable success.

Mr. A. was a middle-aged man with a stable marriage, a responsible job, and three children aged 17 to 22. I worked with him for fifteen once-weekly sessions, ten with Mr. A. alone, one with his wife alone, and four with husband and wife together.

When I saw Mr. A. for the first time, he had recently been arrested. His molesting impulses had diminished somewhat but were still present. . . .

In order to reduce the cues for molesting, Mr. A. agreed to my request to stay away from the major stimulus situation—that is, [to stay away from] shopping centers when alone. We then began the aversive imagery procedure, of which the first step is training in deep muscle relaxation. Mr. A. reached an adequate level of relaxation skill after daily practice at home for two weeks. The imagery was then begun. To do this, the therapist and patient together agree in advance on two images to use, and [then] work out exact details for each of them. In Mr. A.'s molesting image he had a girl in a car, and could feel himself becoming erect. In the aversive image, two policemen poked their guns in the window of the car, arrested him, and took him off in their car. The aversive image is always presented as soon as the molesting image is vivid, and dismissed as soon as substantial fear is aroused. When the sequence was vivid for Mr. A., after a half-hour of training in my office, he was asked to practice it daily at home for half an hour. He was to vary both images, using other similar situations. In doing this, he was told to work out the imagined details in advance and then to systematically relive them, like a vivid dream.

After several sequences at home with a particular molesting image, he usually became unable to create it again. At that point he was instructed to shift to an image [that] he could imagine vividly. Over a period of several weeks, it became more and more difficult for him to get molesting impulses in imagery. When it became practically impossible to develop a molesting image, Mr. A. was told to use any possible thoughts or memory that might lead to an image. After about five [more] weeks the impulses were completely extinguished. . . .

The next task for Mr. A. was to begin deliberately trying to experience a molesting thought or impulse in real life. He was instructed to attempt to do so in "safe" situations; for example, when riding in a bus, or when walking along the street with his wife. Whenever he developed a thought or im-

*pulse he was instructed to follow it immediately with the most highly aversive image he could achieve. After three weeks of daily practice, Mr. A. was completely unable to generate any molesting impulses no matter how hard he tried. At this point, therefore, I instructed him to return to the original shopping center and to try to develop an impulse there. He was instructed to initially have his wife nearby, and gradually have her remain further and further away as he showed himself unable to generate molesting impulses. If he experienced the slightest impulse, he was instructed to punish it swiftly. He experienced no impulses, no matter how hard he tried. . . . Four months later, there had still been no impulses. (Lanyon, 1978, pp. 9–13)**

Behavior therapies focus on the immediate problem; they try to eliminate the problematic behavior as directly as possible and ensure that it does not recur. To eliminate the undesired behavior, therapists have typically relied upon counterconditioning, in which presentation of the unwanted erotic stimulus is accompanied by an aversive event. This breaks the chain: The deviant sexual stimulus is no longer reinforced by sexual arousal and orgasm because it is linked instead to punishment. An alternative strategy is covert sensitization, in which the individual's mental imagery provides both the stimulating scene and the aversive response (Barlow et al., 1969; Callahan and Leitenberg, 1973). For example, a voyeur might imagine being caught in the act by an enraged husband, arrested, scorned by his family and friends, and sent to prison.

Wickramasekera (1972, 1976) developed a variant of the aversive strategies for use with some exhibitionists. In **aversive behavior rehearsal**, the patient exposes himself in the clinic at a preplanned time and place to staff who know him. During the exposure, the therapist asks the patient to report his feelings, fantasies, and physical responses. In this way, the fantasies that inspire exhibitionistic behavior can be brought out and demythologized. Wickramasekera reports that this approach has been used with twenty patients, with no reported relapses for up to seven years. Using a variant of covert sensitization, Maletzky (1980a, b) has also had remarkable success in changing exhibitionist behavior.

The next step is to condition the deviant to a new, more appropriate way to obtain sexual gratification. This is extremely important since, if no new behavior replaces the old one, chances are very good that the person will soon start to respond to the same deviant stimuli that caused trouble before. Therefore therapist and client must together decide on what new acceptable behavior will be instituted, and then, through the principles of respondent and operant conditioning, the behavior becomes a conditioned response.

Orgasmic reconditioning (Marquis, 1970) is a one-step process to eliminate the old habits and to ensure that the patient can obtain sexual arousal from the appropriate stimuli. The person masturbates to mental imagery of the deviant stimulus until just before orgasm, and then he switches his masturbatory fantasy to one involving appropriate imagery. If the imagery is switched on the brink of orgasm, the individual is not likely to lose his arousal, and the socially acceptable imagery can begin to acquire arousing quality. The switch from the deviant to the normal imagery is gradually moved back to earlier and earlier points in the arousal process until appropriate imagery, and not deviant imagery, creates arousal.

Any successful behavior change strategy must ensure that the individual has the ability and the opportunity to obtain sexual gratification from normal, socially acceptable relationships; otherwise the undesired behavior may recur or another undesired pattern of behavior may develop. Behavior therapy for the sexual variations therefore often includes teaching appropriate social and sexual skills; it also attempts to reduce the patient's anxiety. These methods have not succeeded in all cases, but so far they have had more positive results than any other treatment strategy. In fact, behavior therapy has had remarkable success in treating sexual disorders, and it is now almost universally used.

* Reprinted by permission of the author.

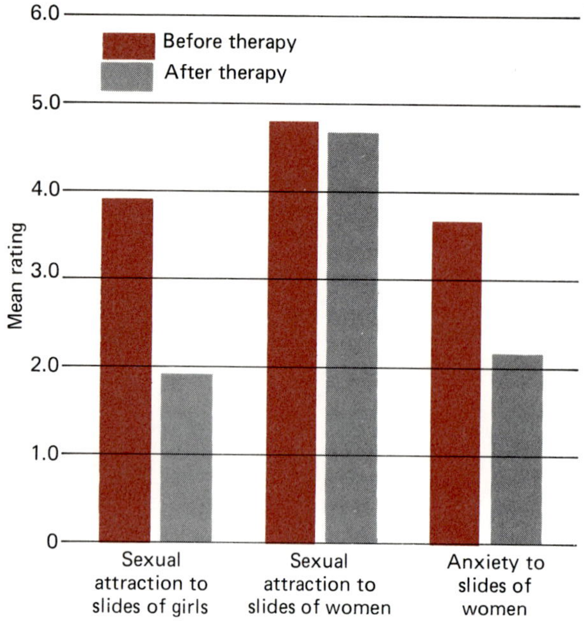

Figure 8.4. *Effectiveness of therapy on a pedophile's attraction to women and girls. From Levin et al., 1977.*

SUMMARY

Before Kinsey conducted his scientific inquiry into human sexual practices, very little was known about normal human sexuality. Masters and Johnson went even further in dispelling the many myths surrounding sexual behavior by conducting scientific laboratory studies of the human sexual response. Largely as a result of these efforts, the discipline of sex therapy has emerged to help people understand sex and deal with the problems related to it.

Sexual problems may be grouped into two broad categories: **dysfunctions** and **deviations**. Sexual dysfunctions result from a disruption in the natural flow of arousal through the phases of excitement, plateau, orgasm, and resolution. Dysfunctions that are not attributable to physical causes often involve a problem in the relationship between the partners. Masters and Johnson developed an effective treatment program for couples that is based on a series of graduated assignments that teach the partners first to communicate with each other and then to overcome their dysfunction through the use of specific techniques.

Sexual deviations are sexual variations considered to be abnormal and maladaptive by social and legal standards. There are many diverse sexual deviations. This chapter focused on eleven: voyeurism, exhibitionism, pedophilia (child molesting), fetishism, sadism, masochism, incest, rape, transsexualism, ego-dystonic homosexuality, and transvestism. Unlike dysfunctions, deviations involve an inappropriate choice of sexual object or goal. The concept of "appropriate" sexual behavior, however, is largely determined by cultural bias, and what is considered "perverted" in one culture may be considered perfectly acceptable in another. The forms of sexual deviance discussed usually involves compulsive behavior that serves as the individual's primary source of arousal or gratification. A man who is "turned on" by stroking a woman's hair is therefore not a fetishist, nor is the woman who enjoys being spanked during foreplay therefore a masochist.

Although many attempts have been made to explain the origins of sexual deviance, no simple answers have been found. The Freudian notions of fixation at an early developmental stage or an unresolved Oedipal (or Electra) complex cannot be validated. Psychoanalysis has also had little success at reorganizing personalities in order to solve sexual difficulties or change sexual preferences. Some learning theorists maintain that repeated masturbation to a memory or fantasy of an early image or experience serves to reinforce the erotic value associated with that particular stimulus; thus the individual learns to associate arousal and sexual gratification with inappropriate stimuli. No therapeutic strategy has proved universally successful at treating deviations, but various forms of behavior therapy have been very effective. Whether or not any deviant behavior performed in private by consenting adults should be a matter of social and legal concern remains an unresolved issue. There are also sensitive ethical issues related to treatment.

Conversation 3

The two young women in this interview, Ali and Candi, are lovers, a fact that has not made their life together easy. They live in an East Coast city that prides itself on being avant-garde and broad-minded, yet the true nature of their relationship is best kept secret from family and colleagues. Their professional worlds are different—Candi is a corporation administrator and Ali is a scientific researcher—but they've found many people in both who may not accept them if they "come out of the closet." Despite these problems, their relationship has lasted more than two years, and they are confident that it will last much longer still.

Interviewer: When did you recognize that you were not heterosexual?

Ali: I had considered myself heterosexual until I found myself acting upon my feelings with a woman, and that really floored me.

Candi: I disagree with labels. I guess you'd say I'm a homosexual biphile, a person who loves both sexes but tends to respond right this minute to one of the same sex.

Int.: Do your families know?

Candi: They have not been told in so many words.

Int.: What is their attitude toward homosexuality?

Ali: It's frowned upon.

Candi: God forbid their children should be homosexual! My mother is not concerned about me or herself but her image: What would the neighbors think?

Ali: I think my father would be concerned with religion. My mother would be disappointed because she would have liked me to get married and have kids.

Int.: Do your colleagues know?

Ali: They definitely suspected. The only people from whom I receive telephone calls are females, and I don't play Monday morning pronouns.

Candi: *Monday Morning Pronouns* is a film about how gay women have to say "he and I" instead of "she and I" to remain in the closet. I have told my closest female associate. I work in a very conservative company where successful women are automatically labeled "queer." I think that if I were out I would be discriminated against, although it would be very difficult to prove.

Int.: Your lives are very restricted.

Ali: Only within work, and I guess I'm saying that for Candi because when I came out at work, for a little while people said, "Oh!" and now we're back to our usual routines.

Candi: Well, I don't feel all that restricted by not being out in my professional life. That fact doesn't stop me from being the person I am, and I'm not going to change. If I were straight I wouldn't tell everybody at work about my private life.

Int.: What are lesbian bars like?

Ali: I just shy away from bars in general. Some of them are meat racks.

Candi: I'm not so sure of that. I've been going for ten years; it was an after-meeting thing to do if you were a member of the Daughters of Bilitis. Like singles' bars, people do a lot of looking, but I would say that there's more to it than just sex. Men may look for the one-night stands and the purely sexual relationship; I don't think women do. If you're asking me are they like a straight bar, no. Women who aren't comfortable with their own sexuality are going to feel threatened.

Int.: How do the women react when men come in?

Ali: I remember one time: The whole place quieted down, all eyes stared at this male and there were a lot of whispers—"What's a man doing here?" But it makes a difference if he's accompanied by an obvious gay couple.

Candi: I would feel violated. There are all sorts of men's clubs where women are not welcome. Well, turn about is fair play, and we deserve space that's just ours as much as they do! Also there's the feeling that a straight man is just looking for the big notch on his belt, you know? There's always that feeling about women: All a woman needs is a good lay, and a lesbian needs a better one. So making a lesbian is a big thing for a man. I would feel very threatened if a straight man came in on the make.

Int.: Are your friends predominantly homosexual?

Ali: Most of them are straight but among them are a couple of gays. Most of my closest friends are women, but there are a couple of men friends in there, too.

Candi: Mine are fifty-fifty lesbian and feminist. Most of my friends are straight. I don't know any gay men; I don't particularly like them. Maybe I've met the wrong sort, but the ones I meet more or less caricature femininity rather than being the people they are.

Int.: What do you see as the primary differences between gay men and lesbians?

Candi: Gay men look for sex and lesbians look for relationships.

Int.: In most studies of the male homosexual world, this seems to be true—until they get older.

Ali: The two gay friends with whom I've spoken at length about this say it is true about other men.

Candi: A young straight man is expected to sow his oats for a certain length of time, but I think that time is longer in the gay world—as long as they can keep their looks. But I think that as gay men get older they acquire the courage and self-confidence to defy the cultural norms, which are sex for sex's sake, the one-night stands, and the idealization of youth. They can see the fallacy and the frustration inherent in that kind of philosophy.

Int.: Where do you see yourselves five years from now?

Ali: We're both thinking of moving someplace out in the country.

Int.: But doesn't that mean confronting the silent majority?

Candi: Oh, but that's not true! I know of a number of women who live together, and one of them dresses completely in "drag": man's haircut, suit, tie, shirt, shoes. She is regarded as eccentric, but in the country you get a lot more acceptance for eccentricity than you do in the city.

Ali: In addition, I think that economic pressures are making it a lot easier for people of the same sex to live together, to buy a house together.

Candi: It's always been OK for two women to be roommates. Well, if they happen to buy real estate together, then they're just a little more economically aware. But women aren't taken seriously in this culture so there's less censure than there would be if two men bought property together. Two women who live together are considered "marking time" until husbands appear.

Int.: What's the hardest part about keeping your true relationship secret?

Ali: Exactly that. You can't bubble over with enthusiasm about certain things.

Candi: Your self-esteem suffers. You can't be accepted as just who you are.

Int.: How do you compensate for this?

Candi: Get angry!

Int.: Do you take it out on each other occasionally?

Candi: Yes, I'm sure we did. But now we're becoming more aware of the sources of our anger so it's happening less frequently.

Int.: Do you think there will come a time when you can be more open?

Ali: I think the time is coming closer and closer when I'm going to tell my family because I am so sick of playing games and I like being open with them.

Candi: My mother is 70; there's no sense in telling her because verbalizing it would only upset her. I have her complete acceptance without being overt.

Ali: The only way we can come out is when it is legal to come out. For example, gay people cannot get government security clearance because they can be blackmailed for being gay. If they're out they can't be blackmailed, but since being gay is not legal, they can be fired for blackmail potential: the classic Catch 22.

Candi: It's also against the law for two people of the same sex to be married. I remember a test case in which a male couple tried to get married for tax and inheritance considerations and couldn't. So the older male partner adopted the younger. Well, the courts overturned it, because they said it's a farce to adopt someone over 21.

Int.: What do you think is better about your relationship than a heterosexual relationship?

Candi: Well, for me it's that women sharing a common cultural background tend to be more aware of the things that men deny them or put them down for.

Ali: I would answer that I have found in Candi those qualities that I was looking for in a person. I think we complement each other very nicely.

Candi: We like our strengths instead of harping on each other's weaknesses. You know, I can find all those same good qualities in a man, but he's going to be threatened by them in me. I think men have a long way to go before they accept women as equals. Of course, there are still women who have relationships based on gender identification. I had a relationship with a woman who insisted on carrying the groceries because she was "butch" and I was "femme" and therefore it wasn't my role. It didn't last long.

Ali: We keep switching roles. Candi uses the word "androgynous" for it.

Candi: I think we are not representative of the kind of woman who discovers early in her life that she likes just women; we look for qualities rather than gender. I have known since I was seven that I like women sexually, but that doesn't mean I like men any less. I had a predominantly straight woman lover once who said, "It just boils down to enjoying sex. It doesn't matter what the plumbing is." For Ali and me, it just boils down to enjoying each other.

CHAPTER 9

Drug Abuse Disorders

On every corner there's a man who stands
And waits for guys like me
And I can bet that he's got everything I need
He can keep me awake
Or he can make me fall asleep
He can almost bring the stars within my reach
Pantomime . . .
I get so high that I can't make words rhyme
So on that note I don't bother trying
Nothing matters when you're flying
Border line
It all depends upon your state of mind
But lately I've been more than less inclined
to get blown away.

Allen Estes, "Blown Away"*

Throughout history, people have experimented with mind-affecting substances that they believed would help them to have fun, calm down, wake up, fall asleep, or explore the perimeters of their perceptions. The study of these substances and of the physiological, psychological, and social disorders associated with their use and misuse are primary topics of public and private research in the United States today.

The term *drugs* as used in this context is a common name for chemical substances that are known to alter mood, consciousness, or perception in human users. In this chapter, we shall investigate the use of **psychoactive** (mind-altering) drugs, specifically alcohol, barbiturates, tranquilizers, amphetamines, cocaine, heroin, marijuana, hallucinogens, and nicotine.

Drugs are newsmakers. Demographic studies and surveys by public and private research services chart the use of drugs in the United States as carefully as the popularity of political candidates, and information on various drugs is plentiful. Nearly 25 million people admit to having tried marijuana, and millions more use stimulants and tranquilizers without prescription. Cocaine has become a very popular drug—and a particularly expensive habit. Heroin users are blamed for a high percentage of the petty crimes in the United States. Yet by far the most widely used drugs are the legal ones: nicotine and alcohol.

In a drug-centered culture such as our own, drug use surely cannot be considered abnormal behavior—as long as the use is moderate and there are no apparent harmful consequences for users and the people around them. But millions of people do suffer harmful consequences or inflict harm on other people as a result of drug abuse. And public opinion about drugs tends to be contradictory—seeming acceptance of drug use, public censuring of drug abusers. Our society's definitions of the problem are inconsistent. Are drug abusers weak, lazy people who refuse to take control of their own lives, or are they physically ill? Should they be sent to jail or mental hospitals? Are they victims of impoverished, unstable, or repressed environments who should be nourished back to health? Each school of thought has its defenders—and the drug user who seeks help will thus find a bewildering variety of attitudes and treatment philosophies. Nonetheless, we can pin down some basic facts about the psychoactive drugs and the people who use them.

DEFINING DRUG ABUSE

Most people can use drugs solely for occasional diversion without experiencing more than temporary consequences—perhaps an evening of relaxation or heightened awareness, sometimes a little more than that. DSM-III offers these guidelines for the onset of **drug abuse:**

1. The use of a substance persists for over a month.
2. Its use affects a person's ability to function in the family or larger social setting or on the job.
3. The pattern of use can be seen as pathological—that is, excessive or uncontrolled.

Drug abusers believe that drugs are essential to their ability to function, which is the reason they take the drug, not necessarily because of any physical need. This psychological need is termed **dependence.** By the time users become dependent on the drug, they have often become

Table 9.1 *Major Psychoactive Drugs*

Drug Group	Type of drug	Legal status	Major effects	Psychological dependence potential	Addiction potential	Tolerance potential	Overall abuse potential	Withdrawal problems
Alcohol	Depressant	Legally available	Euphoria, drowsiness, impaired motor function and sensory perception, slowed reaction time	High	High	Yes	High	Moderate
Major tranquilizers (sedatives, barbiturates, Quaaludes)	Depressant	Legally available only by prescription	Drowsiness, impaired motor function and sensory perception, slowed reaction time	High	High	Yes	High	Severe
Minor tranquilizers (Valium, Librium)	Depressant	Legally available only by prescription		Moderate	Moderate	Yes	Moderate	Moderate
Heroin, morphine, methadone	Depressant	Some are strictly illegal; others are legally available only by prescription	Euphoria, drowsiness	High	High	Yes	High	Moderate to severe
Cocaine	Stimulant	Strictly illegal	Intense stimulation, excitation, talkativeness, insomnia	Moderate	Possible	Possible	Moderate	Mild
LSD, PCP, mescaline	Hallucinogen	Strictly illegal; sometimes available for scientific research	Illusions, hallucinations, euphoric, distorted time sense	Minimal	None	Yes	Minimal	Mild
Marijuana	Unclassified	Illegal in most states; sometimes available for scientific research	Euphoria, distorted time sense, drowsiness, increased appetite	Moderate	Unknown	Possible	Moderate	Mild
Amphetamines	Stimulant	Legally available by prescription	Hyperactivity, excitation, nervousness, insomnia, decreased appetite	High	Possible	Yes	High	Mild
Nicotine	Has both depressant and stimulant properties	Legally available	Combination; both calming and exciting	High	Moderate	Yes	High	Moderate

addicted as well. **Addiction** represents a physiological need: The user's body has reached the point of **habituation** to the drug (resistant to its effects at a certain dose) so that even greater doses are required to obtain the desired effect. In this way, the user develops increasing **tolerance** for the drug. If the drug use is discontinued after addiction has been attained, **withdrawal** occurs, during which the user experiences a variety of unpleasant or painful effects, ranging from headaches and nervousness after withdrawal from nicotine, to convulsions and hallucinations after withdrawal from alcohol or heroin.

Not all drugs are addictive. As far as we know for sure, regular users of cocaine, hallucinogens, and perhaps marijuana do not develop tolerance to these drugs, although they can become dependent on them. However, most of the other drugs we shall discuss in this chapter do lead to addiction as well as dependence. The development of addiction depends a lot, of course, on the size and strength of the dose taken. Doses are categorized as effective, toxic, or lethal, depending on the user's reaction to them. An *effective dose* provides the user with the desired effect; a *toxic dose* may provide the desired effect, at least initially, but also causes undesired side effects, such as convulsions or unconsciousness; a *lethal dose* kills.

Our discussion of drug abuse is divided into three sections: a description of the types of drugs and their effects on the human body; the explanations for abuse offered by various schools of thought; and a survey of the methods for managing these disorders. For ease of explanation, we have grouped the drugs together in three categories: depressants, stimulants, and distortive drugs.

Depressants

Depressants have a sedating effect on the central nervous system. They reduce anxiety and tension, and they sometimes induce sleep. Tolerance to depressants develops very quickly, which means that the dose must be continually increased in order to achieve the desired effect. Unfortunately, all of the depressants—including alcohol, the narcotics, and the barbiturates—are addictive when used regularly, and withdrawal from them is likely to be difficult.

Alcohol

This man that I see, we've talked about it. If he's alone, he doesn't drink, and when we're out he tries, though I know it sounds patronizing, to get me off of it. He'll say, "You don't really need another one, do you?" The other night, this crazy thing happened. I wanted a drink and so we went to this bar and it was late, after a movie, and it was closed. So we went to this other place where they knew us and it was closed too, so we knocked on the door to see if they'd let us in. But there was no answer. So we went around to the kitchen because we knew the cook and we asked him to let us in. But he wouldn't and we started to get a little bit . . . pushy. Finally, it dawned on me what we were doing. I turned to my friend and I said, "Hey, are we alcoholics or something, we got to have a drink?" He said, "Yeah, it's pretty pathetic, isn't it?" (Langone and Langone, 1980, pp. 41–44.)*

It is obvious that the young woman in this case has a problem—a drinking problem. She is not alone. Conservative estimates suggest that there are ten million Americans with the same need for alcohol; other estimates go as high as seventeen million. Of these, roughly one-fourth are alcoholics on the order of Jack Lemmon and Lee Remick in *The Days of Wine and Roses:* tormented by the need to drink, unmindful of anything but the bottle, satisfied only when completely inebriated, gradually experiencing fewer and fewer sober periods. The other three-fourths are spread out on a continuum of dependence: Some need only one drink a day; others have needs similar to those of the girl described here; but all of them need alcohol to keep going.

Interestingly, only a small percentage of problem drinkers (3 to 5 percent) fit the stereotype of the "skid-row drunk." The remainder

* Reprinted from *Women Who Drink* by John and Dolores Langone, © 1980, with permission from Addison-Wesley Publishing Co.

An anti-alcohol poster circulated during the nineteenth-century temperance movement.

are generally decent, respectable, middle-class citizens, with nice homes, good jobs, and loving families. How did these otherwise fortunate people get caught on such a terrible treadmill?

History and prevalence. Alcohol can claim the longest known history of any addictive drug. Humans apparently discovered alcohol early in their evolutionary development; archeologists have established its presence in all but three prehistoric cultures. As ancient written records indicate, modern humans are simply carrying out an old tradition: enjoying the effect of alcohol but not knowing how to control it.

History has witnessed many efforts to curtail the use of alcohol. Perhaps the most well known was the American Volstead Act of 1919, which made the sale of alcoholic beverages illegal and thus ushered in the Prohibition Era. During the next decade, the national fondness for drinking fostered the reactionary development of a highly organized—and illegal—supply network not unlike the present drug supply network. This attempt at enforced control ultimately failed: In 1933, the manufacture and sale of alcoholic beverages were legalized again and placed under the jurisdiction of state governments. Today, it is an $83-million-a-year industry.

Drinking alcoholic beverages is a generally accepted part of the social routine for most Americans. Although drunkenness—behaving wildly or stupidly, passing out, or becoming ill—is not usually rewarded, it is often overlooked or forgiven, especially among young drinkers, a group that grows alarmingly more numerous every year. Many young people see that their parents' social lives center on liquor; not surprisingly, they want to find ways to imitate this adult behavior.

Today's social acceptance of drinking—and the refusal to recognize it for the social problem it is—have made alcohol the most abused drug in the United States. Since 1971, the per capita consumption of alcohol for those fourteen and older has climbed to an average of 2.69 gallons per year. Seven percent of the 145 million adults (over eighteen) are alcoholics. Approximately 205,000 alcohol-related deaths occur each year, especially motor vehicle accidents (National Institute on Alcoholism and Alcohol Abuse, 1978).

Nevertheless most alcoholics somehow lead what appear to be normal lives. It is estimated that 6 percent of the American work force are alcoholics; American business loses twenty billion dollars annually to the decreased productivity that results and to treatment and rehabilitation programs. The sickness and accident benefits paid to alcoholics by company insurance programs are three times greater than those paid to the average worker.

The most common abusers of alcohol tend to shift with trends in overall drug use. In the late 1960s and early 1970s adolescents preferred other drugs, but they have recently returned to alcohol. Globetti (1977) found that by the seventh grade, 63 percent of the boys and 54 percent of the girls had already used alcohol. By the twelfth grade, these percentages were 93 percent and 87 percent, respectively; 5 percent reported becoming intoxicated at least once a week, and 23 percent did so four to five times a year. Nineteen percent of youths between 14 and 17 years old are classified as problem drinkers.

Although more publicity is given to the drinking problems of American young people, many of the elderly also have a significant problem, particularly elderly males. People over 60 years old make up approximately 10 percent of those treated in alcoholism programs, and it is estimated that fully 10 percent of the elderly male population of the United States are addicted to alcohol.

Studies indicate that more alcoholics live in urban areas than in rural areas. They are also more likely to be divorced or separated from their spouses. Alcohol-related problems underlie about 20 percent of all the divorce cases in the United States. Unemployment and low socioeconomic status are also more common among alcoholics than among the general population, but no study has yet shown a correlation between these trends and the inherent difficulties of maintaining a life-style whose primary activities are securing a supply of liquor and getting drunk.

Defining alcoholism. A person can drink frequently—even every day—and become drunk occasionally without being an alcoholic. **Alcoholism** is drinking that impairs life adjustment in terms of health, personal relationships, and/or occupational functioning. People who are alcoholics have no control over their drinking; once they begin, they continue until intoxicated (Chafetz and Demone, 1962; Plaut, 1967). DSM-III specifies that alcohol dependence consists of long-term, pathological use that frequently results in lack of control during intoxication, and impairment of social and occupational functioning.

Alcoholism can be approached in many ways, a useful method being to view it as a progressive illness with stages of increasing deterioration. Jellinek proposed a four-stage model based on his study of 2000 male alcoholics. In the *prealcoholic* or *symptomatic phase* (1952, 1971), drinkers are impressed by alcohol's ability to relieve tension and, believing that they have more than a fair share of troubles, may justify drinking for that reason. Eventually, after months or even years, drinkers come to rely more and more on alcohol to cope with tension, and drinking becomes a daily habit.

In the next stage, the *prodromal* phase of alcoholism, drinkers experience **blackouts,** or loss of memory, following intoxication, probably because they are now more susceptible to the effects of alcohol. They may begin to drink in secret, stocking up on their alcohol supply to ensure that they are not caught short. Drinkers also begin to gulp down—rather than sip—their liquor. And, as a manifestation of guilt, they avoid conversations about drinking.

Drinkers progressing through these stages abstain less often, become less able to control intake, and show more and more physical symptoms. By the time the *crucial phase* has set in, whatever psychological problems precipitated the use of alcohol have become unimportant. Such people drink until they are too intoxicated or too sick to drink any more. But even at this stage, they can still decide not to take a drink at all and will often go "on the wagon" for short periods. The longer periods of intoxication usually affect work performance and attendance, perhaps even resulting in job loss—or at least provoking angry ultimatums from the boss.

Some physiological changes now appear. There is a loss of appetite, since long-term alcohol consumption leads to disinterest in food. Malnutrition becomes a very real danger. There is also a phenomenon called the "alcohol jealousy syndrome": For example, the drinking husband may blame his now poor sexual appetite and performance on the imagined infidelity of his wife. Late in the crucial phase, alcoholics begin drinking in the morning in order to steady themselves.

During the *chronic phase,* alcoholics are often drunk all day, for days at a time, to a point of total incapacitation. They may drink *anything* to get drunk, including hair tonic, rubbing alcohol, and even mouthwash. Because of the deterioration of the liver by this time, the alcohol is easily absorbed into the system and immediate intoxication is possible. Alcoholics *must* drink now; otherwise, they will be besieged by indefinable fears and uncontrollable tremors, which occur during periods of sobriety. Rational thought processes begin to break down, although even at this late stage some alcoholics may realize the hopelessness of their condition and seek medical or psychological help.

Jellinek's categories are by no means rigid or all-inclusive. Some individuals completely bypass the prealcoholic phase and become "instant" alcoholics. Some people who drink only occasionally nonetheless report having occasional blackouts. And some alcoholics are capable of abstaining for very long periods—but will suddenly respond to stress by drinking until they wind up in a hospital or jail. Despite such variations, classification of alcoholism into stages is extremely helpful in simplifying the problem of management.

Effects of alcohol. Although alcohol is a depressant—that is, it has a sedating effect on the central nervous system—its first effects are often stimulating. Initially it quickens certain physiological processes, such as heartbeat and cellular activity; at the same time, it suppresses those parts of the brain that inhibit responses, thus causing psychological stimulation. But as alcohol reaches and affects more areas of the nervous system, it begins to behave more like a depressant. It slows heartbeat and cellular activity, constricts blood vessels, and deadens the appetite. It also impairs vision, speech, coordination, and balance—the familiar signs of intoxication—and confuses or distorts thought. Its stimulating abilities may be the reason for alcohol's popularity, especially at social gatherings. But its depressing powers are what people who overindulge actually get.

Unlike foods, alcohol can be absorbed into the blood not only from the small intestine but also from the stomach, rectum, and lungs. Once absorbed, the alcohol travels in the blood until it is *oxidized*—that is, combined with oxygen to make other chemicals, such as water and carbon dioxide. The liver is the major oxidizing organ, but the lungs also process a small amount of the blood alcohol, which allows police to gauge a person's level of intoxication by measuring the alcohol content of the air that is exhaled. The rates of absorption and metabolism, and ultimately the specific effects of the drug, depend on such variables as how much was drunk and how quickly; the presence and type of food in the digestive tract; the drinker's weight, rate of metabolism, and liver condition; and the form of the alcohol itself. Wine and beer are absorbed more slowly than hard liquor, such as whisky and vodka; and liquor, in turn is absorbed more slowly when diluted with water and more rapidly when diluted with carbonated liquids.

The liver oxidizes alcohol slowly, about one-half ounce (the amount in a full ounce of 100-proof liquor) per hour. The unmetabolized quantity left circulating in the blood is what causes persistent and increasingly severe physiological and psychological reactions. Alcohol abuse eventually damages the liver, causing it

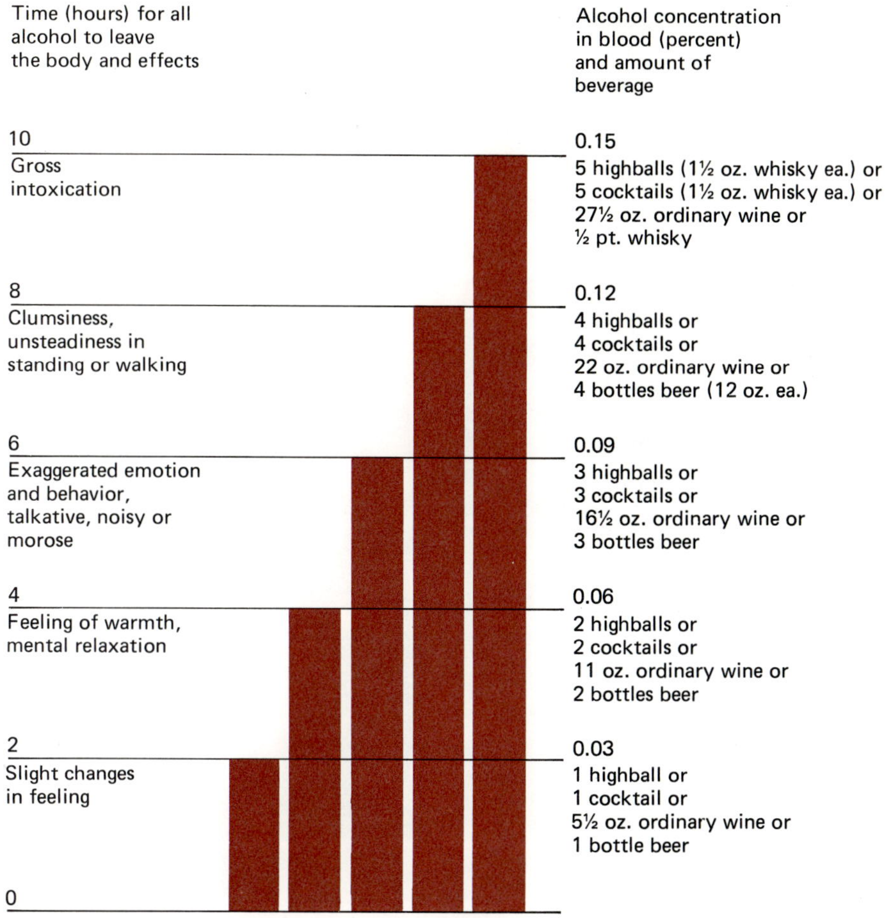

Figure 9.1. *Alcohol levels in the blood of a 150-lb. person after drinking on an empty stomach. From Hortens, 1974.*

to oxidize the drug even more slowly, so that intoxication lasts longer.

Problem drinkers develop a tolerance for alcohol as their systems become habituated to the drug. To obtain the desired physical and psychological effects, they must thus consume increasingly large amounts of alcohol. During periods of abstinence, when the blood alcohol level decreases, they suffer the **withdrawal syndrome.** Typical withdrawal symptoms range from a craving for alcohol, muscle tremors, weakness, excessive perspiration, and anxiety in cases of moderate addiction, to appetite loss, nausea, fever, convulsions, hallucinations, and **delirium tremens** (an acute psychosis, also called the DT's) in more severe cases. The nausea, fatigue, shakiness, and headache of the infamous hangover, suffered by even the casual drinker after intoxication, may be a mild form of withdrawal.

The side effects of alcohol abuse can be as harmful as the addiction itself. The most common side effect is the liver disorder called *cirrhosis,* in which the liver's working cells are replaced by nonworking tissue. Alcohol abuse is implicated in 90 percent of all cases of cirrhosis of the liver, which in turn is the sixth most frequent cause of death in the United States. A 1974 report by the U.S. Department of Health, Education and Welfare suggested that excessive alcohol consumption may somehow restrict white blood cells from fighting infection;

In small quantities, alcohol acts as a stimulant, increasing feelings of pleasure and releasing inhibitions. These students are enjoying alcohol in a typical social situation—it makes them feel freer to act as they want, to say what they please, and to feel less responsible for their behavior.

the report linked alcohol abuse with an increased risk of cancer.

Probably the most serious adverse side effect takes place in the brain: Heavy alcohol abuse causes premature and irreversible destruction of brain cells. Alcohol seems to inhibit their production of proteins and ribonucleic acid (RNA), both of which are believed to affect learning and memory capacity. Two or three drinks a night on an empty stomach over a period of twenty or thirty years may be sufficient to permanently impair learning ability.

Alcohol's effect on the drinker's personality is neither predictable nor fully understood. The motivation for drinking is psychological to begin with—to ease stress, reduce shyness, and relieve depression—but as drinking increases, it may affect the brain in other ways as well. Although alcohol does immediately relieve tension and anxiety, it can have the opposite effect, especially after prolonged use. When intoxicated, a drinker may be tense, irritable, even belligerent. Social drinkers may succumb to depression when drunk, a reaction that is quite common among alcoholics. The psychological effects of alcohol multiply and feed on each other as a drinker progresses through the stages identified by Jellinek. Paranoia, compulsive lying, aggression, jealousy, obsession—all of these may be experienced by the alcoholic in increasing severity. But the person will still drink, even in the face of these unpleasant psychological effects, because the physical effects of withdrawal are much worse. Furthermore, blackouts commonly erase the alcoholic's memories of all the unpleasantness that occurred during intoxication, so there are no real psychological restraints to inhibit drinking.

Narcotics

It was 10:30 and the last patient had finally left the office. . . . He paused wearily at the door trying to figure out what it was he had forgotten. He turned back to the treatment rooms and turned on the lights in each as a final check. To his horror, he found he had left the syringe and the morphine ampule on the table and had not locked the drug cabinet. His office nurse would have found it in the morning, and he would have been hard put to explain why it was there. It had happened once before a week ago and he recalled stammering and stuttering as he tried to explain it away.

*He dropped into the chair again and started to worry about his increasing sloppiness in the last few weeks. He had been caught in a number of oversights that could have been dangerous. He had covered them up, but he knew that the floor nurses at the hospital had begun to give one another meaningful glances when they thought he was not watching. He smiled and noted that while doctors might be heroes to their patients they could not fool a working nurse for two minutes. They always knew, and all the charm in the world would not change their minds. He knew too. They thought he was a lousy doctor. (McNeil, 1967, pp. 137–140)**

* Elton B. McNeil, *The Quiet Furies: Man and Disorder.* © 1967. Adapted by permission of Prentice-Hall.

Although humans can become dependent on or addicted to many substances, the word "addiction" suggests narcotics to most people. Like alcohol, **narcotics** are depressants; their name is from the Greek word *narkoun,* "to make numb." The best-known narcotics are opium, morphine, and heroin—all of which are also called **opiates** because they are derived from the opium poppy, native to the Middle East, Southeast Asia, and Mexico. **Opium** is a raw, natural drug, made of the dried juice of the unripe poppy blossom. Its active ingredient is **morphine.** A powerful means of intensifying morphine's effect as a painkiller was discovered in 1898: Exposing morphine to heat in the presence of acetic acid produces **heroin,** which is by far the most popular narcotic.

History and prevalence. Opium has been used for at least six thousand years to treat most known physical and psychological problems, from diarrhea to depression. Morphine was extracted from opium in the early nineteenth century and widely used to relieve pain and tension. During the American Civil War, doctors administered the drug so freely (aided by the newly invented hypodermic needle) that many soldiers returning home from the battlefield were addicted to it. Although scientists began to study the effects of morphine with some concern, the drug remained as obtainable then as aspirin is today. When heroin was first produced, it was believed to have none of the addicting properties—yet all of the sedating and painkilling abilities—of morphine. In addition, it produced a more intense euphoria much more rapidly than either opium or morphine. Before long, however, heroin was recognized to be even more addictive than morphine; by the early twentieth century scientists and government agencies were taking steps to restrict its use. The Harrison Act of 1914 made criminals of the estimated 175,000 narcotic addicts then living in the United States as well as all other drug users who were not addicts. Addicts and users went underground, and a profitable if illegal business developed to fulfill their needs.

Heroin was first associated primarily with the black subculture and later with the Beat

Generation of poets and musicians; it attracted widespread notice and concern in the 1960s and 1970s, when it became a problem among middle-class adolescents and returning Vietnam veterans. The federal government made its first renewed moves to control heroin in the 1970s, by attempting to stop the drug's flow into the United States. The effect was to reduce supply and raise prices, but the market for the drug did not appear to decline.

The number of opiate addicts today—almost all of them heroin addicts—is estimated to be around 800,000, about half of them in New York City alone. The new users—white, middle-class, young—can more easily afford heroin, which is usually the most expensive drug. They are often veteran abusers of drugs—particularly alcohol and cocaine—who turn to heroin in search of more intense drug experiences. Some people who use heroin—particularly those who sniff it rather than inject it—are able to do so without becoming addicted. But in most cases heroin is believed to lead to addiction—about 80 percent of those who try it will get hooked.

The mortality rate is high among heroin addicts, primarily because of its illegal status. Although it is smuggled in pure form, it is usually diluted with sugar, cornstarch, or some other substance before being sold on the street. Users have no way of knowing what that other substance is and whether the substance itself is harmful. Nor do they know how much pure heroin the dose actually contains—with every use they risk an overdose. The only way to measure the drug's potency is to take it. Addicts face more risks when they inject a full dose into their veins, a method called **mainlining.** If the syringes and needles used for injection are not sterilized, they can contract an infectious disease like hepatitis. And generally, despite concerted efforts, disease does strike. It can hardly be helped: The economics of a narcotic addict's life dictate that every spare cent go toward more of the drug. That leaves little for such things as a clean living environment or food. Besides, when addicts have just had a "hit" and are feeling euphoric, or when they are shaky and in desperate need, cleanliness doesn't really matter.

Defining narcotic addiction. Like alcohol, narcotics can lead to both abuse and dependence. Abusers develop a pathological pattern of frequent and/or excessive use, and control over the drug wanes. Eventually, social relationships and job performance are adversely affected. The heroin-dependent person who shows signs of tolerating the drug will need larger doses to achieve the desired effect, and will therefore experience the withdrawal syndrome when the drug supply is curtailed or stopped.

Heroin withdrawal is extremely severe. After four to six hours of abstinence, desire for the drug will begin. Within eight to fourteen hours the user yawns a lot, sneezes, perspires, and becomes tearful. The symptoms then begin to intensify, and appetite loss and tremors are experienced. After 36 drug-free hours, muscles twitch uncontrollably; legs, stomach, and back cramp up; restlessness intensifies; sleep will not come; blood pressure and pulse rate rise; and vomiting and diarrhea occur. These symptoms peak after 48 hours of abstinence and last another 72 hours. They then diminish slowly over five to ten days. The severity and length of the withdrawal syndrome varies, depending on the size and strength of the last dose taken.

Because the initial withdrawal symptoms are so unpleasant and prolonged, there is plenty of motivation to take another dose. Thus the good intentions that may have prompted a user to stop taking the drug are slowly overridden. Furthermore, because of **cross-tolerance,** a heroin addict can lessen withdrawal symptoms by simply taking another narcotic derived from opium. Morphine-based painkillers or cough syrups containing **codeine** (another opiate) will maintain the addiction because they are all derived from the same source and produce similar effects.

Effects of narcotics. The effects of narcotics vary with the amount taken, the user's experience, and the method of administration. Heroin especially is used in many ways. Recreational users may eat or sniff heroin, or breathe in its vapors. None of these methods is reportedly as

Mainlining heroin produces an immediate "rush"; however, collapsed veins and abscesses may develop from numerous injections.

effective as **skin popping,** injecting the drug under the skin, and skin popping is not as effective as mainlining. Mainlining makes the drug work almost instantly; by the time the needle is removed the heroin has spread through the body. The user experiences a very intense euphoria (a "rush"), which is followed by relaxation and less intense euphoria.

Opiates, like all the depressants, have a sedating influence on the central nervous system. Scientists have recently learned that opiates produce their *analgesic* (pain relieving) effect by acting on so-called opiate receptors in certain brain cells. The function of these receptors may be to receive chemicals that are produced naturally by the body. Besides relieving pain, heroin also tranquilizes and induces sleep. In addition, it provides relief from coughing and diarrhea. The main side effects are constipation, constriction of pupils, nausea, vomiting, dizziness, and shortness of breath. But an overdose can cause coma and eventual death from respiratory failure. Fortunately, an antidote called Nalline (nalorphine) has proved successful in treating patients who overdose on heroin—if they can receive medical attention in time. What is perhaps strange for such a powerful drug is that heroin does not appear to have any long-term adverse effects on the body of the user—as long as the dose is continued.

Heroin abuse can cause a host of psychological and social problems. Regular users are usually lethargic from the effects of the drug, a state that may impair the ability to function in a family or social setting or on the job. At the same time, however, tolerance for the drug is increasing, so users must devote more time and energy to getting money and maintaining a supply. Since the addiction renders them unable to hold down a steady job, they almost inevitably turn to theft to support a habit that can cost 100 dollars a day or more. At first, they may start pilfering cash or saleable items from relatives and friends, but eventually they are almost forced to seek money from whatever sources present themselves. And when they are desperate for a "fix," addicts are not likely to be very selective about how they obtain that money.

Barbiturates

The **barbiturates,** the third group of depressants, are synthetic sedatives derived from organic barbituric acid. They may be obtained legally with a doctor's prescription and illegally from the black market drug trade. There are two types: long-acting and short-acting. The *long-acting* barbiturates, such as phenobarbital, are generally prescribed for daytime sedation and usually do not lead to dependence. Addiction is much more likely with prolonged use of the *short-acting* barbiturates, such as pentobarbital (Nembutal) and secobarbital (Seconal), which go to work on the central nervous system immediately after ingestion and are thus prescribed most often for inducing sleep.

History and prevalence. During the late nineteenth century, researchers sought a safe, nonaddicting substitute for addicting or otherwise dangerous substances such as alcohol, the opiates, and bromides. In 1903, barbital was introduced to the medical profession as a sleep inducer and relaxant and by 1912 an anticonvulsant drug called phenobarbital was introduced. The new barbiturates received an enthusiastic welcome from the medical community and from the patients who used them. They were odorless, tasteless, and came in measurable doses. When taken as directed, their action was generally predictable and they had few side effects. By the 1930s an estimated billion grains of barbiturates were being taken in the United States each year.

It is estimated that one person in every six takes one of the barbiturates regularly. Doctors now write about 100 million prescriptions for barbiturates every year, and about 3 million people a year use barbiturates without proper medical supervision. Barbiturates are abused more often than heroin and all other drugs except alcohol (Wesson and Smith, 1977); 18 percent of the drug-related deaths in the United States are caused by barbiturate overdose.

Barbiturates are commonly prescribed for legitimate medical treatment of anxiety, insomnia, depression, mood alterations, and major motor seizures. However, those who hold prescriptions—and those who do not—often take them for other psychological problems or to relieve insomnia; barbiturates also counteract the irritability, paranoia, and anxiety resulting from amphetamine use. In addition, many people experiment with barbiturates to achieve varied intoxicating effects.

Defining barbiturate addiction. Most patients who are prescribed barbiturates do not become addicted to them. But many of those who do become dependent abuse the drugs because of their intoxicating potential. Many more, who first took the drugs to overcome insomnia or reduce anxiety or tension, become unable to sleep at all or to face any stress without the aid of a barbiturate dose. Barbiturate dependence is almost identical to alcohol dependence: Users develop a tolerance for the drug and undergo a similar progression and range of withdrawal symptoms, including delirium tremens. Barbiturate withdrawal is further complicated by the fact that the users often confuse the withdrawal symptoms (anxiety and sleeplessness) with the symptoms that initially led them to take the drug. Such people will often travel from doctor to doctor seeking new prescriptions.

Kolb (1973) states that any barbiturates taken daily for three to six months in eight or more times the usual effective dose will produce addiction. Barbiturate addicts tend to be confused, forgetful, inattentive, and giddy; slurred speech is common. The route back from barbiturate addiction is one of the most difficult. The symptoms of withdrawal usually begin within twelve to twenty-four hours of the last dose and increase in severity over the next one to three days. Between the third and seventh days, hallucinations may develop. Supervised barbiturate withdrawal is done slowly, with gradually decreasing doses, because abrupt withdrawal can be fatal.

Effects of barbiturates. Like all of the depressants, the barbiturates act as a sedative on the central nervous system. They can relax not only nerves but also skeletal muscle, smooth muscle, and coronary muscle. The extent of their effect depends on the type of barbiturate, the amount consumed, the method of administration, and the nervous system's state of excitability. Depending on these, barbiturates can produce anything from mild sedation to coma.

A small amount of barbiturate, like a small amount of alcohol, will leave a person relaxed and sociable but less alert. Increased amounts may cause sluggishness, gloominess, or even belligerence. Still higher doses lead to deep sleep and coma. And because barbiturate addicts eventually come to tolerate a near-lethal dose, barbiturates are more dangerous than alcohol. An overdose of alcohol causes vomiting, which removes some of the toxin from the body (Williams, 1967). The only hope for a person in barbiturate coma is to pump the drug out of the stomach. Many cases of barbiturate overdose are intentional, a means of painless suicide. But many more are accidental because the toxic or lethal dose is so unpredictable.

Prolonged use of barbiturates for treatment of insomnia often can cause brain deterioration, permanently impaired motor functioning, and severe vitamin deficiency. In a syndrome called *drug-induced insomnia,* repeated use of barbiturates to overcome sleeplessness backfires to produce fitful, dreamless sleep. Because barbiturates inhibit the REM (rapid eye movement) stages of sleep, during which dreams occur, the regular user who tries to sleep without barbiturates may experience *REM rebound,* a restlessness often accompanied by nightmares and fragments of dreams. Inevitably, the user returns to the drug or increases the dose in an attempt to get a night's rest.

A special problem with barbiturates is that they interact easily and unpredictably with alcohol. Some interactions between alcohol and other drugs, such as antibiotics or anticoagulants, are **antagonistic:** Alcohol reduces the effect of the drug and vice versa. But the interaction between barbiturates and alcohol is more likely to be **supra-additive:** The total effect of the two drugs is greater than the sum of their separate effects. For instance, when alcohol combines with a short-acting barbiturate, the result is an intoxication level that far surpasses the usual effects of either one. The user appears "super-drunk," with greater mental and motor impairment than usual but an elevated mood. To the intoxicated person, everything seems normal, so it is especially dangerous to operate machinery after combining alcohol and the barbiturates. Blood levels of only 0.5 percent barbiturate and 0.1 percent alcohol can kill. Hospitals admit almost 50,000 patients a year who suffer from barbiturate-alcohol overdose—a combination that kills 2500 people a year.

Stimulants

Stimulants activate and arouse the central nervous system. Users describe feeling excited and having renewed energy but complain of sleeplessness and extreme irritability. The most commonly used stimulants are cocaine and the amphetamines. However, nicotine—the active drug in tobacco—is often categorized as a stimulant.

Nicotine

Since tobacco is so commonly used and causes no visible ill effects or impaired functioning, many experts argue that **nicotine** should not be lumped with addictive drugs. Nevertheless, heavy users of tobacco do develop a tolerance to nicotine and suffer withdrawal symptoms if they stop smoking. Accordingly, it is an addictive drug by our definition.

History and prevalence. Tobacco use originated in North America and was transported to Europe by the English explorers who had followed Columbus to the New World. Until the twentieth century, most users smoked tobacco in pipes or cigars, chewed the leaves, or inhaled tobacco-based snuff. The modern cigarette was introduced in this century to encourage smoking among young people and women. It was an instant hit.

In 1942 Lennox Johnston isolated nicotine as the addicting substance in tobacco. In 1964, the U.S. Surgeon General stated that smoking contributed to lung cancer, heart disease, emphysema, and other major illnesses. Except for a few remaining skeptics, scientists now agree that smoking is harmful; yet despite wide publicity of that fact, one half of the adult men and one third of the adult women in this country still smoke. Although about 30 million people have stopped smoking since the publication of the Surgeon General's report in 1964, 55 to 60 million people are addicted to nicotine.

Defining nicotine addiction. Although it is a subject of much dispute, evidence shows that smoking can lead to addiction to nicotine. The habit is a particularly difficult one to break; all smokers have probably tried to quit at least once, and most have failed. Although people generally choke their way through their first cigarettes, tolerance develops very quickly. Average smokers consume about a pack a day, and very heavy smokers "light up" continuously, making nicotine the most frequently abused of all drugs.

The smoker who gives up a habit totalling half a pack or more a day may experience a

Close-up: *Freud's Addiction*

At around the age of 40, Freud was diagnosed as having a heart condition. His attending physician quite naturally insisted that his eminent patient stop smoking the twenty cigars he consumed each day. Freud made many valiant efforts to comply, but withdrawal was always too difficult. Already afflicted with bouts of depression, he found these periods to be intolerable when deprived of his favorite cigars. His habit continued.

Almost thirty years passed before he discovered sores in his mouth that would not heal. Cancer began to eat away his jaw and palate. Thirty-three operations later, Freud emerged with an artificial jaw and an undiminished need to smoke. When he died at the age of 83, the cancer had spread to his cheek, but he was still smoking "an endless chain of cigars."

withdrawal syndrome consisting of decreased blood pressure and pulse rate, headaches, drowsiness, digestive problems, social discomfort, anxiety, depression, compulsive overeating, intellectual impairment, and sleep disturbances. A group of former heroin abusers who gave up smoking reported that giving up heroin had been easier: The heroin withdrawal symptoms had lasted only days, but the smoking withdrawal symptoms lasted up to six months (Brecher et al., 1972).

Effects of nicotine. Nicotine stimulates the central nervous system and elevates blood pressure and heart rate. Nicotine itself (and/or tobacco smoke) can cause heart disease, gastrointestinal ailments, lung, mouth and throat cancer, and emphysema in long-term and heavy smokers. In 1979, a follow-up to the 1964 Surgeon General's report claimed that male smokers are eleven times more likely to contract lung cancer than male nonsmokers.

Studies with test animals and humans prove that nicotine produces EEG changes that can be interpreted as arousal (Eysenck, 1973b). Although nicotine is thus physiologically arousing, regular smokers clearly see smoking as psychologically relaxing, controlling tension rather than producing it (Nesbitt, 1973). The only other psychological effect of nicotine is that heavy smokers may become anxious, irritable, and inattentive when they must stop smoking for a while. Since it was discovered that "sidestream" smoke (the smoke not inhaled by the smoker) is just as toxic to nonsmokers as cigarettes are to smokers, many public places now request that people not smoke. Action by nonsmokers has brought about laws in some cities and states that prohibit smoking in certain areas, usually enclosed spaces such as elevators. Many restaurants now have separate sections for smokers and nonsmokers.

Amphetamines

The synthetic **amphetamines**—notably Benzedrine, Methedrine, and Dexedrine—stimulate the nervous system. Although they are abused (that is, a user can develop a pathological pattern of their use that affects social and occupational functioning), and although a user may also develop tolerance for them, amphetamines are not believed to be addictive because discontinuance does not produce a regular withdrawal syndrome.

History and prevalence. First synthesized in 1887, Benzedrine was used to treat asthma and *narcolepsy,* a disease that causes its victims to fall asleep constantly. It also cleared clogged sinuses, relieved mild depression, and controlled appetite—all of which are still treated by amphetamines today. Many people in the United States use prescribed or over-the-counter amphetamines to help them lose weight. It was also discovered that amphetamines are, paradoxically, an effective treatment for hyperactive children (see page 462).

Effects of amphetamines. Amphetamines affect the sympathetic nervous system, decreasing appetite, increasing heart action and metabolic functions, and stimulating mucous membranes. Sleeplessness and a dry mouth result, and sometimes diarrhea, nausea, stomach cramps, and chest pain. These physiological changes can be accompanied by feelings of euphoria, alertness, and competence (the desired psychological effect) or by restlessness, tension, and panic. Emotional changeability is quite common among amphetamine users (Honigfeld and Howard, 1973).

Frequent and heavy amphetamine users generally develop high tolerance for the drug and thus must take extremely large doses to achieve the desired "high." For maximum effect, amphetamines can be mainlined like heroin but this method can cause convulsions, coma, or cerebral hemorrhage, which sometimes occur with amphetamine overdose. A more common consequence of large doses of amphetamines is the development of acute paranoid psychosis, with delusions of persecution or of reference (that is, the belief that everyone is talking about you) or feelings of omnipotence.

Though amphetamines have no associated withdrawal syndrome, some ex-users have reported experiencing disturbed sleep patterns and ravenous hunger when they stopped using the drug. Others have become extremely depressed or even suicidal (Glatt, 1974). Amphetamine abusers may be inclined to experiment with addictive drugs such as heroin or the barbiturates. Some abusers will switch between depressants and stimulants, achieving a seesaw effect from the sedation of one and the exhilaration of the other.

Cocaine

Cocaine, a white crystalline powder derived from the leaves of the coca plant, is an increasingly popular recreational stimulant. It too can be abused, but it is not considered addictive, since the frequent user develops no tolerance to it and shows no physical signs of withdrawal.

History and prevalence. South American Indians had been using coca leaves as a stimulant for perhaps thousands of years before Europeans arrived. The Europeans did not popularize coca as they did tobacco, so cocaine remained relatively unknown until the nineteenth century, at which time cocaine was used as an anesthetic, to numb small areas of tissue. Freud found the drug very helpful and used it to combat his own depression. One original ingredient of the soft drink Coca-Cola was coca leaves (and therefore cocaine); to this day, both Coca-Cola and cocaine are nicknamed "coke."

Although the 1914 Harrison Act made cocaine illegal, the drug remained very popular and was considered the most abused drug until the 1930s. It then went out of fashion until the 1960s, when its nonaddictive nature and stimulative effects earned it a new following. Today it is estimated that many thousands of people in the United States use cocaine at least once a month. Sold at over 100 dollars a gram, cocaine is one of the most expensive drugs, and was known for a time as the "rich man's high."

Effects of cocaine. Although some heavy cocaine users inject the drug, most users sniff or

Table 9.2 *Effects of Cocaine*

Effects	Percentage
Euphoria	100
Stimulation	82
Reduced fatigue	70
Restlessness	70
Loss of appetite	67
Talkativeness	59
Sensitivity to light	44
Anxiety	34
Hyperexcitability	28
Hallucinations	18
Irritability	16
Sexual arousal	13
Paranoia	5

From Siegel, 1977.
Based on a study of 85 male recreational users.

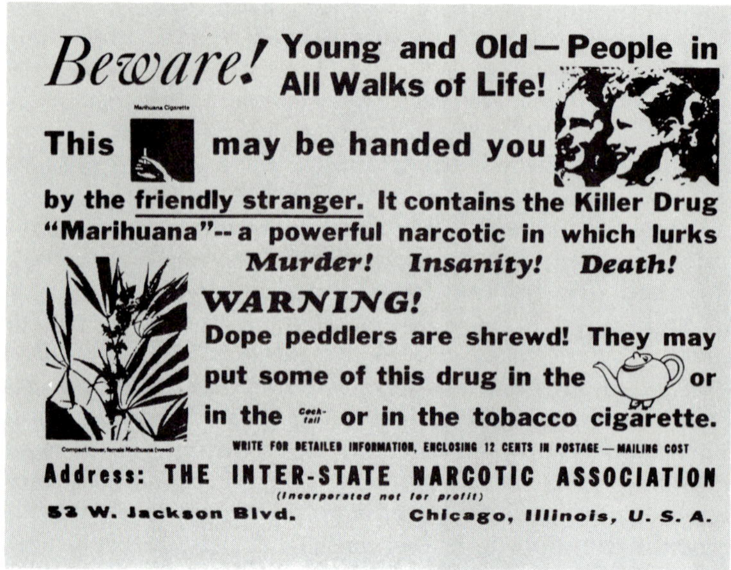

A 1930s billboard warns the public of the dreadful fate awaiting those who experiment with marijuana. From D. D. Girdano and D. A. Girdano, Drugs, A Factual Account, *2nd ed. Reading, Mass.: Addison-Wesley, 1976.*

"snort" the powder through their noses. When it makes contact with the mucous membranes of the nostrils, it usually produces anesthesia. But when the drug enters the bloodstream, it produces the pleasant sensations that make it so popular: euphoria, elation, energy, self-confidence, and gregariousness. Sensory and emotional experiences are intensified. The effects are similar to those of the amphetamines but milder and more transient.

Cocaine activates the hormone governing the sympathetic nervous system, which therefore signals the body to be on the alert. This interaction produces the physical changes experienced as emotional excitement. Cocaine dilates the pupils; it constricts the blood vessels in the skin and mucous membranes; it raises blood sugar, blood pressure, heart rate, and temperature; it inhibits digestive processes; and it increases sexual appetite.

Prolonged heavy use of cocaine may cause insomnia, depression, agitation, paranoia, and frightening hallucinations. If the drug is sniffed, the mucous membranes of the nose may become inflamed.

Like heroin, cocaine is usually smuggled as a pure powder and then diluted or "cut" with other substances to increase its bulk and price. The other substance may be anything: powdered milk, cornstarch, a local anesthetic (such as lidocaine and benzocaine), even *phencyclidine*, commonly called **PCP**, an extremely dangerous animal tranquilizer. Users generally do not know how much cocaine is in their dose or what else it contains, and they therefore risk overdose and poisoning with every use; this does not stop them, however.

Distortive Drugs

Much controversy surrounds the use of the distortive substances, which alter the user's perceptions and may alter mood or behavior as well. The distortives include marijuana and hallucinogens like peyote (which is a natural substance) and LSD (which is synthetic). None of these drugs have any reliably reported withdrawal syndrome (Brecher, 1972; Glatt, 1974), so they are not considered addictive.

Marijuana

Marijuana is derived from the dried leaves, seeds, and flowers of the Indian hemp plant, *Cannabis sativa*. **Hashish,** made from the dried resin of the same plant, is five or six times more potent than marijuana.

History and prevalence. Records mentioning cannabis date back to the third millennium in China, where it was listed in the herbal compendium of the emperor Sheng Nung. The early settlers at Jamestown, Virginia, used the strong fibers of the hardy plant to make excellent rope. George Washington grew the plant as a crop on his plantation, presumably also for rope-making, but people of his day also used marijuana as a folk remedy, muscle relaxant, pain reliever, and asthma preparation.

Marijuana began to gain popularity as a recreational drug early in the twentieth century, when Mexican farmers smuggled their potent strains into the United States. By 1930 the drug was popular in most American cities, particularly among musicians and artists (Nahas, 1973). At that time it was still being marketed as a medicine called "extract of cannabis." When the Marijuana Tax Act of 1937 banned the drug except for use in making rope, marijuana went underground. There it stayed, among certain population groups, until the late 1960s, when it surfaced as a widely popular if illegal social drug.

Though marijuana is still used by many fewer people than are alcohol and cigarettes, it has a considerable following for an illegal drug. In 1973, about 8.3 million Americans used marijuana regularly. Twenty-four million people over the age of eleven (15 percent of adults over 18, and 14 percent of those aged 12 to 17) had tried the drug (Nahas, 1973). In a 1970 Gallup poll, 43 percent of college students, half of whom were under 21, reported using marijuana.

Marijuana use, possession, and sale are still illegal everywhere, but classification of these crimes varies widely. In some states, possession of less than an ounce is a civil offense, comparable to a parking violation; in others it is a felony punishable with up to twenty years in prison. The National Organization for the Reform of Marijuana Laws (NORML), a strong lobby for legalizing the drug or at least reducing sentences, has received support from various legal and social agencies, including the American Bar Association, the National Council of Churches, the American Medical Association, and the National Association for Mental Health.

Effects of marijuana. A low dose of marijuana's active chemical, *tetrahydrocannabinol* (THC), usually results in contentment, a ready flow of ideas and imagination, and a distorted sense of time and space. Marijuana also increases the pulse rate and blood pressure, reddens the eyes and inner eyelid, dilates the pupils, dries the mouth and throat, and increases the appetite. Depending on the user's experience and the amount smoked, it can lead to laughter, excitement, or depression. The user's mood and expectations seem to affect the experience with the drug (Miller, 1974). Since marijuana impairs reaction time, visual perception, and motor coordination, it is unsafe to drive or operate machinery while "high" on the drug. Although some users have described adverse reactions to marijuana, including feelings of panic and frightening hallucinations (Halikas, 1974), toxic reactions are apparently a rare occurence.

The fact that THC does not disappear from the body after a period of intoxication has bolstered claims that prolonged marijuana use has long-term negative effects. Some researchers suggest that brain damage, disruption of cell metabolism, genetic damage, and reduced production of testosterone (the male sex hormone) are linked with marijuana use. But there is no conclusive evidence that prolonged use of marijuana is physically dangerous over the short or long term. Nor is there much evidence in support of the *amotivational syndrome,* the apathy, sluggishness, lack of goals, and general moral decline once thought to result from heavy marijuana use.

Marijuana has also been accused of leading people to other, more dangerous drugs. It is true that marijuana users are fairly disdainful of drug laws and therefore are possibly tolerant of all drug use. It is also true that trading in the illegal drug market may expose the users to people who sell heroin, amphetamines, and the like. However, no evidence exists that using marijuana inevitably leads to using harder drugs (Goode, 1974).

Close-up: Angel Dust

Phencyclidine, or PCP (an abbreviation given to the "PeaCe Pill" popular in the Haight Asbury district of San Francisco during the 1960s), is a barbiturate that was developed as a tranquilizer in the 1950s. It was discontinued for human use, however, because of its unpredictable and sometimes violent side effects, which include delirium and disorientation.

Recently PCP has reemerged under street names such as angel dust, busy bee, and tic tac, with lethal results. Users may smoke the drug by sprinkling it on marijuana, tobacco, mint, or parsley; it can also be snorted or ingested orally. Although many users experience a pleasant sensation the first time they try PCP, subsequent experiences may be frightening. A moderate dosage may produce an apathetic condition or coma. Reactions vary, however, and psychotic hallucinations, self-mutilating behavior, and impaired motor skills are common. These symptoms may remain long after use of the drug has been discontinued.

PCP has also been implicated in several violent crimes. When Ira Attenby engaged the police in a gun battle during a San Antonio parade in 1979, two spectators were killed and some 50 others injured. Attenby finally committed suicide, and the autopsy revealed traces of PCP in his blood. Although Attenby had suffered paranoid delusions (possibly the result of a 1971 automobile accident), the medical examiner felt his bizarre behavior could be ascribed to the influence of PCP.

In some cases, minor tranquilizers such as Valium and Librium have been used to reduce the effects of PCP, yet other reports indicate these same drugs may actually intensify the unpleasant symptoms. Perhaps the most successful way to control its influence is the administration of high doses of vitamin C to hasten the excretion of PCP from the body via the urine.

Hallucinogens

The drugs that produce profound effects on the mind—altered states of consciousness, perceptual distortion, and frequent changes in behavior or mood—are known as **hallucinogens.** There are several: **peyote,** derived from cactus; **mescaline,** derived from peyote or produced synthetically; the mushroom **psilocybin;** and some potent synthetic substances, such as **STP.** The effects of all these drugs depend on many factors regarding the user: stability of personality, expectations of the drug experience, and mood at the time of ingestion. The setting in which the drug is used can also be important. Our discussion of hallucinogens will focus on **LSD** (*lysergic acid diethylamide*), the most common hallucinogen. LSD is an alkaloid synthesized from lysergic acid, which is one component of a fungus that grows on rye, wheat, and the blossom of the morning glory.

History and prevalence. In 1943, Swiss scientist Albert Hofmann accidentally embarked on history's first "acid trip." Five years earlier, Hofmann and a colleague had first synthesized LSD. They were manufacturing the substance in their lab when Hoffman ingested some by mistake. His experience attracted attention, and over the next two decades, researchers experimented with the possible uses of LSD and other hallucinogens in psychotherapy. Much of that research came to naught, but LSD has been used to ease the pain and improve the mental state of people with terminal cancer (Kurland, 1967).

Beginning in the early 1960s, the profound psychological effects of these drugs made them

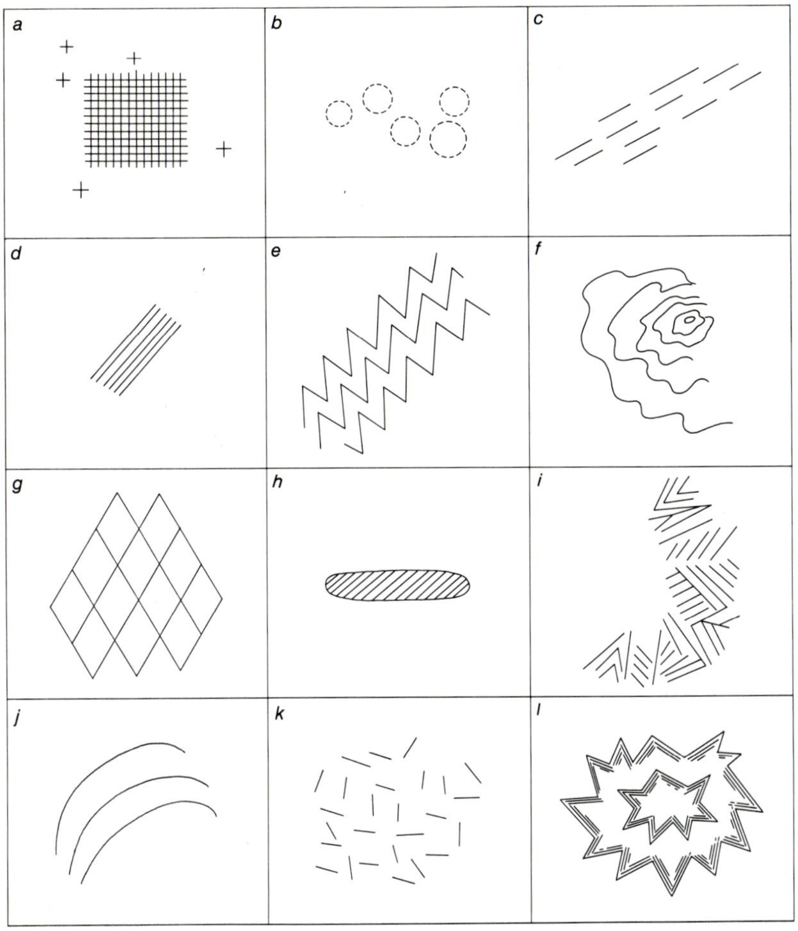

These patterns reportedly appeared in the peripheral field of vision after chronic use of cocaine. Interestingly, patterns f, i, *and* l *are identical to patterns that appear during migraine auras and may reflect common mechanisms of central nervous system excitation.*

increasingly popular recreational drugs. Although their use was restricted by law in 1963, illegal use of the drugs flourished and reached a peak in the late 1960s. LSD seemed to be the perfect drug for exploring the limits of perception. Psychedelic, the popular term applied to the drugs, meaning distortive or hallucinatory, was widely used to describe styles of art, music, and even clothing.

Effects of LSD. LSD is extremely potent—an amount the size of an aspirin tablet contains about 3200 average doses. It stimulates the central nervous system, causing increased heart rate, pulse, and blood pressure, tremors, flushing, and irregular breathing. Depending on the size of the dose, on the user's personality, mood, and expectations, and on the setting, the psychological effects may include euphoria, rapid shifts in mood and attitude, altered awareness and time perception, slowed reflexes, an inability to concentrate, impaired judgment, and heightened suggestibility. The perceptual changes are the most dramatic: Colors seem more vibrant; inanimate objects seem to come alive; textures, smells, and sounds become deep and rich. These effects usually peak two to three hours after ingestion and wear off four to six hours later.

Adverse reactions to LSD, called "bad trips," may include anxiety or panic, acts of aggression, paranoia, and acute depression that may lead to thoughts of suicide—and even to actual attempts. LSD-related deaths have not been caused by the chemical per se but by suicide or accident while users were "under the influence." For instance, a young man on a "trip" who perceives the air to be tangible and able to support his weight may step out a window, expecting to walk. Another adverse effect of LSD is the **flashback,** a return of the perceptual distortions long after the drug has been taken—even after its use has been stopped completely. The sudden onset of a flashback can be terrifying for the victim, whose subsequent behavior may so resemble psychosis that hospitalization becomes necessary.

Polydrug use

That combination, Valium and alcohol, was something I liked to do a lot. And I didn't even know it was that dangerous, can you believe it? It gave me a big boost . . . it was the best thing I had found of all the things I had tried. It felt the best to me. And I didn't know it was dangerous. I got into it in junior high school. Then the Karen Ann Quinlan thing happened, and it scared the hell out of me, that I had done something so dangerous. . . .

You know, I did everything you weren't supposed to do. . . . I did Valiums ten to twenty times, and I'd get it by lying about myself a lot to doctors. I'd call them and make up stories. A woman goes to a doctor, though, and it's easy. She's nervous, she says, and she's going to get Valium, no question about it. I also had a prescription I could refill, of fifty, and I could do that five times if I wanted. I also sold it.

I stopped taking Valium because I discovered speed and that was a lot nicer. I'd mix it with alcohol, and that's kind of neat because your head is . . . asleep, and your body is awake. You know what I mean? You can do things you can't do when you're drunk. Like dance all night. With Valium and alcohol, you're most likely to pass out. Later I did Quaaludes and alcohol, but only a couple of times because I knew that that was very dangerous. Those times, I remember, I could see everything but I couldn't react. It's like looking through a fish bowl, everything is so distorted and you feel like you can't do anything. (Langone and Langone, 1980, pp. 41–44)

As this passage suggests, mixing drugs has become increasingly common today. In the past, such drug abuse probably involved simple ignorance: No one was informed of the possible dangers involved. Now, however, since such tragedies as the Karen Quinlan case have become publicized, more people are aware of the fact that mixing chemicals is not safe.

As we have already mentioned, the combination of alcohol and barbiturates is a particularly volatile mixture, but it's not the only one. Even some over-the-counter drugs are dangerous in certain combinations. Consumer groups advocate more extensive warnings on drug labels, but informing the public about the dangers of polydrug use is the first step toward avoiding potential hazards.

EXPLAINING DRUG ABUSE

Why do some people avoid drugs? Why do others use—or abuse—them? Why can't some people stop using drugs—even nonaddictive ones—once they begin? Various biological, psychological, social, and interactional explanations for drug abuse have been offered, and each explanation fosters its own type of treatment.

Biological Explanations

One biological theory of alcoholism attributes it to genetic factors. Goodwin and colleagues (1973) compared 55 male children born to alcoholic parents with 55 male children born to nonalcoholic parents. All 110 children were adopted. Of the test group, 20 percent became alcoholics later in life, compared with only 5 percent of the control group. The study could not control different environmental factors, and most of the children of alcoholics did not become alcoholics. But Goodwin's study is generally accepted as evidence that a genetic influence affects the development of alcoholism (Armor et al., 1978). Other studies suggest that an inherited nutritional deficiency (notably of the B vitamin, thiamine) may be at fault.

A variant genetic theory is built around evidence that certain ethnic groups show hypersensitivity to alcohol. For instance, Fenna and colleagues (1971) and Wolff (1972) documented

Table 9.3 *Drug Use Statistics*

	AGE 12 TO 17		AGE 18 TO 25		AGE 26 OR OLDER	
	Used at all	Used in last 30 days	Used at all	Used in last 30 days	Used at all	Used in last 30 days
Alcohol	52.6%	31.2%	84.2%	70.0%	77.9%	54.9%
Marijuana and/or hashish	28.2	16.1	60.1	27.7	15.4	3.2
Hallucinogens	4.6	1.6	19.8	2.0	2.6	*
Inhalants (such as glue sniffing)	9.0	0.7	11.2	*	1.8	*
Cocaine	4.0	0.8	19.1	3.7	2.6	*
Heroin	1.1	*	3.6	*	0.8	*
Other opiates (morphine, codeine, methadone)	6.1	0.6	13.5	1.0	2.8	*
Stimulants†	5.2	**	21.2	**	4.7	**
Sedatives†	3.1	**	18.4	**	2.8	**
Tranquilizers†	3.8	**	13.4	**	2.6	**

From Abelson, Fishburne, and Cisin, 1977.
* Less than 0.5%
** Statistics not available
† Nonmedical use

that Orientals and Eskimos experience allergic reactions to alcohol; both cultures have a very low incidence of alcoholism. Other researchers suggest this is due to their naturally higher rates of metabolism, which would indicate that their systems burn off alcohol much more quickly. However, if certain ethnic groups cannot tolerate alcohol, it is clearly conceivable that other groups may have the opposite characteristic: a heightened susceptibility to alcoholism. Certain cultural groups do have very high alcoholism rates—the Irish, for example—but whether this is a genetic factor or a sociocultural one has yet to be determined.

A biological theory of heroin addiction proposes that the brain and pituitary gland produce a morphine-like family of substances called **endorphins,** which affect the body's ability to withstand pain. The opiate receptors of the cell membrane may also be susceptible to endorphins. If a human body is deficient in endorphins or unable to produce them adequately, it may need narcotics to relieve pain. The only strong evidence for this theory is a study by Su and colleagues (1978), which found that endorphins reduce the symptoms of withdrawal from methadone, a morphine substitute.

The **cellular adaptation theory** of heroin addiction maintains that the body may respond to the depressing effects of heroin by signalling cellular mechanisms to restore the body to homeostasis. Each time the drug is taken, the mechanisms strengthen; soon *they* offset equilibrium, so that increasing amounts of heroin are needed to restore the balance. Theoretically, these cellular mechanisms cause the withdrawal syndrome because they remain active after the abstinence begins (Kolb, 1973).

Wikler (1968) suggests that taking a drug just once leads to a "subtle derangement of homeostasis" that necessitates taking the drug again. He believes that these symptoms are associated with environmental stimuli, so that even after the withdrawal syndrome has passed, the environment can elicit the symptoms and the addict will again take the drug. Ausubel (1961) objects to using withdrawal symptoms to establish a physiological cause. He believes that no one would continue drug use and possibly damage their lives just to avoid short-lived symptoms that resemble a bad case of the flu. Since up to 90 percent of cured addicts return to drug use (Hunt and Odoroff, 1962), Ausubel feels that other factors are involved.

Psychological Explanations

Psychodynamic and related theories link drug abuse in various ways with the character of the user. One suggestion is that the drug abuser's personality is not and never was well-adjusted, since the tendency toward abuse itself indicates an imbalance of personality development and function (Kolb, 1968). In support of this theory is the fact that people with disorders are overrepresented among drug users. Chronically depressed people, schizophrenics, and people with schizoid and antisocial personalities are more likely to abuse drugs. However, both depression and antisocial personality may also result from addiction and its life-style (Pradham and Dutta, 1977). Other research suggests that drug abuse may be a form of self-medication for people with these disorders (Williams, 1967).

Another psychological approach avoids labeling the abuser as disordered, but still searches for personality traits that may reliably distinguish the abuser from the general population. Alcoholism research in particular seeks these constitutional traits. One assumption is that alcoholism is a defensive maneuver some people use to deal with conflicts; therefore those conflicts may be similar in people with similar traits. No personality constellation for alcoholics has yet been discovered (Zwerling and Rosenbaum, 1959), but a number of traits have been found to recur in alcoholic populations.

For men, these traits include personal power deficiencies, low stress tolerance, a negative self-image, dependency, isolation, insecurity, depression, a tendency toward self-punishment, anger, impulsiveness, tolerance of deviance, emotionality, poor reality testing, and sensitivity to criticism. For women alcoholics, the traits include narcissism, extraversion, and mistrust of interpersonal interaction—all traits that reflect immaturity, vulnerability, dependency, low self-esteem, and problems in social adjustments. Traits among abusers of other drugs are less well-defined but often include hostility, passivity, dependency, immaturity, desire for arousal or thrills, antisocial feelings, and instability (Cohen, 1977; Dunn, 1973; Eysenck, 1973b; Williams, 1967).

Psychodynamic theory, which deals less with drug abusers than with other types of disorder, holds that the psychosexual development of the male drug user was arrested at a passive, dependent stage because he had a weak father (if the father was present at all) and a mother who alternated between overindulgence and rejection. Living in a drug-induced "high" continues that passive and tensionless state, with all needs met effortlessly by the one external source (Chein et al., 1964; Williams, 1967). Similarly, alcoholism is caused by an early deprivation that leads to fixation at the oral stage. As children, alcoholics were enraged and disappointed by parental treatment; they drink in an attempt to return to a pre-weaning state before they were disappointed. Most theorists also agree that self-destruction is a potent motivator in excessive drinking (Zax and Cowen, 1976).

All definitions of drug abuse and dependence stress a loss of control over behavior. The behavioral approach to abuse suggests that excessive drinking or drug use is learned behavior. The basic idea is that drug abuse results from operant conditioning: Taking the drug is followed by a desirable consequence (the positive reinforcer) that inclines the person toward more use. Reduced fear, tension, or anxiety is generally thought to be the desired consequence (Kolb, 1973). Secondary reinforcers such as peer approval can also foster drug use. With drugs, the reinforcement is very strong because it is so immediate. Support for this learning theory has been obtained from studies in which animals learned to accept the most commonly abused drugs as positive reinforcers (Pradham and Dutta, 1977).

Some two-stage theories of drug abuse are

more thoroughly worked out. In one, alcohol use is initially positively reinforced by its ability to make social interaction easier and more pleasant for some people. Gradually, these social reinforcers are replaced by the physiological reinforcers of increasing tolerance and uncomfortable withdrawal symptoms. A conditioned stimulus (addiction) has developed. If alcohol is taken again, the feelings of comfort that result reinforce its use as a conditioned response to the conditioned stimulus of physical need.

Another two-stage, operant-conditioning model is that of Bandura (1969). First, drug use is rewarded by euphoria and loss of tension; the user then learns to turn to the drug for its stress-reducing properties. However, this habit, thus strengthened, can lead to more stress, such as losing a job and having family problems—which naturally leads back to the drug. In this first stage, behavior is ruled by immediate stimuli; there is no regard for future consequences. The second stage is addiction, when withdrawal symptoms occur if the drug is not taken. As in the previous model, addiction is now a conditioned stimulus that elicits further drug use, which is then reinforced by symptom relief.

Social Explanations

The social explanations of drug abuse attribute the problem to factors other than the physical or psychological characteristics of the user. In one view, the amount of drug abuse in a society is determined by the amount of societal pressure to either abstain from or partake in drugs. A society that demands and enforces total abstinence has few drug abusers. At the other extreme, a society that allows drug use and exerts few controls on it is likely to have many. For example, the incidence of alcoholism is very high in France, where alcohol is readily available, even to children. Among Jews, however, alcohol use is tolerated but controlled by rituals, and alcoholism is relatively infrequent, although it may be on the rise (Glatt, 1974).

Obviously, American society supports and even encourages the use of some drugs, particularly alcohol and nicotine. Many drugs—even barbiturates and amphetamines—are fairly easy to obtain legally, even though they are controlled somewhat by laws limiting their use to adults or requiring a doctor's prescription. Moderate users of these drugs, and even addicts as well, do not feel deviant or alone because they see thousands of others like themselves. Advertising plays a big role in this cultural acceptance of drug use, even to the point of appealing to an individual's tension or low self-esteem by presenting an attractive, relaxed, self-confident role model who supposedly uses a particular drug.

Another social approach views the abuser as an integral part of the immediate network of family and friends. For example, the families of alcoholics may experience more conflict than the families of nonalcoholics, so they may thus rely more on alcohol to alleviate stress. Studies indicate that smoking, too, occurs more often when other family members smoke (Estes and Heinemann, 1977; Mausner and Platt, 1971). Peer influence is also considered critical: The regular members of a group can make drug use a part of the group's norms and then "selectively recruit" new members who will be just as likely as the original members to use and therefore abuse drugs (Miller, 1974). Being a drug user also helps individuals define themselves socially. Smoking and drinking, for example, are common activities of adolescents who want to show the world, their friends, and themselves that they are mature and sophisticated. Smokers smoke more when others around them are doing it, too—which indicates the importance of social context in cigarette smoking, and possibly in other types of drug abuse as well.

Interactional Explanations

No single theory, whether biological, psychological, or social, satisfactorily explains all types and aspects of drug abuse. Researchers have therefore devised interactional theories that integrate biological variables, the personality traits and prior learning of individuals, and the cultural and social context in which they live. Drug dependency is then attributed to a complex blend of factors: cultural and familial forces that determine the availability of the drug as well as the opportunities to use it, and the biological and psychological characteristics that may predispose an individual to abuse (Kolb, 1973).

There are five interactional factors that may influence a person's disposition toward drug use:

1. Emotional characteristics of the potential user, especially anxiety and anger.
2. Cognitive orientation, particularly low self-esteem.
3. Biological elements, such as heredity and low tolerance for withdrawal symptoms.
4. Social conditions that may create excessive stress.
5. Situational variables, such as peer pressure and role models.

Of course, these factors will be weighted differently in each person. For example, an American female may live in a city where alcohol is plentiful and its use commonplace. Her family may then use alcohol extensively, and she herself may be the kind of person who seeks quick and easy ways to cope with stress. Thus she turns easily to alcoholism. In contrast, a Chinese male may be influenced by very stressful social and psychological factors that outweigh the strong physiological constraints of his ethnic group—the Oriental's hypersensitivity to alcohol mentioned earlier. An Irish male may have fewer biological or psychological problems but a strong peer group that expects him to join them nightly at the corner pub (Kissin and Begleiter, 1977). Such a multifaceted approach suggests that rigorous diagnosis of all the factors causing and maintaining drug abuse are necessary in order to manage the problem.

MANAGING DRUG ABUSE DISORDERS

The opinions of how best to manage drug abuse are even more diverse than the theoretical views of what causes the problem. The old (but not yet dead) view that abuse is a moral problem requiring punishment led to incarceration as the chief means of treatment, especially if the abuser stole, destroyed property, or "disturbed the peace." Jailing the offender served the dual purpose of stopping (at least temporarily) use of the drug and protecting society. However, in the more current views ascribing abuse to biological, psychological, and social causes, abusers who commit immoral or criminal acts are thought to be that much more desperately in need of the drug.

The focus of all the different management approaches is basically to try to eliminate—or at least weaken—that pathological need. Generally, the first step is biological: to clear the person's body of all traces of the drug. After that, many different treatments are available.

Detoxification

The first and most important treatment is **detoxification**—removing the drug from the user's body. This is often done by simply waiting until the drug has been eliminated naturally by the body itself, although sometimes—especially in emergencies—pumping the stomach can help clear out some drugs much faster. When the user is addicted to the drug and the withdrawal symptoms are painful or dangerous, detoxification must deal with these symptoms as well. The techniques used depend on the drug involved.

Narcotic withdrawal can be accomplished fairly quickly (although not suddenly) in about ten days, by reducing the dose each day. The patient will be uncomfortable; indeed, anyone who does not experience distress probably has secret access to the drug (Kolb, 1973). Barbiturate withdrawal must occur more slowly or seizures may develop (Williams, 1967). One technique replaces the abused barbiturate with phenobarbital, which is safer, easier to withdraw from, and has more predictable effects (Wesson and Smith, 1977).

Detoxification of alcoholics is the most thoroughly studied and most performed. Alcohol is removed entirely at the start, and a sedative like Librium or Valium is prescribed in the early stages to lessen the withdrawal discomfort. Complete detoxification does not occur until use of the drug has also ceased. Fructose (a simple sugar) or insulin may also be used to speed up

American society encourages the use of some drugs, particularly alcohol and nicotine, through advertising campaigns that link a product with self-confidence and physical attractiveness. Photograph © 1971 Bettye Lane.

metabolism of alcohol in the blood. Since alcoholics are often malnourished, a balanced diet is usually part of detoxification as well (Becker et al., 1974; Estes and Heinemann, 1977).

Detoxification should always occur in a supervised medical setting, usually a hospital. Besides ensuring the availability of medical help, hospitalization also removes the user from the source of the drug and the social setting that may have been fostering its use. When the individual is "clean" of the drug, other biologically based treatments are available.

Biological Methods

One treatment involves the controlled use of other drugs either to counteract the effects of the abused substance or to transfer the user's dependence to a less harmful, more easily managed addicting drug. The most common application of **counteractive drugs** is used in the treatment of alcoholism. **Antabuse** (disulfiram) produces an intolerance for alcohol. By itself, the drug has few effects; in combination with alcohol, however, it makes the drinker very uncomfortable within just a few minutes: The face flushes, the throat becomes irritated, and coughing begins. When combined with a large amount of alcohol, Antabuse may produce more serious effects, such as nausea, vomiting, dizziness, breathing problems, and blurred vision. Managing alcoholism with Antabuse requires cooperation and motivation, for the patient must voluntarily and regularly take the drug if it is to have any effect. Nonetheless, the treatment is very widely used and seems to be effective at least for the short term. One longitudinal study showed high rates of abstinence over the first six months but less success after eighteen months (Armor et al., 1978).

Antabuse and other similar counteractive drugs are criticized because they treat only the symptoms of problem drinking and leave untouched the underlying motivators. However, it does seem effective in breaking the drinking cycle of a less self-motivated person and is useful for older, nondepressed alcoholics who have no heart disease. Furthermore, simply halting alcohol consumption—and with it the acute problems drinking can cause—may facilitate more extensive work on the drinker's underlying problems.

The best example of substituting a safer, more controllable addicting drug is **methadone maintenance.** A synthetic analgesic available since the end of World War II, **methadone** is a central nervous system depressant similar to morphine, but its effects develop more slowly and persist longer. Though it is addictive, its withdrawal symptoms are generally less severe than those of other narcotics. A relatively low dose does not produce the euphoric high and heavy sedation of other narcotics, but it has cross-tolerance with them—that is, it is chemically similar and produces the same effects—and so can be used as a substitute. In fairly high doses, it can even block the effects of heroin.

Methadone maintenance has become very common in this country. In 1972 about 50,000 drug abusers were believed to receive methadone in place of other drugs, mainly heroin. Most programs require only that the user be over eighteen and have a history of narcotic abuse for at least two years. In a typical program, users are assigned a counselor and a methadone dose is determined; they must then report to the clinic frequently (more than once a week) for one year, while gradually resuming a normal life. Then they check in about once a week until free of all drugs; they must also prove capable of holding a job and show other signs of normal functioning.

Evidence that methadone use does foster normal functioning is quite strong. In addition, participants in methadone programs who have criminal records have shown a sudden and dramatic decrease in illegal behavior, which suggests that their criminality originated with using an illegal drug (Zax and Cowen, 1976). Nevertheless, there are those who object to methadone maintenance on the grounds that it merely replaces one addiction with another. Many people feel that an addict should become strong enough to live completely drug-free. There is a possibility, as yet not fully explored, that addicts can move through methadone use to abstinence. But even if methadone is not the route to a drug-free life, its success in helping drug users function usefully in society makes it a valuable resource in treatment.

Psychological Methods

The major criticism of the biological methods is, as we have stated, that they treat symptoms, not what actually causes them. Psychological management attempts to discover what motivated the abuse in the first place, and what can be done in the future to keep this same maladaptive behavior from reappearing.

Perhaps the most common method of managing drug abuse is the group approach, in which much of the therapeutic effect is derived from peer support within the group itself. This approach has evolved from both a psychological and a social approach to substance abuse: It accepts that the characteristics of the individual may lead to abuse while it also recognizes that the social milieu has an important effect. The group establishes its own set of norms, the essential one being that use of the drug—sometimes of any drug—is prohibited. In addition, the group provides a new social network for support and companionship; new role models—people who have already stopped using drugs—are also available. These groups are a form of therapeutic community.

The prototype of this approach is **Alcoholics Anonymous (AA),** the best-known treatment for alcoholism. Founded in 1935 by two alcoholics, a physician and a stockbroker, AA is a self-help fellowship with no fees or professional staff. Although not a religious organization, AA does consider spiritual strength to be critical in achieving sobriety. Its members share a belief in the adage, "God helps those who help themselves." In 1972, there were over 17,000 AA groups worldwide, with over 575,000 members (Glaser et al., 1978).

The idea behind the AA program is that alcoholism is an incurable disease and that once sober, the alcoholic must never again touch alcohol. The goal of all members is to help others achieve sobriety and to continue to maintain it themselves. When new members join, they are assigned *sponsors,* veteran AA members who are reliably sober and available for counseling and support whenever the new members feel the urge to drink. All members must pass through

Rehabilitation centers, such as Odyssey House, provide support for residents attempting to shake their dependence on alcohol and other drugs.

twelve steps, beginning with the admission that when exposed to alcohol, they are helpless and that their life is unmanageable because of this helplessness. Each AA group meets often to hear members recount their life stories and their road to sobriety. Anonymity is crucial in AA; members are known only by their first name and last initial.

The anonymity of its members has made it very difficult to study AA, but the program seems reasonably successful. Between 20 and 40 percent of its members stay with the program into full or at least partial sobriety. The one third of AA members who are women have a particularly high rate of success: Of those who stay in the program, 50 percent stay sober, 25 percent have relapses but sober up again eventually, and the remainder at least continue to attend the meetings. The reasons for AA's success seem to be threefold (Chafetz and Demone, 1962):

1. It provides a warm and accepting community for people often shunned by society.
2. In somewhat the same manner as biological methods, it focuses on symptoms rather than going into deep psychological influences, an approach many alcoholics prefer.
3. It directs (or redirects) alcoholics toward a more adaptive life-style along a religiously oriented path that offers forgiveness for past mistakes.

Some other drug management programs based on the AA method provide residential therapeutic communities, at least in the early stages of treatment. Perhaps this helps ensure that members will stay drug-free until their motivation to change gets stronger. Examples of such communities for drug abusers are Phoenix House, Exodus House, and Daytop Village. Modeled after Synanon, which is no longer an abuse-control center, these are generally run by former addicts and require round-the-clock participation and commitment as well as total abstinence. In many communities, members must submit to a daily urinalysis to check for the presence of drugs. The members progress through ranked levels as they become less and less dependent. Most programs involve various amounts of confrontation, but physical violence and sexual relations between members are forbidden. The basic accepted norm of each of these groups is a hatred for all drug use (Rosenbaum, 1973). Although studying these groups is difficult, as it is with AA, research does show encouraging results, with fairly high rates of abstinence among those who remain in the program (Zax and Cowen, 1976).

Table 9.4 *Success of Controlled Drinking Therapy*

Results	Test group* (20)	Control group** (19)
Maintained abstinence	63%	37%
Controlled their drinking	23	6
Became drunk	12	49
Were jailed or hospitalized	3	8

From Sobell and Sobell, 1977.
* Alcoholics attempting to drink socially.
** Alcoholics not trying to control their drinking.

Other psychological approaches to management focus on the individual abuser, although a group program may be used as an adjunct (Kissin and Begleiter, 1977). Traditional psychotherapeutic approaches have had little success in treating drug abuse disorders, however, probably because the slowness and intellectualism of insight therapy contrasts markedly with the abuser's general reliance on instant gratification (Armor et al., 1978; Glatt, 1974). But some behavioral approaches show more promise. Based on the idea that abuse is learned and can therefore be unlearned, they concentrate on using behavior modification techniques to change specific symptoms rather than attempting to reorganize the living situation or entire personality of the abuser. The effects are generally immediate—a fact that may partially explain the success of behavioral methods. Users see themselves improving quickly, and this provides motivation for staying with the treatment.

Aversive conditioning, pairing a noxious stimulus with the drug, is a common behavioral technique. Administering Antabuse to alcoholics is a form of aversive conditioning; its unpleasant effects, particularly nausea and vomiting, may lead the person to expect to feel sick from drinking alcohol and thus to stop drinking altogether. But aversive conditioning has not proved generally effective as the sole method of abuse management, in part because the aversive stimulus is so very unpleasant that the drinker, who must medicate himself, may give in to the temptation not to use it.

In covert sensitization, the user internalizes a particularly vivid and repugnant image of the effects of drug use—such as being very sick from alcohol or dying from a heroin overdose—that will become linked with thoughts of the drug (Cautela, 1966). This method is fairly effective but may still rely too much on the user for its success. Aversive conditioning is probably the more successful technique, if it is combined with other approaches.

One that combines well with either of the two just mentioned is based on the belief that drug abuse is a response to high anxiety: Eliminate the source of anxiety and the drug abuse will cease; better yet, teach the abuser a more adaptive way to cope with anxiety. If the source of anxiety is known, the drug user can be trained in systematic desensitization, which pairs relaxation with the fear-provoking stimulus, so that eventually the stimulus no longer makes the user anxious (Kraft, 1969).

In **contingency management,** users earn rewards or privileges by behaving in ways that are inconsistent with the drug abuse; the user's family may be actively involved in this treatment. **Skill training** has a somewhat different goal. For example, alcoholics have been taught to drink in a controlled situation by being trained to sip rather than gulp their drinks, to socialize while sober, and to pace their drinking over a period of time. Some programs set up a bar in order to train people in appropriate drinking behavior after the maladaptive abuse has been extinguished (Estes and Heinemann, 1977). The controlled drinking study by Sobell and Sobell (1977) proved that, for alcoholism at least, former abusers don't have to abstain from the drug forever; they can learn to control their use.

SUMMARY

Psychoactive drugs include depressants, drugs that have a sedating effect on the central nervous system; stimulants, drugs that increase central nervous system activity; and distortive drugs, substances that can alter the user's state of consciousness and perception. Common examples of depressants include the narcotics (natural drugs such as opium, morphine, and heroin), alcohol, and the barbiturates (synthetic drugs such as Seconal and Nembutal). Stimulants include the amphetamines, cocaine, and nicotine, the active ingredient in tobacco. The most popular distortives are marijuana and LSD.

Most drugs can lead to dependence, a state in which there is a psychological need for the drug in order to function, and many of them lead to addiction, a state of physiological need characterized by the withdrawal syndrome if the drug is discontinued. An effective dose of a drug produces the desired effect; a toxic dose produces undesired side effects as well. A lethal dose kills. Addiction to or abuse of alcohol is one of the nation's leading social problems, perhaps because of the legality of alcohol and the social acceptance of its use—and even its occasional abuse. Despite past attempts such as Prohibition to control drinking, alcohol remains the most abused drug in our society.

The narcotics and barbiturates started as medical sedatives, to kill pain or induce sleep. The narcotics are now illegal, and can be obtained only on the black market. Their illegal status more than likely leads to an increased crime rate and probably a higher overdose death rate, as well. The barbiturates are still obtainable by prescription and are probably over-prescribed in this country. In combination with alcohol, their effects are supra-additive—that is, the effect of each drug is strengthened by the presence of the other.

Although most users consider nicotine to be a calming influence, it also acts as a stimulant, and it is addictive. Amphetamines are popular today for the help they provide in losing weight. Cocaine, the "rich man's high," seems not to be addicting, but people can still become dependent on its use. Marijuana is a very popular natural distortive drug that is generally smoked. Although LSD was very popular in the late 1960s, it seems not to be as widely used as before. Both these drugs heighten awareness, distort the user's sense of time and space, and can lead to mood changes.

Genetic and physiological explanations for abuse have not had a great deal of support. Personality theories indicate that certain characteristics may recur in abuser populations, among them immaturity, low self-esteem, and poor interpersonal relations. The most likely theory is interactional, accepting these elements but also emphasizing the influence of environmental factors, such as stress and peer pressure.

Detoxification—eliminating the drug from the user's body—is the first step in any treatment program, a process that requires time and care to deal with painful withdrawal symptoms. Biological managements stress the use of either less addicting, more controllable substitutes or counteractive agents—drugs that make the abuser intolerant of the abused drug. Antabuse, given to alcoholics, is an example of a counteractive drug.

Psychotherapy has not been successful in the individual treatment of drug abuse disorders, perhaps because it is a slow process and most abusers seem to want instant gratification. Behavior modification—a technique that focuses primarily on quick behavior changes that keep the abuser motivated—has shown more promise. However, since behavior therapy and biological treatments have been criticized for dealing only with symptoms and not with the underlying cause, the best solution is probably a combination of the two.

Self-help groups, such as Alcoholics Anonymous, have also been successful in changing the behavior of drug abusers. Most of these groups advocate abstinence, but some recent reports indicate that for alcohol at least past abusers can learn to control their use of the drug.

Conversation 4

Alcoholism can very often destroy a family; less often it can make that family more aware of the needs of its members and of its own needs as a working unit. But a lot of pain must be endured in overcoming the problems presented by alcoholism. This interview is with three members of the Potter family: Tim, a middle-aged executive; Bev, a horticultural enthusiast; and their youngest child, David, 23, out of college and living at home until firmly established in his new career. Their two daughters, Judy and Teri, live away from home. This established, respectable, and well-to-do family faced the problems of alcohol and survived.

Interviewer: How long has alcohol been a problem?

Tim: I drank for some 35 years. I was an alcoholic probably the last ten. I've been sober about three and a quarter years.

Bev: I didn't know he was an alcoholic. He kept saying that we had different styles of drinking. And I never saw him drunk at a party—it was only here at home. I wondered if it was my fault.

Dave: I wasn't aware that he was pretty badly affected by alcohol until I was eighteen and drinking too.

Tim: I was extremely fortunate in that I never had trouble with the law or on the job. Our troubles were almost entirely in the family.

Int.: Were there any family confrontations?

Dave: There wasn't very much communication at all. People might have been hurt or upset but they never said anything. At least I never did. I was defending him a lot.

Bev: Our family before this was very noncommunicative. Our way of coping was to retreat to our own little corners.

Tim: Well, there was one early family confrontation. Our oldest daughter Judy was the prime mover but everybody told me I was drinking too much. I just denied it right up to the very end. It was Bev's problem—I wasn't having any problem. She was going to Intervention and to Al-Anon. If that made her feel better, why that was swell.

Int.: What was the intervention like? It sounds unusual.

Bev: I made the initial contact. When I went I did nothing but cry. I just didn't know what end was up or down or in the middle. The counselor there said, "I think he's crying for help." I told the children what was going on and they all agreed to be in the intervention. We were each asked to write down a list of all the things we could remember that Tim had done that had hurt us in some way. Then the day before the intervention we met with the counselor and practiced reading our lists. We all agreed that we love Tim, and we all wanted him to get help, so we were learning how to phrase it so it was clear that we loved him and yet were worried. He agreed to meet us at Intervention the next day to hear what we had to say.

Int.: How was the intervention different from the earlier family confrontation?

Tim: The intervention was professionally organized. They had done a lot of homework in remembering specific instances. And the big difference was that it was done lovingly instead of accusingly. It was very loving.

Bev: Everybody was crying. It was very difficult. This was the first time that everybody in the family had said these not very pleasant things to his face.

Dave: It was *very* difficult. I didn't think it would be, but it hit me. It really hurt to say it; it hurt to hear other people say it. He was my father—there couldn't be anything wrong with him. I didn't want to bring any shame to him.

Tim: The weight of all the instances began to pile up. Towards the end, the counselor asked the two questions commonly asked of a person who's in trouble with alcohol: "Tim, are you having a problem with alcohol?" I said, "Well, maybe I am." The second question was "Do you want to do something about it?" Then it flashed in my mind, well by golly, the thing to do is go into the hospital and get dried out so I can start drinking normally. No way was I admitting to myself that I was an alcoholic. In the hospital I used the words "I am an alcoholic," but it took me months to understand what I was really saying.

Int.: I'd like to know what you used to think the word "alcoholic" meant and what you think it means now.

Bev: I felt it was a moral issue. Drinking was a way of coping with pain, but people could control it if they really wanted to. But I learned about alcoholism. We're taught that it's a three-fold illness—mental, emotional, and physical—that can be arrested. Now I think of alcoholics as people with an addiction over which they have no real control.

Dave: I pictured alcoholics as people who woke up in the morning and drank, drank at lunch, and were just generally a real mess. Now I view alcoholism as much more involved with feelings toward others—love, sharing—the whole personality.

Tim: My perception of an alcoholic was somebody who was completely out of control, "in the weeds" as the expression goes—the skid-row bum. I did not appreciate that an alcoholic can hold a job. I thought I still had control, but I had the obsession, the compulsion, to drink, and was unable to face that. I would try to cut down—and would for a few days, but I couldn't help it: I *had* to drink. Still, I wasn't an alcoholic, I was a heavy drinker.

Int.: There is a lot of emotional meaning to the word "alcoholic."

Tim: Oh, yes. There's still a stigma attached to it. But we feel the opposite: I've been public from early on. Everybody at work knows, and everybody in the neighborhood, and many, many people in town. It's a wonderful life—so much better than when I was drinking. The friendships in AA and Al-Anon are second to none. If an alcoholic stops drinking and stays dry, his life changes. It's a very potent change: He begins to feel a lot better physically, spiritually and mentally. It's quite easy for him to feel he's completely recovered, and he can't understand why other people around haven't recovered, too. But the family has been taking an awful lot of abuse and pain and suffering. I think that AA doesn't fully recognize the damage that we alcoholics have done to other people. Typically, there's an awful lot of resentment.

Bev: Anger and resentment are discussed quite frequently at Al-Anon. I've heard it said—and I think it's true of me—that the nonalcoholic is sicker than the alcoholic after the alcoholic stops drinking.

Dave: When Dad was drinking, she could always blame any problems she might have had on the alcoholism. But when he stopped, the problems continued and she lost her scapegoat.

Bev: After the years of alcoholism some of the other problems that were there all along were bared and needed to be addressed. We were in therapy with a psychiatrist for five years while Tim was still drinking. We learned a lot about ourselves, but he did nothing about the situation with alcohol.

Tim: He was of the school that thinks alcohol is a symptom of something else. It's my own feeling that alcohol becomes a problem in itself and requires its own appropriate treatment.

Bev: But alcoholics have to grow emotionally and spiritually—they can't just rest on getting over the physical addiction. A "dry drunk," a person who stops drinking and stays dry, still has the same basic self-centered personality.

Tim: Self-centeredness is quite typical among alcoholics. I was a very self-centered person, but I think I feared knowing myself better.

Dave: I still don't realize what my parents have been through, what my father has been through. I'm trying to get to know them as people, to be friends with them. I still don't think we communicate really well, but it's a hell of a lot better than it was. I feel more relaxed, more comfortable in the house. I feel safe; I have total trust in my parents. I don't go to Al-Anon, I just want to get to know them better.

Int.: What are the basic differences between Intervention and Al-Anon?

Bev: Intervention deals one-to-one with your particular case. At Al-Anon, we're there to help ourselves. We talk more about how to detach emotionally from the alcoholic, how to gain back our self-worth. Al-Anon is like a growth group, a support group. I have never felt as at home and able to identify with other people the way I do with them. No matter what mood you're in, everybody has had that feeling at some time. It's a tremendous support.

Int.: Do you try to get others to come to meetings?

Bev: We have the same basic tenets at AA. If we discover someone bothered by alcoholism in the family, the only thing we can do is give some literature and talk about it.

Tim: Nobody can make an alcoholic stop drinking. We're powerless over alcoholics just the way alcoholics are powerless over alcohol. They have to want to stop.

Bev: What often happens is that the nonalcoholic who attends Al-Anon meetings learns to stop doing the enabling things. Nagging and taking responsibility for the alcoholic just enable that person to drink more. When these stop, it can spur the alcoholic to seek treatment.

Int.: How has this affected your drinking?

Bev: I drink when we go out and when we have friends here.

Dave: My sisters drink only occasionally. I probably drink more than anybody in the family just because I get into drinking situations more. But I'm very cautious and don't let myself go overboard at all. I'd like to say that I will never be a problem drinker, but of course I can't. I do feel that drinking can be a safe and acceptable and moderate practice.

Int.: Can you drink at all?

Tim: No, I'm one drink away from a drunk.

Int.: What about the recent attempts to establish controlled drinking?

Tim: I've heard too many people who've tried it say that it's not better, it's much, much worse. It's so much harder to come back the second time. For the first, say, six months, I kept away from drinking on a day-to-day basis, mainly out of fear, but the fear leaves you. Most people come to find a higher help. (I like to call it inner help.) I feel now that I have a choice: I don't have to pick up a drink today. But I take it one day at a time.

CHAPTER 10

Personality Disorders and Criminal Behavior

Dan F . . . was a well-known actor, a "personality" who had appeared on national television a number of times. . . . He made a lot of money, had a handsome wife, a big house in an exclusive suburb, drove a beautifully appointed Mercedes, and couldn't care less that there were other people in the world. . . . The list of incidents I witnessed and the long succession of stories he related painted a grisly picture of life-long abuse of people for Dan's amusement and profit. He was adept at office politics and told me casually of an unbelievable set of deceptive ways to deal with the opposition. Character assassination, rumor-mongering, modest blackmail, seduction, and barefaced lying were the least of his talents. He was a jackal in the entertainment jungle, a jackal who feasted on the bodies of those he had slaughtered professionally.

Elton McNeil, *The Quiet Furies: Man and Disorder**

The man psychologist Elton McNeil calls Dan F. suffered from antisocial personality disorder—though "suffered" is perhaps the wrong word. Others suffered from Dan's disorder; Dan himself seems to have been enjoying life.

DESCRIBING THE PERSONALITY DISORDERS

Personality disorder is a diagnostic category that encompasses a wide range of behavioral problems, from a severe lack of self-confidence (dependent personality) to an exaggerated sense of self-importance (narcissistic personality). According to DSM-III, a personality disorder may be said to exist when the basic personality traits by which the person perceives and relates to the environment "are inflexible and maladaptive and cause either significant impairment in social or occupational functioning or subjective distress" (p. 305). In other words, personality disorders reflect a fundamentally distorted view of the self and of the individual's role in society.

Whereas most psychological disorders center on one or a few aspects of a person's life, personality disorders involve pervasive patterns of thought and behavior that color overall self-concept and the way the individual deals with other people. People with these disorders have a hard time establishing and maintaining successful relationships. Their distorted view of life makes it difficult for them to comprehend other people's perceptions and needs, and their own needs are often impossible for others to meet for any length of time. A man with a dependent personality, for instance, may require so much attention, support, and guidance from his wife that she finally gets fed up and leaves him. But this man's personality disorder represents a *pattern* of behavior, not just an inability to function in one situation: His next step probably will be to find someone else to depend on, until that relationship too is exhausted.

As the case of Dan F. suggests, another tendency of individuals with personality disorders is to duck responsibility for the trouble they cause for those around them. The dependent man whose wife leaves him is likely to blame her, not himself. He does not see himself as having any need to change, but may consider that he is well rid of her and eagerly await his next rescuer. Such people are often convincing just because they are so sure they are right—and because they can put together a plausible case excusing their own behavior and condemning those who have been disrupted by it.

Types of Personality Disorders

DSM-III describes eleven personality disorders: **histrionic, narcissistic, dependent, compulsive, avoidant, passive-aggressive, paranoid, schizoid, schizotypal, borderline,** and **antisocial**. In addition, DSM-III includes a category for other or mixed personality disorders. We shall first discuss the eleven major types of personality disorder, with a focus on the antisocial personality, describing their major characteristics and the theories that have developed as to their cause. We shall then discuss criminal behavior, a major social problem that presents another side of abnormal behavior.

* Englewood Cliffs, N.J.: Prentice-Hall, 1967, pp. 83, 86. Adapted by permission of the publisher.

Table 10.1 *Personality Disorders*

Histrionic	Overly dramatic and temperamental
Narcissistic	Self-centered, needs to be admired
Dependent	Unwilling to make decisions
Compulsive	Perfectionistic, rigid, aloof
Avoidant	Hypersensitive to rejection, withdrawn
Passive-aggressive	Deliberately "forgetful," resentful
Paranoid	Suspicious in the extreme; hostile
Schizoid	Completely withdrawn and emotionless
Schizotypal	Shows mild schizophrenic tendencies
Borderline	Unstable—constantly switches from low to high mood
Antisocial	Amoral, cold, but superficially charming

Histrionic

People with this disorder are generally overly dramatic and excitable, tending to exaggerate and always trying to be the center of attention. They seem emotionally immature, giving way to irrational fits of temper and never able to stand routine for long. They form friendships rather easily but then start demanding more than they themselves are willing to give.

According to DSM-III, many of these individuals are quite attractive and are often seductive as well. However, they tend to use their seductiveness to manipulate other people. Ironically, the sexual adjustment of many histrionics is very poor. More women than men are diagnosed as having this disorder.

Narcissistic

The distinguishing feature of this disorder is an exaggerated sense of self-importance. Narcissistic personalities are certain that they are unique and very special. This actually camouflages a very fragile sense of self-worth, which is indicated by their intense need for reassuring admiration.

Narcissistic personalities are overwhelmingly concerned with how others regard them and they are apt to choose their friends according to how socially prominent they are. Their total self-involvement leaves little room for real concern for other people, so most friendships are superficial. They may often demand special treatment but never reciprocate.

Dependent

Due to a pervasive lack of self-confidence, people with dependent personality refuse to take responsibility for major life decisions—indeed, sometimes for even the most trivial decisions, such as selecting a restaurant. They apparently cannot function independently; they must have someone there to direct their lives. This willingness to place the needs of others above their own seems to stem from fear—the fear that, if they did make demands, they would be left alone, with no one to lean on. Many times, they will "justify" turning over the responsibility to someone else on the grounds that they are stupid and couldn't do it well anyway. Interestingly, considering their historically dependent position, more women than men are given this diagnosis.

Compulsive

"Perfectionistic" is a word often used to describe the compulsive personality, a disorder more common in men. The typical compulsive man is picky about everything from neatness to rules, a characteristic that often blinds him to the macro view. On the surface, he appears to be

A rigidly neat desktop such as this may indicate the presence of a compulsive personality.

extremely organized and efficient, but in reality he often gets bogged down in trivial things—forms, for instance. His interpersonal relationships tend to be cool and distant; the unyielding attitude he has toward things and procedures is carried over to people as well. He seems unable to show warmth, nor does he often give gifts or even compliments. He basically doesn't value people as much as his own role at work.

Avoidant

People with this personality disorder withdraw from mainstream society out of intense fear that they will be rejected. Their voluntary self-removal allows them to avoid (hence the name) any humiliating confrontations, at least in their minds. They are extremely unwilling to start up friendships because of the same fear. Yet despite the anxiety they feel when around people, they do want the affection and warmth that go with personal relationships—in fact, they yearn for it. However, their difficulty in communicating with other people in productive ways prevents them from trying to overcome their fear of rejection.

Passive-aggressive

The term passive-aggressive categorizes behavior that is a passive form of otherwise unexpressed aggression. Passive-aggressive personalities resist all demands that are placed on them to perform, but they do this indirectly, never by saying no outright. They tend to procrastinate, to dawdle, to "forget" important meetings or memos or deadlines; whatever it was they did not want to do is not done, or not done well. Since their professional reputation suffers from these actions, they rarely get very far in their careers. Socially, they are generally viewed with disfavor because of all their unkept promises. This in turn leads to a pessimistic view of the future and of life in general, which tends to sour an already resentful attitude.

Paranoid

Paranoid personalities don't trust anybody. They see schemes to undermine them everywhere they look. Their all-pervading suspicion that others are plotting against them leads to an ever-vigilant watchfulness. They guard themselves closely, afraid they will unwittingly aid whoever is threatening at the moment. Not unnaturally, they seem very cold and aloof to others. Consequently, they are left alone, which suits them well. They are extremely serious and don't often have a sense of humor.

They generally pride themselves on their "objectivity," but in actuality they are rigid and defensive when contradicted. They tend to read special meanings in everyday actions—assuming, for instance, that they are being spied upon when a car follows them for a few blocks down the street. Trying to convince them that their mistrust is unjustified simply doesn't work. They will merely ignore any concrete evidence that does not confirm their suspicion, and in fact they will probably assume that the person challenging their beliefs is "one of Them." More men than women are diagnosed as having a paranoid personality.

Schizoid

The distinguishing feature of this disorder is the inability to form personal attachments. Schizoid personalities are usually loners—withdrawn, distant, apparently emotionless. They have very few, if any, close friends, preferring solitude. They seem dull and devoid of any sparkle and are generally indifferent to either praise or criticism. They also seem incapable of expressing any emotion—neither warmth nor anger. Sometimes they appear to be miles away in thought, as if reality is not the place where they want to spend their time.

Schizotypal

A person diagnosed as having schizotypal personality disorder exhibits essentially schizophrenic behavior (see Chapter 11), but not in a severe enough form to warrant the diagnosis of true schizophrenia. Odd speech patterns, bizarre thoughts and fantasies, and recurrent illusions are characteristic of the schizotypal personality. Depersonalization, described in Chapter 5, is often present. In addition, the person frequently displays inappropriate emotions—laughing while discussing some sad event, for instance—and has a strong inclination to remain alone, all of which clearly inhibits personal relations.

Borderline

"Unstable" is the word often used to describe the borderline personality. Impulsive and unpredictable, such an individual—usually a woman—shifts between moods, between pastimes, between lovers, between jobs—and does so often and rapidly. Everything is either very intensely "on" or completely "off" for her. Even her own self-image goes from exceptionally good to exceptionally bad over and over again. The kind of life-style thus led can be very self-destructive—there is no sense of stability, no awareness of goals, and no inclination to get either. Some theorists feel that because this category contains many elements of other personality disorders, borderline is really a level of personality organization (a low level) rather than a true disorder.

Antisocial

This disorder is the focus of a later section, so we shall here give just a brief description of its characteristics. In very general terms, the actions of antisocial personalities seem amoral—they flagrantly and repeatedly violate the rights of other people and very often break the law as well. What is more, they show no compunction for their behavior when they are caught—as they often are—performing an illegal act. Although they can dream up incredible schemes that work for a while, they inevitably fail. They seem incapable of learning from their past mistakes and thus often cannot maintain success for long at whatever their occupation.

General Characteristics

Symptoms of personality disorder usually begin to appear during childhood or adolescence, which was the case with Dan F.:

I can remember the first time in my life when I began to suspect I was a little different from most people. When I was in high school my best friend got leukemia and died and I went to his funeral.

Everybody else was crying and feeling sorry for themselves and as they were praying to get him into heaven I suddenly realized that I wasn't feeling anything at all. He was a nice guy but what the hell. That night I thought about it some more and found out that I wouldn't miss my mother and father if they died and that I wasn't too nuts about my brothers and sisters, for that matter. I figured there wasn't anybody I really cared for but, then, I didn't need any of them anyway so I rolled over and went to sleep. (McNeil, 1967, p. 87)

McNeil notes that although Dan was "as close as I ever got to what I conceived a psychopath [antisocial personality] ought to be" (p. 83), they met not as therapist and patient but through friends. Professionally, financially, and socially, Dan was (and probably still is) highly successful. He did not perceive himself as "disordered" or in need of treatment; quite the contrary. As McNeil concludes rather wryly, "Dan will always make out one way or another" (p. 89).

This paradox points to one of the major differences between personality disorders and most other types of disorder. Most people with personality disorders are quite able to live a fairly normal, though perhaps personally dissatisfying, life. They almost never seek treatment because they don't feel they have a problem, and they have no idea how distressing their behavior is to those around them. Fairly often they come to the attention of a clinician because of some secondary sign, such as alcohol or drug abuse or depression resulting from their inability to enjoy satisfying interpersonal relationships. Even then, the clinician must talk with the individual's family, friends, and business associates in order to appreciate the true nature of the problem.

From the diagnostic standpoint, personality disorders appear to be quite common but are difficult to identify. This situation has led some writers to question the value of personality disorder as a diagnostic category. Some common objections are as follows:

1. *The symptoms that characterize personality disorders are poorly defined.* For most types of personality disorder, too few data are available to serve as an adequate basis for diagnosis. Overall, diagnoses of personality disorders have proved to be inconsistent and unreliable (Spitzer and Fleiss, 1974) and there are no clear-cut, objective criteria to use in distinguishing between normal and abnormal manifestations of symptoms related to personality disorders. Deciding whether an individual is a compulsive personality or merely extremely formal and fastidious, or whether someone else is a histrionic personality or simply given to overdramatizing, is largely subjective.

2. *Personality disorders typically cannot be diagnosed simply on the basis of observable behavior.* Because these disorders are presumed to be long-term functional problems, the diagnostician must examine the patient's past history as well. This often means relying on the patient's own account of past behavior—not an ideal source of data. Moreover, both the patient and the diagnostician may be inclined to focus on those reported memories that seem relevant to the present problem and ignore those that appear irrelevant or contradictory. Generally, reports from past and present friends and associates will confirm any suspicions, but getting them requires extra effort for which most diagnosticians just don't have the time.

3. *Characterizing personality disorders as essentially fixed and consistent over long periods assumes that personality in general is consistent.* Many psychologists take issue with the DSM-III definition of personality on which the concept of personality disorder is based. They contend that to view a personality disorder—or any human behavior—as being based on fixed personality traits is to deny the flexibility and adaptability of the individual in responding to continual changes in life situations.

EXPLAINING AND MANAGING PERSONALITY DISORDERS

As we just stated, there is considerable debate over the issue of fixed personality traits. This in effect stems from different theoretical viewpoints: Psychodynamic therapists are more likely to agree that this category is valid than, say, humanists, who believe that the individual's personality is continually growing and changing. Clearly, then, there is equal debate on the topic of etiology. In the final analysis, however, data on these disorders are so limited that very few studies have been done to determine their possible causes. The one exception to this is antisocial personality disorder, which is to be discussed next.

There may be disagreement over etiology, but there is little dispute over the management of these disorders: By and large, nothing works. First, as we have said, people with personality disorders don't really feel that anything is wrong—with themselves, that is. Therefore they are rarely seen by clinicians. Second, they are all so convinced that their view of themselves and others is the right one that they don't respond well at all to any challenges to their belief systems.

We can speculate on possible match-ups between disorders and therapies. For instance, gestalt therapy might be useful for work with histrionics, since one of its approaches is to make the person more aware of the body's physical signs and what they mean. If a histrionic woman is made to focus on her seductive maneuvers, perhaps the therapist could make her aware of the manipulation involved. Likewise, it seems highly likely that Rogers's client-centered therapy might eventually help an avoidant personality, since the humanist clinician showers the client with nonjudgmental acceptance and approval. But it is not certain that the results of treatment would last outside the therapist's office. However, the chances that a person with paranoid personality disorder could be helped by therapy are very limited; indeed, it is doubtful that the person could put aside all suspicions long enough to enter therapy.

In the next section we shall focus on one particular type of personality disorder: the antisocial personality. While people suffering from most personality disorders may create considerable inconvenience to themselves and the people with whom they come in contact, those with antisocial personality disorder can be responsible for much more serious damage. The antisocial personality is the most extensively researched and reliably diagnosed of the personality disorders. It is also a useful focal point for discussing crime and criminals, whose antisocial behavior often resembles that of people with antisocial personality disorder but also differs from it in several important ways.

THE ANTISOCIAL PERSONALITY

The English psychiatrist J. C. Prichard established the antisocial personality as a behavioral type in 1835 when he described it as "moral insanity." In the late nineteenth century, individuals who were believed to be genetically predisposed to antisocial behavior were labeled *psychopaths,* a term still used by some writers to describe extreme cases, but officially out of favor. As the influence of environmental factors on the development of personality became increasingly evident, the term **sociopath** (Partridge, 1930) began to replace psychopath in most descriptions of antisocial personality. We have endeavored to use only antisocial personality (or, on occasion, sociopath) since we feel that term has the greatest degree of definition.

Primary Characteristics

According to DSM-III, antisocial personality disorder occurs in only about 3 percent of males and 1 percent of females in the general population. Although most of us occasionally exhibit some of the characteristics common to the disorder—for example, self-centeredness and impulsiveness—the true antisocial personality shows these qualities to a degree that is clearly extreme. A detailed portrait of the individual with antisocial personality disorder was presented by Hervey Cleckley (1964) in his book *The Mask of Sanity* and subsequently augmented by McCord and McCord (1964) and Hare (1970a,b). Cleckley's observations can be summarized in the categories that follow.

Inability to feel guilt. People with antisocial personality disorder seem to lack a conscience. Unable to distinguish between right and wrong, they feel no remorse for their harmful acts and may even feel contempt for those who suffer as a consequence of their destructive behavior. They appear to be totally self-centered and feel no guilt when they mistreat or betray people. They often appear incapable of understanding why anyone is disturbed by their antisocial actions.

Inability to learn from experience. Sociopaths do not benefit from their mistakes: Punishment does not affect their behavior. Indifferent to authority, they seem to consider themselves immune from the consequences of their actions and behave as if the laws of society do not apply to them. Their inability to learn from experience may be attributable to their failure to exhibit normal anxiety and fear. Often they repeat the same antisocial acts time after time without apparently fearing punishment.

Impulsiveness. Antisocial personalities live for the present moment. Totally irresponsible and unconcerned with the future, they act impulsively to get what they want whenever they want it. They crave continual change and excitement and, consequently, may have trouble keeping a job or maintaining any sort of regular routine. Casual sex as well as drug and alcohol abuse may play a prominent role in their never-ending search for stimulation. They act on their whims, and they demand instant gratification of their desires.

Any criminal act they attempt is not likely to be well-planned or carefully thought out. Reckless and aggressive, these individuals do not commit crimes merely for financial gain; rather, they seem to engage in antisocial behavior just for the fun of it.

Inability to form personal attachments. Loyalty and affection are not in the emotional repertoire of people with antisocial personality. They invariably are loners, with many acquaintances but no strong personal ties. Manipulative and exploitive, they find it impossible to build close and lasting friendships and show complete disinterest in the problems and feelings of other people. They are chronic liars and thrill-seekers, who are unable to accept responsibility or to fulfill commitments.

Ability to appear charming and intelligent. Despite their long-term failure to sustain close personal ties, antisocial personalities often make wonderful first impressions. They seem intelligent, clever, and likeable. They wear the "mask of sanity" referred to by Cleckley (1964). Their charming manner, combined with their shrewdness at manipulating people and their complete lack of sympathy for their victims, makes them excellent con-artists—if they can stay interested long enough to carry out the swindle.

At age sixteen John was involved in a fight at school, during which he knifed a classmate who said that John was trying to rob him. John was sent to reform school for six months. While there, he organized a small riot that left one guard and two inmates badly injured. When he was released, he moved to another town and got a job as a door-to-door salesman. He never saw his family again. He married when he was eighteen and quit his job. His wife supported him for awhile; then he went back to work, this time taking a job that forced him to travel from town to town. Within six months he was married to two other women in different towns. He was soon arrested for bigamy, and he spent a short time in jail.

Afterward, John began his door-to-door selling again, this time swindling elderly people. He would make them sign phony contracts to have their homes painted, take a cash deposit from them, and then move to another area. He was caught after buying drinks for everyone in the same bar several nights in a row.

After his fourth or fifth release from prison, John obtained a mail-order doctorate of divinity and established a parish. When the congregation found out about his past, they forced him to leave, but he soon found new victims. Now at 40, John is monogamous and still a pastor. The only trouble that he has run in to in the last five years concerned questionable expenditures of contributions; nothing came of it.

John exemplifies many of the features Cleckley and others have described: impulsiveness, inability to profit from experience, a knack for making a good impression, lack of emotional ties, freedom from anxiety and guilt, impatience with boredom. John's case has an additional factor that has not previously been mentioned—as he grew older, he became less prone to cause problems. Many people with antisocial personality disorders settle down as they age.

John probably would be diagnosed by any psychologist as a clear case of antisocial personality disorder. A judge, however, might see it differently. Besides disrupting the lives of those around him, John committed several crimes: fraud, bigamy, assault and battery, and theft, among others. In keeping with the law, he spent a considerable part of his life not in therapy but in jail. John is a typical sociopath; is he also a typical criminal? From the point of view of psychology, the answer is no.

CRIMINAL BEHAVIOR

Although sociopaths are likely to break the law at some time in their lives, by no means are all criminal acts performed by people with antisocial personalities. According to one study, (Gunn et al. 1978), only about one third of convicted criminals appear to be psychiatric cases. The distinction between the "normal" criminal (who, in DSM-III terms, exhibits "adult antisocial behavior") and the psychologically abnormal criminal is not always easy to draw, however. Does it make sense to call a person who has intentionally murdered another human being "normal"? How are we to distinguish between the criminal who merits psychiatric treatment and the criminal who merits life imprisonment? Obviously, the broad area in which psychology and criminal law overlap raises many complex social and moral questions.

Consider the case of John Gayce. Gayce was a prominent citizen of the Chicago suburb in which he lived, the owner of a flourishing construction company. He functioned well in the community, was respected by his neighbors, and was not particularly impulsive. Then he was convicted of raping and murdering more than thirty teenage boys, whom he subsequently buried beneath his house. Gayce's neighbors were shocked to discover that such a well-respected and highly successful businessman was a rapist and mass murderer.

Was Gayce psychiatrically disordered? Most people would say yes—yet he was ordered enough to plan each murder very carefully. And he knew that what he did was wrong (or at least illegal) because he disposed of the evidence equally carefully, though not quite carefully enough. Does this fit some of the characteristics that are typical of the antisocial personality?

Now consider another case—a Mafia "hit man." He is likely to be even more ordered and careful than Gayce was, planning his "hits" months in advance. And he also realizes the legal ramifications of what he does for a living, so he uses every means at hand to avoid capture; but occasionally a hit man does get caught. Like Gayce, he too leads a double life. He probably has a family and a regular job (a "front"); he may even attend church. All in all, he seems quite respectable. Is he disordered?

Cleckley (1964) has argued that there is a fundamental distinction between a person with an antisocial personality and a typical criminal. He calls this second category **dyssocial.** Cleckley feels that criminals plan their crimes carefully to achieve some socially approved goal (such as financial gain), whereas antisocial personalities act impulsively without considering the possible consequences of their actions. This distinction is a useful point of departure for the psychologist. Professional criminals—whether they are burglars or hired killers—do not act to gratify an impulse. They are not unaware of the dangers of their chosen profession, and their activities are carefully planned to optimize their chances of success and escape. Unlike the antisocial personality, they may have close friends and be devoted to their families. Their goals and aspirations are much like those of normal people. They may seem hard and unfeeling in performing their jobs, but they separate that aspect of their life from their nonprofessional activities. They engage in crime for financial gain rather than simply for stimulation; their antisocial behavior does not pervade their entire personality. By this definition of the dyssocial criminal, we see that Gayce does not fit that category, since his crimes did not help him achieve socially approved goals. Still, whether

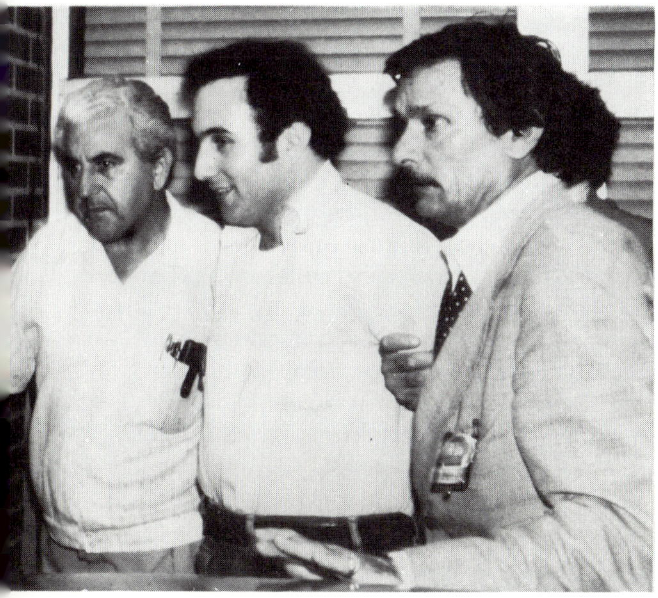

It is difficult to decide how criminal behavior should be categorized. Was Al Capone a classic dyssocial criminal? Were Bonnie and Clyde (here portrayed by Faye Dunaway and Warren Beatty) antisocial personalities? Should David Berkowitz ("Son of Sam") have been declared legally insane?

Gayce was antisocial or had different psychological problems is unknown.

The U. S. Crime Rate

Studies by the Federal Bureau of Investigation indicate that many types of serious crimes are on the increase in the United States. During the first half of the 1970s, the rate of violent crime—including homicide, rape, robbery, and aggravated assault—increased over fifteen times as fast as the population size. In an average 24-hour period in 1977, 53 murders, 180 rapes, 1440 aggravated assaults, and some 30,000 robberies, thefts, and burglaries took place in the United States (Uniform Crime Reports, 1978). Furthermore, the actual crime rate is probably considerably higher than these statistics suggest. It has been estimated that from one third to one half of all serious crimes—a category that includes violent crimes plus burglary, larceny, and auto theft—go unreported. The crime rate in cities is almost three times as high as that in rural areas, although it is increasing faster in the latter. And these figures cannot begin to estimate the amount of criminal activity undertaken by groups like the Mafia. Nor is it clear how much "white collar" crime occurs; some embezzlers today are computer wizards who can conceal their financial manipulations until long after they have actually absconded with the funds. Nevertheless, it is estimated that both mob and white collar activity is extremely profitable for those involved.

Who is responsible for all this criminal activity? Of the more than 10 million Americans arrested each year for the commission of serious crimes, some 74 percent are under 25 (Megargee, 1979). One reason this figure is so high is that over a million of the crimes involved are auto thefts, which are committed mainly by young people. On the other hand, 10 percent of the murders reported in 1977 were committed by people under 18, and 43 percent by people under 25. Most violent crimes involve an assailant and a victim who know each other; a person is twice as likely to be attacked by a relative or an acquaintance than by a stranger. White criminals most often victimize other whites and black criminals, other blacks. The great majority of criminals are male, although the number of serious crimes committed by women has been increasing rapidly in recent years. Altogether, more than half a million Americans—16 percent of them women—are currently serving time in prison, and twice as many more are on probation.

The proportion of both arrests and convictions is highest among the poor and nonwhite. We shall discuss the various sociocultural reasons for this pattern later in the chapter. Another important factor, however, is bias in our legal system—a bias that ranks crimes against person as worse than crimes against property. Yet in financial terms, "white collar" crime accounts for the overwhelming majority of American crime. All the burglaries, robberies, auto thefts, larcenies, and forgeries committed each year cost the public about $1 billion; money stolen by tax fraud alone totals some $25 to $45 billion a year (Akers, 1973).

The legal system is seemingly more tolerant of white collar criminals, such as the corporation executive who steals a few hundred thousand dollars by tampering with the company computer, than it is of the heroin addict who holds up a liquor store for less than five hundred dollars. Since white collar crime can all too easily go undetected, it is a great temptation. And often when it is caught, the corporation involved prefers to avoid the publicity of litigation and decides not to prosecute. But when they do go to court, the white collar defendant usually has the advantages of being able to afford a capable and experienced lawyer and of looking and sounding respectable to the judge and jury. No small point, this psychological edge can make the difference between a suspended sentence and a prison term.

EXPLAINING ANTISOCIAL AND CRIMINAL BEHAVIOR

We shall review the main areas of research on the origins of the antisocial personality, and also look at theories about crime. It is not always

Close-up: Are Criminal Traits Hereditary?

In a now-classic study, *The Jukes: A Study in Crime, Pauperism, Disease, and Heredity,* Richard L. Dugdale argued that immorality, including criminality, insanity, and other forms of deviance, were inherited traits.

With the support of the State Prison Association of New York, Dugdale traced the roots of the "Jukes" family (an alias) back to the mid-1700s, and more specifically to the wife of one Jukes son, whom he dubbed "Margaret, mother of criminals." Of the 540 "blood relatives" and 169 persons related by marriage or cohabitation to Margaret or her progeny, Dugdale concluded that 140 were criminals, 300 were wards of the state, and the remainder were generally debauched and despicable.

It was not until after Dugdale's death that criticisms of his work arose. Many of the Jukeses classified by Dugdale as criminals had never been arrested, let alone convicted of a crime. Instead, the criminal Jukes included "a reputed sheep-stealer," "an unpunished and cautious thief," and even one family member about whom Dugdale noted that it was "impossible to get any reliable information, but it is evident that at nineteen he was a leader of crime." Moreover, later researchers have pointed out the impossibility of tracing family lines of those born illegitimately and the unreliability of poor-to-nonexistent records of insanity, venereal disease, etc., in backwoods America of the eighteenth and nineteenth century.

In his determination to prove his theory, Dugdale ignored or rejected information that did not support his view; he came to view every Jukes as a probable criminal and every criminal as a probable Jukes. This steadfast refusal to study the roots of criminality objectively has made Dugdale's work a classic lesson on the dangers of preconceptions in research.

easy to separate the two: Most research on antisocial personality disorders has drawn its subjects from prisons, and the experience of arrest and incarceration may well affect the attitudes and behavior of those individuals.

Biological Explanations

As with other mental disorders, the major biologically based ideas of etiology can be broken down into genetic theories and physiological theories. We shall discuss them in turn.

Genetic theories

Early in the twentieth century, an Italian criminologist named Cesare Lombroso proposed a hereditary theory of criminality. Lombroso believed that criminality was an inherited characteristic manifested in the shape of the head and facial features, and he devised elaborate mechanisms for measuring the head to determine the degree of criminality inherent in any individual. This line of research is not as eccentric as it may sound. For one thing, we know that criminal behavior does run in families to some extent; it is not unreasonable to suppose that *if* there is a genetic factor in criminality, it might be correlated with one or more physical features. Furthermore, other investigations have suggested a relationship between body type and mental disorder (Kretschmer, 1925) and between body type and personality (Sheldon, 1940).

But while these and subsequent studies have turned up some interesting results, there is no clear evidence at present of any relationship between physical features and criminality or personality disorder.

Other researchers studied identical twins born to known criminals but separated at birth, hoping to discover whether genetically identical individuals raised in different environments would exhibit the same inherited behavioral characteristics (Rosanoff et al., 1941). Unfortunately, their findings proved inconclusive because of the difficulty of distinguishing between hereditary and environmental influences and the failure of the researchers to distinguish between criminal behavior and antisocial personality disorders.

A more recent study in Denmark focused on adopted children whose biological or adoptive fathers or both were known criminals (Hutchings and Mednick, 1974). Among adoptees whose biological fathers were criminals, the crime rate was twice as high (21.0 percent) as the rate for adoptees with no criminal father (10.4 percent) or an adoptive but not a biological criminal father (11.2 percent). Adoptees whose biological and adoptive fathers were both criminals had the highest crime rate of all—36.2 percent. Crowe (1974) found that adopted offspring of antisocial mothers had a significantly higher incidence of antisocial behavior than adopted controls. There seemed to be an interaction between length of time in custodial care and having an antisocial mother.

Subsequent genetic research has focused on the **XYY chromosomal aberration** (Jacobs et al., 1965). Most people have one pair of gender-related chromosomes; maleness is genetically determined by an XY chromosome configuration and femaleness by an XX chromosome configuration. A few men—including Richard Speck, the man who murdered eight student nurses in Chicago in 1966—have an additional Y chromosome. The incidence of the XYY chromosome configuration in the general population is .4 percent; among convicted criminals it is 1.5 percent. However, the relationship of this genetic factor to criminal behavior has not been well established (Hook, 1973; Shah, 1976). Some theorists have proposed that the XYY chromosomal type is linked to an overproduction of the male hormone testosterone and, consequently, a predisposition toward aggressive behavior. This hypothesis has not been substantiated by clinical evidence. Many individuals who have the XYY chromosomal aberration exhibit no criminal tendencies whatever, and the great majority of criminals do not have this abnormality.

Physiological theories

Substantial evidence has been gathered to suggest that people with antisocial personality disorder may be afflicted with a physiological defect. In studying electroencephalograms (EEGs), which show patterns of brain waves, researchers have found a high incidence of abnormality among people with the disorder. Positive spikes, indicating brief and sudden bursts of brain-wave activity, usually occur in 2 percent of the general population: They show up in 40 percent of the EEGs of antisocial personalities with histories of sudden, aggressive behavior (Hughes, 1965). Moreover, about half of those diagnosed as having antisocial personality disorder commonly show slow brain-wave activity in the temporal lobe of the cerebral cortex, which is a normal pattern in young children.

These data have not always been confirmed in later research. One study (Fenton et al., 1974) reported no differences between antisocial personalities and normal controls in slow-wave temporal lobe activity. Syndulko (1975) reported no differences on a wide range of EEG measures. However, the issue is still alive: Harper and colleagues (1972) found that 53 of 100 antisocial personalities had abnormal EEGs.

These studies suggest the possibility of **cortical immaturity**—failure of the cerebral cortex to develop on schedule—as a factor in antisocial personality. The cortex is the part of the brain that controls such higher functions as learning and memory. The temporal lobe of the cortex is close to the *amygdala,* a structure in the limbic system that facilitates aggression and plays a role in the formation of memory. Cortical immaturity could help explain why sociopaths can remain free of fear in extremely upsetting situations and why they have trouble associating past memory with current experience. An inability to connect the results of previous behavior with present behavior might also explain the impulsiveness of such individuals and their inability to learn from experience. Without any connection between past and present events, their behavior occurs in a moral vacuum. According to Mednick (1974), a normal person experiences fear of punishment when contemplating an antisocial or criminal act, and inhibiting that act dissipates the fear. A lower susceptibility to this anticipatory fear, and therefore to its dissipation, would make the sociopath less successful at avoiding antisocial behavior.

The idea that the lack of fear exhibited in antisocial personality disorders is based on physiology has been supported by laboratory experiments. David Lykken (1957) devised a test in which college students, nonsociopathic prisoners, and sociopathic prisoners were subjected to mild electric shocks unless they took certain precautions. Although all three groups were comparable in intelligence, the sociopathic prisoners seemed less capable of acting to prevent the shocks. Apparently the prospect of experiencing a shock did not create enough anxiety to motivate the sociopaths to avoid it. Nygard (1975) found that in a learning task antisocial personalities did not respond differently to two levels of shock, while normal subjects did. Schacter and Latane (1964) provided further support for this hypothesis when they found that sociopathic prisoners performed better on Lykken's test when first injected with adrenaline, which can induce anxiety. However, antisocial personalities have been reported to perform better than nonantisocial subjects at observational learning (Matthey, 1974), which is in keeping with their social adeptness.

The inability to respond normally to fear-provoking stimuli has also been linked to autonomic underarousal. According to Hare (1970), the autonomic nervous system of persons with antisocial personality may be unable to achieve sufficient arousal to induce normal levels of fear. This theory may explain their ability to remain calm in a dangerous or upsetting situation, as well as their failure to learn from bad experiences. Hare's hypothesis was supported by Fenz (1971), who found that sociopathic individuals seem to have an insatiable need for stimulation. Quay (1965) suggested that antisocial personalities engage in impulsive behavior in order to raise their arousal level; however, subsequent research (Siddle, 1977) has failed to substantiate Quay's contention that constant thrill-seeking is actually an attempt to compensate for autonomic underarousal.

Psychological Explanations

The various psychological theories offer explanations of how the antisocial and the criminal or dyssocial personalities develop. We shall examine them in turn.

Psychodynamic theories

One hypothesis presented by Freudian theory is that antisocial personality is the result of an underdeveloped superego. The superego, you may remember, is the part of the personality that controls the aggressive and sexual inclinations of the id—in effect, it is similar to the person's conscience. Normal development of the superego depends in part on identification with the parent of the same sex during childhood. Absence of the same-sex parent from the home or failure to provide the child with an emotionally secure homelife may therefore result in faulty superego development. Because the personality is thought to be formed by the age of six, children who are exposed to antisocial values by their parents are considered unlikely ever to develop a normal superego, which means that they will be unable to profit from experience later in life.

Although this theory cannot be tested directly, research has confirmed the existence of a strong link between antisocial behavior and parental deprivation. A study by Oltman and Friedman (1967) revealed that parental loss—usually involving the departure of the father from the household—was more common among sociopaths than among drug addicts, alcoholics, schizophrenics, and other psychiatric groups. Sociologist Lee N. Robins (1966) substantiated the significance of parental influence in the de-

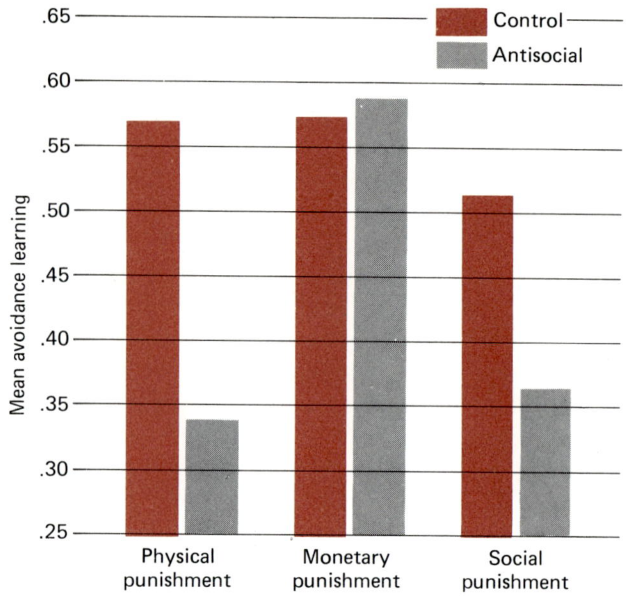

Figure 10.1. *Success of various punishments in reducing antisocial behavior. From Schmauk, 1970.*

velopment of antisocial personality in her follow-up study of 524 children who had been seen in a child guidance clinic over 30 years before. Robins found that the single most reliable predictor of antisocial behavior in adulthood was growing up in a home with antisocial parents. Robins suggested that it is not family disruptions in themselves that cause antisocial behavior; rather, it is the emotional instability of the parents that leads to both the disruptions and the child's subsequent antisocial behavior. Rutter (1974a) reported that although antisocial behavior is correlated with divorce, it results more from the conflict associated with parental separation. McCord and McCord (1964) concluded from a review of research on the subject that parental rejection was the strongest common thread among those with antisocial personality disorder.

Another idea that grew out of Freudian theory relates to the aggressive instinct that may be built up within the ego during the formation of the superego. According to a hypothesis called **catharsis of aggression,** a person who is forced to hold back this pent-up aggression is more likely to engage in violent acts than a person who vents aggressive feelings, whether directly or indirectly. In other words, a person has to let off steam once in a while—or at least enjoy watching someone else letting off steam. This idea has not stood up under scientific scrutiny, however. Contrary to popular belief, individuals who are encouraged to express aggression or who witness other people behaving aggressively tend to be more aggressive as a result. Aside from what this says about gestalt and other aggression-venting therapies, it raises interesting questions about the effects of television viewing on the American public.

Behavioral theories

According to behavioral theories, most normal adults received consistent reinforcement for positive social behavior when they were children—that is, they were rewarded for being good. In contrast, adults with antisocial personality disorders received inconsistent reinforcement as children, sometimes rewarded and sometimes punished regardless of their behavior. Inconsistent reinforcement teaches children that there is no connection between their behavior and its environmental consequences: Children whose parents reward aggressiveness one day and punish it the next are unlikely to perceive any clear relationship between what they do and what consequences are likely to occur. Similarly, children who are beaten every night for no reason are likely to assume that there is no real distinction between right and wrong behavior. This is supported by the case histories of many antisocial personalities.

In some instances, antisocial behavior may be reinforced throughout the course of a person's life. A child may discover that antisocial behavior is an effective way of getting attention. As an adult, the individual finds that aggressive and even criminal acts can lead to financial success, adventure, and personal notoriety. Antisocial personalities may not be well liked, but they are not easily ignored. Schmauk (1970) used a variation of the Lykken study mentioned earlier to investigate the possibility that their ability to learn to avoid making errors relates to the nature of the reinforcement they receive. Schmauk found that when subjects were penalized for errors with physical punishment (electric shock) or social punishment (criticism from the experimenter), they learned less well than the control groups, as they did in Lykken's experiment. But when the punishment was financial (losing money), they learned *more* successfully than the controls.

Social learning theories stress the importance of modeling and reinforcement in the development of antisocial personality disorder. Modeling involves imitation; many sociopaths have grown up with an inappropriate model to imitate, or with no model at all. This theory—that a child whose parents or guardians did not behave according to socially accepted standards is more likely to develop into an antisocial adult—is supported by Robins's analysis (1966).

Social Explanations

Neither biological nor psychological theories, both of which center only on the individual, account for the influence of social variables on the development of antisocial personality disorder and criminality. The fact that both these types of antisocial behavior are so prevalent among the poor and culturally disadvantaged suggests a strong link between social pathology and personal pathology.

Several elements that are frequently found in the background of sociopaths—particularly parental rejection, disrupted family life, material deprivation, and antisocial role models—are fairly common in the lower socioeconomic classes. Growing up in such a situation may predispose a person toward antisocial personality disorder. Many lower-class children live under extreme psychic stress (Masuda et al., 1978; Martin et al., 1978). Parents who are burdened by poverty and stressful living conditions may pay too little attention to their children, discipline them inconsistently or even reject them entirely (McCord and McCord, 1964). Children in such circumstances may well reject the adult world in return. With parents who are absent, abusive, or prone to antisocial activities, they have no opportunity to learn to depend on other people for emotional support and gratification. Lacking both the trust and the social skills necessary to get along with others, they grow up resenting or despising society, in which they feel like outsiders. An outcast from the Great American Dream—a poor person in the most affluent society in the world—they may turn to aggressive behavior to express profound disappointment and anger.

The idea of a social basis for antisocial personality disorder is supported by the fact that some subcultural groups almost never produce sociopaths. Among some religious groups, a powerful sense of communal unity seems to preclude antisocial attitudes and behavior. Family and intergroup ties are strong, norms of behavior are well defined and uniformly enforced, and children are provided with appropriate and consistent role models. Even though such environments are successful in preventing antisocial personality disorders, they have other disadvantages, and they do not seem to represent a realistic model for society as a whole in the foreseeable future.

Broken homes are common to the background of many individuals with antisocial personalities. The trauma involved in parental loss through separation or divorce typically seems to occur before the separation rather than after it, however (Hare, 1970a,b). This is probably because a separation is usually the climax of severe disturbances in the family's emotional life, during which the constant tension between the parents often focuses on the child. After the separation, the absence of one or both parental role models may leave the child confused, struggling to survive alone in the environment in which the only way to get what is needed is to take it. Greer (1964) found that 60 percent of the antisocial individuals he studied had suf-

Many subcultural groups, such as these Amish from Delaware, possess a strong sense of family ties and communal unity that seem to discourage antisocial behavior.

fered parental loss during childhood—significantly more than any other pathological group. Of course, loss of a parent and inconsistent punishment make children feel unworthy and assume that there is no point in trying to live up to parental ideals. Indulged by a doting mother and confused by a stern but emotionally distant father, the child may begin to assume the characteristics associated with antisocial personality disorder.

Criminals appear to be responding to many of the same sociocultural influences as people with antisocial personality disorder, but their response is in fact different. Of course, we should bear in mind that about a third of sentenced prisoners actually are suffering from antisocial personality or some other mental disorder (Gunn et al., 1978), so that to treat criminals as a single group is somewhat misleading. Furthermore, the factors that lead half a dozen young teenagers to steal a car for a joy ride are bound to be different from those that induce a 22-year-old woman to shoot her boyfriend or a 34-year-old man to create a computer program that siphons money out of a bank. The common thread among criminals is their choice of an antisocial life-style (or an antisocial act) rather than one based on those rules and values that middle-class America considers standard. This choice appears to be motivated in many cases by the same childhood deprivations and adolescent or adult frustrations that lead other individuals into antisocial personality disorders.

We do not have enough information about the causes of either of these behavior patterns to say for certain why, given apparently identical circumstances, one person develops a personality disorder, a second turns to crime, and a third lives a normal, well-adjusted life. One important difference, however, seems to be the availability of an alternative set of social standards. Criminals are not necessarily rejecting the whole idea of living by society's standards; they may simply be choosing the standards of a criminal subculture. A number of black writers have commented on the prestige enjoyed by the successful drug dealer who drives a new Cadillac, wears flashy, expensive clothes, and carries a roll of hundred-dollar bills. Such an individual is probably a stronger role model for the children in the community than the successful businessperson blocks away.

I don't know what writer first described the safeman as the aristocrat of the criminal class. . . . They stole clean, with only the slightest potential for violence. They deplored violence and dismissed it scornfully as "rawjaw"—a classless and inartistic crime which needlessly frightened and stirred the ordinary people, which put pressure on the police who made the life of a quiet outlaw more difficult. They were also respected for their traditional knowledge and their craftsmanship. It was generally accepted that any master safecracker could easily earn his bread in the straight world if his sense of honor were not too fine to permit him to disgrace himself by working for wages. More realistically, they were respected because they had the skills necessary to steal very large amounts. (Braly, 1977, p. 125.)

For someone growing up in underprivileged circumstances, crime—dealing drugs, running numbers, cracking safes, or whatever—may seem to provide just as workable a set of rules and values as those of the straight world. It offers financial benefits and social prestige to the successful; and it has the added allurement of being illegal, a special but risky undertaking that allows membership with the "in" crowd. For some people, these attractions outweigh the disadvantages of possible prison sentences, death by violence (or by drugs), and the prospect of being forever an outcast from the rest of society.

Social theories regarding antisocial personality and crime generally propose an interaction between biological and psychological predispositions and environmental circumstances. Unfortunately, aggression seems to be an established way of life in the contemporary American environment. Spanking and other forms of corporal punishment are an accepted

Some researchers believe that children are negatively influenced by the violence they view on television.

Close-up: Can Television Cause Aggression?

Television programs glorifying violence have long been accused of encouraging aggressive behavior in children; now they have been cited as the possible cause of murder. In June 1977, Ronald Zamora, aged 15, shot his next-door neighbor, an elderly Miami Beach widow, who discovered him burglarizing her home. Zamora's defense lawyer, Ellis Rubin, attempted to prove his client innocent by reason of insanity due to "prolonged, intense, involuntary, subliminal, television intoxication."

To convince the jury that Zamora was unable to differentiate between right and wrong at the time of the crime, Rubin intended to present testimony from several psychiatrists that Zamora had been brainwashed and was living in a "television fantasy world." According to Rubin, "pulling the trigger became as common to him as killing a fly." The defense further claimed the crime loosely resembled two episodes of *Kojak* and a Dracula movie that Zamora had watched the night before the murder. The boy's parents were willing to testify that their son was a confirmed TV addict who spent at least six hours a day watching television. His favorite shows were cops-and-robbers series, such as *Kojak, Baretta,* and *Starsky and Hutch.*

During the trial, Judge Paul Baker refused to accept generalized studies linking TV violence to aggression. He allowed as evidence only psychiatric examination reports on Zamora and studies that linked specific television shows to specific acts of violence. The defense had to concede that no such specific studies existed, and the jury convicted Zamora of first degree murder.

part of childrearing in many American homes, and violence between spouses is far from uncommon as a part of the family problem-solving process. The effect of television on children remains controversial, but it is clear from even a casual study of television programming that the viewer is exposed to a continual display of crime and violence. Although justice usually triumphs in the end on television, research suggests that viewers are more likely to remember the deviant behavior than its ultimate consequences (Bandura et al., 1963)—the thrill of the gunshots and the chase lingers on long after the slam of the prison door has faded. Children who model their behavior on that of bickering parents or on that of the television and comic-book characters who figure prominently in their fantasies are likely to conceive of human society as a structure in which violence and brutality have a rightful place.

MANAGING THE ANTISOCIAL PERSONALITY AND THE CRIMINAL

Treating individuals with antisocial personality disorder has not proved highly successful. Because they are not distressed, these individuals rarely seek psychological help. As long as they are functioning adequately in their environment, they are unlikely to be committed involuntarily. Those who are convicted of a crime and sentenced to prison may be seen by prison psychologists, but the majority are never seen for therapy at all.

The psychologist or psychiatrist who attempts to help these individuals faces a formidable task. Sociopaths never accept responsibility for their own behavior and will exert more effort in trying to charm the therapist—often successfully!—than in discussing their actions and attitudes. Therapy seems to offer little benefit to them. Failing to profit from experience, they lack insight into their own behavior. Given the chance, most will avoid therapy sessions. The very characteristics that result in the diagnosis of antisocial personality are the characteristics that impede their participation and progress in therapy.

Biological Methods

Various biological treatments have attempted to alter the genetic defects and physiological abnormalities suspected of causing antisocial personality disorder. Early remedies included the use of electroconvulsive therapy to alter the EEG abnormalities associated with antisocial behavior, and the use of medication intended to raise the individual's arousal level and thus eliminate the compulsive need for thrill-seeking. Unfortunately, neither of these techniques proved very effective. In the 1950s, *prefrontal lobotomy*—the surgical removal of that portion of the brain associated with aggressive activity—was a widely used procedure. Although patients usually did stop behaving aggressively, their personalities were so radically altered that the cure seemed disproportionate to the problem. More recent attempts at controlling behavior through psychosurgery include **stereotaxic surgery,** the implanting of tiny electrodes in the brain to destroy a small number of specific cells in the amygdala. Users of this technique claim clinical and surgical success in controlling antisocial behavior in violent patients (Mark and Ervin, 1970). Major tranquilizers like the phenothiazines and minor tranquilizers like the benzodiazepines have also proved somewhat successful in reducing excitability and aggressive tendencies (Moyer, 1971a,b).

The use of psychosurgery and pharmacotherapy raises serious ethical considerations, however. Critics have called lobotomies and other subsequent efforts to manipulate human behavior mind control and have pointed out that these techniques have most often been used by the rich and powerful to control the poor and defenseless. To alter another person's physiological control systems against that person's will is to interfere with human integrity in a most profound and disturbing way. The implications of mind control as a social and political weapon are frightening: Who is to be entrusted with the right to establish and enforce standards of right and wrong? Should the government or the scientific or medical community have the power to determine how the rest of us think, feel, and behave? There are commonly agreed-upon answers to these questions.

Psychological Methods

Individual psychodynamic therapy has generally not been successful since motivation and insight—the qualities required for progress in such therapy—are so notably lacking in the antisocial personality. Psychodynamic therapy has been used in group homes for adolescents with behavioral problems, the objective being to create an opportunity for the adolescent to begin to trust adults, identify with the therapist, and incorporate the social standards the therapist represents. Unfortunately, these programs have not yet been demonstrated to be effective.

Behavioral techniques have also been applied to adolescents with conduct disorders. Achievement Place, a home for adolescents with behavioral problems, was founded in Kansas and has been imitated across the country (Phillips et al., 1971; Cohen et al., 1968). A highly structured reinforcement program is used to encourage the residents to earn their privileges and to engage in prosocial behavior. Responsibility to other people is taught through group meetings and group decision making, and the individual adolescent is given frequent opportunities to interact with resident adult therapists.

Management techniques based on social learning theories have provided an alternative approach to the problem of controlling aggression. In treating antisocial personality disorder, the therapist attempts to control the environmental situation of patients in order to shape their behavior into more prosocial form. Bandura (1969) suggested three procedures in the modification of antisocial behavior: (1) removing reinforcers and, when possible, using punishment for antisocial behavior; (2) having the individual model prosocial behavior of admired individuals; and (3) phasing out material reinforcement as the individual begins to administer the symbolic rewards that play an important role throughout the program. As with most behavioral problems, the final goal is self-management of behavior.

Some therapists stress the importance of exposing the individual to other antisocial personalities who are more advanced in therapy and can serve as models for clients entering the program. Vaillant (1975) suggests that exposure to peers with similar problems is crucial to effecting changes in behavior, and that outpatient therapy, even if it occurs several times weekly, cannot succeed. According to Vaillant, punishment is ineffective; rather, sociopaths must be supported within the context of a group of peers in order to gain useful insights into their own behavior.

Most of these programs are less expensive than maintaining "reform schools" and have been highly successful at reducing antisocial behavior and increasing prosocial behavior while the individual is at the residential center. The relapse rate once the residents leave the home seems, however, to be about the same as that of adolescents leaving reform school. The gains shown at the residential home do not seem to last after the individual returns to a nontherapeutic environment.

This points to a perennial problem in treating antisocial personality disorder and other antisocial behavior: It is virtually impossible to control the patient's environment outside of treatment. Even if individuals learn new motivation and attitudes, the stresses and reinforcements they must return to are still very powerful. The adolescent boy who goes home to the same old pattern of parental abuse or neglect is likely to fall back into his old patterns of coping. Sometimes the parents can be persuaded to come in for therapy; but if one of them has antisocial tendencies—as is often the case—then treatment is likely to be avoided. It

Sterile, dehumanizing conditions in prisons and mental hospitals do little to prepare prisoners or patients for their return to normal society.

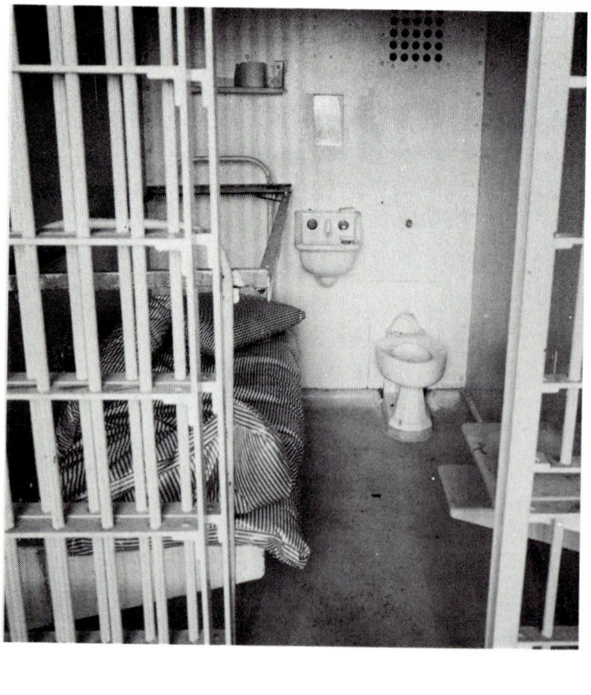

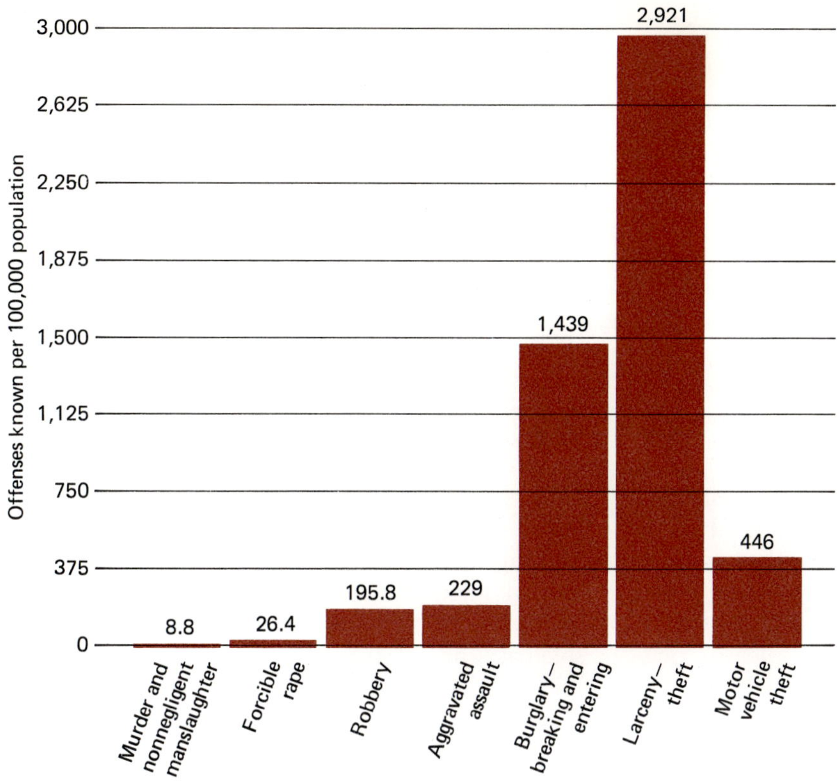

Figure 10.2. *Index crime rates. From* Statistical Abstract of the United States, *1977.*

is not practical to try to change the patient's whole network of relationships with friends, teachers, and so forth. The best way to ensure against relapse is to teach patients skills that will make success possible in the straight world, and keep them in a supportive environment until those skills have brought reinforcing success. This is ordinarily a long, involved process, one that few, if any, therapeutic programs are equipped to provide.

Prisons and Mental Hospitals

Most people who are caught violating the laws of society do not receive psychological counseling and rehabilitation. Unless they can afford very good lawyers, they are usually locked up in a prison. Rehabilitation and treatment play a very small role in the day-to-day reality of prison life. The overwhelming majority of prison personnel are not rehabilitation workers but rather administrators and guards. The chief functions of imprisonment are to remove criminals from society for a while and to punish them for their transgressions. Preparing them for life after they are set free is low on the list of priorities.

The inhumane conditions of prison life have been well publicized in recent years. Public indifference to the welfare of the convicted criminal has resulted in penal institutions that are overcrowded and understaffed. Furthermore, prisons surround criminals with antisocial models on which to pattern their own behavior—what better place than prison to learn the latest advances in the arts of burglary, arson, rape, and murder? Insufficient funding and overcrowding make therapy programs grossly inadequate in most prisons; the only nonconvict many prisoners see each day is an underpaid and discontented guard. On the whole, prisons serve as warehouses for the temporary storage of malfunctioning human beings and not as rehabilitation centers designed to help offenders return as productive members of society

Perhaps the deplorable conditions of prison life could be justified if they served as an effective deterrent to crime—but they do not. "Ex-cons" have little chance of succeeding on the outside: They are no better equipped to deal with society when they are released from prison than when they went in—except, of course, that they have had an excellent opportunity to sharpen their skills as criminals. Over 80 percent of major crimes in America are committed by persons who have already been incarcerated (Leinwand, 1972), and the probability of recidivism, or being jailed again, seems to increase with the length of time previously spent in prison (Glaser, 1964).

Involuntary confinement to mental institutions has not proved to be a satisfactory alternative to imprisonment. Individuals confined to either a prison or a mental hospital often receive indeterminate sentences—that is, they are supposedly confined only until they prove ready to return to society. In practice, however, the use of indeterminate sentences leaves prisoners or patients completely at the mercy of those in power. They cannot simply serve out the necessary time and await release. In effect, any failure to conform to the demands of the authorities can result in a life sentence.

The use of surgical and pharmaceutical techniques on involuntary subjects confined to mental hospitals raises more problems than it solves. Such mind control techniques have not yet advanced technologically beyond the point where subjects could be considered much more than human guinea pigs. Technological limitations notwithstanding, does society have the right to protect itself from criminal behavior by violating the individual's right to biological integrity? The dangers inherent in allowing the government to use medical technology to control human thought and behavior are too great to be casually condoned for the treatment of convicted criminals.

SUMMARY

Personality disorders include a variety of long-term problems involving a maladaptive self-image and distorted ways of relating to other people. Personality disorders tend not to be sharply defined, and it is often difficult to determine whether a person has a personality disorder or is merely eccentric in some aspect of behavior. The personality disorder that has been the most consistently diagnosed and extensively studied is antisocial personality disorder. Individuals with this disorder, sometimes referred to as sociopaths, are unable to control their behavior. They act impulsively, with little or no regard for the possible consequences of their actions. They have no fear of punishment, and they feel no remorse for the damage they do. Rather, they blame their victims for being so gullible.

Not all criminals are sociopaths. Although many criminals suffer from psychiatric problems, some choose crime simply as a way of making a living. Not surprisingly, the majority of convicted criminals come from lower socioeconomic backgrounds. By far the most expensive category of crime, however, is "white collar crime." Legal penalties for businessmen or politicians caught with their hands in the cookie jar are nevertheless rarely as severe as those imposed on thieves who steal in a less elegant fashion.

Little is known about the underlying causes of antisocial behavior. Distinctive EEG patterns and other clinical research suggest that the sociopath may be suffering from faulty development of those parts of the brain controlling learning and memory. Antisocial personality has also been linked to parental rejection, absence of appropriate models, and inconsistent reinforcement of behavior in childhood. Individuals deprived of cultural and economic advantages may engage in antisocial acts to vent their feelings of resentment and alienation, especially if they have learned to use aggression as their primary means of self-expression.

Criminals seem different from sociopaths. Although their backgrounds may be similar, criminals usually adopt the norms of an alternative subculture rather than the accepted social standards.

The treatment of antisocial personality disorder has been largely unsuccessful. Attempts at behavior modification through group interaction have proved to be of little enduring value once the individual is back on the street. Some success has been achieved in modifying behavior through the use of drugs and surgery, but these practices raise serious ethical and political questions about the right to experiment with mind control using involuntary subjects. Prison rarely rehabilitates criminals; instead it usually establishes them more firmly in their antisocial attitudes and behavior patterns. Ultimately, it may be our overly aggressive and socioeconomically unbalanced society itself that must be set straight before the problems of antisocial behavior and crime can be reduced to manageable proportions.

CHAPTER 11

Schizophrenic Disorders

DESCRIBING THE SCHIZOPHRENIC DISORDERS

Symptoms of Schizophrenia

Schizophrenic Logic

Types of Schizophrenia

Diagnostic Problems

EXPLAINING THE SCHIZOPHRENIC DISORDERS

Biological Explanations

Psychological Explanations

Social Explanations

Interactional Explanations

MANAGING THE SCHIZOPHRENIC DISORDERS

Biological Methods

Psychological Methods

Interactional Methods

Things were still unbearably beautiful. I got this giddiness in my stomach and walked around completely overwhelmed by the incredible loveliness of the trees and the sky and the moss, infinitely delicate worlds within worlds, and people's faces and the way they moved and my own body and what a perfect machine it was and the stove and the floors and our funky house. And everything fit together so perfectly. . . .

. . . The idea of purpose cracks me up. The only thing that puzzles me is why it took me so long to catch on. How did I manage to keep a straight face for as long as I did? I vaguely remember pain and struggle but it seems so remote, so unnecessary, so absurd.

And then one night, after several days of pure Eden, as I was trying to get to sleep, marveling at the fullness of each moment, feeling that I was living whole lifetimes within each moment, I started listening to and feeling my heart beat. Suddenly I became terribly frightened that it would stop.

And from out of nowhere came an incredibly wrinkled, iridescent face. Starting at a small point infinitely distant, it rushed forward, becoming infinitely huge. I could see nothing else. My heart had stopped. The moment stretched forever. I tried to make the face go away but it mocked me. I had somehow gained control over my heartbeat but I didn't know how to use it. I was holding my life in my hands and was powerless to stop it from dripping through my fingers. I tried to look the face in the eyes and realized I had left all familiar ground.

Mark Vonnegut, *The Eden Express*, p. 74*

Mark Vonnegut's *The Eden Express* is a powerful account of the battle between a thoughtful, intelligent young man and the disorder we call **schizophrenia.** This description of the onset of his disorder points to one of the aspects of schizophrenia that psychologists find most fascinating and frustrating: Every case is unique. For Vonnegut, a dedicated member of the countercultural movement, the schizophrenic experience was shaped by his philosophy and his familiarity with altered states of consciousness. His reaction to the startling changes in his mind was one of curiosity as well as fear, which led him to some insights that we shall return to later.

The schizophrenic disorders are the most commonly diagnosed mental disorder in the United States today. It has been estimated that about 1 percent of Americans, or roughly two million people, are currently diagnosed as schizophrenic (Dohrenwend and Dohrenwend, 1974). Approximately 20 percent of all first admissions to mental hospitals are diagnosed as schizophrenics. Many of these individuals will return to the hospital repeatedly; thus, almost half the mental hospital population at any given time consists of persons diagnosed as schizophrenic (Taube and Redick, 1973). It has been estimated that the incidence of schizophrenia is about 150 new cases per 100,000 population per year (Crocetti and Lemkau, 1967), although there may be more that go undiagnosed. With so many cases, it is not surprising that schizophrenia has been heavily researched. It has, however, remained an extremely perplexing disorder.

One conclusion most psychologists now agree on is that schizophrenia probably is not one disorder but several, with overlapping symptoms and perhaps different causes. The reason for using the single term schizophrenia rather than the more accurate **schizophrenic disorders** is that the word has been in use since the early days of psychology, and the group of disorders it referred to was recognized long before that.

DESCRIBING THE SCHIZOPHRENIC DISORDERS

The nineteenth-century German psychiatrist Emil Kraepelin described a collection of symptoms—disturbed thought and perceptual processes, inappropriate emotional expression, and other characteristics—that are still associated today with schizophrenia. Kraepelin used the term *dementia praecox* (coined by Morel in 1857) because he maintained that the disorder began

Eugen Bleuler, the Swiss psychiatrist who introduced the term schizophrenia to replace dementia praecox.

early in life (praecox), typically during adolescence, and that it involved irreversible mental deterioration (dementia). He also believed it had an organic cause.

In 1911, Eugen Bleuler, a Swiss psychiatrist, introduced the term *schizophrenia* to replace dementia praecox. Bleuler argued that not all cases of the disorder ended in complete disintegration, and further, that many of the affected individuals did not manifest the symptoms until their middle twenties or later. "Schizo" means splitting off of functions, and "phren" refers to the psyche or mind. Thus Bleuler proposed that schizophrenia was a fragmentation of the normally integrated mental processes of thought and emotion. The popular term "split personality" is very likely a descendant of the term schizophrenia. However, "split personality" refers to multiple personality, a completely different disorder (see page 153).

The current view of schizophrenia is not far removed from Kraepelin's and Bleuler's ideas. According to DSM-III, schizophrenia always involves a deterioration from a previous level of functioning. That is, individuals become unable to work, relate socially, or engage in daily activities as well as they did before the schizophrenic episode. The disorder usually begins during early adulthood. Most schizophrenics admitted to mental hospitals for the first time are between 20 and 40 years old; the highest rate of first admission for any ten-year period occurs among people between ages 25 and 35 (Yolles and Kramer, 1969). It occurs about equally among males and females. The psychotic symptoms must persist at least six months before a diagnosis of schizophrenia is appropriate; cases lasting less than six months are classified as *schizophreniform disorder*.

Symptoms of Schizophrenia

Bob also began to miss days at work and give vague excuses for his absence. Later I learned that he had spent this time watching his own house in a rented car parked inconspicuously down the street and shadowing his fellow employees home from work to see where they went and what they did. He began to keep a little black book in which he scribbled cryptic notes during the day. Whenever he did this, he would look around the room knowingly as if to say "I've got the goods on you now. You'd better stop what you are doing and be quick about it." He would then lock it in a box, place the box in a locked desk drawer, and head for the water cooler where he would pretend to drink while surveying the group to see if anyone looked guilty or frightened.

Bob's work began to suffer as he became obsessed with the idea that the enemy was closing in on him. He was sure there was a hidden message in routine requests whenever the slightest departure in procedure occurred. He was sure he was being checked so he could be proved incompetent and fired. At one point he brought me routine vouchers to ask if the signature on them "didn't look a little funny."

During this period of psychological decline, Bob was totally humorless. The elasticity of life had gone out of him. Everything worried him, the smallest things had great significance, and he began to lose weight rather markedly. He was eating only one meal a day, and he chose the meal he would eat by a system designed to outwit anyone studying his personal habits. He had even made an attempt to hire a private detective to help him discover who was after him, but the detective agency told him it was all in his imagination and to go home and forget it. He at once was convinced that they were in on it too.

*The world had indeed closed in on Bob H. After an explosive scene in the office one day, he became quite agitated and could not be reassured or calmed down. His superior told him to take several days off and get some rest. The fear that prompted this action communicated itself to Bob, so he left that day and never returned. His wife told us he came home in a rage, went to his room, locked the door, and wrote a detailed account of the day's events. Bob did not sleep that night. He wandered the house mumbling incoherently and woke his wife and children early to help him do what was needed. He kept the children home from school that day, locked all the windows and doors, and pulled the shades down at every window. Bob's vigil was kept all that day and night and he allowed no one to turn on the radio or television set since it was necessary for him to hear everything going on outside the house. He armed himself and by 4 a.m. was so agitated that he roared out of the house firing shots in the air and daring his enemies to come and get him. (McNeil, 1967, 170–171)**

This passage bears little resemblance to Mark Vonnegut's description of schizophrenia. Bob H. was suffering from paranoid schizophrenic delusions that apparently had been going on for some time. He was not aware that he himself was the center of the problem; indeed, he was convinced that everyone else was at fault.

One cannot say that the experiences of Bob H. or Mark Vonnegut are typical of schizophrenia. The disorder manifests itself differently in every person who has it, and it may even change considerably over time in the same person. In a hospital ward of schizophrenics, most patients may see through (or see the unreality of) the delusions of everyone else—without yielding an inch on their own delusions. As we look at schizophrenia, we must thus bear in mind that, with the exception of disordered thought, which is always present, the symptoms of the disorder represent a broad range of possibilities that cannot be summarized by a single case or group of cases.

Deteriorated functioning

An essential characteristic of schizophrenia is the deterioration in a person's previous level of functioning, generally involving behavior at work, at home, or with friends; it may take place gradually or suddenly. The main thing is that those close to the person notice that "he's not himself" or "she's turned into a different person." This is the aspect of schizophrenia that led Kraepelin to believe that the disorder involved some kind of organic degeneration.

Disordered thought

The odd ways schizophrenics think, communicate, and relate to other people represent what is perhaps their most striking characteristic. This is what Bleuler was referring to when he spoke of a splitting off of mental functions. To an observer, the schizophrenic's thought processes appear irrational, completely unlike those of normal people. In addition, schizophrenics typically show deficits in abstract thinking and conceptualization (Wright, 1975). They tend to be overinclusive in their thinking, which

* Elton B. McNeil, *The Quiet Furies: Man and Disorder.* © 1967. Adapted by permission of Prentice-Hall.

means that they have trouble excluding irrelevant material in problem solving or concept-formation tasks (Chapman and Taylor, 1957; Cromwell and Dokecki, 1968). They seem to be more susceptible than nonschizophrenics to drawing illogical conclusions from information. We shall look more closely at schizophrenic logic and illogic later in this chapter.

Delusions. The primary thought disturbance of schizophrenia is **delusions,** beliefs that run counter to reality. A delusion is not simply an unusual opinion, a nonconformist idea, or a superstition, but an irrational or exaggerated notion that contradicts obvious facts. Even in the face of strong evidence against their beliefs, schizophrenics cling tenaciously to them, turning to irrelevant information for support.

Delusions assume many different forms and can involve a variety of themes. One of the most common is the delusion of being controlled, in which individuals think that their thoughts, feelings, or behavior have been taken over and are being directed by some external force. In the delusion of *thought broadcasting,* they believe that their thoughts are being broadcast into the environment so that others can hear them. *Thought insertion* refers to the delusion that, somehow, thoughts that are not the schizophrenic's own are being inserted into the mind against the person's will. *Thought withdrawal,* on the other hand, is the belief that thoughts are somehow being drained from the individual's head.

The delusions of schizophrenia are characterized by unusual content as well as unusual form. Grandiose, hypochondriacal, melancholic, and persecutory (paranoid) delusions are the most common types (Shean, 1978). The man with a delusion of *grandeur* believes that he is a powerful, famous, or highly skilled person. Rokeach (1964) brought together three schizophrenics who believed that they were Jesus Christ. Despite the obvious fact that all three of them could not be Christ, since by their own admission there is only one son of God, all three schizophrenics refused to give up their grandiose delusions. Individuals with *hypochondriacal* delusions believe that they are afflicted with some bizarre physical illness in spite of having no substantiated symptoms.

Individuals with *melancholic* delusion are convinced that they are dead, a difficult belief for a nonschizophrenic to imagine, but to someone suffering from the extreme disorientation that comes with severe schizophrenia, being dead may be viewed as a perfectly plausible state to be in. The delusion of *persecution* involves the false belief of being hunted, followed, watched, harassed, pursued by one, or several, persons. Such schizophrenics may believe that someone is trying to poison their food or burn down their house; Bob H. thought he was under surveillance by his colleagues at work.

To summarize, a delusion is an obviously erroneous personal belief that is held tenaciously and directs a significant aspect of the afflicted person's behavior. It does not usually appear out of the blue—someone does not just wake up one morning believing he is Napoleon. A schizophrenic delusion is usually the result of inadequate attempts to explain puzzling events or relationships in the person's life. But the explanations are rather extraordinary because of the characteristics of schizophrenic thinking and perceptions.

Disordered communications

Closely related to the schizophrenic's disordered thought processes are disturbances in speech. In conversation, schizophrenics frequently come out with utterances that seem nonsensical, and their train of thought is often difficult or impossible to follow. The reason for this incoherent speech typically includes an inability to exclude irrelevant details, a preoccupation with events and ideas unknown to the listener, and obscure or unusual associations between words and concepts. For example, the schizophrenic might hear the word "pen," meaning a fenced enclosure, but then use this same word to mean a writing tool. The following conversation with a schizophrenic illustrates the point.

Interviewer: Have your views changed since I last talked to you?

Patient: No. I can't study my mind. I can't study a word. If I see something big, if I see it in my mind I spell a word and it drops big. If I stud-

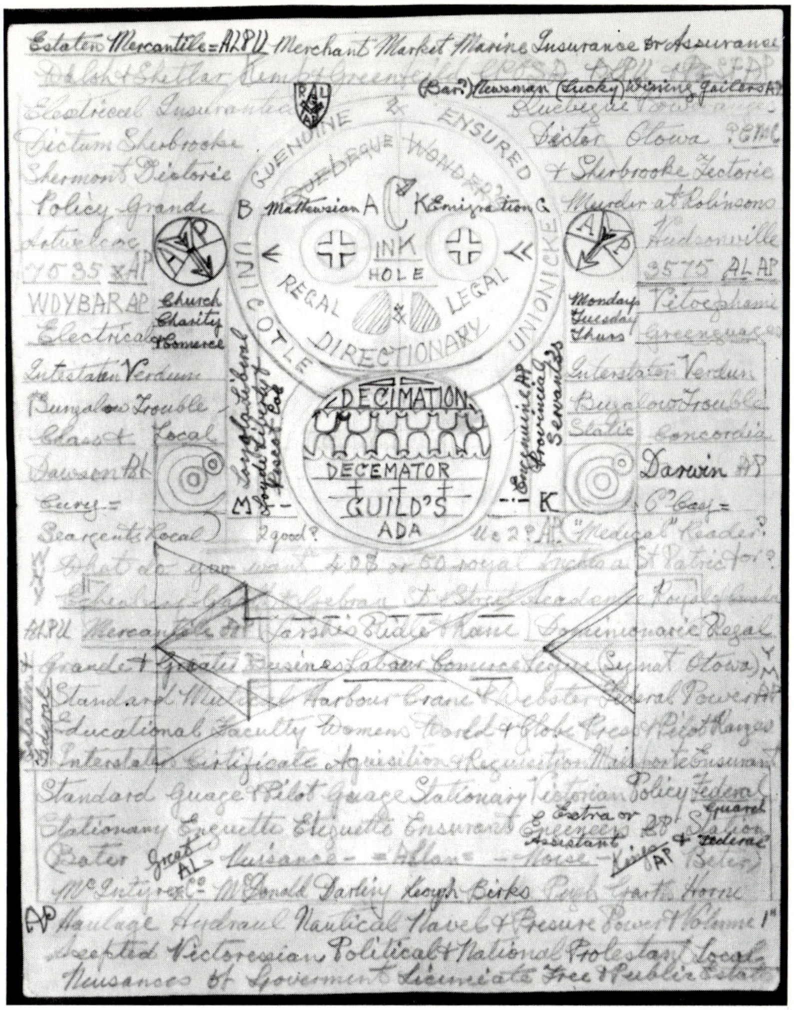

This message was created by a 42-year-old man diagnosed as schizophrenic. It shows the characteristic disordered thought processes and seemingly nonsensical associations between words and symbols.

ied a big motor or something, it would drop—so I don't study my mind because it would build up.

Interviewer: I don't follow.

Patient: The motor, or a house, or a world. If I study it, it may drop. A tree or car, I drop cars all the time. A bulldozer fell out of my mind you know, so I stopped fooling with it.

Interviewer: It fell out of your mind?

Patient: Yeah. Anything will fall. If I get a notion to study a car or tree or something, anything might fall. I got a building mind. I got more bulldozers and things in my mind right now. I'll tell you Doc, my building mind is so big it can make anything you want to build. But people that don't have no building mind, they could put down a little food or a tract or something like that, if they get electrocution into their minds—they can reach off the abyss you know. I went over the whole world putting down beans and meat. My body dropped food all the time. It builds the trucks traveling along the highways. My mind is real smart, real smart, real smart, man. (Shean, 1978, p. 69)

The patient has connected his thoughts and sentences through remotely related words: "bulldozer," "car," "building," "tract," "highways." He also jumps to other topics that do not seem to be even remotely related, such as "beans and meat." Note that this patient has woven an intricate story that has little meaning, which illustrates another characteristic of schizophrenic speech: *poverty of content.* The individual may deliver a long speech but convey little or no real information. Utterances sometimes take the form of *word salad,* a string of words unrelated to each other that make no sense to the listener.

In some cases, schizophrenics make up their own words, called *neologisms,* often by condensing or combining several existing words. Some examples are "spectroautorotation," "relaudation," and "circlingology" (Forrest, 1969), all of which were definable to the patients who used them. Relaudation, for instance, means "praising over and over." The reason for inventing new words usually seems to be to represent concepts for which no term—and no previous need—exists.

Other unusual speech patterns exhibited by schizophrenics include *echolalia* (repeating part or all of what another speaker has just said); and *perseveration* (repeating one word or phrase senselessly for hours or even days); and using one concept repetitively in response to varying questions. Some schizophrenics engage in what is called *clang association,* which is the pairing of unrelated words on the basis of sound rather than meaning ("mister sister"). Others practice *mutism,* a refusal to speak at all.

Distorted perceptions

Schizophrenics also experience distortions of perception. A common problem appears to be a defective perceptual filter—the inability to screen out irrelevant sights, sounds, smells, etc. The schizophrenic is constantly deluged with sensory input and thus has great difficulty focusing on any one perceptual task. Such a fundamental inability to sort out and process information obviously affects the ability to function at other levels. Some of the other symptoms we have noted—for instance, overinclusive thinking and clang association of words—may be due to the schizophrenic's faulty perceptual filter.

The other primary perceptual problem of schizophrenics, which is probably related to the difficulties they have in dealing with sensory input, involves **hallucinations**—sensory perceptions that have no real-world source. Auditory hallucinations are the most common, especially voices. The schizophrenic may hear one voice or many, familiar or unfamiliar, perhaps giving orders or commenting on behavior, usually in an insulting manner. Mark Vonnegut has described his auditory hallucinations:

> At first I'd had to strain to hear or understand them. They were soft and working with some pretty tricky codes. Snap-crackle-pops, the sound of the wind with blinking lights and horns for punctuation. I broke the code and somehow was able to internalize it to the point where it was just like hearing words. In the beginning it seemed mostly nonsense, but as things went along they made more and more sense. Once you hear the voices, you realize they've always been there. It's just a matter of being tuned to them.
>
> . . . "You know you're in hell, don't you?" The voices said that a lot.
>
> "All I know is that I don't like it much."
>
> "You know Virginia's dead. You know your father's dead. You know the world is ending. You know you're dead. You know you've killed a lot of people. You know you're responsible for the California earthquake, the death of the planet. You know you have a mission. You know you're the messiah." (1975, pp. 106–108)

Less often, the hallucinations are tactile—electrical, tingling, or burning feelings. Strange bodily sensations are occasionally reported, such as the feeling of snakes crawling inside the abdomen. Hallucinations of vision, taste, and smell occur sometimes but not as frequently as auditory hallucinations. There may also be the perception that part or all of the body is distorted and out of proportion. Other people and objects, too, may look strange—people may appear to be wearing masks, or objects may seem farther away or smaller than they are.

Disturbed affect

Many schizophrenics experience a general reduction in emotional response referred to as *blunted affect.* In its extreme form, *flat affect,* there are almost no signs of emotion; the in-

A patient in a mental hospital completing his self-portrait. Schizophrenics often perceive part or all of their bodies as distorted.

dividual speaks in a monotone without facial expression or movement. Sometimes the lack of emotion takes the form of *anhedonia,* an extreme state of apathy in which the individual appears unable to experience pleasure in any form.

Another type of affective disturbance involves responses that are inappropriate to the situation. For example, when told of the death of a relative, the schizophrenic patient might laugh; in another situation extreme anger or sadness may be shown without any provocation. Sudden and unpredictable changes in emotion may also occur, often in the form of inexplicable outbursts of anger. Schizophrenics sometimes show emotional ambivalence—that is, simultaneously reacting both positively and negatively to the same situation.

Disordered behavior

One of the most common features of schizophrenia is social withdrawal. Schizophrenics are typically oversensitive to potential rejection by others. Finding social relations painful or frightening or, at best, difficult, they withdraw into their self-created delusional world and avoid social contact, a condition referred to as *autism* (but not the same as childhood autism, which is discussed in Chapter 14). The bizarre behaviors that are the result of the disturbed thoughts and feelings of schizophrenia may be obnoxious to other people; schizophrenics will thus be rejected by them, and their fears about social relations will be confirmed.

Social withdrawal, disordered thinking and speech, perceptual distortion, and disturbances of affect all take their toll on the ability of schizophrenics to carry out social roles. Schizophrenia usually disrupts or completely prohibits their social activities as well as their functioning at work, at school or at home. In addition, coworkers and relatives may find their behavior embarrassing and distracting at best, offensive at worst, which makes it even harder for schizophrenics to function effectively.

An occasional symptom of schizophrenia, particularly among those who are more severely affected, is disturbances in motor behavior. In **catatonic schizophrenia,** individuals may show a marked reduction of movement and activity (*catatonic stupor*), or maintain a rigid posture even when others try to move them (*catatonic rigidity*). They may move in purposeless and stereotyped ways unrelated to external stimuli—facial grimacing, pacing, and performing inflexible rituals are common examples. Other behaviors include assuming bizarre or inappropriate postures and imitating the movements of others.

Schizophrenic Logic

Before Kraepelin's time, schizophrenia was called "madness" or "insanity." Today, schizophrenia is still interpreted as "craziness" by the average person. As we have noted, the schizophrenic's perceptions, thoughts, speech, and behavior are all likely to be disordered, so the physical appearance tends to be disordered as well. How would you react if an unkept, wild-eyed man ran up to you and demanded that you get him out of the hospital because the world is about to end and he is the only one who can stop it? This man may not be talking or acting randomly. His powers of logic may very well be the same as ever—only the input has suddenly changed. Flooded by a deluge of sensations, with his old processing system no longer doing its job, he must find some new way of coping, of explaining why everything is suddenly so different.

Schizophrenics may be aware that they are acting abnormally, but their senses and logic persuade them that it would be crazy to go along with other people's ideas of proper behavior under the circumstances. McNeil (1967) reports the following argument from a paranoid schizophrenic:

> Sure, it looks like there is some other good explanation for everything that happens. That's the way they would arrange it if they are smart and they are. They have tricks most of us never heard of and there are more of them than you can imagine. You watch them for a while and you learn their secret signals of recognition. They know who's what but nobody else knows it. I'm onto them and they don't know it yet. Everything looks innocent, sure. But that's the way they operate. You can't tell me that all the things that have happened are nothing but accidents. I know better. (p. 169)

The schizophrenic disorders are so varied that it would be rash to conclude that all schizophrenics are operating according to a precise and consistent logic of their own. But it is evident that the symptoms of schizophrenia are not merely a random collection of crazy behaviors. Some of them appear to be a logical—we might even call it rational—response to drastically altered perceptions of the world (which may include hallucinations). The variations of schizophrenia are as distinct as the patterns of snowflakes—and it is possible that the structure of schizophrenia, if we can ever find the means to decipher it, may prove to be just as orderly.

When a therapist *can* discern the logic behind a schizophrenic's speech or actions, it may facilitate treatment. Hofling (1975) describes the case of a young woman:

> [*She*] *was noticed to be pounding her pillow, muttering obscenities, and repeatedly using the phrase, "the all-seeing eye." The head nurse knew that a visit from the patient's mother was expected that day, and despite the fact that the patient had occasionally called her mother's name, she wondered if the patient's behavior might be expressing hostility to and fear of her mother.*

The nurse informed the psychiatrist, who thought that the interpretation might well be correct. He asked the patient if she were not upset at the prospect of a visit from her mother. The patient immediately confirmed the idea and expressed relief when the doctor told her that the visit would be postponed indefinitely. (p. 378)

Types of Schizophrenia

As we have noted, the various manifestations of schizophrenia suggest that it may actually comprise several fairly distinct disorders. These differences have led observers as far back as Kraepelin to suggest categories for schizophrenia according to similar symptoms. DSM-III uses three of Kraepelin's categories of schizophrenia—**disorganized** (formerly called *hebephrenic*), **catatonic,** and **paranoid**—plus a fourth, **undifferentiated** schizophrenia, a sort of catch-all category roughly comparable to Kraepelin's simple schizophrenia. There is also a category called **residual** schizophrenia, which is where patients who seem to be on the way to recovery—like Arnold in Chapter 1—are classified.

Disorganized schizophrenia

The primary features of disorganized schizophrenia are marked incoherence of speech, flat affect, and incongruous or silly behavior. People diagnosed with disorganized schizophrenia may, for no apparent reason, have long spells of uncontrollable giggling. They commonly experience hallucinations and delusions that have no systematic theme. They are prone to stereotyped gestures, inappropriate emotional responses, and bizarre movements or mannerisms. Social withdrawal and role impairment are usually extreme. They often behave in ways that are immature or socially unacceptable—eating with their fingers, for example, or urinating on the floor. Most have had an adolescence characterized by maladjustment and social isolation. The *active phase* (when all symptoms are at peak severity) is likely to begin earlier in life and have

Table 11.1 *Types of Schizophrenia*

CATEGORIES	FEATURES: Essential	FEATURES: Associated
Disorganized	Incoherence; flat or silly affect; fragmented, unassociated delusions	Unusual expressions and mannerisms; extreme social withdrawal; onset early and gradual; process traits
Catatonic	Psychomotor disturbance—stupor, rigid posing, bizarre posturing, purposeless excited movements	Mutism; waxy flexibility; rarely diagnosed today
Paranoid	Highly evolved delusions or hallucinations of persecution or grandeur	Anxiety; anger and hostility; argumentativeness; onset later in life; process traits
Undifferentiated	Psychotic schizophrenic symptoms that do not fit any other category *or* that fit all three	General psychotic signs—bizarre behavior, delusions and hallucinations, disordered thought and speech, social withdrawal
Residual	Nonpsychotic schizophrenic symptoms that occur after at least one psychotic episode	Mild signs—social withdrawal, inappropriate emotional expression, illogic and loosened associations

a more severe onset than in other types of schizophrenia, and the symptoms may persist for years with few remissions. For these reasons, the prognosis is poor.

An example of a disorganized schizophrenic is a young woman called K.A., whose case was recorded in the 1920s (Thorpe and Katz, 1948, pp. 619–621).

> Poorly adjusted since childhood, at 25 K.A. was single and had a tedious job in a hosiery factory. The other young women she worked with teased her, calling her an old maid and talking constantly about topics related to sex. Despite her extreme prudishness, K.A. did indulge in self-abuse [masturbation].
>
> The onset of her illness came after a visit to the dentist, which left her claiming that the dentist was in love with her and had some influence over her. "He made me do things." She became careless of her appearance and very untidy, at times exposing herself. Later she began hearing voices which made her confess onanism [another pejorative term for masturbation], claiming that she was a bad girl. The other girls in the factory continued to disturb her in various ways, and she imagined she must be making people crazy. She had prolonged periods of laughing and smiling to herself; at other times she was depressed, and relatives said she threatened suicide. At one point she felt that she was facing death, but stated she was willing to die in order to "leave some pleasure in the world" and "save the world."
>
> On admission to the hospital, K.A. was impulsive, antagonistic, resistive, and at times abusive to those around her, whom she accused of torturing her in various ways. Her speech was extremely irrelevant. At one time she spoke of Catholics and Jews being "against her" and said she had to die. At other times she expressed the idea that her food had been tampered with and something put in it to make her sexually excited. She felt that she was under the control of electricity and also under a mental spell due to telepathy and thought waves. Emotionally she seemed apathetic, though she tended to laugh and be silly when asked about her invalid father's condition. Her intellectual functioning appeared unimpaired. She had no insight into her condition, however; she insisted, there was "nothing wrong" and that she should be discharged at once.
>
> In the hospital K.A. quickly deteriorated. She became increasingly careless of her appearance and eventually refused to go to the toilet. At the table she was sloppy, frequently eating with her fingers. She developed delusions about the ward doctors; she thought they were tempting her in various ways, and felt she was under their influence through mental suggestion which caused her to masturbate shamelessly during the day as well as at night. She continued to smile and laugh to herself.*

Catatonic schizophrenia

The most notable feature of catatonic schizophrenics is their bizarre motor behavior. Two behavior patterns—rigid immobility and wild excitement—alternate during the early stages of the disorder. Later, one or the other pattern becomes dominant. Catatonic schizophrenics who are immobile appear to be in a stupor, even though they may be fully aware of what is going on. They respond to other people oppositionally or not at all. A phenomenon called *waxy flexibility* may also occur—for example, if an attendant picks up a patient's arm and lets go, the arm may stay in the new position. A schizophrenic in the wild excitement phase is frenzied, often raving incomprehensibly and experiencing hallucinations and preposterous delusions.

The onset of catatonic schizophrenia is usually sudden, which has led some professionals to conclude that this type offers a better

* Reprinted by permission.

prognosis for recovery than the disorganized type. Schizophrenics in a catatonic stupor or state of excitement need careful supervision, however, and may even need emergency medical attention to prevent them from becoming exhausted, starving, or injuring themselves or others.

Kolb (1977) has described a case of catatonic schizophrenia:

> Two months before commitment the patient began to talk about how he had failed, had "spoiled" his whole life, that it was now "too late." He spoke of hearing someone say, "You must submit." One night his wife was awakened by his talking. He told her of having several visions but refused to describe them. He stated that someone was after him and trying to blame him for the death of a certain man. He had been poisoned, he said. Whenever he saw a truck or a fire engine, the patient stated that someone in it was looking for him in order to claim his assistance to help save the world. He had periods of laughing and shouting and became so noisy and unmanageable that it was necessary to commit him.
>
> On arrival at the hospital, the patient was noted to be [a] . . . poorly nourished man with dilated pupils, hyperactive tendon reflexes, and a pulse rate of 120 per minute. In the admission office he showed many mannerisms, lay down on the floor, pulled at his foot, made undirected, violent striking movements, again struck attendants, grimaced, assumed rigid, attitudinized postures, refused to speak, and appeared to be having auditory hallucinations. Later in the day, he was found to be in a stuporous state. His face was without expression, he was mute and rigid, and paid no attention to those about him or to their questions. His eyes

A drawing by a schizophrenic patient fusing several strong images—including ancient warrior, horse, mythical bird, mountains, and people—in an attempt to convey an ideal of strength and grandeur. The drawing is a good example of schizophrenic condensation, fusion, and abnormal cognition. From Interpretation of Schizophrenia, *2nd edition. Revised and expanded by Silvano Arieti, M.D. © 1974 by Silvano Arieti. © 1955 by Robert Brunner (Basic Books, Inc. N.Y.).*

> were closed and the lids could be separated only with effort. There was no response to pinpricks or other painful stimuli.
>
> On the following morning an attempt was made to bring him before the medical staff for the routine admission interview. As he was brought into the room supported by two attendants, he struggled, grimaced, shouted incoherently, and was resistive. For five days he remained mute, negativistic, and inaccessible, at times staring vacantly into space, at times with his eyes tightly closed. He ate poorly and gave no response to questions but once was heard to mutter to himself in a greatly preoccupied manner, "I'm going to die—I know it—you know it." On the evening of the sixth day he looked about and asked where he was and how he came there. When asked to tell of his life, he related many known events and how he had once worked in an airplane factory, but added that he had invented an appliance pertaining to airplanes, that this had been stolen and patented through fraud and that as a result he had lost his position. He ate ravenously, then fell asleep, and on awaking was in a catatonic stupor, remaining in this state for several days.*

An explanation given by some catatonics for their rigid immobility is that they are so afraid of something terrible happening that they don't dare move. One man later explained that, like Atlas, he had been balancing the world on his shoulders and was convinced that the least movement would allow it to fall to destruction.

Paranoid schizophrenia

The most prominent characteristic of this category is delusions. Such schizophrenics may believe that they are being harassed or followed (delusions of persecution), or that their behavior or thoughts are being directed by some outside force (delusions of control), or that they are famous people on important missions (delusions of grandeur). Related to the delusions are *ideas of reference:* Paranoid schizophrenics believe that overheard conversations, newspaper articles, and TV and radio broadcasts are meant for them personally. In general, they are suspicious and mistrustful, obsessed with a sense of being the center of attention for some or all other people. Such individuals can be dangerous if they decide to take action against those who are perceived as the enemy. Otherwise, they are usually closer to normal in speech and behavior than disorganized or catatonic schizophrenics. Paranoid schizophrenics tend to be hospitalized for briefer periods, and they are readmitted less often.

DSM-III distinguishes other forms of paranoia in addition to paranoid schizophrenia. Some of these are discussed in the Close-up on paranoia.

Undifferentiated schizophrenia

The person who is clearly schizophrenic but does not fall into the paranoid, catatonic, or disorganized category—or could fall into all three—is classified as undifferentiated. Typical symptoms of undifferentiated schizophrenia include incoherent speech, loose associations, grossly disorganized behavior, and evidence of pronounced delusions, hallucinations, and social withdrawal.

Diagnostic Problems

About ten years ago, a rather unusual study took place. Eight people—five men and three women—were admitted to mental hospitals after complaining of hearing voices that seemed to be saying "empty," "hollow," and "thud." The hospitals ranged from aging, understaffed, state institutions to modern, expensive, private hospitals. The eight patients were, in reality, normal; they were not hearing voices. Other than this single misrepresentation for the sake of the study, they gave their true life histories (though under false names) and behaved as they ordi-

* Reprinted from *Modern Clinical Psychiatry (9th ed.)* by L.C. Kolb, p. 407. © 1977, W.B. Saunders Co., Philadelphia.

Close-up: Paranoia

Paranoia is very similar to paranoid schizophrenia, the one distinguishing feature being that most people with paranoia do not experience hallucinations. Meissner (1978) believes that this distinction is probably given too much weight and that the fact that the two disorders are virtually identical is undervalued.

The chief feature of both is a strong, generally complex, and often logical (to a degree) delusional system. Most often, persecution is the major theme. The paranoid individual is being hounded, maligned, undermined, spied upon, injured or cheated by virtually everybody. Sometimes jealousy is the core. Occasionally, this deep suspicion can lead to violent behavior, but the more typical response is social isolation: The paranoid person prefers to be alone, and most acquaintances are very willing to comply.

Still, paranoia involves very little life disruption apart from whatever results from the delusional system. People with this disorder do not exhibit any of the more unusual behaviors, such as peculiar mannerisms or twisted speech patterns, that are common to schizophrenia. But when paranoia hits, it generally stays for life. Like people with paranoid schizophrenia, paranoid individuals don't believe they have any problems—everyone else has the problem.

An interesting feature of paranoia is that the delusional system of one person can occasionally be passed to another person, or even to more than one. Called *folie a deux* (or *a trois,* or *en famille,* depending on how many others are involved), this form of paranoia is usually shared by women, especially sisters. Genetic influence may be at work, but researchers have noted that in most cases when the dominant person (the one with true paranoia) is separated from the other for an extended period, the second person's delusions weaken and eventually disappear.

narily would. All were diagnosed psychotic, and all but one were diagnosed schizophrenic (Rosenhan, 1973).

This study points to a question that often arises in connection with schizophrenia: How valid are the diagnoses? The schizophrenic disorders are the most commonly diagnosed mental illnesses in the United States—but is this a true representation of their prevalence? For some time now, the schizophrenic population in this country has held steady at around 1 percent. In Europe and Asia, on the other hand, the incidence of schizophrenia is reported at between .2 percent and .9 percent (DSM-III, 1980). Are Americans more prone to schizophrenia than people in other countries, or just more prone to diagnosing it?

Murphy (1976) concluded that the incidence of schizophrenia probably holds fairly steady all around the world—it is the diagnoses that vary. A series of studies comparing diagnoses in the United Kingdom and the United States supports this conclusion. Given the same group of patients to diagnose, American doctors diagnosed them as schizophrenic far more frequently than their British counterparts did—in one instance, *nine times* more frequently (Cooper et al., 1972). Even within the United States, clinicians do not always agree whether a given patient is schizophrenic (Schmidt and Fonda, 1956), and reaching agreement on the *type* of schizophrenia is harder still.

During the past 30 or 40 years, efforts have been made to tighten up the diagnostic criteria

Table 11.2 *Reactive vs. Process Schizophrenia*

Reactive	Process
Onset: sudden, usually after visible stressor	Onset: gradual, with no clear precipitating stressor
Premorbid adjustment: good	Premorbid adjustment: poor
Hospitalization: short, with less severe symptoms; readmission less likely	Hospitalization: lengthy; symptoms indicate great deterioration of functioning
Effective treatment: phenothiazines (Thorazine)	Effective treatment: phenothiazines (Thorazine is especially effective)
Prognosis: good	Prognosis: poor

for the schizophrenic disorders, since most of the discrepancies in diagnosis could be traced to differing ideas of just what constitutes schizophrenia. This is partly because the schizophrenic disorders involve a great variety of symptoms, and any one patient may have some or all of each, but only one—thought disorders—is exclusive to schizophrenia. In the United States, the category of undifferentiated schizophrenia has often been used whenever a patient shows any kind of psychotic reaction or bizarre behavior that is difficult to classify; it is probably the most often diagnosed category. DSM-III has attempted to narrow the diagnostic criteria for schizophrenia; it will be interesting to see whether the proportion of diagnoses changes over the next few years.

Differentiating between categories is one way to bring order to the schizophrenias. Another is to make a distinction between reactive and process schizophrenia, the difference between the two being related to the onset of the disorder: **Reactive** schizophrenia comes on suddenly, following some stressful environmental event, whereas **process** schizophrenia involves gradual deterioration that seems to connote a malfunction of the brain. Individuals suffering from process schizophrenia are characterized by a lower level of social adjustment before hospitalization (called **premorbid adjustment**). Poor premorbid adjustment usually means the person was socially withdrawn during late adolescence, has had trouble holding a job for any length of time, shows sexual maladjustment (either inactivity or promiscuity), and probably has never married or had a significant romantic involvement. Good premorbid adjustment, associated with reactive schizophrenia, typically means normal romantic involvements, a good work record, and successful social activity.

Several studies (Higgins, 1969; Neale and Cromwell, 1970) show that at first hospitalization the symptoms of good premorbids (reactive schizophrenics) tend to be less severe than those of poor premorbids (process schizophrenics). Reactive schizophrenics usually stay in the hospital a shorter time and they are discharged sooner and are less likely to be readmitted (Strauss, 1973). Process schizophrenics seem to respond better to treatment with antipsychotic drugs (the phenothiazines) than reactives (Goldstein et al., 1969), which again seems to suggest an organic dysfunction.

It is unclear whether process and reactive schizophrenia constitute two different disorders, or simply represent a continuum that can be used to describe the degree of a patient's premorbid social impairment. The issue is a controversial one; resolving it will require further research on the differences—etiological, physiological, biochemical, and so on—between process and reactive schizophrenics.

EXPLAINING THE SCHIZOPHRENIC DISORDERS

Although volumes of research have been published on schizophrenia, no one has yet been able to say for sure what causes the disorder. This is partly because, as noted earlier, we are not even certain whether the various categories of schizophrenia are actually one or several disorders. Another problem is that some theories seem to fit our observations about schizophrenia but lack empirical data to back them up, while some of the most effective treatment methods work for unknown reasons. In this section we shall review the three main areas of inquiry into schizophrenia: the biological, the psychological, and the social.

Biological Explanations

Biological research on schizophrenia falls into two main areas: genetic, which investigates the possible role of heritability, and biochemical, which seeks to explain how the disorder works. In both areas some highly promising results have been obtained.

Genetic theories

It now appears very likely that either schizophrenia itself or a pronounced susceptibility to schizophrenia is inherited. The evidence comes from three types of studies: family psychiatric histories of schizophrenics, the occurrence of schizophrenia in twins of schizophrenics, and adoption studies in which the offspring of a schizophrenic parent were reared by other than their biological parents.

Chances of developing schizophrenia are considerably higher among the blood relatives of schizophrenics than among the general population. The incidence of schizophrenia among the first-order relatives (siblings, parents, and children) of schizophrenics is higher than among second-order relatives (aunts, uncles, nieces, and nephews). Zerbin-Rudin (1972) reported that between 9 and 16 percent of children with a schizophrenic parent become schizophrenic themselves. In a study by Slater and Cowie (1971), 12.9 percent of children with one schizophrenic parent were found to be schizophrenic also; for children with two schizophrenic parents, that figure rose to 46.3 percent.

Still stronger evidence that schizophrenia is genetically transmitted—as well as excellent opportunities for researchers to test hypotheses of heredity—comes from studies of twins. If schizophrenia is genetically based, we would expect a high concordance rate for schizophrenia among monozygotic twins and a lower rate among dizygotic twins (twins sharing the same proportion of genes—approximately 50 percent—as nontwin siblings). Rosenthal (1970), reviewing twin studies of schizophrenia, found that the concordance rate for monozygotic twins is indeed considerably higher than the rate for dizygotic twins. The results of several studies indicate that the average concordance rate of schizophrenia is almost 50 percent for monozygotic twins, compared with 9 percent for dizygotic twins and 8 percent for nontwin siblings. All of these rates are, of course, higher than the 1 percent occurrence of schizophrenia in the general population.

The concordance rate for schizophrenia in monozygotic twins, as well as the rate for first-order relatives, provides support for a genetic theory of schizophrenia. The picture is clouded, however, by the fact that family members (and twins in particular) are exposed to similar environments, and they also have many opportunities to learn from each other. It is plausible that children of a schizophrenic parent are adversely affected by the parent's disturbed behavior, or that one twin imitates the odd behavior patterns of the other. One way of separating the effects of heredity from those of environment is to study children with a high genetic risk of schizophrenia who are adopted by nonschizophrenic families. Rosenthal (1971) compared such a group with a control group of adoptees whose biological parents had never been hospitalized for psychological problems, and found that there was in fact a greater incidence of schizophrenia among the adoptees born to schizophrenic parents.

Table 11.3 *Twin Concordance Rates in Five Major Studies*

	IDENTICAL TWINS		FRATERNAL TWINS	
STUDY	Number of pairs	Concordance rate	Number of pairs	Concordance rate
Rosanoff et al., 1935, United States and Canada	41	61%	101	10%
Kallman, 1946, New York	37	65–74	115	11–14
Slater, 1953, England	55	36–60	17	6–12
Gottesman and Shields, 1966, England	24	41	33	9
Tienari, 1975, Finland	17	0–36	20	5–14

From Rosenthal, 1970, and Gottesman and Shields, 1976.

A more extensive study began with a sample of 5000 adults who had been adopted early in life by persons not biologically related to them (Kety et al., 1968). Having identified 24 schizophrenics in the group, the researchers found that 13.9 percent of the biological relatives of those individuals were schizophrenics, whereas 2.7 percent of their adoptive relatives were schizophrenic. Heston (1966) followed up 47 individuals who had been born to schizophrenic mothers but raised in orphanages, comparing them with 50 children of nonschizophrenic mothers from the same orphanages. As adults, none of the individuals in the control group were diagnosed schizophrenic, but 16.6 percent of the offspring of schizophrenic mothers were. The latter group also showed a much higher incidence of other mental disorders—66 percent versus 18 percent in the comparison group.

In general, adoption studies have reported a higher incidence of schizophrenia among the biological relatives of schizophrenics than among relatives who were not biologically related but with whom the adoptees shared rearing and other environmental experiences (Heston, 1966; Karlsson, 1966; Rosenthal, 1971). This is to say not that environmental factors do not also play a part, but rather that genetic factors cannot be ignored.

Still, we should keep in mind the limitations of this type of research. Many of these studies are handicapped by having to work backward, investigating possible causes after the disorder already has developed. Samples are usually small, and they are often biased in some way. One large gap is the *second* parent of children designated as having "a schizophrenic parent." What kind of person would be a likely mate for a schizophrenic? An obvious answer: another schizophrenic. In Rosenthal's (1973) investigations of spouses and lovers of schizophrenics whose children were given up for adoption, a high proportion were found to have either schizophrenia or some other psychopathological disorder. Other factors often unaccounted for in adoption studies include any medication a schizophrenic mother may have been taking during pregnancy, problems with the birth, the child's age at adoption, and possible negative expectations on the part of the adoptive parents.

In family and twin studies, it is worth noting that the concordance rates for schizophrenia are not exactly what we would expect if a single gene were involved. First, not all identical twins of schizophrenics develop schizophrenia. More significantly, 90 percent of schizophrenics do not have parents diagnosed as schizophrenic. A possible explanation is that schizophrenia may be controlled by more than one gene, making the hereditary picture somewhat complicated. Another strong possibility is that a diathesis (a susceptibility or weakness) for schizophrenia rather than schizophrenia itself is genetically transmitted, an idea we shall explore further when we discuss interactional theories.

Biochemical theories

If the transmission of schizophrenia is genetic, the disorder itself must be biological rather than psychological in nature. Even if it is proved that heredity is not a key to the disorder, biochemistry may still be a major factor. The idea that schizophrenia involves some kind of internal biochemical imbalance is attractive for several reasons. For one thing, it presents the theoretical likelihood that what is caused by chemicals can be cured by chemicals—that is, it greatly improves the prospects for treating schizophrenia medicinally, which may thus enable the schizophrenic to return to a normal life. For another, it lets schizophrenics—and their families—off the hook, so to speak. If the disorder is biochemically based, then they have no cause to blame themselves for leading the wrong kind of life or being the wrong kind of person. In the same vein, parents cannot be blamed for their child's body chemistry the way they can be for their faulty upbringing, which has often been proposed as a cause of schizophrenia.

On the empirical side, biochemical theories are attractive because they explain the success of antischizophrenic drugs such as chlorpromazine, which we shall explore when we turn to the management of schizophrenia. Biochemical theories also address the similarity between schizophrenia and the altered states of consciousness produced by hallucinogens such as LSD (lysergic acid diethylamide). At one time, it was thought that these *psychotomimetic* (producing psychotic symptoms) drugs could be used to mimic the psychotic symptoms of schizophrenia and thus to study them. It has turned out, however, that the similarities between schizophrenia and drug experiences were not as close as researchers first thought.

Biochemical theories of schizophrenia are numerous, and research investigations have touched on just about every physiological function that could possibly be connected with schizophrenia. Some studies have analyzed the chemical composition of schizophrenics—the makeup of their blood, urine, and other substances that reflect chemical activity in the body. Other studies have focused on physiology—how certain substances are produced or inhibited within the body. Still others have examined functioning—the schizophrenic's eye tracking patterns, electrical conductivity of the skin, and the interaction between right and left sides of the brain. In each of these areas, researchers have come up with interesting results. We shall concentrate here on a few of the most promising avenues of investigation.

Chemical composition. A favorite theory of many researchers is that a schizophrenic's body produces some toxic substance that causes the disorder. Heath and Krupp (1967) hypothesized that a protein in the blood called **taraxein** was the culprit. Supposedly taraxein interferes with physiological activity in certain parts of the brain and causes psychotic behavior, an idea for which Heath gained support by injecting the substance into nonschizophrenics and producing schizophrenic symptoms.

Years of attempts to replicate Heath's experiments have been unsuccessful, however. Investigators who found it impossible even to isolate taraxein from the blood of schizophrenics suggested that the antibody's existence might be due to some factor as subtle as the tap water Heath and his colleagues used in their process, or the diet of the patients he studied, rather than to schizophrenia. Schizophrenics are often hospitalized, and therefore lead a much quieter life than most nonhospitalized people; typically, they take more medication, follow a more regulated diet, and often drink more coffee and smoke more cigarettes than the average person. Therefore any biochemical differences between them and control subjects may well reflect differences in these other factors rather than the presence of some toxic substance.

Other researchers have speculated that the "success" of Heath and colleagues in producing psychotic symptoms in nonschizophrenics using taraxein could be the result of suggestion—the subjects *expected* the injections to make them act schizophrenic. At present, taraxein is not con-

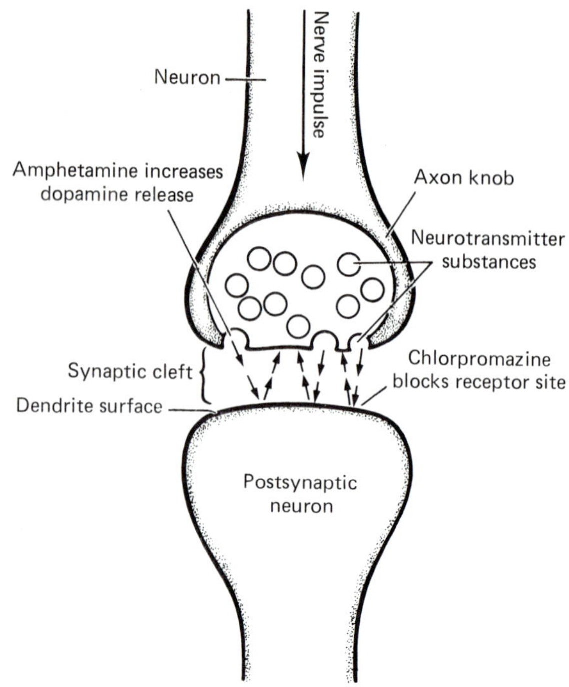

Figure 11.1. *Electrical impulses traveling from neuron to neuron trigger the release of neurotransmitters such as dopamine. Too much dopamine is released under amphetamine use, resulting in schizophrenic-like signs. The presence of chlorpromazine in the synaptic cleft, however, blocks the dopamine from being absorbed and transmitting the impulse, thus reducing these symptoms. From Goldstein et al., 1980.*

sidered a likely candidate for explaining schizophrenia. The possibilities of a toxic substance in the blood or elsewhere in the body still exist, though—and so do the potential pitfalls involved in tracking it down.

The body chemistry approach also favors the idea of an internal imbalance, but casts it at a more individual level. The idea here is that each of us has a somewhat different biochemical makeup—even monozygotic twins are not identical in this respect. Various types of schizophrenia thus might be related to a deficiency or a surplus of certain substances that affect the individual's physiological functioning. The onset of schizophrenia often does follow a drastic change of diet or chemical intake; and massive doses of vitamins and a carefully controlled diet have helped some schizophrenic patients. There are not enough data in this area yet, however, to warrant any general conclusions.

Physiology. The most promising biochemical theory of schizophrenia at present is the **dopamine hypothesis** (Meltzer and Stahl, 1976). Essentially, this theory holds that schizophrenia is related to an excess of the neural transmitter **dopamine** in the brain. Apparently, when there is an unusually high concentration of dopamine in the synapse between neurons, the neurons' rate of firing speeds up. This theory therefore logically supports reports made by some schizophrenics that too much sensory input is coming in too fast.

One source of support for the dopamine hypothesis is the fact that amphetamines, which appear to work by increasing the level of available dopamine in the brain, produce symptoms similar to schizophrenia—and can make a schizophrenic's symptoms worse (Angrist, Lee, and Gershon, 1974). Amphetamines evidently act on the nervous system either by releasing dopamine or by preventing it from being deactivated. Phenothiazines, in contrast, reduce schizophrenic symptoms by apparently lowering the dopamine level. Phenothiazines also produce side effects similar to the symptoms of Parkinson's disease, an illness partly caused by insufficient dopamine in one area of the brain. Exactly how the phenothiazines work to reduce dopamine levels is uncertain. Phenothiazine molecules are similar in structure to dopamine molecules, so it may be that phenothiazine blocks the neuroreceptors that are sensitive to dopamine. In any case, there is no direct evidence as yet that schizophrenics actually do have higher levels of dopamine in their brains than other people. Pending further research, the theory remains speculative.

Functioning. It has been suggested that schizophrenia may be related to abnormalities in the functioning of the autonomic nervous

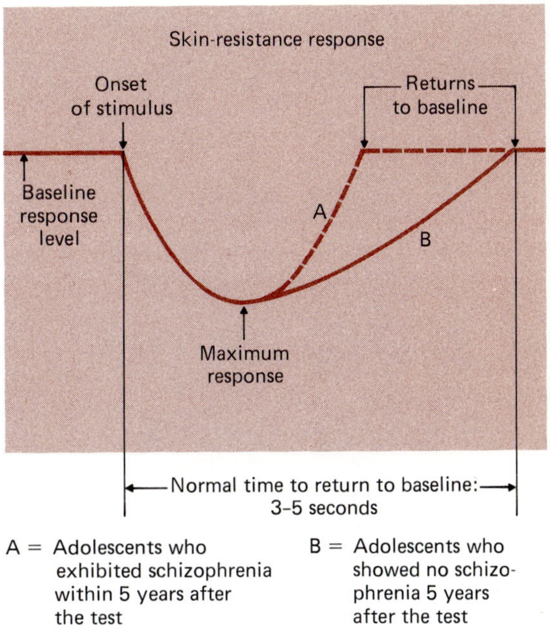

Figure 11.2. *Galvanic skin response and schizophrenia. Note that those who did exhibit schizophrenic symptoms returned to a base rate much more quickly. From Mednick and McNeil, 1968.*

system. That is, the physiological responses of schizophrenics to stimuli are perhaps different in some way from the responses of other people. If this is the case, the other biochemical theories would not necessarily be ruled out. Indeed, it may help explain how a fundamental biochemical difference in one part of the nervous system is manifested as specific schizophrenic symptoms in another part.

For instance, Holzman and colleagues (1973) discovered that the eye tracking patterns of schizophrenics are generally much less regular and smooth than that of other people. They recorded the eye movements of subjects who were asked to watch a pendulum swing back and forth. The pattern of the schizophrenic group showed more sudden changes and full stops in tracking than is found in a normal pattern. In addition, it was determined (Holzman et al., 1974) that this disordered pattern was often shared by first-degree relatives of the schizophrenic group—people who had never themselves been schizophrenic.

Various other studies have found that the ordinary levels of autonomic nervous system arousal of schizophrenics are unusually high. Measures of their heart rate and **galvanic skin response** (a sudden change in the electrical conductivity of the skin indicating an emotional reaction to some stimulus) suggest that schizophrenics may respond more strongly to their environment than the rest of us. These findings bring us back again to a picture of the schizophrenic as someone who is hypersensitive to sensory input and highly distractible.

Another recent hypothesis is that schizophrenics may have some impairment of the *corpus callosum,* one set of communication lines linking the left and right hemispheres of the brain. The two halves of the cerebral cortex govern opposite sides of the body; to some extent they also control different mental and physical functions. Fully coordinated thought, speech, and movement is dependent on the functioning of the two hemispheres. Green (1978) found that when schizophrenics were asked to perform a simple mechanical task, the right hand literally did not know what the left hand was doing—perhaps indicating "faulty wiring" in the corpus callosum.

Psychological Explanations

Whether schizophrenia has biological roots or not, its form can be very different for each individual. The delusions and other symptoms any one schizophrenic experiences relate to personal history. This is most evident in reactive schizophrenia, which appears to be triggered by stress. Most of the psychological theories are thus useful in identifying not only the general causes of the disorder but the particular causes for a given individual. We shall look at three psychological theories: psychodynamic, behavioral, and family interactions.

According to some psychodynamic theorists, painful early childhood experiences can lead to a pattern of distortion and withdrawal characteristic of schizophrenia.

Psychodynamic theory

Although most of Freud's psychoanalytic theories concerned the neuroses (anxiety-related disorders), he did also comment on schizophrenia. Freud saw schizophrenia as a regression to the oral stage of development, in which the infant ignores external reality, and id, ego, and superego are poorly differentiated. The disorder occurs when id impulses (particularly infantile sexual impulses) gain in strength, and the individual experiences anxiety and guilt because gratifying those impulses is socially unacceptable. By regressing to the infantile oral stage and breaking from reality, the schizophrenic avoids the anxiety and guilt.

Arieti (1974) has proposed a more recent psychodynamic view of schizophrenia which emphasizes the psychological effects of early childhood experiences. Arieti maintains that painful or traumatic events can sensitize a child to negative interactions within the family, creating a negative self-image and chronic feelings of being inferior, unwanted, and unloved. As family tensions cause the child increasingly intense anxiety, refuge will be taken in withdrawal and distortions. In this way the child represses from consciousness the true characteristics of the parental relationship and also diverts the blame for unpleasant feelings to the external world. That is, by redesigning the world in a less threatening (and more unrealistic) way, the schizophrenic escapes a negative self-image. According to Arieti, the schizophrenic deliberately regresses to successively lower levels of cognitive functioning and integration to reduce unbearable anxiety and stress.

Because psychodynamic theories of schizophrenia generally do not offer testable hypotheses or predictions, there is little empirical evidence either for or against them. Nothing we know of schizophrenia rules out any of these psychodynamic views, but the most we can say in favor of them is that they sound plausible.

Behavioral theory

Ullman and Krasner (1975), the primary proponents of the learning view of schizophrenia, maintain that all behavior, including schizophrenic behavior, is learned. In their view, schizophrenia is the result of failing to receive reinforcement for reacting to stimuli the way other people do. For example, a boy whose family life has not taught him to interact successfully with others will avoid other children when he goes to school rather than seek their company and approval. As the other children recognize this, they may make fun of him for being different. This reinforces his inclination to withdraw—and may cause teachers, too, to respond negatively to him, perhaps labeling him "maladjusted." This lack of successful interactions also deprives the boy of opportunities to receive feedback from others on his general behavior or beliefs. If he assumes that fire hydrants grow out of the ground like trees, or that jumping up and down will keep bugs away, no one is likely to correct his misconception. As a result, he grows up with a highly individual view of the world.

According to Ullmann and Krasner, social withdrawal, disorganized thought, apathy, and inappropriate affect are all consequences of this type of failure to attend to the same environmental cues as other people and thus failing to be socially reinforced. Further, because other people do not reward schizophrenics for attending to appropriate stimuli, they learn instead to attend to idiosyncratic stimuli, such as internally generated sensations and thought-images. In this way, hallucinations and delusions can gradually become more valid to the schizophrenic than external reality.

In view of the biological data presented earlier, it is unlikely that schizophrenia can be entirely accounted for by learning. Undoubtedly, some aspects of schizophrenic behavior are learned, and certainly much of it is influenced by the person's interpretation of environmental stimuli. Behavioral theory alone, however, does not explain why some individuals develop schizophrenia and others in the same environment do not.

Family theory

Many theorists implicate early childhood experiences—particularly as they are related to family relationships—in the development of schizophrenia. The **schizophrenogenic parent,** a term coined by Fromm-Reichmann (1948), reflects the idea that parents may create enough disturbance in the family to cause schizophrenia in the child. The schizophrenogenic mother has been described as cold, domineering, insensitive, and inconsistent. She proclaims affection but actually rejects the child. At the same time, she is overprotective and encourages the child to remain dependent on her. The schizophrenogenic father is described as passive, ineffectual, and equally insensitive to others. Both parents may be covertly seductive with their opposite-sex children. Although the notion of the schizophrenogenic parent appears to have some validity, it has not been substantiated as *the* cause of schizophrenia. Children of parents who match the schizophrenogenic description do not necessarily grow up to be schizophrenic, and not all schizophrenics have such parents.

The **double-bind hypothesis** of Bateson and colleagues (1956) focuses on a faulty communication pattern between at least one parent, or some other equally important figure, and the child. The parent says one thing but the accompanying expression or gestures say the opposite. The confused child doesn't know which message is real and therefore doesn't know how to respond. At the same time, the parent makes it clear that commenting on this contradiction is forbidden. Unable to just ignore the message, the child is caught in a no-win situation. For example, a mother may continually complain that her son doesn't love her, but she never shows him any affection, and she rebuffs all his attempts to hug or kiss her. No matter what he does, he loses. Bateson then speculates that retreat into bizarre behavior and distorted thought is the child's only way to cope with this difficult situation.

Lidz (1973) has suggested that the parents of children who develop schizophrenia have failed to provide the necessary amount of nurturance. His research indicated that two family relationship patterns in particular, which he terms **marital schism** and **marital skew,** are involved. In schism, the parents have openly declared war: They battle constantly and insist that the children choose sides. In skew, there is little discord, because one parent is willing to be dominated by the other. In fact, the entire family is submissive. Usually, the dominant parent is at least highly eccentric; often, psychopathological problems exist. Either way, the family caters to every strange whim.

Clearly, under both marital schism and marital skew, children cannot obtain their full share of attention. In both situations, the family is too preoccupied with fighting or with fulfilling the needs of one of its members to worry about whether the children are maturing properly. Therefore the children never learn the skills needed to become independent. Nor can they work in social roles other than those they see at home, where the only role models are very poor and interpersonal communication is, at best, quite unusual.

The child who has schizophrenogenic parents, who is caught in a double bind, or who lives with schism or skew is deprived the chance to learn the normal balance of love, trust, and independence that would lead to successful relationships with other people later in life. What the child *does* learn is that social interactions are a source of pain and anxiety. Thus there develops neither the ability nor the willingness to relate to others.

Nevertheless, there is no convincing evidence at present that schizophrenogenic parenting, double-bind communications, or marital schism or skew is a primary cause of schizophrenia. There is no supporting evidence that *all* children brought up by such parents become schizophrenic—in fact, it's just the reverse: Most children who are brought up by parents in these situations do *not* become schizophrenic, and those who do often have normal brothers and sisters.

A number of studies have found distinct communication styles in families with a schizophrenic child (Mishler and Waxler, 1968; Wynne and Singer, 1965), and it appears likely that modeling in such situations influences the child's behavior. Whether the child is actually developing the disorder or merely acquiring some of its characteristic symptoms is unclear, however. It is also possible that the disturbed communication pattern is more a result of the presence of the schizophrenic member than a cause of the disorder. Most studies of family interaction and schizophrenia have focused on relationships between parents and the already diagnosed schizophrenic (Fontana, 1966; Jacob, 1975); few data exist on what family interaction is like *before* a child becomes schizophrenic. For these reasons, it is not possible to say with certainty what role family factors play in the development of schizophrenia.

Social Explanations

In urban areas, schizophrenia is diagnosed most frequently in the lowest socioeconomic classes (Kohn, 1968). One explanation that has been suggested for this is that low socioeconomic class is in effect a cause of schizophrenia. As we saw in Chapter 5, people at the bottom of the socioeconomic scale struggle continuously with economic deprivation, lack of rewards and opportunities, poor education, and unpleasant physical surroundings. The stress created by these disadvantages may contribute to the development of mental disorders, including schizophrenia.

A second explanation takes the opposite view—that people drift into lower-class urban areas because their disorder keeps them from holding a job or earning enough money to live elsewhere. The **drift hypothesis** (Myerson, 1941) suggests that schizophrenics are downwardly mobile. Various studies designed to test this hypothesis by comparing the occupations and socioeconomic levels of young schizophrenic men with those of their fathers have turned up conflicting data, however; so it is not clear at present what relation, if any, socioeconomic drift has to the incidence of schizophrenia.

A third explanation implicates differential diagnosis. Advocates of this hypothesis contend that doctors treating patients from the higher classes are relatively reluctant to diagnose them as schizophrenic because of the potential stigma. Conversely, doctors treating lower-class patients may be quick to use that label because overcrowded, underfunded state hospitals can now manage schizophrenics more easily than patients with most other disorders, as we shall see in a later section. Another factor may be the quality of treatment available to someone with money and influence compared with what is generally available to a poor person. Improvement, early release, and readmission probably are all affected—which in turn affects statistics on the prevalence of schizophrenia at each socioeconomic level.

Finally, we must also consider the motivations patients have to get well—or at least to get out of the hospital. There is evidence that chronic patients, like chronic prisoners, may prefer the relatively peaceful hospital environment to the stresses of an underprivileged life on the outside. One patient put it this way:

> "Look, doc," he said, "I have no family, no job skills, and nothing waiting for me on the outside. I first got sick in the Navy and they have been putting me up ever since. In here I get my meals, my room, and any doctoring I need. We got a bowling alley, a swimming pool, a movie theater, and a nine-hole golf course. I get $400 from the government every month, tax-free, and they let me go into town every once in a while. If I get out of here, they take away my money, I got no job, and no place to go. Now, are you gonna tell me I'm crazy for not wanting to leave?" (Mahoney, 1979, p. 448)

Szasz (1960) maintains that mental illness is a myth used by psychiatry and society to "explain" and control the deviant behavior of individuals. Ullmann and Krasner (1975) have pointed out that many people make their living from the whole mental hospital process—psychiatrists, psychologists, social workers, nurses, attendants, administrative staff, cooks, custodians, security guards, and so on—all of whom have a strong vested interest in the continuation of the present system. The most controversial of the social explanations of schizophrenia is known as **labeling.** The most extreme interpretation of this theory, which is held by existentialist Laing, views schizophrenia as a sane reaction to a sick society.

Earlier in the chapter we mentioned Rosenhan's 1973 study in which several normal people claiming they heard voices were admitted to psychiatric hospitals. All patients but one, who was diagnosed manic-depressive, were diagnosed schizophrenic. Their stays in various hospitals lasted an average of 19 days; no staff members suspected that the pseudopatients were not disturbed, though many of the other patients did. While hospitalized, the pseudopatients received more than 2100 pills. Contact with staff was infrequent and mostly superficial. At discharge, the diagnosis was schizophrenia in remission.

Rosenhan maintains that this study demonstrates the problem of inappropriate (and potentially destructive) labeling. A psychiatric diagnosis of schizophrenia should not be made on the basis of one symptom in the face of otherwise successful adjustment; yet the diagnosis *was* made on this basis, and the patients were stuck with it when they were discharged. On the other hand, it has been argued that if someone comes to a mental hospital complaining of auditory hallucinations and seeking admission for treatment, it is not unreasonable to assume that a disorder exists and to try to find a diagnosis that fits such a symptom.

Laing (1964) sees schizophrenia as a label that society applies to certain sets of behaviors devised by ordinary people in an attempt to adapt to difficult life situations. Laing's own experiences working in a mental hospital and subsequently studying schizophrenics and their families led him to conclude that what appear to be psychotic symptoms are in fact attempts to cope with irrational, impossible, or conflicting demands in the family. Ironically, the family that engenders the schizophrenic behavior may then assist in getting the individual labeled schizophrenic and committed for treatment. Laing has observed that when therapy is successful during the patient's hospital stay, its effects are often quickly counteracted by returning home.

R. D. Laing has attracted much attention with his theories on schizophrenia. He believes that the disorder is a desperate attempt of the individual to find wholeness as a human being within an irrational world.

Gruenberg and Zusman (1964) hypothesized in greater detail how social labeling might create chronic schizophrenia. To begin with, individuals who lack self-confidence and inner standards regarding rules of behavior are considered vulnerable to the **social breakdown syndrome,** which means that their concept of who they are and how they are supposed to act is easily disturbed. For example, a man who lands in a mental hospital following some intense disturbance is, for a while, unusually dependent on others for guidance on how to act and think. But his very presence in the hospital gives him the label "crazy." He may be ridiculed by others, subjected to legal proceedings, and forced to participate in the hospital's treatment regimen. Gradually, he begins to fit that label: He is a mental patient, weak in the mind, passive, and helpless, with little chance of improvement. There are few if any opportunities to use his previously acquired skills of everyday living—even such skills as shopping, cooking, and driving—so the person's capacity to function outside the institution atrophies. He has become a more-or-less permanent institutional resident.

In some situations, where symptoms are mild or the diagnosis is questionable, labeling may be involved in schizophrenia. However, labeling alone does not account for severe cases, for those patients who function very poorly, and who are unable to work, socialize, reason, or relate to family members and friends.

Interactional Explanations

From the evidence we have at present, the most likely explanation for schizophrenia appears to be an interaction of two or more factors, probably including both heredity and environmental influences. Accordingly, many researchers lean toward the diathesis-stress model mentioned earlier, in which some external event interacts with a genetic predisposition for the disorder. Meehl (1962) has proposed one such model. He theorizes that an inherited brain defect is a necessary but not sufficient condition for schizophrenia. That is, without the genetically determined brain defect, schizophrenia would not develop, but the presence of the defect alone does not produce schizophrenia.

The constitutional defect, which Meehl calls **schizotaxia,** leads to a personality that he calls *schizotypic* (see also schizotypic personality disorder, Chapter 10). All schizotypic individuals show mild thought and affective disturbances, but most of them do not become schizophrenic because their environment is not particularly stressful and they seem to be able to resist some degree of stress. Those individuals who do develop schizophrenia are less resistant than others to the stresses of everyday life, or they may have been exposed to particularly severe stress.

Another diathesis-stress model has been proposed by Mednick (1970), who suggests that the key stress may come before or during birth. Mednick supports the theory of a genetic predisposition for schizophrenia; he asserts that schizophrenics have an inherited tendency toward high levels of anxiety. But he has also found evidence that a high proportion of the offspring of a schizophrenic parent who grow up to be schizophrenic themselves experienced birth complications—prematurity, oxygen deficiency, prolonged labor, umbilical cord complications, breech birth (baby emerging feet first instead of head first), and so on.

Mednick pioneered a method of studying the development of schizophrenia called the **high-risk method.** Unlike traditional retrospective studies, high-risk research is a good way to examine the interaction of biological and environmental factors. The high-risk study begins with a sample of children known to have a parent diagnosed as schizophrenic. These children are then studied over the years; some of them become schizophrenic and some do not. The ones who develop schizophrenia are compared as adults with the ones who do not, with particular attention paid to differing childhood experiences and characteristics. In one such high-risk study, Mednick (1970) found that the two groups differed in specific ways:

1. The mothers of subjects who became disturbed were hospitalized earlier in their children's lives, and their symptoms were more severe, than the mothers of the subjects who did not become disturbed.
2. The fathers of the disturbed offspring were more disturbed than the fathers of the nondisturbed offspring.
3. The disturbed group had been perceived by their teachers during childhood as more aggressive, domineering, and disruptive in class.
4. The disturbed group showed greater anxiety on a physiological test during childhood.

There are several high-risk studies now in various stages of progress around the country (Garmezy and Streitman, 1974). They focus on the everyday functioning—school adjustment, academic performance, family and peer relations—of children with a disturbed parent as well as on cognitive functioning, physiological characteristics, exposure to environmental stress, and other features of development. The search is for any common factor that may be a precursor of schizophrenia. So far, although the children of schizophrenic parents are not grossly debilitated during childhood, they do have some discernible problems. For example, Weintraub, Prinz, and Neale (1978) have reported that a relatively high proportion of these children are perceived by their classmates as less likable and sociable than other children, and as either aggressive or socially withdrawn.

The high-risk studies will undoubtedly shed considerable light over the next several years on the causes of schizophrenia. These studies are particularly useful in that they enable researchers to look for various components of an interactional model. Until now, it has not been possible to identify the exact nature of the relationship between constitutional factors (genetics, biochemistry, physiology) and environmental factors (social learning, family influence, stress).

A chronic problem with this kind of study is trying to discern what, if any, influence the very fact that they are being studied will have on these subjects. It is conceivable that knowing they are under surveillance can alter the way they act as well as the attitudes and expectations of others (teachers, for instance) who are aware of the study. Perhaps some may come to exhibit schizophrenic symptoms simply because it is expected of them—the self-fulfilling prophecy again.

MANAGING THE SCHIZOPHRENIC DISORDERS

Ideally, the treatment we select for any disorder would follow from what we know about its causes. Schizophrenia is an excellent example of how things often work just the opposite. One of the best reasons for hypothesizing a biological factor in schizophrenia is that a biological therapy—drugs—has such success in treating it. Not all cases respond to drug therapy, however, a reminder that schizophrenia probably comprises more than one disorder.

Back when schizophrenia was considered synonymous with madness, the usual way of managing patients was to lock them up. This approach is by no means extinct, but other more constructive methods of treatment have gained preference over the years. Several different types of intervention have been used with schizophrenics, with varying results. The main biologically based method at present is pharmacotherapy (drug treatment). Different psychological methods are used also, especially techniques built around the operant conditioning model of the behavioral school. Hospitalization is almost always the first step, however, so the methods we shall describe are primarily programs used for a large community of patients. Individual therapy is attempted in some programs, but for the most part, the very nature of the disorder precludes that kind of therapy.

Biological Methods

In the 1940s and 1950s, when a new age of science and technology was coming into flower, dramatic attempts were being made to cure schizophrenia. One of these was lobotomy, in which certain connections in the brain were surgically severed. Some patients did indeed calm down as a result, but there were undesirable side effects; in several cases, personalities tended to vanish along with the schizophrenic behavior. Another fairly drastic treatment was electroconvulsive therapy (ECT), which involves passing a brief electrical current via two electrodes through the patient's temples. The current was strong enough to induce an epileptic-like seizure (hence the term *convulsive*) and to render the patient unconscious. The theory was that epilepsy was incompatible with schizophrenia, so that inducing seizures would make it impossible for the patient to continue being schizophrenic. Although ECT is still used occasionally to treat other disorders, such as severe depression, it has proved ineffective in the treatment of schizophrenia.

Pharmacotherapy

In the mid-1950s, after the discovery of reserpine and chlorpromazine, pharmacotherapy came into use, and it quickly supplanted the older biological approaches. Today, the major tranquilizers in general, and phenothiazines in particular, are the most widely used treatment for schizophrenia. The most commonly used phenothiazine is chlorpromazine (also called Thorazine), which has proved moderately effective at reducing confusion, agitation, incoherent speech, hostility, and reports of hallucinations, and at increasing social participation and self-care behaviors. Hogarty and Goldberg (1973) studied schizophrenics who, when released from the hospital, were maintained on either chlorpromazine or a placebo. At the end of one year, 72 percent of the placebo group had returned to the hospital, compared with 31 percent of the chlorpromazine group. While these results do demonstrate that chlorpromazine is more effective than a placebo, 31 percent is still a substantial relapse rate. For those schizophrenics who did not require rehospitalization, adjustment in many cases was only marginal.

Chlorpromazine sometimes produces side effects such as drowsiness, constipation, nausea, dizziness, jaundice, dryness of the mouth, blurred vision, and symptoms similar to those of Parkinson's disease—muscular tremor and rigidity and some loss of muscular control. Patients treated with chlorpromazine also report that it seems to reduce schizophrenic symptoms by diminishing their overall level of mental functioning, including their imagination and responsiveness to their environment. Despite the side effects, however, the phenothiazines are at present the primary treatment for schizophrenia. This is not to say that they are viewed as an outright cure for the disorder. A more realistic assessment is that they decrease schizophrenic symptoms enough for the person to function outside a hospital. Drug treatment has thus caused a dramatic decrease in the number of long-term, institutionalized patients. However, it replaced institutionalization with a "revolving door" treatment policy: Admit patients briefly, treat them with drugs, and send them out to the community again; when problems arise, repeat this procedure.

Psychological Methods

The various psychological therapies have only recently started to play a major role in the management of schizophrenia, largely because most schizophrenics were too disturbed to reach effectively and there were too few trained professionals available. When chlorpromazine was introduced, the situation changed somewhat. The drug calmed the patients down and made them accessible to therapy, although not all therapies have proved successful.

Psychodynamics, for instance, has been found to produce no significant changes in behavior. Freud himself believed that psychoanalysis was better suited to what he termed the neuroses, although a few therapists reported having some success treating schizophrenia (Fromm-Reichmann, 1948). The insight into hidden motives and conflicts typically offered by psychodynamic therapists appears to be less valuable than the moral support they can provide to bolster the self-esteem of their patients (Gunderson and Mosher, 1975). But just getting the patients interested in establishing the all-important therapist-client relationship is still a major difficulty.

Other psychological therapies have been more successful, particularly behavioral methods, and we shall discuss the major treatments in use today. However, since almost all of these methods are used in hospitals—because schizophrenia almost always requires a hospital stay—we shall first describe the environment of a typical institution.

Hospitalization

Over the course of a lifetime, the typical schizophrenic will spend anywhere from a few weeks to several years in a mental hospital. About half of all patients admitted to mental hospitals are diagnosed schizophrenic. Under ideal conditions, hospitalization gives the schizophrenic a chance to get away from environmental pressures that may be contributing to the disorder, as well as access to professional assessment, counseling, and specialized treatment. It also relieves the burden that the person may have placed on family and friends. Unfortunately, few hospitals are able to meet the needs of patients as consistently as would be desirable. Most mental hospitals in the United States are funded by the federal or state government. Many of them are old, grim, and somewhat removed from metropolitan centers. Private hospitals, which have more money, are generally superior to public hospitals; patients receive more staff attention and the surroundings are more pleasant. However, they also cost more.

The average patient in a mental hospital has very little contact with psychiatrists or clinical psychologists. In the previously mentioned study of hospitalization by Rosenhan (1973), the "patients" were asked to keep track of staff responsiveness. On several occasions, they approached psychiatrists, nurses, and attendants with straightforward questions. In 71 percent of the contacts with psychiatrists, the doctors kept moving without making eye contact; 23 percent of the time they made eye contact but did not stop to talk; 6 percent of the time the doctors stopped to chat. Nurses and attendants moved on without making eye contact 88 percent of the time; 10 percent of the time they made eye contact but did not stop to talk, and 2 percent of the time they stopped to chat.

For many patients, the hospital experience is lonely, boring, and dehumanizing. Given the difficulties most schizophrenics have relating to those around them, such an environment may be far from therapeutic. Imagine, for instance, the effect on paranoid schizophrenics of being forced to take mind-dulling shots or pills, while the whole hospital staff seems to be involved in a conspiracy not to acknowledge their existence. But then, as we have stated, most hospital programs are now oriented to getting all but the most psychotic cases on drug treatment and back out in the community again. The most severely disturbed, those who remain in the hospital for long periods, are the ones who fall prey to all the ills of hospitalization. However, it may be argued that although they don't receive much personal attention, they may never notice the lack.

For the majority, the drugs work and allow them to return to their homes after only a brief stay—or to remain at home and receive treatment at outpatient facilities (that is, where the patient does not spend the night). These clinics can monitor medication and make sure the person has a social worker, psychiatrist, or psychologist to talk with during stressful periods. For patients who need closer supervision, the hospital may provide aftercare in the form of follow-up visits from social workers.

Sometimes, if living at home is not practical, living in a halfway house is a solution that provides a step between hospitalization and complete return to the community. Following release from the hospital, patients live together in a boardinghouse, usually under the supervision of staff members. Residents share responsibilities but are not left entirely on their own. Some schizophrenics eventually make the transition from the halfway house to their own homes, while others stay in the halfway house for long periods.

The basic idea is to provide a supportive and constructive alternative to the mental hospital. Rather than being thrown directly from total dependence on hospital care to total self-sufficiency, the patient has a chance to practice self-care and effective social skills under supervision. This method has not been a total success, however. Many schizophrenics find that phenothiazine treatment enables them to function only marginally outside the hospital; they may be unable to participate satisfactorily in family life or take complete care of themselves—a situation that traps patients in the "revolving door."

Milieu therapy

If traditional hospitalization is not helping schizophrenics to improve, and if they have trouble functioning in the community outside the hospital, maybe the answer is to create a therapeutic community *inside* the hospital. This is the reasoning behind **milieu therapy,** an approach that became popular in the 1950s and 1960s. The aim of milieu therapy is to provide patients with an atmosphere of acceptance and respect that can raise their self-esteem and to encourage them to take an active part in their own rehabilitation. In this therapeutic community, staff members are encouraged to interact with the patients just as they would with peers. Patients are permitted to come and go within the ward as they please, to maintain a reasonable level of privacy, and to wear their own clothes instead of uniforms. They are also encouraged to participate actively in hospital routine.

Milieu therapy has been implemented in modified form in some hospitals, and it does make a mental hospital a more humane place to be. Unfortunately, although it is simple in conception, a successful milieu therapy community is expensive to set up and difficult to maintain properly on a 24-hour-a-day basis. However, the most serious drawback is that when milieu therapy has been implemented, its results are unclear.

Behavior therapy

Therapists who believe schizophrenic behavior is established and maintained by environmental reinforcements generally believe it can be modified by the same means. O'Leary and Wilson (1975) have described successful attempts to alter schizophrenic behavior by using operant conditioning. Many behaviors are affected by the social consequences they cause, such as the verbal attention they elicit from other people.

Close-up: Laingian Therapy

Existential psychiatrist R. D. Laing's unique theory of schizophrenia led him to a rather unusual therapy for the disorder. Believing that schizophrenia is the way the individuals so labeled have chosen to try to get in touch with their true selves, he contends that experiencing the disorder is essential for reintegration. Therefore "treatment" consists of helping the person through what can be a living nightmare, as the person attempts to penetrate layer after layer of facade looking for the long-hidden core.

At Kingsley Hall, a now-defunct residential center in London, therapists were expected to monitor the progress of the residents. The most important part of the therapists' role was to encourage the patients in whatever direction they might be headed, to establish a relationship in which both participants were seekers *and* guides. A resident who smeared his own feces on a wall would more likely receive praise for his creative urges than censure for bad conduct. This is similar to Carl Rogers's humanistic concept of giving unconditional positive regard, but the intent is not only to build up the person's self-concept and self-esteem but also to discover what messages are hidden in each act.

However, Laingian therapy is not directed only at the person diagnosed as schizophrenic. In accordance with Laing's belief that irrational life situations—most notably in the family—are at the root of the problem, therapy sessions with the family are regarded as essential for understanding the maladaptive interactions that led to problems for at least one of its members. In short, if schizophrenia is a nonpathological result of pathological family dynamics, the real treatment lies in correcting the environment that awaits the newly reintegrated person.

By reacting to schizophrenics with a positive response (a smile, praise, eye contact) when they utter a sensible remark, and withholding attention when they make a statement that is silly, psychotic, or irrational, hospital staff members have been able to dramatically decrease schizophrenic speech and increase appropriate verbalization. Social withdrawal, apathetic behavior, and refusing to speak can be altered by similar methods, although stronger reinforcers (such as cigarettes or access to desired activities) are sometimes required.

This clearly runs counter to the basic approaches used by insight therapists and others who try to understand what may be underlying the behavior. For example, the woman mentioned earlier whose behavior worsened when the time for her mother's visit approached is a case in point. A behaviorist might say that preventing the mother's visit would reinforce the bizarre behavior shown by the patient without questioning the long-term nature of their relationship.

Token economies. One comprehensive system of reinforcement, the **token economy,** has been used with hospitalized schizophrenics. First, target behaviors are specified. For schizophrenics, these may include work tasks on and off the ward; self-care activities such as grooming, bathing, and appropriate care of clothing; and social interactions such as appropriate conversations, cooperative responses, and participation in rec-

Figure 11.3. The effect of token reinforcement on schizophrenic behavior. From Ayllon and Azrin, 1965.

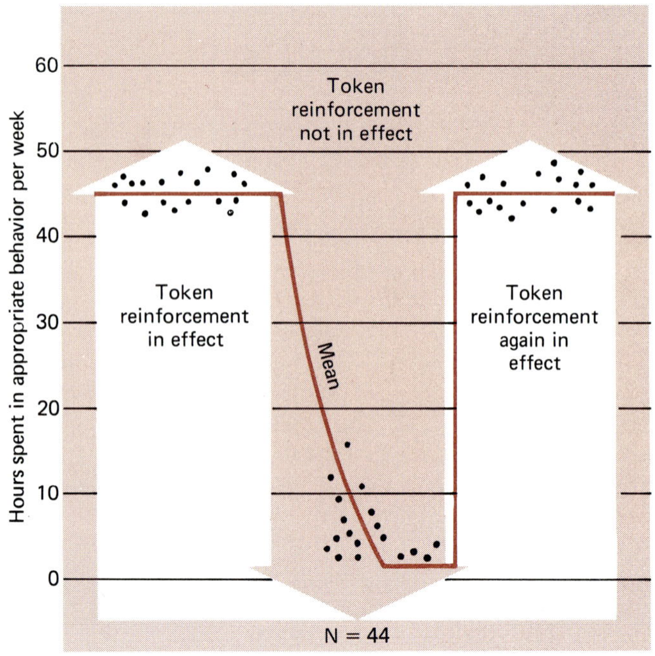

reational activities. When patients engage in one of these behaviors, they receive one or more tokens, either on paper or in the form of poker chips or some other symbolic object. With these tokens, patients can buy activities, privileges, material items (such as cigarettes or sodas), and other things. A popular purchase is privacy—more free time or a private room, for example.

Applying a token economy in a Veterans' Administration hospital ward of chronic schizophrenics, Atthowe and Krasner (1968) reported significant changes in behavior. Patients became less apathetic and socially withdrawn, interacted with other people more often, and followed ward rules more closely. In addition, the staff's morale improved and the proportion of patients discharged from the hospital went up. Still, such a program is not effective with all schizophrenics; extremely socially withdrawn patients and those who seem to have little interest in any type of reinforcer do not usually fare well.

Another problem is how to maintain the behavioral improvements when the patient is discharged. Obviously, the token economy cannot practically be transferred into the person's home, which may limit its long-term effects. Kazdin and Bootzin (1972), reviewing various token economy programs, concluded that patients' accomplishments rarely last outside the hospital. Others have drawn more positive conclusions.

A well-controlled, six-year-long study by Paul and Lentz (1977) compared the effectiveness of milieu therapy, token economies, and traditional hospital care. Their data show conclusively that token economies do lead to successful releases into the community: More than 90 percent of those who had lived under a token economy while hospitalized still lived in the community a year and a half after release. Milieu therapy was not quite as successful; 30 percent of the released patients had been readmitted. Traditional treatment fell far behind, with more than 50 percent returning to the hospital.

Although merely altering a schizophrenic's behavior is viewed by some as attacking the symptoms rather than the underlying disorder, it is clear that reinforcement and the token economy can help reduce the aberrant behaviors that prevent some schizophrenics from coping successfully with their environment. Whether or not this is a cure may not be the most important consideration; that certainly has not been the prime consideration of the pharmacotherapies in use today.

The other question often raised about the token economy and other reinforcement techniques for treating schizophrenia involves ethics. Does our ability to shape people's behavior give us the right to substitute behaviors we decide are desirable for those chosen by the subject? Is it reasonable to withhold things a patient wants and needs—food, privacy, cigarettes, opportunities to participate in enjoyable activities—until our behavioral standards are met? (For that matter, what are the ethics of encouraging cigarette smoking as a means of altering other behaviors?) It has been argued that the token economy is unfair and demeaning to patients because it denies their basic human rights to pleasure. Again, the usual response is a practical one: If a token economy can help schizophrenics to function more effectively in society, it is obviously beneficial to them in the long run.

Social skill training. Token economies typically teach the patients certain basic skills to help them cope with life outside the hospital. Social skill training is very similar, but the skills involved are generally more complex. A token economy will concentrate on such things as making eye contact, talking to other people even briefly, and keeping clean and neat. In the next step, they learn to assert themselves in stores and restaurants, to participate in discussions, to go on job interviews, to ask someone to go to a movie.

Staff members break down each skill into its component parts, then carefully and thoroughly coach patients through each component, beginning with the simple ones. Teaching methods include modeling the staff member, repeated practice by the patient with and without prompting, and frequent reinforcement. The whole process requires many sessions and much patience on the part of the instructor. In one study (Meichenbaum and Cameron, 1973), the experimenters modeled appropriate cognitive skills out loud to teach patients to monitor their own "crazy talk." Patients in the training group showed more improvement than controls.

Although social skill training programs can obviously help schizophrenics learn to interact more confidently and effectively with other people and decrease their abnormal behavior (King et al., 1960), the problems with the method are similar to those of token economies: A good program is time-consuming and expensive, and the improvements are hard to maintain once the patient leaves the hospital. Another major problem with both programs is that although they are designed by professionals, they are usually administered by attendants. This has at least two serious drawbacks:

1. Attendants are usually not motivated to be consistent in their treatment and attitudes; they may not understand the importance of the treatment nor care about the end results to the patients.
2. The turnover among attendants is quite high because of generally low salaries for a heavy and emotionally draining workload, which also hurts the consistent treatment aim.

Interactional Methods

Research on the effectiveness of various therapeutic approaches to schizophrenia strongly suggest that two are usually better than one. The phenothiazines can reduce schizophrenic symptoms enough to make the person more receptive to behavior therapy, and in turn behavior therapy may strengthen more effective patterns of behavior and help the person gain confidence.

The best indicator of a given patient's likelihood of recovery is not the form of treatment used, however. The type of schizophrenia is still the most important element: A reactive schizophrenic—that is, someone who had been functioning well but broke down in response to a

Figure 11.4. *Type of aftercare and its impact on relapse rates. From Goldstein et al., 1978.*

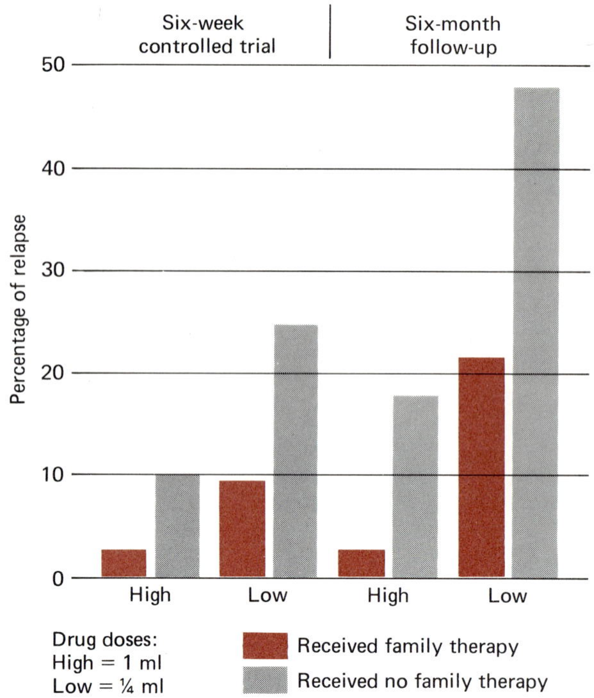

stressor—has a much better chance of returning to normal functioning than a process schizophrenic, a person who deteriorated gradually. But even if recovery is out of the picture, the likelihood of any schizophrenic living a successful life at home is greatly strengthened by family therapy.

Family therapy treats the whole family as a unit rather than just the schizophrenic member. This can help ease the adjustment of having a potentially disruptive family member back at home. The family can learn the reinforcement techniques that were used in the hospital and can continue the esteem-building process.

If inadequate communications or bizarre interactions between members have contributed to the disorder, analyzing those patterns and trying to alter them is essential. Otherwise, when patients return home, they are liable to fall back into old habits because the family interaction patterns have not changed. Then the gains made during therapy will be lost. Family therapy and drugs have proved more successful when used together (Goldstein et al., 1969).

For the reactive schizophrenic, continued pharmacotherapy and counseling may be the means to a normal and happy life. With long-term schizophrenics, treatment is more likely to lead to improvement than to cure. Patients may learn to get along successfully in a low-pressure situation, such as a hospital or halfway house, but may never be completely self-sufficient.

SUMMARY

Schizophrenia is a severe group of psychotic disorders that affects approximately 1 percent of the population. It is characterized by a deterioration of functioning; the person no longer operates as effectively as in the past. Specific symptoms typically include disordered thought (often including delusions), disturbed speech, perceptual distortions (often including hallucinations, especially auditory hallucinations such as voices), decreased or inappropriate emotions, and bizarre actions. To an observer, the schizophrenic's thought patterns appear random and illogical, but evidence suggests they follow a logic of their own. Delusions, for instance, may be the person's attempts to make sense of these disordered perceptions.

DSM-III lists five types of schizophrenia: disorganized, catatonic, paranoid, undifferentiated, and residual. Disorganized schizophrenia is characterized by incoherent speech, silliness, inappropriate emotional responses, fragmented delusions, and bizarre movements or mannerisms; social impairment is usually extreme. Catatonic schizophrenics display bizarre motor behavior, alternating between rigid immobility and wild excitement. Paranoid schizophrenics suffer from delusions of persecution or control; they may have other schizophrenic symptoms as well but usually function more normally than the disorganized or catatonic schizophrenic. Undifferentiated schizophrenics show various schizophrenic symptoms, such as delusions, social withdrawal, and disordered speech, but no specific patterns place them in the other categories. Residual schizophrenics are in the process of recovery and have only mild symptoms. Another distinction that can be made is between reactive schizophrenia, which comes on suddenly and follows a good premorbid adjustment, and process schizophrenia, which involves long-term deterioration.

Studies of twins, adoptees, and family psychiatric histories provide strong evidence for a genetic factor in the etiology of schizophrenia. The mechanisms of the disorder appear to be biochemical. One promising avenue of research concerns the hypothesis that schizophrenia is the result of an excess of the neurotransmitter dopamine in specific areas of the brain. Psychodynamic theories of schizophrenia emphasize regression—the individual is believed to be returning to an early childhood level of functioning. Environmental factors appear to play a role in the development of the disorder, though their precise influence is not understood. Social learning, disordered communications within the family, socioeconomic status, and labeling all are related to schizophrenia, but whether they contribute to causing the disorder or merely help determine a given individual's pattern of symptoms is unclear. Interactional theories such as the diathesis-stress model suggest that schizophrenia is the result of a complex interaction between biological and environmental factors.

The management of schizophrenia is limited by our lack of comprehensive knowledge about its causes. Pharmacotherapy (drug treatment) is the most widely used form of treatment; the major tranquilizers, particularly the phenothiazines, have largely replaced earlier biological methods such as lobotomies and electroconvulsive therapy (ECT). Hospitalization can relieve schizophrenics from the pressures of their previous environment, but it is often more custodial than therapeutic. Constructive alternatives include outpatient community care, milieu therapy, token economies, and skill training. Psychotherapy and family therapy may be of some help, particularly if used along with pharmacotherapy. Prognosis for recovery, however, is more closely related to the onset of the disorder and the patient's premorbid adjustment rather than to the therapy used.

Conversation 5

Schizophrenia is a horrifying experience for those who are ill as well as for those who observe from the sideline. But some fortunate few fight their way out of it. Mary, the middle-aged woman in this interview, struggled back from what she was convinced was hell to become a counselor for other psychotic patients. The account of her return is truly incredible.

Interviewer: You had a very rough life. What was the beginning?

Mary: I was adopted at age five by a couple in their fifties—not really elderly, but old enough to be my grandparents. They'd never had any children and didn't understand them; they were very rigid; didn't understand the need for play and so forth. I lived in fear of my father, who was a seaman and very stern and aggressive and demanding. And my adopted parents were quite well off, so there was a lot of animosity from the relatives because I, who was not related by blood, might inherit some of the money. I was very, very unhappy. I felt very, very much alone. I wasn't allowed to play with other children, so I read voraciously. I was a fairly religious child, too, and I set pretty high values for myself. I also had a sensitivity that I think played into the illness.

During my teen years the pressures got worse. I ran away from home overnight and went to a friend's house. The next day, when I and my family and friends talked about what to do, I told them I wanted to go to a boarding school. I was in the boarding school for a while, but I wound up in the hospital because by that time I was pretty depressed and suicidal.

Once I hit the hospital, where people took care of me, I didn't want to leave. I did everything to stay there. The state hospital experience back in the 1940s was pretty bad—seclusion, beatings—yet there was just enough security to lasso me. And some people were very caring; I got some positive attention and some negative attention. I wasn't really psychotic, just very depressed.

Later, when I was at home again, my father returned from a fishing trip and dropped dead in my arms when I greeted him. Then I started experiencing severe anxiety. Two years later my mother died and I experienced the first psychosis. That was pretty bad: I felt the floors tipping over, everything looked really weird—like looking through glass. It felt like the world was crumbling.

Int.: Did just being in the hospital have anything to do with the severity of that episode?

Mary: I don't think so. I think the fact that I was so insecure was more influential. Don't forget, when my parents died, there was nobody. I had never taken care of myself and I was totally alone in the world. You can't say that circumstances or stress cause a psychosis. We don't know how much is biological and how much is environmental. But I don't think it was just the hospital environment. I think the previous environment plus the biological changes of adolescence induced the psychosis.

But don't forget that I played many games in the hospital, too. I didn't want to get well. I didn't want to be part of life. Until I became catatonic, I was not really psychotic enough to be uncomfortable. Then I got psychotic to the point where I was really suffering. I was in a totally different world: Colors were psychedelic; people looked like monsters. It was horrendous, and I was paralyzed with fear.

Int.: What were you thinking?

Mary: I thought I had died and gone to hell. I had no feelings in my hands. My face was distorted. I was catatonic: An invisible force was controlling me, raising my hands into a set position and keeping them there. It was almost like an LSD trip. I felt the effects physically, too. I couldn't eat and went down to 86 pounds. I was in bed for almost two years. They didn't think I would survive. But at that lowest ebb—that's when I started on the road to recovery.

Int.: What happened?

Mary: I can remember sitting up in bed and seeing the whole horror, and I thought, my God! This is that other world I heard about. We talked about catatonics being in another world, but I never associated it until then. And I thought, I don't like this world; I want to come out of it. But is that possible? I started thinking, and I formed my own treatment plan. I knew that physical things could help a patient get well. So I thought, if I get in touch with the real world by touching, maybe the real world will eventually come back to me. I started playing with cards, shuffling them, to get the feelings back in my hands. I took my first steps; I made a bed. I just gradually started doing physical things around the unit. It took a long time before it worked.

Int.: How did the staff and other patients react?

Mary: They didn't know what I was doing. I wasn't verbal so I couldn't tell them. But you know, they didn't care at that point. They felt I was hopeless. Well, I started getting better, so I went to the doctor and asked to talk to her. The fact that I opened my mouth was enough to make her say yes. I told her I'd been trying to get well, but had done all I could on the unit. I needed her permission to go off the ward, to go outdoors, and I didn't want anyone to interfere with what I was doing.

Int.: What did she say?

Mary: She gave me permission. The staff thought she was crazy, but I went out. I went up to the canteen for a cup of coffee. I knew interaction was important, so I sat with some patients at a table, saying to myself, "Even if you can't talk, you're there and making progress." Afterward I went to the chapel and prayed. I told God I didn't expect miracles, but I would do everything in my power to get well and I asked Him to not make my efforts be in vain. And I vowed to dedicate my life to mental health if I succeeded.

I did everything I could in the ward and then went to the doctor again. I said, "It's time for me to move on to an open ward." The staff couldn't understand it—they took 25-cent bets that I would be back on the closed ward in two weeks. It's been fifteen years!

Int.: You were stubborn!

Mary: It wasn't easy. I had to constantly keep at it. Trying to grow caused awful anxiety. But the doctor was on my side—I still see her. I told her that if I was ever going to get out of the hospital I had to learn to support myself. So she made arrangements for me to go to a workshop, where I made shoes. Then I graduated into working in the office and started interacting with people. A rehab counselor wanted to work with me, but I said no: I had to learn to be independent. I knew that was crucial to making it.

Then I went back to the doctor and said it was time for me to go out into the world. It was hard. But I got a job in a hospital, got my own apartment, and signed up for a college course, remembering my vow. After I passed the course I wanted to go full-time, but I didn't know how to pay for it. I talked to a counselor at the college and painted the blackest picture. But I said that if he found a way for me to attend, I would give it everything I had. He turned out to be not only a counselor, but also the Financial Aid Director!

Int.: Not bad!

Mary: In college, I started giving to everybody. I became more outgoing and made a lot of friends, including my future husband; I did outreach work with psychotic patients at the hospital I'd been in; I developed the first internship program for the psychology department in that school. I made *Who's Who in American Colleges and Universities.* Then my husband died when I had only one more semester to go. I got a job and worked full-time, took six courses, and graduated with a 4.0 average. I've been working in mental health ever since.

Seven months ago I implemented this program, a residential center for deinstitutionalized schizophrenic patients. We have eight residents, male and female, mostly younger people. I created this program model based on my own philosophy—it's never been duplicated. We've got quite a reputation; it's considered one of the best programs in the region.

Here there is no external sign of control: no chore charts, no bulletins, no keys to lock the doors, no rules on the walls. There's nothing programmatic to rebel against. The control and the structure are there but they're not visible. This allows for less rebellion and for internalization of the way of life here. When they internalize the structure, it becomes a natural environment. It's like your own home: You don't have rules printed up at home. There's also no separation between staff and residents—everybody takes turns with chores. It's working. We've had a recidivism rate of one in seven months: a 58-year-old woman who was in the hospital for 42 years. They pushed her onto me too quickly. She needed more transition time. The others are original residents.

Int.: How does the community react?

Mary: We haven't had any problems. The residents go downtown, to the sub shop, to the ice cream parlor, to the park. They go to church. Plus we're in the YMCA, where the community is in and out all the time. We've had not one complaint in seven months.

Int.: What was different about you that enabled you to overcome your schizophrenia?

Mary: I suffered, but chronic cases become comfortable with their illness. Also, I didn't lose total insight; I knew I was sick. I could work my way through it. But you have to look at each one as an individual. We can't expect them to do what I did necessarily, but we should bring them to their own best potential.

Int.: Yours is a really amazing story. You're an extremely self-motivated person. Not everybody could do what you've done with your life.

Mary: I think they could if they wanted it badly enough. God's been very good to me, too. But in spite of all the bad things, I'm so happy to be a part of life. To me it's a privilege to be out in the world and to live with people and have the same pressures. I'm just like everybody else: I shed my tears, I laugh when I'm happy, I get mad, other times I'm very caring. I'm glad to be part of the struggle. I just got accepted to Harvard University Graduate School; I'm starting in September to get my master's degree. Then we'll see how motivated I am. But it's a new challenge and I'll be able to contribute even more. My philosophy is that suffering doesn't have to be a negative aspect of your life. If you just succumb to it it will be; but if you do something positive with it, it becomes a positive part of your life.

CHAPTER 12

Affective Disorders and Suicide

DESCRIBING THE AFFECTIVE DISORDERS

Major Depressive Disorder

Bipolar Disorder

Diagnosing Affective Disorders

EXPLAINING THE AFFECTIVE DISORDERS

Biological Explanations

Psychological Explanations

Social and Cultural Influences

MANAGING THE AFFECTIVE DISORDERS

Biological Methods

Psychological Methods

SUICIDE

Explaining Suicide

IDENTIFYING POTENTIAL SUICIDES

PREVENTING SUICIDE

My mind is rambling rambling
It's just like some rolling stone
Since that nightmare's come to stay
My thoughts just don't belong
They say the blues is just a bad dream
They say it lives inside your head
But when it's lonely in the morning
You're bound to wish that you were dead.

James Taylor, "The Blues Is Just a Bad Dream"*

DSM-III's description of the depressive syndrome sounds a lot like James Taylor's description of the blues:

> An individual with a depressive syndrome will usually describe his mood as depressed, sad, hopeless, discouraged, down in the dumps . . . Thoughts of death or suicide are common, as is the belief that the individual or others would be better off dead. (pp. 210–211)

All of us occasionally feel depressed. After a personal setback or tragedy—being fired from a job, losing a loved one—the depression may be so severe that we begin to wonder if life will ever seem worthwhile again. Ordinarily, time eventually heals the wound. Indeed, some observers believe that depression is not only a natural reaction to stress but an adaptive one—a way for us to conserve and regenerate our physical and psychological resources. But when depression persists months after the event that sparked it—or when it occurs for no apparent reason at all—then it can be destructive to the individual and may require the intervention of professional help.

In this chapter, we shall investigate depression and the related disturbances that DSM-III classifies as affective disorders—the various types, the explanations that have been proposed for them, and the methods used to treat them. We shall also review what is known about suicide, including its relation to depression.

DESCRIBING THE AFFECTIVE DISORDERS

An **affective disorder** is a disturbance of mood or emotions, in contrast to the thought disorders, such as schizophrenia, that were discussed in Chapter 11. According to DSM-III, the term *mood* refers to a prolonged emotion that colors all aspects of life. The disturbance almost always involves periods of depression; it may also include swings to wild enthusiasm, euphoria, and self-confidence. Most of us experience mood swings. We have moments of wild exhilaration and power, when we feel on top of the world: falling in love, winning a big sports event, graduating *summa cum laude.* At these times we feel unstoppable—but eventually we calm down and go back to feeling normal again.

What is the difference between normal swings of mood and moods that are considered affective disorders? In general, depression and mania become clinically significant when they are debilitating to the individual—when they interfere with the person's ability to function. At the extreme, they involve the total personality and entail a substantial or complete loss of contact with reality.

DSM-III divides the affective disorders into two general categories: **major affective disorders** and **other specific affective disorders.** The second category is comprised mostly of milder forms of the major disorders, including cyclothymic disorder and dysthymic disorder, which will be briefly discussed in later sections. Because the symptoms of the milder forms are by and large identical to those of the more severe forms, we shall focus on the major affective disorders.

There are two general types of major affective disorder. The first is major depressive disorder, which involves serious mood disturbances characterized by continuing or recurrent depression—sadness, hopelessness, what psychologists call a *dysphoric mood.* The second type, bipolar disorder, involves both depressive and manic episodes—*manic* (from "mania") referring to a mood that is highly exuberant or irritable. Both types of disorder will be later examined in detail.

In attempting to define and classify affective disorders, we must keep a broad perspective of the diagnostic categories and what they mean to the people they describe. For the individual patient—and for society as a whole—the affective disorders inflict a serious burden. In the early seventies, depression was identified by the National Institute of Mental Health as the number one mental health problem in the United States, rivaling even schizophrenia (Secunda et al., 1973). A decade later, depression is still the major mental health problem in the country. Well over a million and a half individuals are currently being treated for depression, and it has been estimated that three to five times that number are in need of treatment (Berger et al., 1978). The results of one nationwide study suggest that 15 percent of all adults between 18 and 74 may have significant depressive symptoms. The cost of treating depression has been estimated at $4 billion per year (Secunda et al., 1973).

Depression has been called "the common cold of mental illness" (Seligman, 1975)—yet it often goes undiagnosed and untreated. We have no way of telling how many people suffering from depression turn to alcohol or drugs for temporary relief, and how many more cases, like Elaine in Chapter 1, remain hidden behind the picture windows of lovely suburban homes. Perhaps this accounts for the fact that depression is one of the few mental disorders with a significant mortality rate. Among people with bipolar disorder, the suicide rate is about 14 percent, compared with .01 percent for the general population in the United States (Becker, 1977). Previous research suggests that of the approximately 26,000 Americans who commit suicide each year, about 80 percent manifested major depressive symptoms (Flood and Seager, 1968).

Relatively few depressions lead to suicide, however. In most cases, the dysphoric mood eventually lifts on its own, especially if it arose in response to a specific circumstance. Those depressions that do persist usually can be treated. We shall review the most common and successful treatment methods later in this chapter.

As we have noted, milder depressions arise in response to some stressful incident or situation, and fade as the circumstances change again or the person recovers or adjusts. The stressor may be a major event, such as the death of a loved one, but often it is less dramatic. The parent whose last child has gone off to college, the dedicated worker forced to retire at 65, the graduate confronted for the first time by the need to earn a living, all may face depression. Nor is the stressor always negative. Mothers who have just given birth often suffer from **postpartum depression.** After spending nine months in anticipation of a joyful event, they often experience a great deal of guilt because they believe their new baby should bring nothing but happiness. Novelists (and writers of textbooks and term papers) sometimes experience the same mixed feelings when a major project is finally finished.

If we think of mood as running along a scale or continuum that ranges from mild depression to euphoria, the position of any individual at either end depends on three things: the type of symptoms, their severity, and their duration. At one end of the continuum might be the depression that hits a college student who has just come back from Christmas vacation to a bleak campus, a cold room, and a new term. For a few weeks, the student may spend a lot of time in bed listening to the stereo; but she manages to come down for most meals and some classes, and by February she is ready to go off on a ski trip. Farther along the scale would be a classmate who never gets out of bed, who refuses to eat, talk to people, wash, or change clothes. This student's symptoms involve more aspects of her personality, and as the weeks go by, her condition grows worse instead of better. When a friend finally drags her out to see the school psychiatrist, she is likely to be diagnosed as suffering from an affective disorder.

In the most extreme cases, the disturbance of mood is so severe that the patient's whole personality is affected. Physiology, behavior, and cognitions all are greatly altered, and loss

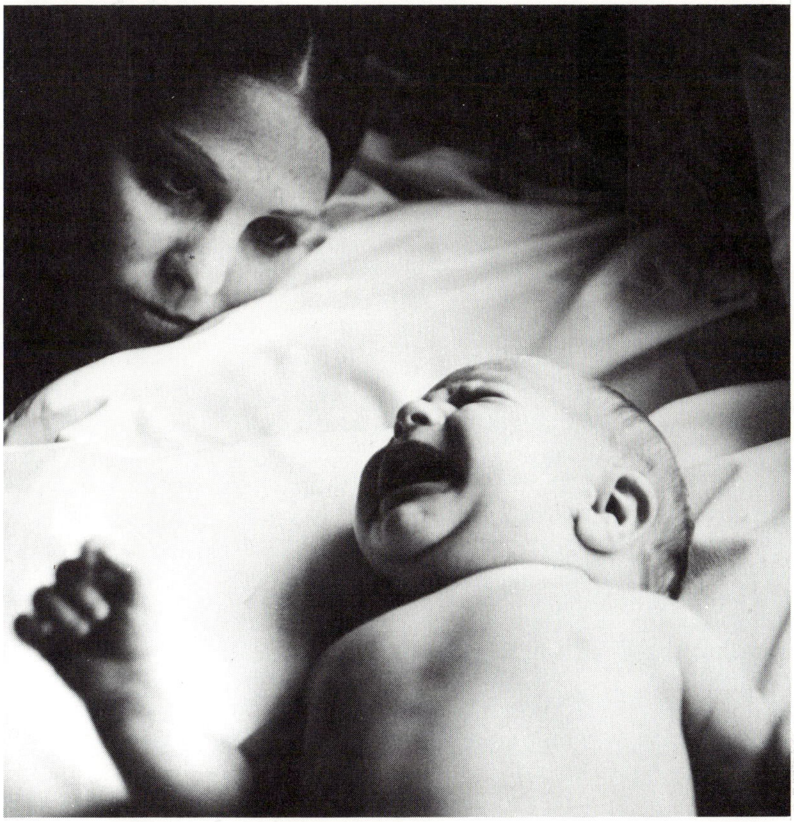

Some women may suffer from temporary post-partum depression, triggered by the physiological and psychological stresses of new motherhood.

of contact with reality may be almost complete. In the sections that follow, we shall see some examples of the devastating impact the affective disorders can have.

Major Depressive Disorder

The most common of the major affective disorders is the **major depressive disorder,** sometimes called *clinical depression.* Once known as *melancholia,* it has been recognized as a clinical syndrome for over two thousand years. In the Old Testament Job lamented:

> When I lie down, I say, When shall I arise, and the night be gone? and I am full of tossings to and fro unto the dawning of the day. My flesh is clothed with worms and clods of dust. . . . My soul chooseth strangling, and death rather than my life. (Job 7:4–5:15)

Shakespeare's Hamlet uttered his famous "To be or not to be" speech as he was contemplating suicide after his father's death. Queen Victoria, Tchaikovsky, Lincoln, even Freud—all are known to have suffered from recurring bouts of depression.

The most prevalent symptom in the major depressive disorder is the dysphoric mood—unhappiness, hopelessness, apathy. The individual often has a negative self-concept—"Nobody cares about me, and why should they?"—involving feelings of worthlessness, guilt, futility, and emptiness. Thinking processes are slower and poorly focused, and concentration is difficult. The depressed person may report an inability to feel pleasure in life—a condition called *anhedonia.* There is usually a withdrawal from interactions with others and from participation in normally pleasant activities. Loss of appetite and an accompanying weight loss are very common; sometimes the opposite pattern—a weight gain—develops. The person is likely to wake early and sleep irregularly. Doing anything at all is an effort; some individuals feel constantly tired, move sluggishly, and speak and respond more slowly than usual. For others, movement is agitated: They are unable to sit still—they may pace, wring their hands, burst into shouts.

Of course, no one of these symptoms alone characterizes a major depressive disorder. Nearly all of us have experienced at least one of them, and probably several, at some time in our lives. What distinguishes a major depressive disorder from the less severe forms of depression is the presence of most or all of these symptoms to the degree that they seriously impair the person's ability to cope with life. Journalist Percy Knauth described depression vividly in his autobiographical work, *A Season in Hell* (1975):

> My life turned inside out so that everything I saw was a photographic negative. . . . Where life with its continuing promise should have sustained me, only the oblivion of death attracted me now, for living had become a hell on earth. . . . Day and night, I was swept by fears and agonies that left me reeling.
>
> I ached for sleep. Would I ever know restful sleep again? Even pills gave me only restless snatches in which I tossed and trembled, racked by doubts and horrors that surfaced from my unconscious mind. And always I awoke in the darkest hours, just before dawn. . . .
>
> When I think back now over that terrible time, it seems to me that for long periods I was living in an entirely different world. There was a real world all around me, but I seldom saw it. I walked familiar streets in the lovely Connecticut village where I lived, but I saw no friendly houses and heard no children's cries; there was only the echo of my own footsteps in an empty gloom. . . .
>
> Every morning I fought down panic to get out of bed, and from then on it ruled everything I said or did. A simple question—"Daddy, what time is it?"—would send me into a helpless paroxysm of doubt, bewilderment, confusion, and guilt. Why was it asked? Why was I responsible for answering? Where was I? Why *couldn't* I answer? What *was* the matter with me, that I could not answer a simple question from my child? Look at your watch, you blind and helpless fool—*look at your watch!* (pp. 2–3, 5–7)*

In the most severe types of depression, symptoms such as retarded movements and feelings of guilt are exaggerated. Some patients may have delusions—for example, that they are responsible for some catastrophe, or that the body is disintegrating. Hallucinations may occur; suicidal thoughts increase. At the extreme, the patient may lose all willingness to respond, speak, eat, or even move.

Dysthymic disorder

In **dysthymic disorder,** many of the common depressive symptoms are present, but they are milder and do not last as long. Generally, the person's functioning is only moderately impaired, and there may even be brief periods of positive feelings. Certain characteristics appear more often in dysthymic disorder than in major depression. One of these is a tendency to be irritable or to get excessively angry over small things. Another is a tendency to break into tears very easily. Feeling slowed down but restless at the same time is also common.

Dysthymic disorder seems to occur about equally among the sexes (DSM, 1980) and is quite possibly the single most common mental disorder.

Bipolar Disorder

The major depressive disorder is characterized by continuous or recurring depression. In the other type of major affective disorder, the **bipolar disorder,** depressive episodes alternate with periods of *mania*—a highly elated or irrit-

* Specified excerpts abridged from pp. 2–9. © 1975 by Percy Knauth. Reprinted by permission of Harper & Row Publishers.

able mood, accompanied by heightened physical activity and thoughts that jump rapidly from one topic to another. Mania is almost a mirror image of depression, hence the name *bipolar,* which implies a switch back and forth between two extremes. This syndrome is more generally known as **manic-depressive illness,** the name it was given by German psychiatrist Emil Kraepelin in 1899 and that was used by the American Psychiatric Association through the publication of DSM-II.

Like the major depressive disorder, the bipolar disorder has been with us for thousands of years. Hippocrates wrote a complete description of the symptoms of both mania and melancholia in the fourth century B.C. Both King Nebuchadnezzar of Babylon and King Saul of Israel apparently suffered from manic periods. In a series of fascinating biographical explorations, psychiatrist Ronald Fieve (1975) speculated that many historical figures, including Abraham Lincoln, Theodore Roosevelt, and Winston Churchill, fought lifelong bouts with bipolar disorder.

Today, about 600,000 cases are treated in the United States each year (Berger et al., 1978). Estimates of the total number of Americans afflicted with the disorder vary: Some researchers believe the incidence is as high as 2 to 4 percent (Fieve, 1975), whereas others place it around 1 percent (Klerman, 1978; Weissman and Myers, 1978). Accurate figures are hard to come by for several reasons, perhaps the main problem being that because acute manic symptoms are much like those of paranoid schizophrenia, bipolar disorder is often misdiagnosed as schizophrenia. Also, some individuals have manic episodes that take on the very mild form known as *hypomania.* They are highly productive and appear almost normal, so that they may never be diagnosed at all.

Mrs. B.D. had been depressed for three to four months prior to the manic episode; her symptoms were apathy, social withdrawal, tearfulness, insomnia, and weight loss; she neglected her home and frequently expressed feelings that she was a burden to the family. Her husband, a politically and financially powerful man in the county, arranged that she be appointed as a delegate to a national political convention, "to snap her out of her depression."

At the convention her mood was different from what it had been at home. She was active, aggressive, and interested in the proceedings; and, to the surprise of her family, she made several speeches before the state delegation. During the last and most hectic nights of the convention, she slept only one to two hours per night and uninhibitedly took part in several demonstrations for her candidate. Her behavior was not considered unusual for a delegate.

On her way home, the patient and her husband stopped off to visit with her daughter . . . and her behavior, which was appropriate at the convention, did not change. She continued to make speeches, place calls, and send telegrams on behalf of the candidate. She refused to sleep, and on the next day, the day prior to admission, she began to notice references in the Bible and on TV to her "man" which indicated that she and the candidate would together save the world. (Winokur, Clayton, and Reich, 1969, p. 59)

In the setting of a political convention, Mrs. B.D.'s manic symptoms—expansive mood, heightened activity, unusual confidence, decreased need for sleep, loss of inhibitions, aggressive speech—appeared perfectly normal. Only when the context changed was her behavior recognized as unusual. This is often the case with hypomanic individuals. Their confidence and happiness can be contagious; and with their unlimited energy, they often get a lot more done than other people. Beneath this rather appealing veneer, however, they are likely to show up as impatient, intolerant, easily diverted, unrealistic, and undependable.

In *The Quiet Furies,* psychologist Elton McNeil described the case of Joe A., a clear illustration of many of the symptoms of a typical manic-depressive patient. Having developed—overnight—an elaborate plan for a nationwide telephone dating service, Joe began to fall apart when his business failed. He responded by working harder and faster, eliminating food, sleep, even trips to the toilet. At last, agitated

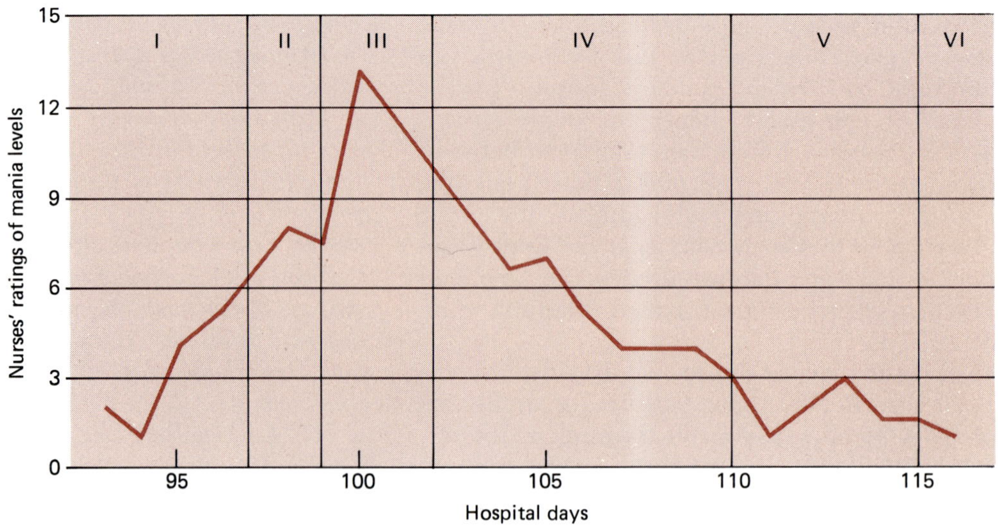

Stage I: Hyperactive and happy
Stage II: Paranoid, grandiose, paces and talks a lot, hyperreligious
Stage III: Delusional—reports having talked with dead father, suspicious, angry, sexually preoccupied, somewhat disoriented
Stage IV: Paranoid but more cooperative, manipulative, still angry and sexually preoccupied, restless
Stage V: Quieter and more organized, seductive
Stage VI: Seems normal—shows realistic emotion and cares about others

Figure 12.1. *Description of a manic episode. From Carlson and Goodwin, 1973.*

and disheveled, he was escorted by the police to the local mental hospital. McNeil overheard part of Joe's rapid-fire, barely intelligible appeal to the policemen who brought him in:

> You look like a couple of bright, alert, hardworking, clean-cut, energetic go-getters and I could use you in my organization! I need guys that are loyal and enthusiastic about the great opportunities life offers on this planet! It's yours for the taking! Too many people pass opportunity by without hearing it knock because they don't know how to grasp the moment and strike while the iron is hot! You've got to grab it when it comes up for air, pick up the ball and run! You've got to be decisive! decisive! decisive! No shilly-shallying! Sweat! Yeah, sweat with a goal! Push, push, push, and you can push over a mountain! Two mountains, maybe. It's not luck! Hell, if it wasn't for bad luck I wouldn't have any luck at all! Be there firstest with the mostest! My guts and your blood! That's the system! I know, you know, he, she, or it knows it's the only way to travel! Get 'em off balance, baby, and the rest is leverage! Use your head and save your heels! What's this deal? Who are these guys? Have you got a telephone and a secretary I can have instanter if not sooner? What I need is office space and the old LDO [long-distance operator]. . . . (p. 147)*

* Elton B. McNeil, *The Quiet Furies: Man and Disorder.* © 1967. Adapted by permission of Prentice-Hall.

As Joe's case suggests, the mood of someone in a manic period may be just the opposite of the typical depressive mood. Instead of feeling hopeless, such individuals are overly optimistic and self-confident, full of wildly ambitious plans and brimming with energy to put them into action. They may pour resources—psychic and financial—into some bizarre scheme that anyone else would recognize was doomed from the beginning. When these great ambitions are thwarted, the exultant mood may turn quickly into annoyance and anger. In this respect, the manic phase is similar to the depressive: The person has lost touch with reality. The more acute the disorder, the greater the gap between perceptions and the real world; more and more of the person's personality is being affected. It has been speculated that mania may be the individual's last-ditch defense against depression.

In a severe manic episode, restlessness increases; movement is rapid, often purposeless, sometimes violent. Speech becomes faster and more incoherent. The *flight of ideas*—thoughts jumping from one topic to another—speeds up. The person is easily distracted, thought processes are disordered, judgment is poor, and grandiose delusions are common. The individual's mood may change abruptly from elation to rage. The need and desire to sleep decrease drastically, while energy increases. Inhibitions vanish, replaced by open sexual references and behavior. Hallucinations may occur.

Cyclothymic disorder

Cyclothymic disorder is to bipolar what dysthymic disorder is to major depressive: a milder, less debilitating form of the serious disorder. The person experiences mood swings from depression to hypomania, which is a mild form of mania, but neither mood is extreme, and there are often normal periods between the swings.

Very often, the person will exhibit exactly opposite behaviors in the different moods, so that these actions seem paired. For instance, when in a hypomanic episode, the individual may have an inflated sense of self-esteem, may rarely sleep, and may constantly seek out people for companionship. In the depressed episode, there may be feelings of personal inadequacy, excessive sleeping, and withdrawal from others.

Diagnosing Affective Disorders

It is difficult to decide what an affective disorder is and who has it; trying to pinpoint its cause is even harder. Does the patient's depression seem to spring from a recent unhappy event, such as a broken marriage? Or is there a family history of depression that may lie behind the disorder? Is the problem an inherited one or is it the result of learning from family members? Perhaps the cause is not one unhappy event but a series of them that have made the patient give up hope that life can ever be enjoyable.

An affective disorder involves so many aspects of the person's life that it is hard to reach general conclusions about causation. We shall look at a few of the models researchers have proposed in their attempts to explain or at least classify affective disorders and then examine in detail the major approaches to diagnosis and treatment in use today.

Some diagnostic issues

Over the years, investigators have suggested numerous approaches to understanding the affective disorders. An early distinction was first proposed by Kraepelin and used through DSM-II: **Endogenous** depressions are defined as those with internal biological causes, whereas **exogenous** (or *reactive*) depressions are those caused by external stressors, such as bereavement or financial losses. The advantage of this scheme is that it makes a useful distinction between depressions brought on by specific external circumstances and those with no readily identifiable cause.

The exogenous classification assumes that the patient or the therapist can reliably pinpoint some stressful event in the recent or distant past as the cause of a given depression, which is by no means always true. Some researchers believe *all* depressions are precipitated by stressors, whether obvious or hidden, and that the endogenous category is essentially meaningless.

At the peak of her popularity, Janis Joplin died a tragic death from a drug overdose. Was her compulsive overindulgence in drugs and alcohol an attempt to cope with loneliness and chronic depression?

The category also has the disadvantage of focusing on the patient's history rather than the present situation, which opens the way for a degree of interpretation and speculation that many therapists consider inappropriate. Furthermore, it fails to account for causes that may be neither biological nor entirely external, such as social or psychological factors (Beck, 1967). For the present, the drawbacks appear to be too many, and the exogenous-endogenous distinction does not appear in DSM-III.

Kraepelin also suggested that the agitated depression many people experience in middle age is a unique clinical entity. He called it *involutional melancholia* because it occurs during the period known as the *involutium* (menopause), when significant endocrinological changes are taking place. For women, this period is around ages 40 to 55; for men it is about ten years later (Henderson and Gillespie, 1969). As Mendels (1970) has pointed out, however, these years are also a time of personal changes:

> For a woman, it usually marks the stage of life when her children, to whom she may have devoted a major portion of her time, become independent and prepare to leave the home; at the same time, childbearing is no longer possible for her. . . . [For both men and women] after twenty years or more of adult life, there is frequently a questioning of role and purpose, and the realization that many ambitions have not been fulfilled and are unlikely to be. (p. 30)

It appears, then, that involutional melancholia may not be significantly different from other types of depression in its nature and cause. At present, it is not considered distinct enough to warrant a separate classification, and the category involutional melancholia has been dropped from DSM-III.

Another model that does not appear in DSM-III is the psychotic-neurotic distinction. Psychotic depressions were distinguished mainly by a loss of the ability to function and a tendency toward delusions—ideas and perceptions that seriously distort reality. But considerable question arose as to whether the difference between psychotic and neurotic depressions was really one of substance or only of degree. In particular, the distinction was found to be of little use for treatment (Klerman, 1978). DSM-III has categorized them into major depression, which may or may not have psychotic symptoms, and dysthymic disorder, a mild form roughly equivalent to the old depressive neurosis classification of DSM-II.

One diagnostic distinction that is still regarded as valid and important is that between unipolar and bipolar disorders. As we have seen, *unipolar disorders* involve only episodes of depression, whereas *bipolar disorders* include both depressive and manic episodes. Cases of manic episodes without periods of depression are extremely rare—so rare, in fact, that most research and clinicians believe manic episodes are always part of a bipolar disorder.

People with bipolar disorder have periods of mania much less often than periods of depression. According to Klerman (1978), only about 15 percent of patients who are diagnosed with manic-depressive illness show the presenting symptoms of a manic episode or indicate a history of previous manic episodes. This presents an obvious difficulty for diagnosis: How do you know whether a depressed patient is simply depressive, or a manic-depressive who has not yet had a manic episode?

On the surface, this distinction may not seem very important. Research suggests, however, that the two disorders may be quite different. Studies have shown that unipolar and bipolar patients differ in several dimensions, including family history, biochemistry, and response to various forms of treatment. Bipolar patients more often have family members who have suffered from the same disorder than do unipolar patients, for instance. People with bipolar disorder also tend to have their first episodes earlier in life—generally in their twenties to mid-thirties, compared with the mid-thirties to forties for unipolar patients. We shall consider the possible genetic implications of these and related findings later in this chapter.

EXPLAINING THE AFFECTIVE DISORDERS

Trying to isolate the origins of the affective disorders is a complex task indeed. For one thing, it is very difficult to do reliable, comprehensive research. What we know about causes generally comes from working backward: The typical sample population is a group of patients, which creates a bias from the outset, and data on their histories may consist largely of what they can tell us. Matters are further complicated by the fact that every therapist asks patients different questions and interprets the answers somewhat differently. A more ideal situation for research would be to select and study subjects who will later develop affective disorders—obviously not a practical possibility.

Even if we could design some method for scrutinizing the life of every person who may someday suffer from an affective disorder, we would still face the problem of untangling all the diverse influences on those lives. Take the case of Robert, a young man who left his hometown and moved to a city several hundred miles away. Now Robert is seeking treatment for depression. He tells the therapist that he came to the city to get away from a broken engagement, unreasonable demands from his parents, and a dead-end job. As soon as he arrived he caught the flu and spent two weeks in bed in a cheap rooming house. Now he is looking for a job, worried that his money is running out, missing the friends and familiar places he left behind. He has lost weight—is that because of the flu, because he dares not spend much money on food, or because he is depressed? Is he depressed because he cannot find a job, or has he failed to find a job because he acts so depressed when he goes for an interview? Was the broken engagement back home a cause or a result of his depression? As we consider the various explanations researchers have proposed for the affective disorders, we should keep in mind the complex network of relationships they are trying to analyze.

Biological Explanations

The term "biological" can be applied to a number of different types of internal and external influences. Heredity is a biological factor, obviously—but so are the foods we eat, the air we breathe, the drugs we take, and the illnesses we experience. For convenience, we use biological here to refer only to those influences that are largely or exclusively internal—the endogenous factors, as they have been called. These fall into two general categories: genetic and biochemical.

Genetic factors

Research on the heritability of affective disorders has turned up some interesting correlations, as we noted earlier. People with bipolar disorder in particular often show that disorder in at least two previous generations of their families (Secunda et al., 1973). Parents and siblings of such patients have a 20-percent chance of having the disorder, according to one report, whereas family members of a unipolar patient have only a 12- to 14-percent risk of being diagnosed as depressive (Slater and Cowie, 1971). The two disorders do not overlap: Families with a history of unipolar disorder do not tend to produce bipolar children, and vice versa (Pincus and Tucker, 1978).

Winokur, Clayton, and Reich (1969) suggested that bipolar disorder is genetically transmitted by a dominant gene on the X chromosome, meaning that only women can pass it on (men give only a Y chromosome). In support of this theory, a study they did indicated that female relatives are at much higher risk (about 50 percent) than males, who averaged about 20 percent. However, more recent studies (Goetzl et al., 1974; Hays, 1976) have found father-son cases of bipolar disorder.

But are these relationships necessarily genetic? Might it be that children learn depressive (or manic-depressive) behavior from their families? Another finding, that correlations are higher between mothers and children than between fathers and children, is similarly ambiguous. It could mean that affective disorders have a sex-linked component or that the early closeness between mothers and their offspring encourages learning of the disorder.

Evidence from twin studies supports a genetic interpretation. For both unipolar and bipolar disorder, there is a high concordance rate among twins: that is, if one twin develops the disorder, chances are the other one will, too. Monozygotic (identical) twins have a higher concordance rate than dizygotic (fraternal) twins; and the concordance rate for both is higher with bipolar disorder than with unipolar disorder. If one identical twin has bipolar disorder, the chances are 50 to 100 percent that the second twin also has it. For nonidentical twins, that likelihood ranges up to about 40 percent (Berger et al., 1978).

Still, the mechanisms of heredity are complex, and it is impossible to say exactly how and to what degree they may be responsible for affective disorders. One popular hypothesis is that individuals can be genetically predisposed to a disorder, but whether and when they get it depends on other influences, such as psychological stress.

Biochemical factors

One of the most promising areas of current research into causes of the affective disorders has been the biochemical. Investigations have suggested a strong link between depression and certain chemical changes in the body's nervous and endocrine systems. This is not surprising, since we know that all human thought, feeling, and behavior involve activity in these systems. What researchers have been trying to determine is which biochemical processes are related to the affective disorders, and how. Among the areas currently under study are biogenic amine metabolism, electrolyte balance, and adrenocortical hormone metabolism.

Biogenic amines are neurotransmitters, substances that play a crucial role in the central nervous system's transmission of messages. When an electrical impulse travels along the *axon* (the body) of a neuron, it triggers the release of one of these amines. The neurotransmitter travels across the *synapse,* the space between neurons, and either inhibits or excites the next neuron. It is then reabsorbed, mostly by the neuron it came from. There are two types of biogenic amines: **catecholamines** and **indolamines.**

Two early clues to the relationship between the biogenic amines and depression came from clinical observations. In the 1950s, a **monoamine oxidase (MAO) inhibitor** that was being used to treat tubercular patients was found to alleviate depression as well. What such an inhibitor does is restrain the biochemical action

Table 12.1 *The Major Neurotransmitter Theories*

Name	Theory for depression	Theory for mania
Norepinephrine (NE) theory (Catecholeamine hypothesis)	Not enough NE	Too much NE
Serotonin (S) theory	Not enough S	Too much S
Permissive theory	Not enough NE Not enough S	Too much NE Not enough S

From Fann et al., 1977.

of MAO, which ordinarily metabolizes biogenic amines after they have played their part in transmitting nerve impulses. Patients receiving this treatment can thus be assumed to have higher levels of unmetabolized biogenic amines in the brain than they normally would.

Around the same time, it was found that about 15 percent of patients who were being treated for hypertension with the drug reserpine developed depressive symptoms. Animal studies showed that reserpine decreases the level of certain biogenic amines in the central nervous system.

The catecholamine hypothesis. These findings led to a major biogenic amine theory, the **catecholamine hypothesis.** This hypothesis stated that depression is related to a deficiency of catecholamines, principally *norepinephrine,* while manic episodes are related to an excess of these neurotransmitters at important sites in the brain (Bunney and Davis, 1965; Schildkraut, 1965).

It has not been practical to measure levels of biogenic amines in the human brain directly, but animal studies and measures of metabolic products of norepinephrine in urine, plasma, or cerebrospinal fluid have produced indirect support for the catecholamine hypothesis (Wehr and Goodwin, 1977). Bunney and colleagues determined in two different studies (1970, 1972) that the norepinephrine level increases in the manic stage of bipolar disorder and that it decreases during depression. Many investigators currently believe, however, that this hypothesis is too simplistic.

The serotonin hypothesis. Another major biogenic amine theory is based on the indolamines, particularly *serotonin.* The **serotonin hypothesis** asserts that low levels of that neurotransmitter in the brain cause depression. Mendels et al. (1972, 1975) did indeed find markedly decreased levels of serotonin in the cerebrospinal fluid of depressives. When treated with drugs that increased the serotonin, their conditions improved.

The permissive amine theory. Prange and colleagues (1974) have tried to incorporate both models—the catecholamine and serotonin—into an interactional biochemical theory. They suggest that a low level of serotonin is a necessary predisposing factor for affective disorders in general. The norepinephrine level will then determine the form of the disorder—low norepinephrine will lead to clinical depression and high levels will yield mania. This is called the **permissive amine theory.**

Two other points are worth noting. First, even if it could be demonstrated that depression is related to abnormalities in biogenic amine mechanisms, we still would have to face the question of whether those abnormalities are a cause or an effect of depression—that is, has the depressed mood led to the physiological changes? Second, biogenic amine processes may not be related specifically to depression but rather to a general stress reaction (Mendels, 1970). For example, general stress has been shown to lower the level of norepinephrine in animals (Bliss, Wilson, and Zwanziger, 1966).

Electrolyte balance. Another major research area is **electrolyte balance.** Electrolytes are electrically charged substances that are present both inside and outside neurons. The balance between the concentration of electrolytes inside and outside a nerve cell influences the cell's excitability. Research suggests that a high concentration of the electrolyte sodium within neurons is related to depression: Depressive patients were found to have an intracellular sodium concentration of about 50 percent above normal, which in manic-depressive patients jumped to 200 percent above normal during manic episodes (Coppen, 1967). The effectiveness of lithium carbonate in treating some cases of manic depression adds support to these findings, for lithium apparently decreases the concentration of intracellular sodium (Mendels, 1970).

Hormone metabolism. Another biochemical factor that may be involved in the affective disorders is **adrenocortical hormone metabolism.** The body's various endocrinological systems—the adrenal glands, the pituitary, the thyroid—release hormones into the blood or lymph that regulate distant organs and tissues. One of these is a steroid hormone called *cortisol,* produced by the adrenal glands. Several studies have found depressed patients to have higher levels of cortisol than nondepressed patients (Rubin and Mandell, 1966). Other steroid hormones may also play a role in depression; as with the biogenic amines, it is not clear, however, whether steroid hormone imbalances relate specifically to depression or to a general stress reaction (Sachar, 1975).

Circadian rhythms. One of the most recent biological theories concerning the affective disorders focuses on **circadian** (daily) **rhythms,** our biological "clocks." Many physiological processes follow regular patterns, and it is possible that depression is among them. Recent reviews of studies examining the course of affective disorders have concluded that 80 to 100 percent of cases of depression are recurrent (Zis and Goodwin, 1979; Zis et al., 1980). Grof and colleagues (1978) found a striking pattern of relapses among the bipolar subjects they studied. It is possible, then, that depression is related to a defect in one or more of the "pacemakers" in different systems of our body, resulting in a desynchronization of bodily functions. For example, biogenic amines have recently been found to vary in concentration in relation to circadian rhythms, suggesting that previous biogenic amine research, based on measurements made at the same time each day, may have been misleading. Disturbances in the sleep cycle, especially early morning sleep, are a classic symptom of depression, and manic phases are often preceded by drastic changes in sleep patterns (Bunney, 1977). It has been suggested that disruption of the various stages of sleep, such as the REM (rapid eye movement) period, may result from some dysfunction in a patient's activity-rest cycle (Wehr and Goodwin, 1977).

Psychological Explanations

Long before anyone was aware of biogenic amines or intracellular electrolyte concentration, explanations were being sought for mania and depression. Recent advances in biochemical research have given us new insight into the affective disorders, but they do not by any means rule out the psychological and social theories originated by earlier investigators. In this section we shall consider current ideas about psychological influences on the affective disorders—keeping in mind that these ideas are a supplement rather than an alternative to the biological theories. The psychological approaches fall into three general categories: psychodynamic, behavioral, and cognitive.

Psychodynamic theories

In 1911, Karl Abraham, a student of Sigmund Freud, proposed an interpretation of depression that became the basis for Freud's own theories. Abraham believed that depression is a reaction to the loss of a loved one in early childhood— either an actual loss or an imagined one. The young child has ungratified unconscious sexual drives toward the loved person that turn into inward-directed hostility, self-hatred, and a predisposition toward depression as the child grows up. Freud (1950) distinguished depres-

Infant monkeys reared without mothers and without normal social interaction developed the withdrawal symptoms characteristic of depression.

sion from ordinary grief on the basis of these mixed feelings. Grief—open, outward, and subsiding over time—is the typical reaction to losing someone with whom one has a fairly straightforward positive relationship. If the relationship is complicated by unconscious hostility, however, the individual reacts to the loss much more personally, with feelings of guilt, self-blame, and diminished self-regard.

The classic psychoanalytic view of depression thus is that it is a pathological response to losses (either real or symbolic) that is rooted in a predisposition for depression arising from early childhood experiences. The depressed individual is characteristically oral—a fixation that manifests itself clinically as excessive dependence with exaggerated needs for affection and support (Chodoff, 1974).

Because psychodynamic explanations are impossible to test in any detail, there has been little research support for them, although they continue to be intuitively attractive to many practitioners. The crucial role of loss has, however, been confirmed by a number of investigations. A study of babies separated from their mothers and held in relative isolation found that the infants developed severe depressive symptoms (Spitz, 1946). Extensive observations of monkeys deprived of their mothers in infancy have shown that they too take on depressed postures and behaviors (Harlow and Suomi, 1974). Other research suggests that an individual who loses a parent at any age up to fifteen is prone to later psychiatric problems, including depression.

An interesting recent twist to psychodynamic theories of depression is the idea that the central impact of loss is not the absence of the loved one per se but the damage to the bereaved person's self-esteem. For instance, a man whose wife has left him may be devastated not by the loss of his wife as an individual but by feelings of rejection and by the prospect of remaining alone and wifeless. A woman whose mother has died may grieve, even though she hardly ever saw her and did not enjoy their few visits together, because she sees herself as having failed to achieve a good relationship with her mother.

Behavioral theories

B. F. Skinner's work in operant conditioning used reinforcement to shape behavior. Behavioral theorists believe a similar process underlies the affective disorders. Ferster (1973) has suggested that, compared with other people, depressed individuals emit fewer behaviors that are likely to elicit positive reinforcement. An example might be the student who is so obsessed with her studies that she never goes out with friends, never leaves campus on weekends, and considers any activity but studying a waste of time. With the opportunities for positive reinforcement limited to schoolwork, she gets relatively little reinforcement and becomes depressed. Or take the student who allows himself to be bullied into going to a party, but is so afraid of making a fool of himself that he stands close to the door all evening and talks to no one. By avoiding any risk of being "shot down," he ensures that he will also miss any chance for enjoyable interactions with other people.

Lewinsohn has elaborated on these ideas. Using data from his class study, he outlines the

Close-up: The Pleasant Events Schedule

The idea behind the Pleasant Events Schedule was to test the hypothesis that depressed people have few reinforcements and little pleasure in their lives. Devised by MacPhillamy and Lewinsohn in 1973, it is a good example of how difficult it can be to study something as complex as the possible causes of depression. It is also a good example of how ingenious psychologists can be at putting an intangible subject into a form they can study.

The study divided 120 community volunteers into three groups—depressed, nondepressed, and control—on the basis of their scores on an abbreviated MMPI and a structured clinical interview. The researchers then administered the Pleasant Events Schedule to measure the subjects' activity levels and their potential for being reinforced by a wide variety of events.

"Pleasure" was operationally defined as any occurrence or event that elicited a positive emotional response from the individual. The schedule listed a range of activities and events that most people would find reinforcing—plus a few that most people might *not* find too pleasing—and the subjects were asked to identify the items they considered pleasant. The pleasant events were quite varied, from "shaving" and "driving fast" to "taking powerful drugs" and "going to a party." The respondents were then scored on the basis of how many of these items they had experienced in the 30 days just prior to this test. As predicted, the depressed group scored significantly lower than the two control groups, which did not differ significantly from each other.

following assumptions as underlying the learning model for depression (Lewinsohn et al., 1969):

1. *A low rate of response-contingent positive reinforcement acts as an eliciting stimulus for some depressive symptoms.* That is, a person whose life offers few opportunities to earn reinforcement is likely to show signs of depression. The point here is not that such people are never reinforced, but that the rewards in their lives do not appear to them to come from any effort they may make to earn them. Many rock musicians, for example, describe themselves as seriously depressed even though they are showered with admiration and applause everywhere they go. When the audience's approval no longer seems to be contingent on their giving a good performance, applause loses its reinforcing quality and eventually ceases to be viewed as a sign of appreciation.

2. *Certain environmental events, such as a loss through death or separation, and various individual traits and states, such as social skill deficits, can result in a low rate of positive reinforcement.* The behavioral emphasis on loss echoes that of the psychodynamic theorists, although here the loss is seen as a removal of opportunities for positive reinforcement. The idea that a lack of social skills also limits potential reinforcements seems logical: however, there is some question whether it really is a cause of depression. Most depressed people show a marked deficit of social skills only while they are in the depressed state—before onset and after recovery, they get along quite adequately with other people.

3. *The depressed individual is considered to be on a* prolonged extinction schedule—*that is, the low rate of reinforcement leads to more behavioral symptoms of depression, such as a low rate of activity and verbal behavior.* In other words, as the person receives fewer reinforcements for behavior, there

is less and less inclination to do anything at all. Why bother?

4. *Interaction between the depressed individual and the social environment may turn into a vicious circle—others may find the behavior of depressed individuals aversive and avoid contact with them, which increases the depression.* This has been an intriguing question for investigators of the affective disorders. Manic behavior seems to be fairly straightforwardly aversive: The manic person is not seeking reinforcement in the form of friendliness or sympathy from others, but appears to *want* to alienate them—it's almost as if reinforcement lies in a sense of being in control, of being able to throw other people off balance. Depressive behavior, on the other hand, seems to repel and attract at the same time.

Coyne (1976) has postulated that some stressful experience or set of experiences initially leads a person to seek personal support from others. This can be just about any life crisis or major change—the loss of a loved one, retirement, even a positive change, such as a promotion or a major accomplishment. Neither the particular event nor the possibility that the person may be predisposed in some way to depression is of critical importance. What is important is the depressive behavior displayed by individuals seeking support—behavior that both repels others and arouses their guilt. The depressed person's persistent demands for reassurance and sympathy elicit annoyance and hostility; but they also elicit some sympathy and a reluctance to reject the appeal for support directly. A likely outcome is verbal expressions of warmth and approval ("You poor thing! How could they do that to you?") combined with behaviors such as avoidance or hasty withdrawal that express the opposite message. The depressed individual, sensing the mixed message, pushes for greater reassurance by conveying a more intense level of depression, which causes spiraling ambivalence in whoever is approached.

In another study (Howes and Hokanson, 1979), college-age subjects interacted with a confederate in a waiting room setting, supposedly while waiting to participate in a psychology experiment. Three different confederates pretended to be depressed, normal, or physically ill. The "waiting room" interactions were recorded, and the subjects' responses were categorized by various dimensions, for instance, whether they gave direct supportive statements, direct negative statements, or no response at all. The subjects responded to the "depressed" person with a higher rate of silences and directly negative statements. In addition, the subjects described the "depressed" confederates in more negative terms and were more likely to reject them.

All these hypotheses have received some support from research. Truly definitive research is of course impractical; it would be unethical to intentionally demonstrate that depressive behavior can be intensified by differential reinforcement. Other lines of research have consistently shown, however, that social reinforcement patterns have a major impact on an individual's behavior (Kanfer and Phillips, 1970; Bandura, 1969).

Cognitive theories

Depressed individuals are characteristically negative about themselves and their future. The theories of depression we have considered so far all view such negative cognitions as symptoms—results—of depression. In contrast, the cognitive theories of depression see the negative cognitions as the cause and the depression as the result. The question for the cognitive theorist is: Why do certain types of individuals develop negative views about themselves, their world, and their future that lead them to become depressed?

Martin Seligman's theory of **learned helplessness** (1974) is similar in many ways to the behavioral and social learning models we have just reviewed. Seligman found that dogs placed in a box and given electric shocks normally struggled to escape. If they could not get out, however, they gradually gave up trying. Once they had learned to wait passively through the shock, the dogs would not make any attempt to escape, even after the situation was changed and they could have gotten out. Only when the experimenters repeatedly urged them and dragged them to safety did the dogs catch on and learn to avoid being shocked.

Numerous studies have shown that learned helplessness can be produced in a variety of situations, with different kinds of aversive stimuli, and in a wide range of species (Seligman, 1975). Seligman hypothesized that a similar process underlies depression in humans: When people learn that reinforcement is not contingent on anything they can do to earn it, they stop trying, and their resulting negative cognitions about their ability to control their situation lead them to become depressed. Experiments in which college students could or could not turn off an obnoxiously loud noise showed that humans can learn helplessness (Hiroto, 1974) and that those who did learn it performed worse than others on a subsequent problem-solving task (Hiroto and Seligman, 1975). Attempts to link learned helplessness to depression also yielded some success, but the results caused Seligman and his associates to make some changes in the model (Abramson, Seligman, and Teasdale, 1978). It now appears that helplessness occurs on two levels: *personal* ("I have no control over my life") and *universal* ("Nobody can straighten out this mess"). A person may also perceive a situation of helplessness as either *global* (applying to all circumstances) or *specific* (applying to one particular circumstance), and as either *stable* (lasting or recurrent) or *unstable* (temporary or intermittent).

How the person *attributes* a given state of helplessness influences whether depression occurs. A woman whose car has been hit by a reckless driver will generally attribute her helplessness to external sources and see it as limited to one situation; that is, she views it as universal, specific, and unstable. She will therefore react with anger and frustration rather than with negative cognitions about herself. In contrast, a man who expects an important promotion that is given to someone else may view his failure as proof of personal inadequacy and helplessness. If he has a series of such failures, he is likely to adopt a negative self-image and become depressed.

Another pioneer in cognitive theory is Aaron Beck, whose model grew out of his early work in psychoanalytic theory (Beck, 1967). It was Beck who first suggested that depression results from distortions in thinking rather than the other way around. He sees these distortions as occurring within what is called the **cognitive triad** of depressive thought: The person's view of self, the outside world, and the future.

On the basis of clinical observations, Beck has listed several types of distorted thought that he found to be common among depressed patients. These include the following:

1. *Arbitrary inference.* The person draws a conclusion from a situation or experience that is unsubstantiated by the evidence. Beck gives the example of a patient who, while riding an elevator, made the unsubstantiated conclusion, "He [the elevator operator] thinks I'm a nobody." Beck suggests that a depressed person is likely to draw arbitrary inferences when a situation is ambiguous. He speculates also that the depressed individual does not consider alternative explanations for events, but immediately chooses a negative interpretation.

2. *Selective abstraction.* The person focuses on only one aspect of a situation, taking it out of context and ignoring other features that are equally or more important. A typist who is criticized for misspelling a word may conclude that his boss dislikes all of his work, even though the boss's comments in the past have been very positive.

3. *Overgeneralization.* On the basis of only one, perhaps trivial, event, the person makes a sweeping self-evaluative generalization. An example is a woman who forgets to thaw the chicken in time for dinner and then berates herself for being a failure as a homemaker.

4. *Magnification and minimization.* The individual underestimates personal performance and abilities and exaggerates the significance of problems or of some unpleasant event. This is not unlike Ellis's notion of *catastrophizing,* in which minor events are interpreted as signaling impending doom (Ellis, 1962). Beck suggests

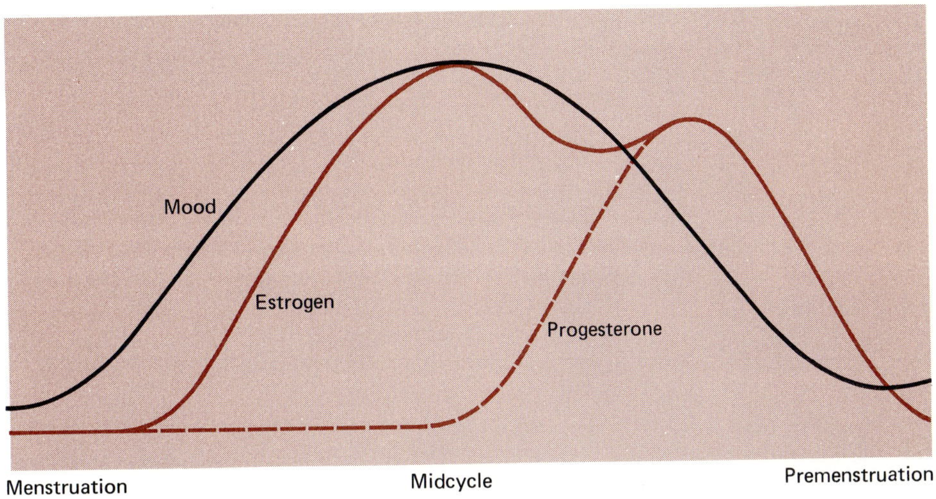

Figure 12.2. *Although there is still no clear-cut evidence linking the menstrual cycle with clinical depression, this chart indicates a definite relationship between mood and hormone level. From Allman and Jaffe, 1978.*

that the person may be labeling situations incorrectly. For instance, a girl may decide that if her boyfriend really loves her, he will bring her flowers for Valentine's Day; when he gives her a book instead, she feels sure their relationship is fated to end soon.

Beck has suggested that the origins of the depressed person's distorted thought patterns may lie in a loss or setback which has been interpreted as a personal failure. For example, a man taking the blame for a single incident may come to see other incidents too as "his fault." He falls into the habit of interpreting every ambiguous remark someone makes, every little situation that might have been handled more efficiently, as confirmation that he is dismally inadequate. No wonder other people feel contempt for him and reject him—he is such an unworthy creature. Thoroughly depressed, the individual sees no hope that things will ever improve: "As he looks ahead, the patient sees an indefinite continuation of his present difficulties and a life of unremitting deprivation, frustration, and hardship" (Beck, 1974, p. 71).

Social and Cultural Influences

Most of the theories and data we have examined come from research in the United States and from studies using heterogeneous samples of subjects. Investigators have naturally been curious, though, about whether certain social and cultural factors may be important in the affective disorders. As we saw earlier, age seems to be significant—bipolar disorder tends to strike earlier than unipolar, and the involutional period (menopause) may be a time of particular vulnerability to depression. In the following sections we shall review evidence regarding two other possible factors in affective disorder: gender and nationality or culture.

Sex differences

Data have shown fairly consistently that in the United States about twice as many women suffer from depression as men. The difference in susceptibility appears to hold true throughout the world and for all time periods. Possible explanations are numerous: Perhaps women have a sex-linked genetic vulnerability to depression; hormonal differences may make women more prone than men to this disorder; the social role of women in our culture may increase their chances of becoming depressed. Radloff and Rae (1979) have suggested that the difference may be due to both biological mechanisms and psychological factors or learning. Mendels points to the possible influence of steroid hormones:

Close-up: Women and Depression—One Theory

Science writer Maggie Scarf recently published a book entitled *Unfinished Business: Pressure Points in the Lives of Women.* This work describes the results of her study examining why for every man suffering from depression there are two to six women afflicted with the same disorder. After observing and interviewing women patients in hospitals and clinics over a four-year period, Scarf found that many depressed women were unable to cope with the loss of a relationship, such as a separation from a child or parent or the loss of a husband or lover. She concluded that depression among women often springs from their dependency on life-or-death attachments to other people. Expected by society to be competitive and aggressive, men are more likely to become depressed over matters relating to work. In fact, many of the hospitalized men whom Scarf saw were of retirement age.

According to Scarf's study, women tend to assess themselves by their intimate relationships with others, while men measure their self-worth by their degree of career success. Whether this preoccupation is due more to hereditary factors than to cultural conditioning has not been determined. Scarf believes that in their efforts to maintain important relationships, women are prone to examine their own feelings, while men are oriented more toward problem solving. This emphasis is a crucial one since depression, by its very nature, arises from negative feelings that are turned inward. Scarf discovered that many women will harm themselves rather than endanger important relationships by expressing anger against those who may be causing them pain. Some women even prefer death to the prospect of being alone.

Some of Scarf's premises have been disputed, particularly her claim that for every man who suffers from depression there are two to six women with this disorder. To those who dispute her findings on the basis that her figures do not include alcoholics (who are assumed to be depressed), Scarf points out that in countries where alcohol is not consumed, there is still a significantly higher number of depressed women than men.

One of the most serious criticisms of Scarf's conclusions is that she repeatedly references a study by psychologist Wendy Stewart, whose findings were based on interviews with only eleven women. The credibility of broad generalizations based on such a small sampling is highly questionable. Nevertheless, one should not overlook the fact that apparently little scientific research has been done on women passing through life crises. Certainly those issues of power and dependency, the need to care for and be cared for, and the ability to survive on one's own emotional resources are problems faced by many women.

Depression is more frequent in women than in men; depression in both men and women frequently occurs during the involutional period when there are significant changes in various hormones; and there are reports that oral contraceptive compounds (usually a combination of estrogen and progesterone, two steroid hormones) both cause depression, and paradoxically, relieve depressive symptoms. (1970, p. 174)

Depressed women tend to turn to someone close for support, whereas men try to deal with depression on their own. Photo at top © 1975 Bettye Lane.

According to a more recent analysis, however, the data do not support any consistent relationship between hormone levels and depression (Weissman and Klerman, 1977).

We have noted that many bipolar patients have a history of manic-depressive disorder in at least two previous generations. In such families, significantly more females than males were affected (Winokur, Clayton, and Reich, 1969). At first, this seemed to clearly indicate a sex-linked—and specifically an X-chromosome-linked—etiology. However, there have been cases where both father and son were disturbed. Although the evidence that bipolar disorder is passed through women is strong, it is by no means conclusive. And it does not begin to explain the overwhelming number of women with unipolar disorder.

Hammen and Peters (1977) have suggested that one reason more women than men show depressive symptoms is that other people react more negatively to such behavior in men than in women. The fact that men are more inclined than women toward alcohol use and abuse—which is considered to be an alternative for depression—accords with this idea. It is possible that men find those around them to be more sympathetic toward a drunk than a depressive, whereas the opposite is true for women; such differential reinforcement thus encourages different behavior. The results of a recent study (Funabiki et al., 1980) that examined sex differences in depressive experiences suggested that when depressed, women may tend to withdraw socially more than men. This may relate to additional findings that women are also more likely than men to seek out others on a one-to-one basis.

Cultural differences

A number of cross-cultural studies have confirmed that the affective disorders occur all over the world. The studies have also pointed out some of the difficulties of conducting such comparative research. One investigation found that only about 10 percent of patients admitted to a hospital in Malaysia were diagnosed as suffering from affective disorder, a rate low enough to suggest that these disorders are less common in Malaysia than in Western countries. Later studies took a closer look at the findings, however, and raised other possible explanations. For example, it was pointed out that the hospital ward under study contained only 32 beds, although it was the only psychiatric facility serving roughly two million people. Patients with affective disorder thus were less likely to be admitted than those with more dramatic problems such as schizophrenia or organic psychosis (Tan, 1977).

A 1961 study by the National Institute of Mental Health found that of patients admitted to a hospital for the first time, about 80 percent fewer were diagnosed manic-depressive in the United States than in England and Wales. In contrast, diagnoses of schizophrenia ran about one third higher in the United States than in England and Wales, a point that was raised in the previous chapter. Subsequent studies using carefully controlled diagnostic interviews in London and New York suggested that the incidence of manic-depression is probably similar in both countries, and that the difference could be due to a tendency among American psychiatrists to misdiagnose manic-depressives as schizophrenics (Fieve, 1975).

Other cultural differences influencing the incidence of affective disorders appear to come from differing attitudes. Spiro observes that Burmese Buddhists are taught from childhood that pessimism and suffering are a necessary part of life, and that the answer to problems can be found in meditation. As Spiro points out, "The person who in our society might well end up in a psychiatrist's office or a mental institution with the pejorative label of 'sick' may in Burma end up in a monastery with a honorific label, 'monk' or 'meditator'." (1974, p. 264). A researcher investigating what behaviors are perceived as indicators of mental disorder in the Japanese and Portuguese communities in Hawaii found that the Japanese viewed agitated, paranoid behavior as socially deviant, whereas the Portuguese viewed depressive behavior such as helplessness, nervousness, and hyperactivity as indicating a mental problem (Katz, 1971). Depressed members of the Japanese-Hawaiian community were thus more likely to be tolerated and less likely to be hospitalized than Portuguese-Hawaiians with similar symptoms.

MANAGING THE AFFECTIVE DISORDERS

Unlike many psychological problems, a large proportion of affective disorders disappear almost as quickly as they appear. Yet it is impossible to say when a patient arrives for treatment whether this will turn out to be one of the fortunate cases that clears up by itself. Particularly because of the risk of suicide connected with depression, most therapists will try biological therapy, psychological therapy, or both.

Biological Methods

We have seen that even psychological explanations for affective disorders give an important role to physiological factors. For example, animal studies have demonstrated that inducing learned helplessness appears to reduce the level of the biogenic amine norepinephrine in the animal's brain. In the context of theories emphasizing loss of reinforcement, Costello (1972) noted that biochemical and neurophysiological changes may influence the degree to which external reinforcers are attractive to a person. Consequently, most therapists rely heavily on biochemical therapies and electroconvulsive therapy in treating the affective disorders.

Pharmacotherapy

Antidepressant drugs are extremely popular as a treatment method. However, different drugs affect these disorders in varying ways, and many of them have serious limitations, such as harmful side effects or a delayed therapeutic effect.

Tricyclic antidepressants. At present, the **tricyclic antidepressants** are the most popular drugs for treating depression. Of these, the most common is *imipramine* (Tofranil). Studies suggest that these drugs work by increasing the availability of norepinephrine at receptor sites in the brain (Schildkraut, 1965; Mendells and Stinnet, 1973). They also have a sedative effect and help to regularize the sleep cycle, which may contribute to their antidepressant quality. Beck (1973) reports that about 60 to 65 percent of depressed patients gain at least some improvement from tricyclics.

Unfortunately, the tricyclics usually take three to four weeks of treatment before they have any therapeutic effect (Klerman, 1978). Clearly, in an emergency—if the person is so depressed that the will to live is gone, for instance—these drugs are almost useless. Another problem is that the effective dose for each person must be found by trial and error.

MAO inhibitors. Although drugs that inhibit monoamine oxidase (MAO) have been shown to be more therapeutically effective than a placebo, they are generally less effective than the tricyclics (Klerman, 1978). They are used much less often in the United States because they have more adverse potential side effects than the tricyclics, a narrow range of effectiveness according to dosage, and high toxic interactions with a variety of foods. MAO inhibitors are useful with some patients who do not respond to tricyclics, though, and some clinicians believe that certain depressed persons are responsive to only the MAO inhibitors (Klerman, 1978).

Lithium salts. Tricyclics have not been found to work well as a treatment for bipolar disorder. In fact, some case studies have reported that manic episodes may be precipitated by the tricyclics. In recent years, **lithium salts,** primarily *lithium carbonate* (Eskalith, Lithane, and Lithonate) have been found to be considerably more effective for treating hypomanic and acute manic episodes. One pharmacological review indicated improvement rates of 70 to 80 percent in ten to fourteen days (Baldessarini, 1978). In addition to preventing recurrence of mania, lithium also appears to be useful in subduing the depressive side of bipolar disorder. It thus "dampens" both the manic and depressive episodes, and, in some cases, prevents recurrence of either kind of episode (Fieve, 1975).

Table 12.2 *Treatments for Depression*

Treatment	Mechanism	Effect
Tricyclic antidepressant	Presents reuptake of norepinephrine (NE), thus increasing NE level in the synapse	Relieves depression
MAO inhibitor	Inhibits metabolism of NE by the MAO, thus increasing NE level	Relieves depression
ECT	Facilitates NE synthesis	Relieves depression

From Fann et al., 1977.

Electroconvulsive therapy

In severe cases of depression where emergency measures are required, particularly to prevent potential suicide, electroconvulsive therapy (ECT) is often the fastest effective treatment. An electrical current lasting less than a second is passed through the brain via electrodes fastened to the patient's scalp, thus inducing a seizure. To prevent possible bruises or broken bones, a muscle relaxant is also administered. Normally ECT works in three to six sessions, although some cases may require more treatments. Recently, however, a technique called **multiple-monitored ECT** has become popular. Patients receive a large enough dose of muscle relaxant to completely block peripheral seizures; they are then given several ECT treatments within a session, monitored by an electroencephalogram (Salzman, 1978).

Although originally used to treat schizophrenia, it was noted that a side effect of ECT—a more positive frame of mind—might prove beneficial for depressed patients. Before long it was widely used. One of the attractions of this procedure was that it could be easily and inexpensively applied, allowing quick treatment for many patients at a time when mental hospitals were overcrowded and understaffed.

It was (and is) a relatively violent means of intervention, however. It produces, in addition to the muscular convulsions that resemble epileptic seizures, temporary confusion and sometimes fairly extensive memory loss. Although ECT works faster than any other method and has proved quite successful as a means of treating severely depressed patients, it is typically used today only in desperate situations. For one thing, no one knows exactly how it works, and there is some question that it may cause permanent brain damage (Fink, 1979).

Psychological Methods

In most cases, psychological therapy is not used *instead* of biological treatment but along with it. As with other disorders, biologically based treatments may be prescribed to alleviate the patient's symptoms, while psychotherapy aims at changing the attitudes or habits that have been contributing to the disorder. Two psychological approaches have been successful with affective disorders: behavioral and cognitive.

Behavior therapy

Behavioral approaches to treating depression begin with the hypothesis that the disorder is a result of being on the prolonged extinction schedule mentioned earlier—that is, as individuals fail to receive reinforcement from their activities and interactions, they make less and less effort to act or interact, and in turn receive less and less reinforcement. Behavioral therapists reason that since the person's level of reinforcement is determined to a large extent by interactions with the social environment, an important goal is to identify and change the depressed person's deficits in social skills.

Social skill has been defined as "the ability to emit behaviors that are positively reinforced by others" (Lewinsohn et al., 1976, p. 120). In one study, Lewinsohn and colleagues (1970) used group therapy sessions to provide depressed patients with feedback about their behavioral difficulties. Comments from peers in the group helped the patients to identify their own interpersonal behaviors and become aware of the effect of those behaviors on others. The objective was to enable patients to develop more effective ways of behaving that would result in fewer negative reactions and more positive reinforcement from others.

The family of the depressed person is often included in therapy so that treatment can be continued at home. If family members ignore depressed behaviors and reinforce positive ones, the therapy is more consistent and works much faster. Although some successful results have been reported from these approaches, not enough data have been accumulated yet to warrant any clear conclusions about the effectiveness of behavior therapies.

Cognitive therapy

In recent years, cognitive therapy has been gaining widespread acceptance as a means of treating depression (Beck et al., 1979). Cognitive theories of depression characterize depressed individuals as having certain dysfunctional attitudes and assumptions that influence the way they interpret events, and thus influence their mood and behavior. Cognitive therapy for depression involves a set of techniques designed to identify and change these distorted belief systems. Some typical "depressogenic" assumptions are offered by Beck and colleagues (1979, p. 246):

1. In order to be happy, I have to be successful in whatever I undertake.
2. To be happy, I must be accepted by all people at all times.
3. If I make a mistake, it means that I am inept.
4. I can't live without you.
5. If somebody disagrees with me, it means he doesn't like me.
6. My value as a person depends on what others think of me.

In cognitive therapy, the therapist and the patient work together at identifying the specific irrational assumptions that are contributing to the patient's depression. Many of these assumptions have become so fundamental to the patient's belief system that they are accepted automatically until they are brought into question by the therapist. Using reinforcement techniques borrowed from behaviorism, the therapist focuses on reinforcing positive, nondepressed thoughts and statements, especially about the individual. Sometimes the clients are instructed to write down and read out loud positive statements about themselves, which when repeated, may help them think more positively about themselves.

Some recent studies suggest that cognitive interventions alone, without antidepressant medication, are effective with a substantial proportion of hospitalized depressed patients. In one case, cognitive therapy was found more effective than imipramine in the treatment of 41 depressed outpatients (Rush et al., 1977); additional research involving a total of 44 patients indicated that 78.9 percent of those treated with cognitive therapy showed "marked" improvement or complete remission by the end of treatment, compared to 20.0 percent of the pharmacotherapy patients (Beck et al., 1979).

SUICIDE

As we have noted, one reason why psychologists treat severe depression as such an urgent problem is the risk of suicide that may accompany it. Whether any given patient is seriously contemplating suicide is of course impossible to know for sure. Suicide attempts are significantly more frequent among people with affective disorders than in the general population, however—around 13 to 30 percent for those with bipolar disorder, and as high as 35 percent for people suffering from depression (Klerman, 1978). Although the annual world death rate from suicide, at 13 per 100,000, is lower than that for cancer (210 per 100,000) or coronary heart disease (250 per 100,000), the fact that suicide is deliberate—and therefore presumably

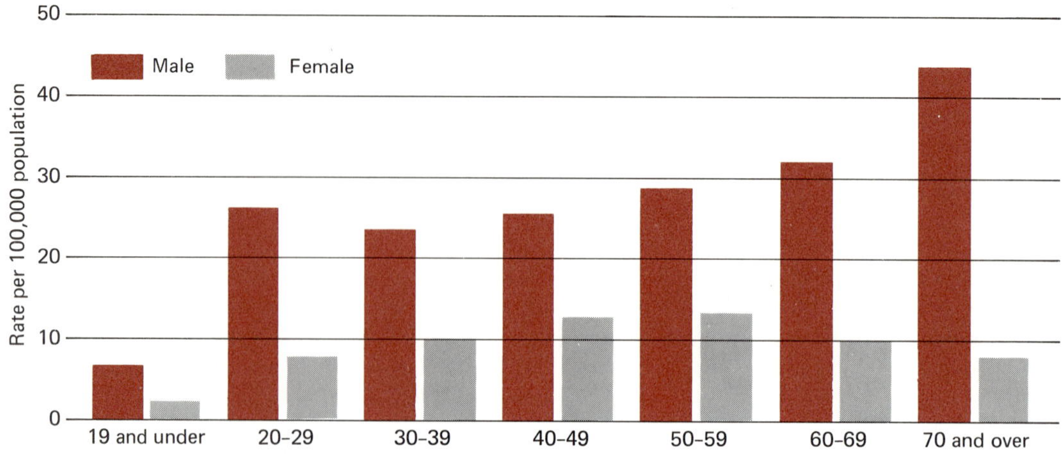

Figure 12.3. *Suicide rates for men and women by age group. From the U.S. Department of Health, Education, and Welfare, 1976.*

preventable—makes it a cause for very serious concern.

In the United States, at least 25,000 deaths each year are attributed to suicide (Shneidman and Mandelkorn, 1970). The actual rate is thought to be as much as two to four times higher. For one thing, because of the stigma attached to suicide and the anguish it causes those left behind, there is a tendency not to attach that label to any questionable death. Also, deaths due to high-speed highway driving, to drug overdoses, and to various other ambiguous causes commonly are classified as accidental rather than suicide. The only obvious way of identifying a death accurately as suicide is if the person has left a note, and only about one third of suicides do so (Shneidman and Farberow, 1961). Furthermore, these figures represent only successful suicides—the rate of unsuccessful suicide attempts is believed to be at least eight times as high (Resnik, 1968; Shneidman and Farberow, 1961).

Explaining Suicide

One of the reasons suicide shocks us is that it seems so inexplicable. Self-destruction cannot by definition be reinforcing; nor is it in keeping with the human tendency to find some way, however bizarre, of managing reality. Researchers have tried to identify possible causes of suicide, and several hypotheses have emerged. Their efforts are limited, however, by the unavailability of their subjects for comment, and by the difficulty of reconstructing what probably happened from suicide notes and interviews with family and friends. Studying people who have attempted suicide and failed is another method; but the very failure of those individuals suggests that they may differ in important respects from those who have succeeded. Nor is it reasonable to expect their observations to be an impartial, reliable source of information.

Who commits suicide?

Suicide attempts are most common between the mid-twenties and mid-forties. In recent years, the rate for adolescents and children has increased alarmingly, while the rate for those over 45 has decreased. The rate for blacks and whites is fairly similar, although among black men aged 20 to 35 it is about twice as high as among whites the same age. If we were to establish the profile of someone whom most psychologists probably would classify as a high suicide risk, the person would be a middle-aged white man, divorced and living alone, who has a history of previous suicide attempts. However, only a

Close-up: Student Suicides

The adjustment to college life can often be overwhelming. The demands of the work load, pressures from parents to succeed, problems in sexual relationships, competition and peer pressure, exposure to drugs and alcohol, and a student's well-intentioned but often overly intense drive to succeed may all contribute to the difficulties. Frequently the result of such problems is depression; increasingly, it is suicide.

Recent reports on suicide among college students suggest that it is the second leading cause of death in the young adult age group; only accidents take more lives. These reports indicate that student suicide is also on the rise. One counselor estimates that the rate has tripled in the past decade. Presently some 40,000 young people (students and nonstudents) attempt suicide each year; about 5000 succeed. As is true of the general population, three times more women students than men students attempt suicide, but more men succeed, apparently because men tend to use more violent means, whereas women use slower methods that allow time for rescue attempts. In most cases of college suicide, the young person has been hit by several stressors at once: a poor grade plus the loss of a close relationship; a failed test after intense studying; a rejection notice from all graduate schools applied to.

How can you tell if a classmate is a potential suicide? First of all, suicide threats should not be ignored. In eight out of ten cases of successful suicide, the person *did* talk about death as an escape, *did* tell others that suicide was being contemplated. Other danger signs are excessive sleeping or insomnia, severe depression, overeating or total loss of appetite, physical complaints such as violent stomachaches without physical cause, withdrawal, and giving away cherished belongings. After a long period of depression, a suicidal person may become extremely cheerful and energetic. Psychologists recognize this as the person's relief that the decision to end the suffering has been made.

The increasing number of college suicides has prompted schools to improve their programs for crisis prevention and intervention. Harvard University, for example, offers an extensive mental health service including counselors on duty 24 hours a day, seven days a week, and a student-staffed hotline. Resident advisors and others who deal directly with students are trained to recognize and deal with potential suicides.

It is difficult to assess the success of suicide prevention programs. But any such effort made to help a troubled person seems to be important in deterring some suicides. As one psychologist pointed out, "Often, just listening or holding someone's hand will make all the difference in the world. It is the difference between living and dying."

small percent of men fitting this description actually do attempt suicide.

About three times more men than women kill themselves. However, about three times more women than men *attempt* suicide. Part of the reason for this rather startling difference is that men tend to choose more drastic methods, such as shooting themselves; women are more inclined to try drug overdoses, for example. But even when allowances are made for the contrast in methods, the general difference in attempts versus successes reveals the same findings in other cultures as well. There has been considerable speculation about why this is so. Do women turn to suicide as a means of calling attention to their problems, as a way of reaching out for help? Do men resort to it only when they are determined to end their lives? Is it possible that officials are more likely to label ambiguous deaths as suicide for women and accidents for men? Do men turn to liquor and a fast car in situations where women turn to pills? Not enough evidence exists for any of these hypotheses for us to know the answers for sure.

What causes suicide?

The possibility that biological factors may predispose certain people to suicide has intrigued a number of investigators. So far, though, neither genetic nor biochemical influences have been documented. Psychoanalytic explanations—that each of us maintains a balance between a life instinct (*libido*) and a death instinct (*thanatos*) that can be thrown off if society prevents us from expressing aggression—have had no significant support from data, either. Nor has any convincing behavioral theory emerged.

There is some evidence that a lack of cognitive resources for problem solving may be related to a tendency toward suicidal behavior—for example, suicidal individuals were found to do worse at problem-solving tasks than nonsuicidal individuals (Levenson and Neuringer, 1971). People who have attempted suicide in the past are more likely to try it again later (Bagley and Greer, 1971; Buglass and McCulloch, 1970). Similarly, Funabiki (1977) found a significant relationship among college students: Those who reported having attempted suicide in the past believed they would try it in the future if their life circumstances were severe enough. These findings suggest that further research would be valuable to examine patterns of problem solving and general coping among suicidal and nonsuicidal groups.

Sociologist Emile Durkheim (1951, originally published in 1897) suggested that suicidal behavior has to do with the levels of social integration and regulation within a society. Specifically, Durkheim suggested that there are three types of suicide: **egoistic**, **altruistic**, and **anomic** (from the term *anomie,* which he coined, meaning normless, without standards, chaotic).

1. *Egoistic.* People who kill (or attempt to kill) themselves out of a feeling of isolation are considered to be egoistic suicides. Whether in actuality or in their own imagination, they feel alienated from other people. They lose their ties to the community and to society at large, feeling utterly alone.
2. *Altruistic.* Some people willingly sacrifice their lives "for the good of society." These are altruistic suicides. The Japanese kamikaze pilots in World War II and the Buddhist monks who committed self-immolation during the Vietnam War are clear examples of altruistic suicides.
3. *Anomic.* When the familiar world seems to be falling into pieces at our feet, most of us feel shocked and numbed but then try to fit the pieces together again. Others are so overwhelmed by a feeling of anomie that they give up living. The people who killed themselves when the stock market collapsed in 1929 were anomic suicides—completely shattered by the sudden changes in their life situations.

Some theories today continue to center on Durkheim's ideas; however, none of these theories have been able to explain why some people in the situations Durkheim outlined commit suicide and others do not.

We do know that suicide rates are high among depressed people, though major depression probably does not account for more than 40 percent of suicides. Suicide rates seem to be highest in late spring and early summer; but no specific meteorological or cosmic factors, such as month, latitude, weather, barometric pressure, humidity, precipitation, or day of the week, have been found to be consistently related to suicide rates.

IDENTIFYING POTENTIAL SUICIDES

The topic of suicide is somewhat complicated by the fact that not everyone who thinks about

Table 12.3 *Precipitating Factors in Childhood Suicide**

	Boy	Girl	Total
Disciplinary crisis	8	3	36%
Quarrel with peers	3	1	13.33
Fight with boyfriend or girlfriend	1	2	10
Fight with parent	1	2	10
Being dropped from a school team	2	0	7
Fantasy "model"	1	1	7
Psychotic parent	2	0	7
Precipitant unknown	3	0	10

From Shaffer, 1974.
* Under age 15.

suicide attempts it, not everyone who attempts it truly wants to succeed, and not everyone who wants to succeed actually does so. At least occasional thoughts about suicide are likely to occur to each of us. The relationship between suicidal ideation and actual suicidal behavior, however, is as yet unclear. For instance, although thoughts of suicide are quite common among depressed individuals, actual intent to commit suicide is much less so (Klerman, 1978). Beck (1967) has reported a high correlation between the degree of depression and the tendency toward suicidal thoughts. He found that 74 percent of severely depressed patients, 53 percent of moderately depressed patients, and 31 percent of mildly depressed patients reported wanting to commit suicide. Interestingly, 12 percent of *nondepressed* patients also reported suicidal wishes.

While suicidal thoughts in themselves are, therefore, not unusual, the communication of suicidal thought to others appears to be an important indicator of serious intentions. Communicating these thoughts appears to indicate that the person is severely distressed and in need of some form of mental health support. Approximately two thirds of patients who voluntarily admit themselves to psychiatric hospitals express suicidal ideas to others (Delong and Robins, 1961). In spite of the common belief that people who discuss suicide will not commit it, two thirds to three fourths of people who do kill themselves communicated thoughts about death or suicide to others before they acted (Murphy and Robins, 1968). As McCulloch and Philip (1972) have cautioned, "It is now well known that people who talk about attempting to kill themselves frequently do so, *and that all such threats should be taken with great seriousness*" (p. 26).

Other indications that someone may be seriously considering suicide include sudden moves to tidy up loose ends: having a will drawn up, or giving someone an expensive gift for no apparent reason. A sudden mood change—for example, from sadness or depression to happiness, as if a great personal burden had suddenly been lifted—also may be a warning signal, an indication of relief at having made the decision.

This brings up an unusual point about the relationship between depression and suicide: There is what might be called a suicide-prone time in the depression cycle. Contrary to what might be expected, however, the peak time is not when individuals are sunk in the depths of despair, but when they seem to be on the road to recovery. Why people should kill themselves when they've recovered a small portion of their formerly positive outlook is unknown. Perhaps they recover only enough to let themselves believe they are now seeing reality—but not enough to make that reality more hopeful.

Identifying individuals who are on the brink of suicide obviously is a question of considerable urgency for psychologists. Therapists cannot afford to ignore any indication patients may give that they are considering suicide. On the other hand, so many people do give such indications without ever going on to attempt to kill themselves that if therapists deal with all of them, they risk missing the person who takes action without warning signals. If there were some way of narrowing down potential suicides, the chances of intervening in time would be greatly increased.

But how to approach the problem? Clearly, demographic factors, such as the greater probability of suicide among certain age groups, are too general to be much help. Researchers have tried to develop a profile of a suicidal personality, but their sources of information are severely limited, as we noted earlier. Nor do personality tests given to people who have threatened or unsuccessfully attempted suicide, for instance, necessarily tell us much about those who succeed in killing themselves. Scales have been devised that weigh data about personal histories and demographic qualities against attributes that are believed to be associated with suicide (Brown and Sheran, 1972), and this approach may have some promise. Still, as one observer has summed up, "There are no valid psychological test indicators capable of predicting with any degree of accuracy whether an individual will commit suicide in the foreseeable future" (Piotrowski, 1968, p. 198).

PREVENTING SUICIDE

The dilemma of suicide is more than a simple issue of trying to stop people from doing it. Sometimes suicide may seem justified: People with painful terminal diseases, for instance, may prefer to die while still in some control of their faculties. On a more philosophical level, it has been argued that the right to choose when to die should be as respected as any other human right (Szasz, 1976). This is the concern of an association known as EXIT.

Most people who try to commit suicide, however, do not succeed, and most of those who survive do not make a second attempt. Seiden (1974) has noted that attempted suicide usually reflects a crisis in a person's life, not a long-term wish. In this regard, Farberow and Litman (1970) have identified three classes of suicidal behavior:

1. Those who are serious and determined to kill themselves.
2. Those who use the attempt to draw attention to their desperate need for help.
3. Those who seem ambivalent about dying, so leave it to fate.

Farberow and Litman determined that the second group is the largest—they make up about two thirds of all attempted suicides. The third group is next in size, accounting for about 30 percent. The determined group comprises only 3 to 5 percent of suicides. Perhaps, then, we should not look at suicide prevention as the attempt of cultural norms to override individual choice but as society giving another chance to someone who is momentarily desperate.

In the past twenty years or so, suicide prevention centers have sprung up to try to help people contemplating suicide. Such centers usually function as a "hotline," handling telephone calls anonymously; only about 2 percent of first contacts are face to face. The main goal is to create a positive and supportive relationship with the caller. This then becomes the basis either for on-the-spot intervention or for arranging ongoing therapy.

The Los Angeles Suicide Prevention Center is the prototype on which most others are based. This center has listed five components it uses in providing emergency intervention (Shneidman and Farberow, 1968, p. 370):

1. Establishing a relationship, maintaining contact, and obtaining information.
2. Identifying and focusing on the central problems.
3. Evaluating the "lethality" of the threat.
4. Assessing the individual's resources and mobilizing outside resources.
5. Formulating and initiating therapeutic or rehabilitative plans.

Following this general guideline, the people staffing the telephone attempt to, first, stop the person from carrying out the threat. For the most part they are successful, since the very fact that these people have called means (usually) that they would prefer to be talked out of the idea. If the staffer can keep them talking and then talk them through the immediate problem, chances are good that—this time, at least—the threat will not be acted upon.

Many callers prefer not to give their real names, but the staffer tries to obtain as much

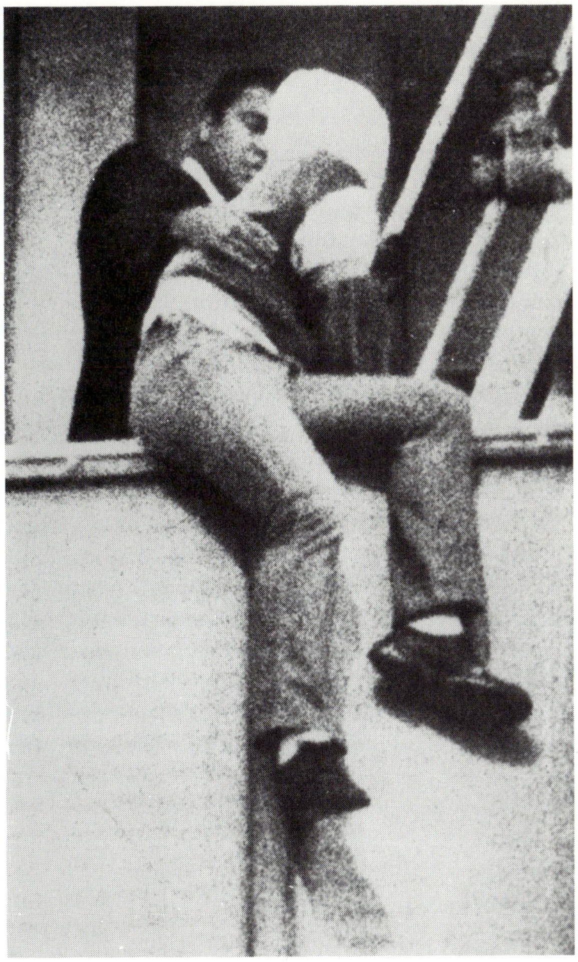

Muhammad Ali talks to an undentified man threatening to jump from the ninth floor of a Los Angeles building. Ali was able to persuade the man to return into the building.

factual data as possible about each caller. This helps determine what resources are available to the individual that could intervene at an earlier stage should another crisis arise; it also helps gather information toward a working suicidal profile.

It's impossible to say how many callers act on suggestions made by staffers to initiate therapy or work out some other way to cope more adaptively. Some callers, however, do call again to say thanks and report on their rehabilitative plans and process; likewise, some callers also call back with another suicide threat.

Another interesting point is that many become "regulars"—they become well known to the staffers because they call often, sometimes just to chat. Clearly, being alone—or simply perceiving themselves as being in isolation—has a strong impact on their desire to live. What is amazing is that a mere voice on the telephone, unconnected to anything familiar, can have such a profound influence on the will to live.

SUMMARY

The affective disorders are disturbances of mood or emotions. DSM-III divides them into two general categories: major affective disorders and other specific affective disorders. The major affective disorders are those that are severe enough to impair the person's ability to function. They fall into two types: major depressive disorder, characterized by continuing or recurrent depression, and bipolar disorder, in which periods of depression alternate with manic periods of great exuberance or irritability.

In its various forms, depression is one of the most serious health problems in the United States. Over one and a half million individuals are currently being treated for it, and perhaps as many as three to five times that number need treatment. Major depression may be directly responsible for up to 40 percent of suicides, and about 80 percent of the more than 25,000 Americans who commit suicide each year have some depressive symptoms.

Whether a depression is serious enough to be classified as a major affective disorder depends on three things: the type of symptoms, their severity, and their duration. The depressed individual typically suffers from a dysphoric mood—unhappy, hopeless, and apathetic. To do anything at all requires too much effort; life seems weary, stale, flat, and unprofitable. Loss of appetite is common, and sleep may be irregular. In extreme cases, the patient's whole personality is affected, and a loss of contact with reality may be almost complete. A milder and briefer form is called dysthymic disorder.

Patients with bipolar disorder (also known as manic-depressive illness) swing from depression into episodes of intense physical and mental agitation. Their mood is often euphoric, and in the mild form of mania called hypomania, they may be very cheerful, highly motivated, and efficient. An acute manic phase is marked by flight of ideas, rapid and incoherent speech, decreased need for sleep, loss of inhibitions, quick and often purposeless movements, delusions, and sometimes hallucinations. DSM-III lists cyclothymic disorder as a mild version of a manic episode.

In many cases, depression seems to be brought on by stress, but other factors appear to have a significant role. Some depressions may be due at least partly to hereditary predisposition, or to biochemical malfunctions involving biogenic amine metabolism, cellular electrolyte balance, or adrenocortical hormone metabolism. Circadian rhythms—the "pacemakers" that govern various cyclical bodily functions—may also be involved. Many researchers believe biological factors determine a person's threshold of vulnerability to depression, but that stress, learned patterns of behavior, or negative cognitions probably precipitate most affective disorders.

Psychodynamic theories propose that depression is a pathological response to a real or symbolic loss, rooted in a predisposition caused by a loss in early childhood. Behavioral theorists contend that depressed people are on a prolonged extinction schedule: they emit few behaviors that yield positive reinforcement, so that they become less and less likely to emit any behavior. A social learning slant on this model is that depression results when the reinforcement that individuals do receive is no longer perceived as contingent on their behavior. Also, although others may offer the depressed person verbal support, they simultaneously withdraw, which increases depression. Cognitive theorists believe depression is caused by negative cognitions—the distorted ideas certain people have of themselves, their world, and their future.

Both biological and psychological therapies have proved helpful in treating the affective disorders. In emergencies, electroconvulsive therapy (ECT) often produces marked improvement; its potentially harmful side effects make it undesirable for less severe cases, however. The drugs most commonly used to treat depression are the tricyclic antidepressants. Monoamine oxidase (MAO) inhibitors may also be effective, though less so than the tricyclics, and with more disadvantages, such as adverse side effects. For bipolar disorder, the usual treatment is lithium salts.

Behavior therapy strives to identify and improve deficits in social skills—that is, to increase those behaviors that are likely to be positively reinforced. Cognitive therapy, which has been quite successful in treating depression, focuses on identifying and changing the patient's distorted assumptions and attitudes.

One of the risks of severe depression is suicide. It appears that the actual annual suicide rate in the United States may be two to four times higher than the reported rate of around 25,000; the rate of suicide attempts is higher yet. Although numerous demographic data have been gathered about people who attempt and commit suicide, there is no way at present to identify such individuals beforehand. Nor has any biological or psychological theory been found to explain why certain individuals decide to kill themselves. Suicide prevention centers try to help depressed individuals through the brief crisis period that usually precipitates and accompanies a serious contemplation or threat of suicide; but whether such centers have actually succeeded in lowering the suicide rate is not now certain.

CHAPTER 13

Organic Mental Disorders and Mental Retardation

THE HUMAN BRAIN

Functional Divisions

THE SYMPTOMS OF BRAIN DAMAGE

EXPLAINING THE ORGANIC MENTAL DISORDERS

Head Trauma

Infections

Brain Tumors

Dietary Deficiencies

Toxic Agents

Cerebrovascular Problems

Endocrine Disorders

Degenerative Disorders

MANAGING ORGANIC MENTAL DISORDERS

EPILEPSY

Types of Epilepsy

Treating Epilepsy

DESCRIBING MENTAL RETARDATION

The AAMD Definition

EXPLAINING MENTAL RETARDATION

Organic Factors

Environmental Factors

MANAGING MENTAL RETARDATION

WHAT MENTALLY RETARDED MEANS

Someone being slow, they are way down low,
Some of them might be alone, in darkness.
These are the severely retarded children and
adults.
They may not talk. Some have difficulties
in learning how to walk. Some may not hear.
Some may not see. They do have this fear
of darkness
It is hard, this disaster is going too far
for mental
Retardation is a condition, in the brain, or
a disease,
Which we do not see.

But we the people, can help the Retarded on
to a
"Brighter World!"
For Retarded people can learn and earn
The facts of life for their lives.
Some may learn faster than the severely retarded
But they are all under retardation. They all need
A special helping hand. You've got to understand.
Won't you help, with your special-guided hand?

Roger Meyers*

When people think about abnormal behavior, the most common image is of one of the syndromes we have discussed so far: schizophrenia, depression, multiple personality. We tend to think of people like Arnold and Elaine and Tommy, the three cases that opened this book. But what about the young soldier who gets shot in the head and never fully regains his previous level of ability? What about the man with a brain tumor who can barely move or speak? What about the child born with Down's syndrome who will never attain full intellectual maturity? These people all exhibit abnormal patterns of thought and/or behavior, but in each case there is a definite known and verifiable cause—organic brain impairment.

There is one factor common to all organic mental disorders: They reflect biogenic damage to neural tissue or a physiologically based disruption of normal brain functioning. Why, then, are they included in this book? Because another common factor is that simply because the damage is in the brain, the problems may very often mimic those that we classify as psychogenic. In fact, it is sometimes extremely difficult to determine whether a given group of behavioral symptoms represents a psychological or a purely organic problem, or some combination of the two. Of course, when the clinician is faced with a bullet wound in the skull, or a personal history that shows a syphilitic parent, or a patient with Down's syndrome, it is safe to assume—at least for the moment—that the person's difficulties are biogenic. However, some organic mental disorders give distressingly few hints that they are, indeed, organic. In treating and diagnosing such cases, extremely subtle clues must be recognized to determine what is occurring unseen in the labyrinth of the human brain.

Another problem is that the symptoms of organic brain impairment are incredibly varied. After all, the brain is the center of action, thought, and emotion; it controls everything we do. Symptoms of impairment can range from mild to startling, from headaches and dizziness to partial amnesia or the sudden inability to move specific muscles. And certain disorders, such as tumors, will produce different symptoms depending on their location and rate of development.

In addition, the diagnostician must try to distinguish the direct effects of the problem from its indirect effects, as is the case with psychogenic disorders. Are a woman's irritability and depression caused by brain dysfunction—which is quite possible—or are they secondary effects, her emotional response to unexpected and untimely memory lapses that leave her confused and embarrassed? Obviously, when the workings of the brain are disrupted, the effects are seldom simple. In order to make our discussion of organic disorders a little more clear, it will be useful to review the structure and functioning of the master organ of the human body—the brain.

* From Robert Meyers, *Like Normal People*. © 1978 McGraw-Hill Book Company. Reprinted by permission.

THE HUMAN BRAIN

The brain is a gelatinous mass of tissue about the size of a large grapefruit, weighing about three pounds and situated inside the bony protective cavity of the skull. Between the skull case and the brain tissue itself is a watery cushion of cerebrospinal fluid and three layers of membrane called the **meninges.** The brain needs all this protection because its ten to fifteen billion cells are extremely vulnerable. Most of them have quite limited regenerative powers, so any damage to brain tissue is usually permanent. Luckily, only a small percentage of the available brain cells are needed for normal functioning, and when an area of the brain is damaged, unused cells in the same section can often be used in replacement. In some cases, a function governed by a damaged area can be relearned in a new area of the brain.

Sometimes, however, the damage may be so extensive that an entire area of the brain stops functioning. When this happens, a wide range of debilitating physical and mental symptoms may result. Usually, the greater the area of the brain that is severely damaged, the greater the effects of the damage. Enough is now known about the brain's functional divisions that a given set of symptoms in an adult can often be linked to damage in a general area. But because the brain operates as a total unit, not as a group of independent tissues, it is difficult to make assumptions about the exact locations of brain dysfunctions. Likewise, if a person receives damage to a specific part of the head, it is not easy to predict the exact effects of the injury.

Functional Divisions

The largest part of the brain is the **cerebrum,** which is divided by a deep *lateral fissure* into two similar but not identical **cerebral hemispheres.** The outer layer of the cerebrum is the convoluted, gray cerebral **cortex;** underneath this, the brain is composed of white matter. The two cerebral hemispheres are joined in the interior by three networks of interwoven nerve fibers, one of which is called the **corpus callosum.** This allows a constant interchange of information

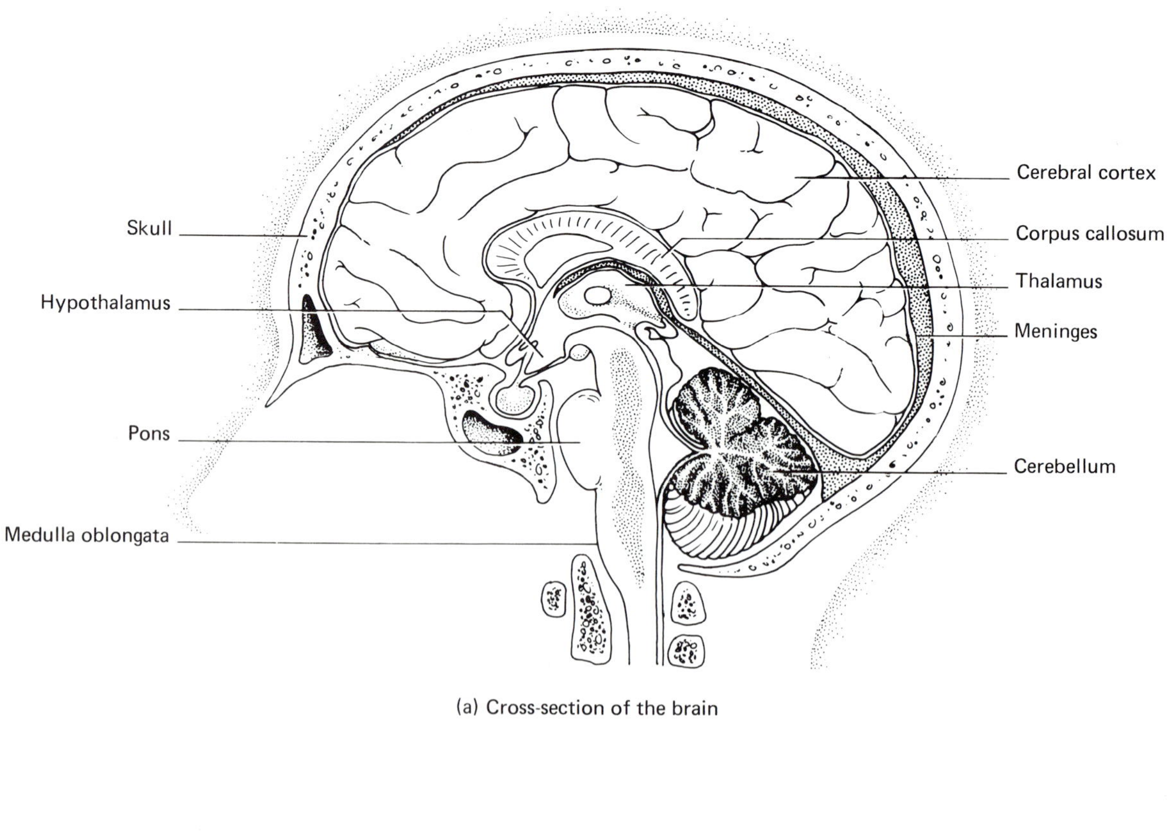

(a) Cross-section of the brain

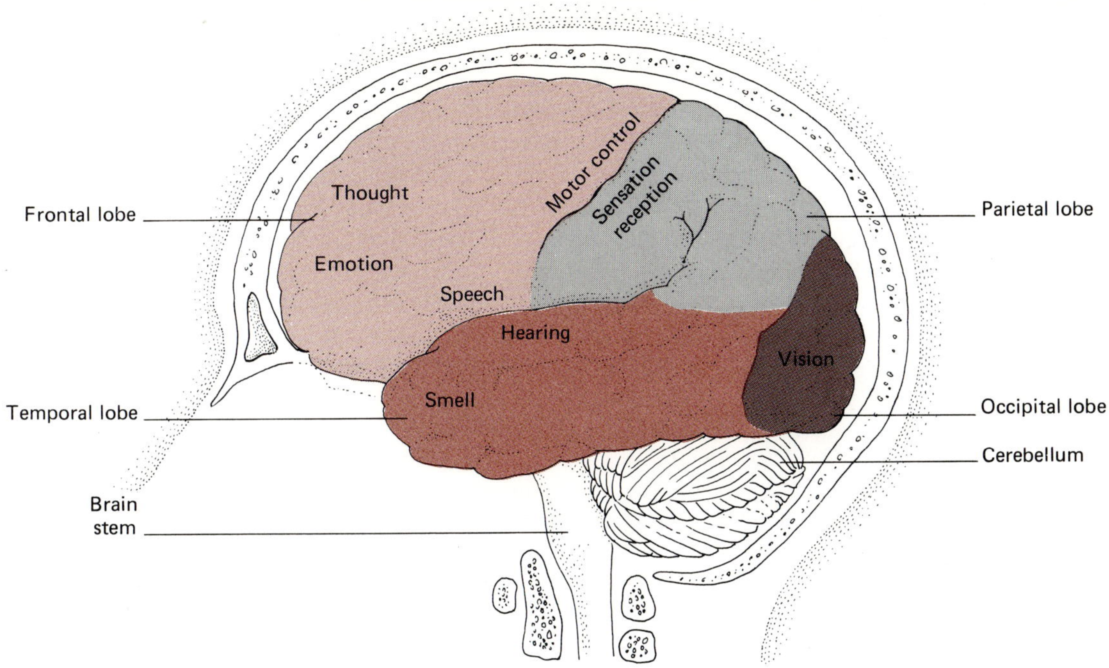

(b) The left hemisphere

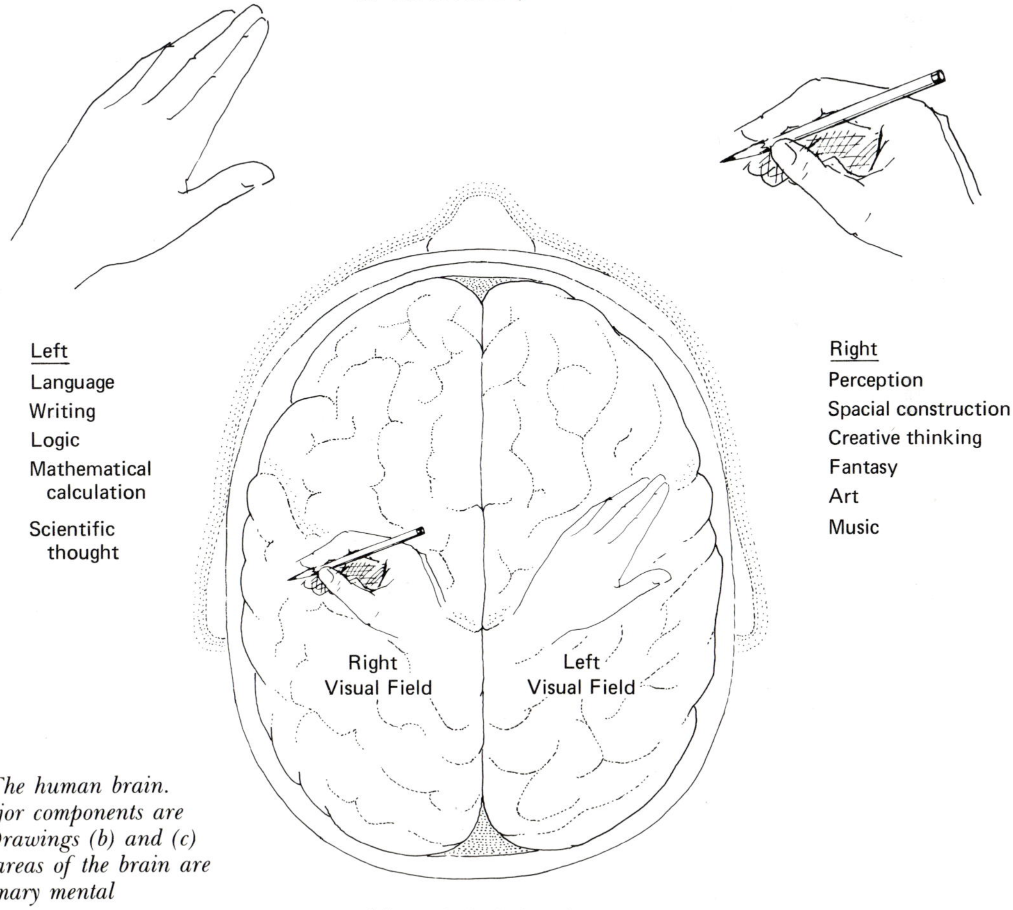

(c) Hemispheric functions

Figure 13.1. *The human brain. Some of the major components are shown in (a). Drawings (b) and (c) indicate which areas of the brain are involved in primary mental functions.*

between the two halves. For the vast majority of people, the left hemisphere of the brain has **dominance**—that is, the left side controls logic and language skills, especially reading, writing and speech. The right hemisphere in contrast, is the center for visual-spatial constructional abilities.

Both hemispheres are divided into four major areas called *lobes,* arranged front to back. Each lobe has functions that are linked to the abilities of the corresponding lobes in the opposite hemisphere. The role of the **frontal lobes** is to integrate complex motor tasks, to coordinate language skills, and to sort information for

Close-up: *The Split-Brain Phenomenon*

Although the two hemispheres of the cerebral cortex are in many ways similar to each other, over the course of human development each has developed specialized functions. The degree to which each half is capable of functioning independently of the other becomes dramatically apparent in studies of people who have had their corpus callosum surgically severed to relieve epileptic seizures.

After split-brain surgery, two consciousnesses emerge, each capable of learning on its own and able to control different parts of the patient's body. These two "minds" are almost identical in temperament, attitude, and general intelligence, and they go to sleep and wake up at the same time. Important differences do exist, however. The dominant hemisphere (usually the left, which controls the right side of the body) governs logical thinking and controls the ability to speak and write. The right hemisphere is the center for perceptual and spatial abilities and for creative thinking and emotion.

By setting up experiments in which information can be communicated to only one side of the brain, researchers have determined that once neurological feedback between the hemispheres has been cut off, neither side of the brain has direct knowledge of what the other is doing. Each hemisphere possesses somewhat independent memories; moreover, patients often verbally deny responses generated by the right, or monitoring, hemisphere. For example, when a picture of a nude woman was shown to a woman's right hemisphere, the right consciousness produced a laugh, but the left consciousness—which governs speech but had not perceived the nude—caused her to say she hadn't seen anything.

Having no control over speech, the right hemisphere can still cause a person to communicate nonverbally—for example, by pointing or acting oddly in ways that disrupt the pattern of behavior produced by the dominant left hemisphere. One patient reported that every so often the left half of his body seemed to be possessed of a will of its own. He was right-handed and while his right hand would zip up his pants as usual when he dressed, during more emotional situations his left hand might casually unzip them again, or follow up with even more embarrassing actions.

It is hard to believe that we have two similar but different minds controlling our behavior, yet even split-brain patients are not consciously aware that anything is "missing" after their operations. Sometimes the dominant half of the brain gains control; sometimes neither side ever learns to coordinate all movements of the body. In general, however, both hemispheres learn to cooperate, and the younger the patient at the time of the operation, the more successful the adjustment is apt to be.

referral to memory or reasoning areas. Damasio (1979) suggests that the frontal lobes first evaluate perceptual information received from the different senses via other brain areas, using both memory and emotion for reference, and then formulate an appropriate response. The **temporal lobes** are involved in interpreting auditory stimuli, such as distinguishing one song from another, and the pitch and tone of each. They are also the center of *olfaction,* the sense of smell. Some researchers believe that the temporal lobes may be involved in memory recall as well, since damage in this area can result in loss of memory. In many people, some parts of the left temporal lobe are larger than the corresponding parts on the right side, possibly due to differences in language functions (Wada, 1977), since the speech center in most humans lies very near the left temporal lobe.

The **parietal lobes** are the brain's major somatosensory areas. Sensory stimuli are received and integrated along the central *sulcus* (fissure) that separates the frontal and parietal lobes. These are also believed to help with motor control and orientation, since injury in these areas can result in difficulty with coordination and walking. At the base of the cerebrum are the **occipital lobes,** the primary visual perception centers.

Deep within the brain lie other, more specialized parts (Carpenter, 1976). The **hypothalamus,** near the center of the brain, regulates body metabolism, appetite, and emotions. The **thalamus** is a central relay system that sorts out messages arriving from all parts of the nervous system and routes them to their proper destination. The **cerebellum,** a large area at the back of the brain, beneath the occipital lobes, is responsible for the overall maintenance of balance and motor control. The **pons** is part of the brain stem, which reaches down to the base of the skull, where the spinal cord joins the brain. The brain stem also includes the **medulla oblongata,** which governs the vital life signs—heartbeat, blood pressure, and breathing—and the **reticular formation,** which regulates sexual arousal.

From this brief description of the brain, it is easy to see why damage to cerebral tissue can be so far-reaching. Although specific areas may control certain functions, the brain as a whole is involved in every integrated thought, action and emotion. If the separate parts cannot work together as a unit, many different human functions can be affected.

THE SYMPTOMS OF BRAIN DAMAGE

Most people with severe brain damage have disruptions of at least one of the following functions:

1. *Memory.* Memory problems are the most common symptoms of organic mental disorders. Sometimes brain-damaged people have trouble remembering things that happened to them long ago. More often, they have gaps in their recent memories.
2. *Orientation.* Brain-damaged patients may be easily confused. they tend to lose track of time and may become progressively frightened by the periods of confusion—sometimes to the point of losing touch with their personal identity.
3. *Emotion.* The moods of such patients may alternate abruptly, for no apparent reason. At other times they may seem apathetic. But these emotional swings may be simply a secondary effect—a psychological symptom that can interfere with the diagnosis of the organic cause.
4. *Reasoning and judgment.* Some patients face the dilemma of being unable to muster even the most basic powers of reasoning. They find it impossible to make a decision. In addition, they may lose the ability to do simple arithmetic or to reason out logical sequences. Comprehension of written or spoken language may also be affected.
5. *Social behavior.* Sometimes, brain-damaged people seem to change character. They may begin to lie or cheat or steal, even though such behavior goes against their normal code of ethics. If confronted with questions about why they are acting so strangely, they are likely to seem confused.

As we stated earlier, these general signs of organic impairment are remarkably—and distressingly—similar to symptoms of psychologi-

Figure 13.2. *The drawings show the relative size of Phineas Gage's skull and the tamping iron that penetrated it. The fact that he survived at all is remarkable. From Harlow, 1868.*

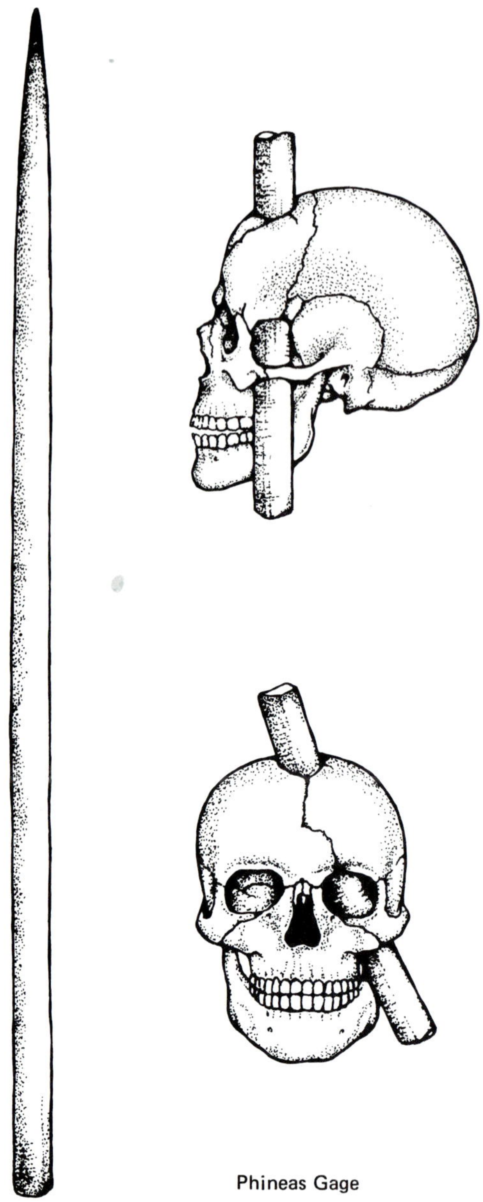

Phineas Gage

cal disorders. How, then, can a clinician determine whether these disruptions are biogenic or psychogenic? Fortunately, modern technology has developed several ways to check the functioning of the brain. Brain x-rays, angiograms, pneumoencephalograms, chemical analysis of the cerebrospinal fluid, electroencephalograms (EEGs), neuropsychological tests and especially computed axial tomography (CAT) scans are some of the tests that a diagnostician can use. Sometimes the cause can be determined from the person's medical history, such as a father with syphilis, or a severe attack of meningitis during childhood. And there are some cases in which the cause is self-evident:

Phineas P. Gage, aged 25 and strong and healthy, was the popular foreman of a railroad excavation crew. While he was working at a site, a premature explosion drove a tamping iron into the left side of his face and up through his skull. Gage, thrown onto his back by the force of the blast and by the entry of the rod, convulsed. However, he quickly regained speech and was placed in a cart, in which he rode in a sitting position for three quarters of a mile to his hotel. He got out of the cart by himself and was able to walk up a long flight of stairs to his room. Although bleeding profusely, he remained fully conscious during the doctor's ministrations, and soon afterward he appeared to be completely recovered physically.

However, his personality had undergone a radical change. The equilibrium between his intellectual faculties and his impulses seemed to have been destroyed. He was now inconsiderate, impatient, obstinate, and capricious and vacillating in decision-making. He also began indulging in profanity. The change in temperament was so extreme that his employers had to replace him as foreman.

The process of testing for the cause, if it's not obvious, can be lengthy, since there are so many avenues for search. But our knowledge of the divisional functions of the brain combined with improved technological testing methods and equipment can often cut time considerably. And although many of the organic syndromes share similar general signs, most of them have individual characteristics that do set them apart for easier identification, which also helps.

Once an organic mental disorder is diagnosed, the diagnostician must go one step further and determine the extent of the damage. An *acute* disorder is one that shows severe signs but may have a chance of improving with time. A *chronic* disorder is one that has developed gradually and is stable; it involves irreversible damage to the central nervous system. However, some acute conditions can accelerate so quickly that they prove fatal to the patient. But even if the acute symptoms clear up, there is always the chance that some kind of residual or chronic deficit will remain. On the other hand, some chronic problems have occasionally shown improvement over a period of years.

EXPLAINING THE ORGANIC MENTAL DISORDERS

By definition, organic mental disorders reflect either damage to normally healthy brain tissue or a physiological breakdown in the normally efficient workings of the various parts of the brain. However, the damage can result from an extraordinary number of different factors. An injury to the head, such as that received by Phineas Gage, an inborn biochemical deficiency, exposure to certain toxic elements—these are just a few of the things that can adversely affect neurological functioning. In the next section, we shall briefly describe several ways in which an organic problem can arise.

Head Trauma

Just as an apple bruises when you drop it, so the brain can be injured by a blow or fall. Even though nature has designed the skull and cerebral fluid to be protective, the brain can still be injured or at least negatively affected by accidents.

Head injuries are by far the most common source of damage to the brain. It is estimated that in the United States, 60 to 70 percent of all head injuries are sustained in car accidents. In fact, head injuries resulting from automobile accidents in which the driver was intoxicated or not using seat belts are the number one cause of death for adults under 30 (Rimel, 1979). However, most head injuries are mild enough not to result in serious damage. In fact, it is probable that most people will receive a blow

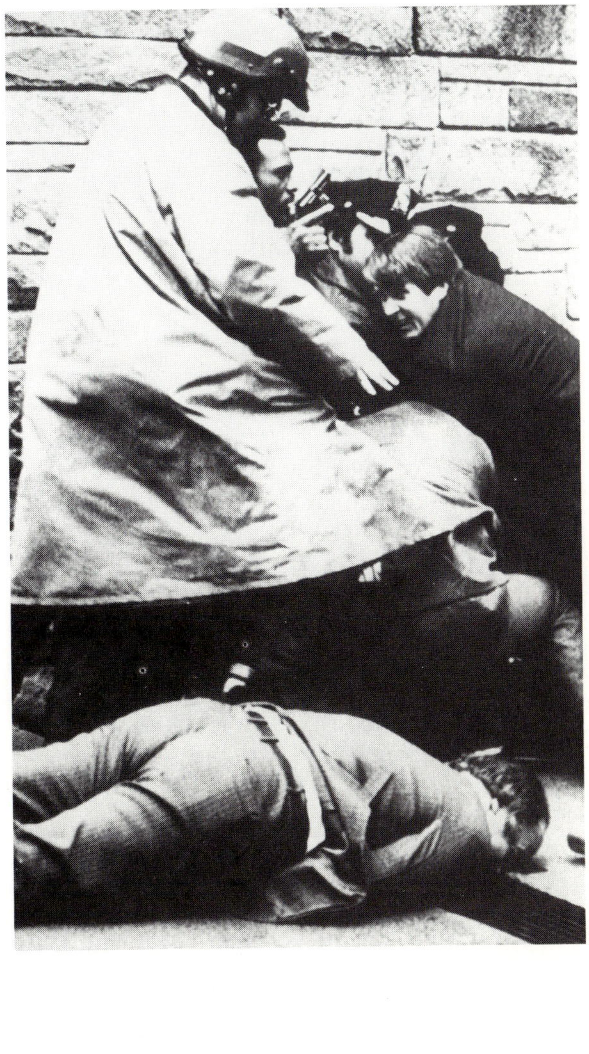

Early in 1981, Presidential Press Secretary James Brady suffered massive brain damage when he was struck by an assassin's bullet meant for President Ronald Reagan. The full effect of such traumas on physical and intellectual functioning are not always known immediately.

to the head at least once in a lifetime, yet the majority will suffer nothing more than a headache and some soreness. Only severe head injuries are likely to result in an organic mental disorder.

Concussions

One type of head injury is a **concussion,** which occurs when the head is struck sharply. The blow jars the brain inside the skull, temporarily disrupting its regular functioning and causing at least temporary loss of consciousness; in many cases, unconsciousness can last longer.

Concussions are common in boxing matches, where the object is to "knock out" the opponent. A boxer knocked down by a punch that is hard enough to make him lose consciousness usually comes around in a few seconds and struggles to his feet, but he may stagger a bit and appear dizzy. Concussions received outside the ring follow the same pattern. When the person comes to, there is usually confusion and disorientation. *Retrograde amnesia*—loss of memory for events preceding the injury—may also be experienced. Other effects of a concussion may be dizziness, headache, nausea, and difficulty concentrating. Concussions ordinarily have no permanent effects. After a short period of rest, the person easily regains the previous level of functioning. The longer the person remains unconscious, however, the greater the chance of aftereffects.

Contusions

Contusions are similar to concussions, but more severe. Not only is the head jarred inside the skull, but the blow is sharp enough to compress the brain against the side of the skull. The result is a bruise in the brain tissue, caused by the rupture of tiny blood vessels. The patient loses consciousness and may go into a **coma** (a deep, unresponsive unconsciousness), which can last anywhere from several hours to several days—and sometimes, in a few cases, several months or even years. Upon awakening, the person's confusion and disorientation are more severe than that experienced after a concussion, and they last longer. The individual may also temporarily lose control of speech, a condition called aphasia.

Unlike concussions, contusions can cause permanent neural damage. Even after recovery seems complete, the person may experience residual deficits in memory, sensorimotor, intellectual, and emotional functioning.

Lacerations

The most severe form of head trauma are **lacerations,** the penetration and tearing of brain tissue. This occurs when a contusion has a shearing effect on the brain tissue, or when a foreign object—such as a bullet—pierces through the skull and punctures the neural tissue. Some lacerations are severe enough to cause death; others result in coma. When the person comes out of the coma, intellectual and sensorimotor functioning may be permanently impaired by the injury, depending on where and how extensive the damage is.

Infections

Infections are most often caused by microorganisms, such as bacteria or viruses, that invade the body and travel to the brain via the circulatory system. When a set of microorganisms becomes established in the brain, they attack the neural tissue, causing it to swell and become inflamed. This condition is generally termed *encephalopathy*.

Meningitis and encephalitis

Meningitis is an inflammation of the meninges, the three outer layers of membrane surrounding the cortex. It can be caused by the presence of viruses, bacteria, fungi, or protozoa. These disease carriers may enter the brain through the bloodstream or through a head wound.

When the meninges become inflamed, the brain literally swells up and flattens against the wall of the skull. Patients usually become depressed, irritable, have difficulty concentrating, and suffer memory loss. In the acute phase of meningitis, there is delirium and disorientation. In the most severe cases, the patient lapses into a coma and may die very quickly.

Adults generally have a good chance of recovering from meningitis, though some may have permanent sensorimotor deficits. For infants, meningitis can be more serious: Sometimes the outcome is mental retardation.

Encephalitis is a general term for an inflammation of the cerebral cortex. One form is called *epidemic encephalitis,* also known as "sleeping sickness." This disorder is caused by a protozoan that is carried by insects, such as flies and mosquitoes. Epidemic encephalitis has become rare in the United States, but it still is a major health problem in certain parts of Africa and Asia. Symptoms are the same as those of acute meningitis: irritability and delirium, sometimes accelerating to seizures and hallucinations. The outstanding symptom, however, is the afflicted person's tendency to sleep for long periods—sometimes even for days or weeks at a stretch (hence the name). The aftereffects of epidemic encephalitis vary widely, but severe personality change is fairly common. A child who contracts epidemic encephalitis may have personality difficulties lasting into adulthood.

Abscesses

Brain **abscesses,** like any other abscess, occur when an area of tissue becomes infected by bacteria. Connective tissue seals in the infection, causing liquid from lymph and bacteria to build up in the area. For healing to begin, the liquid has to be drained off.

An abscess can form in the brain when bacteria enter through a puncture wound, usually a bullet wound. Or the abscess can be the central point of an infection elsewhere in the body, or an extension of an infection in the ears or sinuses. Abscesses do not spread; they are self-contained. Their effect comes from the pressure they exert on surrounding tissue as the volume of fluid builds up.

The clinical symptoms of an abscess vary according to where the infection occurs. Generally, they include headache, nausea, vision problems, and sometimes personality changes. Medical treatment of abscesses generally includes both administration of antibiotics and surgical drainage.

Neurosyphilis

As we mentioned in earlier chapters, syphilis is now known to be caused by the spirochete *Treponema pallidum,* which invades the body through the mucous membranes of the mouth or the genitals during intercourse or oral-genital contact. Sometimes the disease is passed from an infected mother to her unborn child. It can be treated successfully with antibiotics if caught at an early stage. Unfortunately, the signs are often hard to recognize. If it is not treated, syphilis can turn into **neurosyphilis,** also called *general paresis,* in which brain tissue is destroyed. Once that happens, the disorder permanently disables and may even kill its victims.

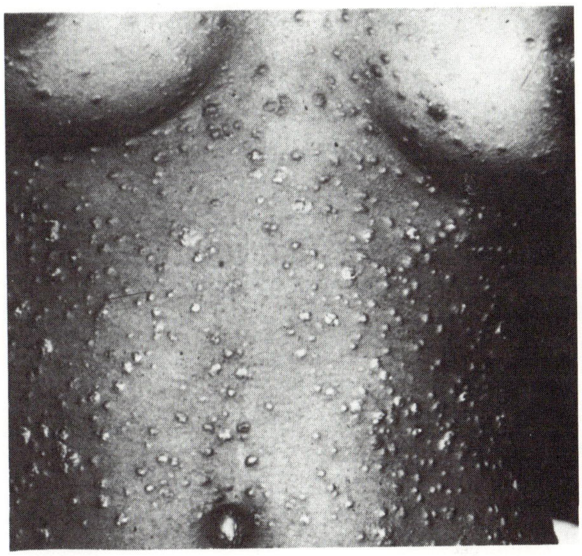

A syphilis rash, occuring during the secondary stage that follows healing of the chancre.

Syphilis has four stages:

Stage 1: Ten to twenty days after contact with an infected person, a hard sore called a *chancre* appears at the site of the infection. The chancre is painless and generally disappears without treatment; thus it can easily not be recognized as a sign of disease.

Stage 2: Three to six weeks after the chancre disappears, more obvious signs of the disease begin to show—a copper-colored skin rash, sore throat, fever, headache, hair loss. Like the chancre, these signs will also disappear without treatment. At that point, the disease may dissipate or it may go into incubation.

Stage 3: During this stage, which can last anywhere from two to forty years, there are no visible symptoms of the disease. Within the body, though, the spirochetes are merely latent, waiting to attack any of the vital systems: heart, bone marrow, spleen, brain.

Stage 4: In the final phase, the spirochetes carry out the invasion, and the damage they create begins to surface. At this point the outcome is either death two or three years after the mental symptoms appear or, if treated with antibiotics, a permanent state of mental impairment.

Depending on where the spirochetes have been at work, the person may be struck by a sudden heart attack, blindness, or loss of motor coordination. If the brain is the victim, which it is in about 3 to 5 percent of untreated cases, mental disturbances result, usually showing up first as personality changes. The person becomes careless and inattentive; personal habits begin to deteriorate; memory starts to lapse. There may be trouble speaking clearly, words are slurred. Emotions become blunted; depression is common. The person may appear vacant and silly and make constant errors in judgment that will be blamed on others. Ultimately the person may go into delirium, an extreme disorganization of the mental processes that makes it impossible to function most of the time.

If a clinician suspects the presence of neurosyphilis, there is a test—though not a conclusive one—for determining that fact. This test involves what is called the *Argyll Robertson pupil.* If neurosyphilis is present, the pupil of the eye contracts and expands normally to changes in perceptual distance, but it does not react to light.

Fortunately, early detection of syphilis is possible by other means. The Wasserman and VDRL tests detect the presence of antibodies against the spirochetes; the TPI blood test and the fluorescence antibody test are better able to detect the disease itself. In addition, penicillin provides an effective cure.

In the 1950s, medical authorities were able to bring syphilis under control in the United States. Recently however, the number of untreated cases has risen dramatically to an estimated 100,000 per year (Beneson, 1975). This means that in about twenty years, hundreds of thousands of people may suffer the advanced stages of syphilis. Hospitals will be full of syphilitics, and the chance of these people transmitting the disease to offspring is a serious threat.

Brain Tumors

Brain tumor is the common name for what is medically termed an *intracranial neoplasm.* Intracranial means "inside the head," and neoplasm means "new growth." A tumor develops when something goes wrong in the control center of a cell-production area. A few cells begin to grow incredibly quickly. As they multiply, they may also destroy the normal, healthy cells and tissue in that part of the organ.

There are two kinds of tumors, *benign* (noncancerous) and *malignant* (cancerous). Benign brain tumors do not destroy tissue, but as they grow, they may press against other areas, or cause an increase in pressure inside the skull. It does not take much pressure to disrupt the brain's normal functioning. In contrast, malignant tumors spread out and destroy the tissue around them. A malignant tumor can develop from the brain cells themselves, or it can spread to the brain from tumors elsewhere in the body, such as the lung, breast, or prostate.

The symptoms of a brain tumor vary according to the severity and location of the damage, like all organic mental disorders. Brain tumors have three classic physical symptoms: headaches, vomiting, and *papilledema,* or "choked disk." That is, pressure inside the skull flattens the optic disk, causing swelling at the back of the retina.

Whether it is benign or malignant, a brain tumor that continues to grow unchecked will produce more severe symptoms, including personality changes that may be extreme. Without treatment, the patient may eventually exhibit some psychotic behaviors. Coma and death are the end result. The surest way of removing a tumor from the brain is with surgery, although many doctors prefer to try chemotherapy and radiation treatment.

Dietary Deficiencies

Like all the cells in the human body, brain cells need the proper types and amounts of nutrients to stay healthy. Too much or too little of certain elements, such as the B-vitamins, can affect the functioning. Although deficiencies caused by malnutrition and simple starvation are less common in the United States than in many other countries, organic brain disorders can nevertheless develop from chronically inadequate or unbalanced diets.

Korsakoff's psychosis

Korsakoff's psychosis is a disorder that strikes alcoholics. Patients develop small lesions in the brain stem and limbic system, apparently because of a deficiency of B-complex vitamins. The deficiency may be due either to faulty body metabolism or to an inadequate diet, both of which are common results of alcoholism. The primary symptoms of Korsakoff's psychosis are an inability to remember recent events (*anterograde amnesia*) and a tendency to fill in these memory gaps with very unlikely rationalizations (*confabulation*). Patients are usually pleasant and appear in control of their faculties, but they lack practical sense and good judgment. In extreme cases, they may become very confused and disoriented. Sometimes the behavioral symptoms can be reversed by megavitamin therapy with vitamin B_1 (thiamine).

Beriberi and pellagra

Both of these disorders are now rare in the United States. **Beriberi,** like Korsakoff's psychosis, is caused by a thiamine deficiency, which damages the peripheral nerves. Symptoms include irritability, fatigue, insomnia, weak muscles, and extreme lassitude. Beriberi is most prevalent in parts of the Far East where polished rice is the main diet staple and little thiamine is available.

Pellagra is a deficiency of niacin, another B vitamin. Physical symptoms include diarrhea and reddening of the skin on the neck and the back of the hands. Psychological symptoms are irritability, depression, inability to remember recent events, and difficulty in concentration. In the southern United States in the early 1900s, nearly 10 percent of all admissions to state mental hospitals were due to pellagra. The chief reason for this was that one staple of the diet—especially among the poor—was corn meal, which does not provide niacin. Pellagra can be effectively treated with a diet rich in protein and vitamins. If it is untreated, however, delirium and hallucinations develop, and eventually the patient dies.

Toxic Agents

Two hundred years ago, the greatest dangers people faced from toxic agents in their environment came from poisonous plant life. Eating mushrooms of the genus *Amanita* or *Galerina* might cause hallucinations, delirium, or death. Belladonna, a useful herb (in small doses) that relieved spasms in whooping cough or pain during fevers, would kill anyone who took more than a small quantity. Hemlock, a common wild plant, was used as a sedative and anesthetic, but its juice was given to the Greek philosopher Socrates for his death sentence.

All these plants are as deadly today as they ever were, but they have been overshadowed by a new generation of poisons. Lead poisoning from paint, toxic gas leaks, mercury poisoning, chemical and radioactive wastes—the newspaper headlines of today reflect a dramatic change in health hazards. A number of substances—among them heavy metals, gases, and drugs—can cause serious damage to the human nervous system.

The effects of exposure to a toxic agent are often temporary. Sometimes, however, permanent brain injury and even death can result. Difficulties in concentration, emotional instability, and psychotic delusions and hallucinations are common symptoms of toxic agents in the nervous system.

Two cooling towers at the Three Mile Island nuclear plant overshadow a residential area of Harrisburg, Pennsylvania. A serious accident at the plant in the spring of 1979 sparked widespread debates over the dangers of increased use of nuclear energy.

Heavy metal poisoning

The heavy metals, which include lead, mercury, and manganese, among others, are poisonous to human beings. When too much lead enters a person's system, it causes the brain to fill up with fluid, increasing pressure inside the skull—a condition called *hydrocephalus*. The person may have abdominal pains, hallucinations, convulsions, even delirium. Workers in lead smelting plants or other manufacturing facilities using this metal are prone to lead poisoning from the dust they breathe. Children, particularly in ghetto areas, often develop lead poisoning when they eat crumbling paint and plaster, a behavior known as **pica.** Although lead is no longer an ingredient in household paint, old houses and apartment buildings that have not been renovated in recent years may contain dangerous quantities of lead. Typical early symptoms of lead poisoning in children are a pale complexion, vomiting, and excessive crying. Continued exposure causes at least temporary mental problems, although these may disappear over time if exposure stops.

Mercury and manganese also are toxic. Most poisoning by these metals occurs among people who work with them daily in an industrial setting. However, small amounts can be found in the food we eat, in the containers in which the food is shipped and stored, and in certain prescription medications. In Japan, where fish is a staple of the diet, there was a severe outbreak of mercury poisoning about 25 years ago when the fishing waters were polluted with mercury from nearby factories. Americans too have been warned from time to time to avoid fish believed to be contaminated with mercury. Unfortunately, little research has been done on human tolerance levels for metals, so there is no way of knowing how safe the government's guidelines are.

Early signs of mercury poisoning include the memory loss, irritability, and concentration problems common in other organic mental disorders. *Tunnel vision*—an inability to see things to the side—develops soon afterward, along with problems in coordination, speech, and hearing. Manganese poisoning, which affects the spinal cord as well as the brain, interferes with motor ability and causes emotional disturbance.

Gases and bromides

Carbon monoxide is one of the subtlest toxic agents capable of causing brain damage. This gas, which is colorless, odorless, and tasteless, is found in the exhaust fumes of motor vehicles (and also in cigarette smoke). When inhaled, it gets into the bloodstream and prevents oxygen from being absorbed by the red blood cells. The brain is particularly vulnerable to the resulting lack of oxygen. People who survive carbon monoxide poisoning generally have memory defects and problems with apathy and confusion which may last for years.

The fumes from certain paints, hairsprays, and glues—which were for a time a popular way to get "high"—can in large amounts be lethal; others can lead to temporary or permanent impairment.

Over-the-counter sleeping pills are made up of bromides, a common and traditional sedative. Desperate insomniacs may take pill after pill from the bottle—and end up poisoning themselves. A toxic dose of bromides can cause extensive brain damage. The symptoms range from apparent drunkenness to "bromide psychosis," which may involve hallucinations and can induce a withdrawal syndrome.

Cerebrovascular Problems

The cerebrovascular system is a complex network of veins, arteries, and capillaries that constantly supply the brain cells with nutrients and oxygen and dispose of waste materials. There are two problems that can cause this system to malfunction and disrupt the brain: an **occlusion,** in which a blood vessel is blocked, and a **hemorrhage,** in which a blood vessel ruptures. When either occurs in a major blood vessel, the result is a **cerebrovascular accident** (CVA) or, in common terms, a **stroke.** Strokes are the third highest cause of death in the United States. Symptoms of a CVA can include paralysis of the limbs and sensory impairment on the side of the body that is controlled by the injured side of the brain. If a CVA occurs in the language center (near the junction of the frontal, parietal and temporal lobes of the dominant hemisphere) the result is **aphasia**—the loss or impairment of the ability to express symbols or ideas in words, whether spoken or written.

An occlusion has two possible sources. One is a *thrombus,* a blood clot that forms in a blood vessel already narrowed by fatty deposits. The other is an *embolus,* a clot that has formed elsewhere in the body (or a foreign element that has been introduced into the bloodstream) and is then carried by the blood to a spot in the brain where it lodges. Both have the same effect: The blocked blood vessel prevents blood and the nutrients it carries from reaching cells farther down the line.

The network of blood vessels in the brain is similar to the network of branches on a tree. If an occlusion happens in a very small branch of an artery, it will have specific effects on that part of the brain and may be contained there. But if an occlusion blocks a major pathway through the brain, all the little branches off it are affected. The results are fast and serious. Without an adequate supply of oxygen and glucose, the brain cells cannot survive for long. Then the brain tissue begins to soften as the cells die off.

In a cerebral hemorrhage, a rupture in a blood vessel causes blood to spill out into the brain. When the blood comes into contact with neural tissue, it destroys the tissue's functioning ability. A frequent cause of hemorrhage is an **aneurysm,** a weakened portion of a blood vessel. Much like a weak spot in an inner tube, the wall of the blood vessel bulges out from the force of the blood inside. Ruptured aneurysms and severe head injuries are the most common causes of hemorrhaging.

The patient, John W., is a married 59-year-old man who completed a standard high school education and, until a year and a half ago, owned and operated a catering service. His wife reports that one morning he woke up with a severe headache. After taking several aspirins, he went to work only to call her three hours later stating that he had gotten lost and could not find his way home. His headaches persisted, especially in the mornings, and he frequently stayed home. At first, his wife merely thought he was avoiding going to work, but as time progressed he became more sullen and irritable, and he began forgetting simple things such as what program he had just watched on television. When he could not recall the answer to a question, he would make up wild stories. Mrs. W. recalls that on one occasion when she asked him what he had been doing outside, he replied in all seriousness "visiting with Sara"—their daughter living in another state.

After about three months, Mrs. W. finally persuaded him to go to the hospital. In the emergency room, he told the attending physician that it was his wife who was sick and not him. He then proceeded to tell the doctor that he had been "in a restaurant like this" when he was stationed in Europe two years ago. The physician's first impression was that the patient was delusional and suffering from a psychotic break with reality. He admitted Mr. W. to the psychiatric ward, but ordered a neuropsychological evaluation to rule out the possibility of an organic brain syndrome. The results of the neuropsychological tests, however, suggested that the patient had a severe memory deficit and was functioning well below the level expected for a man of his age and education. Mr. W. was transferred to the neurology ward and underwent a complete neurological examination. Laboratory tests revealed that he had an aneurysm lying deep between the frontal lobes.

He underwent surgery for clipping of the aneurysm, which apparently had begun to bleed. Following surgery, he made a good recovery and was discharged, but although his mental status has improved somewhat, he still has severe memory difficulties, and becomes disoriented and confused when he leaves familiar surroundings. Currently, he is not competent to live independently or to assume the major responsibility of any important decisions concerning his welfare.

Sometimes, a cerebral hemorrhage can happen very quickly, but its effects depend on the importance of the ruptured vessel. When a major vessel ruptures, all functions of the brain—speech, memory, reasoning, orientation, consciousness, motor abilities—are likely to suffer. The person may have seizures and quickly lapse into a coma. Those people who recover may be handicapped by paralysis, speech difficulties, and psychological difficulties such as memory problems and confusion. Most people who suffer massive cerebral hemorrhages die within two to fourteen days.

Endocrine Disorders

The endocrine system is composed of the various glands in the human body that secrete hormones into the bloodstream. These hormones play a major role in maintaining steady metabolism and growth. The hormonal balance in the body is very delicate, and it must be carefully maintained for optimum performance. When the endocrine system over- or under-produces, the body—including the brain—is instantly affected. Thus, several organic mental disorders are linked to endocrine malfunction.

Thyroid syndromes

The thyroid gland, located in the neck, controls overall metabolism. It secretes a hormone called **thyroxin,** which carries the message to speed up or slow down to all parts of the body. If the thyroid is manufacturing too much thyroxin, a disorder called **hyperthyroidism,** or *Grave's disease,* develops. The body begins to act like a 33-RPM record played at 78 RPM: Everything speeds up. The person feels restless, confused, irritable, and may even suffer from delusions and hallucinations.

When the thyroid is underproductive, the opposite occurs. **Hypothyroidism** produces a condition in adults called **myxedema.** Metabolic processes, including speech and intellectual functioning, slow down. The person feels depressed and exhausted; there may be hair loss and cracked skin. In infants and young children, hypothyroidism can cause **cretinism,** in which the entire metabolism is interrupted, resulting in stunted physical growth and mental retardation.

One form of hypothyroidism, which results from insufficient iodine, is now rare because of the use of iodized salt. However, not all forms have been as easily curbed.

Adrenal syndromes

There are two **adrenal glands** in the human body. Both are located just above the kidney. When the adrenal gland fails to produce enough **cortisone,** the result is **Addison's disease.** The patient loses weight, the skin turns bronze, blood pressure drops, and fatigue and depression may occur. Overproduction of cortisone, in contrast, causes **Cushing's syndrome.** This is a rare disease that most often strikes young women. The main psychological symptom is unpredictable mood swings—the emotions may switch from depression to irritability to anxiety. Physical symptoms may include obesity, muscle wasting, skin discoloration, and spinal deformities.

Degenerative Disorders

Organic mental disorders that are classified as degenerative involve deterioration of tissue in the brain and sometimes elsewhere in the central nervous system. As the tissue breaks down, so do the functions associated with it. How quickly the deterioration takes place varies from disease to disease, and the sites affected also play a part. Most degenerative disorders strike people over 40 years old. With age, the symptoms intensify. There are, of course, certain signs of aging that show up in almost all adults, and these should not be confused with the degenerative disorders. Most people grow old without any breakdown of the brain and its functions.

Degenerative disorders are classified as either **senile** or **pre-senile.** Senile disorders generally strike people over the age of 60. Many people experience a gradual loss of memory and motor skill as they become older; the senile disorders are characterized by an extreme breakdown of these functions. Pre-senile disorders show generally similar symptoms, but they strike younger people, usually those between the ages of 30 and 60.

Pre-senile disorders

Pick's disease and Alzheimer's disease are both rare syndromes, and not much is known about their etiology. Parkinson's and Huntington's diseases are more common, but a lot remains to be learned about how to treat them effectively and perhaps prevent them.

Pick's disease is named after Arnold Pick, the physician who first described it in 1892. It is characterized by **atrophy** (wasting away) of the frontal and temporal lobes of the brain. Initial symptoms vary from memory and reasoning impairment to confusion and emotional indifference. As more and more brain tissue is destroyed, the psychological symptoms intensify. The person becomes increasingly distracted and confused, and eventually loses speech coordination. Finally, only the vital life processes function; the person may lie in a vegetative state for several years before death.

Alzheimer's disease was first described by neurologist Alois Alzheimer in 1860, and it too involves an atrophy of brain tissue. It is not centralized in the frontal and temporal lobes, however, but affects the entire cerebral cortex and some of the interior structures of the brain. Alzheimer's disease strikes three times more women than men. It generally begins between the ages of 40 and 60, and it usually results in death four to five years after it starts. Victims initially complain of having difficulty concentrating, remembering, and maintaining a pleasant expression; later, they become irritable. As the disease progresses, intellectual functioning rapidly breaks down, and the person becomes very disoriented and agitated. In the final stages, occasional convulsions, twitching, and speech impairment precede death.

Parkinson's disease and Huntington's chorea are two pre-senile degenerative disorders that affect the **basal ganglia,** nerve-cell bunches deep inside the brain. The basal ganglia relay messages to all parts of the body to oversee posture and muscle tone. Any disorder that affects their functioning produces a disjointed movement symptom called **dyskinesia.**

Parkinson's disease, which usually begins after age 50, is also known as "shaking palsy." It was first described in 1917 by James Parkinson, an English surgeon. Its most outstanding characteristic is severe muscle tremors that shake the arms, legs, hands, neck, and face of the victim when the muscles are relaxed. When the muscles are in action, they almost always show no signs of tremor, nor is there any tremor during sleep. Later symptoms of Parkinson's disease are rigid muscles, an expressionless and mask-like face, and a stiff, forward-leaning walk. Psychological symptoms range from depression and social withdrawal to memory deficits and intellectual deterioration.

The cause of Parkinson's disease is uncertain, although encephalitis, heredity, viruses, and deficient brain metabolism have all been suggested. The process by which the disease works is known, however. Neurons in the basal ganglia that produce the neurotransmitter dopamine start to deteriorate. The subsequent deficiency of dopamine makes it impossible for neural messages to be adequately transmitted. A drug called L-dopa can boost the production of dopamine and control the tremors of Parkinson's disease, although it cannot cure the disease.

Huntington's chorea is one of the few degenerative organic mental disorders that is known to be hereditary. The disease is carried in a dominant gene, so that the offspring of a victim have a 50-50 chance of developing the disorder. Huntington's chorea usually appears around the age of 30. Like Parkinson's disease, it is centered in the basal ganglia and involves a breakdown of muscle function. Instead of the shaking or tremors that characterize Parkinson's disease, however, victims are plagued by involuntary spasmodic twitches in the legs, arms, and body. The Greek word *chorea* (dance) in the disease's name refers to this twitching. Behavioral, emotional, and personality changes appear with these physical symptoms. The person may become moody, slovenly, and unpredictable; memory and judgment begin to deteriorate. As the disease intensifies, the spasms set in, sometimes accompanied by delusions and hallucinations. Eventually, the person loses all control of body functions and will die, but this may take ten to twenty years.

There is no cure for Huntington's chorea. The best program seems to be genetic counseling that would prevent new cases. However, since the symptoms do not appear until after a person is well into or past the childbearing years, the disorder is often not diagnosed until it is too late to advise the person not to have children.

Senile disorders

It is very difficult to distinguish between the two senile degenerative disorders, senile dementia and multi-infarct dementia. They often have overlapping symptoms and may even be present in the same person at the same time. Sometimes the proper diagnosis is reached only after an autopsy.

Senile dementia involves extensive brain atrophy similar to that of Alzheimer's disease. It too does not attack one specific area in the brain, but spreads throughout. Usually the disorder develops slowly, marked by gradual changes in personality and a growing neglect of dress and grooming. Afflicted individuals begin to have erratic memory losses; they may be able to recite a poem learned years before but cannot remember where they now live. This malfunction of memory intensifies as their disorder progresses. They are likely to have judgment difficulties, perhaps at times acting impulsively or foolishly. Other symptoms include emotional lability and skepticism about new or different things or ideas. People with senile dementia may seem to always be "talking to themselves." This symptom, called *logorrhea,* is not really talking, but the constant repetition of a jumbled string of syllables. The person may or may not be conscious of the mumbling.

Multi-infarct dementia is a series of small

Individuals afflicted with senile dementia suffer a variety of symptoms, among them apathy, hallucinations, rambling speech, and an inability to think abstractly.

embolic strokes in certain parts of the brain that eventually close down some of the brain's functions. The symptoms are nearly identical to those of senile dementia—loss of memory, lack of concern for personal hygiene, and lapses into confused or emotionally labile states. However, the psychological impact of multi-infarct dementia is more severe and complex than that of senile dementia. Mental functions can fluctuate unpredictably, and there may also be such dramatic physical symptoms as blackouts, heart attacks, hypertension, and *retinal sclerosis* (scarring of tissue in the eye).

MANAGING ORGANIC MENTAL DISORDERS

Because the primary problem in an organic mental disorder is biological, treatment is usually medical. Of course, since the early symptoms often seem psychological—memory lapses, personality changes, disorientation—the person may be seen first by a psychologist. And the patient may eventually come back to a psychologist, particularly if there is trouble adjusting to the physical limitations imposed by the disorder. However, the treatment generally lies entirely within the realm of medicine. Medication, special diets, radiation treatment, surgery, and physical therapy are some of the main ways of treating organic mental disorders.

Special diets and medication are commonly prescribed for disorders with a known etiology. Disorders that stem from dietary deficiencies, such as Korsakoff's psychosis, beriberi, and pellagra, often respond to dietary supplements. In cases of endocrine disorder, too, a special diet may be able to reverse the progress of the disorder. For infections, such as syphilis, encephalitis, and brain abscesses, penicillin or another antibiotic can effectively clear the infection, although the damage they cause remains. Medication may also be part of the treatment for disorders in which the person suffers from anxiety, irritability, or mood swings.

A growth or lesion in the brain may have to be treated directly. Chemotherapy and radiation treatment can be used to retard the development of brain tumors, often successfully substituting for the surgery. In other cases, surgery is the treatment of choice—or the only possible treatment. A tumor may have to be removed or an abscess drained to prevent further damage, either from the disorder itself or from the pressure it has created in the brain. Some physicians prefer surgery to chemotherapy and radiation therapy because of the side effects of those two forms of treatment. Loss of hair, mood changes, alterations in skin texture, and loss of bladder or bowel control are just a few of the possible side effects. The danger of an overdose of radiation is another.

If the organic cause of the disorder can be brought under control, the patient still may be left with a deficit of skills or motor abilities. A stroke, for instance, can cause paralysis of one side of the body. Patients may be able to regain some or all of the lost functions through **physical therapy,** a progressive exercise program

Close-up: Diagnosing Fetal Abnormality

About 5 out of 100 babies born in the United States have a serious birth defect or will develop mental retardation. Twenty percent of birth defects are hereditary—passed on through genetic inheritance; the remaining 80 percent are congenital—acquired during development in the uterus. Examples of causes of congenital defects are use of drugs and exposure to diseases or x-rays during pregnancy. The age of the mother has also been linked to fetal abnormalities. Babies born to women over the age of 35 are more prone to birth defects, and after 40 the incidence rises dramatically. For example, Down's syndrome is found in only 1 out of 2000 babies born to mothers 25 years of age, but in 1 out of 50 babies born to mothers over age 45 (Rugh and Shettles, 1971).

In recent years a new technique has been developed for detecting a number of severe hereditary or chromosomal disorders. This procedure, called *amniocentesis,* is simple, reliable, and carries relatively little risk to mother and fetus. It is performed between the fourteenth and sixteenth weeks of pregnancy. First, a photographic scan of the position of the fetus in the uterus is made by means of sound waves (ultrasound). Then a hollow needle is inserted through the abdominal wall into the uterus and a sample of the amniotic fluid is extracted. Analysis of the amniotic fluid can reveal a range of chromosomal abnormalities including Down's syndrome, Tay-Sachs' disease (a fatal genetic disease found primarily among Jews), cystic fibrosis, and Rh incompatibility (in which Rh-negative antibodies from the mother destroy Rh-positive blood cells of the fetus).

If a fetal abnormality is found (which is the case in 4 percent of fetuses of women undergoing amniocentesis), the woman may choose to have an abortion. However, since the results of the chromosome analysis may not be complete until the twentieth to twenty-fourth week of pregnancy, the abortion procedure is more dangerous than abortion during early pregnancy and is more emotionally and physically taxing for the pregnant woman. Amniocentesis is now recommended for pregnant women who are 35 years of age or older; it is not routinely performed on women under 35.

aimed at strengthening and building up the person's limited capacities. The same is true of loss of speech following a stroke. Speech therapists teach patients how to do exercises that will gradually help them recover the lost function.

Blood tests and other analyses can help people who suspect they may have a disorder that could be passed to their offspring. Neurosyphilis, for instance, should not be ignored by anyone planning to have children. The spirochetes that cause the disease can be transmitted from a mother to her unborn child and ruin the child's chances for a healthy life. The blood tests required before marriage are intended to prevent this problem, but obviously not all pregnancies occur shortly after marriage. Huntington's chorea, which is genetically transmitted, is a more difficult disease to confront. Because it may not show up until after the childbearing years, someone with a family history of the disorder is likely to know only that it might be present. In such a case, **genetic counseling,** which explains the mechanism of the disease and can give the odds of its transmission, can be helpful. If you knew that you had a 50-50 chance of carrying the dominant gene, would you take the risk of having children? Testing is also possible for unborn children, to detect problems that might exist. Of particular use in this area is **amniocentesis,** the analysis of amniotic fluid—the liquid that surrounds and protects the fetus in the womb. Another good preventive test is to study the fetal cells that can be found in the mother's bloodstream.

Many organic mental disorders cannot be reversed or even arrested, and many patients (and their families) are faced with learning to live with physical or mental handicaps: Dad will never again be able to shave by himself; Grandma will always confuse her grandchildren with her children. For most of these people, the best option is to return to as normal a life as possible with the loving support of family and friends. Continued medical treatment may be advisable, and psychological counseling for the family group may help those involved find ways to get around these limitations—or at least cope with the frustration they can cause. Specific rehabilitation or social treatment programs also can be useful for bolstering the person's skills and self-confidence. One possibility is participating in a training program during the day and returning home at night.

EPILEPSY

Epilepsy is the term used collectively for a group of disturbances characterized chiefly by **seizures,** sudden and often dramatic changes in the brain's electrical rhythms. Whether these disturbances are a separate organic disorder in and of themselves or merely signs of some other physiological dysfunction is open to debate. Regardless, they often present serious problems that must be managed in order to prevent injury to the person who experiences the seizures.

In severe episodes, the seizure can be an extremely violent spasmodic convulsion, followed by a period of unconsciousness. Often, however, it is quite mild—a momentary period of distraction in which the individual seems to be in a trance. In these instances, the person may never even realize that a seizure has struck. Precipitating factors also range from one extreme to the other: Excitement and emotional stress can bring on a seizure—but so can the periods of calm that immediately precede and follow sleep. Other precipitators are alcohol consumption, menstruation, and fatigue.

Current statistics (Goldenson, 1978) estimate that around two million people in the United States have epilepsy—one out of every hundred. About half this number are younger than fifteen. Epilepsy can develop at any age, but certain forms are more common among children and teenagers. As these youths mature, there is a chance that their seizures will eventually cease; however, there is an equal chance that they will remain for life.

The EEG of an epileptic seizure is pretty distinctive, as Figure 13.3 shows. There are periods of erratic, jagged lines instead of the usual series of S-curves. This is not a foolproof test for epilepsy, however; 15 percent of tested epileptics have normal EEGs. This may be because the abnormal electrical discharges in the

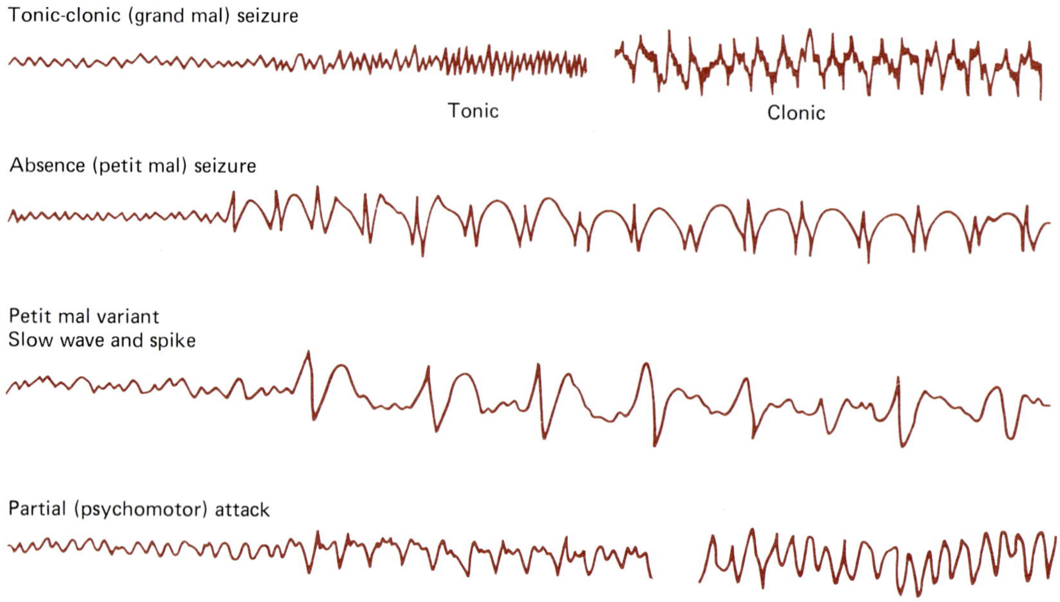

Figure 13.3. *The EEG patterns of four kinds of epileptic seizures. From Gibbs et al., 1939.*

brains of some epileptics are too faint or infrequent to be accurately measured; or perhaps the discharges are happening too deep inside the brain to be picked up by surface electrodes. Epilepsy apparently involves different parts of the brain in different people. Furthermore, 10 percent of normal people have brain-wave patterns that could be interpreted as epileptic.

Types of Epilepsy

The International Classification of Epilepsy system has recently revised the traditional categories of this disorder into four categories: **generalized, complex partial, elementary partial,** and **idiopathic** (a residual category). Generalized seizures include absence seizures, formerly called *petit mal* ("small illness") and tonic-clonic seizures, formerly called *grand mal* ("great illness").

Absence seizures are very mild. They are much more common in children than adults (Hughes, 1980), and they affect more girls than boys. Absence seizures taper off after a child reaches puberty and usually disappear totally by the age of twenty. If you were to watch a child going through an absence seizure, you would have a hard time describing any definite symptoms. The child just seems to stare into space, as if lost in a daydream. Sometimes the facial muscles twitch slightly, or the eyelids may blink again and again. But some children show no outward signs at all beyond appearing "far away"—hence the name "absence." Children having such seizures may not even be aware of them. They do not move during the seizure and are not conscious of their surroundings. Ordinarily, the seizure lasts only a few seconds and as soon as it passes the child goes on with previous activities. Some children have as many as 300 of these seizures in a day.

The **tonic-clonic seizure** is the violent, unpredictable form of epilepsy that is most common among adults. Sixty percent of all epileptics experience this type of seizure. Fortunately, drugs are available that can usually control the seizures and allow the epileptic to live a normal life.

Tonic-clonic seizures have four phases, although the first phase may be absent or unrecognizable in some cases. First comes the *aura phase,* a warning sign that a seizure is on the way. The aura might consist of a funny smell, a wild flashing of lights and colors, or a feeling of dizziness—it varies from one person to another. The aura is quickly followed by the *tonic phase.* The muscles contract so strongly that the arms flex, the legs stretch out straight, and the hands curl up into tight fists. The person stops breathing and falls to the floor, unconscious. Within half a minute the *clonic phase* begins: The person is still unconscious, but breathing starts again. As air enters the lungs and oxygen starts toward the brain, the body reacts by going into generalized muscle spasms. The jerks can be so violent that the person may be injured in this phase, which usually lasts about 60 seconds. The final *coma phase* begins with a deep sleep, from which the person usually awakens fully conscious. Muscles are relaxed and calm again, but movements are very slow; many people feel confused and exhausted after a seizure, and they may have a headache.

Complex partial seizures, which used to be called *psychomotor seizures,* strike 10 percent of epileptic children and 60 percent of epileptic adults. They are different enough from generalized seizures that some observers believe they represent a separate disorder. People having one of these seizures seem to go into a trance. They retain motor control but lose contact with reality. Sometimes, they may go right on with whatever they were doing; more often, though, they become engaged in some repetitive and apparently meaningless activity—patting the arm of a chair, for instance. The seizure can last a few seconds or a couple of minutes; when it has passed, the person has no recall of what happened. Another distinctive feature is that there is not always a warning aura before this type of seizure, except for an occasional feeling of *deja vu* or a shift in time perception. Some reports suggest that people may be prone to bizarre or even criminal behavior during a complex partial seizure, but a recent review concludes that there is no persuasive evidence of this (Lewis, 1975).

Elementary partial seizures primarily affect sensory motor control. Individuals experiencing a seizure of this type might notice a tingling sensation in a hand or foot; often, a muscle or a connected group of muscles can twitch uncontrollably. But they will remain fully conscious throughout the seizure. This kind of seizure is not very common—only about 10 percent of those with epilepsy experience elementary partial seizures.

The cause of epilepsy is still pretty much a mystery. The presence of epileptic seizures of any type is clear-cut evidence that something somewhere in the brain is not working correctly, but there are no clearer indications. Some clinicians suspect a hereditary factor, but this has yet to be proved. Epilepsy presents such a varied array of symptoms that it is often impossible to even conjecture about which type is being exhibited, much less what's causing the problem. In fact, idiopathic epilepsy is diagnosed more frequently than any other type because of this difficulty. The descriptions of the different types given earlier are of the classic symptoms, but only rarely does a person present a classic case.

Treating Epilepsy

Eighty percent of all epileptics can control the occurrence of seizures or lessen their effects with drugs (Howell, 1978). For those who are not helped by medication, surgery may provide some relief. Biofeedback has also had some positive results. However, the greatest problems may arise from the social stigma and personal embarrassment of having epilepsy. Personal shame and frustration, coupled with the fear and discomfort that other people may feel, can cause psychological problems. This is especially likely among epileptic children, for whom the normal difficulties of growing up are made worse by this barrier between them and their peers. There may also be more direct secondary psychological symptoms. When a person comes out of a seizure—especially a tonic-clonic—there is usually confusion and disorientation. These feelings are sure to be compounded if such a seizure takes place in public. These factors coupled with somewhat more limited mental functioning between seizures can leave people with epilepsy feeling at a disadvantage; despite (usually) normal social skills, some may prefer fewer social contacts—or to socialize in small doses.

DESCRIBING MENTAL RETARDATION

Mary Lou is a neat, attractive 20-year-old woman who lives at home with her family. Every morning, instead of going off to a job, Mary Lou goes to a special school, where she is learning how to operate a cash register. She also attends classes in gymnastics, home economics, and art.

Mary Lou is sometimes lonely. People her own age have always scorned her as a playmate because she acts so much younger. She likes to play with children; she does not show much interest in the activities of adults, except that she is anxious to please her parents and teachers.

Mary Lou is a mildly retarded adult. She thinks and acts like a young teenager. She has difficulty comprehending and assimilating new ideas and skills, and she will never be as alert and bright as a normal adult. When she finishes her course of study at the special school, she will probably hold a permanent job, preferably at a health food store.

To most people, **mental retardation** conjures up an image of people who are at best a little slow mentally. At worst, they are viewed as being dumb, stupid, even crazy. Few of us really understand what mental retardation means for society as well as for the individual concerned. Yet mental retardation is not uncommon: By one definition of its criteria, the mentally retarded population has been estimated at 6.5 million—more than 3 percent of the U.S. total (Dunham and Dunham, 1978).

Mental retardation is classified as a mental disorder because it almost always involves patterns of behavior that are considered to be abnormal. In many—if not most—of these cases this is due to an abnormal pattern of development as well. Although we have grouped it here with organic syndromes, it should be noted that the problem is not always organically caused. In fact, for most cases, the cause is unknown.

The AAMD Definition

As we mentioned, there is more than one definition of mental retardation, and each can influence how we view and deal with people who are mentally retarded. For instance, we just stated that according to one estimate, the mentally retarded population totals about 6.5 million. However, if estimated according to another set of criteria, that figure is reduced by almost half. Clearly, the guidelines of the definition can yield widely varying results.

The *Manual on Terminology and Classification in Mental Retardation,* which was published by the American Association on Mental Deficiency (AAMD) in 1963, 1973, and 1977, is now being revised again. Each edition of this document has presented a fairly good working definition of mental retardation. The 1977 version states that mental retardation is "significantly subaverage" general intellectual functioning that exists concurrently with adaptive behavior problems, both of which are manifested during the infant and childhood developing years.

This fairly recent definition is much reduced from previous versions. Because most mental health professionals are now more aware of the potentially harmful effects that can arise from labeling people mentally retarded, they have tried to sharpen the criteria for inclusion. By these newer standards, the estimated population of mentally retarded is only about 1.5 percent of the U.S. total. The big difference in the two figures we have quoted stems from the second part of the AAMD definition—deficits in adaptive behavior.

A full understanding of the AAMD definition is important to a full understanding of mental retardation. The definition can be explained by looking at it more closely.

Significantly subaverage general intellectual functioning. According to David Wechsler, compiler of the Wechsler Intelligence Scales (see Chapter 2), intelligence is the individual capacity to act purposefully, think logically, and deal effectively with the environment (Matarazzo, 1976). Intellectual functions include reason, perception, comprehension, and memory—all

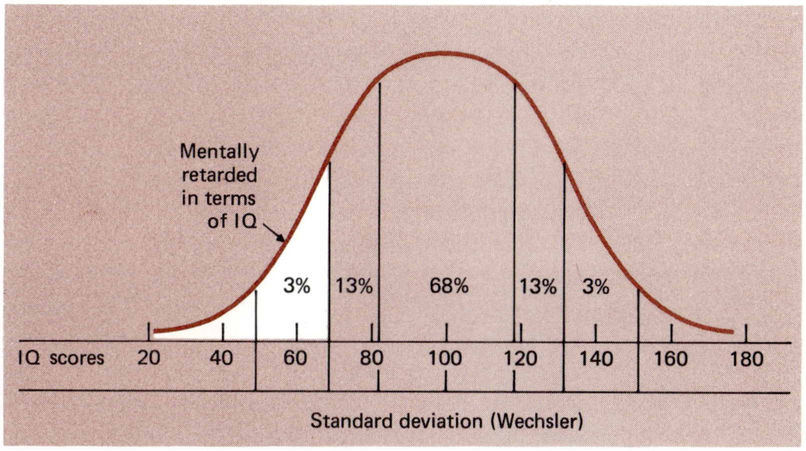

Figure 13.4. *Distribution of intelligence quotients (IQs). The divisions represent standard deviations by the Wechsler Scales. The figures inside the curve are percentages of the total population. From Gottesfeld, 1979.*

of which are commonly assessed by standardized tests, such as the Wechsler Scales.

Newer versions of intelligence tests no longer use the concept of mental age made popular by the pioneering Stanford-Binet test. Instead, they derive deviation IQs using the same general system that teachers use when grading tests "on a curve": All the scores of a same-age population are plotted to show the bell curve; the average for that group is then clear, as are the standard deviations both above and below normal. According to AAMD criteria, "significantly subaverage" is any score two standard deviations below normal, or an IQ of less than 70.

Generally, a low level of intellectual functioning is suspected if a child consistently performs poorly at school. Once a teacher expresses concern, most parents will seek testing to determine the exact nature of the problem. Certain physical handicaps—notably hearing impairment and such vision difficulties as *dyslexia*—must be eliminated before the child can be diagnosed as mentally retarded. In addition, the clinician would check for certain specific learning problems (see Chapter 14) that are suspected to be psychogenic. When all alternatives have been ruled out, the child is diagnosed as mentally retarded for educational purposes.

Deficits in adaptive behavior. The ability to function adequately despite mental limitations is a very important factor. Some people who have significantly subaverage IQs are quite able to care for themselves at home and can handle certain social situations. Those who test at the high end of the retardation spectrum may function at an even more typically adult level—holding a job, for instance, is often a possibility.

The AAMD has its own test for adaptive behavior, and others (such as the Vineland Social Maturity Scale, which is also being revised) are also available. Whatever measurement is used, however, a person must score poorly on both the general intelligence scale and a general level of behavior (adaptability) test to be considered mentally retarded by the AAMD definition. However, the broader picture indicates that generally there is at least some behavioral deficit even for this group, and lower IQ scores usually go hand in hand with greater deficits.

Onset during the developmental period. Human development proceeds in an orderly way from birth to adulthood. The developmental period is usually considered to run from birth to age eighteen. If something happens during that time to prevent the acquisition of social and intellectual functions or to cause those learned to be lost (an accident that leaves permanent injury, for example), the person's progress slows down. Interruptions after age eighteen are less likely to affect overall development, since physical and psychological maturation are essentially complete by then.

It should be noted that being classified as mentally retarded is not necessarily a lifetime status. Officially at least, the status can change. Training can help improve adaptive behavior, for instance, and education in fundamentals can help improve test scores. Often the increase is minimal, but for those people with marginal scores to begin with, a minimal increase may be significant. Of course, it must be emphasized that an official change in status may not—and probably will not—alter any real life circumstances. People formerly labeled mentally retarded are usually treated much like former mental patients or former convicts. They are often looked upon with skepticism and have to spend a lot of time "proving" themselves.

Levels of retardation

The abilities of retarded people may vary significantly, as do their social and behavioral deficits. Of the 6.5 million retarded people in the United States, about 275,000 are institutionalized (Dunham and Dunham, 1978)—an alternative that is turned to in cases of extremely severe retardation, physical disability, or inadequate home care or facilities. This still leaves a sizable number of mentally retarded people who live at home with their families, or in group homes; a lucky few are even able to live independently within the community.

Because of such differences, mental retardation is commonly divided into four levels—*mild, moderate, severe,* and *profound*—that are related to IQ and adaptive test scores. Each level represents one standard deviation (15 points) below the mean on the normal intelligence curve—but the picture is not fixed or static and there is a great deal of room for varying abilities. The levels help professionals classify mentally retarded people into homogeneous groups so that they can plan programs for them according to common abilities and potential.

Mild retardation (Wechsler IQ 55 to 69). Nearly 90 percent of all mentally retarded people are in this category (Dunham and Dunham, 1978). Most of them are normal in appearance, but they are likely to learn tasks such as dressing and feeding themselves more slowly. They may also begin to speak and be sociable a little later than their nonretarded peers. In many cases, mild retardation can be so borderline that the child goes through the preschool years without anyone detecting the condition.

Once the child starts school, the mental deficit soon becomes apparent. It is very difficult for a retarded child to keep up with a classroom full of normal children, since academic skills develop so much more slowly. Still, with proper attention, most average, mildly retarded individuals should be able to master the equivalent of a sixth grade education: By adolescence, they can usually carry on everyday conversations, read and write simple communications, make change correctly, and do other tasks considered normal for late childhood. In adulthood, most mildly retarded people can master the skills of a simple job, interact cooperatively and competitively with others, and enjoy certain recreational activities. Some may live in group homes; others, with their families. Those who can live alone have the occasional help and advice of a counselor or advisor.

Although all those who are classified at this level are capable of fulfilling their personal potential, it is sometimes difficult to accomplish. The everyday frustrations of being just outside the normal range are depressing and the support and understanding of family, social workers, and employers are thus very important.

Moderate retardation (Wechsler IQ 40 to 54). Those mentally retarded people who are unable to take care of themselves and communicate without some help are classified as moderately retarded; they make up about 6 percent of the total population of retarded people (Dunham and Dunham, 1978). Many of them are further handicapped by secondary physical problems.

During the preschool years, moderately retarded children can learn how to use a spoon; they can help dress themselves and can cooperate with toilet training. In other words, development in general is fair. During later childhood they function at the level of a typical three to four year old. For instance, they are slow to distinguish dangerous objects and to learn what things are edible. They can speak

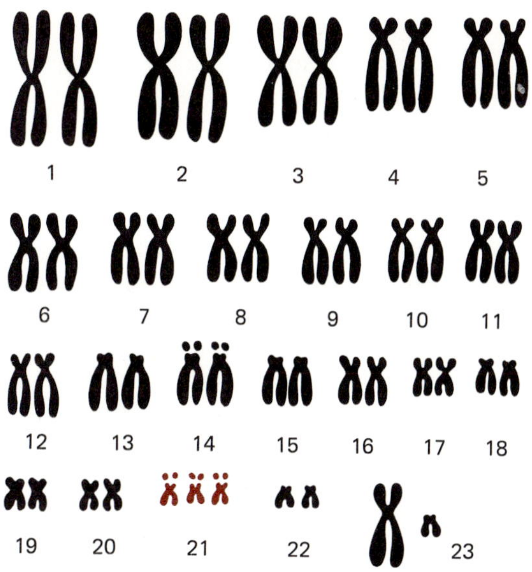

Figure 13.5. *The chromosomes of a male child with Down's syndrome, showing the extra one in pair 21. In rare cases, the trisomy occurs in pair 22.*

in short, crude sentences, but most of them do not understand nuances. They have poor social awareness and need very structured training programs. Although they are not likely to progress beyond the level of second or third grade, they can be trained to master certain social and occupational skills.

An unskilled or semiskilled job is the best prospect for moderately retarded adults. With the support of a group home or their families, they can generally care for themselves, travel alone over familiar routes, and maintain good work and social habits. Although they can contribute to a family or communal living situation, they do need guidance to get them through times of emotional stress and to assist them with everyday financial matters.

Severe retardation (Wechsler IQ 25 to 39). Three and a half percent of mentally retarded people are classified severely retarded (Dunham and Dunham, 1978). These people, who are sometimes referred to as dependent retarded, are quite limited in their potential functions and need considerable supervision. They often have impaired sensory, motor and speech functions, and their early childhood development is slow and quite limited.

By the time they reach school age, most are able to talk and express emotions and desires. Education for this group is most likely to center on whatever limited self-help and personal hygiene skills they are capable of learning. As adults, the severely retarded have difficulty performing even simple functions in a work setting, but under supervision they can participate in the life of a sheltered group home.

Profound retardation (Wechsler IQ below 24). Less than 2 percent of all retarded people fall into this category (Dunham and Dunham, 1978). Most profoundly retarded people die while young because they are prone to diseases and are likely to have multiple physical handicaps. Of those who survive, most need constant nursing care; many spend all their adult lives in hospitals. Some never develop the ability to speak; others learn speech only in adulthood. Profoundly retarded people can respond to training of simple responses, but their limited development is likely to be interrupted constantly by medical problems.

These are the four official levels of mental retardation, but most mental health professionals tend to view the retarded population as two broad groups. One group—the larger by far—truly seems to represent the low end of the intelligence curve; those in the other group have experienced an overwhelmingly unlucky throw of the dice.

The first group, which used to be called "cultural familial" (or "retarded by psychosocial disadvantage") is composed almost entirely of people in the mildly retarded category described earlier. In fact, they can and often do blend imperceptibly with the borderline population because they are actually the lower continuation of it. The greatest proportion of mentally retarded people make up this group, and most of them are able to lead fairly average lives because of their borderline position. The school years are generally the most difficult for them because their disabilities are likely to stand out and set them apart from their peers.

These people come for the most part from marginal families—both economically and socially. Many factors in their background may thus have contributed to a lower intelligence: poor nutrition, poor pre- and post-natal care, lack of support for cognitive growth, a family history of similar circumstances, inherited characteristics—and many more things that make it nearly impossible to identify a single cause.

The second group is handicapped because of some genetic or environmental catastrophe—an extra chromosome, a bad set of genes, prenatal infection. People in this group represent all economic levels, although the poor are again generally overrepresented simply because catastrophies happen to the poor more than to the rich. Usually, the retardation level of this group is high, but mild cases can also result.

This group includes the "interesting" medical syndromes, the highly unusual cases that generally excite the most professional and public interest, but it should be remembered that they represent the minority of mentally retarded people. Paradoxically, these handicaps are potentially more preventable because they tend to be caused by accidents or genetic errors; retardation in the larger group is inextricably bound to poverty.

EXPLAINING MENTAL RETARDATION

The four levels of mental retardation serve as a useful system for psychologists and teachers who deal with retarded people. These categories focus on what the individual can be expected to learn. The AAMD also uses a medical classification system that identifies ten categories of mental retardation by cause to help evaluate a person's condition:

1. Chromosomal abnormalities
2. Metabolic and nutritional disturbances
3. Infections and intoxications
4. Trauma and physical agents
5. Gross brain disease occurring after birth
6. Unknown prenatal influences
7. Gestational disorders
8. Psychiatric disorders
9. Environmental influences
10. Other conditions

This classification system is obviously more useful for research than for day-to-day management. Two people who are mentally retarded because of the same reason may well have entirely different levels of ability. Still, knowing the cause can be useful for the families involved, especially if they are planning to have more children.

The existence of this list does not mean that a good diagnostician can identify the cause of every case of retardation. Quite the opposite. You will notice that the AAMD list covers just about every imaginable factor that might affect a person's mental capacity yet still includes an "other" category. We know that these factors are involved in some cases of mental retardation, but which factors are involved in a particular case can be very hard to say. Sometimes it is fairly easy to relate a retarded person's problem to one or more of these influences; often it is impossible. Much of the time, the best anyone can do is make an educated guess.

Some of the potential causes of the AAMD list have already been examined in the section on organic mental disorders. Others are too vague or too speculative to warrant discussion here. In this section our emphasis will be on those factors that are unique to mental retardation and those that are generally considered to be most influential. These can be divided into organic factors and environmental factors, but keep in mind that interaction between the two is very likely to be the root of the problem.

Organic Factors

A fairly high proportion of cases of mental retardation at the moderate, severe, and profound levels appear to have biological origins.

Many children with Down's syndrome achieve a higher level of functioning with the help of early training and the support of a loving home environment.

Some observers believe that as investigations continue, organic causes will be found to underlie most or all cases. Here we shall look at just three categories of biological influences: chromosomal aberrations, metabolic errors, and infections and intoxications.

Chromosomal aberrations

Ten to twenty percent of the U.S. children annually classified as moderately to severely retarded are born with a chromosomal abnormality called **Down's syndrome.** Whereas most people have 23 pairs of chromosomes, people with Down's syndrome have an extra (or forty-seventh) chromosome in the twenty-first pair. This results in the familiar physical symptoms of this disorder: a flattened face and nose, eyes slanted upward and outward, an overly large and fissured tongue, coarse hair and skin, low muscle tone, and general physical underdevelopment.

There is a clear correlation between the age of the parents—especially the mother—and the incidence of Down's syndrome: One out of every 50 babies born to mothers older than 45 is born with the syndrome (Holvey and Talbott, 1972).

It was once believed that Down's syndrome led inevitably to severe retardation, probably because it was also believed that efforts to train or educate any retarded group were futile. However, current efforts toward early education and training combined with the trend to keep these children at home with supportive families have resulted in a higher average level—generally in the moderate range.

A second type of chromosomal abnormality linked to mental retardation is **Klinefelter's syndrome.** The chromosome configurations that determine gender are XX for a female and XY for a male. Sometimes a male child is born with an extra X chromosome (XXY), which results in a sterile male with small testes and developed breasts. Only about one out of every five children born with Klinefelter's syndrome is mentally retarded, however.

Table 13.1 *Pre- and Post-natal Prevention Measures*

Before planning your pregnancy, check for inherited forms of retardation in your families.
Before the pregnancy, check for Rh compatibility.
Before the pregnancy, get a vaccination against German measles (rubella).
Avoid becoming pregnant after age 40.
During the pregnancy, try not to smoke or to do anything else that might affect the oxygen supply to the fetus.
Maintain a balanced diet during pregnancy and breast-feeding.
Avoid using drugs during pregnancy and breast-feeding.
Minimize your exposure to radiation (x-rays) during pregnancy.
Before and during pregnancy, check for the presence of venereal diseases or other complications.
If your physician suspects deformity, request amniocentesis (analysis of the amniotic fluid).
Plan for a delivery at a hospital that is well prepared for emergencies.
Make sure your newborn is tested for phenylketonuria (PKU).
Become familiar with the normal patterns of infant development, and contact your pediatrician if you are concerned.

Medical science has developed a highly sophisticated method of early diagnosis for chromosomal disorders called *amniocentesis.* There are enough cells of the fetus in this fluid to be checked for the extra chromosome that would cause either Down's or Klinefelter's syndrome, or for many other chromosomal and biochemical abnormalities. Amniocentesis is costly and entails a slight risk to the fetus, however, so it is currently being used only with those women for whom the risks of an abnormal fetus are high.

Metabolic errors

Another source of retardation is metabolic disorders related to defects in the gene pairs that oversee the production and distribution of specific enzymes. One of these disorders is **phenylketonuria (PKU).** Although a child with PKU has a normal appearance at birth, the liver is unable to produce the specific enzyme that breaks down the amino acid *phenylalanine,* found in proteins. Phenylalanine and its derivative *phenylpyruvic acid* then build up in the body fluids, which can cause irreversible brain damage and severe mental retardation. Fortunately, PKU can be identified by laboratory tests early in a child's life. A special diet low in that amino acid will prevent the brain damage, and by the time the child is about six years old, the danger is over.

Two other metabolic disorders that can lead to mental retardation are caused by an inability to metabolize *lipids* (fats). These are **Tay-Sachs' disease** and **Neimann-Pick's disease.** Tay-Sachs is an inherited disorder, carried in a recessive gene; it is found in Jewish people whose ancestors lived in a certain region in Eastern Europe. Children born with Tay-Sachs never advance very far in developing: Before they are a few months old, their muscles weaken and eyesight begins to fail. If they live long enough, they will be blind and helpless, but most victims die before the age of three. Neimann-Pick's disease leads to gastrointestinal disturbances, malnutrition, and progressive metabolic dysfunction.

The accompanying mental retardation worsens as the disorder progresses, and the child eventually dies.

Infections and toxic agents

Sometimes mental retardation is caused by an infection, poison, or disease that strikes a pregnant woman and affects the brain of her unborn child. These disorders are not genetic in origin but rather are contracted during the gestation period. Syphilis, as we have seen, can be passed from mother to child in this way, as can **rubella,** also known as German measles. The earlier in the pregnancy—especially during the first three months—a woman contracts rubella, the greater the likelihood and the probable extent of damage to the child. Many other physical defects besides mental retardation can be caused by rubella. Lead poisoning also can be transferred from a woman to a developing fetus, although most cases of mental retardation linked to lead poisoning involve older children.

Research indicates that many drugs can cause mental retardation when used by pregnant women. Probably the most serious problem is presented by alcohol abuse. Although no exact figures have been published, it is well established that a pregnant woman who consistently drinks more than small amounts of alcohol increases her chances of giving birth to a child of low birth weight who may be mentally retarded or physically deformed. Pregnant women who are alcoholic may give birth to children with **fetal alcohol syndrome (FAS).** In FAS, there is a consistent pattern of underdevelopment that includes growth deficiency, malformation, and retardation. Very often, the head is small in proportion to the body, caused by premature hardening of the skull. The entire frame is smaller than normal, too. And defects in the muscular walls between the heart chambers and cervical spine fusions have been found (MacLeod, 1979). In a recent study (Jones, 1973), the average IQ of FAS children was found to be 63; the range ran from below 50 to only the middle 70s.

According to one report (Smith, 1979), the incidence of FAS is greater than one per 1000 live births. Streissguth and colleagues (1980), however, have put the figure at one out of every 750. They also claim that of all those children born to alcoholic mothers, about 33 percent have the full syndrome; another 76 percent will show partial symptoms.

Environmental Factors

Most cases of mental retardation, especially mild retardation, are never definitively diagnosed. When no organic cause is verifiable, the alternative is that the source of the person's deficiency lies in the environment. As we mentioned earlier, the problems of poverty can contribute greatly to retardation, and the largest group of retarded people—the mildly retarded—do indeed come from the lower socioeconomic classes; often they are also racial minorities.

One environmental factor that has been implicated in retardation is isolation. Some children are born into life situations so bad that their already desperate parents abandon them. These children are usually brought up in institutions, under the care of nurses and other paid personnel instead of within a family unit. Clearly, they will not receive the love and attention that most families lavish on their members; certainly they will also suffer a lack of stimulation and support for cognitive development that usually is fostered by the family. Studies have found that children who grow up in institutions tend to be less advanced than noninstitutionalized children the same age (Heber, 1978), and they have particular difficulty with language development. However, this process can be reversed if the children are given more attention and stimulation. Heber noted that a number of children transferred from institutions to foster family care showed an increase in mental development.

Most mildly retarded children have not grown up in an institution, however, and have never been especially isolated. How then can environment figure in their condition? The answer for many is a home life that is unstable or poverty-stricken, or very likely both. In such conditions, there may be little intellectual stimulation, and relationships between family members may be poor. The children may be starved for affection and mental stimulation—and also for proper nutrition. These children naturally suffer at school. Their test scores and general performance show subaverage achievement. The problem does not seem to be organic; rather, it could be called **mental impoverishment.** These children have not learned background skills at home—no one has read aloud to them or helped them practice counting. Nor have they been encouraged to develop the kind of aggressive curiosity that facilitates learning. When they start school in the same classroom with children who have been stimulated and encouraged—and of course well fed—mentally impoverished children typically lag far behind. Unless they are taken aside from the start and given special attention, their problem is likely to intensify as the school years go on.

With mental retardation, as with most psychological disorders, it appears likely that two or more factors acting simultaneously are a more potent influence than one factor acting alone. The poor diet and medical care that a lower-class mother receives during pregnancy might well compound the negative influence of the surroundings into which her child is born. Insufficient medical attention is viewed as the cause of many premature births, birth defects, and illnesses of babies that can lead to mental retardation. Many specialists feel that raising the standard of living in the United States and setting up programs to help eradicate the side effects of poverty could eliminate most cases of mental retardation—especially the milder forms. However, the possibility of successfully attacking poverty is extremely small. Saying that children from unstable and impoverished homes need extra help is a lot easier than supplying it. Even though certain government programs, such as Head Start, have had good results in trying to make up for the lack of mental stimulation in the lives of underprivileged children, fiscal problems, such as inflation, continually threaten the existence of these programs.

Nor are psychologists in agreement that special assistance is the answer for these children. Psychologist Arthur Jensen created a storm of controversy when he published his conclusion that blacks, on the average, are genetically less intelligent than whites. This notion is rejected by the majority of mental health professionals, but it does represent another obstacle to providing special assistance: If some professional people believe it wouldn't help anyway, why bother to do it? Clearly, the issue goes beyond socioeconomic environment and mental ability—it becomes a question of our society's values.

MANAGING MENTAL RETARDATION

Mental retardation is a disorder for which "management" is definitely a more appropriate term than "treatment." In most cases, there is no hope of the person's condition improving significantly. Usually, the goals are to help the person to become as self-sufficient as possible, and to work on any subsidiary problems, such as physical handicaps, that are adding to the difficulties.

Most medical forms of intervention are aimed at either preventing mental retardation or minimizing it. Drug treatment for syphilis or rubella, for example, may keep a pregnant woman's illness from endangering her child. Medication and special diets often can reduce the potential impact of metabolic disorders like PKU.

Another medical treatment that can be helpful is physical therapy. Many of the disorders associated with mental retardation involve physical handicaps, along with low immunity to infections, which add further complications. When a child burdened with these disabilities is helped to overcome at least the physical problem, new possibilities are opened up. Speech therapy in particular is usually a necessary part of a moderately or severely retarded person's education.

Still, most management techniques for mental retardation are psychosocial rather than medical. The first premise for educating retarded people is that all people, no matter how severely handicapped, have at least the potential

Close-up: *The Retarded: Helping Each Other*

Paraprofessionals—people with no official qualifications beyond light training in a particular field—have been found to be extraordinarily effective counselors. Some assert that this is because they have experienced life situations and problems similar to those described by the clients seeking advice, which gives them a special insight that often leads to better communication. This same concept has been put to work in programs for the mentally retarded.

Whalen and Henker (1971) described a case in which a mildly retarded young woman acted as the behavior therapist for an eleven-year-old severely retarded boy in the same hospital. During the course of their sessions together, she had to go through a series of tasks to help him respond appropriately and on cue. To do this effectively, she had to learn how to get and keep his attention, how to elicit his responses, and how and when to reward him for correct responses. This might have been a trying experience for a therapist, but it was not for the young paraprofessional and she made considerable progress. The little boy, who previously had rarely interacted with anyone and almost never spoke, learned to imitate some gestures and to respond to simple requests. More important, perhaps, he established a positive and rewarding relationship with another person.

The young woman also benefited from this arrangement. Once considered a hard case because of her poor conduct and long history of institutionalization, she developed several valuable skills. She became punctual, carried out her responsibilities efficiently and well, managed her salary appropriately, and was proud of her work. Her irresponsible behaviors dropped off dramatically and she was eventually deinstitutionalized.

to learn and grow, even if there are very strict limits to what can be learned or how quickly. Second, retarded people have more or less the same sensitivities, emotions, and needs that we all have and should be treated accordingly. Today, most mental health professionals believe that mentally retarded people can contribute to society, despite their social and intellectual immaturity.

The 1975 Education for All Handicapped Children Act requires all states that receive federal aid to develop and implement plans to educate handicapped children until they are 21 years old. The system used should be the least restrictive that is appropriate for individual needs. For some children, this means attending public schools instead of special institutions; others who are more severely handicapped may have to stay in special schools. The idea behind this act is to normalize the children's situations as much as possible. Practical courses in vocational preparatory skills, daily living skills, and social skills are also important parts of the education programs for retarded children.

The last resort for a retarded person is institutionalization. About 275,000 mentally retarded people in the United States are in hospitals and institutions (Dunham and Dunham, 1978). Some of these are strictly custodial and do not offer any educational or training programs. Others now provide positive enrichment programs and a supportive therapeutic environment in several different kinds of residential care programs. Community foster homes and group homes in particular offer retarded people the security of a home environment plus the opportunity to interact with others like themselves and with nonretarded community members. This alone can often have a rehabilitative and motivating effect.

Roger Meyer on the job and at home with his wife, Virginia, sorting trading stamps. Through supportive counseling and perseverance, the Meyers overcame societal prejudice against marriage for the mentally retarded.

The book *Like Normal People* tells the story of Roger Meyers and Virginia Hensler, retarded adults who met in a group home, fell in love, married despite a lot of initial opposition, and moved out on their own. One of the goals that Roger knew they would have to reach in order to marry was to find a way of supporting themselves. He responded to the challenge by getting a job as busboy in a restaurant and working steadily, a fact of which he was understandably proud.

> During my several visits to the restaurant to interview people, I often sat with Roger at a table in the back of the bar. He would introduce me to people he worked with—the waitresses and busboys and some of the steady customers—but he

> was always pretty cool about it, holding back the emotions I know he feels. But when he saw Warren Mays come into the room, he got visibly excited, then sort of casually waved "Hi" to him. He had to literally choke back his enthusiasm. I realized that a brother is always a brother, but having a boss is an achievement. (Meyers, 1978, p. 165)

In most cases, jobs for the mentally retarded are hard to come by. Many employers still maintain that mentally retarded people are unproductive and need constant supervision. Roger disproves that belief: When *Like Normal People* was first published, he had been on the job—a job his own boss said had a turnover rate of over 200 percent—for more than five years. He was also popular with both staff and customers.

Many jobs that other workers scorn could be done easily and with enthusiasm by retarded people. The government has started an incentive program to encourage employers to take advantage of this potentially important labor pool. In some cases, the government will reimburse the employers one-half of the first month's salary paid to a retarded employee. Government counselors will help retarded citizens find work, and they keep in touch with the situation to be on hand should any problems arise. Sheltered workshops, such as those run by Goodwill Industries, have training programs that teach the mentally handicapped to perform simple skills and to develop good work habits. The emphasis is on helping individual workers reach their potential and to move toward a time when they will be able to support themselves, at least partially.

SUMMARY

In this chapter we have examined the nature, causes, and management of three categories of brain disorders: organic mental disorders, epilepsy, and mental retardation. Organic mental disorders are linked to specific biological damage or dysfunction in the brain. It is not always possible to pin down the cause, location, nature, or extent of the damage, however. The primary symptoms of organic mental disorders are impairments of orientation, memory, intellectual functioning, emotional control, and social behavior, all of which mimic the signs of certain psychological disorders.

The primary underlying causes of organic mental disorders are head trauma, infections, dietary deficiencies, toxic substances, tumors, vascular disorders, degenerative diseases, and endocrine disorders. Treatment is divided into two areas: medical and psychosocial. Since the organic mental disorders always have an underlying organic cause, they are primarily approached as medical problems. Medication, diet, surgery, and physical therapy are used to help people who are suffering the effects of an organic mental disorder.

Epilepsy is characterized by abnormal electrical discharges in the brain. Various external and internal stimuli can set off major discharges that are manifested as seizures. A seizure may have minimal physical symptoms or may involve violent muscle tremors or convulsions. In most cases, medication can either prevent seizures or reduce their intensity.

Mental retardation can be generally defined as subnormal intellectual development and adaptive functioning. In most cases, no specific cause can be identified, although the significant factors are known to include genetic abnormalities, metabolic and nutritional deficiencies, infections and toxic agents, head trauma, prenatal and environmental influences. The AAMD has established four levels of impairment—mild, moderate, severe, and profound—that are based on IQ and the ability to function adequately in more or less normal situations. Most cases of mental retardation are mild, and researchers suspect that the problems associated with poverty are to blame. In only a small percentage of all cases of mental retardation is the cause known to be a biological problem. Mental retardation is essentially untreatable; however, the mentally retarded can be educated and trained to various levels of self-sufficiency and can sometimes lead productive and rewarding lives on their own.

Conversation 6

When a newborn baby is brought home from the hospital, the family generally feels a lot of happiness and excitement. But sometimes—when the baby is born with Down's syndrome, for instance—the reaction is different. Meri, the sister of a 24-year-old mentally retarded brother, tells how this experience helped shape her life. Just four when her baby brother was born, she, her two older brothers, and their parents discovered that although they had to face some sorrow and some life-style problems, the presence of this unusual family member also brought a great deal of joy.

Interviewer: Did your mother have any kind of difficulty with that pregnancy?

Meri: She was constantly sick with every pregnancy, but there was no indication of a real problem. And since she is a nurse, I think she would have known if she had been in any danger or done anything differently from her other pregnancies. And she was only 35 when she conceived.

Int.: What was it like when your brother was first brought home?

Meri: It was very tense; I can remember it being very strange. But I'd like to stress that my parents were never ashamed of him. And they explained everything that they knew and that we could understand about the situation. Still, they also realized that there were a lot of people who didn't know beans about retardation and who thought he was insane, so they did not take him out a great deal at first. But my parents were never bitter. I never remember any talk of "Why did this happen to us?" We have a real identity as a family—we're very proud of our family, and we accepted this as part of our life, as in a sense normal for our family. This was God's will for us. I think our belief in God definitely had a bearing on our attitude. But I don't think anything or anybody was left unchanged. For one thing, he could never be left alone—he has always lived at home, and somebody always had to be in the house with him. That was pretty much my job.

Int.: What about your brothers?

Meri: They helped to some extent, maybe 30 percent of the time. But I generally stayed at home after school and helped around the house, so it just sort of happened that way. The only thing that really bothered me was that every Saturday for a year (when I was in fifth grade, I think) I had to stay home all day and take care of him. My parents attended a class to learn about mental retardation, and my older brothers were very involved in sports and activities.

Int.: What was it like taking care of him?

Meri: He played with his blocks or whatever, and I just read. When he was little I loved caring for him—getting him up and changing his diapers and doing that kind of thing. But I had trouble later on. I remember sometimes getting very angry with him because he did things that a normal child would not have done that I had to put up with. When he was ten or eleven he would pick up any piece of paper he could find—my homework, my letters, any little thing I had—and hide it. This would infuriate me! I was fourteen or fifteen, which is a rough age—your papers are very private—and I can remember screaming at him that I hated him. He understands when someone is angry with him and sometimes he would get mad at me in return. Sometimes my parents intervened.

Int.: Did they protect him too much because of his handicap?

Meri: Oh, no. They had always disciplined him. They treated him in most respects like they treated us. But they would never punish him for his very different behavior. They felt I was wrong in getting angry with him for being retarded. You can't punish me for having blue eyes.

Int.: What capabilities does your brother have?

Meri: He's been evaluated as severely retarded, which means he's capable of being trained to do very simple things: He can dress and feed himself, take a bath alone, dry the dishes, fold the laundry, set the table. He's on the level of about a five-year-old. He's still learning new simple tasks—he just learned to wash the dishes—but he won't get beyond that. Our family has tried to train him to do other things, but he just isn't capable. Communication is very poor with my little brother. He speaks in phrases and he gestures. We have all tried to get him to speak in sentences, and either he can't or he won't. That has been most frustrating.

He thrives on routine. In winter his school is in session. He didn't start school until around 1964 or 1965, which is when my parents took that class—it was the first time it was offered. It seemed then that the whole world kind of opened up; there were programs for children and awareness programs for parents. Anyway, his first program was more like a day-care center with activities, but as time went on, it became a very well organized learning environment. He's very happy in that kind of setting, with other children like him, activities, and a routine.

In the summer he has very little to do. He's home all day and helps my mother with chores. He watches some TV, but that's not generally interesting—first, because his eyesight is very poor so he can't see very well; second, he can't understand most of what's going on. He doesn't enjoy playing with other retarded children outside of school. He likes listening to music, especially rock music—he loves that beat. He still colors and plays with certain toys.

Int.: Is it strange to see a 24-year-old man playing with toys?

Meri: He doesn't look that old. He looks like he's about twelve. He's shorter than I am—barely five feet. He has the typical Down's syndrome face, but he has an excellent physique. My mother's a nutrition nut so he gets an excellent diet. He's strong and not at all overweight. I think a lot of parents try to compensate by overfeeding their children. My parents have really kept him very healthy.

Int.: It sounds like your family's attitude, for whatever reasons, was very unusual for the times.

Meri: He's always been an integral part of our family. He always goes to church with us—he's very accepted there. He's always gone on family vacations when we camped all over the eastern United States and Canada. And my parents take him to concerts: He likes the music and the color. They said he loved a Russian group that did dances.

Int.: What is going to happen with him in the future?

Meri: Originally, my oldest brother was going to take him—that's what my parents wanted. But that's all changed now. About three or four years ago, my little brother went through an unbelievable stage: He was continually irritable, whereas before he had the most placid, affectionate, easygoing personality. His messages were basically "I don't want you to bother me. Just fix my meals and leave me alone." I really think it was a sort of late adolescence, because he did many of the things that teenagers do.

During this time he started exhibiting violence, which can happen with retarded children. My mother tried to get him to do something—take some medicine, I think—he didn't like it, and he turned on her and started hitting her—and he's very strong. My father had to restrain him. This was repeated another time, again to my mother because she is the primary care person. That's when my parents decided that he would not live with any of us. Instead, he'll be put in a home—not a public institution, but a well-run and well-staffed private home. My parents had lately heard many positive things about some of them and felt that my brother would be happy there. But as long as they're capable of taking care of him and he has a good school program to attend, things are fine. He's at home now, and we would all like it to remain that way as long as possible.

I'd have to say that we've been extremely fortunate. The majority of our experience has been very good. I'm sure there are a lot of people who haven't found this to be true; I'm sorry that it has been overwhelmingly negative for them to have a retarded individual in the family. But there are worse things—there are worse ways of being malformed.

Yet when I meet people who find out about my brother, they immediately say "Oh, that's too bad!" or "Oh, how awful that must be for you!" I understand where they're coming from, but unfortunately they have missed the fact that children like my little brother have some very good effects on family life. They can bring a lot of joy into the family.

Int.: What kind of joy did it bring into your life? How did it help your family?

Meri: My little brother has been a unifying force. My family is made up of highly individualistic people who don't do much of anything alike: We live in different parts of the country, we enjoy different kinds of things, we have different life-styles, we have very different talents. But we were all fairly intellectually oriented. And my brother, with his simplistic outlook on life, was so balancing. He always brought us back to the fundamentals. It's a wonderful purpose in life. These children have very few aims in life: to eat, sleep, enjoy the few things that give them pleasure—and to give and receive affection. They're *very* affectionate—it's a trait of Down's syndrome children in general. And this creates an atmosphere of affection. I've seen it in other homes—a schoolmate of mine had a little brother who was very much like my brother, and they gave him the same sort of response. I realize that there are problems that need to be dealt with, but for the most part it's been wonderful having him there. He's just a jewel.

And also, because of my responsibilities with him, I realized sooner than a lot of people in my generation that life was not all fun and games, which I think was one of the best things I could have learned early. I grew up with a greater sense of duty, and this has enabled me to see other circumstances in my life as challenges—as duties—rather than as problems. That's how my parents were: This child came their way—they didn't ask for it, but it happened—and they did their duty lovingly and well.

Sometimes I'm torn over whether the fact that my brother is retarded is ultimately tragic, for him alone. Someone else in my family recently did something unbelievably horrible, and all I could think was how lucky my brother is: He will never have to face this decision. Still, I feel that he *is* ultimately unlucky in that he is not given the chance to make choices. And he can't enjoy life: He will never be able to read a good book or appreciate beautiful scenery; he will never experience married love.

I don't think this is really him, though. I feel that he has a personality and an intellect that I see only parts of—they're hampered by a malformed body. But his spirit and soul are not malformed, and they will be released in heaven to enjoy eternity as much as anyone else. The thought that someday I will see him as he really is fills me with real joy.

CHAPTER 14

Disorders of Childhood and Adolescence

THE VULNERABILITY OF YOUTH

DESCRIBING THE CHILDHOOD DISORDERS

Pervasive Developmental Disorders

Specific Developmental Disorders

Disorders with Physical Symptoms

Anxiety Disorders

Hyperactivity

Obesity

DESCRIBING THE ADOLESCENT DISORDERS

Anorexia Nervosa

Conduct Disorders

EXPLAINING THE DISORDERS OF CHILDHOOD AND ADOLESCENCE

Biological Explanations

Psychological Explanations

Social Explanations

Interactional Explanations

MANAGING THE DISORDERS OF CHILDHOOD AND ADOLESCENCE

Biological Methods

Psychological Methods

Institutionalization

Hugging his knees to his chest, watchful and suspicious, he sits in the center of the [*room*] *and can see all about him, how blank and open everything is, how much empty space surrounds him.*

Joyce Carol Oates, "Wild Saturday," in *Where Are You Going, Where Have You Been?**

The young boy described in Joyce Carol Oates's short story "Wild Saturday" perceives the world as a barren, threatening place and himself as alone and isolated. This is in sharp contrast to normally developing children, who view their environment as exciting, filled with interesting and desirable objects. Most children are eager to explore their surroundings; but some withdraw, becoming trapped inside crippling or bizarre behavior patterns. In "Wild Saturday," ten-year-old Buchanan is surrounded by adults who are either uninterested in him or unable to respond to his needs. As the story progresses, all these adults, including his father, barely acknowledge his presence. It is no wonder, then, that Buchanan feels hopeless and alone.

Children are very vulnerable, being totally dependent on adults—usually their parents—for love and physical care. When these primary caregivers are incapable of adequate nurturing, the children, unable to distinguish their own feelings of rejection from the inadequacies of their parents, are likely to blame themselves. To most children, parents are the ultimate source of knowledge and authority. When problems arise, children have no way of knowing that their parents may be at fault. Nor is it possible to seek reassurance, as adults often do, from the idea that this is a difficulty other people have, too. Rejected children typically assume that they are bad, unworthy of love—and that there is no way out.

THE VULNERABILITY OF YOUTH

Emotional deprivation is one of many factors contributing to disorders that occur in childhood and adolescence. In this chapter, we shall examine those disorders, which cover almost as wide a range as adult disorders. At one end of the spectrum are specific maladaptive behaviors, such as speech and learning problems, which affect an otherwise integrated individual. At the other end are severe disorders that involve the whole personality, including both affective and cognitive functions. A good example of a severe adolescent disturbance comes from the semi-autobiographical novel *I Never Promised You A Rose Garden* by Hannah Green. Deborah, a young schizophrenic, lives in a private, internal world—the Kingdom of Yr—over which she experiences little conscious control. In this world, the balance between calm and terror is very precarious—but far more real than the external, physical world.

> The Kingdom of Yr had a kind of neutral place which was called The Fourth Level. It was achieved only by accident and could not be reached by formula or an act of will. At the Fourth Level there was no emotion to endure, no past or future to grind against. There was no memory or possession of any self, nothing except dead facts which came unbidden when she needed them and which had no feeling attached to them. . . . In the world where she was most alive, the sun split in the sky, the earth erupted, her body was torn to pieces, her teeth and bones crazed and broken to fragments. (pp. 12–13)

How many children and adolescents are affected by disorders? It is estimated that approximately a million and a half children in the United States suffer from severe mental disorders. Researchers have found that of fifty million elementary school children, between 10 and 12 percent have moderate to severe emotional problems that require at least some mental health care. Among economically deprived children, the statistics are even more alarming, indicating that one out of three youngsters has emotional problems that need attention (National Institute of Mental Health, 1970b).

These figures are far from precise, for clinicians are by no means agreed as to what constitutes a childhood or adolescent disorder. It

* Greenwich, Connecticut: Fawcett, 1974.

Because they lack the experience of adults, children may cope with stressful situations in intense and indirect ways; often their anger and fright are expressed as "problem behavior."

is only in this century that childhood disorders have been recognized as needing special attention and investigation. It is not surprising, then, that different classification systems include different behaviors as disorders. Even the most conservative statistics, however, are startling.

Although there is no conclusive evidence that childhood disorders are etiologically different from similar adult problems, certain variations are obvious. Children and adolescents are developmentally different from adults—cognitively, emotionally, and physically. They have only begun to acquire the understanding and coping mechanisms they need to face stress and crisis. Their stresses and life situations are also different. If a parent dies, an adult daughter may feel the loss to be very great, but she has probably already dealt with separation from that parent and may have faced many other stressful situations—losing another relative or close friend, attending a new school, starting a new job, or moving to a new home. In contrast, a five-year-old child confronting a major stress-producing situation may have little prior experience to draw on for reference and guidance. Children, therefore, are more vulnerable than adults in similar situations and may react more intensely or less directly than adults.

For example, a young boy who loses a father through divorce may seem to accept the situation with little difficulty. Months later, however, his grades may drop, or he may suddenly get into fights at school or just feel "bad" for no reason. Children may be aware that they feel uncomfortable, that something is wrong, but they do not have the knowledge and experience needed to understand and solve their problems, or even to identify them as problems that can be solved. Therefore children—unlike adults—do not usually seek psychological assessment and treatment. Instead, it is generally a parent or teacher upset by the child's behavior who calls attention to a problem. Buchanan might go on to become increasingly withdrawn and depressed, but if the adults in his world do not notice, he is likely to suffer for months, or even years, without help.

There is much excitement and adventure in a child's early and adolescent years, but there is also inexperience and ignorance accompanied by periods of rapid growth and change. It is no wonder that author Flannery O'Connor once told prospective writers wondering where to get material that "anybody who has survived his childhood has enough information about life to last him the rest of his days" (1961, p. 84).

In this chapter we shall examine children and adolescents who did *not* survive childhood unscarred. Some of them, those suffering from *autism,* will never leave childhood—or even infancy. We shall look first at the disorders of childhood, then at those of adolescence; explanations and management of both will also be discussed.

DESCRIBING THE CHILDHOOD DISORDERS

It can be argued—and it often is, particularly by psychodynamic theorists—that *all* mental disorders begin during infancy or childhood. The problems usually classified as "disorders of childhood" are those that not only originate in the person's early years but impair functioning during that period. Two of the best known, and most disruptive, childhood disorders are *autism* and *hyperactivity*. A number of other maladaptive behavior patterns, such as running away and anorexia nervosa, are more likely to begin during adolescence. Few disorders are entirely exclusive to one age group, however, and some overlapping exists.

Pervasive Developmental Disorders

DSM-III uses the term **pervasive developmental disorders** for those disorders that involve severe impairment of basic psychological functions. Inevitably, more than one function is affected. For example, a child may have language difficulties, impaired motor development, and an inability to interact appropriately or affectionately with family or peers. The abnormal behaviors or symptoms that characterize these disorders are not considered normal for any stage of development; that is, they are clearly not a delay but a *distortion* in development.

Autism

Jason, a four-year-old white male, first came to the attention of the clinic at age 30 months. His parents became concerned over Jason when by 20 months of age he failed to develop any language and would spend most of his day rocking in his playpen, making strange babbling noises to an empty milk container or twirling pieces of paper up in front of his eyes. His mother described him as being a passive infant with few demands. By the age of two years he made his wishes known to his parents by pulling at them and would go into "a wild, hysterical rage" if his demands were not met. He did not seem to understand things that were said to him and seemed oblivious to most attempts at getting his attention. He hardly ever looked at anybody.

By the time he was seen at the clinic, the picture had not significantly changed. He had not developed speech, and his temper outbursts had intensified, especially when any aspect of his routine was changed. He began to be fascinated with numbers and mechanical objects. During clinical examination, he became engrossed in examining a digital clock radio and resisted all attempts by the examiner to free his attention from the clock and have him play with toys in the office.

Jason exhibits several of the distinctive features of **infantile autism.** As babies, many autistic children are undemanding, not requiring much attention. As time passes, however, they become involved in bizarre, self-stimulating activities

A therapist plays a body contact game in order to help an autistic child improve his communication skills.

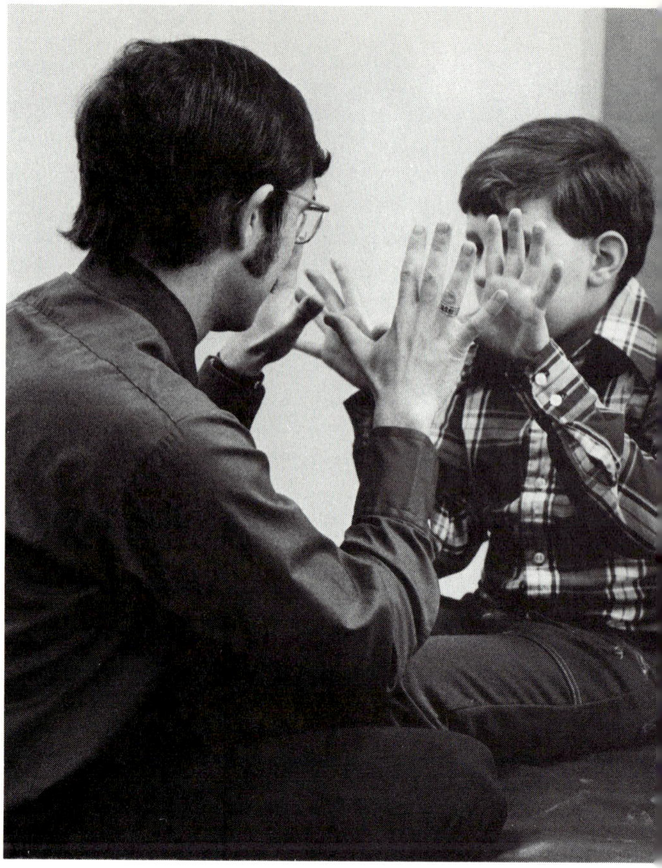

and seem to be off in their own world. They may rock back and forth or snap their fingers; head banging, hand flapping, and spinning are also common. Some autistic children, such as those who repeatedly bang their heads against walls, floors, or furniture, have to be prevented from injuring themselves.

The aloofness of autistic children is one of the most striking characteristics of the disorder. The Greek root *auto* means *self;* autistic children appear unresponsive to other human beings and uninterested in interpersonal contacts. Parents may notice that their child stiffens when picked up, doesn't cuddle, and doesn't seek affection. The child may even fight or scream if held or hugged. Appropriate smiling and eye contact never seem to develop. When autistic children do smile, it is for no apparent reason. Although they are sometimes attentive to what people are doing around them, they rarely respond to verbal or nonverbal communication. They often become attached to animals and inanimate objects rather than other children or adults. Jason preferred an empty milk carton and mechanical objects; other children may be fascinated by light switches or tools. A child might become obsessed with a hair dryer, for example, unable to leave a room or eat a meal without it.

The vocalizations of autistic children are usually random and meaningless, often involving repetition of familiar phrases or rhymes. These language disturbances—specifically, the failure to use language for communication—are an essential part of the picture of autism that was first described by child psychiatrist Leo Kanner in 1943. Kanner originally focused much attention on these language problems, but he later modified this conception, stating that language disturbances are secondary to the underlying disturbance in human relations (Eisenberg and Kanner, 1956; Rutter, 1965).

A closer look at the way autistic children use language reveals that in the rare instances when they do use language to communicate, it is only to give yes or no responses to questions. Therapists have also observed confusion of personal pronouns. For example, one young girl always referred to herself as "you" or "she" or even "Sally" instead of "I." *Echolalia*—a parrotlike repetition of what has just been said by another person—occurs in many cases. Some children repeat television jingles; others recite nursery rhymes or sing verses of songs. Ironically, these unusual feats of memory or musical ability helped Kanner (1943) demonstrate the strong intellectual potential of autistic children, leading him to differentiate infantile autism from mental deficiency.

Another defining characteristic of autism is

that the child anxiously insists on maintaining sameness in the environment. Many autistic children want to be dressed in a specific way. If a little girl is used to having her socks put on first, she probably would scream if her mother began with a T-shirt. Kanner discovered that children begin to display these symptoms early, usually within the first two years of life.

The incidence of autism is relatively low. It affects approximately 80,000 American children, or about one child in 2500 (Schreibman and Koegel, 1975). As with other childhood psychotic disorders, many more males than females are autistic—by a ratio of four to one. The children come from all socioeconomic levels, ethnic backgrounds, and family patterns, although DSM-III indicates that autism is somewhat more common in the upper class.

When we examine developmental delays and specific learning disorders later in this chapter, the differences between the characteristic behaviors of autistic children and those found in hyperactive, anxious, or dyslexic children will be obvious. The differences between autism and childhood schizophrenia are less clear. In fact, Bender (1968) suggests that autism and childhood schizophrenia are the same disorder beginning at different developmental stages. However, one striking difference between the two disorders is that the schizophrenic child tends to develop normally until the onset of symptoms. As Bettelheim (1969)

Table 14.1 *Shared and Unique Characteristics of Childhood Psychoses and Adult Schizophrenia*

Characteristic	Known neurological impairment	Autism	Childhood schizophrenia	Adult schizophrenia
Odd since birth or early infancy	Occasional	Common	Rare	Rare
Extreme aloneness	Common	Common	Rare	Rare
Mental retardation	Common	Common	Rare	Rare
Boys affected more than girls	Common	Common	Common	Rare
Ritualistic behaviors	Common	Common	Occasional	Occasional
Delayed speech	Occasional	Common	Rare	Rare
Pronoun reversal	Rare	Common	Rare	Rare
Echolalia	Occasional	Common	Rare	Rare
Disordered thought	Rare	Rare	Common	Common
Hallucinations	Rare	Rare	Common	Common
Blunted or inappropriate emotions	Rare	Rare	Common	Common
Perceptual disturbances	Common	Common	Rare	Rare
Abnormal EEG and/or seizures	Common	Common	Rare	Rare
Strange motor behavior	Common	Common	Rare	Rare
No improvement	Common	Common	Rare	Rare
Antipsychotic drugs reduce symptoms	Unknown	Rare	Common	Common

From Hanson and Gottesman, 1976.

has stated, "While the schizophrenic child withdraws from the world, the autistic child fails to ever enter it" (p. 21). This distinction is taken as a meaningful one by many researchers and clinicians. It will be examined more closely as we investigate the dynamics of childhood schizophrenia.

Childhood schizophrenia

The boy was brought to the clinic at age five years, eleven months, when his mother sought help because the child embarrassed her by his peculiar behavior, and because of certain purposeless movements of the upper extremities. She stated that there was something definitely wrong with him because he did not act like other children his age. She mentioned his fondness for examining women's purses, his running into rest rooms looking under commodes to explore the pipes, his getting on his knees to examine women's legs, and his desire to rub his hands over the hair of other children and then smelling his hands. Because of these actions, as well as a tendency to strike other children on the head, the mother stated that he needs "watching all the time." She added that the boy prefers to remain at home and to play by himself. When he occasionally joins other children, the shooting of a cap pistol creates intense fear in him. In playing hide-and-seek, he screams when the other child comes out of hiding and when it is his turn to hide, he insists that his mother accompany him.

During subsequent interviews with the mother, further "strange behavior" was reported. The boy likes to listen to the radio and seems to prefer popular music with a pronounced rhythm. He is extremely preoccupied with the daily mail delivery and will ask constantly whether the mail has come and accosts the mailman when he arrives at the house. Fender aprons of trucks are of particular fascination to him and he will crawl under trucks to examine them. He calls these aprons "rainwater" and when he sees a vehicle without them, he'll get upset and cry, "Put the rainwater on, Mommy, put the rainwater on." (Ross, 1974, pp. 224–225)

There are many reasons why this boy would not be diagnosed with autism. The first immediate clue is the boy's age. His mother seems appropriately alarmed about his behavior, which suggests that she would not have silently tolerated these disruptive actions for years. It appears likely, then, that her son developed fairly normally for several years and only recently began to show signs of being severely disturbed. In addition, unlike an autistic child, this boy does seek out human contact, although his approach is strange, inappropriate, or negative. For example, he rubs women's legs, strikes children on the head, and makes odd demands of his mother. We also notice that he uses speech to communicate, something an autistic child rarely does. His communication, however, is bizarre and inappropriate. He calls the fender apron of a truck "rainwater" and asks his mother to "put the rainwater on" when he sees a truck without the apron.

The boy in this case study displays many of the typical features associated with **childhood schizophrenia.** His thoughts are disordered, he has perceptual problems, and he is emotionally unstable—one moment he is irritable, the next highly excited, and then just as suddenly he goes into a temper tantrum. Childhood schizophrenics tend also to be phobic, to experience extreme anxiety, and to have problems with motor control and body perception. Another common symptom exhibited by the boy in this case is an excessive response to a stimulus. During hide-and-seek, he screams when a playmate comes out of hiding. Other schizophrenic children exhibit an apparent insensitivity to pain—a child might be burned by hot coffee, for example, and not respond. Deborah, the young adolescent schizophrenic in *I Never Promised You A Rose Garden,* deliberately cut herself with a tin can:

> The edges were rippled and sharp. She dragged the metal down the inside of her upper arm, watching the blood start slowly from the six or seven tracks that followed the metal down below the elbow. There was no pain, only the unpleasant sensation of the resistance of her flesh. (Green, 1964, pp. 57–58)

We should note at this point that childhood schizophrenia probably is not simply a juvenile version of adult schizophrenia (although Deb-

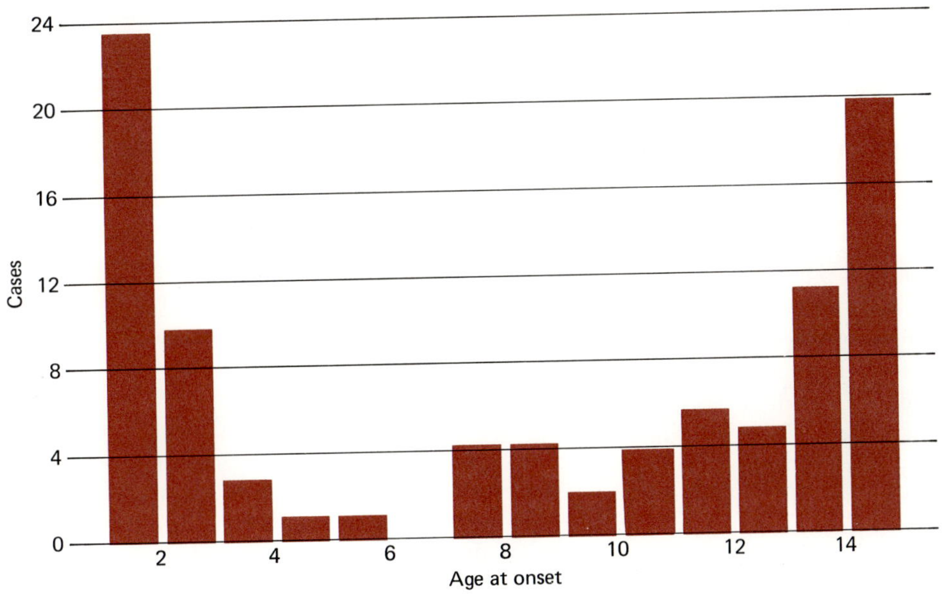

Figure 14.1. *Incidence of childhood psychosis by age. From Rutter, 1974.*

orah's disorder was typical of schizophrenia as described in Chapter 11). The relationship between autism, childhood schizophrenia, and adult schizophrenia is not entirely clear. This is perhaps not surprising, considering that it is not even certain whether and how the various types of adult schizophrenia are related. An alternative term for this disorder, **childhood psychosis,** lumps it together with virtually all the severe mental disturbances that might affect a child, and in that regard childhood schizophrenia is somewhat more precise.

In a follow-up study of 100 childhood schizophrenics, Lauretta Bender found that 94 of them showed schizophrenic symptoms as adults (Bender, 1970, 1973). Bender believes that adult and childhood schizophrenia *are* closely related. Other researchers have questioned Bender's classification system, however, and other studies have come up with distinctly different results and conclusions (Lockyer and Rutter, 1969). For one thing, the childhood schizophrenic does not ordinarily have hallucinations, as does the adult schizophrenic. With respect to interpersonal relationships, the adult schizophrenic may actually resemble the autistic child more closely than the schizophrenic child; the first two usually withdraw from social contacts, whereas the childhood schizophrenic may be closely attached to one or both parents or to some other caretaker. DSM-III has addressed this problem by using the term *childhood onset pervasive developmental disorder,* but thus far it has proved too cumbersome a term to catch on. Remember, then, that when we refer to a childhood schizophrenic we are speaking of someone with a disorder of childhood, who may or may not be schizophrenic as an adult.

As with autism, the incidence of childhood schizophrenia is relatively low. Researchers estimate there are 4 or 4.5 cases per 10,000 children (Lotter, 1966). Kessler (1966) reported that of 6869 children evaluated at various psychiatric outpatient facilities in Ohio, only 277 were diagnosed as having this disorder. Childhood schizophrenia is much more common among boys than girls; according to one recent study, three to four times more males than females are diagnosed with this disorder (Werry, 1979a).

Specific Developmental Disorders

In the pervasive developmental disorders, the child acts in certain ways that are noticeably different from most other children. In contrast, the **specific developmental disorders,** as defined by DSM-III, involve the *absence* of certain normal behaviors when they would ordinarily be expected. Rather than learning all the new skills appropriate to a particular age group, the child continues in a previous pattern. These disorders are therefore seen as relating to biological maturation. That is, symptoms of specific developmental disorders are normal for some stage in a child's development—usually for very young children.

The child with a specific developmental disorder generally has problems learning a particular competency—reading, articulation, arithmetic—which causes most children little or no difficulty. Such children usually show just one outstanding symptom rather than a more pervasive maladaptive pattern, although occasionally the same child will have more than one of these problems. Because there are often no signs of psychopathology other than the specific affected function, DSM-III's classification of these difficulties as "mental disorders" is somewhat controversial. It does not necessarily follow, however, that these children will just "catch up." Although many of them do, many others continue to exhibit disturbances into adolescence and adulthood.

Language

An African prince wrote of his first encounter with books and the written word, "I gradually came to understand that the marks were trapped words. Anyone could learn to decipher the symbols and turn the trapped words loose again into speech" (McLuhan, 1964, p. 84). In a rudimentary way, preschool children experience something similar. They become interested in and capable of using symbols and language to represent objects in their world (Lidz and Fleck, 1960). They learn, for instance, that different combinations of sounds represent their favorite animal or food. If children are not speaking recognizable words by the age of 24 months and phrases by 36 months, they are considered to have a speech delay. There are a number of causes for delayed speech, including mental retardation, deafness, brain injury, and early infantile autism. We shall now explore the speech delays generally associated with developmental delay.

Delayed development accounts for a sizable percentage of late talkers (Bakwin and Bakwin, 1966). An otherwise normal child with no other observable difficulties may not use words with meaning until the age of three to three and a half. Motor and social development appear on time, but meaningful language is absent. Once the child does begin to speak, speech development may be slow; speech may be confused, not well articulated, and not easily comprehensible. Some children do not speak easily until the age of six or eight. There is no relation between this type of delay and intelligence—Albert Einstein is a striking example of someone highly intelligent who did not speak a word until he was three years old. When the onset of language is delayed beyond three and a half years of age, however, a developmental delay probably is not the cause, and a more serious problem may exist.

Children with developmental delays in speech generally do not have difficulty with other functions. Most appear undisturbed by this inability to speak, but some may become angry because they are unable to express themselves. DSM-III explains that an *expressive language disorder* affects only the ability to speak; understanding or decoding skills remain intact. In some cases reading disability is associated with language lag, adding further stress to the child's adaptation (Chess and Hassibi, 1978). Like the African prince, children with expressive language disorder may feel that their words are "trapped." This can be especially frustrating when a child reaches school age and comes into contact with other children and unfamiliar adults. For example, a little girl who wants a friend to play with or who may be afraid or sick, is unable to express her wants and needs except in a very awkward and unsatisfactory way. As adults, many of us have encountered this problem visiting a foreign country. If we do not know the native language, we may have to resort to crude tactics like hand motions or facial expressions to express complex ideas or feelings.

A related language disorder of childhood is *elective mutism,* a label reserved for children who have the ability to speak, but for some reason or other choose not to. Their early speech development is normal, but as time passes they stop talking in certain situations. Emotional factors are a possible explanation, since many children who are elective mutes are also negativistic, shy, withdrawn, and timid.

Articulation

Defects in articulation involve faulty sound production or faulty use of sounds. A common example is lisping. In most cases, this involves the inability to articulate common sounds, such as "s," "z," and "ch." A child might, for example, say "cool" instead of "school," or "waf" instead of "wash."

In five- and six-year-olds, problems in articulation are common and not a cause for great concern. Researchers have found that faulty articulation occurs most often in younger children and lower school grades; only about 2 percent of college freshmen have these problems (Bakwin and Bakwin, 1966). Most often the difficulty seems to be caused by faulty learning, and it clears up as the child gets older. However, problems may also relate to structural defects of the organs of articulation (lips, jaws, tongue). When the difficulty does persist into adolescence or adulthood, it may cause emotional problems for the individual. The person may become extremely shy or withdrawn, or self-conscious when speaking. Any situation that involves being asked to speak or address a group may be avoided.

Reading and arithmetic

A young girl with a high IQ is unable to write down directions given by her teacher. She adds extra vowels to certain words and omits other words entirely. The dictated directions, as a result, look like nonsense, puzzling both the teacher and the girl's parents.

If this girl were evaluated, her problem would probably be called a **learning disability.** Researchers describe a child with a learning disability as one who appears to have adequate intellectual potential and adequate instruction, yet for some reason performs poorly in one or more academic areas. Clinicians may examine the child's intellectual ability, emotional development, social maturity, and family background. However, they are almost always unable to discover the cause for a learning problem in any one specific area.

In a class of 30, a teacher has four children who have a mild to severe *reading disorder.* One child has serious difficulty, and the other three read slower and less well than their classmates. According to recent research, this could be classified as a statistically average classroom. Schroeder and colleagues (1978) found that between 10 and 15 percent of elementary school children in the United States have reading skills one year or more below their expected grade placement. They also estimated that two thirds of all children who are referred for learning disabilities have reading difficulties. The most common of these reading disorders is **developmental dyslexia.**

Bakwin and Bakwin (1966) describe the following characteristics of dyslexia:

1. Difficulties in comprehending written language
2. Unusual clumsiness
3. Emotional disturbances arising out of the subject's inability to read

DSM-III further indicates that faulty oral reading typically occurs in dyslexia, that words are omitted, added, or distorted. Like the dyslexic girl who could not take dictation, these children may make numerous or bizarre errors that cannot be explained by phonetics or simple reversal of letters.

Some dyslexic children are only mildly affected, but others have more severe difficulties that continue into adolescence. This creates obvious and widespread problems in the person's academic life. The ability to accurately comprehend written material is essential to successful learning experiences at school, so children with reading problems are at a decided disadvantage. Their friends may be no more intelligent, but their achievements may be greater and made with less effort. Children with a reading difficulty may then begin to withdraw, or they may become restless and irritable. Thus the problem becomes evident not only in intellectual accomplishments but in the child's emotional life as well. Researchers do not agree on any particular syndrome associated with reading difficulties, but they do believe that these disabilities create many problems for a child, particularly during the school years.

A much less studied communication difficulty is *arithmetic disorder*. Children with this problem show no profound neurological disturbances, yet their arithmetic skills are significantly below their intellectual capacity. This difficulty is much less common than the types of reading disturbances discussed above, but it may at times be associated with a reading disability, particularly in the more advanced grades when complex operations are called for (Bakwin and Bakwin, 1966). Arithmetic learning disabilities appear to relate in some cases to more general visual (spatial) difficulties—the child has trouble differentiating a figure from the background, recognizing reversed or inverted letters and forms, or perceiving forms consistently. Such visual problems create difficulties for the child in the very early grades. When children are introduced to math concepts for the first time, they may be unable to make sense of the numbers. If they see a 9 as a 6, or a 3 as an 8, for example, this visual difficulty will interfere with the acquisition of basic math skills.

Disorders with Physical Symptoms

Another group of disorders related to biological maturation are those classified by DSM-III as **disorders with physical symptoms.** Among them are stuttering and the disorders of elimination, which include enuresis (bed-wetting) and encopresis (uncontrolled defecation). A third disorder with physical symptoms is somnambulism, or sleepwalking.

Stuttering

Stuttering is a speech disorder consisting of a disturbance in the rhythm of speech. Typically, it involves repetitions or prolongations of sounds, syllables, or words, and frequent hesitations or pauses. The person may begin talking in a slow and hesitant way, pause, and then "explode" with a final word or phrase, speaking very rapidly. For example, a stutterer may say "D-d-d-don't go in . . ." and after a long pause nearly burst out the word "there" as if spitting something out. Other times the person may be unable to produce any sounds at all.

Some stutterers have no difficulty speaking under normal, everyday circumstances but they develop difficulties when called on to make an important or stressful communication. For example, a student may stutter occasionally when talking to her friends, but she may be completely unable to give an oral report in front of a small class. She repeats the beginning of certain words, unable to complete them without much difficulty. At other points in her presentation she becomes speechless, her face turning red as she tries to continue her thoughts. Finally, in a rapid-fire torrent of words, she finishes a sentence. Yet this same student may appear in the chorus in a school musical, singing before a large audience, with no observable problems. When singing, whispering, or imitating other voices, there is usually no sign of the stutter.

It is estimated that in the United States some 2 to 3 million individuals—1 to 2 percent of the population—stutter (Bakwin and Bakwin, 1966; Sheehan, 1970). Stuttering generally begins during the preschool years, usually before age six. There are four to eight times as many male as female stutterers.

Hesitation in speech is common in children, and many people can remember an instance of stuttering at a moment of sudden anxiety or surprise. DSM-III indicates that between 50 and

Entertainer Susan Anton and Mel Tillis, the country-western performer who works to enlighten the public about the problem of stuttering. Tillis himself stutters when speaking but not when singing.

80 percent of children recover from the disorder spontaneously. This is most likely in mild cases. If stuttering does not decrease by adolescence, it becomes complicated and compounded. At that time, social interactions become more important and more stressful; as adolescents become more anxious, their speech becomes more disturbed, which makes interactions with peers still more difficult. Acquaintances may become impatient with or embarrassed by individuals with speech problems and may begin to avoid them. Interpersonal relationships may thus become strained, and the adolescent may begin to feel isolated and alienated. These secondary emotional problems may very well dominate the clinical picture in adult stutterers, causing even simple communication to be extremely painful and embarrassing.

Enuresis and encopresis

Enuresis, the more common of these two conditions, is diagnosed when someone three years of age or older does not have control over urinary functioning. There are two types of enuresis, *nocturnal* or nighttime wetting, the more common form, and *diurnal* or daytime wetting, which is less frequent and more apt to be associated with organic factors. A second distinction is made between *primary* or *persistent* enuresis, which describes an individual who has never had control over this functioning, and *secondary* or *acquired* enuresis, which is usually associated with a transient environmental factor or a developmental crisis (Sours, 1978). An example of secondary enuresis would be a young boy used to living in the city who moves to a new home in the country. He may be especially upset at bedtime when he stands at his bedroom window and sees few lights and hears strange sounds. As a result, he begins to wet his bed at night. However, once he becomes accustomed to his new surroundings, the bedwetting stops.

Enuresis varies in frequency, from every night to occasionally to only when the individual is under considerable stress or extremely tired. Usually it occurs from two to five times a week. Although the incidence of the disorder is unknown, it has been estimated that four to five million children and adolescents in the United States suffer from enuresis (Turner and Taylor, 1974). Different researchers and authors interpret criteria differently, so that estimates vary considerably.

Organic factors are involved in some cases of enuresis; however, faulty learning appears to be a more likely explanation in most instances. Before the age of about two, most children are unable to voluntarily control bladder functions. Occasional bedwetting in a preschool child thus is not cause for concern. However, nightly wetting by a school-age child merits attention, if only for the embarrassment, discomfort, and shame it causes. At this point, parents or professionals need to acknowledge the problem and help the child to deal with it. Fortunately, all but 2 percent of enuretic children spontaneously stop wetting by the age of fourteen.

Experts disagree on the relationship of enuresis to other psychopathological disorders of childhood. However, many children seen at mental health clinics display symptoms of enuresis as part of their presenting problem. Kanner (1972) reported that approximately 26 percent of children referred to a clinic for psychiatric or psychological services were enuretic. Of this group, 62 percent were male and 38 percent were female—again emphasizing the greater percentage of males affected by childhood disorders.

Kanner (1972) defines **encopresis** as an involuntary act of defecation that is not directly due to organic disease or deformity. Werry (1979b) points out that although persistent "soiling" after age two is generally referred to as encopresis, only 50 percent of children achieve bowel control by that age. He feels that age four is a more realistic one for identifying encopresis as a clinical problem since 90 percent of children have achieved control by then. Bowel control usually occurs before bladder control, and unlike bladder control, nighttime control is typically achieved before daytime control. Although encopresis is rarer than enuresis, most clinicians regard it as more serious. Like enuresis, encopresis can be categorized as primary or secondary depending on whether the child has never achieved control or originally achieved but then lost control.

Somnambulism

DSM-III describes **somnambulism** as repeated episodes of sleepwalking—that is, getting out of bed while asleep and walking about for several minutes, sometimes for half an hour. During sleepwalking, the face is blank and the eyes are usually open or half open. The individual does not respond to other people while walking but generally avoids objects. A child may in fact carry out many purposeful actions, such as getting dressed, making a sandwich, or going to the bathroom. However, coordination is poor and injury can result. For example, children can lose their balance or mistake a window for a door.

Sleepwalking may be linked with fatigue or stress. For example, a college freshman living away from home for the first time, taking many difficult courses and involved in several time-consuming extracurricular activities, may become anxious and tired. She begins to sleepwalk, but neither she nor her roommate are aware of it. Instead, they are aware of a peculiar mystery: Food, particularly sweets, have begun

Table 14.2 *Undesirable Childhood Behaviors by Age Group, as Reported by 275 Parents*

BEHAVIOR	AGE GROUPS (YEARS) 5–7	8–10	11–14	15–18
Disobedience	52.6%	39.8%	33.3%	28.0%
Temper tantrums	10.5	9.7	5.6	4.0
Shy, uncommunicative	7.9	7.1	20.4	20.0
Thumbsucking	10.5	13.3	5.6	2.0
Bedwetting	9.2	2.6	1.8	0.0
Many fears	14.5	23.0	7.4	10.0
Overconscientiousness	15.8	18.6	37.8	14.0

From Long, 1941, 43–62.

to disappear during the night. Finally the mystery is solved when the roommate stays up all night to study and finds her friend, still asleep, sitting at her desk eating.

When individuals awaken during sleepwalking episodes, they generally do not remember getting up and may feel briefly confused. If they do not awaken during the "walk," they may go back to bed unaware that the episode has occurred.

Anxiety Disorders

DSM-III divides childhood anxiety disorders into three categories: separation anxiety disorder, avoidant disorder of childhood or adolescence, and overanxious disorder. Children with separation anxiety disorder and avoidant disorder are afraid of specific situations, whereas a child with an overanxious disorder is more generally anxious or fears several different situations.

Separation anxiety disorder

Children with **separation anxiety disorder** are afraid of being away from their parents or home. They are afraid to travel, to visit or sleep over at friends, to go away to camp, or even to attend school or run errands. Such children cling to their parents, fearing that any separation will be permanent. They may believe that their parents will die or abandon them; or they may believe that they themselves are likely to die. For this reason, some of these children go to great length to stay at home. A boy might vomit after breakfast, for example, to prove to his parents that he is too sick to go to school. A girl might run outside in her nightgown on a cold day and hide in her backyard in order to miss the school bus. Unlike a psychotic child, this girl is quite sensitive to pain and cold, but she prefers that discomfort to the terror of leaving home without her parents.

Avoidant disorder

Avoidant disorder is more commonly referred to as *shyness disorder*. In a mild case, a child with this difficulty may blush and become tongue-tied when spoken to; more severe cases may be similar to the following:

Mark was a rather small, slender six-year-old boy who was the only child in a white middle-class family. He was in the first grade at school and described by his teacher as quiet, timid, and withdrawn. He had no friends in the classroom, seemed to prefer to sit quietly alone at his desk at recess and lunchtime and seldom participated in classroom activities. When forced to do so, he would become extremely upset to the point where he vomited twice within the first three weeks of school. The kindergarten teacher described a similar picture of Mark during his first year at school. Although intellectually adequate, he was severely underachieving at school as he failed to complete assignments and appeared preoccupied with his own thoughts and fantasies most of the time. His mother reported that this was typical of Mark whenever she took him out although he proved to be no problem at home as he was "a nice, quiet boy who likes to play alone with his toys."

Overanxious disorder

Children who are **overanxious** have many worries and fears and are generally very nervous. They are inclined to expect perfection from their efforts and may become upset when they find a mistake. They might draw beautiful pictures or play musical instruments with unusual skill, and yet still doubt their abilities, feeling nothing they can do is "good enough."

Such children usually appear immature, self-conscious, and inhibited. They may be afraid to be alone, but they are also afraid to be in a room filled with people. Overanxious children may be afraid of drowning in the bathtub or being killed when riding their bikes; they may be afraid of going to new places because they could get lost or hurt. They consequently do not play freely with friends or even siblings—they are too busy watching out for danger.

How many children suffer with anxiety disorders? Jenkins (1968) found that 287 out of 1500 clinical cases (approximately 19 percent) involved anxiety reactions. Again, more males than females are affected. However, since it is difficult for clinicians to agree when a child should be diagnosed as *excessively* anxious or fearful, statistics are difficult to interpret. Every normal child experiences some anxiety over the course of growing up. Nearly all of us can remember experiencing childhood fears—even intense, unrealistic fears—that would be considered developmentally normal.

As was mentioned earlier in this chapter, environmental influences also must be taken into consideration when we apply "deviant" labels. Buchanan, the child in "Wild Saturday," became uninterested in his world and withdrew into an empty, unstimulating room. However, the world he was withdrawing from was chaotic and unsupportive. In that sense, his reaction might actually be considered healthy—although he himself might become psychologically unhealthy as a result. Sex role expectations, too, may play an important part in whether behavior is considered maladaptive. Our culture still expects males to be "braver" than females, which may have a bearing on why more boys than girls have anxiety disorders. Unrealistic demands may be placed on a male child to approach rather than avoid a fear-evoking situation. For the child who is not very adventuresome, this may prove very stressful and could aggravate rather than alleviate fearfulness.

Perhaps the most crippling effect of anxiety disorders is the way they limit the child's world. Children who refuse to go to school or camp or out with friends miss many pleasurable and learning activities as well as opportunities to form meaningful and rewarding friendships with peers.

Hyperactivity

Hyperactivity, or **hyperkinesis,** has received much attention in both professional and lay publications in the last ten years. Hyperactive children are hard not to notice, for they disrupt their environments, causing problems at home and at school. There are constantly "on the go," wearing out teachers, parents, and siblings. They seem unable to sit still or stop talking. These children may jump out of their seats during a lesson or interrupt classmates. These symptoms have been given a variety of labels including *hyperkinetic syndrome* and *minimal brain dysfunction.* DSM-III classes hyperactivity as an **attention deficit disorder.** There are two categories of this disorder: attention deficit disorder with hyperactivity (excessive motor output), and attention deficit disorder without hyperactivity. In both types, the essential feature is that the child has a short attention span and is unable to concentrate on anything for more than a few minutes; hyperactivity may or may not be present.

Although children with an attention deficit disorder *without* hyperactivity do not move about constantly, they do have difficulty completing tasks, they cannot organize or plan activities, and they turn in sloppy schoolwork done in a haphazard manner. In contrast, hyperactive children constantly run around the room at school or home, and when forced to sit down, may constantly fidget, perhaps tapping their feet or fingers or just wiggling. They are also demanding and disruptive, constantly interrupting the activities of others or even their own activities. Such children may be described as a "whirlwind" or "tornado," for their energy seems endless and furious.

There is no evidence of subnormal intelligence with attention deficit disorders. However, researchers do not agree on whether or not a neurological problem is involved. Neurological signs often associated with this condition include poor fine motor coordination, impaired visual motor coordination, poor balance, clumsiness, and poor speech. These are referred to as "soft" signs (in contrast to "hard" signs, such as paralysis or loss of sensation, that clearly indicate neurological damage). Thus the label minimal brain dysfunction (MBD) is often used to describe this condition. However, Wender (1971) points out that about half the children classified with MBD are "neurologically intact." Wender further states that hyperactivity can appear without any indication of neurological problems. This question will be examined again in a later section when we consider some of the explanations for childhood disorders.

Hyperactivity usually starts early. Many times parents report that their child has always had problems with attention, almost since birth. Generally, a diagnosis is not made until children reach school age, however, and their behavior can be compared with that of other children the same age. Hyperactive children often are unable to tolerate the demands of formal or structured learning, for it is difficult for them to remain sitting or to concentrate for any length of time on one subject.

Researchers have estimated that more than two million children in the United States—between 5 and 10 percent of elementary school children—have attention deficit disorders (Soloman, 1972). Again, many more males than females display these symptoms. After age eight there is a decline in the incidence of attention deficit disorders, which very often clear up by the middle teens, although the reason for this change is not clear. However, Soloman has found that children with these disorders who are not treated are more likely than others to become involved in delinquent or other maladaptive behaviors during adolescence and adulthood. He suggests that this may be due to repeated school failure and family tensions arising from the time the individual exhibited the problematic behavior.

Table 14.3 *Classroom Behavior of Hyperactive Children*

Behavior	Percentage reported in 37 subjects
Overactive	100
Fidgets	84
Doesn't complete projects	84
Can't sit still	81
Doesn't stay with games	78
Talks too much	68
Wears out toys and furniture	68
Doesn't follow directions	62
Fights	59
Unpredictable	59
Unresponsive to discipline	57
Gets into things	54
Has temper tantrums	51
Defiant	49
Unpopular	46

From Stewart et al., 1966

Obesity

Irene Wintertree, an intelligent Native American child, received good grades throughout school but was very much overweight. Her father left the home and her mother was an alcoholic who many times was unable to respond to her daughter's physical and emotional needs. The family was poor and their diet consisted of starch and fatty foods. Irene's *grandmother made a special fried homemade bread, and it was the custom in their culture to eat this bread with meals and for snacks. Since the other children at school teased her and called her names because of her large size, Irene did not participate in activities with them but generally stayed home, watching television or doing schoolwork. Her mother was fairly involved with alcohol and other men, and her sister sought solace with her friends away from home, so often Irene was lonely and bored. During these times, and at times when she was upset by her mother's erratic behavior or taunts by peers, she found some solace in food. This pattern increased her weight even more, however, and she continued to be teased and rejected by potential friends. A nurse at school finally referred Irene to a clinic, where a psychologist discovered Irene was a very unhappy girl, crying out for help. (Leon, 1977, pp. 161–174)**

In categorizing **obesity** as a disorder of childhood and adolescence, we are diverging from the DSM-III classification scheme in two ways. First, although there is a category called eating disorders under the general childhood classification, obesity is not included. Second (but possibly more significant), DSM-III does not list obesity as a disorder *anywhere*.

DSM-II (1968) classified obesity as a special symptom with no evidence of mental disorder. This was the case with Irene, who was a good student with no overt problem other than obesity. But it's clear that food was a problem for Irene. In her case (as in many others) there were several additional factors that probably influenced her emotional state, so it's hard to lay the blame on her eating habits alone. Nevertheless, food is intimately involved, much as alcohol or cigarettes can be, and we feel that it merits discussion—especially since it is such a widespread problem. We include it in this chapter because the problem very often begins in childhood.

Technically, a child is considered obese if body weight is 25 to 40 percent greater than the average weight of children the same height. As Irene's case shows, however, obesity is typically both a cause and a result of emotional problems. Physically, an obese child not only looks different from other children but also may be unsuccessful in certain activities because of size. Heavy children typically cannot run as fast as their peers; they may be less agile in general. Thus they are often the last ones chosen to play many team sports or games, which may cause them to feel unwanted and disliked.

In addition, our society presently idealizes the thin person. Thin people are considered more attractive than heavier ones. Children teased Irene and called her "fatty" perceiving her as ugly and undesirable. In some cultures, however, being fat is not considered unattractive. In countries where there is widespread poverty, people who are overweight may hold a high status, heaviness being considered synonymous with wealth. In Irene's Native American culture, large individuals were not thought to be less attractive. In fact, it was the custom to eat a high-calorie bread several times a day—a practice certain to promote weight gain.

As Irene's case shows, cultural and ethnic factors have a great influence on the relationship between obesity and emotional problems. What is considered normal in one family or culture is regarded as abnormal in another. And children, who are learning these distinctions along with the other rules of their society, tend to be particularly intolerant of differences. Irene's obesity caused her to be rejected by her peers; this in turn retarded her social development and distorted her self-image.

But Irene's weight was a result as well as a cause of her social problems. Eating was a way for her to occupy her time and to feel better. Perhaps when she was an infant her mother held and cuddled her during feeding, so that she associated eating with emotional satisfaction. In emotionally distant families, food may be more available than physical affection, and children may turn to eating as a substitute for human love. Irene could not turn to her mother, sister, or peers, so she turned instead to the refrigerator.

* Adapted from Gloria Rakita Leon, *Case Histories of Deviant Behavior: An Interactional Perspective*, 2nd ed. © 1977 by Allyn and Bacon, Inc., Boston. Used with permission.

DESCRIBING THE ADOLESCENT DISORDERS

A young Australian boy, a member of the Arunta tribe, gave the following description of his initiation ceremony: "An old man produced a sharp kangaroo bone (ntjala). He stabbed my thumb with it and pushed the bone deep beneath the nail . . ." (Weyer, 1959, p. 237).

Most of the initiation rites that take place in remote societies are not as severe and painful as this one. But even in this tribe, where some of the rites are horrifying, most boys looked forward to the experience because they knew it was the way to manhood. When the initiation ceremony was over, they knew they would be adults, with adult responsibilities and privileges.

In our own society the transition from childhood to adulthood is not as clear. Many children reach puberty around thirteen or fourteen, a time marked by dramatic growth spurts and sexual maturing. They become what this society terms *adolescents.* Adolescents may be "men" or "women" enough to have adult jobs outside the home, yet their parents may still have control over their activities and schedules. This creates confusion. Where do adolescents fit in? On one hand, they may crave independence and resent having to obey their parents, yet on the other hand they may be reluctant to give up the security of childhood. These are some of the many issues an adolescent has to face and solve.

The demands placed on an adolescent, along with physical and psychological changes, may be disruptive for both the individual and the family. For some adolescents the disturbances are minor and transient; for others, difficulties may become severe enough to be seriously debilitating. In this section we shall examine both transient and severe disorders that generally occur during adolescence.

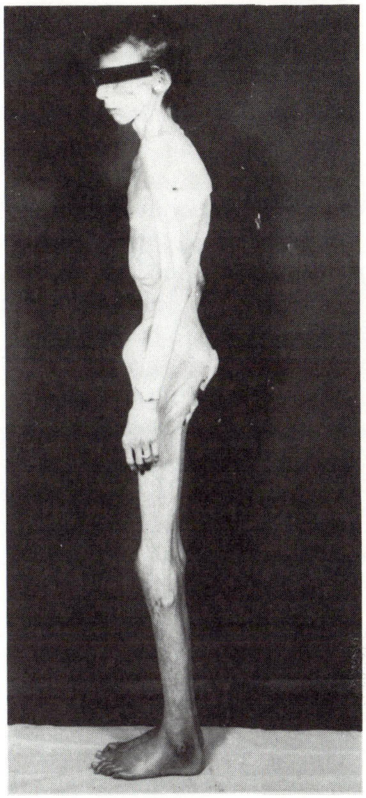

A woman suffering from anorexia nervosa, weighing only 47 pounds; after a year and a half of treatment, her weight had risen to 88 pounds.

Anorexia Nervosa

Janet Caldwell at fourteen was five feet two inches tall and weighed 62 pounds. She was a bright "A" student, but physically she was emaciated, her face hollow and her bones protruding through her skin. At twelve she had been 115 pounds, and her family had teased her about being "pudgy." She was quite upset by these comments and began to diet. She was quite pleased when she began to lose weight. Each time she reached a weight loss goal she decided to lose "just a few pounds more." After the first year of dieting her weight was 88 pounds. During the second year her mother tried to tempt her with favorite foods and attractive meals, but she insisted food disgusted her. Her father ordered her to eat, but she ran from the table in tears, unable to swallow the food she had put into her mouth. (Leon, 1977, pp. 145–9)

Janet's case illustrates several features of **anorexia nervosa.** Janet was very conscious of wanting to be thin and horrified at being called "pudgy." She lost a significant amount of weight, but then refused to maintain even a minimally healthy body. At the point where anyone else would have stopped dieting, Janet still wanted to lose "just a few more pounds." Generally, individuals with this disorder carry with them distorted body images. The mirror may reflect a bony, frighteningly thin body, but the girl may still see a fat or chubby figure.

This puzzling and at times dangerous psychological disturbance is found primarily in young girls. Some boys do become anorexic, but this is one of the few disorders of childhood and adolescence in which girls outnumber boys—in this case ten to one (Werry, 1979b).

Puberty is the most frequent time for anorexia to begin, although an individual may develop the disorder either later or earlier in life. Clinicians have occasionally discovered anorexia in children as young as nine years old. One adolescent may experience a mild "transitory" form of anorexia (with occasional relapses), while another individual may be severely and chronically ill for a number of years.

Female anorexics cease to menstruate, and both males and females may experience other endocrinological, electrolyte, and tissue changes due to deliberate starvation (Werry, 1979b). The term anorexia (loss of appetite) appears to be a misnomer, as patients do not really lose their appetite until late in the illness. For this reason, some authors (Crisp, 1970) prefer to describe the condition as a *weight phobia,* since the individuals are very concerned with their body images, deny they are thin, and go to great lengths and pains to avoid food or eating.

Conduct Disorders

At fifteen, Jeff has been expelled from school several times for aggressive behavior. He pushes and shoves his classmates for no particular reason and swears at his teachers. He doesn't seem to have any significant relationships with any of his peers or teachers. A psychologist would probably diagnose him as having a **conduct disorder.**

Individuals with conduct disorders manifest behavioral excesses (Bijou and Redd, 1975): Instead of withdrawing, like the children or adolescents who become over-anxious, they act out their frustrations and anxiety. If a boy feels suddenly upset or worried about an upcoming test, he may start a fight with a classmate or make cuts in a desk with a pocket knife. Conduct disorders are one of the subjects of a popular 1970s television show called "Welcome Back, Kotter." Kotter's "sweathogs" occasionally acted in aggressive, defiant, or childishly demanding ways.

DSM-III lists two basic types of conduct disorders: *undersocialized* and *socialized.* In addition, each type can be classified as either *aggressive* or *nonaggressive.* The undersocialized aggressive is the classic bully—perhaps cruel, hostile, defiant, and physically abusive to others. Such individuals must appear "tough," whatever the cost, and frequently steal or lie.

Individuals diagnosed as undersocialized nonaggressive are more childish in nature—rather than throw a brick through a window, they throw a tantrum or whine. They often feel rejected and mistrustful. Also in this category are adolescents who are exploitive and detached. They appear unaffectionate, may lie or steal, and lack guilt feelings. They are more likely to *cause* a fight than to *start* one—for instance, they may provoke peers by exploiting them or lying to them until finally a physical or verbal battle results. In general, their behavior resembles that of the adult with antisocial personality disorder (see Chapter 10). Males tend to have conduct disorders more often than females. They may be precocious sexually; often they are reckless drivers, and usually they begin to drink and smoke at an early age.

How many adolescents have conduct disorders? In a study of the behavior problems of 1500 children seen at the Institute for Juvenile Research, Jenkins (1968) diagnosed nearly one third of these individuals as falling into the undersocialized aggressive category. However, this may not reflect the actual incidence of the disorder in the general population, since the symptoms are more easily recognized and less tolerable to adults than those of most other disorders. A teacher or parent is more likely to be aware of the boy who is constantly in trouble at school or has been arrested for minor crimes than the boy who is anxious and disturbed but withdrawn. Even so, the number of cases of conduct disorders is great, calling for serious attention from professionals concerned with juvenile mental health.

Running away

What causes young people to leave the security of home and family? What makes them feel that they just can't go back home? The reason is often a difficult or unpleasant home life. Sometimes a father or stepfather has made sexual advances to a teenage girl. Other times a parent is physically or verbally abusive. The adolescent's parents may be unable to handle their own stress in an appropriate manner and the home becomes a battleground. Therefore even though many adolescent **runaways** feel confused and scared "out on their own," they don't want to face the misery or difficulties of their home environment.

Occasionally a particular crisis precipitates the decision to run away. A girl who learns she is pregnant may feel that she cannot tell her parents and instead leaves home. For her, running away is likely to be a one-time event, whereas for others it may be a recurrent one. In a small minority of cases, running away becomes a way of life—the adolescent wanders from place to place looking for adventure, or perhaps just for love and nurturance.

Sometimes a runaway does return home, only to leave again. This was the case with Rose.

Rose was an attractive, blue-eyed, blonde fourteen-year-old who came for treatment on the strong recommendation of Juvenile Court with which she was involved because of her repeated pattern of running away from home; she was termed a child "out of control" and in need of services. This was her third time "splitting," although the first two instances were not reported to the authorities as she left home and spent several nights at a girlfriend's house. The most recent episode involved her leaving with a male friend for another state, where she remained for eight days.

Rose lived at home with her mother and eighteen-year-old sister; her parents had divorced two years ago. She was having numerous problems at school, including academic and discipline difficulties. She had left home because she couldn't take her mother's yelling and constant bickering any longer. She described herself as miserable, lonely, and depressed.

It is hard to know how many boys and girls in the United States run away from home because many—or perhaps most—runaways are not reported. For those that are reported the average age is about fifteen, although an increasing number are considerably younger (between ten and fourteen years old). An equal number of girls and boys run away from home each year.

Delinquency

In *The Quiet Furies*, a mother talks about her son Tim's gang: "They steal stuff and sass folks who wasn't bothering them at all. They hang around that store and mouth everybody that's there on real business" (McNeil, 1967, p. 100). Tim is a fifteen-year-old male labeled as a **juvenile delinquent.** He has been in and out of juvenile detention homes and has recently been arrested for armed robbery. He sees the situation differently: "I cruise out cool on the street and look out for whose ass I know I can whip. I'm 'bad' man. I'm mean . . . they know mess with me and you die" (pp. 101–102). Tim has stolen many cars and threatened both a gas station attendant and his own doctor with a gun. He is the leader of a gang and "rises every morning prepared to fight."

Is juvenile delinquency a mental disorder? Technically, delinquency is a legal term, not a mental health term. Juvenile delinquents are lawbreakers whose behaviors would be crimes if they were adults. However, adolescents who run away, whose actions or words are considered menacing or disruptive, or who are labeled

Two delinquents attack a 52-year-old man who has just cashed his welfare check. The victim was prepared in this case: Suspecting a robbery, he was armed with a six-inch knife and eventually succeeded in frightening off his attackers.

Table 14.4 *Juvenile Arrest Rates for Index Crime Offenses, 1974*

Charge	Arrests	Increase 1960–1974
Murder	5.3%	224%
Aggravated assault	10.5	211
Forcible rape	10.1	147
Robbery	17.8	307
Burglary	34.3	139
Larceny-theft	37.4	166
Motor vehicle theft	35.3	33

From *Uniform Crime Reports*, 1974.

ungovernable—in other words, those with conduct disorders—may also be called juvenile delinquents. Tim's mother describes her inability to discipline her son or influence his actions: " He goes out after supper and won't tell me where he's going and I never know when I'm going to see him again" (p. 101). How many mothers have said or thought that same thing? Adolescents searching for a separate identity rebel against parental demands and control. Some of them steal or harass others; some merely refuse to obey their parents. Depending on the local laws and the attitudes of the police, court, and parents, it is possible for an adolescent to be labeled a delinquent for very trivial misbehaviors or for serious crimes.

Researchers have identified some differences in the behavior patterns of female and male delinquents. Bakwin and Bakwin (1966) found that male delinquents typically commit crimes against property: For example, they tend to steal cars, burglarize homes, rob stores, and vandalize schools more than they attempt murder, rape, and assault against other people. According to the Bakwin study, only about 10 percent of the offenses committed by young males were crimes against people. Young women are often labeled delinquent if they are runaways. Other common charges are larceny, sex offenses, and just being ungovernable.

Recent research indicates, however, that both the seriousness and the frequency of offenses by juveniles is on the rise, especially for females. Polk (1974) estimates that if current trends continue, about one in three juveniles will have a police record by the time they are eighteen years old. Juvenile delinquency thus is a major concern in the United States today. It has always been a problem, however, affecting nearly every culture and country. Delinquency is about three times more prevalent in urban areas than rural areas. Although most delinquents are adolescents, their antisocial behavior pattern usually begins early in life. Many delinquents commit their first offense before the age of ten (Clarizio and McCoy, 1976).

The backgrounds and family situations of delinquents vary, but most come from the lower socioeconomic groups, where they face poverty and other social deprivations. These difficulties are usually compounded by stressful home environments. For example, Tim had an alcoholic father who consistently beat his wife until he finally deserted the family. Tim's mother then began to drink more and more and became involved with other men. Many times the family could not pay the rent, and they were evicted. Tim describes their situation: "You get kicked out of one place and you move a couple of blocks to the next pig pen. One of my 'uncles' gets a truck and we load up all we got and go somewhere else" (McNeil, 1967, p. 101).

Of course, these statistics reflect only part of the problem. A family's attitude and circumstances may also influence the delinquent process. For example, according to Tim's mother, her husband saw Tim as "a punk who wouldn't listen to him and had no place to go but Jackstown [Jackson Prison]" (p. 101). In contrast, parents in the upper socioeconomic groups are typically unwilling even to think of their children as delinquents or potential delinquents, much less to have them identified or reported as delinquents. Regardless of actual incidence, however, there is little doubt that delinquency poses an increasingly serious problem to society.

EXPLAINING THE DISORDERS OF CHILDHOOD AND ADOLESCENCE

Why is Deborah schizophrenic? Why is Jason autistic? Why does one child have trouble reading and another one lie and steal? As is the case with adult disorders, there are several explanations. Some emphasize the internal life of the individual—these are the biological and psychological theories, which have figured most prominently in other chapters. Others stress the person's external life, pointing to a bad home environment, while others take into account the play between the individual's personal characteristics and the environment. Most of the explanations that are currently proposed for the disorders of childhood and adolescence are very similar to those for related adult disorders. Accordingly, our discussion here will focus on the most promising areas of investigation and any important differences between the adult and juvenile disorders.

Biological Explanations

As with adult disorders, the evidence for a biological influence is strongest for the most severe disorders of childhood and adolescence. It appears likely that biological factors are involved to some degree in childhood schizophrenia, autism, and hyperactivity. In addition, some researchers suggest that biological factors may play a part in learning disorders, conduct disorders, and anorexia nervosa. However, since this latter research is controversial and speculative, we shall concentrate on the possible role of biological factors—genetic and neurological—in the pervasive developmental disorders and hyperactivity.

Close-up: *The Controversial Feingold Diet*

The publication of the book *Why Your Child is Hyperactive* in 1975 drew widespread public attention to the issue of how to treat hyperactivity in children. Its author, Dr. Ben Feingold, an allergist at the Kaiser-Permanente Medical Center in San Francisco, advanced the theory that food additives—in particular, food coloring, artificial flavoring, and salicylates (substances similar to aspirin found in various fruits and vegetables)—cause hyperactivity and that the way to alleviate the disorder is through a carefully controlled diet free of the offending substances.

Feingold's theory has had substantial appeal among parents of hyperactive children who were concerned about the use of amphetamines such as Ritalin to treat hyperactivity. By 1980, an estimated 200,000 children were on the diet and many of their parents were convinced that it was working. However, there has been considerable controversy in the scientific community among researchers who have tried to test Feingold's theory.

The study that most researchers accept as valid was performed by Harley and his associates at the University of Wisconsin in 1976. Forty-six hyperactive boys (36 school age and 10 preschoolers) were observed over an eight-week period by parents, teachers, neurologists, and trained observers. Some of the children were placed on the Feingold diet and some were not, but only the University of Wisconsin researchers knew which child was following which diet. The results generally failed to confirm the effectiveness of the Feingold diet, although the ten preschoolers were rated as improved by their parents.

Even though researchers are skeptical of the benefits of the diet, many parents continue to swear by it, and their experience cannot simply be dismissed. Some psychologists believe that the beneficial effects the diet seems to have on some children can be accounted for by behavioral changes related to the diet, such as increased parental attention to the children. If this is true, it would suggest that parents of hyperactive children might look more closely at how the family situation may be contributing to the problem and how patterns can be altered to help their hyperactive child.

Genetic factors

Although genetic studies have not been extensive enough to justify any firm conclusions, their results for childhood schizophrenia, at least, have been fairly dramatic. One twin study showed a very high concordance rate—88.2 percent—among identical twins (Kallman and Roth, 1956). The weight of the data in favor of a genetic hypothesis for adult schizophrenia adds additional support. However, keep in mind that childhood schizophrenia and the adult schizophrenic disorders may not be the same.

Genetics appear to play no role in the etiology of autism (Hanson and Gottesman, 1976). But this does not rule out the possibility that a defective gene may have some influence. Most clinicians believe that the basis of autism *is* an inborn defect, but just where it lies and how it came to be are still anybody's guess.

There is some evidence that hyperactivity may be genetically influenced (Gross and Wilson, 1974). According to Morrison and Stewart (1971), 20 percent of hyperactives had a parent with the same problem; the average rate for controls was 5 percent. An adoption study by Cantwell (1975) confirmed these findings. However, other areas of research have been more fruitful, so genetics are usually not considered of major importance in the development of hyperactivity.

Neurological factors

For the most part, neurological studies for all three of these disorders have yielded very interesting results, making this the favored area for research. Researchers have found a relatively high frequency of pregnancy and birth complications for schizophrenic children, although the actual number of children affected amounted to only a little more than a third of the sample in one study (Gittleman and Birch, 1967). Schizophrenic children commonly have an abnormal EEG (electroencephalogram). A large percentage also show "soft" signs of neurological damage, such as poor motor coordination.

Many researchers suspect that autism is also related to neurological impairment. Kanner (1943), for example, suggested that autism results from an inborn affective disturbance, which, as indicated in Chapter 12, is strongly influenced by neurological functioning. In a highly significant study, Werry (1979a) found that autistic children, like childhood schizophrenics, do in fact exhibit "soft" neurological and EEG abnormalities. He concluded that at least in some cases, autistic children appear to have severe brain damage, either inborn or suffered during the birth process. Rutter and Lockyer (1967) reported that a significant percentage of cases (14 to 20 percent) went on to experience epileptic-like seizures as adults. There is now wide, though not unanimous, agreement that *some* cases of autism, particularly those that begin early in infancy, probably are caused by brain malfunction.

Another prevalent opinion is that the autistic child's odd behavior is due to a highly unusual approach to the world. It appears that such children explore their surroundings not by looking and listening, as most children do, but by tasting, smelling, and most of all by touching and feeling. When they flap their hands or bang their heads against the sides of the crib, these may be ways of gathering sensory information. Autistic children seem to depend heavily on their *kinesthetic sense;* in other words, they use sensorimotor rather than visual or aural data to orient themselves.

As we noted earlier, hyperactivity has been attributed to minimal brain dysfunction because some hyperactive children display neurological "soft" signs—clumsy speech, for example, or impaired fine or even gross motor control—that may imply at least minor damage to the brain. So far, no specific brain defect has actually been demonstrated, but brain damage is not easy to identify. Some research has indicated that a higher-than-average number of hyperactive children were premature or were born after difficult pregnancies (Pasamanick et al., 1956). More recent studies (Satterfield et al., 1974; Grunewald-Zuberbier et al., 1975) found a higher incidence of abnormal EEGs in hyperactive children than in controls, so neurological damage is definitely implicated.

Biochemical investigations also are taking place, pointing to possible abnormalities of neurotransmitter substances. These include studies on serotonin (Greenberg and Coleman, 1976) and the catecholamines (Shetty and Chase, 1976). Feingold (1975) found a relationship between hyperactivity and food additives, suggesting that some people are born with or develop central nervous system (CNS) sensitivity to certain biochemicals. He and other clinicians (Hawley and Buckley, 1974) have treated some children successfully with a controlled diet, but many others have failed to respond to this program (Goyette and Conners, 1977).

Psychological Explanations

Most psychological explanations for adult disorders focus on early experiences—childhood relationships with parents and peers, the patterns of behavior learned over the years, the cognitive view developed of the world and the self. In childhood, most life experiences still lie in the future. The impact of toilet training may show up in the compulsive cleaning behavior of a 35-year-old, but can this explain why an infant who is still in diapers screams while being held?

The answer is: probably not. The biological elements are so strongly indicated for the childhood psychoses and for hyperactivity that it seems almost irrelevant to search for another answer in faulty learning or negative cognitions. This is not to say that psychological factors play *no* role in the psychotic disorders; that would be a totally false conception. Perhaps the answer closest to the truth is that some biological factor (an inborn defect or CNS sensitivity) interacts negatively with certain psychological and environmental elements (being considered strange, for instance, or living in poverty), thus producing the disorder.

For the less debilitating disorders of childhood and adolescence, however, this situation may well be reversed: Psychological elements may be more important. Whether we focus on the Oedipal complex, learned responses to stimuli, or cognitions about self-esteem, any child in question is looking at the experience directly, without the filter of years that affects the adult's perceptions. Children have not had time to mull things over, try out new approaches, compare notes with friends, interpret and reinterpret. Most of their time is spent simply experiencing. Nor can they draw on the physical, psychological, or emotional maturity of the adult to cope with problems. Their view of the world is highly biased and extremely narrow. Even the adolescent is still caught up in the metamorphosis from self-centered and parent-directed youngster to independent adult. This means that the child's or adolescent's methods of processing external information are much less refined than the adult's, and the verbal information they are able to give to a psychotherapist is equally limited. Therefore interviews must often be supplemented by consultations with parents as well as with behavioral and psychological data.

The major psychological theories—for example, psychodynamics, behavior therapy and such related branches as the cognitive and social learning models—all have their particular focus. However, the theoretical lines of research are less clear for disorders of childhood and adolescence than for adult disorders because of two obvious factors: relationship between parent and child and the learning that consumes so much energy in childhood. Our discussion will focus on these two areas of the young person's experience rather than on the theoretical orientations of research.

The parent-child relationship

The parent-child relationship is of central importance to psychodynamic theorists; it has also been extensively studied by researchers of many different orientations. The most dramatic and tragic impairment of parent-child relations occurs when a specific loving caregiver is not present. Clearly, the loss of a beloved parent could make the child cling more strongly to the one who remains. If no nurturing adults are present, the situation could be much worse. Rene Spitz (1945) found that children reared in a foundling home and given little personal attention showed progressive and profound deterioration. Harry and Margaret Harlow (1966) reared baby monkeys on wire and cloth "mothers" with similar results. Given a choice, the monkeys would cling to a terrycloth dummy in preference to a wire one, even if they were fed on the wire dummy. The babies reared by these impersonal "mothers" did fairly well at first, but as adults they were asocial, sexually incompetent, and inept and cruel parents.

One major theory of childhood schizophrenia is the schizophrenogenic parent hypothesis, described in Chapter 11. Briefly, this hypothesis suggests that the behavior of a parent (usually the mother) can be the primary cause of schizophrenia in a child. The schizophrenogenic mother is described as overprotective but insensitive to the emotional needs of others. The schizophrenogenic father is generally passive and ineffectual. While mothers of schizophrenics have been found to exhibit more abnormal behavior than mothers of normal children, they do not necessarily follow the schizophrenogenic or any other clear pattern (Mednick, 1970). It is also quite conceivable that the strange behavior of a schizophrenic child can in turn cause the parents to respond strangely.

Kanner (1943) concluded that an innately caused disorder in the child is aggravated by

A loving parent-child relationship is important in encouraging a child's feelings of confidence and self-esteem.

a cold and unresponsive parent, resulting in autism. Bruno Bettelheim (1969) extended this theory, describing the parents of an autistic child as rejecting and cold from the outset. However, most investigators today feel that this description is not valid, and studies have not corroborated Bettelheim's theory (Schreibman and Koegel, 1975).

There is somewhat more agreement among researchers on the importance of parent-child relations in nonpsychotic disorders, such as anxiety and conduct disorders. Studies of undersocialized aggressive children have turned up significant evidence that their families were rejecting and harsh. The parents were generally frustrated and had difficulty setting limits; many times they were either unable to live together harmoniously or had separated or divorced. They also tended to be emotionally disturbed or antisocial and gave their children little guidance or affection. Juvenile delinquents tend to have similar rejecting and disturbed parents.

In a similar vein, children with anxiety disorders—especially overanxious children—usually have parents who are themselves anxious and overprotective. They tend to smother their children and may be reluctant to let them venture out on their own. Such overprotectiveness may also cause children to think their parents lack confidence in them and doubt that they could cope with complex or difficult situations. The child may assume, "They think I'll get hurt because I'm stupid or clumsy. Probably they're right, and I am."

Learning

The parent-child relationship may be susceptible to behavioral as well as psychodynamic interpretations. Anxious and concerned parents probably reward avoidance and withdrawal responses. They may realize that a child is missing opportunities for fun and learning, but on the grounds that it is "better to be safe than sorry," they may set punitive limits on "dangerous" behavior. A more social learning theory suggests that the child models the anxiety and fearfulness exhibited by parents and can become overcautious and suspicious as a result. Always anticipating the worst clearly limits the ability to participate in and enjoy activities.

For Jean Piaget, an eminent developmental theorist, mental development plays an important part in how children perceive a situation and how they react emotionally to it at a given time. Before children can develop fear about being separated from their parents, they must develop the notion of **object permanence**—that is, understanding that Mother or Father still exist when they are out of sight. Perhaps children who are afraid to leave home have not completely mastered this concept but believe a separation might in fact threaten the continued existence of their parents. For example, a little girl may follow her father from room to room, fearing that if she loses sight of him, he will mysteriously vanish.

Exactly how cognitive developmental factors color childhood pathology is still speculative at this time. An increasing number of clinicians are carefully and enthusiastically examining these theories, however, and we can expect more ideas and data as investigations continue.

Social Explanations

A clear distinction between psychological theories (especially those stressing parent-child relations) and social theories is difficult. The examples cited in this section stress the individual's external environment: How do the members of a child's family relate to each other? Are they affectionate or emotionally distant? Are the parents helpful teachers or rigid disciplinarians? In what kind of neighborhood does an adolescent live? Do the neighbors generally respect each other or do they constantly violate each other's rights and property? Finally, how do cultural values affect our perception of a behavior as abnormal? Data on these questions fall into two general categories: family patterns and sociocultural rules.

In recent years, researchers have begun focusing less exclusively on traditional explanations for maladaptive behaviors, such as impaired relations between a parent and a child; they now focus on overall family systems and patterns. For example, researchers are now studying the schizophrenogenic family. Lidz and Fleck (1960) believe that the individual personality characteristics of the parents do not foster the development of schizophrenia in a child, but conditions of perpetual stress and strife in the family can. According to these theorists, schizophrenia may result from a blurring of the age or sex structure in the family. For example, a mother might assume the role of a child and be unwilling to feed or care for her children. Therefore a young son may have to take on responsibilities that he is neither prepared for nor capable of handling. The resulting stress and confusion make it difficult for the child to learn appropriate behaviors for his true role. The child may even need to "get sick" to avoid an impossible and threatening situation. Disorder may be the only defense.

Again, the major emphasis here is on the environmental context in which children find themselves. The various familial and sociocultural roles the child is expected to play are important in this context. Are they reasonable roles or will they limit or frustrate the child? In some cases of juvenile delinquency, adolescents appear to be reacting to impossible or extremely frustrating roles. Cohen's (1955) early theory of "status deprivation" addressed this point. According to Cohen, the lower-class child is exposed to middle-class values of achievement and success but is hindered in efforts to achieve them. For example, an adolescent boy from a poor background might watch endless hours of television shows that all identify the advantages of success and wealth, yet he has none of the resources or training to actualize these dreams. Cohen suggests that this deprivation of status and resulting frustration lead to rebellion. The adolescent begins to develop alternative values and means, such as antisocial behavior, to achieve these ends.

A similar theory points to a poor adolescent's limited opportunities and the resulting alienation from society. Poor neighborhoods generally don't have the better schools, which means that the children who attend them don't acquire an adequate education. This in turn limits their chances of finding a job—and certainly of moving up and out of the lower classes. They then feel like misfits. McCandless and colleagues (1972) studied approximately 200 institutionalized male delinquents and determined that most of them could not read at the high school level.

In some situations and subcultures, a male may not be considered a man if he is not a member of a gang, which may be involved in criminal activities. Again, expected roles may be crucial in determining whether a child or adolescent will develop maladaptive or destructive behaviors considered deviant by the dominant culture.

Interactional Explanations

Having examined biological, psychological, and social explanations, we can see that no single theory entirely accounts for the development of any one disorder of childhood or adolescence. Many personal characteristics and situational stresses contribute to possible explanations. Is a child neurologically impaired or the product of an emotionally deprived environment? There are probably no simple answers. Our bodies, minds, emotions, and environments interact in very complex and subtle ways. Unfortunately, no interactional theory to date has proved comprehensive enough to win wide acceptance.

Certain theories do incorporate various factors. For example, one of the most popular explanations for schizophrenia is the diathesis-stress theory, which hypothesizes a genetic susceptibility to schizophrenia that can be activated by stresses in the individual's environment. Other theories of this type (Mednick, 1958; Meehl, 1962) also suggest that schizophrenia may be caused by an interaction of genetic and environmental factors. Still, we are far from being able to propose interactional models that incorporate all the factors that appear to influence any one disorder. Researchers are continuing to look for explanations both in new theories and in unexpected combinations of old ones.

MANAGING THE DISORDERS OF CHILDHOOD AND ADOLESCENCE

Research on the treatment of childhood and adolescent disorders has accelerated greatly in recent years. There is still considerable disagreement, however, over which approaches are best. First of all, treatment is always directed at a unique individual in a unique environment. Also, practical constraints frequently limit the therapist's options. As with adults, management—coping with the problem, trying to find the easy way out—often takes precedence over a thorough analysis of the individual's needs and best interests. The patient's legal status as a minor may also be a consideration.

Two main types of intervention will be presented in this section. The first is biological treatment, which consists mainly of the use of drugs. The second and more predominant type includes the various psychological therapies: play therapy, group therapy, skill training, institutionalization, parent and teacher training, and family therapy. Again, we shall avoid repeating information covered in earlier discussions of adult disorders, emphasizing instead the techniques that are most common for, or unique to, this age group.

Biological Methods

Physicians frequently prescribe various kinds of medication to relieve or at least lessen troubling behaviors. Although the mechanisms by which these drugs work are not fully understood, the method is popular because there is usually a beneficial effect on the problematic symptoms. Pharmacotherapy is used most often with those disorders that seem to have a strong biological influence—autism, childhood schizophrenia, and hyperactivity.

Drug therapy for young people is somewhat different from that used for adults. The major tranquilizers, a common treatment for adult schizophrenia, are prescribed much less frequently for children. Aside from their potentially harmful side effects, most of these drugs are not as effective on young children as they are on adolescents or adults (Chess and Hassibi, 1978), another indicator of the difference between childhood and adult psychosis. Phenothiazine derivatives have been helpful for children, however, because of their sedative and antianxiety effects. They are prescribed for autistic and schizophrenic children more than any other major tranquilizers.

For hyperactive children, the most common and effective treatment surprisingly involves stimulants, such as the amphetamines. Roughly 75 percent of hyperactive children are helped with these drugs. Stimulants may not decrease the child's amount of activity, but they usually increase the attention span, coordination, and control. *Methylphenidate,* marketed under the name of Ritalin, has been used extensively to help children become more attentive. At present, some researchers advocate using Ritalin for all children with attention disorders. The short-term results of pharmacotherapy are positive; but the children involved do not generally show any long-term improvement.

The widespread use of stimulants to treat hyperactivity, however, raises many questions. Does drug treatment encourage teachers and psychologists to focus on eliminating bothersome symptoms and therefore ignore the underlying problem? And what about the attitudes of the children involved? Many of them apparently assume that taking medicine relieves them of responsibility for their behavior: "It's not my fault, Mom forgot to give me my pill." Children who perceive things this way may well become careless about how their actions affect others. More generally, they may develop a distorted view of the world that impairs their ability to set and achieve personal goals. Parents, teachers, and peers are also likely to reinforce this perception since they, too, are aware that the child's behavior is not completely self-determined. They may simply see the hyperactive child as "sick," and therefore as special.

The practical usefulness of stimulants in managing hyperactive children probably ensures that they will continue to be used for the present time. The problem that remains is that these drugs must be used with as much attention as possible to the overall adjustment of each child who receives them.

The other childhood disorder commonly given medical treatment is enuresis. The antidepressant compound imipramine (Tofranil) is now the most popular of the many drugs used with this condition. The drugs apparently work by direct action on the bladder reflex rather than through their antidepressive effect. So far, though, they have been successful with only a limited number of children.

Psychological Methods

Most treatment of the more common nonpsychotic disorders is psychological rather than biological. In recent years, the trend has been away from long-term psychoanalysis, the traditional favorite, toward behavior therapy. This shift is evident both in inpatient or institutional settings and in outpatient clinics. The main reason is that long-term psychotherapy has had limited success (shorter-term psychotherapy does appear helpful for a variety of disorders in certain situations, however).

The problem with psychoanalysis is that children and even adolescents lack the perceptive skill needed to achieve the necessary in-

Table 14.5 *Success of Various Psychotherapies in Treating Childhood Disorders*

Disorder	Number of studies	Number of cases	Total improvement
Psychosis	5	252	65%
Neurosis	3	230	61
Acting-out	5	349	55
Special symptoms	5	213	77
Mixed cases	6	697	68
Total	24	1741	65

From Levitt, 1963.

sights. Because children's perceptions of themselves and the world tend to be more immediate and concrete than those of adults, they do not always appreciate the value of analyzing problems, and they may also have a hard time supplying the kind of information an analyst seeks. Moreover, both children and adolescents are usually brought in for treatment—they do not seek it voluntarily. They may view therapy as one more adult attempt to control them, and resist it. Nevertheless, certain methods have had some success.

Play therapy

One way of dealing with the difficulties just described is to use nonverbal methods. Child psychologists often begin their sessions by suggesting that the child pick out a toy to play with. This **play therapy** puts children into a more relaxed and familiar situation, which may increase their willingness to "open up" to the therapist. This opening up is not usually direct. The child begins to play actively with a toy, moving it, perhaps talking to it, and frequently hitting it or using it to hit other toys. The therapist can infer from this behavior the child's attitudes toward important situations and people. If the mommy doll scolds the daddy doll for coming home drunk every night, for instance, or if the baby doll is always alone and never gets a kiss or a hug from the mommy or daddy doll, the therapist has clues to possible sources of the child's problems. If the child's favorite game is smashing toy trucks into each other, this too is a clue. Sometimes violent play seems to serve as a safety valve; it can calm some children in general or help them to talk more easily with the therapist. The therapist may ask children to describe what they are doing, or suggest possible interpretations of their play, or simply observe them.

Group therapy

A popular alternative or supplement to play therapy is the group session, in which half a dozen or so young people meet every week for a period of play or discussion with the therapist. As with adults, group therapy for children and adolescents has both practical and therapeutic advantages: It enables the therapist to see more people in less time, and it helps the clients to work on their social interaction skills, which often are central to their problems. A typical group might bring together several third-grade boys who are aggressive or uncooperative in class, or seventh- and eighth-grade girls with negative self-images, or a mixed group of similar-aged children trying to cope with divorce.

The goals of these groups are similar to those of adult groups. The main difference, again, is likely to be that much of the young people's communication with each other and the therapist is nonverbal. The therapist has the

Close-Up: An Experiment in Helping Autistic Children

The world of autistic children seems so isolated and so different from what most of us consider normal that few people would seriously consider mixing autistic children with nonautistic children in a classroom. Yet integrating the two was tried recently in a limited program reported by McHale and Boone (1980).

Six second and third graders visited a special class of six autistic children aged six to nine for half an hour every day for a week, at which point another group of school children took over. When the program began, five of the six autistic children were nonverbal and all displayed moderate to severe disorders of social, affective, cognitive, and perceptual functioning. The nonautistic children were told beforehand that the autistic children did not know how to play and that it would be their duty to teach them. This element of responsibility made the visits more appealing, and the second- and third-grade teachers used the visits as an incentive for good class work.

In the special classroom the two groups of children were introduced to each other and the teachers mentioned the toys or games that each autistic child preferred. The nonhandicapped children were reminded of their job to teach and were told that the best way to do this was to be "bossy" (directive). During the half hour the teachers reinforced the play by praising specific behaviors exhibited by both groups.

Over time the autistic children began to interact with others more often and also became more familiar to the other teachers and children in the school so that greetings in the hall and other social interactions occurred more frequently. The normal youngsters in the program expressed positive attitudes toward the autistic children and indicated that they would like to continue participating in the program.

The positive outcomes of this program seemed to be linked to several factors in its structure:

1. The sessions took place in the special classroom, which was familiar to the autistic children and therefore may have helped them exhibit less "disturbed" behavior that would have frightened the nonautistic children.
2. The visits were brief and dealt only with play. In the play setting the autistic children may have appeared less deviant than they would have in a task-oriented situation. In addition, the normal children may have been more adaptable in a play situation.
3. The short period of time and the instructions given the nonautistic children seemed helpful. Aware that their purpose was to help, the nonhandicapped children may have tried harder. Also their energy and quickness were valuable aids.

This program, which is being tried in other schools, suggests that under carefully structured circumstances integration of normal and autistic children can help to enhance the social skills of both groups.

Two high school students work out a problem by role-playing in a group setting.

tricky task of keeping the level of problem behavior low enough to prevent physical or psychological injury while at the same time trying to interpret that harmful behavior. Over the course of the group meetings, the therapist also works to help members improve their adjustment, sometimes with verbal questions or observations and sometimes with behavioral techniques such as shaping (reinforcing the person's behavior more as it gets closer to the target behavior).

Skill training

A more structured form of treatment is social skill training, in which the therapist teaches the child or adolescent in a direct and active way how to cope with some specific behavioral problem, such as a speech difficulty or violent temper. Using such techniques as role playing, behavior rehearsal, modeling, and shaping, the child or adolescent can establish various new behaviors as alternatives to the old maladaptive ones.

Behavior therapy techniques have been successful with both autistic and schizophrenic children as well, helping them to increase or improve their language and speech as well as develop specific self-help skills. Children with habit disorders such as enuresis and encopresis also have been shown to benefit from skill training. A clinician or parent might help a child develop appropriate toileting skills by using instruction, practice, guided rehearsal, and reinforcement (Azrin et al., 1974). In a typical case, the desired behavior is broken down into a series of steps: The child is shown how to do each one, rewarded as each step is learned, and rewarded further when it is done without coaching. Enuresis is especially responsive to behavior therapy in which a device that is sensitive to even minimal moisture is worn to bed. When activated, it sets off a loud alarm, awakening the enuretic child. Once awake, the child can reach the toilet in time, and since the awakening was unpleasant, the behavior is reduced.

Parent and teacher training

Another important development in managing the disorders of children and adolescents is parent and teacher training. Behavior modification and similar programs can be considered truly successful only if their results carry over to the child's general environment. Most often this means the therapist must involve the parents in the program, and also teach them to use the same techniques at home. The therapist may also train the child's teachers to use behavioral techniques at school. Typically this is done by teaching the parents and teachers how to assess problem behaviors, develop and implement simple change strategies, and then monitor and modify the programs. The actual training may be done either individually or in a group, such as a workshop or in-service training.

This approach has several long-term advantages. First, parents and teachers are significant individuals in a child's life, and the child is more likely to respond to them. Second, they are generally attuned to the child's behaviors and can readily detect problems. Kazdin (1980) further emphasizes the importance of their attention and affection in bringing about a change in a child's maladaptive behaviors. The effectiveness of this type of training is well supported (O'Dell, 1974), and its use continues to grow.

Family therapy

Even more comprehensive than parent and teacher training is family therapy, in which one or both parents, the child, and any siblings are all involved in the process of change. The form of family therapy varies according to the therapist's theoretical understanding of the problem and the approach to solving it. Nearly all clinicians agree, however, that the family plays a vital part in the development and resolution of childhood problems. Family therapy is not always practical to implement, but it has had notable success with many children and adolescents, from schizophrenics to runaways.

Institutionalization

Clearly, the most extreme way of managing a psychological disorder is to commit the child or adolescent to a residential institution. The impact on both the child and the whole family is great—often financially as well as emotionally. Although a family may feel guilty about placing a child in a residential program, there are times when institutionalization is necessary and advisable.

The children who are most often institutionalized are those whose behavioral disorders are so severe that they pose a threat to themselves or to others. Severely autistic and psychotic children who cannot be managed at home make up a sizable portion of residential cases. These children ordinarily require long-term care (two years or more) since their prognosis is extremely poor even with the best treatment efforts. The other major group usually institutionalized is children and adolescents with conduct disorders, particularly delinquency. Most often they are committed by the state, though sometimes by their families. Their stays may be as brief as one to three months, and depending on the type of institution, they may show considerable improvement on release.

Residential treatment centers vary considerably in the types of services they provide, and thus the types of problems they treat. Treatment philosophies also vary. Some centers function as therapeutic milieus, while others use token economies; some are oriented mainly toward individual counseling and others toward group psychotherapy. All treatment centers aim to provide for the social, educational, and interpersonal needs of their charges—with widely varying degrees of success.

It is very difficult to assess the results of institutionalizing children with psychiatric problems. There is great diversity between treatment centers, and no uniform standard exists for evaluating their effectiveness (Chess and Hassibi, 1978). Furthermore, because most children are institutionalized for a psychological disorder only when the problem is so severe that the parents cannot manage them, there may be little that even the best institution can provide, other than supportive custody. For juvenile delinquents the difficulties are more complex. In both cases, however, the trend today is away from large residential institutions toward more community-based residences. One such project is Achievement Place, a group house in Topeka, Kansas, that provides a homelike setting for predelinquent boys (Fixsen et al., 1978).

SUMMARY

A number of disorders typically begin, or are most prevalent, in childhood or adolescence. Children with pervasive developmental disorders (autism or childhood schizophrenia) have severely impaired emotional and perceptual relations with their families and environments. Autistic children are unable to use language for communication; they are emotionally aloof and insist on maintaining sameness in their environment. These patterns appear to begin at birth. Schizophrenic children develop symptoms later in their development; they do speak and interact with others, but in ways that are bizarre.

Children or adolescents with specific developmental disorders fail to pick up some specific skill at the appropriate age. Their deficiency might be a learning disorder that involves speaking, reading, or arithmetic; or it might involve a physical problem, such as stuttering, enuresis, encopresis, or somnambulism. Children with anxiety disorders suffer from irrational fears: They may be afraid to go to school, to camp, or anywhere that involves leaving home and parents. Hyperactive children are unable to focus their attention on an activity long enough to enjoy it or learn about it.

Obesity, which often begins in childhood, and anorexia nervosa, which starts in adolescence, both seem to relate to problems of self-esteem and poor relationships with others. Adolescents with conduct disorders are virtually guaranteed poor social relationships by generally abusing peers and adults. Runaways physically sever their ties to significant people and places. Delinquents may not be as isolated as other troubled children or adolescents, but their world may be limited to a few city blocks and a small group or gang, and their emotional problems compounded by legal ones.

The first step in dealing with the disturbed child or adolescent is to identify and accurately assess the problems. This can be a difficult task. A boy who is terrified that monsters inhabit his room after dark may simply be overimaginative or may have an anxiety disorder. A bright, restless, independent adolescent might be labeled hyperactive or even delinquent. On the other hand, parents and teachers may not notice when a quiet, obedient child becomes withdrawn and retreats into a private fantasy life; the child may just seem shy or self-sufficient. The attitudes of parents, authority figures, the community, and the society all help to determine both what behaviors are labeled abnormal and what is done about them.

Explanations for the disorders of children and adolescents are as varied as those explaining adult disorders, and often quite similar. A genetic predisposition appears to be involved in certain disorders, most notably schizophrenia. Some disorders may be caused, and many are exacerbated, by emotional neglect. Change also seems to play a part—many children and adolescents develop symptoms of a disorder during or immediately after a crisis or a disruption in their environments. Problems like bedwetting, sleepwalking, and stuttering may vanish when the crisis is past. The physical and psychological changes of puberty—and its social pressures—contribute to most adolescent disorders. Because very few disorders can be explained by just one theory—biological, psychological, or social—researchers are beginning to consider combinations of causal factors. For the most part, these interactional theories are still undeveloped, but they suggest enlightening possibilities.

Biological management techniques center on the use of drugs. The phenothiazines have had some success with childhood schizophrenia, but the most common drug treatment is the use of stimulants, especially Ritalin, for hyperactivity. Most disorders in young people are treated psychologically. Behavioral techniques have had considerable success. Among the most popular therapeutic approaches are play therapy, group therapy, skill training, parent and teacher training, and family therapy. Institutionalization is usually seen as a last resort.

The number of children who are not able to adapt to their environments in healthy, productive ways is a disturbing statistic. Only in this century have researchers become aware of the seriousness of childhood and adolescent disorders and their implications for individuals and society. Children with problems may become adults with problems. Even in cases where spontaneous recovery seems likely, it should still be the responsibility and aim of adults to relieve or reduce the suffering of children.

CHAPTER 15

Problems of Adulthood and Aging

STAGES OF ADULT DEVELOPMENT

Erikson's Psychosocial Stages

Levinson's Developmental Model

The Midlife Crisis

The Elderly

THE AGING PROCESS

Physiological Changes

Psychological Changes

Responses to Aging

MANAGING THE PROBLEMS OF AGING

Disengagement Theory

The Family's Role

Institutionalization

Fighting the Institutionalization Syndrome

PREPARING FOR DEATH

Caring for the Dying

A boy at first is the man; unripe;
then he casts his teeth;
Milk-teeth befitting the child
he sheds in his seventh year.
Then to his seven years
God adding another seven,
Signs of approaching manhood
show in the bud.
Still, in the third of the sevens
his limbs are growing; his chin
Touched with fleecy down,
the bloom of the cheek is gone.
Now, in the fourth of the sevens
ripen to greatest completeness
The powers of the man,
and his worth becomes plain to see.
In the fifth he bethinks him that
this is the season for courting,
Bethinks him that sons will preserve
and continue his line.
Now in the sixth his mind,
ever open to virtue,
Broadens, and never inspires him
to profitless deeds;
Seven times seven, and eight;
the tongue and the mind
For fourteen years together
are now at their best.
Still in the ninth is he able,
but never so nimble
In speech and in wit as he was
in the days of his prime.
Who to the tenth has attained,
and has lived to complete it,
Has come to the time to depart
on the ebb-tide of Death.

Solon*

The material to be covered in this chapter is not (or is not yet) included in DSM-III or any other official listing of disorders. Yet the problems people encounter as they mature and approach old age can be severe. Indeed, most of the disorders that have been described in this book are at least partially the result of the stresses of various life stages. It's entirely possible that as more and more research is focused on these problems, they too will become part of future revisions of the DSM. Freud's theory of psychosexual development generated an interest in childhood development; now perhaps research will turn to the opposite end of the human development process: adulthood and aging.

* Translated by A. L. Vischer in *Old Age: Its Compensations and Rewards.* Hemel Hempstead, England: George Allen and Unwin, Ltd., 1947.

STAGES OF ADULT DEVELOPMENT

The idea that we develop by stages is not particularly new: Solon, after all, lived in the seventh century B.C. But it has only been in the last two decades that we have become more actively aware of some of the problems that regularly strike older age groups in our society. This in turn has led to a slight increase of data about adulthood stages, but our knowledge is still far from complete. Nevertheless, some theories about adult development have been proposed. Of particular interest are the theories of Erikson and of Levinson and colleagues.

Erikson's Psychosocial Stages

Erikson was a student of Freud who did not accept Freud's conceptualization of the psychosexual stages of personality development. Instead, he thought that the emphasis should be on social interactions rather than on libidinal energy; that human personality continues to develop throughout life; that each development stage is characterized by a particular conflict that must be at least partially resolved in order for growth to succeeding stages to continue.

Erikson (1959) postulated eight stages of development from birth to death. Although the later stages are of primary interest to us now, a brief description of all eight is essential for an understanding of Erikson's process:

1. Trust vs. mistrust (to age 1). The kind of care given to an infant determines whether trust—or mistrust—will eventually be part of the adult personality. Through loving attention,

the infant learns to trust other people and to view the environment as orderly; if such care is denied, the opposite happens.

2. Autonomy vs. doubt (ages 2 and 3). As the child's mental and motor abilities emerge, so does the sense of independence. Given the freedom to explore new abilities—and thus the world—children develop a sense of personal adequacy from the control they wield over their own small universe. If restricted, doubt sets in, which generally leads to loss of control and often to shame over personal inadequacy.

3. Initiative vs. guilt (ages 4 and 5). During the next two years, the child continues to explore an ever-widening world. If parents respond positively to activities initiated by the child, initiative results; otherwise, the child will feel that an intrusion has been made on a closed adult society.

4. Industry vs. inferiority (ages 6 to 11). In the last years of childhood, the child becomes more interested in how things work, in organizing groups, in establishing rules. If adults continually joke about these efforts, the child develops a sense of inferiority.

5. Identity vs. role confusion (ages 12 to 18). Beginning to look at the world from many different perspectives, the adolescent learns to change behaviors and attitudes for different situations. This can cause a great deal of confusion about which aspect of the personality is "real," leading to what Erikson termed an **iden-**

The decisions to marry and become parents mark turning points in the development of many young adults; an important issue involves forming a variety of intimate relationships without losing one's sense of personal identity.

tity crisis. The more balanced adolescent learns to integrate the many facets into an acceptable and coherent whole.

6. Intimacy vs. isolation (young adult years). In early adulthood, the person attempts to form close personal relationships even though at times the newfound identity seems likely to be engulfed. The positive resolution is to redefine that identity to incorporate the relationship; the negative is to withdraw.

7. Generativity vs. self-absorption (middle age). At midlife, the person's focus should be on extra-personal concerns: family, society, future generations. If previous conflicts have not been resolved positively, however, the person becomes absorbed in personal matters, such as health and material comfort.

8. Integrity vs. despair (old age). The final state is one of reflection on the past and on the "last adventure": death. Ideally, it should be rewarding and lead to a sense of fulfillment. Those who feel cheated, who feel that life was not satisfying, cannot hope to experience that sense of personal integrity.

According to Erikson, it is not necessary to resolve each stage ideally in order to achieve later stages; an infant who learns mistrust can go on to become autonomous, for instance. But the manner in which each stage is resolved colors each succeeding conflict resolution.

Levinson's Developmental Model

An even more descriptive framework that defines stages in adult male development has been proposed by Levinson and colleagues (1976). According to these researchers, there appear to be six distinct periods within adulthood, each involving a particular developmental task the person must accomplish. Most adults seem to pass through these stages fairly smoothly. When a person does run into difficulties or fails to achieve the goals of a given stage, those unresolved problems can impede further development.

Stage one. The first stage is the transition from adolescence to adulthood, which ordinarily lasts three to five years. The person's developmental task in this stage is to separate from the family and establish an independent, self-sufficient life-style. This typically involves becoming less financially dependent on parents, entering new social roles and living arrangements, and taking on greater responsibility for personal actions and needs. Some young adults accomplish this task by taking jobs; others enter a transitional institution, such as the military or college, where the process is more gradual.

Stage two. Once independence has been achieved, the individual begins the work of being an adult. The second stage involves the exploration and development of adult friendships, sexual relationships, and career responsibilities, through which individuals develop a sense of identity and purpose. Although they need not be absolutely certain of the course of their life at this stage, it is necessary to fashion a temporary life structure that links them to adult society and provides a set of priorities for further growth.

Stage three. This stage, which usually begins in the early thirties, involves settling down and creating a stable adult life-style. During this period individuals establish a place in society, making and pursuing more long-term plans and goals. At this point they also develop a set of expectations for the future.

Stage four. During this stage, which usually occurs in the middle to late thirties, their major task is to become established as truly autonomous and self-sufficient adults. Social recognition and success are sought.

Stage five. This is a transitional stage between earlier phases and later periods of greater stability. In their early forties, people begin to question the value of their accomplishments. Whether or not there has been success in achieving the goals set earlier, most people perceive a gap between their achievements and what they really want from life. This is an interval of doubt and self-examination, which is resolved in the final developmental period.

Stage six. Restabilization occurs during this stage. Individuals accept the successes and failures of earlier periods and develop a life struc-

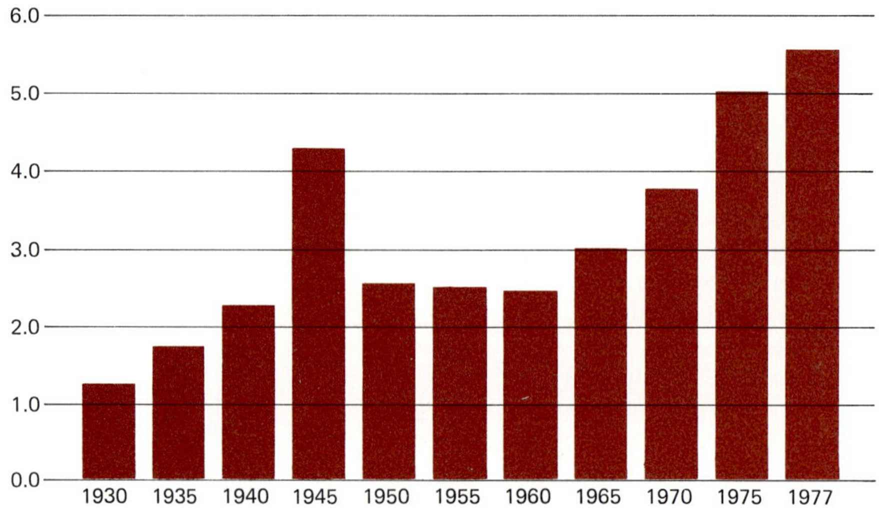

Figure 15.1. *According to Erikson, a major difficulty of the young adult years (his Stage 6) is establishing close personal relationships, such as that of marriage, without losing the sense of personal identity. These divorce rates (per 1000 population) indicate just how serious that problem can be. From Statistical Abstract of the United States, 1977.*

ture consistent with their age and accomplishments. They become resigned to reality and to the decreasing likelihood that they will make any further major changes. The result is a greater acceptance of self, spouse, family, and friends that allows them to move contentedly into old age.

Erikson's stages, formulated nearly twenty years ago, seem vague and nonspecific when contrasted with Levinson's—which clearly indicates how much more complete our knowledge is now. In the past decade, books like *Passages* and *Transitions*, which translate for public consumption the recent notions of adult phase growth, have gained popularity. The fact that they were published in a time when personal identity was an extremely important concept probably enhanced their appeal. Another important factor is that the population of maturing adults is burgeoning, a point that will be developed in a later section.

Another difference between these two models is that, as we noted previously, Levinson feels that when the goals of a given stage are not met, the person cannot proceed into the next stage. In addition, of course, this can also produce considerable stress. If in the fifth stage, the *midlife transition*, the person sees only a life of failure, this period becomes so tension-filled that it turns into a **midlife crisis.**

The Midlife Crisis

The term "midlife crisis" was first used in 1965 by Elliott Jacques, a London psychologist who studied the lives of several renowned artists. Jacques found that many of them began or ended their careers around the age of 40. Paul Gauguin, for example, left a lucrative banking career to begin life as a painter at age 35. Others "burned out," either creatively or literally. In *The Crack Up,* F. Scott Fitzgerald wrote about his realization that he had been draining his physical and spiritual resources far too long. Yet he did not slow down, and five years after writing that book, at the age of 44, he died.

This critical life period is similar in some ways to adolescence. It is a contradictory time: On one hand, the responsibilities of parenthood lighten; professional obligations become less demanding; and more time, energy, and money are available for leisure activities. On the other hand, it can be a time of stressful adjustment to change—children leave home, the physiological changes of aging become more pronounced, career development peaks. Sometimes a parent dies, confronting the middle-aged person with mortality. More often, however, comes the realization that time to make a mark on the world is running out. The person who has not yet published a novel or won the corporate presidency may suddenly find those goals out of reach.

Some middle-aged people respond by acting almost like adolescents—seeking a new identity, becoming involved with a younger partner, whatever seems likely to strengthen their hold on their vanishing youth. This generally results in further life upheavals, such as divorce or a career change, which can thrust individuals into new challenges that it may have been better to avoid. Rona Jaffe (1980) has described the difficult position of women this age who suddenly find themselves in the job market for the first time. A classmate of Jaffe's laments:

> I am worth about as much as yesterday's newspaper. I am told "go support yourself." Prospective employers say I have no work experience. My success as a mother doesn't count, even though it is supposed to be the most sacred job on earth. My volunteer work doesn't count, even though it was the "right" thing to do. My Radcliffe degree doesn't count because it's 25 years old. My husband tells me I "failed." (p. 138)*

Whether middle age is perceived as a time of stressful change or of new-found freedom, most researchers agree that it is usually marked by reflective introspection (Rappaport, 1976). People begin to evaluate the past and present and decide how to best utilize their remaining time. For some individuals the midlife crisis can result in depression and a sense of futility; for others it can lead to personal fulfillment. The people who are most successful during this period are those who critically and realistically reassess their lifetime aspirations, renouncing some and readjusting others (Rayner, 1971). In other words, they are not afraid to face the challenges of growing old.

* Rona Jaffe, "A real-life class reunion," *Ladies Home Journal*, June 1980.

The Elderly

Growing old is a prospect most people will have to face. For many, the realization that youth is gone can be very bitter. They deeply regret what they view as negative changes in their bodies, in their life-styles, in their social status, and see old age only as the last phase before death. For others this prospect is bittersweet. They too may be saddened by those things left behind, but they recognize that, even with limitations, life can still be pleasurable and rewarding. All of us have seen examples of these two different attitudes toward aging. On one hand, we see people like painter Georgia O'Keeffe and President Ronald Reagan—well past their supposed prime but still living vital and active lives. On the other hand, we see the elderly in dreary nursing homes who spend their days doing nothing in particular—except wishing that things were better.

Most of us probably have the wrong idea about how the typical elderly person lives. The reality is that most elderly feel good about their aging, look forward to each new day with enthusiasm, and are generally happy (Harris,

Table 15.1 *The Elderly Population*

Year	Total population (millions)	Number of aged (millions)	Percent of total population
1960	180.7	17	9.4
1965	194.3	18	9.2
1970	204.9	20	9.7
1974	211.9	22	10.4
1975	213.5	22	10.3
1976	215.1	23	10.7
1980*	222.3	25	11.2
1985	233.5	27	11.6
1990	244.8	30	12.2
2000	263.0	32	12.2

* Total population estimates for 1980–2000 were arrived at by taking an average of three separate Bureau of the Census projections.

From U.S. Bureau of the Census, 1977.

1975). Many misconceptions about aging and about the elderly population have been largely accepted as fact in the past, mainly because not much research was conducted to find out the truth. That picture is now in the process of changing.

The demographic profile

According to statistics compiled in 1977 by the U.S. Bureau of the Census, 23 million Americans—11 percent of our population—are 65 or older, which is the official definition of elderly. However, that same report projected that this group will comprise 20 to 25 percent of the population by the year 2030. This is the result of several factors, primarily that the post–World War II "baby boom" children are now hitting middle-age. Also, modern medical technology and a better standard of living have cut the mortality rate of every age group and lengthened the average life span.

A quarter of the population is an incredibly large percentage of elderly—the largest in U.S. history (Crandall, 1980). We must become more knowledgeable about the special needs and problems of this rapidly growing segment of society. First of all, however, we need to understand the aging process.

Close-up: Controlling the Aging Process

People have dreamed of eternal youth since earliest history. The old Gaelic idea of heaven was Tir Nan Og, the Land of the Young, a shadowy land somewhere west of Ireland in the mists of the North Atlantic. In the Middle Ages, alchemists searched for the formula for eternal youth in *this* life rather than waiting for the next. The sixteenth-century explorer Ponce de Leon trekked through the wilds of the New World searching for the legendary Fountain of Youth. The scientific age has not dimmed that zeal, but it has changed the focus of attention. Now, researchers studying cell dynamics believe that in the future it may be possible to control the aging process.

As noted in the text, one biological explanation of aging is error theory, which states that the sensitive DNA present in each individual cell becomes damaged by the cell's activity and by external agents (x-rays, for instance). Over a period of time, the cell may start to malfunction from an accumulation of errors. The cell has the capability of repairing mistakes in the DNA code, but eventually the errors proliferate too fast for the cell to repair itself in time. The result is aging. In support of this hypothesis is the fact that almost all diseases linked to DNA repair deficiency mimic aging. Werner's syndrome is such a disease; it results in gray hair, arthritis, and cataracts, no matter what the sufferer's age.

Recent laboratory experiments have shown that it is possible to improve a cell's ability to repair these mistakes. In one test, the DNA from paramecia (a type of protozoan) was purposely damaged and then quickly repaired by the experimenter. The cell's repair genes, triggered by the damage from outside, went into action, but with that damage repaired, they went to work on other problems. As a result, the paramecia survived 50 percent longer than their normal life span. What is especially intriguing is that animals with longer life spans are better at repairing cell damage. The white-footed mouse, which lives eight years on the average, repairs mistakes almost three times faster than the house mouse, which lives only three and a half years. The much longer human life span means that our ability to repair cell damage is also greater and, therefore, so is our potential for longer life.

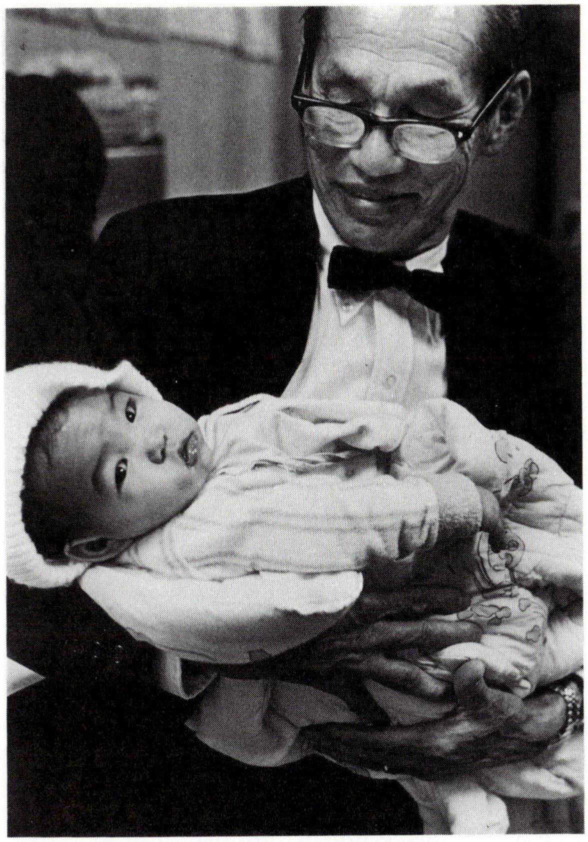

Grandfather and grandchild. Researchers have been unable to agree on a specific cause for aging or whether the phenomenon itself should be defined as a disease or merely a complex but normal physiological process.

THE AGING PROCESS

Why do people age? What causes the physical decline that humanity has tried to avoid for thousands of years? No one knows for sure. There is no single theory of aging. Until recently, researchers believed people aged because of progressive **cell loss.** (Vander Zanden, 1978). This process was thought to be responsible for certain physical changes in the body, such as decreased muscular strength and impaired brain functioning. Although this theory is still of some importance, it is generally felt that cell loss alone cannot adequately explain normal aging. A second theory involves **cellular aging.** In a young person's body, dead cells are quickly replaced by the steady division of healthy cells. The cellular aging theory suggests that as the person grows older, cell division slows down. Thus dead cells are not replaced as readily.

The **error theory** states that as a person's cells divide or reproduce, they accumulate "errors" in the genetic matrix of the cell. In other words, defects or mutations become a greater part of an aging person's cells. These imperfections increasingly interfere with the biochemical support systems and result in the changes we call aging. Another theory of aging is the **auto-immune theory.** A youthful, well-functioning body includes a natural immune system that rejects foreign matter. The auto-immune theory suggests that as a person ages, cells change in certain ways that make them appear foreign. Thus older people's bodies reject more and more of their own cells, causing bodily deterioration. Finally, some researchers contend that the waste products of normal cell metabolism eventually accumulate to the point where they interfere with healthy cell functioning, which increasingly disrupts the functioning of a person's organs and leads to aging.

These biological explanations of aging are not mutually exclusive—any number or combination of them may contribute to the aging process. In addition, aging may be accompanied by disease, which further complicates the search for an accurate explanation. According to most theories, aging is not considered to be the same as disease, but some researchers do state that aging itself is a pathological condition and, therefore, a particular type of disease (Rosenfeld, 1976).

Physiological Changes

In Joyce Carol Oates's novel *Unholy Loves,* Albert St. Dennis, a man in his eighties, describes himself as "elderly, hard of hearing, short of leg and of breath, dim visioned, uncomfortably warm, slightly sick to (my) stomach. . . ." (p. 103). As a person ages, the body begins to function less efficiently: Albert could not see or hear as clearly as he had as a young man; he also had less endurance and physical stamina. These biological changes are a natural consequence of the aging process. In this section we shall review some of the structural and functional changes in the human body that occur as a result of growing old.

In the aged, the skin and connective tissue generally lose their firmness and become less elastic, often resulting in wrinkling and sagging. The muscles decrease in size while the amount of fatty tissue increases, diminishing the person's strength and generally causing a weight gain. In addition, researchers have found that after age 30, muscular strength gradually decreases; the person may then develop a stooped posture. In some people, this creates an illusion of shortness, causing friends and relatives to describe an older person as having "shrunk." The hair often becomes thinner, turning grey and then white. Aging individuals may also lose their teeth and have to wear dentures. In addition, they take in less oxygen and give off less carbon dioxide and their pulse rate does not increase as much with exertion as does the pulse of a younger person. In some cases, elderly people may actually collapse during vigorous activity.

Increased reaction time is a characteristic change of aging (Botwinick, 1967). According to Birren (1974), all behavior associated with the central nervous system slows down as a person ages. Researchers believe that the slowing of central nervous system activity is a consequence of **primary neural aging:** The speed of neural transmissions decreases; thus the speed of all CNS activity is reduced, which increases reaction time. A daughter may feel it necessary to repeat her words to an aging mother when, in fact, the woman has heard everything but is slow to respond. An older man may still be able to do a complex dance step or win at chess, but he may dance more slowly or take longer turns during the game.

Bromley (1974) points out that this delayed reaction time can limit elderly people most in performing what he calls *maximum performance tasks*, such as driving a car or operating intricate machinery. When driving, for example, an older person may be unable to respond quickly enough to avoid sudden danger. Therefore our complex and fast-paced society—unlike more leisurely, less industrialized ones—can present special problems to the slowed-down pace of a person's later years.

Many people experience sensory difficulties during old age. Although all five senses may be affected, the most common and most crucial sensory impairments are of sight and hearing, which can naturally make life more difficult. With age, pupil size tends to decrease, reducing the amount of light that reaches the retina (Chapanis, 1950). In addition, the eye reacts more slowly to changes in light. An elderly person entering a dimly lit room may be unable to see clearly for several minutes; at night, leaving a well-lit house or building, the person may miss a porch step or trip over something. Visual discrimination is also impaired: As people age, they need greater contrast between figure and background. For example, an older person watching a black and white television may prefer a sharp contrast between darks and lights, but to the person's grandchild, the picture looks harsh. Changes in color vision with aging are not as well understood, but there is some evidence that an older person may find it harder to distinguish blues, greens, and violets.

The change in hearing is often so gradual and subtle that the person is unaware of it. An older man who continually asks others to speak up may believe everyone else speaks too softly, not realizing that it is he who cannot hear well. The main changes in hearing occur in the upper frequencies; in general, an older person can hear low sounds more easily than high sounds. However, at any frequency, the intensity of sounds must be greater for an older person to hear them readily. Most important, the older person's ability to hear the frequency range of speech is reduced, which can make communication difficult or stressful.

Aging has also been defined as a decline in the body's ability to avoid or combat the effects of disease and illness (Timiras, 1972). Researchers indicate that 46 percent of people over 65 suffer from some type of chronic illness or disability that restricts their activities. The most common limiting complaints are arthritis and heart conditions—almost 25 percent of the total elderly population listed one of these as a chronic problem (U.S. Bureau of the Census, 1978). The inability to combat illness has other consequences, too. A minor fall may cause a fracture in the more brittle bones of an older person, and this can take months to heal. Therefore the elderly must be more cautious and alert to the environment, since an accident can have disastrous results.

This description of the general physiological changes of aging does not support the commonly held myth that most elderly are ill, confined to beds or wheelchairs, or unable to care for themselves simply because they are old. It is true that as the body ages its functioning slows, but it does not cease. Most elderly—a full 85 percent—are active and healthy (U.S. Bureau of the Census, 1978).

Psychological Changes

The primary psychological element for adaptive functioning—intelligence—is almost universally thought to decrease with advancing age. The proof behind this idea was that most intelligence tests given in the past did demonstrate such a decline. However, researchers are now challenging both the results of those tests and the tests themselves. Among the points at issue are the following:

1. A declining score may result from some pathological condition—a damaged cardiovascular system, say—that is more common among the aged, but not from aging per se.
2. Many previous tests are *cross-sectional*—they compare the elderly with younger people—rather than *longitudinal,* which study one set of individuals from an early age to old age. Thus any discrepancies may reflect generational differences in education.
3. The tests—and the testing situations—may be age biased, especially if there are timed trials (the elderly take longer to do the same task).
4. Recent studies have shown that elderly people can substantially increase their scores on intelligence tests through experiential training (Labouvie-Vief and Gonda, 1976), which challenges an older idea that intelligence losses cannot be regained (Baltes and Labouvie, 1973).

Other factors (motivation, education level) have also been mentioned (Crandall, 1980). It should be noted in addition that in recent years the age at which intelligence supposedly begins its decline (or at least its leveling off) has increased. In the past twenty years it has moved from age 17 to age 50—and some studies now speculate that age 70 is the critical time (Troll, 1971).

Clearly the loss of intelligence in the elderly is another misconception that should now be put to rest. The truth is that as people grow old, they do not *de facto* become senile. *Senility* (from senile dementia) is a misnomer that many people use for a general behavior pattern sometimes evident in elderly people. Common behaviors include confusion, rigid behavior, memory lapses, and mood swings. Many elderly people with senile dementia act childishly, which probably has led to the idea that there is a psychological regression to a less advanced mental state in old age.

True senile dementia is an organic disease (see Chapter 13) that strikes only a very small portion of elderly. Nevertheless, what often happens is that *any* inappropriate behavior exhibited by an aged person gets labeled senility. When an elderly man gets confused in a conversation that he can hardly hear, much less follow, he may be considered senile. To complicate this situation, several physiological problems that could easily be remedied—vitamin deficiencies, anemia, adverse reactions to medication—sometimes resemble senile dementia (Butler, 1975). Inappropriate behavior may also be generated by extremely stressful conditions or a severe emotional crisis (Kiritz and Moos, 1974). But if everyone claims senility is the cause, nothing is done and the problem continues.

Older people are also said to be less adaptable, less willing or able to change their ways of doing things. They may resist change, becoming annoyed with the behavior of younger generations and insisting on attitudes and behaviors that are no longer necessary or even appropriate. For example, a grandmother may insist that her grandchildren dress formally when she takes them out, even though children today dress more casually. An elderly uncle may regard dancing as a sin even if the religion he practices no longer adheres to that belief. Older people are therefore often described as "stubborn" or "set in their ways."

However, researchers again indicate that this is not usually the case (Barrett, 1972). Butler (1974) cites the inflexibility of older people as a common myth held about aging. According to him, although the structure of a person's character is fairly well established by old age, people can and do change up to the time of death, unless severely hampered by brain damage, low intelligence, or lack of education. "Cautious" is a better description of elderly people than "inflexible" or "rigid." Older individuals may be less likely to take risks because of the greater potential hazards to their health and well-being. But in unambiguous and familiar situations they function very well (Barrett, 1972).

Maintaining continuity

Nevertheless, some elderly people do react to the stresses and frustrations of aging by becoming "more as they have been." An elderly woman originally from another country may revert to speaking only her native tongue, even if she knows the language of her adopted country and has lived there much of her adult life. In such cases, rigid thinking and behavior may be seen as the person's attempt to recreate the stability and certainty of earlier years.

It is difficult for elderly people to adapt to changes in attitudes and values, even when they are positive and not very extreme. This is especially true in a society where there is rapid social and technological change. In such cultures young people are generally the first to adopt new styles. The values and beliefs held by older people and their families for many generations may then be quickly discarded by the society that once supported them—the person's children or grandchildren may even be among the vanguard. A young Amish male may turn his back on tradition and enter a profession that requires driving a car, a practice that is banned by the Amish. Likewise, a young Moslem woman may renounce wearing the veil, without which her mother and grandmother will not leave the house.

In order to maintain effective functioning and stability in old age, an elderly person needs to feel a sense of continuity. The adult identity is in part related to basic values and beliefs. When these are challenged—or worse yet, ridiculed—stress and confusion result. Nevertheless, those elderly who fail to integrate the changing values of society with their own beliefs face many difficulties. They may be scorned or ignored, and can even experience hardship as a result of their resistance. For example, an aged and ill woman may suffer unnecessarily because she refuses to go to a doctor's office, insisting that "in her day" doctors never asked sick elderly women to come to them.

Responses to Aging

How do individuals react to the changes in appearance, physical health, and behavior brought about by aging? Each person reacts in a unique way depending on values, beliefs, life circumstances, and adaptability. A person who greatly values a youthful appearance and body and whose job may depend on these qualities will react differently from someone who places little value on physical appearance. For example, a model who earned her living and won widespread admiration solely because she was beautiful would probably be distressed as her body aged; likewise, an athlete would probably be depressed by increasing physical limitations. In our youth-oriented society, all age-related physical changes are potentially disturbing and can be disastrous to the self-image and security of

Many older individuals successfully cope with increasing physical limitations and continue to live active, satisfying lives.

elderly individuals. Will older people be rejected because they have less energy and endurance or because they are considered less attractive?

Research indicates that a person's psychological adjustment to later life is strongly influenced by how well the person has functioned at younger ages (Reichard et al., 1962). Have life changes been appropriately dealt with? Has the individual adapted well or functioned poorly in new situations? However, even if prior life adjustments have been good, it does not necessarily follow that the adjustment to aging will be easy. The older person in our society faces many severe and simultaneous stressors that fight against successful psychological adaptation.

But we have seen that the physiological and psychological changes of aging are not in themselves particularly debilitating, so why is aging fraught with problems? What are the "severe stresses that fight against successful adaptation"? The answer is that the rest of us make assumptions about how the elderly behave, about what they can and cannot do, about how they think and feel—and they respond accordingly. Unfortunately, most of our assumptions and expectations about the elderly are negative. Our society is presently structured so that the aged—except for rare individuals—are not valued or held in much esteem; usually they are benignly ignored or neglected. Clearly this can undermine self-esteem, and lead to a number of problems, especially depression and withdrawal. We shall now examine some of the psychological consequences of aging.

Loss of self-esteem

A raise in salary; a promotion; the birth of a child; the publication of an article; an exhibition of paintings; the discovery of new love—these are the things that increase confidence and self-esteem, that make people feel that they belong, that they have a positive impact on others and on society. In old age there are fewer rewards. After retirement, a person usually no longer has the support and encouragement of employers and co-workers. There are no more pay raises or promotions. Ill health can create boundaries between old friends as well as new ones; it can also lead to the permanent separation of spouses through death. Financial problems from a reduced income can restrict participation in activities that might offer support and reinforcement. Those elderly people who still work may discover that they are not as effective or efficient in their labors as they once were, thus limiting potential rewards.

Older individuals adapt differently to these changes. Some people are able to transcend their physical and social limitations and remain happy in spite of their altered situations. Others deeply regret the loss of the comfort, pleasure, and physical well-being equated with their past youthfulness. For these individuals, the changes associated with aging become tremendous sources of stress and their self-esteem may be affected. As a result, their psychological adaptation to old age may be very painful; in some cases, they may develop symptoms that further limit or upset them.

At such times an individual's self-perception in relation to the environment gradually shifts. During their youth, people feel strong and capable of taking risks and overcoming obstacles; during old age, they may view the world as a complicated and potentially dangerous place no longer within their control (Gutmann, 1964). In some sense, of course, the world *is* more complicated—an arthritic and partially deaf elderly man will naturally have more trouble maneuvering in traffic than will a young man in his prime. Sometimes, just realizing that previously simple tasks are no longer easy decreases a person's self-confidence. Some older individuals experience temporary feelings of self-doubt and depression; others begin to feel totally helpless and impotent. Unfortunately, many well-meaning attempts to help an elderly person with tasks just increases the person's sense of incompetence, worthlessness, and powerlessness.

Depression

Edgar spends hours sitting in a chair in his living room, not moving, just staring into space. Often he drops into a light sleep in the same position. He used to spend most days working in his garden, but now it's filled with weeds; many of the plants have died from neglect. He's lost his appetite and has dropped about ten pounds in the last month. When his daughter drops in to see how he's doing, she tries to get him to eat, to go outside, to move out of the chair. Edgar hardly seems to notice her.

Edgar is a clear example of depression. He has somehow lost the motivation to participate in activities or conversations or even to remain awake. Researchers have found that depressed elderly are no different from depressed adolescents or younger adults. They have the same feelings of sadness and hopelessness: The present and future look bleak and barren. They can find no reason to exert themselves. There is nothing to look forward to, nothing interesting or stimulating in their worlds. Researchers have also found that most depression experienced by older people is *reactive*—that is, it develops in response to some particular loss or threat of a loss (Post, 1965). And here, of course, lies the chief hazard, because in old age there is so much that can be lost. We have already discussed the physiological losses of aging—agility, strength, endurance, youthful appearance. But there are many more losses.

One of the first losses involves retirement. Sixty-five is no longer a mandatory retirement age in this country, but old customs die hard, so most people still look upon this as the time to move out. But when the job is gone, often so is the life-style, since income is reduced; so are the social contacts that were made through work; so is the sense of self as an effective and productive worker. In our work-oriented society these can be devastating losses. We define ourselves by our professions; we set great store on the material possessions that money can buy. When these are gone, so is a large chunk of self-esteem.

Although adult mortality is lower than it once was and the average life span has increased, old age is still a time when death strikes more often. Good friends, close relatives, even a spouse may die, leaving behind a bleak empty feeling, a sense of isolation. In fact, Paul (1966) stated that the majority of elderly who sought assistance at community mental health clinics were suffering from unresolved grief. Those who cannot accept or adapt to the deaths of loved ones and companions may begin to engage in strange, almost ritualized behaviors, acting as if the dead person were still alive and well—setting the dinner table for two or buying the favorite flowers or foods of the deceased.

Sometimes they never recover: Kraus and Lilienfeld (1959) reported that often when one spouse dies, the other dies soon afterward. The death of someone close more or less compels elderly people to face the prospect of their own death, now much more imminent. If people are alone, which happens more and more, the withdrawal can be complete, until like Edgar, they just sit waiting for the end. If there are any added complications—a move to an unfamiliar environment, for instance, or increasingly bad health—the end may not be too long in arriving.

One elderly Eastern European man had extreme difficulty leaving his native land. His son later recalled that "it had never occurred to him that he would leave that place." His ancestors had lived there all their lives, as had the man himself. The move was so traumatic that the man lost his zest for life. His son describes their last visit to the town cemetery and his father's reaction and appearance:

> I couldn't stand to [walk] too close to him. I loved him but the pain that was coming out from him kept me away. First he walked up and down. Finally, he gave the Rabbi there some money to say prayers and keep up the graves. Then he walked over to the grave of his father. He cried, tears coming down and down his face. His hair was black and grey. Old as he was, there was a youthfulness about him, very remarkable. At this time, I saw that youthfulness go out from him forever, like the departure of a spirit. (Myerhoff, 1979, p. 77)

Suicide

In many cases, severe depression in the elderly—as in any age group—can lead to suicide. A conservative estimate is that in the United States there are between 25,000 and 30,000 suicides each year, which yields an overall rate of about 13 percent. However, the elderly, who make up only 10 percent of the total population, account for 25 percent of the total suicides (Patterson et al., 1974). Of this group, white males are the leaders—almost 40 percent of all suicides are committed by white males 65 and over (U.S. Bureau of the Census, 1978).

There are several factors contributing to this higher rate for white males. First is the fact that they probably have the hardest time adjusting to the second-class status of the elderly. Minority racial groups and women face more discrimination at earlier life stages, and are therefore not as dismayed by the change in position wrought by aging. Second, if men are widowed, the likelihood that they will at least attempt suicide goes up even more. There are two reasons for this:

1. Widowed men must assume the domestic duties formerly performed by their wives. This can be extremely frustrating, since most men in our society do not learn basic cleaning and cooking skills (Berardo, 1970).
2. Men do not ordinarily maintain social contacts and most do not have any confidants. Therefore they are more likely to be socially isolated after the death of a spouse.

A third factor in the high white male suicide rate (and also for the high elderly rate in general) is simply that more often than not, an attempt that would not kill a younger person does kill an older person, even if it is not immediately. This is a natural result of aging: The body simply cannot respond as swiftly and as efficiently to trauma.

MANAGING THE PROBLEMS OF AGING

How do the aged cope with their often less than ideal situation? Fortunately, the majority, as we have stated, do adapt to their new physical, psychological and environmental limitations. They recover from mourning; they become more involved in family or community affairs; they remarry; they set new goals and pursue them. Some would assert that they *disengage* from their prior level of involvement with the social structure.

Disengagement Theory

Disengagement theory is a controversial yet persistent idea. Basically, the theory states that the elderly must be gradually phased out of major social roles in order for the society at large to continue to function. Through disengagement, younger people are continually being prepared to assume those roles vacated by the aged. Therefore the sudden death of an important older person does not totally disrupt the social order, and at the same time, new generations are assured of future responsibilities.

Disengagement theorists, like Cumming (1963), believe that this process is mutually satisfactory—it is desired by both the overall social group and the elderly population that must withdraw. This is clearly a controversial issue. Do the aged withdraw by choice or because society forces them to? The disengagement process does seem to have been incorporated into many social structures—witness mandatory retirement. But there are major exceptions, such as President Ronald Reagan. Obviously, not all elderly individuals are content to withdraw quietly into old age.

In fact, one study (Roman and Taietz, 1967) found that, if given the chance to continue their engagement, emeritus professors preferred this to disengagement. Other research contends that the changes associated with aging—poorer health, loss of status, reduced finances, etc.—are actually what effect withdrawal. Therefore given the opportunity to avoid or overcome these changes, disengagement would not take place. This is in fact the case for many elderly individuals. Disengagement theorists would call those people still engaged in satisfying and meaningful social roles "unsuccessful disengagers." Perhaps their timing is off, or maybe they simply constitute an elite.

The Family's Role

But disengagement theory aside, not all the elderly fit this model. A sizable group (though fortunately a minority) cannot adapt to the stresses of being old in our society. For these people there are fewer options, and more often than not, decisions about their lives are made by others—family, friends, the community, the courts. No matter how well-meaning, these groups are usually more interested in their own welfare than in that of an aged individual who can no longer contribute to society.

In the past, responsibility for such people lay clearly with the family. **Extended families**—in which three and sometimes four generations live together—were and still are common to agrarian societies. But this kind of arrangement is no longer as popular in Western society. The geographic mobility requirements of industrialization and technological advances have created what researchers call a **modified extended family:** several nuclear families that do not share the same household but do live near one another and have strong ties of affection and interaction.

Most elderly prefer to live "independently" in a modified extended family arrangement. Studies indicate that living in separate households tends to result in generally better and more stable personal relations (Johnson and Bursk, 1977). Thus the aged can maintain close ties and obtain support when necessary but do not have to feel that they are a burden to their families. **Filial maturity** is the term some researchers use for the role reversal that commonly takes place when an adult child willingly assumes caretaking responsibilities for one or

(a) Affluent senior citizens may select from a variety of living arrangements—from luxury retirement hotels to leisure communities for the elderly. (b) Life in a nursing home can become more meaningful if residents are kept active and are encouraged to maintain social roles.

both elderly parents. Some writers speculate that this kind of arrangement, though still fairly standard, may be diminishing in importance in this country. Treas (1977) has offered several reasons for its decline:

1. For the past several decades, the number of children born per family has declined, which means that many elderly today—and more in the future—will not have an adult child to turn to for help.

2. More younger women are marrying, so that there are fewer "maiden daughters" to live with and care for elderly parents.

3. More women are now in the work force, which means that they are unavailable to provide for their parents. Since women are usually the direct source of help, this is an important factor.

One other factor that has bearing on the living arrangements of the elderly is whether or not they live as a couple. A couple that is married (or simply cohabiting) will remain independent longer than a single individual. Here the sex ratio among the elderly plays an important role.

In 1977 the ratio of elderly men to elderly women was approximately 69, meaning that for every 100 women there were only 69 men. Clearly, once a woman is widowed—or if she has never married—she is more likely to remain alone. If she has few or no children and cannot fully support herself, chances are that she will be institutionalized (Treas, 1977). This happens less often with elderly men simply because there are fewer of them and because the life span for men is not as great as that for women. However, it does happen.

Institutionalization

Very often, the elderly who have physiological or psychological difficulties that their families cannot or will not face—as well as the elderly who are alone—are admitted to convalescent care facilities. More than one million elderly people share this fate: According to the U.S. Bureau of the Census (1978), almost 5 percent of all those 65 and older live in nursing homes. This number is increasing, however, which may substantiate Treas's theory that filial maturity is on the wane. But the fact that there are more nursing homes to choose from may also have prompted more people to take advantage of them.

Nursing homes are not the first choice of most elderly as a place in which to spend their last years. Indeed, most families view institutionalization as a last resort (Brody, 1978). Generally, three variables are important in the decision to place someone in a nursing home:

1. The increasing physical deterioration of the aged individual
2. The inability or unwillingness of responsible people to continue providing care
3. The lack of community services to help the elderly person live independently

Why is institutionalization viewed with such disfavor? Beyond the recent discoveries of scandalous treatment in some nursing homes, there are certain factors common to the general experience of being institutionalized that occur even in those that give the best care.

The impact of nursing homes

Relocating to an unfamiliar environment can be quite traumatic and may lead to a decline in health or negative behavior. Most of the nursing home populations have been described as poorly adjusted, disoriented, unresponsive, dependent, and just generally unhappy (Dudley and Hillery, 1977). Of course, since most of those who are admitted to nursing homes are, as we have indicated, ill, poor, alone, and unable to fend for themselves, chances are that their negative behaviors are not something new. Still, the move to strange surroundings would only make them more unhappy. Lieberman (1961) found that many elderly die during the first year in a home—they were likely to die sooner than those on the waiting list for admission. The exact causes for this increased death rate are unclear, but this research suggests that many older people are unable to recover from the shock of relocation.

Most new nursing home residents are profoundly affected by the nature of their new environment. Suddenly all parts of their daily routine must fit a pattern set by someone else. The loss of autonomy can be extremely distressing (Kalish, 1975). In addition, in strange and confusing surroundings the aged are more likely to make little mistakes such as wandering into the wrong room, which can clearly make them seem worse off than they are. As a result, staff members may be more restrictive. Consequently, the elderly are likely to feel even more helpless and inadequate than they already did.

Other aspects of life in an institution are also rather unappealing. Different studies of typical resident activity found that an outrageous 56 percent of waking time was spent on doing nothing (Gottesman and Bourestom, 1974; Kart and Manard, 1976). The afternoons were generally regarded as the worst stretch; people just sat waiting for dinner time to arrive (Gubrium, 1975).

Probably the final blow comes with the care offered in an institution. Even those that provide good care don't provide very much—Gottesman and Bourestom (1974) discovered that less than 10 percent of the average resident's awake time is spent interacting with the staff, including doctors. The problem seems to originate in attitude: Most staff members see the nursing home as a custodial institution. They also tend to view any problems among the elderly as irreversible (Tobin and Lieberman, 1976) and therefore feel their main duty is to maintain the resident's life at a low level of functioning (Citrin and Dixon, 1977).

Drugs are the institution's major therapy—antidepressants and stimulants to increase their sense of well-being, sedatives and hypnotics to help them sleep, narcotics to kill pain. Physicians often prescribe nonaddictive medications, but used frequently, any drug can produce psychological dependency. And the many elderly who take other kinds of medication for specific physiological ailments may run into complications if all these different chemicals react negatively in combination.

Most nursing homes do not offer rehabilitative therapy. Naturally, treating the residents as if they can no longer do anything for themselves turns them into the helpless and dependent people the residents expect—and thus enables administrators to cite their condition as a justification for the lack of rehabilitative programs. Their final argument is that in view of the elderly's greatly limited life expectancy, expensive rehabilitation efforts would be wasted.

Fighting the Institutionalization Syndrome

All of these factors combined often lead to what has been called the **institutionalization syndrome:** The residents become distracted, despondent, and finally apathetic; they lose interest in the external wrld and the future; they begin to take less care in their personal habits. This decline poses an especially severe threat because so many of those entering nursing homes are already suffering from similar characteristics. The institutional environment accelerates their loss of pride, their contact with the basic elements of day-to-day reality, and their will to live. No wonder then that the elderly view nursing homes as the place where they go to die.

Yet it doesn't have to be this way. Some nursing homes do offer quality rehabilitation programs in an effort to help residents (a) increase their independence, (b) maintain their contact with the real world, and (c) improve their morale and individual self-image. Although not all these programs have been successful, it should be noted that the failures were often conducted by poorly trained staff or were not intensive or long-term enough to have an impact on the participants, who generally had not been stimulated for quite a while. The following sections describe some of the most effective techniques.

Reality orientation

Reality orientation, also called *reality therapy,* is the primary method of reversing the deterioration caused by institutionalization syndrome. The method tries to get the residents more aware of and more involved in various aspects of their environment. The two major techniques are reality interaction and environmental stimulation.

Environmental stimulation is an effort to improve the generally decreased sensory abilities (vision and hearing) of the aged, which otherwise might cause them to withdraw. Big and brightly colored calendars, large clocks, boldly designed announcements on bulletin boards giving such basic information as the weather report keep the residents in touch with day-to-day reality. Interaction between staff and residents, instead of the standard nonconversation (brief, impersonal remarks that no one really pays attention to) is more extensive. The staff is instructed to get a true conversation going as often as possible. They ask questions that call for opinions, that make the residents think, that require them to notice things around them. Sometimes, a staff member joins with small groups of residents to discuss topics of concern in the home, such as how late the television should be on or whether they should have a garden.

Activities therapy

Inaction is another major problem of the life in nursing homes. Once the elderly stop moving, they start vegetating, physically and psychologically. By keeping active and participating in at least one daily activity, a process called **activities therapy,** the aged can renew their interest in life. Some people have to start with activities that are more mental than physical, but when they experience success and satisfaction at one, they are more likely to become involved with others—and with more diverse types. Eventually, they may engage in more physical activities. If the institution offers regular and varied activities, much can be accomplished.

A good example of a mental activity is a writing group. Kenneth Koch taught poetry workshops to very enthusiastic nursing home populations and later published the results in his book, *I Never Told Anybody: Teaching Poetry Writing in a Nursing Home.* It is highly likely that this experience—and especially the recognition of being published poets—increased their sense of identity, usefulness, and accomplishment.

The more physical activities naturally require some mobility, muscle strength, and stamina. Many residents have to work up to this point; many others, however, are admitted in good physical condition and need to continue this kind of sport to maintain their health and well-being. A wide range of programs is essential, from group nature walks, to exercise classes, to a daily trip to the nearest public pool to do laps or just flap around in the water. Still more vigorous activities, such as a dance group or softball, are not ruled out in such programs.

Community contact

A link with the past is very important for all elderly but especially for those who are separated from old friends and close family members. Therefore an effort to keep residents in contact with these important people is essential. Visits from outsiders are encouraged. Unfortunately, in standard nursing homes, visits tend to drop off with time because as the resident debilitates, the visitors become increasingly pained and upset and the visits become more and more unpleasant. With proper rehabilitative programs, however, the visits can continue to be rewarding for all concerned.

Likewise, keeping the residents aware of what is going on in the community can be very positive. Attending events sponsored by the city or town, going to the library and to church or temple services, having outings at public parks—all these help the residents maintain a sense of continuity with the world outside the walls of the institution.

Counseling

Clearly, counseling by a mental health professional can also be a valuable part of rehabilitation. As a greater number of people become interested in the aged and in the problems they encounter, more and better trained personnel will be available to implement and oversee quality programs within institutions.

Life enrichment counseling focuses on helping the older person gain more satisfaction in leisure-time pursuits. The counselor tries to discover which activities are most satisfying to the person and tries to introduce new ones on a periodic basis. Through this approach, the counselor assists the elderly to use leisure time more creatively.

This program is also useful for determining group activities. In fact, the give and take of group interaction and the joint development of plans are fulfilling and growth-facilitating activities in their own right.

In **peer-group counseling,** the elderly residents themselves become paraprofessional counselors. The premise is that the fact that they are elderly and have lived through similar life changes gives them a unique insight into the problems that their fellow residents may be experiencing. A bonus of this system is that the counselors often benefit as well.

PREPARING FOR DEATH

Nearing the end of their lives, many elderly people begin to reminisce about the past. This process has been called the **life review** (Butler,

1963). In the movie *On Golden Pond,* Katharine Hepburn and Henry Fonda play a husband and wife, age 80 and 70 respectively. Aware of their impending deaths, they spend much time remembering past summers and other seasons in their lives, thinking of their children and their accomplishments. The life review may have a positive effect (as it does for the couple in the movie), helping the person to appreciate past times and achievements and thus adjust better to present and future circumstances. In other cases, however, elderly people reviewing their lives may experience intense guilt or depression. These people may become self-deprecating, feeling that their life accomplishments have not measured up to their personal goals.

Part of the life review is thinking about the end of life. People can die or contemplate death at any age or time in their lives, but generally a person does not fully confront it until death is close at hand. Sooner or later, however, in one manner or another, we must all face the fact that we will die. Many people consider the realistic acceptance of death to be the hallmark of emotional maturity. Still, death remains the final mystery, and beliefs about what happens after death are greatly varied. Some people believe that they will pass into another world or into a better state of being; others believe that death is the cessation of being; still others may be uncertain, and this uncertainty can make them fearful.

How much do elderly people think about death? In one study, Jeffers and Verwoerdt (1969) found that 25 percent of the people in the sample thought about it less than once a week, 20 percent said that it came to mind weekly, and 49 percent reported that they considered death in some way at least once a day. Although people often assume that death is more frightening for the elderly than for the young, the evidence indicates just the opposite. Despite the fact that older people think about death more frequently, they seem to be less afraid of it (Kalish and Reynolds, 1975). This seeming acceptance of death is apparently more an indifference to it—an indifference fostered by the feeling that they are valueless, that the future is bleak, that all life is meaningless (Kalish, 1976; Beauvoir, 1972). Ironically, it may be that making life for the elderly more appealing might have the negative side effect of making them more concerned about dying.

Caring for the Dying

Until recently, death was not a topic for discussion. Terminal patients were usually not told they were dying; families were asked to bear the pain of keeping this secret, of not being able to say final farewells to those they loved. In many cases, the dying spent their last hours—sometimes days and even months—in the cold, impersonal atmosphere of an unfamiliar hospital. Contact with their families was limited to visiting hours. Lately, however, people are becoming more aware of the problems this can cause for the survivors as well as for the dying. Now more and more families are returning to the time-honored tradition of caring for dying relatives in the home. This is not an easy task, of course, and it still involves some pain for

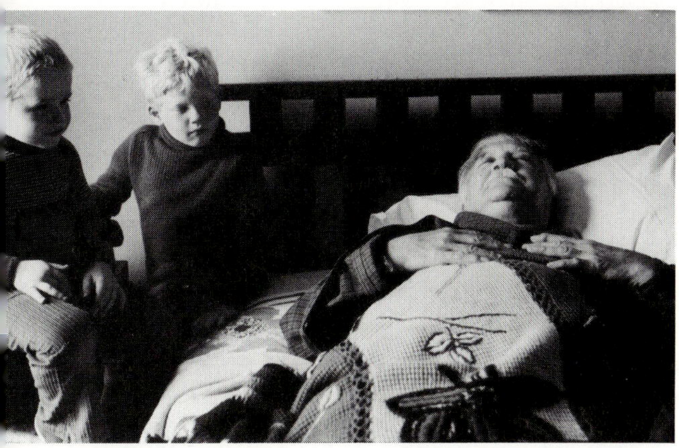

In modern times, people avoided talking about death, but over the last decade there has been a movement to familiarize people, even children, with the realities of dying.

those who must witness the last decline of those who were once strong. But with an understanding of what can and usually does happen, the family can withstand most of the pressures involved.

Elizabeth Kübler-Ross, a pioneer in the study of death, has formulated a five-stage model of dying (1969) in an attempt to help people come to grips with what can be an overwhelming emotional ordeal:

1. Denial. When informed of the fact that they are dying, most people assume it must be a mistake, that somehow the records or lab tests were switched. They can't believe it's true.
2. Anger. Once they are convinced of the validity of the diagnosis, the immediate reaction is "Why me? What have I done to deserve this?" They feel cheated and want to strike back.
3. Bargaining. At this point, they start to offer God, or the doctor, or both a deal: just a little more time and they will be good.
4. Depression. When it's clear that bargaining has no effect, most people become very dejected. They begin to face all the losses imposed by death.
5. Acceptance. In this stage, all other feelings have been expressed; there isn't anything else. They may feel emotionally empty. They have come to terms with death.

Close-up: *The Hospice System*

Until recently, the topic of death was carefully avoided in American society. We glorify youth and most of us try to stay young (or at least young looking) for as long as possible. Discussions of death and planning for this inevitable event are often avoided or considered to be in poor taste. The terminally ill are typically removed from their homes and placed in a hospital where they are isolated from family and friends. Often they are not told that they are dying and family members who are informed of their condition are encouraged to keep it a secret from the dying person.

One attempt to remedy the sense of isolation caused by this approach is the hospice system developed in England. The hospice is a care facility for terminally ill patients, young and old, which is designed to provide medical services in a warm, homelike setting. The focus of the hospice is on helping dying persons to finish their lives as painlessly and with as much dignity as possible. The patients are informed that they are dying, as are the family members. While the hospice staff provides sensitive care, the main support comes from family members who are encouraged to be with the dying person and to share thoughts and feelings. Pain management is also a primary goal, the belief being that problems such as fear and anxiety are often the result of uncontrolled pain. In keeping with the basic hospice philosophy that death is the normal and accepted conclusion to life, there are few life-prolonging machines or other aids. This also has the practical effect of freeing up funds for more personal aspects of care.

Because the hospice system has been only recently introduced into the United States, there are as yet few physical facilities in this country, and hospice care is usually provided for patients who wish to die at home. The research to date indicates that the hospice approach provides a significantly better means of managing death than traditional, depersonalized methods.

Table 15.2 *Kübler-Ross's Five Stages of Dying*

Stage	Expression
Denial	"It's not true! You mixed up my records with someone else's!"
Anger	"It's not fair! Why did this have to happen to me?"
Bargaining	"Just let me make it to Junior's college graduation and I'll go gladly."
Depression	"There's nothing left for me; the world is empty."
Acceptance	"Everything is in order; now I can enjoy my last days in peace of mind."

According to Kübler-Ross, not everyone progresses smoothly from stage one to stage five, and many people can never reach the acceptance of the last stage. Still, this model does seem to fit the majority of cases and it can help promote better communication and understanding between those involved.

More recent research on the dying process has fostered the attitude that prolonging life may not always be in the patient's best interest. This attitude has, in turn, raised the very delicate issue of **euthanasia**—that is, killing those who are mortally sick or wounded out of mercy, to save them from added pain. But it has also prompted the development of the **hospice,** which is a center that cares only for terminal patients without trying to prolong anyone's life (see the Close-up in this section).

SUMMARY

The idea that people mature in stages is very old, but not until recently have professionals started analyzing the stages of adulthood and old age. Erikson proposed eight stages of development from birth to death. These stages were characterized by a conflict that had to be at least partially resolved for personality growth to continue. A later model proposed by Levinson and colleagues was based on studies of men only, but it is more detailed. This model has six developmental stages in adulthood (postadolescence), and Levinson believes that unresolved problems at one level do impede further progress.

A problem that seems more common among adults today is the midlife crisis. This is a period of stress reached around age 40 when people are confronted with the imminence of old age. If they are dissatisfied with their life to date, they may react unpredictably. If they are content with their past contributions, they are more likely to face aging gracefully.

There are many theories of what causes aging. Some attribute it to cell loss or cellular aging; others assert that genetic errors accumulating in the cells have a debilitating effect; still others believe that a person's cells begin to change over time and are then rejected as foreign by the person's auto-immune system. Whatever the cause, the physiological effects—the changes in appearance, endurance, strength, perception, etc.—can often lead to deleterious psychological responses, such as withdrawal, depression, and suicide.

Disengagement theory states that withdrawal is necessary for society and that the elderly prefer it to continuing under the pressure of fulfilling social roles. This idea has been incorporated into many social structures but it is doubtful that the aged withdraw by choice, since so many who can remain engaged in meaningful activity do so. For a minority of older people, however, the changes associated with aging become insurmountable problems. Many of these people are institutionalized.

Nursing homes are generally thought of as last resorts—where the elderly go to die—and many provide only custodial care. Others, however, now offer programs to help fight the effects of institutionalization syndrome. Reality orientation, activities therapy, and peer-group counseling in particular can be very beneficial.

The elderly more than any other age group must face the imminence of death. To this end, the life review can be very rewarding, as can being cared for at home in familiar surroundings among loving family members. Elizabeth Kübler-Ross pioneered the study of dying and established five stages of death. Understanding the trials that are faced by the dying can help all those concerned come to grips with the emotional ordeal of death.

Part Three

Future Goals

CHAPTER 16

Preventing Abnormal Behavior

THE MOVEMENT TOWARD PREVENTION

THE PREVENTION DEBATE

The Three Levels of Prevention

Establishing Goals and Strategies

Theoretical Orientation

APPLICATION OF PREVENTIVE METHODS

Primary Methods

Secondary Methods

PROBLEMS WITH PREVENTION EFFORTS

Ethical Issues

Financial Considerations

A New York street scene around the turn of the century. Public health was to improve significantly with the development of such primary prevention methods as large-scale sanitation systems and widespread inoculation against contagious diseases.

In Chapter 1, we looked at brief case histories of three people—Arnold, Elaine, and Tommy—whose behavior would be considered abnormal. Our purpose was to show the range of their behaviors and, at the same time, to point out the similarities of their situations: disturbing behavior; anxious and upset friends and family; baffled psychologists, psychiatrists, and physicians; wary outsiders. As we have discussed throughout this book, no one has been able to pinpoint specific causes for the majority of mental health problems and, although we can control disorders to a certain extent, we do not have any definite "cures." We have also seen that Arnold, Elaine, and Tommy are not just isolated statistics. Their disorders and a wide variety of other mental problems are faced by a distressingly large number of people. Estimates vary, but it is safe to say that 15 percent of the population in the United States suffers from some form of mental illness. We understand a few of these disorders; a few more we can manage fairly effectively; however, for the most part the picture is a discouraging one.

THE MOVEMENT TOWARD PREVENTION

The problems involved in managing mental disorders have stimulated professionals and nonprofessionals alike to direct their energies toward the possibilities of prevention. Could something have been done to prevent Arnold's schizophrenia, Elaine's depression, or Tommy's autism? Consider the strides we have made in controlling physical disease. There is no question that public health has been dramatically improved by the construction of large-scale sanitation systems, widespread inoculation against disabling diseases, and the other discoveries of modern research.

From any perspective, prevention is obviously attractive, and the concept has received some significant endorsements. At a press conference in 1963, John F. Kennedy issued an unequivocal statement on the subject:

> We must seek out the causes of mental illness and mental retardation and eradicate them. Here, more than in any other area "an ounce of prevention" is far more desirable than "a pound of cure." For prevention is far more desirable for all concerned. It is far more economical and it is far more likely to be successful.

As a result of the former president's drive, Congress passed the Community Mental Health Centers Act in 1963, providing for the establishment of a community mental health center for every 50,000 people in the country. These centers were to provide more than counseling for members of the community; programs were to be implemented for the prevention of mental illness, caregivers and civil servants such as clergy, teachers, and the police were to be educated in preventive methods, and mental health research was to be carried out. More recently, Rosalynn Carter gave the area of prevention her special attention and support.

In spite of the obvious need for preventive mental health programs, widespread endorsements by mental health groups, and promises of financial aid by the federal government, progress in the area of prevention has been distressingly slow. There are no easy explanations for this phenomenon, but perhaps one of the most serious obstacles is the ambiguous concept of prevention itself. Since almost everything has psychological effects on the population, almost everything becomes an appropriate target for prevention efforts. Kessler and Albee (1975) summarize this idea:

> Our reading for a year leads us to the conclusion that practically every effort aimed at improving child rearing, increasing effective communication, building inner control and self-esteem, reducing stress and pollution, etc.—in short, everything aimed at improving the human condition, at making life more fulfilling and meaningful—may be considered to be a part of . . . prevention of mental or emotional disturbance. (p. 557)

Few would argue with the spirit of this statement, but its broad scope only accentuates the enormity of the challenge.

THE PREVENTION DEBATE

Even among prevention experts, there is serious disagreement over just what prevention consists of and how such programs should be implemented. Zax and Specter (1974) suggest that preventive activities should include anything that can improve the human condition. Bower (1967) feels prevention should focus on helping children get through existing social institutions "smelling like a rose" and urges that prevention be directed at prenatal, perinatal, childhood, and adolescent development. Wagenfeld (1972) outlines two basic strategies: (1) intervention in the life crises of individuals and (2) altering the balance of psychological, physical, social, and cultural forces in the community. Cumming (1968) supports two different approaches: (1) discovering and eliminating the causes of mental illness and (2) determing the resistant characteristics of immune populations and how they can be made available to everyone else.

Although the debate spans many distinct views, two basic positions emerge. The first is the positive mental health approach—prevention should include any program that could possibly improve the well being of people. The second is the public health approach—prevention should focus on specific disorders, especially the more serious ones like schizophrenia and the affective disorders.

These two positions can also be seen in the specific programs that are promoted. In the public health approach, prevention stems from the identification of the causes of a particular disorder. For example, if a disorder is clearly hereditary in nature, then genetic counseling is an appropriate preventive measure. If stress is the key factor, then stress management techniques are favored. The obvious problem, as critics of this approach point out, is that our knowledge of the etiology of most disorders is still rudimentary.

Another basic disagreement can also be seen in the issue of *when* intervention should occur. Many experts agree with the popular notion that prevention means literally preventing a disorder from occurring and that any intervention after the onset of a disorder should be regarded as treatment. Efforts geared at reversing the damage are defined as rehabilitation. Yet if abnormal behavior is part of a long continuum, at what point do the warning signs turn into the serious disorder? Perhaps we should consider intervention in the earliest stages of the disorder as a means of preventing more serious emotional disturbances in the future—much as we treat the symptoms of a common cold to prevent it from developing into pneumonia.

The Three Levels of Prevention

At this point it would be useful to consider three distinct levels of prevention (Caplan, 1961), which in public health terminology are called primary, secondary, and tertiary. **Primary prevention** includes any community-wide action taken to anticipate mental disorders, to reduce the risk that people in the community will suffer from mental disorders, and to foster optimal positive mental health in the community. It attempts to build individual and societal coping resources, and its chief tools are those of education and social engineering. **Secondary prevention** involves early diagnosis and treatment of a disorder at a stage when problems may be nipped in the bud. An example is a program in which kindergarten teachers are trained to identify children who exhibit signs of hyperactivity and to see that they are treated with an appropriate intervention.

Tertiary prevention includes efforts to reduce the overall damaging effect of a disorder, to shorten its duration, and to rehabilitate those afflicted for reentry into the community. Typical tertiary prevention programs include halfway houses for released mental hospital patients and sheltered workshops for the mentally retarded. Because tertiary prevention essentially consists of the proper management of disorders that we have been discussing throughout this book, this chapter will concentrate on primary and secondary prevention.

Establishing Goals and Strategies

While the distinctions between primary, secondary, and tertiary prevention are relatively clear-cut, within each approach are a multitude of methodologies for intervention. Needless to say, these different approaches have direct, practical implications for the design and implementation of prevention programs.

The question arises over how prevention should deal with individuals: On a case by case basis? In selected groups of high-risk individuals? Through blanket programs for an entire population? The concept that prevention should encompass whole communities is an outgrowth of the public health dogma, whose proponents hold that no illness can be eliminated by treating only the afflicted parties and that the best approach is one that will inoculate as many people as possible against mental disorder. In their opinion, the community model provides a vehicle that maximizes the effectiveness of trained professionals by extending their therapeutic influence to large segments of the population. Another advantage of this approach is that it eliminates the stigma of being labeled a high-risk individual. Nevertheless, opponents argue that community-wide programs, while cheaper in terms of the cost per person served, are more expensive overall because they serve so many. In addition, an approach that applies intervention to an entire community affects everyone—even those who do not want or need the services offered.

Other major questions arise: Should prevention programs focus on equipping people with personal and environmental resources for coping or should they concentrate on identifying and eliminating those agents that contribute to mental disorder? Is it necessary to have a thorough knowledge of the causes of mental disorders in order to prevent them? Critics of prevention are quick to point out that since so little is known about the etiologies of mental illness, prevention activities are doomed to failure. If they are correct, then prevention programs may have to be abandoned, for little is known about the cause of most mental disorders. To complicate matters further, one agent may produce a range of symptoms. Stress, for instance, produces different, even idiosyncratic problems: One individual might react to marital stress by developing an ulcer, a second might develop panic attacks or agoraphobia, and a third might simply break into hives. As the report of the Task Panel on Prevention (1978) stated: "Most mental disorders are (or will prove to be) multiply caused. It is futile to search for the single, unique cause of every emotional disorder" (pp. 145–146).

Other concerned individuals are more optimistic in their outlook. If we again borrow from the public health field, we see that throughout history primary prevention programs have been successfully mounted despite a lack of detailed knowledge concerning the precise etiology of various diseases. Caplan (1964), while acknowledging that a complete knowledge of etiology would be helpful, nonetheless argues that both treatment and prevention can proceed with incomplete information:

> Some of the most successful programs of primary prevention were instituted before we had valid etiologies of the illnesses which were prevented. The prevention of smallpox by vaccination and the prevention of scurvy by eating limes and fresh vegetables preceded by many years our knowledge of the causes of these illnesses. In fact, the major advances in the control of epidemics or infectious diseases in our cities in the latter part of the nineteenth century predated the germ theory and the discovery of the microbial agents responsible for the disease. The sanitary programs were based on the belief of the hygenic reformers that dirt, squalor, and congestion were "unnatural" and "unhealthy" and by a desire to introduce the pure conditions of country life into the towns. . . . (p. 29)

Theoretical Orientation

Another source of disagreement on the subject of prevention is related to theoretical orientation. As discussed in Chapter 3, there are major differences in the way each theoretical approach explains abnormal behavior, a situation that has distinct implications for prevention.

The biogenic theorists suggest that research should focus on identifying the organic factors that lead to mental disorders and eliminating them from the environment. In this context, prevention might include a broad spectrum of programs: educating prospective mothers on prenatal care and maternal nutrition; eliminating toxins from the environment (for example, the banning of lead-based paint); introducing safety measures to prevent head injuries that might result in brain damage (through installation of seat belts, air bags, and baby car seats in automobiles); sponsoring anti-drug and anti-smoking campaigns on television and radio.

Many advocates of the psychogenic view who believe that early childhood experience is critical to the development of psychopathology in adults suggest that prevention efforts concentrate on the period between birth and young adulthood. Prenatal education, family planning, day-care centers, Headstart programs, and television shows such as *Sesame Street* that increase competence in young viewers—all of these focus on this early period of development.

The sociogenic theorists seek to alleviate stress by changing social systems: the family, the community, places of employment, legal and social services. Welfare, day care, unemployment benefits, and health care facilities all attempt to reduce levels of stress in society. Other preventive interventions based on this model include training various segments of the population to cope better with environmental stress. Toward this goal, many community mental health centers offer support and self-help programs for those going through crises such as divorce or the death of a family member.

Additional arguments are offered by other theoretical groups who say that we should emphasize "wellness" rather than illness. In other words, we should promote positive mental health through measures that increase social competence and coping ability, decrease stress, and improve ego strength.

APPLICATION OF PREVENTIVE METHODS

It is clear that most people believe prevention is important and worthwhile. Unfortunately, conceptual debates hamper the formulation of an overall strategy based on such an approach. We shall return to other social and political issues later in the chapter, but first let us turn our attention to a specific case study and the various preventive efforts that could be brought to bear on the problems involved.

Nancy was a sophomore in high school when she got pregnant; her boyfriend Mike was a local boy who worked as a garage mechanic. They had been dating for a couple of months, but when Nancy

Quality day-care programs can do much to enhance the learning and social experiences of children and to reduce the stress of working parents.

confided in Mike about her suspected condition, he soon lost interest. Nancy spent the next few months in a panic—afraid to tell her parents but not knowing what to do.

When she started to show, Nancy's parents were outraged and humiliated. She was relieved despite their negative reaction because now she believed she would be taken care of. Although her friends' reactions varied, the overall impact was negative. Some of the kids at school grew distant, and Nancy was occasionally the butt of jokes. She couldn't take it and dropped out in the fifth month of her pregnancy.

Under threat of legal action, Mike reluctantly agreed to assume responsibility for Nancy and the child. They were married just before the baby was born, and Nancy moved into Mike's tiny apartment. The cramped quarters, little money to spend even on necessities, Nancy's physical complaints associated with the pregnancy, and just general frustration kept Mike angry most of the time. Nancy didn't know how to change things; she cried a lot alone at home until the baby came.

Their child, Jimmy, was one month premature and had to be kept in the hospital for a long time. All Mike seemed to think about was where he could get the money to pay the bills. When Jimmy was brought home, Mike started staying out all night because of "the smell and the racket he makes." Nancy suspected he was dating other girls and started accusing him of cheating on her whenever he came home.

When Jimmy was six months old, Mike returned one morning still drunk from the night's activities. Nancy immediately began harping at him about drinking, other women, and not earning enough money. Mike was so angry that he hit Nancy, and then he just couldn't make himself stop; she eventually lost consciousness. Suddenly afraid, Mike threw some things together and left. An hour later, a neighbor, disturbed by Jimmy's constant crying, found Nancy on the floor.

Nancy was almost back to normal within a week, except for occasional memory lapses and what she called "fuzzy" thinking, which did not go away. A month passed, but Mike did not return. Although the police tried to locate him, he appeared to have vanished. Two months later, Nancy went on welfare.

How might Nancy's pregnancy—and the 600,000 similar unplanned pregnancies that occur each year—have been prevented? What secondary measures might have altered the negative outcome of the situation? Let us examine various primary and secondary efforts that might have changed the lives of Nancy, Mike, and Jimmy.

Primary Methods

Education in its broadest form involves more than our brief contact with formal schooling; it encompasses all that we learn through interaction with our environment, through relationships with our families and friends, and through the pursuit of our individual interests. And since education in this sense touches so much of our lives, it seems an appropriate medium for utilizing primary prevention. Anything that teaches us how to be more aware of ourselves, our interpersonal relationships, and the world around us, gives us a better chance of developing a healthy personality. Any experience that helps us acquire a positive sense of self and a solid set of values provides us with the tools to build a stable structure for our lives.

Increasing awareness and exploring options

On the simplest level, if Nancy and Mike had been taught to be more responsible about the consequences of their actions, they might have practiced birth control and avoided an unwanted pregnancy. To go one step further, if they had been exposed to a thorough sex education course, one that went beyond mere facts and stressed fundamental issues such as emotional maturity, marital interactions, and the responsibilities of parenthood, they might have waited until they were older before deciding to become lovers. What if Nancy's parents were more supportive and open-minded and had encouraged the young couple to seek professional counseling before deciding on marriage? A trained therapist would probably have helped Nancy and Mike explore all their alternatives. Perhaps Nancy would have been put in touch with an organization like Planned Parenthood. If she decided to have the baby, a social worker

This school for teen mothers provides many services, from counseling to nursery facilities. Social support systems like this enable young women to complete their high school education, which makes it possible for them to choose from a wider range of career alternatives.

could have discussed with her the pros and cons of keeping the infant or putting it up for adoption.

Social support

Even if Nancy's pregnancy could not have been avoided, social support systems might have alleviated some of the stress that she and Mike and their families experienced. For instance, a government-sponsored day-care program might have accepted Jimmy, thus giving his mother an opportunity to complete high school and acquire the skills to get a job and a steady income. Not only would Nancy have been able to supplement her husband's income, but she might have met new friends and been less dependent on Mike for psychological and social support. He, in turn, with some of the pressure removed, might not have been so quick to go out drinking every night. In other words, a few small but significant changes in the level of daily stress combined with an awareness of alternative courses of action might have made a big difference.

The limitations of this kind of prevention are obvious: Many people lack the financial resources that would enable them to take advantage of existing services. Others are threatened by any new viewpoint that runs counter to their own beliefs. Although we may ask people to rethink their value systems, we cannot ethically force them to accept another. Therefore as innocuous as many new programs are, it may still be a major task to establish them in the community.

The self-help movement

Fortunately, there seems to be a growing awareness of the effect that social stress has on mental health—as the recent explosion of interest in self-help literature and self-help groups clearly indicates. Books offering us advice on how to improve our mental health and how to take care of our emotional needs have sold millions of

Close-up: Assessing Self-Help Books

You Can Change Your Personality and Your Life, Instant Relief, Understanding People or How to Be Your Own Shrink, Spare the Couch: Self Change for Self Improvement. These titles are representative of the many do-it-yourself therapy books currently being published. How does one evaluate them? Are they worth buying? Do they work? Rosen (1981) has identified important questions that should be asked when assessing a book's worth. Although these guidelines are for book reviewers, they can be useful to everyone.

1. Are the claims of the book's title and advertising supported by what is in the book? If the book promises a program of self-change, can a clear, step-by-step program be found in the book?
2. Does the author present empirical support for the program? What research has been done on the effectiveness of the programs? Does the research really support the author's claims?
3. Are the limitations of the program clearly spelled out or are they hidden?
4. Does the book address the issue of individual differences and circumstances? Can readers see how the program may vary with their personal situations?

copies. This phenomenon has been a cause of growing concern among some professionals who are questioning the value of many of these books.

Although self-help groups do not by definition involve professionals, their growth and popularity has generated systematic investigation by researchers (Levy, 1976). The primary purpose of a self-help group is to provide help and support for its members in dealing with their problems, and it relies almost exclusively on the efforts, skills, and knowledge of the members themselves to provide that help. Generally, the members of the group share similar problems. Alcoholics Anonymous, for example, deals with problem drinking, Parents Anonymous with child abuse, and Parents Without Partners with the stress of suddenly being the only parent in the family.

Psychoeducational techniques

A variety of broad-based educational programs have been experimented with. Some of the more interesting can be grouped according to media categories:

1. *Advertising.* Since the goal of prevention is to serve the entire community, advertising campaigns that have wide visibility are a useful tool. The New York State Health Department's Office of Health Promotion recently developed a controversial poster designed to call attention to the problem of teenage pregnancy. In a recent anti-drug campaign in California, rock star Frank Zappa was recruited to capture the attention of the teenage drug user.

2. *Television.* The popular and highly praised television program *Sesame Street* has for years served as a significant educational tool for its youthful audience. In a related example, the Ohio Department of Mental Health and Mental Retardation has developed "Bernard the St. Bernard," a series of TV spots aimed at children under the age of six. The 60-second announcements, which star Bernard, a puppet created by Bill Baird, focus on the stressful situations of childhood and how they can be successfully resolved. The situations have included the birth of a new sibling, mother's pregnancy, starting school, a death in the family, and family arguments (Heller and Monahan, 1977).

3. *Audiovisual materials.* Broussard (1966) developed a film that could be shown to new mothers while still hospitalized during the immediate postpartum period. The purpose of the film is to promote positive mental health in the mother during the crucial period following the birth of the child and positive maternal attitudes towards the child by enhancing the mother's sense of competence and confidence.

Environmental psychology

As a result of their interest in the impact of broad social issues on behavioral disorders, community psychologists have become increasingly concerned with how the physical environment affects human emotions and behavior. Their efforts to control behavior through social design are called *environmental management,* and their study of the effects of social design on people has led to a fascinating, new subdiscipline called **environmental psychology,** or **ecological psychology.** A primary area of study within this field is how alterations of environmental stimuli may damage the survival capacity of the human species and cause identifiable abnormal behaviors.

As we noted in Chapter 14 (see Close-up, p. 456), there are many parents who feel that food additives can lead to hyperactivity in children. Similarly, Mayron and colleagues (1974) have suggested that fluorescent lighting, which is so common in schools, may also be a cause of hyperactive behavior in children. While subsequent research (O'Leary et al., 1978) has failed to support this argument, such thinking is an example of the ecological approach to prevention.

Research does seem to confirm that architectural design and the arrangement of living space have a direct affect on the social interaction and behavior of an area's inhabitants. The difficulty in understanding the complex relationship between all the elements determining social behavior is illustrated by the many unsuccessful attempts made to replace substandard urban housing with massive redevelopment projects. Whole city blocks have been leveled and rebuilt, yet the rehabilitation process only seems to create new problems rather than eliminate old ones. While some failures can be attributed to economic and political factors, psychological factors often play a major role. It is apparent that many projects were set up without taking into account the psychological needs of prospective tenants. In some cases, residents felt isolated from the mainstream of the community, and the elimination of shops and businesses discouraged the steady flow of people in and out of the project and thus made the grounds unsafe. Other developments seemed to invite vandalism and delinquency. One apparent cause was the failure of the overall design of the project to extend the residents' feeling of ownership and responsibility outside their own apartments.

Research in this discipline can certainly have far-reaching repercussions in the areas of design, architecture, and urban planning. Toward this end, the National Institute of Mental Health is sponsoring training and teaching programs involving architects, transportation experts, administrators, city planners, and psychologists. Their goal is to equip urban planners with a broad civic outlook and the knowledge needed to design communities that will prevent social problems by meeting the needs of their citizens.

A major difficulty in the implementation of these planning projects, however, will be gaining the cooperation of the many agencies—public, private, local, state, federal—that inevitably control the allocation of funds, land use, and privilege. Leaders of community mental health programs will have to learn how to function effectively within these tightly structured bureaucracies, a skill referred to as the "politics of mental health" (Connery, 1968).

Community efforts

An increasing number of community-based programs offer help to individuals who are having difficulty coping with the problems in their lives. According to the Community Mental Health Centers Act, community mental health and crisis intervention centers were to perform a primary preventive function by providing **consultation and education (C&E) services.** Through psychoeducational techniques, personnel at these centers would teach skills, such as interpersonal problem solving and relaxation training, that would help individuals deal with future crisis situations. In general, mental health workers in community prevention programs concentrate on determining how various community environments and social institutions induce maladaptive behavior and how these processes can be prevented.

A wide range of services may be included under the terms "consultation" and "education." For example, in 1971 a center in San Francisco set up a program designed to reduce the stress created by mandatory busing to achieve racial balance in the schools. A professional staff person rode on the bus with the children and attempted to alleviate separation anxiety by introducing coloring books containing maps of the territory on the route, by utilizing helpful games and toys, and by talking to the children about their new school and their experiences, both before boarding and on the way home. The same staff member held street-corner meetings with the parents to discuss busing concerns and to act as their representative in relations with the school.

Secondary Methods

The preventive programs we have just discussed are examples of primary prevention because they are aimed at people who have not yet exhibited any signs of emotional disorder. Unfortunately, it is not possible to identify the exact differences between primary and secondary prevention; thus we can only illustrate here the difficulties in distinguishing between the two. Nevertheless, we shall now turn our attention to those programs whose focus rests on early detection and intervention with those individuals who already show signs of a problem, or who are clearly at risk for mental disturbance—children of mentally disturbed parents, for example. It should also be noted that a report by the National Institute of Mental Health indicates that only about 4 percent of the total effort of community mental health centers is devoted to C&E. In this respect, they have failed to live up to their original mandate and have become the primary vehicles for secondary prevention.

Intervention with high-risk groups

Systematic programs for the identification of young children with emotional problems—or the potential for emotional problems—have been instituted in some school systems (Watt, 1979). In these programs, teachers and school counselors are trained to recognize certain key symptoms—poor attention span, inability to get along with other children, withdrawal, aggressive behavior, etc.—and refer the child for appropriate treatment. Since most of these programs have been started only recently, it is still too early to measure their effectiveness. It is clear, however, that there are some possible drawbacks. In one study, Cowen and associates (1963) screened young children for maladjustment and identified those at high risk for emotional problems by placing a red tag on their school folders. By the end of the third grade, these red-tagged youngsters were, in fact, doing significantly less well on a variety of behavioral, educational, and adjustment indices (Cowen et al., 1966). The research group further demonstrated that although these children did improve measurably with intervention, they still remained distinguishable from non-tagged youngsters. These results cast doubts on the effectiveness of secondary preventive efforts and pointed out one of the drawbacks of this type of program—that is, the possible stigma attached to the high-risk label. Results indicated that children seen *least* by the project staff improved the most. It was concluded that if teachers believed those students who were seen more often were in more need of therapy and therefore more seriously disturbed, then their expectations of the children may have resulted in a self-fulfilling prophecy.

Crisis intervention

An individual in crisis will either resolve that crisis in an adaptive (healthy) or maladaptive (unhealthy) way. Crisis intervention can help the individual reach a healthy resolution, thus significantly reducing the probability that mental disturbance will occur. In order to be effective on the community level, however, crisis intervention must be readily available. The key is immediate access to free help for all people at any time. Probably such help should not be viewed as therapy, per se, but rather as **advocacy.**

Sally P. just escaped from her husband who had been beating her on a regular basis during their entire married life, about twelve years. She and her two children left home with no possessions other than the clothes on their backs. She has no money, no job, no place to stay, no one to watch her kids, and she's never been on her own before. Sitting in the social worker's office, she bursts into tears as the realization of how bleak her future looks sinks in. She even mentions going back home to more bruising: "Bob has never touched them (the kids), and at least that way they'll get decent food and clothes."

Advocacy. Sally P. is facing an emotional crisis—her marriage of twelve years is in ruins and she does not know how to handle all the problems confronting her. As often happens when people are overwhelmed by many problems simultaneously and feel unable to cope, Sally may become very depressed. If she gives up and returns to her husband, any number of emotional disorders could strike. It is an extremely bad situation over which she has no control, but it is not an uncommon one. Many battered wives remain in abusive marriages or return to them soon after leaving (Rosenbaum, 1979). How Sally resolves this crisis will have a great impact on the future mental health of not only herself, but also her children and even her husband. While Sally may or may not need psychotherapy, she certainly needs an advocate, someone who will provide psychological support and help her connect with social support systems.

If Sally decides she wants a divorce, an advocate-therapist can direct her to somone who provides legal advice. Since Sally has no resources, her advocate may also direct her to and through the welfare system, perhaps facilitating the process so that Sally can start receiving benefits as soon as possible. If Sally wants to report her husband's behavior to the authorities, the advocate will help her complete the police report. Finding a place to live, a job, and day-care services for the children are all difficult problems, but the advocate-therapist is skilled at handling them.

Clearly, advocacy is a function that can be provided by nonprofessionals. For example, the Victims Information Bureau of Suffolk County in Massachusetts employs a staff of nonprofessional and paraprofessional advocates, many of whom are university students. These advocates help their clients cope with practical problems arising from marital violence and rape. But advocacy is not restricted to these crises: Loss of job, long-term illness, legal problems, and death in the family are just a few examples of situations where advocacy can reduce stress and prevent potential emotional disorders.

Telephone hotlines. The **telephone hotline** is an important innovation in community services that provides immediate advocacy assistance in emergency cases. An outgrowth of the suicide prevention movement, these hotlines developed in response to the fact that 78 percent of calls concerned nonsuicidal crises. While some hotlines deal with specific problems such as suicide, drug abuse, rape, and spouse and child abuse, others cater to specific populations such as youth, students, women, or the elderly. The majority, however, offer advice on almost any subject to anyone in need. Someone who has just taken an overdose, someone who has been assaulted, someone whose child has swallowed a toxic household chemical can call and receive either direct aid or a referral to an appropriate agency for special assistance.

Hotlines are frequently criticized for providing services that are inferior to face-to-face psychotherapy. However, this criticism is invalid because nearly 75 percent of calls come in between six p.m. and two a.m. and on weekends, the times when traditional agencies are closed and their services unavailable. To their credit, hotlines eliminate the forms, the commitments, and the social stigma that deter many clients from seeking help, and since almost everyone

Although telephone hotlines have been criticized for their lack of face-to-face interaction, the anonymity they provide may actually encourage hesitant individuals to seek help.

has a phone at home, the service is quick and convenient. This is an enormous asset in situations where time is critical. In short, hotlines offer free assistance to clients who might not turn to traditional helping agencies.

Offering free round-the-clock service to large populations is an expensive operation, but another advantage of hotlines helps keep the expense down: A small number of professionals can serve a large community by utilizing nonprofessional and paraprofessional workers. Although as many as 90 persons may be needed to staff a hotline each week, those 90 can be effectively supervised by fewer than five professionals. The use of volunteers further reduces costs. The personal qualities required for clinical effectiveness—namely warmth, genuineness, and empathy (Carkhuff, 1968)—are not, after all, the exclusive domain of mental health professionals. In fact, some people allege that professional "armor" makes the professional worker less effective in dealing with crisis situations (Farberow, 1966; Caplan, 1961).

Recent estimates indicate that telephone hotlines serve over ten million callers annually in the United States alone. And despite a lack of evidence proving their effectiveness, hotlines continue to proliferate. Rosenbaum and Calhoun (1977) conclude: "The telephone hotline has the potential to be an important therapeutic instrument and represents a necessary step in the direction of preventive psychotherapy and the development of the community mental health delivery system" (p. 338).

PROBLEMS WITH PREVENTION EFFORTS

Despite sincere efforts to deal with the many problems related to prevention, the fact remains that progress has been distressingly slow. We have already discussed the difficulty in defining prevention; we shall now turn to the practical and ethical issues that hamper us in the pursuit of our goal—namely the elimination of mental illness and suffering.

Ethical Issues

Many primary prevention activities threaten to impinge on human rights, particularly the right to refuse treatment, which has already been tested and upheld in several legal contests.

There has always been talk of governments using drugs or hospitalization as a means of social control, and any Soviet dissident can elaborate on the dangers of allowing the government to decide what constitutes mental illness. This same position is expostulated by Thomas Szasz (1970), who expresses the fears of many that the community mental health movement could be used to make citizens "uncomplainingly submissive to the will of the elites" (p. 224), and that mental health technology may be used for political repression instead of psychological growth and enhancement.

Several states recently placed a nominal tax on marriage licenses in order to collect funds for prevention of spouse abuse projects: Florida implemented a five-dollar-per-license tax in October of 1978, and similar provisions have been made in Montana, Ohio, and Pennsylvania (SANEnews, 1, 7, 1979). While no state has yet mandated a license giving permission to have children, many social workers in the area of child abuse hope that some day couples will be required to pass competency tests before receiving permission to become parents. However, although almost everyone accepts the right of a state to license automobile drivers, the idea of requiring a license-to-parent seems to be going too far, even though such a program might reduce the incidence of child abuse. One has only to consider the public outrage at the fluoridation of drinking water to see how anxious people can get over government attempts to treat large segments of the population, whatever the apparent safety or preventive importance of the procedure. Given such a precedent, how can governments ethically decide which behaviors are psychopathological and justify treatment against the will of the patients? Such a program raises the specter of a totalitarian society.

Unfortunately, primary prevention must by definition blanket a population, thereby denying many individuals the right to refuse treatment. Just one person's refusal could produce negative results. A father who refuses a parenting course and then abuses his child would be a double offender, since the chances would be high that his child would become another abusive parent, and so on through future generations.

Financial Considerations

Almost all prevention programs are expensive, and any new expenditures face new obstacles in our current economic climate. Because primary prevention involves intervening before any real problems are visible, people are often unwilling to support expenditures for disorders that *may* develop sometime in the future. Secondary prevention avoids this issue because the focus is on early detection and intervention when symptoms are already evident. However, if intervention is successful and the more serious disorders avoided, doubt may be cast as to whether intervention was really needed in the first place. This constitutes a dual problem for prevention programs: (1) convincing the public that financial expenditures are warranted and (2) generating enough popular support for application of the program to entire communities in order to ensure that everyone in need is served.

Obviously prevention programs carry a high price tag; how do we justify the cost? Perhaps this issue is best addressed at two levels: (1) justification of preventive efforts in general and (2) justification of specific prevention programs. The first issue concerns the fact that, by definition, prevention is directed at populations presently free of a particular disorder and, therefore, must involve the prediction that if nothing is done, the condition in question will, indeed, develop. This problem ties in with the second issue whereby therapeutic intervention is justified on the basis of outcome research: If the client improves, the intervention was successful. But if our predictive ability is not good, justification is not easy.

The issue of prediction is not a new one. Often both formal and informal commitment to mental hospitals is based on the prediction that certain individuals are dangerous to themselves or to society. The decision to detain someone is, therefore, based on the predictive ability

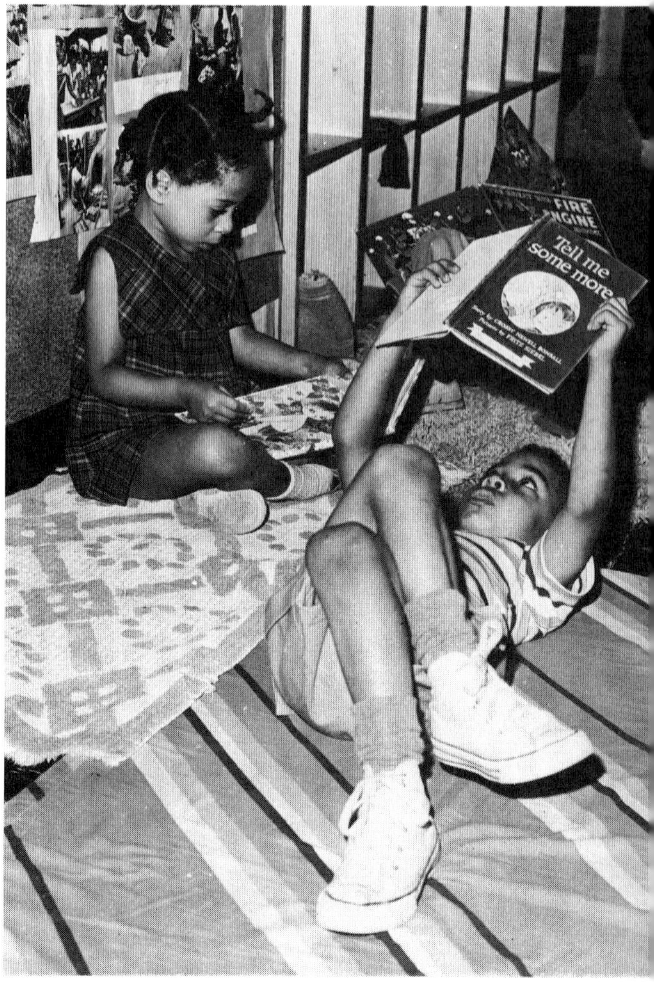

Many of the children selected for Head Start's eight-week summer school program come from homes where there are no books and few chances to learn to read.

of mental health professionals. How good are such professionals at prediction? Based on the evaluation of their performance by several studies (Monahan 1976), the answer seems to be not good. The difficulty was illustrated by New York City's Operation Baxtrom. A thousand mentally ill convicts, who had been placed in maximum security hospitals because of their potential danger to society, were transferred under supreme court order to civil mental hospitals. After one year, only seven required special treatment because they were too dangerous to remain in civil hospitals; 200 had been released.

If the disorder being prevented never occurs, how can we be sure that success was a direct result of the program? The relationship between smoking and lung cancer provides a good analogy. Although it is well known that smoking is strongly associated with lung cancer, it is also known that many smokers will not develop lung cancer, while many nonsmokers will. Such ambiguity may account for the lack of support behind smoking-prevention programs. It is even harder to obtain public support for mental illness prevention programs because our prediction formulas are even more imprecise. The potential problem is less frightening, and the prevention programs are often inconvenient.

Justifying the cost

In order to put the cost of prevention in the proper perspective, it must be compared with the cost of traditional therapy and with the cost of doing nothing. Individual therapy, regardless of its effectiveness, cannot reach all needy people, and the cost per person is high. The cost of prevention is also high but because in theory it reaches a broad range of people, the relative cost per person is low. The cost of not providing any help at all may be beyond computation. In the words of the 1978 Task Panel on Prevention:

> Effective primary prevention programs promise to be less expensive in the long run than the direct (fiscal) and indirect (human) costs to society of not providing such services. (p. 1829)

The Headstart program for children, probably the most popular and widely known of existing prevention programs, illustrates the reality of this statement. During 1978, the United States government spent almost $643 million on Headstart programs, amounting to about $1600 per child per year. What did we get for this money?

The Headstart programs are based on the premise that all children share certain needs and that children of low income families, in particular, can benefit from a comprehensive competency-building program. A ten-year longitudinal study (Heber, 1976) of the effectiveness of an enrichment program for disadvantaged children was directed at high-risk youngsters—those who had mothers with IQs of 75 or less. The study began at birth and ran to age seven. The results? The sample that received Heber's program outpaced the control group and even went beyond expectations for normal populations: At age seven, Heber's special group had a mean IQ of 121; 87 was the mean for controls. Heber concluded that early systematic competency acquisition seems to pave the way for effective adaptation later in life. What dollar value can be put on such dramatic gains?

In the case study of Nancy, Mike, and Jimmy, what would have happened if stress led Nancy to abuse Jimmy, a situation that is more common than we would like to believe? Unwanted children are at high risk for abuse and, therefore, for subsequent placement in foster care. According to recent estimates, foster care costs the government about five thousand dollars per child per year. Since around 400,000 children receive foster care services annually, and each child remains in the program for an average of five years, costs run almost two billion dollars each year.

The fiscal cost of such programs may be exorbitant, but we must also consider the alternative: the emotional effect on abused children and the subsequent social costs incurred in the future. Will Jimmy become a delinquent after being tossed in and out of foster homes? Will he repeat his father's history, passing on his own discontent to yet another generation? Unfortunately, the chances of either alternative—or worse ones—are high. We must thus ask ourselves which alternative will ultimately be the most costly: the cost of prevention or the cost of the problems that may develop in the future—and in future generations.

SUMMARY

Although prevention is an obviously attractive concept that has received widespread endorsement, progress in this area has been distressingly slow. One major obstacle is that there are so many potential targets for prevention. Therefore professionals disagree on the focus of efforts and on the types of efforts to be made. Another major issue is when intervention should occur, a subject that has led to the idea of three levels of prevention. Primary prevention is any action that promotes optimal positive mental health and prevents mental health problems or reduces the risk of their development. Secondary prevention involves early diagnosis and treatment to keep an already established problem from getting worse. Tertiary prevention includes efforts to reduce the seriousness of a disorder, shorten its duration, and rehabilitate the afflicted individual—in other words, most management methods.

There are other issues to resolve in determining the nature of prevention programs: Should the program blanket a population or be restricted to high-risk groups or individuals? Should we try to identify and eliminate the causes of disorder or just teach coping skills to everyone? Different theoretical schools have conflicting opinions on these points. Some favor eliminating the causes; others prefer to focus on children as the highest-risk group. Those who advocate a sociogenic explanation feel that eliminating social stress through changing our social systems is the best prevention; still other groups feel that the major focus should be on promoting "wellness."

Major primary prevention methods center around education: teaching individuals to understand all the ramifications of an act and knowing all possible options. As more and more people—especially in industry and government—become aware of this need, new ideas—for example, using the media to disseminate information, planning more psychologically sound environments, and forming self-help groups—are becoming more common. Community mental health centers are also supposed to be involved with primary prevention through consultation and education services. In reality, however, this service is delegated to last place, and providing secondary and tertiary prevention is the major operation of most community mental health centers. Secondary methods generally revolve around those who already show signs of a problem or who, like the children of mentally disturbed parents, are at extremely high risk. Crisis intervention programs, especially hotlines, are a particularly effective measure: They offer immediate access to free help for anybody at any time—even those times when most public clinics and private offices are closed.

The problems with applying prevention efforts are ethical and financial. In order to provide true primary prevention, the entire population must be blanketed, which clearly overrides the right to refuse treatment of those (the majority) who are not directly affected by mental health problems. And there is always the difficulty of assuring the public that if the preventive measure does not take place, mental disorder will develop, when there is no way of establishing a direct cause/effect relationship. Since most prevention programs are costly, securing public support for programs based on uncertain predictions is a definite obstacle. However, such programs as Headstart indicate that certain prevention techniques do work, and they also illustrate that over the long run it will be more costly for society to do nothing.

Glossary

Abnormal behavior. Maladaptive behavior different in kind or degree from that of most people.

Abscess. An area of infection that has been sealed over by connective tissue.

Absence seizure. A mild epileptic seizure during which the person appears to be "far away" in thought.

Activities therapy. A method of keeping elderly institutionalized patients active and aware by having them participate in daily activities.

Addiction. The physiological need for a substance.

Addison's disease. A disorder of the adrenal glands. Depression can be one of the symptoms of the disease.

Adjustment disorder. An abnormal reaction to an identifiable psychosocial stressor.

Adrenal glands. Hormone-producing organs located above the kidneys. If the glands malfunction, psychological symptoms may result.

Adrenocortical hormone metabolism. An increase in certain hormones—especially cortisol—that may be linked to the affective disorders.

Advocacy. The providing of emotional support and practical coping advice, a function that can often be performed by non- or paraprofessionals.

Affective disorder. An extreme disturbance of mood or emotion.

Agoraphobia. Fear of open places and large crowds.

Alcoholics Anonymous (AA). A self-help group for alcoholics or people who are troubled by their drinking habits.

Alcoholism. A drinking pattern that impairs a person's overall life functioning.

Altruistic suicide. Taking one's own life for the good of society.

Alzheimer's disease. A pre-senile organic disorder of the brain's cortex, characterized by extreme irritability, agitation, and confusion.

Amniocentesis. Analysis of the amniotic fluid (the liquid surrounding a fetus) to determine chromosomal abnormalities.

Amphetamines. Synthetic drugs, such as Methedrine, that stimulate the sympathetic branch of the central nervous system.

Aneurysm. A weakening in the wall of a blood vessel that can balloon out and rupture, causing severe damage.

Anomic suicide. Killing oneself because of overwhelming social chaos.

Anorexia nervosa. An adolescent disorder that usually afflicts young girls who refuse to eat out of fear of becoming fat.

Antabuse. A drug used to treat problem drinking by producing a physiological intolerance for alcohol.

Antagonistic interaction. A type of interaction between different drugs (especially between antabuse and alcohol) in which each substance is pharmacologically contrary to the other.

Antipsychotic drugs. Drugs, particularly chlorpromazine, that reduce the extreme psychotic behaviors of schizophrenia and the affective disorders.

Antisocial personality. An individual characterized by a total disregard for other people, plus the inability to feel guilt, to form close relationships, and to learn from experience.

Anxiety. A general feeling of overwhelming fear, tension, and worry.

Aphasia. The loss or impairment of the ability to express ideas through speech or writing.

Assertiveness training. A therapy designed to increase a person's self-assurance in social settings by expressing needs and feelings. It is frequently used to treat anxiety.

Assessment. The process engaged in by a therapist to determine the nature and scope of the presenting problem of a client.

Associated features. Behaviors that are often—but not always—present in a given disorder.

Asthma. A respiratory ailment commonly believed to be linked with psychological stress and certain personality traits.

Attention deficit disorder. A childhood disorder characterized by an extremely short attention span and a diminished ability to concentrate; excessive motor activity may also be present.

Atrophy. The wasting away of body tissue.

Authenticity. A precept of existentialist psychology that urges the "real" person to surface and direct life according to what the individual believes is valid.

Auto-immune theory. The idea that certain changes in the structure of cells lead them to be rejected by the body's natural immune system, causing deterioration and aging.

Autonomic nervous system. The division of the central nervous system that governs such basic functions as heartbeat, endocrine production, respiration, all of which may be physiological responses to stress.

Aversion therapy. A method of eliminating an unwanted behavior through association with unpleasant or painful stimuli.

Aversive behavior rehearsal. A therapy that has been used for exhibitionism in which the person exposes himself by appointment in order to gradually rob the act of its stimulating properties.

Avoidant disorder. A childhood syndrome characterized by extreme and often incapacitating shyness.

Avoidant personality. An individual characterized by withdrawal from social contact out of fear of rejection.

Barbiturates. Synthetic drugs that depress the functioning of the central nervous system; divided into long-acting (e.g., phenobarbital) and the more addictive, short-acting (e.g., pentobarbital).

Basal ganglia. Bunches of nerve cells located deep in the brain that govern posture and muscle tone.

Becoming. A precept of existentialist psychology that refers to the continual process of growth, awareness, and self-definition.

Behavior contract. A written agreement drawn between two parties to structure and increase the likelihood of a behavior change.

Behaviorism. The branch of psychology that believes all behavior is learned and that the environment is the primary conditioner of human action.

Beriberi. A disease caused by thiamine deficiency; its psychological symptoms include insomnia and irritability.

Biofeedback. A technique that teaches the person to control various autonomic physiological functions.

Biogenic. Having a biological or physiological cause.

Biogenic amines. Substances that help transmit electrical impulses through the brain; divided into catecholamines and indolamines.

Bipolar disorder. An affective disorder characterized by swings from wild mania to deep depression.

Blackouts. Periods of memory loss experienced after heavy or prolonged drinking.

Borderline personality. An unstable, impulsive, and unpredictable, individual who exhibits sudden changes in both mood and life circumstances.

Brain tumor. More correctly called intracranial neoplasm, or cellular growth in the head; may be benign (noncancerous) or malignant (cancerous).

Bruxism. The nonfunctional and maladaptive grinding of the teeth associated with stress or anxiety.

Catatonic schizophrenia. A schizophrenic disorder in which movement and activity are minimal; stupor or rigidity may be present as well.

Catecholamine hypothesis. The theory that depression is caused by a deficiency of the catecholamine norepinephrine, while mania is caused by an excess of norepinephrine.

Catecholamines. Biogenic amines that help transmit neural impulses in the brain.

Catharsis of aggression. An idea stating that a person who represses aggressive tendencies is more likely to explode in violent behavior than someone who gives vent to such emotions.

Cell loss theory. A theory that blames the aging process on the reduction in both the number of functioning cells and the body's ability to reproduce lost cells.

Cellular adaptation theory of heroin addiction. The belief that addiction is a result of the body's increasingly stronger attempts to counterbalance the depressing effects of heroin, attempts that soon offset equilibrium themselves.

Cellular aging. A theory that attributes the bodily deterioration of aging to the decreased rate of activity in older cells.

Cerebellum. A large section located at the lower back of the brain; it controls motor activity.

Cerebral hemispheres. The two major divisions of the cerebrum, designated right and left, that are separated by a deep lateral fissure.

Cerebrovascular accident (CVA). Commonly called a stroke, a CVA occurs when a major blood vessel in the brain experiences either occlusion (blockage) or hemorrhage (rupture), causing severe damage.

Cerebrum. The largest part of the brain, formed of convoluted gray matter called the cortex and divided into two hemispheres that are linked by several networks of nerve fibers.

Childhood psychosis. A collective term for childhood schizophrenia and infantile autism.

Childhood schizophrenia. A severe thought disorder that strikes children at about age 5; although similar in some respects to adult schizophrenia, the relationship between the two is not clear.

Chlorpromazine. A synthetic antipsychotic drug derived from antihistamines that is almost universally used for schizophrenia, with generally good results and few negative side effects.

Chromosomes. The tiny, rod-like structures that form twenty-three pairs in each human cell and contain the genetic code of an individual.

Circadian rhythms. Biological "clocks" that apparently exist in all humans, governing the cycles of various physiological functions; a defect in one or more cycles may be linked with the affective disorders.

Classical conditioning. Also called respondent conditioning, this is a form of learning in which a response comes to be elicited by a stimulus that did not previously elicit the response.

Classic migraine. The most common form of migraine headache, generally striking one side of the head at a time; its onset is often preceded by a warning (aura).

Classification. The organization of data into reasonably similar groups to facilitate communication and prediction.

Client-centered therapy. A humanistic treatment developed by Carl Rogers in which the therapist uses unconditional positive regard to help the client develop a healthier self-concept.

Cluster migraine. A rare form of migraine-type headaches that occur in rapid succession, or clusters, and then may not strike again for some time.

Cocaine. A white crystalline powder derived from the leaves of the coca plant. The illegal stimulant is very popular and very expensive, and it seems to cause no withdrawal syndrome.

Codeine. An opiate used primarily in cough medications. Through cross-tolerance, codeine can maintain a heroin user's addiction.

Cognition. The human thought process.

Cognitive restructuring. A treatment formulated by Aaron Beck that tests a person's beliefs in a logical way, thus exposing any fallacies and breaking down the person's negative cognitive set.

Cognitive triad. A theory that cites a negative view of the self, the world, and the future as a cause of depression.

Collective unconscious. Carl Jung's concept that all humans share certain "primal" memories.

Coma. A deep and unresponsive period of unconsciousness.

Common migraine. Similar to a classic migraine but lacking an aura and less unilateral.

Complex partial seizures. A type of epilepsy characterized by trance-like state and the repetition of some meaningless movement, such as patting a table; formerly called psychomotor seizures.

Compulsion. A repetitive behavior that a person feels compelled to perform in order to avoid feeling anxious.

Compulsive personality. A personality type characterized by perfectionism, rigidity, and coolness toward other people.

Concordance rate. The percentage of twin pairs in which both twins have the same mental disorder.

Concussion. A hard blow to the head that jars the brain inside the skull, causing a temporary disruption of normal functioning and at least a brief loss of consciousness.

Conditioned response. A learned response to a stimulus that has become automatic, as when a driver brakes for a red light.

Conditioned stimulus. A stimulus to which a person has learned to respond automatically.

Conduct disorder. An adolescent syndrome in which the youngster acts out frustrations and anxiety; the disorder can be classified as socialized or undersocialized and aggressive or nonaggressive.

Conscious. The level of mind that Freud believed was used for everyday functioning.

Consultation and education (C&E) services. A primary prevention method developed by the Community Mental Health Centers Act. Services include training in such skills as relaxation and interpersonal problem-solving to help prevent future problems.

Contingency management. A technique from behavior therapy in which consequences for behaviors are controlled so as to extinguish inappropriate behavior and reinforce appropriate behavior.

Continuum of behavior. The idea that the various human behaviors occupy different positions on a continuum and are not different in kind but in degree.

Contusions. A serious head injury in which the brain is knocked against the inside of the skull, forming a bruise; unconsciousness results and a coma may follow.

Conversion disorder. A somatoform disorder in which a physiological function is impaired without organic cause.

Corpus callosum. A network of nerve cells deep in the brain that links the right and left cerebral hemispheres.

Cortex. The convoluted gray matter that forms the cerebrum.

Cortical immaturity. A theory that explains antisocial personality as a failure of the cortex to develop properly, causing the person to act impulsively, like a child.

Cortisone. A hormone produced by the adrenal glands; overproduction can cause Cushing's syndrome, and underproduction Addison's disease.

Counteractive drugs. Drugs used in drug abuse treatments—especially antabuse for alcoholism—that produce undesirable effects when the abused substance is taken.

Covert sensitization. A form of aversion therapy in which the person is asked to imagine something unpleasant or fearful in association with the stimulus that evokes undesirable behavior.

Cretinism. A thyroid disorder caused by hypothyroidism during childhood, resulting in stunted growth and mental retardation.

Cross-tolerance. A relationship that exists between drugs derived from the same source in which the effects produced by each drug are similar.

Cushing's syndrome. A disease caused by overproduction of cortisone; it results in unpredictable mood swings, obesity, and muscle atrophy.

Cyclothymic disorder. A milder, less debilitating form of bipolar disorder, or manic-depression.

Defense mechanism. An irrational way of protecting one's ego, which can include projection, displacement, denial, rationalization, and repression.

Deinstitutionalization. A practice of moving severely disturbed mental patients into the community and focusing their treatment on living outside the mental hospital.

Delirium tremens (DTs). An acute reaction to alcohol withdrawal that includes nausea, fever, hallucinations, and convulsions.

Delusions. A thought disturbance common to schizophrenia and characterized by an irrational or exaggerated notion that contradicts reality, for example, the grandiose delusion of being Napoleon or the melancholic delusion of being dead.

Dementia praecox. Kraepelin's name for what is now classified as schizophrenia.

Dependence. The psychological—but not physiological—need for a substance, especially a drug.

Dependent personality. An individual who out of low self-confidence relies on others to make all major decisions.

Depersonalization disorder. A dissociative disorder that includes distorted perceptions, a temporary loss of control over speech and behavior, and an "out of body" feeling.

Depressants. Addictive drugs, such as the opiates, that sedate the body's central nervous system, reducing anxiety and inducing sleep.

Detoxification. The first step in any drug abuse treatment: clearing all traces of the substance from the body, which can sometimes be very dangerous and painful.

Developmental dyslexia. A reading disorder of childhood that is characterized by faulty comprehension of written language, due to visual/spatial problems, and by awkward speech.

Diagnosis. The initial identification of a presenting problem.

Diagnostic criteria. The behaviors classified in DSM-III that *must* be present for a particular syndrome to be diagnosed.

Diagnostic reliability. The probability that the presenting problem will be correctly classified; interjudge reliability refers to the probability that more than one professional would classify a problem the same way, while temporal reliability is the probability that the classification will hold over time.

Diathesis-stress model. An interactional explanation for deviant behavior, which states that a predisposing biological factor (diathesis) combines with psychosocial stress to form a mental disorder.

Differential diagnosis. The process of using explicit data to distinguish between classifications that have very similar symptoms.

Disaster syndrome. A sequence of typical reactions to a calamity: shock, disorientation, passivity, suggestibility, hypersensitivity to startles, irritability, and talkativeness.

Discordance rate. The percentage of twin pairs in which only one twin exhibits abnormal behavior.

Discrimination. In classical conditioning, the ability to distinguish between very similar stimuli, so that appropriate responses are made only to the correct stimulus.

Disengagement theory. A theory of aging stating that the elderly must be phased out in order for society to continue functioning correctly.

Disorders with physical symptoms. A DSM-III classification for such childhood problems as stuttering, elimination difficulties, and sleepwalking.

Disorganized schizophrenia. Formerly termed hebephrenic, this classification includes incoherent speech, flat affect, silly and bizarre behavior, delusions and hallucinations, and social withdrawal to a marked degree; the prognosis is generally poor.

Disregulation model. Gary Schwartz's theory that malfunction at some point in the body's regular transmission of negative feedback causes stress-related physical disorders.

Dissociative disorders. Disorders characterized by an alteration of consciousness, identity, or motor behavior—specifically, psychogenic amnesia, psychogenic fugue, multiple personality, and depersonalization.

Dizygotic twins. Twins who develop out of two separate eggs; fraternal twins.

Dominant gene. A gene carrying traits that are more likely to be clearly expressed in a person's physiological makeup.

Dopamine. A neural transmitter that may be linked to schizophrenia.

Dopamine hypothesis. The theory that schizophrenia is caused by an excess of dopamine in the synapse between neurons, causing faster and more erratic transmissions that cannot be handled properly.

Double-bind hypothesis. Gregory Bateson's classic theory of schizophrenia: a parent gives a child opposite messages which the child cannot respond to appropriately and so retreats into schizophrenic behavior.

Down's syndrome. A chromosomal abnormality (an extra chromosome in the twenty-third pair) that results in a mentally retarded child recognizable by a flattened nose, slanted eyes, enlarged tongue, and general underdevelopment.

Dream interpretation. An early part of Freud's psychoanalysis in which he tried to uncover the dream's latent content (true meaning) from the symbology used in the manifest content (the dream itself).

Drift hypothesis. A theory explaining the concentration of psychopathology in the lowest socioeconomic classes. It states that people who exhibit deviant behavior "drift" downward on the social scale because they cannot hold a job and maintain a higher standard of living.

Duodenal ulcer. An ulcer that forms in the duodenum, the area between the stomach and the small intestine.

Dyskinesia. Disjointed movements caused by impairment of the basal ganglia.

Dyslexia. Certain types of vision impairments, including seeing things backwards or upside down, that lead to communication problems and reading difficulties.

Dyssocial personality. Cleckley's term for the typical criminal. This personality is distinguished from the antisocial personality by very careful planning and clear desire to obtain socially approved goals.

Dysthymic disorder. A mild form of major depressive disorder, resulting in irritability, a tendency to cry, and moderate life impairment.

Ecological psychology. A new branch of psychology devoted to studying the effects on behavior of altered environmental stimuli.

Ego. According to Freud, the part of the personality mediating between the id and the superego and operating under the reality principle.

Ego-dystonic homosexuality. DSM-III's controversial classification of homosexuality as a behavior that is inconsistent with the person's true sexual inclinations or goals.

Egoistic suicide. Killing oneself because of a feeling of actual or imagined isolation.

Electroconvulsive therapy (ECT). Also called electroshock therapy, this treatment consists of administering doses of electric current to the forebrain, which can be beneficial for severe depression.

Electroencephalogram (EEG). A graphic representation of brain-wave activity; used in assessment.

Electrolyte balance. A higher concentration of electrolytes (charged substances) inside rather than outside neurons has been suggested as a cause of depression.

Electrosleep. A state of deep sleep induced by passing a low electric current through the brain; the treatment is sometimes used to fight anxiety.

Elementary partial seizures. Epileptic seizures that affect sensory motor control; a muscle or a muscle group may twitch, or there may be a tingling sensation, but no loss of or change in consciousness occurs.

Empirical approach. Classifying data by similar and clearly observable characteristics.

Encephalitis. A general term for inflammation of the cerebral cortex.

Encopresis. A childhood disorder involving faulty bowel control but not related to organic or physiological problems.

Endogenous depression. Kraepelin's category for those episodes caused by internal biological malfunction; the classification is not recognized by DSM-III.

Endorphins. Morphine-like substances produced by the human body; narcotics addicts may be deficient in these.

Enuresis. A childhood disorder involving faulty bladder control but not related to organic or physiological problems.

Environmental psychology. See ecological psychology.

Epilepsy. Collective term for a group of disorders characterized mainly by seizures; classified into generalized, complex partial, elementary partial, and idiopathic.

Error theory. The belief that normal cell division accumulates "errors" in the genetic material, thus building up increasingly defective cells that interfere with normal functioning and result in aging.

Essential features. The behaviors of a disorder listed in DSM-III that distinguish it from other syndromes.

Essential hypertension. Chronic high blood pressure with no identifiable organic cause.

Etiology. Cause, or process, of initial development.

Euthanasia. Ending the life of a terminally ill person out of mercy, so that a minimum of debilitation and pain is experienced.

Excitement phase. The earliest stage of sexual arousal.

Exhibitionism. The almost exclusively male sexual deviation of exposing the genitals to strangers in order to become aroused.

Existential anxiety. Anxiety that results when people choose to live inauthentically and then realize that they are spiritually dead.

Existential psychology. A branch of psychology based on existentialism, its main focus being on the relationship between the world and the individual.

Exogenous depression. Kraepelin's category for those episodes caused by clearly identifiable external stressors; the classification is not recognized by DSM-III.

Extended families. Three or more generations of a family living together under one roof; common among agrarian societies.

Extinction. The gradual elimination of a learned response through removal of positive reinforcements or the termination of the unconditioned stimulus.

Factitious disorder. A somatoform disorder in which the person deliberately creates symptoms of illness but usually without conscious intent.

Fetal alcohol syndrome (FAS). A set of characteristics—among them growth deficiency, malformation, and mental retardation—often found in the babies of alcoholic mothers.

Fetishism. A sexual deviation in which the person uses inanimate objects, such as clothing, to obtain sexual gratification.

Filial maturity. A common term for the role reversal that often occurs when adult children take on the responsibility for elderly parents.

Fixation. In psychodynamic theory, an arrest of normal emotional growth at one of the early psychosexual stages.

Flashback. A recurrence of perceptual distortion often experienced by users of LSD long after the drug has been taken.

Flooding. A therapy for anxiety-related problems in which the person is repeatedly exposed to the anxiety-producing stimulus so that it gradually loses the power to evoke anxiety.

Free association. A psychoanalytic technique in which the client talks about whatever comes to mind, eventually freeing repressed memories and emotions.

Freedom and responsibility of choice. A precept of existential psychology stating that all humans can freely choose how to live—but they must accept responsibility for the choices they make.

Frontal lobes. Functional divisions in the forefront of each cerebral hemisphere that deal with complex motor and language skills.

Galvanic skin response. The electrical conductivity of the skin.

Gastric ulcer. A lesion that develops in the wall of the stomach and is strongly linked to stress.

General adaptation syndrome (GAS). Hans Selye's model of bodily reactions to a stressor: alarm, resistance, and exhaustion.

Generalization. In classical conditioning, the tendency for a response to a given stimulus to occur for other very similar stimuli.

Generalized anxiety disorder. A disorder characterized by strong, long-term, and persistent anxiety not due to an identifiable stressor.

Generalized seizures. A broad category of epileptic seizures that includes absence (petit mal) seizures and tonic-clonic (grand mal) seizures.

Genes. The individual transmitters of hereditary trait information carried by chromosomes.

Genetic counseling. Counseling that explains the mechanism of known hereditary diseases to prospective parents, to help them decide about risking parenthood.

Gestalt therapy. Fritz Perls's concept of involving the entire person—and seeking integration of functioning—in treatment.

Habituation. The point at which the body is immune to the effects of a certain dose of a substance; in order to feel anything, the dose must therefore be continually increased.

Hallucinations. Sensory perceptions, such as visions, that have no basis in fact; a phenomenon common in schizophrenia.

Hallucinogens. Drugs, such as mescaline and LSD, that produce altered states of consciousness, perceptual distortion, and changes in mood and behavior; they are generally not addictive.

Hashish. An illegal drug, similar to marijuana but more potent, made from the dried resin of the same plant.

Hemorrhage. The rupture of a major blood vessel in the brain, which lets blood spill out into the surrounding neural tissue, causing a stroke.

Heroin. An illegal narcotic derived from opium; the drug produces an intense euphoria but is highly addictive.

Hierarchy of needs. Maslow's theory of motivation that ranks human needs; until a lower-order need is fulfilled, no progress can be made to a higher order—much less to self-actualization.

High risk method. A technique used to study the development of schizophrenia, pioneered by Mednick; children of at least one schizophrenic parent are followed over time to see which will also become schizophrenic.

Histrionic personality. An individual characterized by always being excitable and overly dramatic and the need to be the center of attention.

Homeostasis. The equilibrium that most living organisms tend to maintain unless some outside influence interferes.

Homosexuality. The desire to have sexual intercourse with a member of the same sex; it is no longer officially classified as a sexual disorder.

Hospice. A medical center for terminally ill patients that does not attempt to prolong life but does try to make dying a less painful experience.

Humanistic psychology. A branch of psychology that aims to emphasize the positive aspects of people and the potential for personal growth; many self-help groups have arisen from this field.

Humors. The term established by Hippocrates for the four vital fluids—phlegm, blood, black bile and yellow bile—that, when present in unbalanced proportions, caused a physical or mental disorder.

Huntington's chorea. An organic mental disorder in which the basal ganglia are impaired, resulting in uncontrollable body twitches and marked personality changes; it is hereditary.

Hyperactivity. The popular term for hyperkinesis.

Hyperkinesis. A childhood disorder, the symptoms of which include a very short attention span, constant motion, inability to sit still or to stop talking.

Hyperthyroidism. Also called Grave's disease, this disorder results from an excess of the hormone thyroxin that causes the body's systems to speed up; a confused, sometimes delusional, state may result.

Hypnosis. The process of inducing a state resembling sleep that still allows the person to respond to spoken suggestion.

Hypochondriasis. A somatization disorder in which the person has a grossly exaggerated fear of becoming ill and insists that every pain means a major illness.

Hypothalamus. A gland near the center of the brain that regulates metabolism, appetite, and emotions.

Hypothyroidism. Underproduction of the hormone thyroxin, which causes myxedema, a general slowdown in all body functions; in children, it results in cretinism.

Id. The part of the personality that Freud thought consisted of instinctual drives and operated under the pleasure principle.

Identity crisis. According to Erikson, the period of confusion about the "real" personality that occurs during adolescence.

Idiopathic epilepsy. A catchall category for those epileptic seizures that do not meet the criteria for the other types of epilepsy.

Implosive therapy. A behavior therapy for anxiety-related problems; the person imagines in vivid detail the feared stimulus so that it will gradually cease to evoke anxiety.

Incest. Sexual intercourse between blood-related members of a family; although taboo in most societies, incest is no longer thought to be rare.

Indolamines. A type of biogenic amine that helps transmit neural impulses.

Infantile autism. A psychotic disorder first evident in infancy characterized by social and emotional unresponsiveness, extreme resistance to environmental change, bizarre self-stimulating behaviors, and meaningless vocalizations.

Inferiority complex. Adler's power-motivation theory that during childhood all humans consider themselves inferior to obviously more powerful adults; as a result they spend their maturity attempting to overcome such feelings.

Inhibited orgasm. A broad category for the various sexually dysfunctional patterns that women exhibit; a similar category exists for men, although this problem is rare among them.

Inhibited sexual excitement. A dysfunctional pattern in which the person is unable to reach or maintain sufficient arousal for intercourse; for men this problem is generally known as erectile insufficiency.

Institutionalization syndrome. A behavior pattern typical of many hospital and nursing home residents: despondency, apathy, and depression often leading to a sharp decline in physical and mental health and sometimes even eventual death.

Intelligence quotient (IQ). In theory, a score indicating the level of cognitive ability that a person possesses as measured by a variety of standardized tests.

In vivo desensitization. A variant of systematic desensitization that uses the actual anxiety-provoking stimulus in the desensitizing process.

Juvenile delinquent. A youth between the ages of 14 and 18 or 21 who engages in illegal and antisocial activity.

Klinefelter's syndrome. A rare chromosomal aberration (an extra X chromosome in the gender-determining chromosome pair of a male child) that can result in mental retardation.

Korsakoff's psychosis. A disorder common among alcoholics that is caused by a deficiency of the B vitamins and impairs memory.

Labeling. A theory proposed by Szasz stating that there is no mental illness, and that society labels certain misfits or potential troublemakers mentally ill in order to control them or remove them from society.

"La belle indifference." A distinguishing characteristic of conversion disorder in which the person seems totally indifferent to his or her disability.

Laceration. The most severe form of head trauma; it includes any injury that penetrates or tears brain tissue.

Law of effect. Thorndike's theory that behaviors with a pleasant consequence are more likely to be repeated than behaviors that have an unpleasant consequence or no consequence at all.

Learned helplessness. Seligman's explanation for depression; a person's negative cognitions about control over life lead that person to cease trying and to become dejected, apathetic, and hopeless.

Learning disability. A controversial DSM-III classification that is based on poor performance in one or more academic areas, especially in reading and arithmetic. The category affects children of at least average intelligence.

Libido. In psychodynamic theory, the constructive side of the id that urges self-gratification in all things, particularly sexual gratification.

Life-enrichment counseling. A treatment that focuses on trying to get elderly patients more involved in leisure activities.

Life review. A process common to the elderly, in which they reminisce about the past, remembering both achievements and failures.

Lithium salts. An effective pharmacotherapy for mania that seems to eliminate depressive episodes; the treatment lends support to the electrolyte balance explanation of depression.

LSD. A strong synthetic hallucinogen that is a popular but illegal recreational drug; time and perceptual distortions, hallucinations, and abrupt and sharp mood changes are typical effects.

Mainlining. A method of administering drugs, particularly heroin, in which the drug is injected directly into the bloodstream, producing immediate effects.

Major affective disorders. A broad category of mood disorders that includes major depressive disorder and bipolar disorder.

Major depressive disorder. DSM-III's classification for clinical depression, which includes such characteristics as hopelessness, apathy, unhappiness, and suicidal ideation and attempts.

Malingering. A somatization disorder in which a person deliberately fakes physical symptoms for a specific end, such as missing a test.

Mania. Hippocrates' original term for wildly excited behavior.

Manic-depressive psychosis. Kraepelin's term for bipolar disorder.

Marijuana. A very popular but illegal, nonaddictive recreational drug derived from the dried flowers and leaves of the Cannabis sativa plant. It produces perceptual and mood changes and a generally contented feeling.

Marital schism. A family pattern characterized by warring parents, which Lidz believes induces schizophrenic behavior in children.

Marital skew. Another family pattern that Lidz feels leads to schizophrenic behavior in children; characterized by the family catering to every strange whim of one dominant parent.

Masochism. A sexual deviation in which the person derives pleasure from pain, whether actual or threatened, inflicted on the body.

Mean. The arithmetic average of a group of scores; the most common characteristics of a given number of things or people.

Medulla oblongata. The part of the brain located at the lower back near the cerebellum and the brain stem that controls the vital life signs, such as heartbeat and respiration.

Melancholia. Hippocrates' original term for depression.

Meninges. The three thin membranes that encase the brain.

Meningitis. An inflammation of the meninges, resulting in depression, memory loss, and other cognitive and emotional changes as well as physical debilitation.

Mental age. A concept formerly used to establish IQ; in theory, the chronological age at which a person functions, which may not match the person's actual chronological age.

Mental impoverishment. A term for what is very likely the cause of most mental retardation: poverty, social instability, poor nutrition, and inadequate social stimulation.

Mental retardation. A classification given to those people whose scores on intelligence tests fall two or more standard deviations below normal and whose adaptive, self-maintenance skills are poor.

Mescaline. An illegal recreational hallucinogen that alters perception and mood but has no withdrawal syndrome.

Mesmerism. An early psychological therapy developed by Anton Mesmer. The treatment used hypnosis to "cure" patients.

Methadone. An addictive drug that has effects similar to heroin. Because it is easier to control, it is often used as a heroin substitute.

Methadone maintenance. A treatment for narcotic abuse that substitutes methadone for more dangerous drugs such as heroin.

Midlife crisis. A period of self-assessment and revaluation of future goals that generally takes place around age 40 and can result in major life-situation changes.

Migraine headache. A broad category for various types of extremely painful headache, all of which generally strike only one side of the head at a time. Studies have linked migraines with an inability to be assertive.

Mild retardation. The first category of retardation—IQ between 55 and 69 (Wechsler)—that overlaps with the low end of the normal intelligence scale; most mentally retarded people fall into this category.

Milieu therapy. A treatment program offered in therapeutic communities, which encourages patient involvement, a relaxed and casual atmosphere, and a blurring of the patient/professional distinction.

Minor tranquilizers. Depressant drugs, such as Librium and Valium, that are prescribed for anxiety; they are addictive.

Modeling. Bandura's social learning variation of conditioning that emphasizes imitation of behavior exhibited by an important role model.

Moderate retardation. The second category of retardation, characterized by adequate adaptive skills requiring supervision, and an IQ between 40 and 54 (Wechsler).

Modified extended family. A modern version of the extended family in which two or more generations live very close to one another and maintain a high degree of contact but do not live in the same dwelling.

Monoamine (MAO) inhibitor. A sometimes successful biochemical treatment for depression that slows down the metabolization of biogenic amines; not widely used in the United States.

Monozygotic twins. Twins who develop from a single egg; identical twins.

Moral therapy. A treatment developed by Pinel that was based on showing kindness and understanding to the client and on instilling a sense of hope.

Morita therapy. A treatment for anxiety-related disorders that moves a person by stages from absolutely no activity or stimulation to full life participation.

Morphine. The active ingredient in opium that is used to produce heroin; an abused drug in itself.

Multi-infarct dementia. A series of minor embolic (blockage) strokes that impair neural functioning and result in memory loss, confusion, and unpredictable changes in emotion and cognition.

Multiple-monitored ECT. A therapy for depression in which the person receives several ECT treatments in one session after being given a muscle relaxant; the brain waves are constantly monitored by an electroencephalograph.

Multiple personality. A dissociative disorder in which two or more distinct personalities—with distinct identities—exist in the same body.

Myxedema. An adult organic disorder of the thyroid (hypothyroidism), in which too little thyroxin is produced, reducing metabolic processes and resulting in a debilitation of the entire body, including mental functioning.

Narcissistic personality. An individual characterized by an exaggerated sense of self-importance and by total self-involvement, although such behavior actually hides a very fragile sense of self-worth.

Narcotics. Drugs, such as the opiates, that sedate central nervous system activity, relieving pain and tension and producing euphoria; they are highly addictive.

Negative cognitive set. Beck's theory that depression is caused by a deeply pessimistic view of the world and by an unrealistically negative evaluation of capabilities and overall life.

Neimann-Pick's disease. A metabolic disorder caused by the body's inability to break down fats, leading to serious physiological problems and sometimes to mental retardation.

Neurosis. A term Freud coined to describe nonpsychotic mental disorders; DSM-III does not recognize it because it implies an etiology (repression of strong desires) that has not been confirmed.

Neurosyphilis. The syphilitic infection of the nervous system that is also called general paresis; gross personality changes, memory lapses, depression, and total debilitation precede death.

Neurotransmitter substances. Biogenic amines that convey neural impulses between neurons in the brain; catecholamines and indolamines are types of biogenic amines.

Nicotine. The active ingredient in tobacco, which has both stimulating and depressing properties and a definite withdrawal syndrome.

Norms. The standards of behavior that a culture or society teaches through socialization to help maintain order.

Nothingness. In existentialist psychology, the ultimate nothing, or death.

Obesity. The state of being grossly overweight due to compulsive overeating; not officially a disorder, but it often leads to severe emotional problems.

Object permanence. A concept in cognitive development formulated by Piaget in which a child learns that people and objects don't cease to exist when they are out of sight.

Obsession. A recurrent thought, impulse, or image that remains in the mind despite repeated attempts to dispel it.

Obsessive-compulsive disorder. An anxiety disorder that is formed around either obsessions or compulsions, which are very similar defenses against anxiety.

Occipital lobes. A functional division of each cerebral hemisphere located just above the cerebellum that controls vision.

Occlusion. The blockage of a major blood vessel that prevents the blood from nourishing the tissue beyond the blockage.

Oedipal complex. The Freudian theory that children in the phallic stage of development desire to take the place of the same-sex parent, which arouses guilt and fear.

Operant conditioning. The type of learning in which a behavior is strengthened (more likely to occur) or weakened (less likely to occur) according to the presence or absence of stimuli that occur as a consequence of the behavior.

Opiates. A group of addictive depressant drugs derived from the opium poppy; the active ingredient, morphine, produces euphoria and sleepiness.

Opium. A natural narcotic made from the dried juice of the poppy blossom.

Orgasm. The peak of sexual arousal.

Orgasmic reconditioning. A therapy for sexual deviations in which the person learns to associate sexual arousal with more appropriate stimuli.

Overanxious disorder. A disorder that affects children who become very nervous and easily upset by unrealistic attempts to be perfect; they are constantly watching out for danger.

Panic attack. An overwhelming feeling of fear that descends very suddenly, without cause or warning.

Panic disorder. An anxiety disorder characterized chiefly by recurring panic attacks.

Paranoid personality. An extremely suspicious and cold personality, convinced of the evil intentions of everyone else.

Paranoid schizophrenia. A schizophrenic disorder characterized by delusions of persecution, and general suspicion; bizarre behaviors are present, but not to the same degree as in other forms of schizophrenia.

Paraphilias. Variations in sexual preference and goals; for instance, voyeurism and fetishism.

Parasympathetic system. The branch of the autonomic nervous system that governs everyday functioning and attempts to maintain homeostasis.

Parietal lobes. A functional division of both cerebral hemispheres, located behind and above the frontal lobes; sensorimotor information is handled here.

Parkinson's disease. A degenerative disorder of the basal ganglia that creates severe tremors in relaxed muscles; depression and withdrawal also occur.

Passive-aggressive personality. A personality that resists all demands to perform, but in a roundabout way; for example, deadlines are "forgotten," or important data "misplaced."

PCP. Phencyclidine, a very dangerous animal tranquilizer popularly known as "angel dust."

Pedophilia. The technical term for the sexual deviation of child molesting.

Peer group counseling. A therapy for patients that draws on the generally similar life experiences of other patients who can relate much better to the special problems being discussed.

Pellagra. A disease caused by a deficiency of the B vitamin niacin; irritability and depression as well as physical signs may be present.

Permissive amine theory. The theory that a low level of serotonin predisposes a person to an affective disorder, the type determined by the norepinephrine level—a low level causing depression and a high level causing mania.

Personality disorder. A broad category of behavioral difficulties due to an inflexible and maladaptive set of personality traits.

Personality tests. An assessment approach that measures a client's responses to specific stimuli that provide information about the typical patterns of behavior of the individual; includes projective tests and self-report inventories.

Pervasive developmental disorders. The broad category DSM-III applies to childhood schizophrenia and infantile autism.

Peyote. A natural hallucinogen derived from cactus.

Phenomenological approach. The humanistic orientation of viewing and understanding each person's idea of reality as true for that person and trying to understand that "reality" in order to understand the person.

Phenylketonuria (PKU). A metabolic disorder in which a specific enzyme is not manufactured in the body, resulting in irreversible brain damage and retardation.

Phobias. Irrational fears that lead to incapacitation.

Phobic disorders. DSM-III's term for phobias.

Phrenitis. Hippocrates' original term for psychosis.

Physical therapy. A progressive exercise program that focuses on strengthening a weakened area.

Pica. The eating of paint and plaster, a disorder mainly affecting children living in ghettos.

Pick's disease. An organic mental disorder in which the frontal and temporal lobes atrophy; eventually, the person cannot talk and may exist in a vegetative state before dying.

Plateau. The second stage of sexual arousal, just prior to orgasm; most dysfunctions occur during this time.

Play therapy. A nonverbal treatment for childhood disorders in which the therapist studies the way a child plays—which toys are selected, what is said or done while playing, etc.

Pleasure principle. In psychodynamic theory, the principle by which the id operates—i.e., the selfish pursuit of pleasure, unconfined by moral or social restraints.

Pons. An enlarged portion of the brain stem near the medulla.

Positive mental health. In general, focusing on the ability to cope with the demands of living and a positive outlook of life.

Postpartum depression. A fairly common period of dejection that many women experience after childbirth.

Post-traumatic stress disorder. DSM-III's classification for the symptoms generally exhibited in response to a disaster; called the disaster syndrome.

Preconscious. In psychodynamics, the level of consciousness in which is stored information that can be recalled at will but is not necessary for daily functioning.

Premature ejaculation. A sexual dysfunction in which a man has difficulty sustaining an erection for as long as he—or his partner—would like.

Premorbid adjustment. The level of functioning and adaptive skills exhibited prior to admission into a hospital or clinic.

Pre-senile disorders. Degenerative organic mental disorders that strike people between the age of 30 and 60.

Primary neural aging. A natural slowdown in the speed of neural transmissions that occurs with age, resulting in increased reaction time.

Primary prevention. Any measures taken to avoid the development of psychopathology.

Principle of reinforcement. Skinner's restatement of the law of effect: reinforcers strengthen responses and therefore can instigate, control, and extinguish behavior.

Process schizophrenia. Schizophrenic behavior that evolves slowly, indicating a long period of gradual deterioration and poor premorbid adjustment.

Profound retardation. The category of retardation that is the most severely debilitating in form; victims either die fairly young because of extensive brain damage or remain institutionalized most of their lives.

Prognosis. The expected outcome after treatment for a disorder.

Psilocybin. A mushroom with hallucinogenic properties.

Psychoactive drugs. Drugs that produce changes in cognitive or emotional states as well as in physiological functioning.

Psychoanalysis. The therapy developed by Freud in which the client is treated by such techniques as free association, transference, and dream interpretation.

Psychoanalytic theory. Freud's original concept of how mental problems developed, how children developed emotionally, and how the human mind operated.

Psychodynamic theory. An alternative name for psychoanalytic theory.

Psychogenic. Having a psychological cause.

Psychogenic fugue. A rare form of dissociative disorder that involves a person's sudden flight from home and identity.

Psychogenic pain disorder. A somatoform disorder characterized by excruciating pain that has no identifiable organic cause.

Psychophysiological disorders. DSM-III's category for disorders that seem to be psychogenic but create clear physiological problems; for instance, asthma and hypertension.

Psychosis. According to Freud, the complete collapse of the ego and a break with reality; a severe form of mental disorder in which the individual's thinking and functioning are severely impaired.

Psychosomatic. Referring to the interaction between mind (psyche) and body (soma); does *not* mean "imagined."

Psychosurgery. A therapy once used for schizophrenia in which parts of the brain were surgically altered or removed to eliminate undesirable behavior.

Rape. An act of violence in which a man forces a woman to have intercourse against her will.

Rape trauma syndrome. A set of typical reactions to rape experienced by many women; fear, anxiety, guilt, and anger are included as well as psychosomatic complaints such as insomnia and headaches.

Rational emotive therapy. Ellis's treatment program, which consists of uncovering and disputing such irrational beliefs as "I must do everything perfectly."

Reactive disorders. A broad category of disorders, including post-traumatic stress disorder and adjustment disorder, characterized by extreme reactions to identifiable stressors.

Reactive schizophrenia. Schizophrenic behavior that develops fairly suddenly, usually due to some stressful event; the prognosis is better for this type than for process schizophrenia.

Reality orientation. An approach used in helping hospitalized persons fight the institutionalization syndrome by making them more aware of and involved in their environment through sensory stimulation and consistent staff interaction.

Reality principle. In psychodynamic theory, the principle under which the ego operates as it mediates between id and superego in trying to conform to the norms and laws of society.

Recessive gene. A gene carrying a trait that is unlikely to be clearly evident in the physiological makeup of an individual but may surface in other generations.

Refractory period. A space of time after the resolution phase of arousal in which men—but apparently not women—cannot be restimulated to orgasm.

Reserpine. An early pharmacological treatment for schizophrenia.

Residual schizophrenia. A category applied to schizophrenics who seem to be on the way to recovery.

Resistance. Identified by Freud, that point in psychoanalysis when a person avoids a painful or threatening revelation by various means, such as changing the subject or missing appointments.

Resolution. The phase in sexual arousal that follows orgasm, when the body's functioning returns to a normal level.

Response shaping. The general term in behavior therapy for learning a new response in which a desired response is obtained by reinforcing successive approximations of that response.

Reticular formation. A part of the brain stem that regulates sexual arousal.

Rubella. Also called German measles, this infection can be extremely dangerous to a developing fetus, especially if exposure takes place in the first three months of pregnancy.

Runaways. Older children and adolescents who run away from the nuclear family because of some conflict.

Sadism. A sexual deviation in which a person becomes aroused by inflicting or threatening to inflict physical or psychological suffering on another.

Schizoid personality. An individual characterized chiefly by the inability to form friendships and an emotionless, withdrawn attitude.

Schizophrenia. A group of thought disorders that always involves deterioration from a previous level of functioning and usually includes delusions, hallucinations, disordered communications, flat or blunted affect, and withdrawal; divided into disorganized, catatonic, paranoid, undifferentiated, and residual.

Schizophrenic disorders. The more correct term for schizophrenia since the different forms probably constitute distinct disorders.

Schizophrenogenic parent. Fromm-Reichmann's concept that a parent—usually a cold, domineering, insensitive, and inconsistent mother or a passive, ineffectual, and insensitive father—who creates enough family disturbance can cause schizophrenia to develop in a child.

Schizotaxia. Meehl's concept of a specific constitutional defect that leads to a personality that will become schizophrenic if exposed to enough environmental or psychosocial stress.

Schizotypal personality. Individuals who exhibit essentially schizophrenic behavior but not severely enough to warrant that diagnosis.

Secondary prevention. The steps taken to intervene as early as possible in the development of a mental or emotional problem.

Seizures. Sudden changes in the brain's electrical rhythms that are often manifested by spasmodic convulsions; the primary characteristic of epilepsy.

Self-actualization. According to humanistic theory, the realization of an individual's full potential; the goal that each person should strive for.

Self-concept. An idea first proposed by James that people have opinions about themselves, their abilities and goals, and their relationships to the world, and that these opinions have a great influence on behavior.

Senile dementia. A senile degenerative disorder that involves extensive brain atrophy and results in gradual personality changes, memory loss, and loss of judgment.

Senile disorders. Degenerative organic mental disorders that strike people over age 60.

Sensate focus exercises. A treatment for sexual dysfunction that teaches both partners how to give and receive pleasure through sensual massage without evoking performance anxiety.

Separation anxiety disorder. A childhood disorder in which the child is afraid to be away from home or parents out of fear of abandonment.

Serotonin hypothesis. An explanation for depression that cites a low level of the indolamine serotonin (a biogenic amine) as a cause of the disorder.

Severe retardation. The third category of retardation, composed of individuals who have quite limited functioning and must be supervised.

Sexual deviation. A sexual practice that is often illegal and does not conform with the socially approved form of intercourse between two consenting adults.

Sexual dysfunction. Any problem arising in the arousal sequence that interferes with the desire or ability to attain gratification.

Sign learning. Mowrer's theory that a person learns to associate neutral stimuli with anxiety.

Simple phobia. Also called specific phobia: the debilitating fear of particular objects or situations, such as claustrophobia (fear of enclosed places) and acrophobia (fear of heights).

Skill training. The behavioral technique used to develop behaviors where there is a deficit—as in social skill training. Also, a therapy that has been used for alcohol abuse that attempts to teach abusers to drink in a controlled fashion by showing them new behavior in situations where alcohol is present.

Skin popping. To self-administer a drug by injecting it into the fatty tissue below the skin surface.

Social breakdown syndrome. The theory that people who lack self-confidence and inner standards are vulnerable to having their self-concept totally shattered by some intense disturbance, which may lead to schizophrenic behavior.

Socialization. The process by which the members of a society learn the norms and laws of that society.

Social phobia. A debilitating fear of public exposure or performance.

Social support hypothesis. An explanation for psychopathology that focuses on the lack of support groups in low-income areas to unify and strengthen the populace, leading to isolation and mental disorder.

Sociopath. A term used for individuals who exhibit typical antisocial personality characteristics.

Somatic weakness theory. An explanation for psychophysiological disorders; each individual's physiological makeup has a weak spot, which eventually becomes disordered under stress.

Somatization disorder. A disorder in which a multitude of physical symptoms are presented, in response to stress or to achieve some end.

Somatoform disorders. A broad category that includes real physical problems that are probably psychogenic, such as asthma and migraine.

Somnambulism. A disorder characterized by repeated episodes of sleepwalking.

Specific attitude theory. The belief, developed by Graham, that certain attitudes can cause specific psychophysiological disorders.

Specific developmental disorder. A controversial DSM-III classification for any age-appropriate skill, such as reading or arithmetic ability, that is absent at the logical point of biological maturation.

Standard deviation. Those groupings that fall directly above and below the mean point of a set of data.

State anxiety. Anxiety that is caused by a specific stressful situation and is generally temporary.

Stereotaxic surgery. An attempt to control antisocial behavior by implanting electrodes in the brain to destroy specific cells in the amygdala.

Stimulant. Drugs such as cocaine and amphetamines that increase the activity of the central nervous system, leading to excitation and emotional arousal.

STP. A potent synthetic hallucinogenic drug.

Stress. A psychological and physiological state of disequilibrium brought on by a stressor.

Stress-inoculation training. Also called self-instructional training, a method developed by Meichenbaum that focuses on changing the statements people make to themselves in a three-step program of cognitive preparation, skill acquisition and rehearsal, and application.

Stressor. An event, situation, or object that offsets a person's equilibrium and results in a state of stress.

Stroke. The common term for cerebrovascular accident.

Stuttering. A disorder first evident in childhood in which the rhythm of speech is disturbed; if not corrected or at least minimized by adolescence, stuttering is likely to continue indefinitely.

Supra-additive. A relationship between drugs—especially between alcohol and the barbiturates—in which the total effect of the combined drugs is greater than the sum of their separate effect.

Sympathetic system. The branch of the autonomic nervous system that energizes functioning in states of emergency.

Systematic desensitization. A therapy for anxiety and specific fears in which, through relaxing, establishing fear hierarchies, and imagining the feared stimulus in increasingly stressful increments, the anxiety is eventually reduced to controllable levels.

Taraxein. A protein in the blood that has been theorized to produce a toxin that interferes with certain neural functions, resulting in schizophrenia.

Tay-Sach's disease. A metabolic disorder common to Jews whose ancestors lived in certain areas in Eastern Europe; it is inherited through a recessive gene.

Telephone hotline. A mental health service that offers emergency advocacy assistance without charge and generally around the clock.

Temporal lobes. A functional division of both cerebral hemispheres located between the frontal and occipital lobes; governs the interpretation of auditory stimuli and with olfaction.

Tertiary prevention. The measures taken to deal with a disorder after it has already created problems for the individual.

Thalamus. A part of the brain that sorts incoming messages and directs them to their appropriate center in the brain for proper handling.

Thanatos. According to Freud, the destructive side of the id, which urges the organism toward death.

Therapeutic community. Another term for milieu therapy, the management method that stresses patient participation in planning and more egalitarian relationships between patients and staff.

Therapeutic specificity. A characteristic of drug treatments in which they work on only one disorder, not a variety of problems.

Thyroxin. A hormone secreted by the thyroid gland that regulates metabolism; too little results in hypothyroidism, while too much leads to hyperthyroidism.

Token economy. A comprehensive system of reinforcement used to extinguish inappropriate behavior and strengthen appropriate functioning.

Tolerance. The state at which the body becomes immune to the effects of a drug.

Tonic-clonic seizure. Formerly called grand mal seizure, this is the violent, convulsive form of epileptic seizure, which has four phases: aura, tonic, clonic, and coma.

Trait anxiety. Anxiety that seems to be a stable characteristic of the personality.

Transference. In psychodynamics, the situation in which the client responds to the therapist as toward a parent or other significant person.

Transsexualism. A disorder in which the person's perceived gender identity—the sex the person feels he or she ought to be—does not coincide with the physical reality.

Transvestism. A disorder in which the person, generally a heterosexual male, achieves sexual arousal from dressing as a member of the opposite sex.

Tricyclic antidepressants. Presently the most common pharmacotherapy for depression; they apparently work by raising the level of norepinephrine and by inducing a more regular sleep cycle.

Type A personality. A category assigned to certain individuals—usually impatient, hard driving, highly ambitious—who seem to have a propensity for certain psychophysiological disorders, specifically hypertension and ulcers.

Ulcer. A lesion or sore, generally in the lining of the stomach (ulcer) or the duodenum (duodenal ulcer), that has been linked to stress.

Ulcerative colitis. A psychophysiological disorder occurring in the intestine and typically causing diarrhea, pain, and bloody stools.

Unconditioned response. Automatic responses to external stimuli, such as blinking in sharp sunlight.

Unconditioned stimuli. Stimuli to which a person reacts automatically without having learned to.

Unconscious. According to Freud, the vast reservoir of memories, thoughts, and desires that have been hidden away, or repressed, because they are too painful or upsetting.

Undifferentiated schizophrenia. A catchall category for episodes of schizophrenic behavior that do not precisely fit the other categories.

Voyeurism. A disorder in which the person receives sexual gratification from watching an unsuspecting person disrobe or engage in sexual activity.

Withdrawal. The effect experienced by a drug addict once use of the substance has ceased; also called withdrawal syndrome.

XYY chromosomal aberration. A very rare configuration in which the gender-determining chromosome pair of a male has an extra Y chromosome attached; some theorists suggest that this may lead to a predisposition to aggressive antisocial behavior.

Photo Credits

8, Henri Cartier-Bresson/Magnum **11,** U.P.I. **13,** (left) Hanna Schreiber/Photo Researchers, (right) Patricia Hollander Gross/Stock, Boston **17,** U.P.I. **20,** Michael Pfleger/Sygma **28,** (a, b, c, d) National Library of Medicine **29,** National Library of Medicine **34,** U.P.I. **39,** (left) The Bettmann Archive, (right) Historical Pictures Service, Inc./ Chicago **43,** John Veltri/Photo Researchers **48,** Van Bucher/Photo Researchers **49,** (top) Van Bucher/Photo Researchers, (bottom) C.P.S., Inc., P.O. Box 83, Larchmont, N.Y. 10538 **62,** Kal Muller/Woodfin Camp and Associates **65,** The Bettmann Archive **70,** A. Maine/Magnum **73,** The Bettmann Archive **77,** Leonard Freed/ Magnum **82,** Carl Rogers **85,** The Bettmann Archive **87,** Nina Leen, Life Magazine, © Time, Inc. **89,** Leo de Wys, Inc. **97,** The Bettmann Archive **101,** The Bettmann Archive **105,** Brown Brothers **110,** The Bettmann Archive **114,** Arthur Schatz/Time Magazine **117,** Don Hogan Charles/NYT Pictures **123,** Paul Fusco/Magnum **138,** U.P.I. **143,** Owen Franken/Stock, Boston **149,** Wide World **151,** (a) The Bettmann Archive, (b and c) U.P.I. **155,** The Washington Post **159,** Jean Boughton **169,** The Bettmann Archive **175,** (left) Robert W. Mitchell/Tom Stack and Associates, (right) Heather Angel, (bottom) D. Krathwohl/Stock, Boston **179,** P. Schuyler/ Stock, Boston **186,** Rocky Weldon/Leo de Wys, Inc. **189,** Sandra Johnson **198,** Eckert/EKM-Nepenthe **200,** (a) White House Collection, (b and c) Wide World **205,** The Bettmann Archive **210,** Rick Smolan **216,** Culver Pictures **221,** U.P.I. **227,** The Bettmann Archive **228,** U.P.I. **231,** Frank Siteman/Stock, Boston **236,** Robert Levin/Black Star **240,** Andrew Brilliant/The Picture Cube **245,** James D. Wilson/Newsweek **249,** (left) The New York Times/Larry Morris, (right) Ken Robert Buck/ The Picture Cube **262,** Historical Pictures Service, Inc., Chicago **266,** J. Berndt/Stock, Boston **269,** Ron Alexander/Stock, Boston **277,** Ronald K. Siegel **285,** Rocky Weldon/Leo de Wys **297,** Sandra Johnson **303,** (top) U.P.I., (right) Personality Photos, Inc., (bottom) U.P.I. **310,** Kent Reno, Jeroboam **311,** Charles Gatewood **314,** (left) Mark Mellett/Taurus, (right) Chris Maynard/Stock, Boston **322,** Historical Pictures Service, Inc., Chicago **325,** Courtesy of Dr. H. E. Lehmann, McGill University, Montreal, Canada **327,** Stern/Black Star **340,** Leonard Freed/ Magnum **344,** Colin Davey/Photo Trends **363,** Arthur Tress/Photo Researchers **368,** Wide World **373,** H. F. Harlow, University of Wisconsin, Primate Laboratory **379,** (bottom) Rick Smolan **389,** U.P.I. **401,** Wide World **403,** David T. Purtilo **406,** Wide World **411,** Abigail Heyman/ Magnum **421,** Bruce Roberts/Photo Researchers **426** (left and right) From *Like Normal People* by Robert Meyers (McGraw-Hill, 1978; New American Library, 1980) **436,** Alice Kendall/Photo Researchers **438,** Burk Uzzle/Magnum **445,** U.P.I. **451,** Environmental Stress Program, Naval Medical Research Institute **454,** Wide World **459,** Jack Prelutsky/Stock, Boston **465,** Miriam Reinhart/Photo Researchers **472,** Suzanne Arms/Jeroboam **477,** Jack Prelutsky/Stock, Boston **481,** Freedman/Sygma **485,** (a) Michael Serino/The Picture Cube, (b) Anestis Diakopoulos/ Stock, Boston **489,** Dick Frank **497,** Library of Congress **501,** Elizabeth Hamlin/Stock, Boston **503,** Wide World **508,** Frank Siteman/The Picture Cube **510,** Wide World

Bibliography

Abelson, H.I., P.M. Fishburne, and I. Cisin. 1977. *National Survey on Drug Abuse: 1977.* Rockville, Md.: National Institute on Drug Abuse.

Abraham, K. 1948. Notes on psychoanalytic investigation and treatment of manic-depressive insanity and allied conditions (1911). In *Selected Papers of Karl Abraham, M.D.,* tr. by D. Bryan and A. Strachey. London: Hogarth.

Abramson, L.Y., M.E.P. Seligman, and J.D. Teasdale. 1978. Learned helplessness in humans: Critique and reformulation. *Journal of Abnormal Psychology,* **87,** 49–74.

Adams, H.E., M. Feuerstein, and J.L. Fowler, 1980. The migraine headache: A review of parameters, theories, and interventions. *Psychological Bulletin,* **87,** 217–237.

Adler, A. 1917. *The Neurotic Constitution.* New York: Moffatt, Yard.

———. 1927. *Practice and Theory of Individual Psychology.* New York: Harcourt Brace Jovanovich.

Akers, R.L. 1973. *Deviant Behavior: A Social Learning Approach.* Belmont, Calif.: Wadsworth.

Allan, W. The inheritance of migraine, 1928. *Archives of Internal Medicine,* **42,** 590–599.

Allman, L.R. and D.T. Jaffe. 1978. *Abnormal Psychology in the Life Cycle.* New York: Harper & Row.

Almansi, R.J. 1949. Psychosomatics in dentistry. *Journal of Dental Medicine,* **4,** 98–103.

American Association on Mental Deficiency. 1977. *Manual on Terminology and Classification in Mental Retardation,* rev. ed. Washington, D.C.

American Psychiatric Association. 1968. *Diagnostic and Statistical Manual of Mental Disorders* (DSM-II). Washington, D.C.

———. 1980. *Diagnostic and Statistical Manual of Mental Disorders* (DSM-III). Washington, D.C.

Amir, M. 1971. *Patterns of Forcible Rape.* Chicago: University of Chicago.

Angrist, B., H.K. Lee, and S. Gershon. 1974. The antagonism of amphetamine-induced symptomatology by a neuroleptic. *American Journal of Psychiatry,* **131,** 817–819.

Antonovsky, A. 1971. Social and cultural factors in coronary heart disease: An Israel-North American sibling study. *Israel Journal of Medical Sciences,* **7.**

———. 1972. Breakdown: A needed fourth step in the conceptual armamentarium of modern medicine. *Social Science and Medicine,* **6.**

Arieti, S. 1974. *Interpretation of Schizophrenia.* New York: Basic Books.

Armor, D.J., J.M. Polich, and H.B. Stambul. 1978. *Alcoholism and Treatment.* Santa Monica, Calif.: Rand.

Atchley, R. 1972. *Social Forces in Later Life.* Belmont, Calif.: Wadsworth.

Atthowe, J.M., Jr. and L.A. Krasner. 1968. Preliminary report on the application of contingent reinforcement procedures (token economy) on a "chronic" psychiatric ward. *Journal of Abnormal Psychology,* **73,** 37–43.

Ausubel, D.P. 1961. Causes and types of narcotic addictions: A psychosocial view. *Psychiatric Quarterly,* **35,** 523–531.

Ayllon, T. and N.H. Azrin. 1965. The measurement and reinforcement of behavior of psychotics. *Journal of Experimental Analysis of Behavior,* **8,** 357–363.

Azrin, N.H., T.J. Sneed, and R.M. Foxx. 1974. Dry-bed training: Rapid elimination of childhood enuresis. *Behavior Research and Therapy,* **12,** 147–156.

Bagley, C. and S. Greer. 1971. Clinical and social predictors of repeated attempted suicide: A multivariate analysis. *British Journal of Psychiatry,* **119,** 515–521.

Bakal, D.A. 1975. Migraine: Intelligence, social class and familial prevalence. *British Medical Journal,* **2,** 77–78.

Bakwin, R.T. and R.M. Bakwin. 1966. *Clinical Management of Behavior Disorders in Children,* 3rd ed. Philadelphia: Saunders.

———. 1978. Chemotherapy. In *The Harvard Guide to Modern Psychiatry,* ed. by A.M. Nicholi, Jr. Cambridge, Mass.: Belknap.

Baltes, P.B. and G. Labouvie. 1973. Adult development of intellectual performance: Description, explanation, modification. In *The Psychology of Adult Development and Aging,* ed. by C. Eisdorfer and M. Lawton. Washington, D.C.: American Psychological Association.

Bandura, A. 1969. *Principles of Behavior Modification.* New York: Holt, Rinehart & Winston.

———. 1976. Social learning and analysis of aggression. In *Analysis of Delinquency and Aggression,* ed. by E. Ribes-Inesta and A. Bandura. Hillsdale, N.J.: Erlbaum.

———. 1977. Self-efficacy: Toward a unifying theory of behavioral change. *Psychological Review,* **84,** 191–215.

———. 1978. The self system in reciprocal determinism. *American Psychologist,* **33,** 344–358.

Bandura, A., E.B. Blanchard, and B. Ritter. 1969. Relative efficacy of desensitization and modeling approaches for inducing behavioral, affective, and attitudinal changes. *Journal of Personality and Social Psychology,* **13,** 173–199.

Bandura, A., D. Ross, and S.A. Ross. 1961. Transmission of aggression through imitation of aggressive models. *Journal of Abnormal and Social Psychology,* **63,** 575–582.

———. 1963. Imitation of film-mediated aggressive models. *Journal of Abnormal and Social Psychology,* **66,** 3–11.

Bandura, A. and R. Walters. 1963. *Social Learning and Personality Development.* New York: Holt, Rinehart, & Winston.

Bannister, R. 1978. *Brain's Clinical Neurology.* New York: Oxford University.

Barlow, D.H., G.G. Abel, and E.B. Blanchard. 1977. Gender identity change in transsexuals: An exorcism. *Archives of Sexual Behavior,* **6,** 387–395.

Barlow, D.H., H. Leitenberg, and W.S. Agras. 1969. The experimental control of sexual deviation through manipulation of the noxious scene in covert sensitization. *Journal of Abnormal Psychology,* **74,** 596–601.

Baron, J.H. 1972. Aetiology. In *Chronic duodenal ulcer,* ed. by C. Wastell. New York: Appleton-Century-Crofts.

Barrett, J.H. 1972. *Gerontological Psychology.* Springfield, Ill.: Charles C. Thomas.

Bateson, G., D. Jackson, J. Haley, and J. Weakland. 1956. Toward a theory of schizophrenia. *Behavioral Science,* **1,** 251–264.

Beauvoir, S. de. 1972. *The Coming of Age.* New York: Putnam.

Beck, A.T. 1967. *Depression: Clinical, Experimental, and Theoretical Aspects.* New York: Harper & Row.

———. 1969. The meaning of depression. *Science News,* **96**(24), 554.

———. 1971. Cognition, affect, and psychopathology. *Archives of General Psychiatry,* **24,** 495–500.

———. 1972. *Depression: Causes and Treatment.* Philadelphia: University of Pennsylvania.

———. 1973. *The Diagnosis and Management of Depression.* Philadelphia: University of Pennsylvania.

———. 1974. The development of depression: A cognitive model. In *The Psychology of Depression: Contemporary Theory and Research,* ed. by R.J. Friedman and M.M. Katz. New York: Wiley.

———. 1976. *Cognitive Therapy and the Emotional Disorders.* New York: International Universities.

Beck, A.T., A.J. Rush, B.F. Shaw, and G. Emery. 1979. *Cognitive Therapy of Depression.* New York: Guilford.

Becker, C., R. Roe, and R. Scott. 1974. *Alcohol as a Drug: A Curriculum on Pharmacology, Neurology and Toxicology.* New York: Medcom.

Becker, J. 1977. *Affective Disorders.* Morristown, N.J.: General Learning.

Bender, L. 1938. A visual-motor Gestalt test and its

clinical use. Research Monograph of the American Orthopsychiatric Association.

———. 1956. Schizophrenia in childhood: Its recognition, description, and treatment. *American Journal of Orthopsychiatry,* **26,** 499–506.

———. 1968. Childhood schizophrenia: A review. *International Journal of Psychiatry,* **5**(3), 211–230.

———. 1970. The life course of schizophrenic children. *Biological Psychiatry,* **2,** 165–172.

———. 1973. The life course of children with schizophrenia. *American Journal of Psychiatry,* **130,** 783–786.

Beneson, A.S., ed. 1975. *Control of Communicable Diseases in Man,* 12th ed. Washington, D.C.: American Public Health Association.

Benjamin, H. 1971. Should surgery be performed on transsexuals? *American Journal of Psychotherapy,* **25,** 74–83.

Benson, H. 1975. *The Relaxation Response.* New York: Morrow.

Berardo, F.M. 1970. Survivorship and social isolation: The case of the aged widower. *The Family Coordinator,* **19** (January).

Berger, P.A., J.D. Barchas, and T.A. Gonda. 1978. Depression: The problem and its treatment. *The Stanford Magazine,* **6,** 12.

Berman, E. 1975. Tested and documented split personality: Veronica and Nelly. *Psychology Today,* August, 78–81.

Bettelheim, B. 1969. Laurie. *Psychology Today,* February, 24–25.

Bijou, S.W. and W.H. Redd. 1975. Behavior therapy for children. In *American Handbook of Psychiatry,* ed. by D.X. Freedman and V.E. Dyvud. New York: Basic Books.

Bild, R. and H.E. Adams. 1980. Modification of migraine headaches by cephalic blood volume pulse and EMG biofeedback. *Journal of Consulting and Clinical Psychology,* **48,** 51–57.

Birren, J.E. 1974. Translations in gerontology—From lab to life: Psychophysiology and speed of response. *American Psychologist,* **29,** 808–815.

Birren, J.E. and J. Renner. 1977. Developments in research on the biological and behavioral aspects of aging and their implications. In *Handbook of the Psychology of Aging,* ed. by J. Birren and K.W. Schaie. New York: Van Nostrand Reinhold.

Blair, C.D. and R.I. Lanyon. 1981. Exhibitionism: A critical review of etiology and treatment. *Psychological Bulletin,* in press.

Blau, Z. 1973. *Old Age in a Changing Society.* New York: New Viewpoints.

Bliss, E.L., B.B. Wilson, and J. Zwanziger. 1966. Changes in brain norepinephrine in self-stimulating and "aversive" animals. *Journal of Psychiatry Research,* **4,** 59–63.

Blum, J.D. 1978. On changes in psychiatric diagnosis over time. *American Psychologist,* **33,** 1017–1031.

Botwinick, J. 1967. *Cognitive Processes in Maturity and Old Age.* New York: Springer.

Bower, E.M. 1967. Preventive services for children. In *Preventive Services in Mental Health Programs,* ed. by B.L. Bloom and D.P. Buck. Boulder, Colo.: Wiche.

Brady, J.V., R.W. Porter, D.G. Conrad, and J.W. Mason. 1958. Avoidance behavior and the development of gastroduodenal ulcers. *Journal of Experimental Analysis of Behavior,* **1,** 69–73.

Braly, M. 1977. *False Starts: A Memoir of San Quentin and Other Prisons.* New York: Penguin.

Brecher, E. and the editors of *Consumer Reports.* 1972. *Licit and Illicit Drugs.* Boston: Little, Brown.

Brenner, M.H. 1973. *Mental Illness and the Economy.* Cambridge, Mass.: Harvard University.

Breuer, J. and S. Freud. 1955. Studies in hysteria (1895). In *Standard Edition,* vol. 2. London: Hogarth.

Brod, J. 1964. Circulation in muscle during acute pressor responses to emotional stress and during chronic sustained elevation of blood pressure. *American Heart Journal,* **68,** 424–426.

Brody, E. 1978. The aging of the family. *The Annals of the American Academy of Political and Social Science,* **438**(July), 13–27.

Bromley, D.B. 1974. *The Psychology of Human Aging,* 2nd ed. Middlesex, England: Penguin.

Broussard, E.R. 1966. Evaluation of anticipatory guidance counseling to primaiparae using the medium of television. Presented at the American Public Health Association Meeting, San Francisco.

Brown, G.W. 1974. Meaning, measurement and stress of life events. In *Stressful Life Events: Their Nature and Effects,* ed. by B.S. Dohrenwend and B.P. Dohrenwend. New York: Wiley.

Brown, G.W., T.O. Harris, and J. Peto. 1973(b). Life events and psychiatric disorders. Part 2: Nature of causal link. *Psychological Medicine,* **3.**

Brown, G.W., F. Sklair, T.O. Harris, and J.L.T. Birley. 1973(a). Life events and psychiatric disorders. Part 1: Some methodological issues. *Psychological Medicine,* **3.**

Brown, T.R. and T.J. Sheran. 1972. Suicide prediction: A review. *Life-Threatening Behavior,* **2,** 67–98.

Brown, W.F. 1942. Heredity in the psychoneuroses. *Proceeding of the Royal Society of Medicine,* **35,** 785–790.

Brownmiller, S. 1975. *Against Our Will: Men, Women and Rape.* New York: Simon & Schuster.

Bucher, B. and O.I. Lovaas. 1968. Use of aversive stimulation in behavior modification. In *Miami symposium on the prediction of behavior, 1967: Aversive stimulation.* Coral Gables, Fla.: University of Miami.

Buckner, H.T. 1970. The transvestic career path. *Psychiatry,* **33**(3), 381–389.

Buglass, D. and J.W. McCulloch. 1970. Further suicidal behavior: The development and validation of predictive scales. *British Journal of Psychiatry,* **116,** 483–491.

Bunney, W.E., Jr., moderator. 1977. The switch process in manic-depressive psychosis. *Annals of Internal Medicine,* **87,** 319–335.

Bunney, W.E., Jr. and J.M. Davis. 1965. Norepinephrine in depressive reactions: A review. *Archives of General Psychiatry,* **13,** 443–494.

Bunney, W.E., Jr., F.K. Goodwin, and D.L. Murphy. 1972. The "switch process" in manic-depressive illness. *Archives of General Psychiatry,* **27,** 312–317.

Bunney, W.E., Jr., D.L. Murphy, F.K. Goodwin, and G.F. Borge. 1970. The switch process from depression to mania: Relationship to drugs which alter brain amines. *Lancet,* **1,** 1022.

Burgess, A.W. and L.L. Holmstrom. 1974. Rape trauma syndrome. *American Journal of Psychiatry,* **131,** 981–986.

Busse, E.W. 1970. Psychoneurotic reactions and defensive mechanisms in the aged. In *Normal Aging,* ed. by E. Palmore. Durham, N.C.: Duke University.

Butler, J.M. and G.V. Haigh. 1954. Changes in the relation between self-concepts and ideal concepts consequent upon client-centered counseling. In *Psychotherapy and Personality Change,* ed. by C.R. Rogers and R.F. Dymond. Chicago: University of Chicago.

Butler, R.N. 1963. The life review: An interpretation of reminiscence in the aged. *Psychiatry,* **26,** 65–76.

———. 1974. Successful aging. *Mental Hygiene,* **58,** 7–12.

———. 1975. *Why survive? Being old in America.* New York: Harper & Row.

Butler, R.N. and M.I. Lewis. 1973. *Aging and Mental Health.* St. Louis, Mo.: Mosby.

Callahan, E.J. and H. Leitenberg. 1973. Aversion therapy for sexual deviation: Contingent shock and covert sensitization. *Journal of Abnormal Psychology,* **81,** 60–73.

Cannon, W.B. 1936. Bodily Changes in Pain, Hunger, Fear and Rage. New York: Appleton–Century.

Cantwell, D.P. 1975. Genetic studies of hyperactive children. In *Genetic Research in Psychiatry,* ed. by R. Fieve, D. Rosenthal, and H. Brill. Baltimore: Johns Hopkins University.

Caplan, G. 1961. *An approach to community mental health.* New York: Grune & Stratton.

———. 1964. *Principles of Preventive Psychology.* New York: Basic Books.

Carkhuff, R.R. 1968. Differential functioning of lay and professional helpers. *Journal of Counseling Psychology,* **15,** 117–126.

Carlson, G.A. and F.K. Goodwin. 1973. The stages of mania. *Archives of General Psychiatry,* **28,** 221–228.

Carlsson, A. and J. Lindquist. 1963. Effect of chlorpromazine and haloperidol on formation of 3-methoxytyramine and normetariphrine in mouse brain. *Pharmacological Toxicologie,* **20,** 140–144.

Carpenter, M.B. 1976. *Human Neuroanatomy.* Baltimore: Williams & Wilkins.

Cattell, R.B. 1963. The theory of fluid and crystallized intelligence: A critical experiment. *Journal of Educational Psychology,* **54,** 1–22.

Cautela, J.R. 1966. Treatment of compulsive behavior by covert sensitization. *Psychological Record,* **16,** 33–41.

Chaftez, M.E. and H.W. Demone. 1962. *Alcoholism and Society.* New York: Oxford University.

Chapanis, A. 1950. Relationships between age, visual acuity, and color vision. *Human Biology,* **22,** 1–31.

Chapman, L.J. and J.A. Taylor. 1957. The breadth of deviate concepts used by schizophrenics. *Journal of Abnormal and Social Psychology,* **54,** 118–123.

Chein, I., E. Gerard, R. Lee, and E. Rosenfeld. 1964. *The Road to H.* New York: Basic Books.

Chess, S. and M. Hassibi. 1978. *Principles and Practice of Child Psychiatry.* New York: Plenum.

Chodoff, P. 1974. The depressive personality: A critical review. In *The Psychology of Depression: Contemporary Theory and Research,* ed. by R.J. Friedman and M.M. Katz. Washington, D.C.: Winston.

Citrin, R.S. and D.N. Dixon. 1977. Reality orientation: A milieu therapy used in an institution for the aged. *The Gerontologist,* **17**(1), 39–43.

Clarizio, H.F. and G.F. McCoy. 1976. *Behavior Disorders in Children,* 2nd ed. New York: Thomas Y. Crowell.

Cleckley, H. 1964. *The Mask of Sanity,* 4th ed. St. Louis, Mo.: C.V. Mosby.

Cobb, S. 1974. A model for life events and their consequences. In *Stressful Life Events: Their Nature and Effects,* ed. by B.S. Dohrenwend and B.P. Dohrenwend. New York: Wiley.

Cofer, C.N. and M.H. Appley. 1964. *Motivation: Theory and Research.* New York: Wiley.

Cohen, A. 1955. *Delinquent Boys.* Glencoe, Ill.: Free Press.

Cohen, D.D. 1974. On the etiology of neurosis. *Journal of Abnormal Psychology,* **83**(5), 473–479.

Cohen, H.L., J. Filipczak, J. Bis, et al. 1968. *Contingencies Application to Special Education—Motivationally Oriented Design for an Ecology of Learning.* Washington, D.C.: U.S. Department of Health, Education, and Welfare.

Cohen, M.L., R. Garofalo, R. Boucher, and T. Seghorn. 1971. The psychology of rapists. *Seminars in Psychiatry,* **3,** 307–327.

Cohen, S. 1977. Profile of a drug abuser. In *Drug Abuse: Clinical and Basic Aspects,* ed. by S. Pradhan and S. Dutta. St. Louis, Mo.: C.V. Mosby.

Connery, R., ed. 1968. *The Politics of Mental Health: Organizing Community Mental Health in Metropolitan Areas.* New York: Columbia University.

Cooper, J.E., R.E. Kendell, B.J. Gurland, et al. 1972. *Psychiatric Diagnosis in New York and London: A Comparative Study of Mental Hospital Admissions.* New York: Oxford University.

Coppen, A. 1967. The biochemistry of affective disorder. *British Journal of Psychiatry,* **113,** 1237–1264.

Costello, C.G. 1972. Depression: Loss of reinforcers or loss of reinforcer effectiveness? *Behavior Therapy,* **3,** 240–252.

Cousins, N. 1979. *Anatomy of an Illness: As Perceived by the Patient.* New York: Norton.

Covi, L., R.S. Lipman, L.R. Derogates, et al. 1974. Drugs and group psychotherapy in neurotic depression. *American Journal of Psychiatry,* **131**(2), 191–197.

Cowen, E.L., L.D. Izzo, H. Miles, et al. 1963. A preventive mental health program in the school setting: Description and evaluation. *Journal of Psychology,* **56,** 307–356.

Cowen, E.L., M. Zax, L.D. Izzo, and M.A. Trost. 1966. Prevention of emotional disorders in the school setting: A further investigation. *Journal of Consulting Psychology,* **30,** 381–387.

Coyne, J.C. 1976. Toward an interactional description of depression. *Psychiatry,* **39,** 28–40.

Crandall, R.C. 1980. *Gerontology: A Behavioral Science Approach.* Reading, Mass.: Addison-Wesley.

Creese, I., D.R. Burt, and S.N. Snyder. 1978. Biochemical actions of neuroleptic drugs: Focus on the dopamine receptor. In *Handbook of Psychopharmacology,* vol. 10, ed. by S.D. Iverson and S.H. Snyder. New York: Plenum.

Crisp, A.H. 1970. Anorexia nervosa: Feeding disorder, nervous malnutrition, or weight phobia? *World Review of Nutrition and Dietetics,* **12,** 452–504.

Crocetti, G.M. and P.V. Lemkau. 1967. Schizophrenia II. Epidemiology. In *Comprehensive Textbook of Psychiatry,* ed. by A.M. Freeman and H.I. Kaplan. Baltimore: Williams & Wilkins.

Cromwell, R.L. and P.R. Dokecki. 1968. Schizophrenic language: A disattention interpretation. In *Developments in Applied Psycholinquistics Research,* ed. by S. Rosenberg and J.H. Koplin. New York: Macmillan.

Crowe, R.R. 1974. An adoption study of antisocial personality. *Archives of General Psychiatry,* **31,** 785–791.

Cumming, E. 1963. Further thoughts on the theory of disengagement. *International Social Science Journal,* **15,** 377–393.

———. 1964. New thoughts on the theory of disengagement. In *New Thoughts on Old Age,* ed. by R. Kastenbaum. New York: Springer.

Cumming, E. and J. Cumming. 1957. *Closed Ranks.* Cambridge, Mass.: Harvard University.

Dahlstrom, W.G. and G. Welsh. 1960. *An MMPI Handbook: A Guide to Use in Clinical Practice and Research.* Minneapolis: University of Minnesota.

Dahlstrom, W.G. and L.E. Dahlstrom. 1972. *An MMPI Handbook, Vol. 1: Clinical Interpretation,* rev. ed. Minneapolis: University of Minnesota.

Dalessio, D.J. 1972. *Wolff's Headache and Other Head Pain.* New York: Oxford University.

Damasio, A. 1979. The frontal lobes. In *Clinical Neuropsychology,* ed. by K.M. Heilman and E. Valenstein. New York: Oxford University.

Davidson, S. 1977. *Loose Change: Three Women of the Sixties.* New York: Doubleday.

Davison, G.C. 1968(a). Elimination of a sadistic fantasy by a client-controlled counterconditioning technique. *Journal of Abnormal Psychology,* **73,** 84–90.

———. 1968(b). Systematic desensitization as a counterconditioning process. *Journal of Abnormal Psychology,* **73,** 91–99.

———. 1976. Homosexuality: The ethical challenge. *Journal of Consulting and Clinical Psychology,* **44,** 157–162.

DeLong, D.B. and E. Robins. 1961. The communication of suicidal intent prior to psychiatric hospitalization: A study of 87 patients. *American Journal of Psychiatry,* **117.**

Deutsch, A. 1949. *The Mentally Ill in America,* 2nd ed. New York: Columbia University.

Didion, J. 1979. *The White Album.* New York: Simon & Schuster.

Dohrenwend, B.P. 1974. Problems in defining and sampling the relevant population of stressful life events. In *Stressful Life Events: Their Nature and Effects,* ed. by B.S. Dohrenwend and B.P. Dohrenwend. New York: Wiley.

Dohrenwend, B.P. and B.S. Dohrenwend. 1965. The problem in validity in field studies of psychological disorder. *Journal of Abnormal Psychology,* **70,** 52–69.

———. 1967. Field studies of social factors in relation to three types of psychological disorder. *Journal of Abnormal Psychology,* **72,** 369–378.

———. 1969. *Social Status and Psychological Disorder: A Causal Inquiry.* New York: Wiley.

———. 1974. Social and cultural influences on psychopathology. In *Annual Review of Psychology,* ed. by M.R. Rosenzweig and L.W. Porter. Palo Alto, Calif.: Annual Reviews.

Dohrenwend, B.S. 1973. Social status and stressful life events. *Journal of Personality and Social Psychology,* **28,** 225–235.

Doobs, A.N. 1971. Deviance: Society's side show. *Psychology Today,* **5** (October), 47–51.

Driscoll, J.P. 1971. Transexuals. *Trans-action,* March-April, 28–31.

DSM-III. 1980. *See American Psychiatric Association, 1980.*

Dudley, C. J. and G.A. Hillery. 1977. Freedom and alienation in homes for the aged. *The Gerontologist,* **17**(2), 140–145.

Dunham, J.R. and C.S. Dunham. 1978. Mental retardation. In *Disability and Rehabilitation Handbook,* ed. by R.M. Goldenson, J.R. Dunham, and C.S. Dunham. New York: McGraw-Hill.

Dunn, W. 1973. Experimental methods and conceptual modes as applied to the study of motivation in cigarette smoking. In *Smoking Behavior: Motives and Incentives,* ed. by W. Dunn. New York: Wiley.

Durkheim, E. 1951. *Le Suicide* (1897), tr. by J.A. Spaulding and G. Simpson. Glencoe, Ill.: Free Press.

Edfors-Lubs, M.L. 1971. Allergy in 7000 twin pairs. *Acta Allergologica,* **26,** 249–285.

Ehrenwald, J. 1960. Neurosis in the family. *Archives of General Psychiatry,* **3,** 232–242.

Eisenberg, L. and L. Kanner. 1956. Childhood schizophrenia. *American Journal of Orthopsychiatry,* **26,** 556–564.

Ellis, A. 1958. Rational psychotherapy. *Journal of General Psychology,* **59,** 35–49.

———. 1962. *Reason and Emotion in Psychotherapy.* New York: Lyle Stuart.

———. 1973. Rational emotive therapy. In *Current Psychotherapies,* ed. by R. Corsinic. Itasca, Ill.: Peacock.

Ellis, A. and R.A. Harper. 1977. *A New Guide to Rational Living,* rev. ed. Beverly Hills, Calif.: Hal Leighton.

Engelhardt, D.M. 1974. Pharmacologic basis for use of psychotropic drugs, an overview. *New York State Journal of Medicine,* **74**(2), 360–366.

Erikson, E.H. 1959. Identity and the life cycle. In *Psychological Issues,* vol. 1. New York: International Universities.

———. 1963. *Childhood and Society,* 2nd ed. New York: Norton.

———. 1964. *Insight and Responsibility.* New York: Norton.

———. 1968. *Identity, Youth and Crisis.* New York: Norton.

———. 1974. *Dimensions of a New Identity.* New York: Norton.

———. 1976. *Toys and Reasons.* New York: Norton.

Estes, N. and M.E. Heinemann. 1977. *Alcoholism:*

Development, Consequences and Interventions. St. Louis, Mo.: C.V. Mosby.

Exner, J. 1974. *The Rorschach: A Comprehensive System.* New York: Wiley.

Eysenck, H.J. 1952. The effects of psychotherapy: An evaluation. *Journal of Consulting Psychology,* **16,** 319–324.

———. 1960. *The Structure of Human Personality.* London: Methuen.

———. 1966. *The Effects of Psychotherapy.* New York: International Science.

———. 1967. New ways in psychotherapy. *Psychology Today,* **1,** 39–47.

———. 1973(a). *Handbook of Abnormal Psychology.* San Diego, Calif.: Robert Knapp.

———. 1973(b). Personality and the maintenance of the smoking habit. In *Smoking Behavior: Motives and Incentives,* ed. by W. Dunn. New York: Wiley.

Fairweather, G.W., D.H. Sanders, D.L. Crissler, and H. Maynard. 1969. *Community Life for the Mentally Ill.* Chicago: Aldine.

Fanon, F. 1967. *Black Skin, White Masks.* New York: Grove.

Farberow, N.L. 1966. Suicide prevention around the clock. *American Journal of Orthopsychiatry,* **36,** 551–558.

Farberow, N.L. and R.E. Litman. 1970. A comprehensive suicide prevention program: Suicide Prevention Center of Los Angeles, 1958–1969. Unpublished final report, DHEW NIMH Grants No. MH 14946 and MH 00128. Washington, D.C.: Government Printing Office.

Faris, R.E.L. and H.W. Dunham. 1939. *Mental Disorders in Urban Areas.* Chicago: University of Chicago.

Federal Bureau of Investigation. 1974. *Uniform Crime Reports.* Washington, D.C.: Government Printing Office.

Federal Bureau of Investigation. 1978. *Uniform Crime Reports.* Washington, D.C.: Government Printing Office.

Feingold, B. 1975. *Why Your Child is Hyperactive.* New York: Random House.

Fenna, D. et al. 1971. Ethanol metabolism in various racial groups. *Canadian Medical Association Journal,* **105,** 472–475.

Fenton, G.W., F.G. Tennent, P.B. Fenwick, and N. Rattray. 1974. The EEG in antisocial behavior: A study of posterior temporal slow activity in special hospital patients. *Psychological Medicine,* **4,** 181–186.

Fenz, W.D. 1971. Heart rate responses to a stressor: A comparison between primary and secondary psychopaths and normal controls. *Journal of Experimental Research in Personality,* **5**(1), 7–13.

———. 1973. A functional analysis of depression. *American Psychologist,* **28,** 857–870.

Fieve, R.R. 1975. *Moodswing: The Third Revolution in Psychiatry.* New York: Morrow.

Fink, M. 1979. *Convulsive Therapy: Theory and Practice.* New York: Raven Press.

Fixsen, D.L., E.L. Phillips, and M.M. Wolf. 1978. Mission-oriented behavior research: The teaching-family model. In *Handbook of Applied Behavior Analysis: Social and Instructional Processes,* ed. by A.C. Catania and T.A. Brigham. New York: Irvington.

Flood, R. and C. Seager. 1968. A retrospective examination of psychiatric case records of patients who subsequently committed suicide. *British Journal of Psychiatry,* **114,** 443–450.

Fontana, A. 1966. Familial etiology of schizophrenia: Is a scientific methodology possible? *Psychological Bulletin,* **66,** 214–228.

Fordyce, W.E. 1973. An operant conditioning method for managing chronic pain. *Postgraduate Medicine,* **53,** 123–128.

Forrest, D.V. 1969. New words and neologisms, with a thesaurus of coinages by a schizophrenic savant. *Psychiatry,* **32,** 44–73.

Fox, R.W. 1978. *So Far Disordered in Mind: Insanity in California, 1870–1930.* Berkeley, Calif.: University of California.

Frank, E., C. Anderson, and D. Rubenstein. 1978. Frequency of sexual dysfunction in "normal" couples. *New England Journal of Medicine,* **299,** 111–115.

Frankl, V.E. 1962. *Man's Search for Meaning.* Boston: Beacon.

———. 1975. Paradoxical intention and dereflection. *Psychotherapy: Theory, Research and Practice,* **12,** 226–237.

Franks, C.M. and G.J. Wilson, Eds. 1974. *Annual Review of Behavior Therapy: Theory and Practice.* New York: Brunner/Mazel.

Frederick, C.J. and H.L. Resnik. 1971. How suicidal behaviors are learned. *American Journal of Psychotherapy,* **25,** 37–55.

Freedman, R., S. Lynn, P. Yianni, and P. Hale. 1981.

Biofeedback treatment of Raynaud's disease and phenomenon. *Biofeedback and Self-Regulation,* **6,** 355–365.

Freeman, T. 1969. Symptomatology, diagnosis and clinical course. In *The Schizophrenic Syndrome,* ed. by L. Bellak. New York: Grune & Stratton.

Freis, E.D. 1973. Age, race, sex, and other indices of risk in hypertension. *American Journal of Medicine,* **55,** 275–280.

Freud, A. 1946. *The Ego and Mechanisms of Defense.* New York: International Universities.

———. 1958. Adolescence. *Psychoanalytic Study of the Child,* **13,** 255–278.

Freud, S. 1932. *The Interpretation of Dreams.* New York: Macmillan.

———. 1947. *The Ego and the Id* (1923). London: Hogarth.

———. 1948. *An Autobiographical Study,* tr. by J. Strachey. London: Hogarth, and the Institute of Psychoanalysis.

———. 1950. Mourning and melancholia (1917). In *Collected Papers,* Vol. 4. London: Hogarth.

———. 1953(a). Beyond the pleasure principle (1920). In *The Standard Edition of the Complete Psychological Works of Sigmund Freud,* Vol. XVIII. London: Hogarth.

———. 1953(b). Three essays on sexuality (1905). In *The Standard Edition of the Complete Psychological Works of Sigmund Freud,* Vol. III, ed. by J. Strachey. London: Hogarth.

———. 1955. Analysis of a phobia in a five-year-old boy (1909). In *Collected Papers,* Vol. 10. London: Hogarth.

———. 1956. A case of paranoia running counter to the psychoanalytical theory of the disease (1915). In *Collected Papers,* Vol. 2. London: Hogarth.

Friedman, M. and R.H. Rosenman. 1974. *Type A Behavior and Your Heart.* New York: Knopf.

Fromm, E. 1941. *Escape From Freedom.* New York: Holt, Rinehart, & Winston.

———. 1955. *The Sane Society.* New York: Holt, Rinehart, & Winston.

Fromm-Reichmann, F. 1948. Notes on the development of treatment of schizophrenics by psychoanalytic psychotherapy. *Psychiatry,* **11,** 263–273.

Funabiki, D. 1977. The behavioral assessment of coping among college students in problematic situations: The development of the College Coping Inventory. Doctoral dissertation, S.U.N.Y. at Stony Brook, University microfilms No. 77-241,322.

Funabiki, D., N.C. Bologna, M. Pepping, and K.C. Fitzgerald. 1980. Revisiting sex differences in the expression of depression. *Journal of Abnormal Psychology,* in press.

Gal. P. 1959. Mental disorders of advanced years. *Geriatrics,* **14,** 224–228.

Gampel, B., C. Slome, N. Scotch, and J.H. Abramson. 1962. Urbanization and hypertension among Zulu adults. *Journal of Chronic Disease,* **15,** 67–70.

Garmezy, N. and S. Streitman. 1974. Children at risk: The search for the antecedents of schizophrenia. Part I: Conceptual models and research methods. *Schizophrenia Bulletin,* **1,** 14–50.

Gayford, J.J. 1975. Wife battering: A preliminary survey of 100 cases. *British Medical Journal,* **1,** 194–197.

Gebhard, P.H., J.H. Gagnon, W.B. Pomeroy, and C.V. Christenson. 1965. *Sex Offenders.* New York: Harper & Row.

Geer, J.H., G.C. Davison, and R.I. Gatchel. 1970. Reduction of stress in humans through nonveridical perceived control of aversive stimulation. *Journal of Personality and Social Psychology,* **16,** 731–738.

Gersten, J.C., T.S. Langner, J.G. Eisenberg, and L. Orzeck. 1974. Child behavior and life events: Undesirable change or change per se? In *Stressful Life Events: Their Nature and Effects,* ed. by B.S. Dohrenwend and B.P. Dohrenwend. New York: Wiley.

Gibbs, F.A., E.L. Gibbs, and W.G. Lennox. 1939. Influence of the blood sugar level on the wave and spike formation in petit mal epilepsy. *Archives of Neurology and Psychiatry,* **41**(6), 1111–1116.

Gibson, J.T. 1978. *Growing Up: A Study of Children.* Reading, Mass.: Addison-Wesley.

Gittelman, M. and H.G. Birch. 1967. Childhood schizophrenia: Intellect, neurological status, perinatal risk, prognosis and family pathology. *Archives of General Psychiatry,* **17,** 16–25.

Glaros, A.G. and S.M. Rao. 1977. Effects of bruxism: A review of the literature. *Journal of Prosthetic Dentistry,* **28,** 149–157.

Glaser, D. 1964. *The Effectiveness of Prison and Parole Systems.* Indianapolis: Bobbs-Merrill.

Glaser, F., S. Greenberg, and M. Barrett. 1978. *A Systems Approach to Alcohol Treatment.* Toronto: Addiction Research Foundation.

Glass, D.C. and J.E. Singer. 1972. *Urban Stress: Experiments on Noise and Social Stressors.* New York: Academic Press.

Glatt, M.M. 1974. *A Guide to Addiction and Its Treatment.* New York: Halstead and Wiley.

Globetti, G. 1977. Teenage drinking. In *Alcoholism: Development, Consequences and Interventions,* ed. by N. Estes and M.E. Heinemann. St. Louis, Mo.: C.V. Mosby.

Goetzl, U., R. Green, P. Whybrow, and R. Jackson. 1974. X-linkage revisited. *Archives of General Psychiatry,* **31,** 665–671.

Goldberg, E.M. and S.L. Morrison. 1963. Schizophrenia and social class. *British Journal of Psychiatry,* **109,** 785–802.

Goldenson, R.M. 1978. Statistics. In *Disability and Rehabilitation Handbook,* ed. by R.M. Goldenson, J.R. Dunham, and C.S. Dunham. New York: McGraw-Hill.

Goldfried, M.R. and G.C. Davison. 1976. *Clinical Behavior Therapy.* New York: Holt, Rinehart, & Winston.

Goldstein, M.J., B.L. Baker, and K.R. Jamison. 1980. *Abnormal Psychology.* Boston: Little, Brown.

Goldstein, M.J., E.H. Rodnick, J.R. Evans, et al. 1978. Drug and family therapy in the aftercare treatment of acute schizophrenia. *Archives of General Psychiatry,* **35,** 1169–1177.

Goldstein, M.J., L.K. Judd, E.H. Roderick, and A. LaPolla. 1969. Psychophysiological and behavioral effects of phenothiazine administration in acute schizophrenics as a function of premorbid states. *Journal of Psychiatric Research,* **6,** 271–287.

Goode, E. 1974. Marijuana use and the progression to dangerous drugs. In *Marijuana: Effects on Human Behavior,* ed. by L. Miller. New York: Academic Press.

Goodell, H., R. Lewontin, and H.G. Wolff. 1954. Familial occurrence of migraine headache. *Archives of Neurology and Psychiatry,* **72,** 325–334.

Goodwin, D.W., F. Schusinger, L. Hermansen, et al. 1973. Alcohol problems in adoptees raised apart from alcoholic biological parents. *Archives of General Psychiatry,* **38,** 238–243.

Gottesfeld, H. 1979. *Abnormal Psychology.* Chicago: Science Research Associates.

Gottesman, I.I. and J. Shields. 1976. A critical review of recent adoption, twin and family studies of schizophrenia. *Schizophrenia Bulletin,* **2**(3), 360–398.

Gottesman, L.E. and N.C. Bourestom. 1974. Why nursing homes do what they do. *The Gerontologist,* **14**(6), 501–506.

Gottlieb, A.A., G.C. Gleser, and L.A. Gottschalk. 1967. Verbal and physiological responses to hypnotic suggestion of attitudes. *Psychosomatic Medicine,* **29,** 172–183.

Goyette, C.H. and C.K. Conners. 1977. Food additives and hyperkinesis. Presented at the 85th Annual Convention of the American Psychological Association.

Graham, D.T., J.D. Kabler, and F.K. Graham. 1962. Physiological responses to the suggestion of attitudes: Specificity of attitude hypothesis in psychosomatic disease. *Psychosomatic Medicine,* **24,** 159–169.

Graham, J.R., and H.G. Wolff. 1938. Mechanism of migraine headache and action of ergotamine tartrate. *Archives of Neurology and Psychiatry,* **39,** 737–763.

Green, H. 1964. *I Never Promised You a Rose Garden.* New York: Holt, Rinehart & Winston.

Green, P. 1978. Defective interhemispheric transfer of schizophrenia. *Journal of Abnormal Psychology,* **87,** 472–480.

Greenberg, A. and M. Coleman. 1976. Depressed 5–hydroxyindole levels associated with hyperactive and aggressive behavior. *Archives of General Psychiatry,* **33,** 331–336.

Greenberg, D.J., S.B. Scott, A. Pisa, and D.D. Friesen. 1975. Beyond token economy: A comparison of two contingency programs. *Journal of Consulting and Clinical Psychology,* **43,** 498–503.

Greer, S. 1964. Study of parental loss in neurotics and sociopaths. *Archives of General Psychiatry,* **11,** 177–180.

Greist, J.H., M.H. Klein, and H.P. Erdman. 1976. Routine on-line psychiatric diagnosis by computer. *American Journal of Psychiatry,* **133**(12), 1405–1408.

Grier, W.H. and P.M. Cobbs. 1968. Black Rage. New York: Basic Books.

———. 1971. *The Jesus Bag.* New York: Bantam.

Grob, G.N. 1965. *The State and the Mentally Ill.* Chapel Hill, N.C.: University of North Carolina.

Grof, P., A.P. Zis, F.K. Goodwin, and T.A. Wehr. 1978. Patterns of recurrence in bipolar affective illness. Presented at the annual meeting of the American Psychiatric Association, Atlanta, Ga. May 1978.

Gross, M.B. and W.C. Wilson. 1974. *Minimal Brain Dysfunction.* New York: Brunner/Mazel.

Gruenberg, E.M. and J. Zusman. 1964. The natural history of schizophrenia. *International Psychiatry Clinics,* **1,** 699–714.

Grunewald-Zuberbier, E., G. Grunewald, and E. Rasche. 1975. Hyperactive behavior and EEG arousal reactions in children's electroencephalograms. *Clinical Neurophysiology,* **38,** 149–159.

Gubrium, J. 1974. Marital desolation and the evaluation of everyday life in old age. *Journal of Marriage and the Family,* **36,** 107–113.

———. 1975. *Living and Dying at Murray Manor.* New York: St. Martin.

Gunderson, J.G. and L.R. Mosher. 1975. The cost of schizophrenia. *American Journal of Psychiatry,* **132,** 901–905.

Gunn, J., G. Robertson, S. Dell, and C. Way. 1978. *Psychiatric Aspects of Imprisonment.* New York: Academic Press.

Gustafson, E. 1972. Dying: The career of the nursing home patient. *Journal of Health and Social Behavior,* **13,** 226–235.

Gutmann, D. 1964. An exploration of ego configurations in middle and later life. In *Personality in Middle and Later Life: Empirical Studies,* ed. by B.L. Neugarten. New York: Atherton.

Halikas, J. 1974. Marijuana use and psychiatric illness. In *Marijuana: Effects on Human Behavior,* ed. by L. Miller. New York: Academic Press.

Hammen, C.L. and S.D. Peters. 1977. Differential responses to male and female depressive reactions. *Journal of Consulting and Clinical Psychology,* **45,** 994–1001.

Hanson, D.R. and I.I. Gottesman. 1976. The genetics, if any, of infantile autism and childhood schizophrenia. *Journal of Autism and Childhood Schizophrenia,* **6,** 209–234.

———. 1970. *Psychopathy: Theory and Research.* New York: Wiley.

Harlow, J. 1868. Recovery from the passage of an iron bar through the head. *Publication of the Massachusetts Medical Society,* **2,** 327–340.

Harlow, H.F. and M.K. Harlow. 1966. Learning to love. *American Scientist,* **54,** 244–272.

Harlow, H.F. and S.J. Suomi. 1974. Induced depression in monkeys. *Behavioral Biology,* **12,** 273–296.

Harper, M.A., M. Morris, and J. Bleyerveld. 1972. The significance of an abnormal EEG in psychopathic personalities. *Australian and New Zealand Journal of Psychiatry,* **6,** 215–224.

Harmatz, M.G. 1978. *Abnormal Psychology.* Englewood Cliffs, N.J.: Prentice-Hall.

Harris, Louis and Associates, Inc. 1975. *The Myth and Reality of Aging in America.* Washington, D.C.: The National Council of Aging.

Hathaway, S.R. and J.C. McKinley. 1943. *Manual for the Minnesota Multiphasic Personality Inventory.* New York: Psychological Corp.

Hawley, C. and R. Buckley. 1974. Food dyes and hyperkinetic children. *Academic Therapy,* **10,** 27–32.

Hays, P. 1976. Etiological factors in manic-depressive psychoses. *Archives of General Psychiatry,* **33,** 1187–1188.

Heath, R.G. and I.M. Krupp. 1967. Schizophrenia as an immunologic disorder. *Archives of General Psychiatry,* **16,** 1–33.

Hebb, D.O. 1958. *A Textbook of Psychology.* Philadelphia: W.B. Saunders.

Heber, F.R. 1978. Sociocultural mental retardation: A longitudinal study. In *Primary Prevention of Psychopathology,* vol. 2, ed. by D. Forgays. New Hampshire: University Press of New England.

Heller, K. and J. Monahan. 1977. *Psychology and Community Change.* Homewood, Ill.: Dorsey.

Helzer, J.E., L.N. Robins, M. Taibleson, et al. 1977. Reliability of psychiatric diagnosis: I. A methodological review. *Archives of General Psychiatry,* **34,** 129–133.

Henderson, D. and R.D. Gillespie. 1969. *Textbook of Psychiatry for Students and Practitioners,* ed. by I.R.C. Batchelor. New York: Oxford University.

Henry, W.E. 1956. *The Analysis of Fantasy.* New York: Wiley.

Henryk-Gutt, R. and W.L. Rees. 1973. Psychological aspects of migraine. *Journal of Psychosomatic Medicine,* **17,** 141–153.

Heston, L.L. 1966. Psychiatric disorders in foster home reared children of schizophrenic mothers. *British Journal of Psychiatry,* **112,** 819–825.

Higgins, J. 1969. Process-reactive schizophrenia. Recent developments. *Journal of Nervous and Mental Disease,* **149,** 450–472.

Hilgard, E.R. 1965. *Hypnotic Susceptibility.* New York: Harcourt Brace Jovanovich.

Hilgard, E.R., H. MacDonald, G. Marshall, and A.H. Morgan. 1974. Anticipation of pain and of pain control under hypnosis: Heart rate and blood pressure responses in the cold pressor test. *Journal of Abnormal Psychology,* **38,** 561–568.

Hinkle, L.E., Jr. 1973. The concept of "stress" in the biological and social sciences. *Science, Medicine and Man,* **1,** 31–48.

Hiroto, D.S. 1974. Locus of control and learned helplessness. *Journal of Experimental Psychology,* **102,** 187–193.

Hiroto, D.S. and M.E.P. Seligman. 1975. Generality of learned helplessness in man. *Journal of Personality and Social Psychology,* **31,** 311–327.

Hite, S. 1976. *The Hite Report: A Nationwide Study of Female Sexuality.* New York: Dell.

Hofling, C.K. 1975. *Textbook of Psychiatry for Medical Practice,* 3d ed. Philadelphia: Lippincott.

Hogan, D.R. 1978. The effectiveness of sex therapy: A review of the literature. In *Handbook of Sex Therapy,* ed. by J. LoPiccolo and L. LoPiccolo. New York: Plenum.

Hogarty, G.E. and S.C. Goldberg. 1973. Drug and sociotherapy in the aftercare of schizophrenic patients. *Archives of General Psychiatry,* **28,** 54–64.

Hokanson, J.E. and M. Burgess. 1962. The effects of three types of aggression on vascular processes. *Journal of Abnormal and Social Psychology,* **65,** 446–449.

Hokanson, J.E., D.E. DeGood, M.S. Forrest, and T.M. Brittain. 1971. Availability of avoidance behaviors for modulating vascular-stress responses. *Journal of Personality and Social Psychology,* **19,** 60–68.

Holmes, T.H. and M. Masuda. 1974. Life change and illness susceptibility. In *Stressful Life Events: Their Nature and Effects,* ed. by B.S. Dohrenwend and B.P. Dohrenwend. New York: Wiley.

Holmes, T.H. and R.H. Rahe. 1967. The social adjustment rating scale. *Journal of Psychosomatic Research,* **11,** 213–218.

Holvey, D. and J.H. Talbott, Eds. 1972. *The Merck Manual of Diagnosis and Therapy,* 12th ed. Rahway, N.J.: Merck, Sharp & Dohme.

Holzman, P.S. and D. Levy. 1977. Smooth pursuit eye movements and functional psychoses: A review. *Schizophrenia Bulletin,* **3,** 15–27.

Holzman, P.S., L.R. Proctor, and D.W. Hughes. 1973. Eye tracking patterns in schizophrenia. *Science,* **181,** 179–181.

Holzman, P.S., L.R. Proctor, D.L. Levy, et al. 1974. Eye tracking dysfunctions in schizophrenic patients and their relatives. *Archives of General Psychiatry,* **31,** 143–151.

Honigfeld, G. and A. Howard. 1973. *Psychiatric Drugs.* New York: Academic Press.

Hook, E.B. 1973. Behavioral implications of the human XYY genotype. *Science,* **179,** 139–150.

Horney, K. 1937. *The Neurotic Personality of Our Time.* New York: Norton.

———. 1939. *New Ways in Psychoanalysis.* New York: Norton.

———. 1967. *Feminine Psychology,* ed. by H. Kelman. New York: Norton.

Horowitz, M.J. 1969. Psychic trauma. *Archives of General Psychiatry,* **20,** 552–559.

Hortens, W. 1974. Chart drawn in *Time,* April 22.

Howell, L. 1978. Epilepsy. In *Disability and Rehabilitation Handbook,* ed. by R.M. Goldenson, J.R. Dunham, and C.S. Dunham. New York: McGraw-Hill.

Howes, M.J. and J.E. Hokanson. 1979. Conversational and social responses to depressive interpersonal behavior. *Journal of Abnormal Psychology,* **88,** 625–634.

Hudgens, R.W. 1974. Personal catastrophe and depression: A consideration of the subject with respect to medically ill adolescents, and a requiem for retrospective life event studies. In *Stressful Life Events: Their Nature and Effects,* ed. by B.S. Dohrenwend and B.P. Dohrenwend. New York: Wiley.

Hughes, J.R. 1965. A review of the positive spike phenomenon. In *Applications of Electroencephalography in Psychiatry,* ed. by W. Wilson. Durham, N.C.: Duke University.

———. 1980. Epilepsy: A medical overview. In *A Multidisciplinary Handbook of Epilepsy,* ed. by B.P. Hermann. Springfield, Ill. Charles C. Thomas.

Hughes, R.C. 1977. Covert sensitization treatment of exhibitionism. *Journal of Behavior Therapy and Experimental Psychiatry,* **8,** 177–179.

Hunt, G.H. and M.E. Odoroff. 1962. Follow-up study of narcotic drug addicts after hospitalization. *Public Health Reports,* **77,** 41–54.

Hunt, J.C. and J.D. Margie. 1979. The influence of diet on hypertension management. In *Hypertension update: Mechanisms, epidemiology, evaluation, and management,* ed. by J.C. Hunt et al. Proceedings of Hypertension Update, 9–11 May, Washington, D.C.

Hunt, M. 1974. *Sexual Behavior in the 1970's.* New York: Dell.

Husted, J.R. 1972. Effect of method of systematic desensitization and presence of sexual communication in the treatment of sexual anxiety by counterconditioning. *Proceedings of the 80th Annual Meeting of the American Psychological Association, Honolulu,* **7,** 325–326.

Hutchings, B. and S.A. Mednick. 1974. Registered criminality in the adoptive and biological parents of registered male adoptees. In *Genetics, Environment and Psychopathology,* ed. by S.A. Mednick, F. Schulsinger, J. Higgins, and B. Bell. New York: Elsevier.

Hyde, J.S. 1979. *Understanding Human Sexuality.* New York: McGraw-Hill.

Imperato-McGinley, J., R.E. Peterson, T. Gautier, and E. Stula. 1979. Androgens and the evolution of male-gender identity among male pseudohermaphrodites with 5α-reductase deficiency. *New England Journal of Medicine,* **300,** 1233–1237.

Jaco, E.G. 1960. *The Social Epidemiology of Mental Disorders.* New York: Russell Sage Foundation.

Jacob, T. 1975. Family interaction in disturbed and normal families: A methodological and substantive review. *Psychological Bulletin,* **82,** 33–65.

Jacobs, J. 1975. *Older Persons and Retirement Communities.* Springfield, Ill.: Charles C. Thomas.

Jacobs, P.A., M. Brunton, and M.M. Melville. 1965. Aggressive behavior, mental subnormality, and the XYY male. *Nature,* **208,** 1351–1352.

Jacobson, E. 1938. *Progressive Relaxation.* Chicago: University of Chicago.

Jaffe, R. 1980. A real-life class reunion. *Ladies Home Journal,* June, p. 138.

Jahoda, M. 1958. *Current Concepts of Positive Mental Health.* New York: Basic Books.

James, W. 1902. *Varieties of Religious Experience.* New York: Macmillan.

Jeffers, F. and A. Verwoerdt. 1969. How the old face death. In *Behavior and Adaptation in Late Life,* ed. by E. Busse and E. Pfeiffer. Boston: Little, Brown.

Jellinek, E.M. 1952. Phases of alcohol addiction. *Journal of Studies on Alcohol,* **13,** 673–678.

———. 1971. Phases of alcohol addiction. In *Studies in Abnormal Behavior,* ed. by G.D. Shean. Chicago: Rand-McNally.

Jenkins, C.D., S.J. Zyzanski, and R.H. Rosenman. 1976. Risk of new myocardial infarction in middle-aged men with manifest coronary heart disease. *Circulation,* **53,** 342–347.

Jenkins, R.L. 1966. Psychiatric syndromes in children and their relation to family background. *American Journal of Orthopsychiatry,* **14,** 65–76.

———. 1968. The varieties of children's behavioral problems and family dynamics. *American Journal of Psychiatry,* **124,** 134–139.

Johnson, E.S. and B.J. Bursk. 1977. Relationships between the elderly and their adult children. *The Gerontologist,* **17**(1), 90–96.

Joint Commission on Mental Illness and Health. 1961. *Action for Mental Health.* New York: Basic Books.

Jones, K.L. 1973. Paper presented at the Conference on Genetics and Birth Defects. Boston.

Jones, M. 1953. *The Therapeutic Community: A New Treatment Method in Psychiatry.* New York: Basic Books.

Jones, M.C. 1924. A laboratory study of fear: The case of Peter. *Pedagogical Seminary,* **31,** 308–315.

Joynt, R.J. and I. Shoulson. 1979. Dementia. In *Clinical Neuropsychology,* ed. by K.M. Heilman and E. Valenstein. New York: Oxford University.

Jung, C.G. 1915. The theory of psychoanalysis. *Nervous and Mental Disease Monograph Series,* **19.**

Kalish, R. 1975. *Late Adulthood: Perspectives on Human Development.* Monterey, Calif.: Brooks/Cole.

———. 1976. Death and dying in a social context. In *Handbook of Aging and Social Sciences,* ed. by R. Binstock and E. Shanas. New York: Behavioral Publications.

Kalish, R. and D. Reynolds. 1975. Death and bereavement in a cross-ethnic context. Unpublished manuscript.

Kallman, F.J. and B. Roth. 1956. Genetic aspects of preadolescent schizophrenia. *American Journal of Psychiatry,* **112,** 599–606.

Kanfer, F.H. and J.S. Phillips. 1970. *Learning Foundations of Behavior Therapy.* New York: Wiley.

Kanner, L. 1943. Autistic disturbances of affective contact. *Nervous Child,* **2,** 217–250.

———. 1972. *Child Psychiatry,* 4th ed. Springfield, Ill.: Charles C. Thomas.

Kantorovich, F. 1930. An attempt at associative reflex therapy in alcoholism. *Psychological Abstracts,* 4282.

Kaplan, H.S. 1974. *The New Sex Therapy: Active Treatment of Sexual Dysfunctions.* New York: Brunner/Mazel, in cooperation with Quadrangle and The New York Times Book Co.

Karlsson, J.L. 1966. *The Biologic Basis of Schizophrenia.* Springfield, Ill.: Charles C. Thomas.

Kart, C.S. and B.B. Manard. 1976. Quality of care in old age institutions. *The Gerontologist,* **16**(3), 250–256.

Kart, C.S., E.S. Metress, and J.F. Metress. 1978. *Aging and Health.* Menlo Park, Calif.: Benjamin Cummings.

Katchadourian, H.A. and D.T. Lunde. 1975. *Fundamentals of Human Sexuality.* New York: Holt, Rinehart, & Winston.

Katz, M.M. 1971. The classification of depression: Normal, clinical and ethnocultural variations. In *Depression in the 70's: Modern Theory and Research,* ed. by R.R. Fieve. The Hague: Excerpta Medica.

Kazdin, A.E. 1980. Advances in child behavior therapy: Applications and implications. *American Psychologist,* **34,** 981–987.

Kazdin, A.E. and R.R. Bootzin. 1972. The token economy: An evaluative review. *Journal of Applied Behavior Analysis,* **5,** 343–372.

Kelly, E. and B. Zeller. 1969. Asthma and the psychiatrist. *Journal of Psychosomatic Research,* **13,** 377–395.

Kempe, C.H. 1962. The battered child syndrome. *Journal of the American Medical Association,* **181,** 12–24.

Kendell, R.E., I.E. Cooper, A.H. Gourlay, et al. 1971. Diagnostic criteria of American and British psychiatrists. *Archives of General Psychiatry,* **25,** 123–130.

Kessler, J.W. 1966. *Psychopathology of Childhood.* Englewood Cliffs, N.J.: Prentice-Hall.

Kessler, M. and G.W. Albee. 1975. Primary prevention. *Annual Review of Psychology,* **26,** 557–591.

Kety, S.S. 1967. The hypothetical relationships between amines and mental illness: A critical analysis. In *Amines and Schizophrenia,* ed. by H.E. Himwich, S.S. Kety, and J.R. Smythies. Oxford: Pergamon.

Kety, S.S., D. Rosenthal, P. Wender, and F. Schulsinger. 1968. The types and prevalence of mental illness in the biological and adoptive families of adopted schizophrenics. In *The Transmission of Schizophrenia,* ed. by D. Rosenthal and S.S. Kety. New York: Pergamon.

Kidson, M.A. and I.H. Jones. 1968. Psychiatric disorders among aborigines of the Australian western desert. *Archives of General Psychiatry.*

Kimmel, D.C. 1980. *Adulthood and Aging,* 2d ed. New York: Wiley.

King, G.F., S.G. Armitage, and J.R. Tilton. 1960. A therapeutic approach to schizophrenics of extreme pathology: An operant-interpersonal method. *Journal of Abnormal and Social Psychology,* **61,** 276–286.

Kinsey, A.C., W.B. Pomeroy, and C.E. Martin. 1949. *Sexual Behavior in the Human Male.* Philadelphia: W.B. Saunders.

Kinsey, A.C., W.B. Pomeroy, C.E. Martin, and P.H. Gebhard. 1953. *Sexual Behavior in the Human Female.* Philadelphia: W.B. Saunders.

Kiritz, S. and R. Moos. 1974. Physiological effects of social environments. *Psychosomatic Medicine,* **36.**

Kissin, B. and H. Begleiter. 1977. *Treatment and Rehabilitation of the Chronic Alcoholic.* New York: Plenum.

Kitano, H.H.L. 1969. Japanese-American mental illness. In *Changing Perspectives in Mental Illness,* ed. by S.C. Plog and R.B. Edgerton. New York: Holt, Rinehart, & Winston.

Kleeman, S.T. 1967. Psychiatric contributions in the treatment of asthma. *Annals of Allergy,* **25,** 611–619.

Klerman, G.L. 1978. Affective disorders. In *The Harvard Guide to Modern Psychiatry,* ed. by A.M. Nicholi, Jr. Cambridge, Mass.: Belknap.

Klove, H. and C.G. Matthews. 1974. Neuropsychological studies of patients with epilepsy. In *Clinical Neuropsychology: Current Status and Applications,* ed. by R.M. Reitan and L.A. Davison. Washington, D.C.: Winston.

Kluger, J.M. 1969. Childhood asthma and the social milieu. *American Academy of Child Psychiatry,* **8,** 353–366.

Kohn, M.L. 1968. Social class and schizophrenia: A critical review. In *The Transmission of Schizophrenia,* ed. by D. Rosenthal and S.S. Kety. New York: Pergamon.

Kolb, L.C. 1973. *Modern Clinical Psychiatry,* 8th ed. Philadelphia: W.B. Saunders.

Konig, P. and S. Godfrey. 1973. Prevalence of exercise-induced lability in families of children with asthma. *Archives of Diseases of Childhood,* **48,** 513.

Kora, T. and K. Ohara. 1973. Morita therapy. *Psychology Today,* **6**(10), 63–68.

Kraepelin, E. 1902. *Clinical Psychiatry: A Textbook for Physicians,* tr. by A. Diffendorf. New York: Macmillan.

Krafft-Ebing, R. von. 1965. *Psychopathia Sexualis* (1886), tr. by F.S. Klaf. New York: Bell.

Kraft, T. 1969. Alcoholism treated by systematic desensitization: A follow-up of eight cases. *Journal of the Royal College of General Practice,* **18,** 336–340.

Kramer, M. 1969. Cross-national study of diagnosis of the mental disorders: Origin of the problem. *American Journal of Psychiatry,* **125,** 1–11.

Kraus, A.A. and A.M. Lilienfeld. 1959. Some epidemiologic aspects of the high mortality rate in the young widowed group. *Journal of Chronic Diseases,* **10,** 207–217.

Kretschmer, E. 1925. *Physique and Character: An Investigation of the Nature of Constitution and of the Theory of Temperament,* tr. by W.J.H. Sprott. New York: Harcourt Brace.

Kronenberger, L., Ed. 1971. *Atlantic Brief Lives: A Biographical Companion to the Arts.* Boston: Little, Brown.

Kübler-Ross, E. 1969. *On Death and Dying.* New York: Macmillan.

Kurland, A.A. 1967. The therapeutic potential of LSD in medicine. In *LSD, Man and Society,* ed. by R.C. DeBold and R.C. Leaf. Middletown, Conn.: Wesleyan University.

Labouvie-Vief, G. and J.N. Gonda. 1976. Cognitive strategy training and intellectual performance in the elderly. *Journal of Gerontology,* **31**(3), 327–332.

Lacey, J.I. 1967. Somatic response patterning and stress: Some revisions of activation theory. In *Psychological Stress,* ed. by M.H. Appley and R. Trumbull. New York: McGraw-Hill.

Laing, R.D. 1964. Is schizophrenia a disease? *International Journal of Social Psychiatry,* **10,** 184–193.

———. 1967. *The Politics of Experience.* New York: Pantheon.

———. 1970. *The Divided Self: An Existential Study in Sanity and Madness.* New York: Pantheon.

Lambley, P. 1976. The use of assertive training and psychodynamic insight in the treatment of migraine headache: A case study. *Journal of Nervous and Mental Disease,* **163,** 61–64.

Lang, P.J. 1975. Acquisition of heart rate control: Method, theory, and clinical implications. In *Clinical Applications of Psychophysiology,* ed. by D.C. Fowles. New York: Columbia University Press.

Langley, R. and R.C. Levy. 1977. *Wife Beating: The Silent Crisis.* New York: Pocket Books.

Langone, J. and D. deN. Langone. 1980. *Women Who Drink.* Reading, Mass.: Addison-Wesley.

Lanyon, R.I. 1978. The treatment of child molesters. Presented at the Sexual Assault Seminar, Phoenix South Community Mental Health Center, Phoenix, Ariz., June 28, 1978.

Lanyon, R.I. 1979. Behavioral treatment of sexual deviations. Presented to the staff of the Scottsdale Memorial Hospital, Scottsdale, Ariz., June 1, 1979.

Lazarus, A.A. 1968. Learning theory and the treatment of depression. *Behavior Research and Therapy,* **6,** 83–89.

———. 1971. *Behavior Therapy and Beyond.* New York: McGraw-Hill.

Leary, T. 1957. *Interpersonal Diagnosis of Personality: A Functional Theory and Methodology of Personality Evaluation.* New York: Ronald Press.

Leinwand, G.L. 1972. *Prisons.* New York: Simon & Schuster.

Leon, G.R. 1977. *Case Histories in Deviant Behavior,* 2d. ed. Boston: Holbrook.

Levenson, M. and C. Neuringer. 1971. Problem-solving in suicidal adolescents. *Journal of Consulting and Clinical Psychology,* **37,** 433–436.

Levi, L. 1972. *Stress and Distress in Response to Psychosocial Stimuli.* Stockholm: Almqvist and Wiksell.

Levin, S.M., S.M. Barry, S. Gambaro, et al. 1977. Variations of covert sensitization in the treatment of pedophiliac behavior: A case study. *Journal of Consulting and Clinical Psychology,* **45,** 896–907.

Levinson, D., C. Darrow, E. Klein, et al. 1976. Periods in the adult development of men: Ages 18 to 45. *The Counseling Psychologist,* **6,** 21–25.

Levitt, E.E. 1963. Psychotherapy with children: A further evaluation. *Behavior Research and Therapy,* **2,** 45–51.

Levy, L.H. 1976. Self-help groups: Types and psychological processes. *Journal of Applied Behavioral Science,* **12,** 3.

Lewinsohn, P.M. 1974. A behavioral approach to depression. In *The Psychology of Depression: Contemporary Theory and Research,* ed. by R.J. Friedman and M.M. Katz, New York: Wiley.

Lewinsohn, P.M. and G. Atwood. 1969. Depression: A clinical-research approach. *Psychotherapy: Theory, Research and Practice,* **6,** 166–171.

Lewinsohn, P.M., A. Biglan, and A.M. Zeiss. 1976. Behavioral treatment of depression. In *The Behavioral Management of Anxiety, Depression and Pain,* ed. by P.O. Davidson. New York: Brunner/Mazel.

Lewinsohn, P.M., M. Weinstein, and T. Alper. 1970. Behaviorally oriented approach to the group treatment of persons with depression. *Journal of Clinical Psychology,* **26,** 525–532.

Lewis, J. 1973. *Atlas of Aesthetic Plastic Surgery.* Boston: Little, Brown.

Lewis, J.A. 1975. Violence and epilepsy. *Journal of the American Medical Association,* **232**(11), 1165–1167.

Lewis, N.D.C. 1941. *A Short History of Psychiatric Achievement.* New York: Norton.

Lidz, T. 1973. *The Origin and Treatment of Schizophrenic Disorders.* New York: Basic Books.

———. 1976. *The Person.* New York: Basic Books.

Lidz, T. and S. Fleck. 1960. Schizophrenia, human interaction and the role of the family. In *The Etiology of Schizophrenia,* ed. by D. Jackson. New York: Basic Books.

Lieberman, M. 1961. The relationship of mortality rates to entrance to a home for the aged. *Geriatrics,* **16,** 515–519.

Lockyer, L. and M. Rutter. 1969. A five-to-fifteen year follow-up of infantile psychosis. III. Psychological characteristics. *British Journal of Psychiatry,* **115,** 865–882.

Long, A. 1941. Parent's reports of undesirable behavior in children. *Child Development,* **12,** 43–62.

LoPiccolo, J. 1978. Direct treatment of sexual dysfunction. In *Handbook of Sex Therapy,* ed. by J. LoPiccolo and L. LoPiccolo. New York: Plenum.

LoPiccolo, J. and W.C. Lobitz. 1972. The role of masturbation in the treatment of orgasmic dysfunction. *Archives of Sexual Behavior,* **2,** 163–171.

Lotter, V. 1966. Epidemiology of autistic conditions in young children. I. Prevalence. *Social Psychiatry,* **1,** 124–137.

Ludwig, A.M., J.M. Brandsma, C.B. Wilbur, et al. 1972. The objective study of a multiple personality. *Archives of General Psychiatry,* April.

Luparello, T.J., E.R. McFadden, H.A. Lyons, and E.R. Bleecker. 1971. Psychologic factors and bronchial asthma. *New York State Journal of Medicine,* **71,** 2161–2165.

Luria, Z. and M.D. Rose. 1979. *Psychology of Human Sexuality.* New York: Wiley.

Lyght, C.E., ed. 1966. *The Merck Manual of Diagnosis and Therapy,* 11th ed. Rahway, N.J.: Merck Sharpe and Dohme.

Lykken, D.T. 1957. A study of anxiety in the sociopathic personality. *Journal of Abnormal and Social Psychology,* **55**(1), 6–10.

MacLeod, P. 1979. Alcohol exposure goes to the bones of developing fetus. *Medical World News,* August, 6.

McCandless, B.R., W.S. Parsons, and A. Roberts. 1972. Perceived opportunity, delinquency, race and body build among delinquent youth. *Journal of Consulting and Clinical Psychology,* **38**(2), 281–287.

McCary, J.L. 1978. *McCary's Human Sexuality,* 3d ed. New York: Van Nostrand Reinhold.

McCord, W. and J. McCord. 1964. *The Psychopath: An Essay on the Criminal Mind.* New York: Van Nostrand Reinhold.

McCulloch, W.J. and A.E. Philip. 1972. *Suicidal Behavior.* New York: Pergamon.

McGuire, R.J., J.M. Carlisle, and B.G. Young. 1965. Sexual deviations as conditioned behavior: A hypothesis. *Behavior Research and Therapy,* **2,** 185–190.

McHale, S.M. and W. Boone. 1980. Play between autistic and nonhandicapped children. *The Pointer,* XXIV (Spring), 28–32.

McLemore, C.W. and L.S. Benjamin. 1979. Whatever happened to interpersonal diagnosis? A psychosocial alternative to DSM-III. *American Psychologist,* **34,** 17–34.

McLuhan, M. 1964. *Understanding Media,* 2d ed. New York: Signet.

McNeil, E.B. 1967. *The Quiet Furies: Man and Disorder.* Englewood Cliffs, N.J.: Prentice-Hall.

Mahoney, D.J. 1972. Research issues in self-management. *Behavior Therapy,* **3,** 173–199.

Mahoney, M.J. 1974. *Cognition and Behavior Modification.* Cambridge, Mass.: Ballinger.

———. 1980. *Abnormal Psychology.* New York: Harper & Row.

Mahoney, M.J. and D. Ainkoff. 1978. Cognitive and self-control therapies. In *Handbook of Psychotherapy and Behavior Change: An Empirical Analysis,* 2d ed., ed. by S.L. Garfield and A.E. Bergin. New York: Wiley.

Maletzky, B.M. 1980(a). Assisted covert sensitization. In *Exhibitionism: Description, Assessment, and Treatment,* ed. by D.J. Cox and R. Daitzman. New York: Gailand.

———. 1980(b). Self-referred versus court-referred sexually deviant patients: Success with assisted covert sensitization. *Behavior Therapy,* **11,** 306–314.

Manual on Terminology and Classification in Mental Retardation. 1977. Washington, D.C.: American Association on Mental Deficiency.

Mark, V.H. and F.R. Ervin. 1970. *Violence and the Brain.* New York: Harper & Row.

Markush, R.E. and R.V. Favero. 1974. Epidemiologic assessment of stressful life events, depressed mood, and psychophysiological symptoms—a preliminary report. In *Stressful Life Events: Their Nature and Effects,* ed. by B.S. Dohrenwend and B.P. Dohrenwend. New York: Wiley.

Marquis, J.N. 1970. Orgasmic reconditioning: Changing sexual object choice through controlling masturbation fantasies. *Journal of Behavior Therapy and Experimental Psychiatry,* **1,** 263–271.

Martin, R.L., C.R. Cloninger, and S.B. Guze. 1978. Female criminality and the prediction of recidivism. *Archives of General Psychiatry,* **35,** 207–214.

Masters, W.J. and V.E. Johnson. 1966. *Human Sexual Response.* Boston: Little, Brown.

———. 1970. *Human Sexual Inadequacy.* Boston: Little Brown.

Masuda, M., D.L. Cutler, L. Hein, and T.H. Holmes. 1978. Life events and prisoners. *Archives of General Psychiatry,* **35,** 197–203.

Matarazzo, J.D. 1976. *Wechsler's Measurement and Appraisal of Adult Intelligence,* 5th ed. Baltimore: Williams & Wilkins.

Matthey, W. 1974. The effects of observational learning and perceived gain on the imitative behavior of sociopaths. *Dissertation Abstracts International,* **34**(9-B), 4669.

Mausner, B. and E. Platt. 1971. *Smoking: A Behavioral Analysis.* New York: Pergamon.

May, R. 1958(a). Contributions of existential psychotherapy. In *Existence: A New Dimension in Psychiatry and Psychology,* ed. by R. May, E. Angel and H.F. Ellenberger. New York: Basic Books.

———. 1958(b). The origins and significance of the existential movement in psychology. In *Existence: A New Dimension in Psychiatry and Psychology,* ed. by R. May, E. Angel and H.F. Ellenberger. New York: Basic Books.

———. 1969. *Love and Will.* New York: Norton.

Mayron, L.W., J. Ott, R. Nations, and E.L. Mayron. 1974. Light radiation and academic behavior. *Academic Therapy,* **10**(I), 33–47.

Mednick, S.A. 1958. A learning theory approach to research on schizophrenia. *Psychological Bulletin,* **55,** 316–327.

———. 1970. Breakdown of individuals at high risk for schizophrenia: Possible predispositional perinatal factors. *Mental Hygiene,* **54,** 50–63.

———. 1974. Electrodermal recovery and psychopathology. In *Genetics, Environment and Psychopathology,* ed. by S.A. Mednick, F. Schulsinger, J. Higgins, and B. Bell. New York: Oxford University.

Mednick, S.A. and T.F. McNeil. 1968. Current methodology in research on etiology of schizophrenia: Serious difficulties which suggest the use of the high-risk-group method. *Psychological Bulletin,* **70,** 681–693.

Meehl, P.E. 1962. Schizotaxia, schizotypy and schizophrenia. *American Psychologist,* **17,** 827–838.

Megargee, E. 1979. An MMPI-based classification system for prisoners. In *New Directions in the Use of the MMPI,* ed. by J.N. Butcher. Minneapolis: University of Minnesota.

Meichenbaum, D.H. 1977. Self-instructional approach to stress management: A proposal for stress inoculation training. In *Stress and Anxiety,* vol. 2, ed. by C. Spielburger and I. Sarason. New York: Wiley.

Meichenbaum, D.H. and R. Cameron. 1973. Training schizophrenics to talk to themselves: A means of developing attentional controls. *Behavior Therapy,* **4,** 515–534.

Meiselman, K.C. 1978. *Incest.* San Francisco: Jossey-Bass.

Meissner, W.W. 1978. *The Paranoid Process.* New York: Jason Aronson.

Meltzer, H. and S. Stahl. 1976. The dopamine hypothesis of schizophrenia: A review. *Schizophrenia Bulletin,* **2,** 19–76.

Mendels, J. 1970. *Concepts of Depression.* New York: Wiley.

Mendels, J., A. Fieve, R.G. Fitzgerald, et al. 1972. Biogenic amine metabolites in cerebrospinal fluid of depressed and manic patients. *Science,* **175,** 1380–1382.

Mendels, J. and J.L. Stinnet. 1973. Biogenic amine metabolism, depression, and mania. In *Biological Psychiatry,* ed. by J. Mendels. New York: Wiley.

Mendels, J., J.L. Stinnet, D. Burns, and A. Frazer. 1975. Amine precursors and depression. *Archives of General Psychiatry,* **32,** 22–30.

Menninger, K. 1938. *Man Against Himself.* New York: Harcourt.

———. 1945. *The Human Mind.* New York: Knopf.

Meyers, R. 1978. *Like Normal People.* New York: McGraw-Hill.

Miller, J.G. 1965. Living systems: Structure and process. *Behavioral Science,* **10,** 337–379.

Miller, L., Ed. 1974. *Marijuana: Effects on Human Behavior.* New York: Academic Press.

Mintz, N.L. and D.J. Schwartz. 1971. Ecological factors in the incidence of schizophrenic and manic-depressive psychoses. In *The Origins of Abnormal Behavior,* ed. by N.L. Corah and E.N. Gale. Reading, Mass.: Addison-Wesley.

Mischel, W. 1976. *Introduction to Personality,* 2d ed. New York: Holt, Rinehart, & Winston.

Mishler, E.G. and N.E. Waxler. 1968. *Interaction in Families: An Experimental Study of Family Processes and Schizophrenia.* New York: Wiley.

Mitchell, K.R. and D.M. Mitchell. 1971. An exploratory treatment application of programmed behavior therapy techniques. *Journal of Psychosomatic Research,* **15,** 137–157.

Monahan, J., Ed. 1976. *Community Mental Health and the Criminal Justice System.* New York: Pergamon.

Money, J. and A. Ehrhardt. 1972. *Man and Woman, Boy and Girl.* Baltimore: Johns Hopkins University.

Moore, P. 1980. Why depression strikes more women than men. *Boston Globe,* October 22.

Morrison, J.R. and M.A. Stewart. 1971. A family study of the hyperactive child syndrome. *Biological Psychiatry,* **3,** 189–195.

Mosher, L.R., J.G. Gunderson, and S. Buchsbaum. 1973. Special report on schizophrenia. *Schizophrenia Bulletin,* **1,** 12–52.

Moss, S. and P. James. 1970. *"Black Rover, Come Over!" The Hypnosymbolic Treatment of a Phobia.* Urbana, Ill.: University of Illinois.

Mowrer, O.H. 1948. Learning theory and the neurotic paradox. *American Journal of Orthopsychiatry,* **18,** 571–610.

Moyer, K.E. 1971(a). The physiology of aggression and the implications for aggression control. In *The Control of Aggression and Violence,* ed. by J.L. Singer. New York: Academic Press.

———. 1971(b). *The Physiology of Hostility.* Chicago: Markham.

Murphy, G.E. and E. Robins. 1968. The communication of suicidal ideas. In *Suicidal Behaviors: Diagnosis and Management,* ed. by H.L.P. Resnik. Boston: Little, Brown.

Murphy, J.M. 1976. Psychiatric labeling in cross-cultural perspective. *Science,* **191,** 1019–1028.

Myerhoff, B. A renewal of the word. In *The Pushcart Prize IV: Best of the Small Presses,* ed. by B. Henderson. New York: Pushcart Press.

Myerson, A. 1941. A review of mental disorders in urban areas. *American Journal of Psychiatry,* **96,** 995–997.

Nahas, G. 1973. *Marijuana—Deceptive Weed.* New York: Raven Press.

Naranjo, C. 1971. Contributions of gestalt therapy. In *Ways of Growth: Approaches to Expanding Awareness,* ed. by H. Otto and J. Mann. New York: Pocket Books.

National Institute of Mental Health. 1970(a). Lithium in the treatment of mood disorders. Washington, D.C.: Government Printing Office.

———. 1970(b). Department of Health, Education, and Welfare, Publ. No. 5027. Washington, D.C.: Government Printing Office.

National Institute of Mental Health. 1973. *Statistical Note #47.* Bethesda, Md.: NIMH, Survey and Reports Section, Biometry Branch.

National Institute on Alcoholism and Alcohol Abuse. 1978. Report on Alcohol and Health.

Neale, J.M. and R.L. Cromwell. 1970. Attention and schizophrenia. In *Progress in Experimental Personality Research,* vol. 5, ed. by B.A. Maher. New York: Academic Press.

Neale, J.M. and M. Katahn. 1968. Anxiety, choice and stimulus uncertainty. *Journal of Personality,* **36,** 238–245.

Nesbitt, P.E. 1973. Smoking, physiological arousal and emotional response. *Journal of Personality and Social Psychology,* **25,** 137–144.

Noyes, R.J., J. Clancy, R. Crowe, et al. 1978. The familial prevalence of anxiety neuroses. *Archives of General Psychiatry,* **35,** 1057–1059.

Nunnally, J.C., Jr. 1961. *Popular Conceptions of Mental Health.* New York: Holt, Rinehart, & Winston.

Nygard, N.K. 1975. A test of Hare's temporal conflict model of psychopathy. *Dissertation Abstracts International,* **35**(7-B), 3590–3597.

O'Connor. F. 1961. *Mystery and Manners.* New York: Farrar, Straus, & Cudahy.

O'Dell, S. 1974. Training parents in behavior modification: A review. *Psychological Bulletin,* **81,** 418–433.

O'Leary, K.D., A. Rosenbaum, and P.C. Hughes. 1978. Fluorescent lighting: A purported source of hyperactive behavior. *Journal of Abnormal Child Psychology,* **6**(3), 285–289.

O'Leary, K.D. and G.T. Wilson. 1975. *Behavior Therapy—Application and Outcome.* Englewood Cliffs, N.J.: Prentice-Hall.

Oltman, J. and S. Friedman. 1967. Parental deprivation in psychiatric conditions. *Disturbances of the Nervous System,* **28,** 298–303.

Orr, D.W. 1949. Psychiatric uses of sodium pentothal. *U.S. Navy Medical Bulletin,* **49,** 508–516.

Osmond, H. and J. Smythies. 1962. Schizophrenia: A new approach. *Journal of Mental Science,* **98,** 309–315.

Ozarin, L.D., R.W. Redick, and C.A. Taube. 1976. A quarter century of psychiatric care, 1950–1974: A statistical review. *Hospital and Community Psychiatry,* **27,** 515–519.

Palmer, R.S. 1950. Psyche and blood pressure. *Journal of the American Medical Association,* **144,** 295–298.

Papalia, D.E. and S.W. Olds. 1975. *A Child's World: Infancy Through Adolescence.* New York: McGraw-Hill.

Parry-Jones, W.W., H.C. Santer-Westrate, and R.C. Crawley. 1970. Behavior therapy in a case of hysterical blindness. *Behavior Research and Therapy,* **8,** 79–85.

Partridge, G.E. 1930. Current conceptions of psychopathic personality. *American Journal of Psychiatry,* **87,** 53–99.

Pasamanick, B., M. Rogers, and M.A. Lilienfled. 1956. Pregnancy experience and the development of behavior disorder in children. *American Journal of Psychiatry,* **112,** 613–617.

Patterson, R.D., R. Abrahams, and F. Baker. 1974. Preventing self-destructive behavior. *Geriatrics,* November, 115–121.

Paul, L. 1966. Crisis intervention. *Mental Hygiene,* **50,** 141–145.

Paul, L. and R.J. Lentz. 1977. *Psychosocial Treatment of Chronic Mental Patients: Milieu versus Social-Learning Programs.* Cambridge, Mass.: Harvard University.

Paykel, E.S. 1974. Life stress and psychiatric disorder: Applications of the clinical approach. In *Stressful Life Events: Their Nature and Effects,* ed. by B.S. Dohrenwend and B.P. Dohrenwend. New York: Wiley.

Peplau, L.A., and S.D. Cochran. Value orientations in the intimate relationships of gay men. *Journal of Homosexuality,* in press.

Perley, M.J. and S.B. Guze. 1962. Hysteria—the stability and usefulness of clinical criteria. *New England Journal of Medicine,* **266,** 421–426.

Perls, F.S. 1970. Four lectures. In *Gestalt Therapy Now: Theory, Techniques, Application,* ed. by J. Fagan and I.L. Shepherd. Palo Alto, Calif.: Science and Behavior Books.

———. 1971. *Gestalt Therapy Verbatim.* New York: Bantam Books.

Pervin, L.A. 1963. The need to predict and control under conditions of threat. *Journal of Personality,* **31,** 575–585.

Peters, J.E. and R.M. Stern. 1971. Specificity of attitude hypothesis in psychosomatic medicine: A reexamination. *Journal of Psychosomatic Research,* **15,** 129–135.

Phillips, D.L. 1963. Rejection: A possible consequence of seeking help for mental disorders. *American Sociological Review* **28,** 963–972.

Phillips, E., E. Phillips, D. Friden, and M. Holf. 1971. Achievement Place: Modification of the behavior of predelinquent boys with a token economy. *Journal of Applied Behavioral Analysis,* **4,** 45–59.

Pincus, J.H. and G.J. Tucker. 1978. *Behavioral Neurology,* 2d. ed. New York: Oxford University.

Piotrowski, Z.A. 1968. Psychological test prediction of suicide. In *Suicidal Behaviors: Diagnosis and Management,* ed. by H.L. Resnik. Boston: Little, Brown.

Plaut, T.F. 1967. *Alcohol Problems: A Report to the Nation.* New York: Oxford University.

Polk, K. 1974. Urban and nonurban delinquency. *Behavior Today,* **5,** 253.

Pomeroy, W.B. 1977. What men fear most about sex. *Cosmopolitan,* May.

Post, F. 1965. *The Clinical Psychiatry of Later Life.* New York: Pergamon.

Pradhan, S. and S. Dutta. 1977. *Drug Abuse: Clinical and Basic Aspects.* St. Louis, Mo.: C.V. Mosby.

Prange, A.J., Jr., I.C. Wilson, C.W. Lynn, et al. 1974. L-tryptophan in mania—contribution to a permissive hypothesis of affective disorders. *Archives of General Psychiatry,* **30,** 56–62.

Prichard, J.C. 1835. *A Treatise on Insanity.* Philadelphia: Hasswell, Barrington & Hassurd.

Prince, V. and P.M. Bentler. 1972. Survey of 504 cases of transvestism. *Psychological Reports,* **31,** 903–917.

Prusoff, B. and G.L. Klerman. 1974. Differentiating depressed from anxious neurotic outpatients. *Archives of General Psychiatry,* **30**(3), 302–309.

Purcell, K., K. Brady, H. Chai, et al. 1969. The effect on asthma in children of experimental separation from the family. *Psychosomatic Medicine,* **31,** 144–164.

Quay, H.C. 1965. Psychopathic personality as pathological stimulus seeking. *American Journal of Psychiatry,* **122,** 180–183.

Rao, S.M. and A.G. Glaros. 1979. Electromyographic correlates of experimentally induced stress in diurnal bruxists and normals. *Journal of Dental Research,* **58,** 1872–1878.

Rachman, S., I. Marks, and R. Hodgson. 1973. The treatment of obsessive-compulsive neurotics by modeling and flooding in vivo. *Behavior Research and Therapy,* **11,** 463–471.

Radloff, L.S. and D.S. Rae. 1976. Adult development: Faster horses . . . and more money. *The Personnel and Guidance Journal,* **55,** 106–108.

———. 1979. Susceptibility and precipitating factors in depression: Sex differences and similarities. *Journal of Abnormal Psychology,* **88,** 174–181.

Rayner, E. 1971. *Human Development.* London: Allen & Unwin.

Rees, L. 1963. The significance of parental attitudes in childhood asthma. *Journal of Psychosomatic Research,* **7,** 181–190.

———. The importance of psychological, allergic and infective factors in childhood asthma. *Journal of Psychosomatic Research,* **7,** 253–262.

Reichard, S., F. Livson, and P.G. Peterson. 1962. *Aging and Personality.* New York: Wiley.

Report of the Task Panel on Prevention submitted to the President's Commission on Mental Health, February 15, 1978.

Resnik, H.L.P., ed. 1968. *Suicidal Behaviors: Diagnosis and Management.* Boston: Little, Brown.

Resnik, H.L. and J.M. Cantor. 1970. Suicide and aging. *Journal of the American Geriatrics Society,* **18,** 152–158.

Rimel, R. 1979. An assessment of recovery following head trauma. Presented at the Third Annual Post-Graduate Course on the Rehabilitation of the Traumatic Brain-Injured Adult. Williamsburg, Virginia.

Robins, L.N. 1966. Deviant Children Grow Up. Baltimore: Williams & Wilkins.

Rogers, C.R. 1951. *Client-Centered Therapy: Its Current Practice, Implications and Theory.* Boston: Houghton Mifflin.

———. 1955. Persons or science? A philosophical question. *American Psychologist,* **10,** 267–278.

———. 1959. A theory of therapy, personality, and interpersonal relationships, as developed in the client-centered framework. In *Psychology: A Study of a Science,* vol. 3, ed. by S. Koch. New York: Basic Books.

———. 1961. *On Becoming a Person.* Boston: Houghton Mifflin.

Rogers, C.R. and R.F. Dymond, eds. 1954. *Psychotherapy and Personality Change: Coordinated Studies in the Client-Centered Approach.* Chicago: University of Chicago.

Rokeach, M. 1964. *The Three Christs of Ypsilanti.* New York: Random House.

Roman, P. and P. Taietz. 1967. Organizational structure and disengagement: The emeritus professor. *The Gerontologist,* **7**(2), 147–152.

Rorschach, H. 1921. *Psychodiagnostik.* Leipzig: Ernst Bircher Verlag.

Rosanoff, A., T.M. Standy, and I.R. Plessett. 1941. The etiology of child behavior difficulties, juvenile delinquency and adult criminality, with special reference to their occurrence in twins. *Psychiatric Monographs,* No. 1.

Rosen, G.M. 1981. Guidelines for the review of do-it-yourself treatment books. *Contemporary Psychology,* **26,** 189–191.

Rosenbaum, A. 1979. Wife abuse: Characteristics of the participants and etiological considerations. Unpublished doctoral dissertation, State University of New York at Stony Brook.

Rosenbaum, A. and J.F. Calhoun. 1977. The use of the telephone hotline in crisis intervention: A review. *Journal of Community Psychology,* **5,** 325–339.

Rosenbaum, M. 1973. *Drug Abuse and Drug Addiction.* New York: Gordon & Breach.

Rosenfeld, A. 1976. *Prolongevity.* New York: Knopf.

Rosenhan, D.L. 1973. On being sane in insane places. *Science,* **179,** 250–258.

Rosenman, R.H., R.J. Brand, C.D. Jenkins, et al. 1975. Coronary heart disease in the Western Collaborative Group Study. *Journal of the American Medical Association,* **233,** 872–877.

Rosenthal, D. 1970. *Genetic Theory and Abnormal Behavior.* New York: McGraw-Hill.

———. 1971. *Genetics of Psychopathology.* New York: McGraw-Hill.

———. 1973. Evidence for a spectrum of schizophrenic disorders. Presented at the Annual Convention of the American Psychological Association, Montreal.

Rosenthal, D., P.H. Wender, S.S. Kety, et al. 1968. Schizophrenics' offspring reared in adoptive homes. In *The Transmission of Schizophrenia,* ed. by D. Rosenthal and S. Kety. Oxford: Pergamon.

Rosenthal, S.H. and N.L. Wulfsohn. 1970. Electrosleep—a clinical trial. *American Journal of Psychiatry,* **127**(4), 533–534.

Rosenthal, T. and A. Bandura. 1978. Psychological modeling: Theory and practice. In *Handbook of Psychotherapy and Behavior Change: An Empirical Analysis,*

2d ed., ed. by S.L. Garfield and A.E. Bergin. New York: Wiley.

Ross, A.D. 1974. *Psychological Disorders of Children.* New York: McGraw-Hill.

Rotenberg, M. 1978. *Damnation and Deviance: The Protestant Ethic and the Spirit of Failure.* New York: Free Press.

Rotter, J.B. 1954. *Social Learning and Clinical Psychology.* Englewood Cliffs, N.J.: Prentice-Hall.

Rubin, R.T. and A.J. Mandell. 1966. Adrenal cortical activity in pathological emotional states: A review. *American Journal of Psychiatry,* **123,** 387–400.

Rugh, R. and L.B. Shettles. 1971. *From Conception to Birth.* New York: Harper & Row.

Rush, A.J., A.T. Beck, M. Kovacs, and S. Hollon. 1977. Comparative efficacy of cognitive therapy and imipramine in the treatment of depressed outpatients. *Cognitive Therapy and Research,* **1,** 17–37.

Ruskin, A., O.W. Board, and R.L. Shaffer. 1948. Blast hypertension: Elevated arterial pressure in victims of the Texas City disaster. *American Journal of Medicine,* **4,** 228–236.

Rutter, M. 1965. The influence of organic and emotional factors in the origins, nature and outcome of child psychosis. *Developmental Medicine and Child Neurology,* **7,** 518–528.

———. 1974(a). Parent-child separation: Psychological effects on children. *Psychiatrie de l'Enfant,* **17,** 479–514.

———. 1974(b). The development of infantile autism. *Psychological Medicine,* **4,** 147–163.

Rutter, M. and L. Lockyer. 1967. A five to fifteen year follow-up of infantile psychosis: I. Description of sample. *British Journal of Psychiatry,* **113,** 1169–1182.

Rycroft, C. 1978. *Introduction to Dissociation of Personality,* by M. Prince. New York: Oxford University.

Sachar, E.J. 1975. A neuroendocrine strategy in the psychobiologic study of depressive illness. In *The Psychobiology of Depression,* ed. by J. Mendels. New York: Spectrum.

Salter, A. 1949. *Conditioned Reflex Therapy.* New York: Farrar, Strauss.

Saltzman, C. 1978. Electroconvulsive therapy. In *The Harvard Guide to Modern Psychiatry,* ed. by A.M. Nicholi, Jr. Cambridge, Mass.: Belknap.

Sameroff, A. and M. Zax. 1973. Schizotaxia revisited: Model issues in the etiology of schizophrenia. *American Journal of Orthopsychiatry,* **43,** 744–754.

Sarason, I.G. 1976. A modeling and informational approach to delinquency. In *Analysis of Delinquency and Aggression,* ed. by E. Ribes-Inesta and A. Bandura. Hillsdale, N.J.: Erlbaum.

Sarason, I.G., Johnson, and Siegel. 1978. Assessing the impact of life change: Development of the life experience survey. *Journal of Consulting and Clinical Psychology,* **46,** 932–946.

Satterfield, J., D. Cantwell, and B. Satterfield. 1974. Pathophysiology of the hyperactive child syndrome. *Archives of General Psychiatry,* **31,** 839–844.

Scarf, M. 1980. *Unfinished Business: Pressure Points in the Lives of Women.* New York: Doubleday.

Schachter, J., J.L. Kerr, F.C. Wimberly, and J.M. Lachin. 1974. Heart rate levels of black and white newborns. *Psychosomatic Medicine,* **36**(6), 513–524.

Schachter, S. and B. Latane. 1964. Crime, cognition, and the autonomic nervous system. In *Nebraska Symposium on Motivation,* vol. 12, ed. by D. Levine. Lincoln, Neb.: University of Nebraska.

Schildkraut, J. 1965. The catecholamine hypothesis of affective disorders: A review of supporting evidence. *American Journal of Psychiatry,* **122,** 509–522.

Schmauk, F.J. 1970. Punishment, arousal, and avoidance learning in sociopaths. *Journal of Abnormal Psychology,* **76,** 443–453.

Schmidt, H.O. and C.P. Fonda. 1956. The reliability of psychiatric diagnosis: A new look. *Journal of Abnormal and Social Psychology,* **52,** 262–267.

Schreiber, F. 1974. *Sybil.* New York: Warner.

Schreibman, L. and R. Koegel. 1975. Autism: A defeatable horror. *Psychology Today,* **8,** 61–67.

Schroeder, C.S., S.R. Schroeder, and M.A. Davine. 1978. Learning disabilities: Assessment and management of reading problems. In *Handbook of Treatment of Mental Disorders in Childhood and Adolescence,* ed. by B.B. Wolman. Englewood Cliffs, N.J.: Prentice-Hall.

Schwartz, G.E. 1977. Psychosomatic disorders and biofeedback: A psychobiological model of disregulation. In *Psychopathology: Experimental Models,* ed. by J.D. Maser and M.E.P. Seligman. San Francisco: Freeman.

Schwartz, R.M. and J.M. Gottman. 1976. Toward a task analysis of assertive behavior. *Journal of Consulting and Clinical Psychology,* **44,** 910–920.

Secunda, S.K., M.M. Katz, and Katz. 1973. *Special*

Report: 1973. The Depressive Disorders. Washington, D.C.: Government Printing Office.

Seiden, R.H. 1974. Suicide: Preventable death. *Public Affairs Report,* **15,** 1–5.

Seligman, M.E.P. 1971. Phobias and preparedness. *Behavior Therapy,* **2,** 307–320.

———. 1974. Depression and learned helplessness. In *The Psychology of Depression: Contemporary Theory and Research.* New York: Wiley.

———. 1975. *Helplessness: On Depression, Development, and Death.* San Francisco: Freeman.

Seligman, M.E.P. and M. Hager, eds. 1972. *Biological Boundaries of Learning.* New York: Appleton-Century-Crofts.

Selye, H. 1956. *The Stress of Life.* New York: McGraw-Hill.

Shaffer, D. 1974. Suicide in childhood and early adolescence. *Journal of Child Psychology and Psychiatry,* **15,** 275–291.

Shah, S.A. 1976. The 47,XYY chromosomal abnormality: A critical appraisal with respect to antisocial and violent behavior. In *Issues in Brain Behavior Control,* ed. by W.L. Smith and A. Kling. New York: Spectrum.

Shean, G. 1978. *Schizophrenia: An Introduction to Research and Theory.* Cambridge, Mass.: Winthrop.

Sheehan, J.G., Ed. 1970. *Stuttering: Research and Therapy.* New York: Harper & Row.

Sheehy, G. 1976. *Passages: Predictable Crises of Adult Life.* New York: Dutton.

Sheldon, W.H. (in collaboration with S.S. Stevens and W.B. Tucker). 1940. *The Varieties of Human Physique: An Introduction of Constitutional Psychology.* New York: Harper.

Shetty, T. and T. Chase. 1976. Central monoamines and hyperkinesis of childhood. *Neurology,* **26,** 1000–1002.

Shields, J. 1968. Summary of the genetic evidence. In *The Transmission of Schizophrenia,* ed. by D. Rosenthal and S. Kety. Oxford: Pergamon.

Shneidman, E.S. and N.L. Farberow. 1961. Statistical comparisons between attempted and committed suicides. In *The Cry for Help,* ed. by N.L. Farberow and E.S. Shneidman. New York: McGraw-Hill.

———. 1968. The suicide prevention center of Los Angeles. In *Suicidal Behaviors: Diagnosis and Management,* ed. by H.L.P. Resnik. Boston: Little, Brown.

Shneidman, E.S. and P. Mandelkorn. 1970. How to prevent suicide. In *The Psychology of Suicide,* ed. by E.S. Shneidman, N.L. Farberow, and R.E. Litman. New York: Science House.

Shoben, E.J. 1957. Toward a concept of the normal personality. *American Psychologist,* **12,** 183–189.

Siddle, D.A.T. 1977. Electrodermal activity and psychopathy. In *Biosocial Bases of Criminal Behavior,* ed. by S. Mednick and K.O. Christiansen. New York: Gardner.

Siegel, R.G. 1977. Cocaine: Recreational use and intoxication. In *Cocaine: 1977,* ed. by R.C. Petersen and R.C. Stillman. Rockville, Md.: National Institute on Drug Abuse, Monograph No. 13.

Singer, M.T. and L.C. Wynne. 1965. Thought disorder and family relations of schizophrenics: III. Methodology using projective techniques. *Archives of General Psychiatry,* **12,** 187.

Skinner, B.F. 1938. *The Behavior of Organisms: An Experimental Analysis.* Englewood Cliffs, N.J.: Prentice-Hall.

———. 1948. *Walden Two.* New York: Macmillan.

———. 1965. *Science and Human Behavior.* New York: Free Press.

Skipper, J.H. and C.H. McCaghy. 1970. Stripteasers. *Social Problems,* **17,** 391–405.

Slater, E. 1968. A review of earlier evidence on genetic factors in schizophrenia. In *The Transmission of Schizophrenia,* ed. by D. Rosenthal and S. Kety. Oxford: Pergamon.

Slater, E. and V. Cowie. 1971. *The Genetics of Mental Disorders.* London: Oxford University.

Slater, E. and E. Glithero. 1965. A follow-up of patients diagnosed as suffering from hysteria. *Journal of Psychosomatic Research,* **9,** 9–13.

Smith, M.L. and G.V. Glass. 1977. Metaanalysis of psychotherapy outcome studies. *American Psychologist,* **32,** 752–760.

Smith, R.S. 1976. Voyeurism: A review of literature. *Archives of Sexual Behavior,* **5,** 585–608.

Snyder, S.H. 1974. *Madness and the Brain.* New York: McGraw-Hill.

Sobell, M.B. and L.C. Sobell. 1977. *Individual Behavior Treatment of Alcohol Problems.* New York: Plenum.

Soloman, J. 1972. Thursday's child. *The Sciences,* **12,** 26–29.

Sours, J.A. 1978. Enuresis. In *Handbook of Mental*

Disorders in Childhood and Adolescence, ed. by B.B. Wolman. Englewood Cliffs, N.J.: Prentice-Hall.

Spiro, M. 1974. On meaning and expression in other cultures. In *The Psychology of Depression: Contemporary Theory and Research,* ed. by R.J. Friedman and M.M. Katz. Washington, D.C.: Winston.

Spitz, R.A. 1945. Hospitalism: An inquiry into the genesis of psychiatric conditions in early childhood. *Psychoanalytic Study of the Child,* **1,** 53–74.

———. 1946. Anaclictic depression. *Psychoanalytic Study of the Child,* **2,** 313–342.

Spitzer, R.L. and J.J. Endicott. 1971. An integrated group of forms for automatic psychiatric case records. *Archives of General Psychiatry,* **24,** 540–547.

Spitzer, R.L. and J.L. Fleiss. 1974. A re-analysis of the reliability of psychiatric diagnosis. *British Journal of Psychiatry,* **125,** 341–347.

Srole, L., T.S. Langner, S.T. Michael, et al. 1962. *Mental Health in the Metropolis: The Midtown Manhattan Study.* New York: McGraw-Hill.

Stampfl, T.G. 1975. Implosive therapy: Staring down your nightmares. *Psychology Today,* **8**(9), 66.

Stark, R. and J. McEvoy. 1970. Middle-class violence. *Psychology Today,* November, 30–31.

Steele, B.F. 1978. The child abuser. In *Violence: Perspective on Murder and Aggression,* ed. by I.L. Katash, et al. San Francisco: Jossey-Bass.

Stengel, E. 1968. Attempted suicides. In *Suicidal Behaviors: Diagnosis and Management,* ed. by H.L.P. Resnik. Boston: Little, Brown.

Sterman, M.B. and M. Shouse. 1980. Quantitative analysis of training, sleep EEG, and clinical response to EEG operant conditioning in epileptics. *Electroencephalography and Clinical Neurophysiology,* **49,** 558–576.

Stern, G.M. 1977. *The Buffalo Creek Disaster.* New York: Vintage Books.

Stern, R.S. and J.P. Cobb. 1978. Phenomenology of obsessive-compulsive neurosis. *British Journal of Psychiatry,* **182,** 233–239.

Stewart, M.A., F.N. Pitts, A.G. Craig, and W. Dieruf. 1966. The hyperactive child syndrome. *American Journal of Orthopsychiatry,* **36,** 861–867.

Stoller, R.J. 1973. Male transsexualism: Uneasiness. *American Journal of Psychiatry,* **130,** 536–539.

Stone, L.J. and J.E. Hokanson. 1969. Arousal reduction via self-punitive behavior. *Journal of Personality and Social Psychology,* **12,** 72–79.

Strauss, M.E. 1973. Behavioral differences between acute and chronic schizophrenics: Course of psychosis, effects of institutionalization, or sampling biases? *Psychological Bulletin,* **79,** 271–279.

Streissguth, A.P., S. Landesman-Dwyer, J.C. Martin, and D.W. Smith. 1980. Teratogenic effects of alcohol in humans and laboratory animals. *Science,* **209,** 353–361.

Su, C.V., S. Lin, Y.T. Wang, et al. 1978. Effects of B-endorphin on narcotic abstinence syndrome in man. *Taiwan I Hoven Hui Tsa Chih,* **77,** 133–141.

Syndulko, K., D.A. Parker, I. Maltzman, and E. Ziskind. 1975. Psychophysiology of sociopathy: Electrocortical measures. *Biological Psychology,* **3,** 185–200.

Szasz, T.S. 1960. The myth of mental illness. *American Psychologist,* **15,** 113–118.

———. 1961. *The Myth of Mental Illness.* New York: Harper & Row.

———. 1970. *Ideology and Insanity—Essays on the Psychiatric Dehumanization of Man.* New York: Doubleday.

———. 1976. The ethics of suicide. In *Between Survival and Suicide,* ed. by B.B. Wolman and H.H. Krauss. New York: Gardner.

Tan, E.S. 1977. The presentation of affective symptoms in non-western countries. In *Handbook of Studies on Depression,* ed. by G.D. Burrows. Amsterdam: Excerpta Medica.

Taube, C.A. and R. Redick. 1973. Utilization of mental health resources by persons diagnosed as schizophrenic. Department of Health, Education, and Welfare Report No. (HSM)73-9110. Rockville, Md.: National Institute of Mental Health.

Thigpen, C.H. and H. Cleckley. 1957. *The Three Faces of Eve.* New York: McGraw-Hill.

Thompson, C.E. 1949. The Thompson modification of the Thematic Apperception Test. *Rorschach Research Exchange,* **13,** 469–478.

Thorndike, E.L. 1932. *The Fundamentals of Learning.* New York: Teachers College.

Thorpe, L.P. and B. Katz. 1948. *The Psychology of Abnormal Behavior.* New York: Ronald Press.

Timiras, P.S. 1972. *Developmental Physiology and Aging.* New York: Macmillan.

Tobin, S.S. and M.A. Lieberman. 1976. *Last Home for the Aged.* San Francisco: Jossey-Bass.

Treas, J. 1977. Family support systems for the aged:

Some social and demographic considerations. *The Gerontologist,* **17**(6), 486–491.

Troll, L.E. 1971. Eating and aging. *Journal of the American Dietetic Association,* **59,** 456–459.

Turk, D. 1974. Cognitive control of pain: A skills training approach. Unpublished manuscript. Ontario, Canada. University of Waterloo.

Turner, R.J. and M.O. Wagonfeld. 1967. Occupational mobility and schizophrenia. *American Sociological Review,* **32,** 104–113.

Turner, R.K. and P.D. Taylor. 1974. Conditioning treatment of nocturnal enuresis in adults: Preliminary findings. *Behavior Research and Therapy,* **12,** 41–52.

Ullmann, L.P. 1970. On cognition and behavior therapy. *Behavior Therapy,* **1,** 201–204.

Ullmann, L.P. and L. Krasner. 1975. *A Psychological Approach to Abnormal Behavior,* 2d ed. Englewood Cliffs, N.J.: Prentice-Hall.

U.S. Bureau of the Census. 1973. *Projections of the Population of the United States: 1977 to 2050.* Current Population Reports, Series P-25, No. 704. Washington, D.C.: Government Printing Office.

U.S. Bureau of the Census. 1977. *Statistical Abstract of the United States: 1977.* Washington, D.C.: Government Printing Office.

U.S. Bureau of the Census. 1978. *Statistical Abstract of the United States: 1978.* Washington, D.C.: Government Printing Office.

Vaillant, G.E. 1975. Sociopathy as a human process: A viewpoint. *Archives of General Psychiatry,* **32**(2), 178–183.

Vander Zanden, J. 1978. *Human Development.* New York: Knopf.

Viscott, D.S. 1972. *The Making of a Psychiatrist.* Greenwich, Conn.: Fawcett.

Vonnegut, M. 1975. *The Eden Express.* New York: Praeger.

Wada, J.A. 1977. Pre-language and fundamental asymmetry of the infant brain. *Annals of the New York Academy of Science,* 470–479.

Wagenfeld, M.O. 1972. The primary prevention of mental illness. *Journal of Health and Social Behavior,* **13,** 195–203.

Waters, W.E. 1971. Migraine: Intelligence, social class and familial prevalence. *British Medical Journal,* **2,** 77–78.

Watson, J.B. 1913. Psychology as the behaviorist views it. *Psychological Review,* **20,** 158–177.

———. 1925. *Behaviorism.* New York: Norton.

Watson, J.B. and R. Rayner. 1920. Conditioned emotional reactions. *Journal of Experimental Psychology,* **3,** 1–14.

Watt, N.F. 1979. The longitudinal research basis for early intervention. *Journal of Community Psychology,* **7,** 158–168.

Webb and Colette. 1975. Urban ecological and household correlates of stress-alleviating drug use. *American Behavioral Scientist,* **18,** 750–769.

Wehr, T. and F.K. Goodwin. 1977. Catecholamines in depression. In *Handbook of Studies of Depression,* ed. by G.D. Burrows. Amsterdam: Excerpta Medica.

Weinberg, M. and C.J. Williams, 1974. *Male Homosexuals: Their Problems and Adaptations in Three Societies.* New York: Oxford University.

Weiner, B. 1972. *Theories of Motivation: From Mechanism to Cognition.* Chicago: Rand-McNally.

Weiner, B., ed. 1974. *Achievement Motivation and Attribution Theory.* Morristown, N.J.: General Learning.

Weiner, H., M. Thaler, M.F. Reiser, and I. Mirsky. 1957. Etiology of duodenal ulcer: I. Relation of specific psychological characteristics to rate of gastric secretion. *Psychosomatic Medicine,* **17,** 1–10.

Weintraub, S., R.J. Prinz, and J.M. Neale. 1978. Peer evaluations of the competence of children vulnerable to psychopathology. *Journal of Abnormal Child Psychology,* **6,** 461–473.

Weiss, J.M. 1971. Effects of coping behavior in different warning-signal conditions on stress pathology in rats. *Journal of Comparative and Physiological Psychology,* **77,** 1–13.

———. 1977. Psychosomatic disorders. In *Psychopathology: Experimental Models,* ed. by J.D. Maser and M. Seligman. San Francisco: Freeman.

Weissman, M. and G. Klerman. 1977. Sex differences in the epidemiology of depression. *Archives of General Psychiatry,* **34,** 98–111.

Weissman, M.M. and J.K. Myers. 1978. Affective disorders in the U.S. urban community. *Archives of General Psychiatry,* **35,** 1304–1311.

Wender, P. 1971. *Minimal Brain Dysfunction in Children.* New York: Wiley-Interscience.

Wender, P., D. Rosenthal, and S. Kety. 1968. A psychiatric assessment of the adoptive parents of schizophrenics. In *The Transmission of Schizophrenia,* ed. by D. Rosenthal and S.S. Kety. New York: Pergamon.

Werry, J.S. 1979(a). The childhood psychoses. In *Psychopathological Disorders of Childhood,* 2d ed., ed. by H.C. Quay and J.S. Werry. New York: Wiley.

———. 1979(b). Psychosomatic disorders, psychogenic symptoms, and hospitalization. In *Phsychopathological Disorders of Childhood,* 2d ed., ed. by H.C. Quay and J.S. Werry. New York: Wiley.

Wesson, D. and D. Smith. 1977. *Barbiturates: Their Use, Misuse and Abuse.* New York: Human Sciences.

Weyer, E., Jr. 1959. *Primitive Peoples Today.* Garden City, N.Y.: Dolphin.

Whalen, C.K. and B. Henker. 1971. Pyramid therapy in a hospital for the retarded. *American Journal of Mental Deficiency,* **4,** 75, 414–434.

Whitlock, F.A. 1967. The aetiology of hysteria. *Acta Psychiatrica Scandinavica,* **43,** 144–162.

Wickramasekera, I. 1972. A technique for controlling a certain type of sexual exhibitionism. *Psychotherapy: Theory Research and Practice,* **9,** 207–210.

———. 1976. Aversive behavior control for sexual exhibitionism. *Behavior Therapy,* **7,** 167–176.

Wikler, A., Ed. 1968. Interaction of physical dependence and classical and operant conditioning in the genesis of relapse. In *Research Publications: Association for Research in Nervous and Mental Disorders,* vol. XLVI. Baltimore: Williams & Wilkins.

Williams, J.B. 1967. *Narcotics and Hallucinogenics.* Beverly Hills, Calif.: Glenco.

———. 1973. Management of the bereavement crisis. In *Crisis Intervention,* ed. by G. Specter and W. Claiborn. New York: Behavioral Publications.

Winokur, G., P.J. Clayton, and T. Reich. 1969. *Manic-depressive Illness.* St. Louis: C.V. Mosby.

Wolf, S. and H.G. Wolff. 1947. *Human Gastric Functions.* New York: Oxford University.

Wolff, H.G. 1950. Life stress and bodily disease—a formulation. In *Life Stress and Bodily Disease,* ed. by H.G. Wolff, S.G. Wolf, Jr., and C.C. Hare. Baltimore: Williams & Wilkins.

Wolff, P.H. 1972. Ethnic differences in alcohol sensitivity. *Science,* **175,** 449–450.

Wolpe, J. 1958. *Psychotherapy by Reciprocal Inhibition.* Stanford, Calif.: Stanford University.

———. 1973. *The Practice of Behavior Therapy,* 2d ed. New York: Pergamon.

———. 1976. *Theme and Variations: A Behavior Therapy Casebook.* Elmsford, N.Y.: Pergamon.

Wolpe, J. and S. Rachman. 1960. Psychoanalytic "evidence," a critique based on Freud's case of Little Hans. *Journal of Nervous and Mental Disease,* **131,** 135–147.

Woodruff, R.A., D.W. Goodwin, and S.B. Guze. 1980. *Psychiatric Diagnosis.* New York: Oxford University.

World Health Organization. 1972. *World Health Statistics Annual, 1969.* Geneva, Switzerland.

Wright, D.M. 1975. Impairment in abstract conceptualization in schizophrenia. *Psychological Bulletin,* **82,** 120–127.

Wynne, L.C. and M.T. Singer. 1963(a). Thought disorder and family relations of schizophrenics: I. A research study. *Archives of General Psychiatry,* **9,** 191–198.

———. 1963(b). Thought disorder and family relations of schizophrenics: II. A classification of forms of thinking. *Archives of General Psychiatry,* **9,** 199–206.

Yalom, I.D. 1960. Aggression and forbiddenness in voyeurism. *Archives of General Psychiatry,* **3,** 305–319.

Yolles, S.F. and M. Kramer. 1969. Vital statistics of schizophrenia. In *The Schizophrenic Syndrome,* ed. by L. Bellak and L. Loeb. New York: Grune & Stratton.

Zax, M. and E. Cowen. 1976. *Abnormal Psychology: Changing Conceptions.* New York: Holt, Rinehart & Winston.

Zax, M. and G.A. Specter. 1974. *An Introduction to Community Psychology.* New York: Wiley.

Zeiss, A.M., G.M. Rosen, and R.A. Zeiss. 1977. Orgasm during intercourse: A treatment strategy for women. *Journal of Consulting and Clinical Psychology,* **45,** 891–895.

Zerbin-Rudin, E. 1972. Genetic research and the theory of schizophrenia. *International Journal of Mental Health,* **3,** 46–72.

Zilbergeld, B. 1978. *Male Sexuality: A Guide to Sexual Fulfillment.* Boston: Little, Brown.

Zilbergeld, B. and M. Evans. 1980. The inadequacy

of Masters and Johnson. *Psychology Today,* August, 29–43.

Zilboorg, G. and G.W. Henry. 1941. *A History of Medical Psychology.* New York: Norton.

Zimbardo, P. 1972. Pathology of imprisonment. *Society,* April, 9.

Zis, A.P. and F.K. Goodwin. 1979. Major affective disorder as a recurrent illness. *Archives of General Psychiatry,* **36,** 835–839.

Zis, A.P., P. Grof, M. Webster, and F.K. Goodwin. 1980. Prediction of relapse in recurrent affective disorder. *Psychopharmacology Bulletin,* in press.

Zubin, J. 1967. Classification of the behavior disorders. *Annual Review of Psychology,* 373–406.

Zwerling, T. and M. Rosenbaum. 1959. Alcoholic addiction and personality. In *American Handbook of Psychiatry,* vol. I. New York: Basic Books.

Index

Stressful events, 172, 220